RELIGIOUS PERSPECTIVES
Planned and Edited by
RUTH NANDA ANSHEN

———————

THE ELUSIVE PRESENCE

RELIGIOUS PERSPECTIVES • VOLUME TWENTY-SIX

THE ELUSIVE PRESENCE

Toward a New Biblical Theology

SAMUEL TERRIEN

1817

Published in San Francisco by
HARPER & ROW, PUBLISHERS
New York, Hagerstown, San Francisco, London

FIRST EDITION

Designed by Paul Quin

Library of Congress Cataloging in Publication Data

Terrien, Samuel L., 1911–
   The elusive presence.

   (Religious perspectives; v. 26)
   Includes index.
   1. Bible—Theology. I. Title. II. Series.
BS543.T37   230   78-7927
ISBN 0-06-068232-9

---

78 79 80 81 82   10 9 8 7 6 5 4 3 2 1

RELIGIOUS PERSPECTIVES
Volumes Already Published

Contents

Religious Perspectives
Its Meaning and Purpose

Religious Perspectives represents a quest for the rediscovery of man. It constitutes an effort to define man's search for the essence of being in order that he may have a knowledge of goals. It is an endeavor to show that there is no possibility of achieving an understanding of man's total nature on the basis of phenomena known by the analytical method alone. It hopes to point to the false antinomy between revelation and reason, faith and knowledge, grace and nature, courage and anxiety. Mathematics, physics, philosophy, biology, and religion, in spite of their almost complete independence, have begun to sense their interrelatedness and to become aware of that mode of cognition which teaches that "the light is not without but within me, and I myself am the light."

My Introduction to this Series is not of course to be construed as a prefatory essay for each individual book. These few pages simply attempt to set forth the general aim and purpose of the Series as a whole. They try to point to the humanistic and transcendent significance of the creative process in the respective disciplines and to the principle of permanence within change as well as to define the essential nature of man as

presented by those scholars who have been invited to participate in this intellectual and spiritual movement.

The justification of RELIGIOUS PERSPECTIVES lies as much in
the positive results of each volume in this Series as in the con-
sistent urge for knowledge in relation to experience at work in
each of these studies, driving them all to a single goal. Every
living being is sharply centered at whatever point in the whole
of natural processes we start to speak of living beings. The life
process of man is a process which reacts as a whole since that
is the nature and the art of being. It is a going out and a
returning to itself as long as it lives. It takes in elements of the
encountered reality and assimilates them to its own centered
whole, or it rejects them if assimilation is impossible.

The process of self-integration of *being* is constitutive of life,
but it is so as a continuous struggle: integrating and disintegrating since these are tendencies ambiguously mixed in any
given moment in man's life. Perhaps the experience of life first
arose in man's consciousness through the experience of death.
The observation of a particular potentiality of beings, whether
of a species or of man actualizing themselves in time and space
has led us to the concept of life—life as the actuality of being.
There is a tension between matter and form in all existence. In
man, however, this experience of life, of being, unites two main
qualifications of being which underlie the entire concept. These
two main qualifications of being are the essential and the existential. Potentiality is that kind of being which has the power to
become actual. For example, there can be no act without potency; no man without manhood.

Modern man is threatened by a world created by himself. He
is faced with the conversion of mind to naturalism, a dogmatic
secularism and an opposition to a belief in the transcendent. He
begins to see, however, that the universe is given not as one
existing and one perceived but as the unity of subject and object; that the barrier between them cannot be said to have been

dissolved as the result of recent experience in the physical sciences, since this barrier has never existed. Confronted with the question of meaning, he is summoned to rediscover and scrutinize the immutable and the permanent which constitute the dynamic, unifying aspect of life as well as the principle of differentiation; to reconcile identity and diversity, immutability and unrest. He begins to recognize that just as every person descends by his particular path, so he is able to ascend, and this ascent aims at a return to the source of creation, an inward home from which he has become estranged.

It is the hope of RELIGIOUS PERSPECTIVES that the rediscovery of man will point the way to the rediscovery of God. To this end a rediscovery of first principles should constitute part of the quest. These principles, not to be superseded by new discoveries, are not those of historical worlds that come to be and perish. They are to be sought in the heart and spirit of man, and no interpretation of a merely historical or scientific universe can guide the search. RELIGIOUS PERSPECTIVES attempts not only to ask dispassionately what the nature of God is, but also to restore to human life at least the hypothesis of God and the symbols that relate to him. It endeavors to show that man is faced with the metaphysical question of the truth of religion while he encounters the empirical question of its effects on the life of humanity and its meaning for society. Religion is here distinguished from theology and its doctrinal forms and is intended to denote the feelings, aspirations, and acts of men, as they relate to total reality. For we are all in search of reality, of a reality which is there whether we know it or not; and the search is of our own making but reality is not.

RELIGIOUS PERSPECTIVES is nourished by the spiritual and intellectual energy of world thought, by those religious and ethical leaders who are not merely spectators but scholars deeply involved in the critical problems common to all religions. These thinkers recognize that human morality and human ideals thrive only when set in the context of a transcendent attitude toward religion, and that by pointing to the ground of identity and the common nature of being in the religious experience of man the essential nature of religion may be defined. Thus, they are committed to reevaluate the meaning of everlastingness, an experience which has been lost and which is the content of that *visio Dei* constituting the structure of all religions. It is the many absorbed everlastingly into the ultimate unity, a unity subsuming what Whitehead calls the fluency of God and the everlastingness of passing experience.

The false dichotomies, created by man, especially by Western man, do not exist in nature. Antinomies are unknown in the realm of nature. The new topology of the earth implies the link between an act and a whole series of consequences; and a consciousness of the individual that every time a decision is made it has distant consequences which become more precisely determined.

Furthermore, man has a desire for "elsewhere," a third dimension which cannot be found on earth and yet which must be experienced on earth: prediction: detailed statement referring to something that is to happen in the future; projection: combining a number of trends; prevision: that which is scientifically probable and likely to happen; prospective: the relation between present activity and the image of the future; plan: the sum of total decisions for coordinated activities with a goal, both spiritual and material, in mind.

The authors in RELIGIOUS PERSPECTIVES attempt to show that to *be* is more important than to have, since *being* leads to transcendence and joy, while having alone leads to apathy and despair.

Man has now reached the point of controlling those forces both outside himself and within himself which throughout history hemmed in decision-making. And what is decisive is that this new trend is irreversible. We have eaten of this new tree of knowledge and what fifty years ago seemed *fate* has not become the subject of our deliberate choices. Therefore, for man, both in the East and in the West, the two basic questions are: What proper use can we make of our knowledge both for the spirit and for the body and what are the criteria for our choices. For the correct answers to these questions which conform to the new reality can the continuity of human life be preserved and the human person related not only to the present but also to the past and therefore to the future in a meaningful existence. The choice is ours—a choice between perfection of performance or, and more important, the acceptance of spiritual and moral conduct.

These volumes seek to show that the unity of which we speak consists in a certitude emanating from the nature of man who seeks God and the nature of God who seeks man. Such certitude bathes in an intuitive act of cognition, participating in the divine essence and is related to the natural spirituality of intelligence. This is not by any means to say that there is an equivalence of all faiths in the traditional religions of human history. It is, however, to emphasize the distinction between the spiritual and the temporal which all religions acknowledge. For duration of thought is composed of instants superior to time, and is an intuition of the permanence of existence and its metahistorical reality. In fact, the symbol[1] itself found on cover and jacket of each volume of RELIGIOUS PERSPECTIVES is the visible sign or representation of the essence, immediacy, and timelessness of religious experience; the one immutable center, which may be analogically related to being in pure act, moving with centrifugal and ecumenical necessity outward into the manifold modes, yet simultaneously, with dynamic centripetal power and with full intentional energy, returning to the source. Through

---

[1]From the original design by Leo Katz.

the very diversity of its authors, the Series shows that the basic and poignant concern of every faith is to point to, and overcome the crisis in our apocalyptic epoch—the crisis of man's separation from man and of man's separation from God—the failure of love. The authors endeavor, moreover, to illustrate the truth that the human heart is able, and even yearns, to go to the very lengths of God; that the darkness and cold, the frozen spiritual misery of recent times are breaking, cracking, and beginning to move, yielding to efforts to overcome spiritual muteness and moral paralysis. In this way, it is hoped, the immediacy of pain and sorrow, the primacy of tragedy and suffering in human life, may be transmuted into a spiritual and moral triumph. For the uniqueness of man lies in his capacity for self-transcendence.

RELIGIOUS PERSPECTIVES is therefore an effort to explore the *meaning* of God, an exploration which constitutes an aspect of man's intrinsic nature, part of his ontological substance. This Series grows out of an abiding concern that in spite of the release of man's creative energy which science has in part accomplished, this very science has overturned the essential order of nature. Shrewd as man's calculations have become concerning his means, his choice of ends which was formerly correlated with belief in God, with absolute criteria of conduct, has become witless. God is not to be treated as an exception to metaphysical principles, invoked to prevent their collapse. He is rather their chief exemplification, the source of all potentiality. The personal reality of freedom and providence, of will and conscience, may demonstrate that "he who knows" commands a depth of consciousness inaccessible to the profane man, and is capable of that transfiguration which prevents the twisting of all good to ignominy. This religious content of experience is not within the province of science to bestow; it corrects the error of treating the scientific account as if it were itself metaphysical or religious; it challenges the tendency to make a religion of science—or a science of religion—a dogmatic act which destroys the moral dynamic of man. Indeed, many men of science are confronted with unexpected implications of their own thought and are beginning to accept, for instance, the trans-spatial and trans-temporal dimension in the nature of reality.

RELIGIOUS PERSPECTIVES attempts to show the fallacy of the apparent irrelevance of God in history. This Series submits that no convincing image of man can arise, in spite of the many ways in which human thought has tried to reach it, without a philosophy of human nature and human freedom which does not exclude God. This image of *Homo cum Deo* implies the highest conceivable freedom, the freedom to step into the very fabric of the universe, a new formula for man's collaboration with the creative process and the only one which is able to protect man from the terror of existence. This image implies further that the mind and conscience are capable of making genuine discriminations and thereby may reconcile the serious tensions between the secular and religious, the profane and sacred. The idea of the sacred lies in what it *is*, timeless existence. By emphasizing timeless existence against rationalism as a reality, we are liberated, in our communion with the eternal, from the otherwise unbreakable rule of "before and after." Then we are able to admit that all forms, all symbols in religions, by their negation of error and their affirmation of the actuality of truth, make it possible to experience that *knowing* which is above knowledge, and that dynamic passage of the universe to unending unity.

God is here interpreted not as a heteronomous being issuing commandments but as the *Tatt-Twam-Asi:* "Do unto others as you would have others do unto you. For I am the Lord." This does not mean a commandment from on high but rather a self-realization through "the other"; since the isolated individual is unthinkable and meaningless. Man becomes man by recognizing his true nature as a creature capable of will and decision. For then the divine and the sacred become manifest. And though he believes in choices, he is no Utopian expecting the "coming of the Kingdom." Man, individually and collectively, is losing the chains which have bound him to the inexorable demands of nature. The constraints are diminishing and an infinity of choices becomes available to him. Thus man himself, from the sources of his ontological being, at last must decide what is the *bonum et malum*. And though the anonymous forces which in the past have set the constraints do indeed threaten him with total anarchy and with perhaps a worse tyranny than he experienced in past history, he nevertheless begins to see that preceding the moral issue is the cognitive problem: the perception of those conditions for life which permit mankind to fulfill itself and to accept the truth that beyond scientific, discursive knowledge is nondiscursive, intuitive awareness. And, I suggest, this is not to secularize God but rather to gather him into the heart of the nature of matter and indeed of life itself. It is also to understand God cosmologically. For just as man is in the universe so the universe is in man.

The volumes in this Series seek to challenge the crisis which separates, to make reasonable a religion that binds, and to present the numinous reality within the experience of man. Insofar as the Series succeeds in this quest, it will direct mankind toward a reality that is eternal and away from a preoccupation with that which is illusory and ephemeral.

As I have said above we are in the presence of a serious crisis of knowledge. The crisis could be defined as the end of social determinism or the end of social fatalism. In other words, our era, for the last two generations, represents a fundamental break with all past history. For we now possess a rapidly growing ability to control the forces which throughout history hemmed in individual decision-making and, even more important, which made the collective social processes appear as inexorable events ruled by pseudo-natural laws.

Up to the middle of the nineteenth century, for example, the population trend was ruled by nothing but biological laws, and the balance of population was regulated by 'natural' events such as Malthus' three horsemen: war, hunger, pestilence. Now a change has been brought about not only by individual control of birth-rates and death-rates, but also by collective application of public health policies and findings of epidemiology. Other examples of equal significance could be mentioned.

Here, however, I wish to refer to a trend which takes us back to the Renaissance. During the last two generations we have made a quantum jump, or, in Hegelian terms, the quantitative changes have altered the quality of our life world. And what is decisive is that this trend of which I speak is *irreversible*. We have eaten of this new tree of knowledge, and what fifty years ago appeared to be *fate* has now become the subject of our deliberate choices.

Thus, I must repeat, if choices are to be made, the first question is: on what foundations of knowledge? And the second question is: what are the criteria for our choices? Therefore, it is the hope of *Religious Perspectives* to try to point to at least some of them, for our dilemma is one of criteria for our judgments.

For man is now confronted with his burden and his greatness: "He calleth to me, Watchman, what of the night? Watchman, what of the night?"[2] Perhaps the anguish in the human soul may be assuaged by the answer, by the *assimilation* of the person in God: "The morning cometh, and also the night: if ye will inquire, inquire ye: return, come."[3]

RUTH NANDA ANSHEN

---

[2]Isaiah 21:11.
[3]Isaiah 21:12.

THE ELUSIVE PRESENCE

A religion which does not
affirm that God is hidden
is not true. *Vere tu es
Deus absconditus!*

BLAISE PASCAL

Preface

The reality of the presence of God stands at the center of biblical faith. This presence, however, is always elusive. "Verily, verily, thou art a God that hidest thyself!" The Deity of the Hebrew-Christian Scriptures escapes man's grasp and manipulation, but man is aware of the presence of that Deity in such a powerful way that he finds through it a purpose in the universe; he confers upon his own existence a historical meaning; and he attunes his selfhood to an ultimate destiny.

In order to examine the Hebraic theology of presence and its direct influence upon the birth of Christianity, one has to analyze those biblical traditions and poems which describe the encounter of God with men. Such a study will reveal the dynamics of interaction between biblical cultus and biblical faith. The patriarchal legends of epiphanic visitations; the Mosaic saga of the Sinai theophany; the psalms of the cultic presence in Zion; the confessions of the prophets on their visions; the poem of Job, together with the proclamation of Jesus as Lord; the "gospel" of Stephen in Acts; Paul's theology of eucharistic communion; the Johannine evocation of the "encamped" Logos; the triple typology of Jesus as priest, offering, and shrine in the epistle to the Hebrews—in brief, the literature of the Bible as a whole presupposes a faith which transcends ritual without ever dispensing with cultic celebration.

The ancient Hebrews anticipated the *Day of Yahweh.* The early Christians celebrated the *Day of the Lord.* Both of them interpreted their historical existence in the light of a theology of presence which reveals at once their affinities and their differences. Moreover, the peculiarity of the biblical theology of presence distinguishes the faith of both Hebrews and Christians from the cults of Near Eastern and classical antiquity. It is the distinctiveness of the Hebraic theology of presence rather than the ideology of the covenant which provides a key to understanding the Bible. This thesis does not fully contradict recent trends in Old and New Testament scholarship, but it seeks to correct their excesses and to go beyond their apparently spent momentum.

One of the consequences of such a study might be to show that Judaism and Christianity fulfill their respective functions only to the extent that they inform the aesthetics of the mystical eye with the demands of the ethical ear. One cannot be divorced from the other. The mystical eye discerns the presence of God through the theological symbol of "glory." The ethical ear responds to the same presence through the theological symbol of "name." When the eye and the ear are separated, the former tends to foment an ethnic, esoteric, sectarian, and even racial exclusivism which promotes a static religion and a "closed" morality. The latter without the former tends to degenerate into a secular activism and an amorphous humanism which in the long run may abandon their proponents to their unfulfilling philosophies of the existential absurd.

The Hebraic theology of presence, which stands at the root of the earliest interpretations of Jesus—as distinguished from the later and eventually normative Christologies—unites the vision of the ultimate with a passion for the service of man. The study of the biblical documents which record this unity makes possible a new approach to the problem of the relationship between religion and ethics.

This essay is a prolegomenon to a genuinely "biblical" theology which will respect historical complexity within, as well as between, the Old Testament and the New. The elements of diversity and of continuity which characterize the modes of presence from Genesis to Revelation will point to an interplay of theological fields of force at the center of Scripture. The recognition of these fields of force may warn contemporary theologians against the risk of abasing Christian faith by attempting to formulate it into intellectual beliefs that reflect only a lower common denominator. Acquiescence to opposition is not the secret of authentic tolerance. This warning may well contribute to the birth of a new foundation for the ecumenical theology of tomorrow.

Portions of these chapters in preliminary form were delivered as lectures at the Concordia Theological Seminary, St. Louis, Missouri; the Bangor Theological Seminary, Bangor, Maine; the Perkins School of Theology, Southern Methodist University, Dallas, Texas; the College of Wooster, Wooster, Ohio; Scripps College, Claremont, California; Hollins College, Hollins, Virginia; and Siena Heights College, Adrian, Michigan. To the students, faculties, presidents, and trustees of these institutions the author expresses gratitude for the warmth of their welcome and for the stimulus of their critical response.

The substance of the Introduction was presented in a lecture given under the auspices of the Women's Committee, Union Theological Seminary, New York, and was subsequently published under the title, "Towards a New Theology of Presence," in the *Union Seminary Quarterly Review*, XXIV (1968–69), pp. 227–37. It was reprinted under the title, "The Recovery of Transcendence," in *New Theology, No. 7*, ed. by M. E. Marty and D. G.

Peerman (New York and London, 1970), pp. 137–51. Thanks are hereby extended to the editors of these publications.

I wish to acknowledge the courteous help which Barbara Reed Robarts and other librarians of the Union Theological Seminary Library, New York, have unfailingly offered me in my research over the years. John Loudon and Dennis Lewis, of Harper & Row, deserve special mention for their expert care in the preparation of the manuscript for the printers.

A note of gratitude to Ruth Nanda Anshen, the editor of the collection in which this volume appears, fails to convey the extraordinary quality of her forbearance in the face of this long-delayed "eschatology."

For my debt to Sara, my wife, I find no adequate word.

Epiphany, 1977.

S. T.

Introduction

The study of Old Testament religion has been profoundly altered in recent decades. Students of the Bible now recognize that Israel's beliefs and cultus were largely influenced by those of the ancient Near East. At the same time, a number of scholars tend to ignore the fulcrum of these beliefs and this ceremonial. Alone in their cultural milieu, the Hebrews developed a unique theology of presence. They worshipped a God whose disclosure or proximity always had a certain quality of elusiveness. Indeed, for most generations of the biblical age, Israel prayed to a *Deus Absconditus.**

In the celebration of her festivals, Israel commemorated the intervention of the Deity in her past, and she anticipated his manifestation in her future, at the end of history. Standing ceremonially between sacred protology and sacred eschatology, she summoned the beginning and the end of time into a liturgical present, but she could remember only a handful of ancestors, prophets, and poets who had actually perceived the

---

*The expression *Deus Absconditus*, although consecrated by usage, is unfortunate because it uses a passive participial adjective. The Hebrew original means "a self-concealing God" (Isa. 45:15).

immediacy of God. The rank and file of her people experienced divine closeness by cultic procuration. Nevertheless, Israel's cultus produced a mode of communion which appears to have been unparalleled in the religions of the ancient world, for it implied a religious reality of a special character, which became semantically associated with the word "faith."

Old Testament religion differed from the religions of classical Egypt, Asia Anterior, and the Mediterranean world precisely because it manifested itself through a unique complex of interaction between cultus and faith.

I

Two main trends have appeared in Old Testament science during the past fifty years. One is represented by the *Myth-and-Ritual* school of Britain and Scandinavia, the other by the *Heilsgeschichte* or *Salvation History* school of Germany and Switzerland. The day has perhaps come when we may try to evaluate the work of both schools and so to indicate eventual developments.

On the one hand, the Myth-and-Ritual school has sharpened special issues which early pioneers in the history of comparative religions, at the dawn of the twentieth century, raised more or less at random. For example, it has called necessary attention to the numinous aspect of Hebrew psychology, the sense of corporate personality, the magical aspects of blessing and curse, the objective quality of speech as ritual, the cultic significance of sexuality, the power of royal ideology, the importance of the feasts, the function of diviners and cultic prophets, and so on. In brief, the Myth-and-Ritual school has stressed the elements of cultural continuity which tie Israel to her Semitic and Egyptian environment.

In spite of its contributions, however, the Myth-and-Ritual school has proved unable to discern those intrinsic features which set Israel's religion apart from the ritual practices and beliefs of Asia Anterior in the Bronze and Iron Ages. It has especially failed to detect those elements which explain the survival of that religion in Judaism and Christianity. An examination of the Hebraic understanding of divine presence reveals that the claims of the Myth-and-Ritual school have to be seriously curtailed.

On the other hand, the *Heilsgeschichte* school has rightly stressed the importance of the covenant for the study of Old Testament religion. It has shown the part played in the national life by the cultic recitals of the "Mighty Acts of God"—*Gesta Dei* or *Magnalia Yahweh*—which brought Israel into historical existence and promoted in her midst a historical awareness. Yet, while the covenant was perhaps "renewed" in some festive celebrations during the twelve centuries of the biblical age, there is little, if any, evidence that covenant consciousness constituted the determinative trait of Israel's religion. It is even doubtful whether the covenant motif provides an adequate principle for the organic presentation of Israel's faith and cultus. The diversity of her responses to the sense of her destiny in the course of a thousand years can hardly be fitted within the reality of covenant consciousness. The notion of covenant is fluid; it ranges from a conditional and historical character (Sinai covenant) to an unconditional and mythical significance (Davidic covenant and priestly covenant). In addition, covenant is conspicuously absent from the wisdom literature of Israel. To explain Israel's religion in terms of covenant may well reflect an anachronistic and alien attitude.

The motif of divine presence, however, unlike that of covenant, constitutes an element of religious homogeneity which respects historical complexity without ignoring coherence and specificity. It is the peculiarly Hebraic theology of presence which explains the importance of covenant in Israel's religion, and not the converse. The motif of presence is primary, and that of covenant is secondary.

II

An inquiry into the Hebraic theology of presence will depend closely on the results of Myth-and-Ritual research, on the one hand, and *Heilsgeschichte* interpretation, on the other. Both methods have shown correctly that religious ideas are not to be understood apart from cultic practices. No historian of Hebrew religion can permit himself to relegate the themes of worship to some appendage on "institutions." Israel knew that her God was both present and elusive whenever she performed her ceremonial of adoration. Moses and individual prophets, priests, psalmists and wise men may have mediated the knowledge of God to the masses, but their activities were always directly or indirectly related to cultus. It may be said that in Israel there would not have been a knowledge of God without the service of God. Theology was bred in celebration. *Theologia* could not be separated from *Theolatreia*.

At the same time, ceremonial proved to be an ambiguous reality for Israel. One may speak of Hebrew cultus at once as the matrix of theological responsibility and religious stagnation, of ethical alertness and moral corruption, of psychological daring and regression, of sociological impetus and disintegration. Yet, cultus was capable of stimulating a faith which in its turn could arouse agents of reform and of renaissance in almost every generation. To recognize the centrality of the theology of presence and the integral mutuality of cultus and faith in ancient Israel opens up the possibility of a new approach to the study of biblical religion.

III

In the twentieth century, theologians have again stressed the relevance of the Old Testament for Christianity and thus raised once more the problem of the relationship between the Old

Testament and the New. Exploration into the interpenetrative character of cultus and faith in Israel may furnish not only a principle of coherence for the understanding of the Old Testament religion but also a solution to the problem of continuity and discontinuity from the Old to the New Testament. It was a new theology of presence, drawn from the Hebraic complex of cultus and faith, which presided over the emergence of Christianity from Judaism.

The public life of Jesus lasted only a few months, probably from the late spring of the year 28–29 to the early spring of the following year, 29–30. The church was born when the disciples of Jesus were transformed by their visions of the risen Lord. These visions included not only the appearances reported in the Synoptics (Matt. 28:11-20, Luke 24:13-49) or the Fourth Gospel (John 20:1—21:25) but also those reported by Paul (1 Cor. 15:4-7), culminating in his own experience on the road to Damascus (1 Cor. 15:8; cf. Acts 9:1-8).

For Christians of the first generation, divine reality was mediated no longer through the temple of Jerusalem but through a living reality—the person of the risen Lord. The ancient mode of Hebraic presence was radically transformed by the experience of the resurrection. The stories of the appearances were couched in a literary form reminiscent of that of the Hebraic theophany. Stephen and Paul developed a theology of presence in which the temple ideology was applied to the spiritual body of the risen Jesus and thus, to the church. Like the prophets and psalmists of Israel, the early Christians waited for the final epiphany conceived as the *parousia.*

It is probable that the first attempts to interpret the person of Jesus were not molded by the form and content of the Messianic prophecies. The traditional figure of the Messiah may have proved to be embarrassing to the early church since it was suggestive of political, military, and racially exclusive manifestations of power. Rather, the Christians of the first generation sought to express their remembrance of Jesus in terms which they borrowed from the Hebraic theology of presence. The Messianic imagery, when applied to Jesus, was radically transformed and interpreted by the motif of cultic presence. This process of reinterpretation appears in the structure of Mark, the synoptic traditions on the Transfiguration, the birth and infancy in Luke, the sermon of Stephen in Acts, the allusions of Paul to the New Temple, the prologue to the Fourth Gospel, and the epistle to the Hebrews.

IV

A genuinely "biblical" theology may arise from a study of the Hebraic theology of presence. It should be neither a theology of the Old Testament nor a theology of the New Testament, for it has to free itself from the historically offensive approach of many traditional Christians who have tended to regard the Old Testament merely as a manual of Messianic predictions embedded within a repository of legal requirements of a racially and ritually particularistic nature.

In both its traditional and modern forms, Christianity has too often distorted the problem of the relationship between synagogue and church. Actually, the Hebrew Bible occupies a complex position in relation to Judaism as well as to Christianity. The Old Testament is not simply a Jewish book. To be sure, it was through the agency of Judaism that the books of the Hebrew Bible were collected, edited, and preserved, but Judaism did not appear in history before the Babylonian exile. As an ethnic religion, Judaism was born when the Judahites who had survived the destruction of the kingdom of Judah in 587 B.C. were transplanted to Lower Mesopotamia and elsewhere in the Babylonian Empire. Unlike the Israelites of the Northern Kingdom, who ethnically and culturally became lost in the Assyrian

Empire after 722 B.C., the Judahites resisted sociological and religious assimilation to a polytheistic culture and thus became the Jews (in Hebrew, *Yehudim,* "men of Judah," a word which came to designate the members of the exilic community and their descendants).

While it is true that most of the books of the Hebrew Bible were written down and published by exilic and postexilic Jews, the core of most of these books was still in the form of an oral—although, fixed—tradition which went back to the early days of Israel and Judah. The bulk of what became the Hebrew Bible represents the faith which created Judaism, but it is not the product of Judaism. The Jews transmitted the Hebrew Scriptures and produced the manuscripts, but their sacred library reflects Mosaic and prophetic Yahwism far more than it reflects the ritual cultus of the Second Temple. From the standpoint of its oral tradition, the Old Testament is more a Hebraic than a Jewish document, for the core of its constituent material existed in a fixed form before the birth of Judaism (sixth century B.C.).

One of the theological issues which has not yet been squarely faced by either Jews or Christians involves the problem of the relationship which binds the Hebrew Bible and post-Maccabean, rabbinical Judaism on the one hand, and the Hebrew Bible and Christianity on the other. An inquiry into the interaction of cultus and faith in ancient Hebrew religion may throw a clearer light on the dialogue between synagogue and church.

V

In a time of rapprochement between Catholic and Protestant forms of Christianity, such a study may also contribute to the development of an ecumenical theology of the Bible. It might remind the conservative wings of the Eastern Orthodox, Roman Catholic, and Anglican communions that, without the radical risk of an insecure and yet secure faith, the church is dead; and it should at the same time warn idealistic, moralistic, sentimentalist, subjectivist, and activist Protestants that faith cannot live or be maintained from generation to generation without the act of sacramental adoration.

VI

The faith of the ancient Hebrews found one of its earliest expressions in the dancing, playing, and singing of Miriam, the sister of Moses, after the passage of the Sea of Reeds (Exod. 15:21). It represents what G. van der Leeuw called "the holy play between God and man."*

The popular quatrain may thus assume a significance which extends beyond its quaintness:

> On Miriam's dance
> And Mary's grief
> Hangs all the brief
> Of Christian stance.

Although they were separated by twelve centuries, the dance of Miriam and the grief of Mary were not far apart ritually and theologically; for, when the temple was empty and Jesus was a derelict on the cross, the Hebraic motif of the elusive God developed into the Hebraic motif of the pathetic God.

The cultivation and the transmission of the faith, with its inescapable discipline of articulate thinking and moral service, springs from the central element of biblical religion, which is the elusiveness of presence in the midst of liturgical fidelity.

---

*G. van der Leeuw, *Sacred and Profane Beauty: The Holy in Art*, tr. by D. E. Green (New York, 1963), p. 265.

1

Cultus and Faith in Biblical Research

Over the past several decades, Old and New Testament scholars have stressed more than ever before the importance of cultus for the understanding of the birth of biblical religion. The complexity of the interaction which apparently operates between faith—with its theological, although poetic, formulation—and the ceremonies of worship has been the object of considerable attention on the part of biblical critics in modern times.

THREE REVOLUTIONS IN BIBLICAL SCIENCE

Not one but three revolutions have taken place in biblical science during the past hundred years, and these came about as a result of three related approaches to the interpretation of the text: literary criticism, form-critical analysis, and traditio-historical method. Present trends indicate an attempt to correlate these different approaches, as well as the emergence of varying emphases on what may be called "rhetorical exegesis," "redaction criticism," and "canonical exegesis." The combination of these factors points to the rise of a new form of biblical theology.

Literary Criticism

The first revolution occurred in the nineteenth century, when the use of literary criticism, born from the humanism of the Renaissance, destroyed the traditional views of a divinely dictated Scripture and conferred upon the literatures of Israel and of the early church a historical concreteness which had been largely unsuspected in earlier times.[1]

In 1876–77, Julius Wellhausen published a series of articles—the culmination of two centuries of meticulous research[2]—on the composition of the Hexateuch, in which he maintained that the first six books of the Bible (Pentateuch and Joshua) grew slowly over a period of five or six centuries through the selective editing of four main documents.[3] As a literary critic, Wellhausen successfully brought attention to the composite character of the Pentateuch and Joshua. As a religious historian, however, he reflected the Hegelian influence of W. Vatke (1835) and viewed Israel's religion in evolutionary terms, tracing its rise from primitive animism during the patriarchal period to lofty ethical monotheism during the exile in Babylon (sixth century B.C.). Wellhausen the critic should be differentiated from Wellhausen the historian.[4]

Moreover, some of Wellhausen's followers have refined the details of the documentary hypothesis so minutely[5] and emended the Hebrew text so freely[6] that the Wellhausen school, in all its aspects, including its literary conclusions, has fallen into disrepute. Confusion should be avoided, therefore, not only between Wellhausen the critic and Wellhausen the historian, but also between the master and the epigonists. Today, the "documentary hypothesis" in a revised form, which conjectures four strata of oral tradition rather than four written "documents," still stands.[7]

Form-Critical Analysis

The second revolution came at the beginning of the twentieth century with the use of an altered method of literary criticism known as form-critical analysis. Its principles are not basically different from those of what the French call *explication de texte*. Modern archaeology, which had been inaugurated by Bonaparte in Egypt in 1798 and Paul-Emile Botta in Mesopotamia in 1842, brought to light from the ancient Near East thousands of literary texts as well as artifacts, but it was not until 1880 or 1890 that these texts were deciphered and published in sufficient number to have an impact on biblical interpreters.

Starting in 1895, Hermann Gunkel, followed by Alfred Jeremias, Hugo Gressmann, and others, attempted to place the Old Testament literature in its newly discovered environment.[8] They did not reject the literary achievements of Wellhausen, but they insisted upon the need to supplement and correct at numerous points the method of literary criticism,[9] through the study of comparative literature and comparative religion.

By investigating Israel's epic narratives and lyric poems in the light of their Egyptian and Mesopotamian parallels, Gunkel was led to pay special attention to rhetorical forms, some of which appeared to be common to Israel and her Near Eastern neighbors. More clearly than Wellhausen,[10] he discerned that oral patterns, literary genres or formal types (*Gattungen*) had acquired a substantial stability long before they had reached a written stage. He sought to place every unit of oral tradition in a precise "situation in life" (*Sitz im Leben*), and he discovered that in almost every instance such a life situation was related to the cultus.[11]

It was in the shrines of Israel and later at the temple of Solomon in Jerusalem that the oral traditions of the Patriarchs, of the Exodus, and of the Conquest of the Land were recited and gradually fixed within the tribal and national memory.[12] Gunkel and his successors have attempted to recapture the spokenness (*Gesprochenheit*) of the biblical literature.[13] Actually, one might even refer to the "singingness" of the literature at its origin as well as in the various phases of its oral transmission, although the cantillating melodies used by the ancient Hebrews are practically lost to modern knowledge.[14] Today, various examples of the application of the method reveal that the analysis of form may not be abstractly divorced from the study of content.[15] A poet's personal intention and inspiration may no longer be brushed aside. Formal patterns do not preclude originality. Today, literary criticism and form-critical analysis are viewed as complementing and correcting each other. In addition, new interest in the dynamics of speech indicates the emergence of a method which may be called "rhetorical criticism."[16]

Traditio-Historical Method

The third revolution was brought about by Scandinavian scholars, especially Sigmund Mowinckel (1922–1924), Johannes Pedersen (1926–1940), and Ivan Engnell (1941–1945) when they initiated what is now known as the traditio-historical method of exegesis.[17] Like form-critical analysts, traditio-historical critics have sought to recapture the oral traditions of Israel which underlie the written text, and to rediscover the cultic situation which gave shape to these traditions.[18] For example, they have tried to show that the narratives of the Exodus were based on the *muthos* or cultic *legenda* of an early form of the Passover celebration,[19] while they maintained that the ethical decalogue originated as an introit ritual at the Jerusalem sanctuary.[20]

Unlike Gunkel and his direct successors, however, a number of traditio-historical exegetes have tended to disregard the results of Pentateuchal criticism and have looked at Israel's literature in its quasi-totality as the product of postexilic Judaism.[21] Furthermore, their concern for comparative religion has led them to assign primary importance to the practices and beliefs of the masses.[22] As a result, their picture of early Israel's religion has conformed largely to the pattern of ancient Near Eastern rituals.[23] At the same time, some traditio-historical critics made outstanding contributions to the study of the prophetic literature.[24] Not only the cycles of prophetic legends, from Samuel to Elisha, but also the later anthologies of prophetic discourses and poems ascribed to the so-called literary prophets were in all probability written down after years of tradition orally preserved in the shadow of a sanctuary[25] and for the purpose of cultic activity.[26] To be sure, some prophets polemicized violently against the abuse of cultus, but they always functioned within the cultic situation of a sanctuary. On the whole, both the rhetorical forms[27] they used and the content of their message reflected the ceremonial of the feasts in the kingdoms of Israel and especially Judah.[28]

Thanks to the pioneering work of Gunkel[29] and of Mowinckel,[30] the Psalter is generally viewed today as an anthology, not of lyric poems and meditations on the spiritual life, but of cultic hymns and laments which correspond closely to the various moments of the ceremonial.[31]

Besides the Psalms, other books within the Hagiographa reveal an intimate affinity with cultus. The books of Chronicles, Ezra, and Nehemiah are dominated by the concerns of the Second Temple, when the splendor of the festivals in Zion became the rallying point of Judaism.[32] It is not impossible that some of the *Megilloth,* or "Five Scrolls," which are still chanted at the feasts of modern Judaism found their oral inception in cultic activity. This appears to be the case at least for Lamentations, possibly for the Song of Songs and Ruth. Even the book of Esther, which in its present form belongs to the Hellenistic Age, probably reflects an early spring festival of the ancient Semitic world.

One may even propose that the poem of Job was first sung

and even pseudo-dramatically acted out in Babylonia during the early years of the Exile by a prophetically influenced wise man who sought to revive the faith of his fellow deportees. In an era when the autumn festival could no longer be observed ritually since temple and altar were no more, the Jobian poet experimented with a paracultic celebration in which the problem of theodicy was displaced by a theatrical representation of the New Year theophany.[33]

Proverbs and Ecclesiastes alone seem to have sprung from a noncultic environment, although the former includes fragments which partake of the hymnic form.

In brief, not only the canonizing process[34] of the three main parts of the Hebrew Bible (Law, Prophets, and Hagiographa) but also the force which led to the editing and the publishing of most of their component books depended chiefly upon the cultic factor. Such a view of the literature of the Bible has had a profound effect upon the historians of Israel's religion. It calls for a re-emphasis on canonical exegesis which sees the growth of the authoritative collections in the context of the cultic and cultural history.[35]

THE MYTH-AND-RITUAL SCHOOL

Biblical scholarship has been increasingly aware of the intricate mutuality of interaction which has linked cultus and faith in ancient Israel and early Judaism.[36] As the narratives of the dialogues between the Deity and individuals of exceptional stature like Abraham, Moses, and Jeremiah were examined in the context of the communal act of worship which preserved them, the biographical aspect of revelation through inspired men of God tended to lose its traditional significance. At the same time, two questions have continually emerged from the discussion: First, what is the origin of Hebrew cultus? Is it a sociological phenomenon which grew anonymously over the ages, or was it indeed devised by special mediators? Second, what is the nature of Hebrew ritual? Does it assume the character of a drama endowed with objective power, as in the nature cults of the ancient Near East, or should it be viewed as a eucharistic act—a rendering of thanks?

To these two questions, which are related, conflicting answers have been offered. Traditio-historical exegetes have stressed the conformity of Israel's worship to Near Eastern patterns of "myth and ritual," whereas form critics have generally maintained that Hebrew cultus—essentially a dramatic recital of *Heilsgeschichte*, or "salvation history"—was based on the memory of distinct events which took place in the nation's past.

In their efforts to go beyond the fragmentariness of the written record, traditio-historical critics have sought to reconstruct the history of the oral traditions in the light of the cultic and cultural picture of the ancient Near East. As early as 1912, Paul Volz conjectured that the worshippers of Yahweh, not unlike the devotees of Marduk in Babylon, celebrated a New Year festival,[37] although no explicit reference to such a celebration could be found in the literary documents before the time of the Exile (Ezek. 40:1). On the "day of Yahweh," the starting point of the yearly cycle, Israel hailed the epiphany of her God. The "head of the year" (*rosh ha-shanah*) was cultically inserted within the myth of creation and sacramentally identified with "the beginning" (*reshith*) of time (cf. Gen. 1:1). Yahweh was exalted above all deities in a ceremony which assumed the amplitude of a cosmic drama.

In reaction to Wellhausen, who had viewed the origin of the feasts of early Israel as purely agrarian, Volz concluded that the annual festival of Yahweh was not a harvest celebration but a historical rite held in honor of Yahweh, the warrior God.[38]

Independently of Volz, Sigmund Mowinckel formulated a strikingly similar theory a few years later.[39] On the day of the

New Year, the ark was brought to Zion in a solemn procession, and Yahweh was enthroned as King in his temple, just as Marduk was solemnly enthroned in his Babylon sanctuary.[40] Such a ritual left its traces not only in the Psalter (Ps. 132) but also in the cultic legends of Jerusalem (2 Sam. 6, 1 Kings 8).[41] When the gates of the shrine opened (Ps. 24), the divine King made his royal entrance and was ceremonially ushered toward his throne. The ritual shout "Yahweh has become king!"[42] constituted the chief response of the participants (Pss. 93, 96, 97, 99).

According to Volz and Mowinckel, the celebration of the New Year festival offers a cultic situation which explains the origin of all the myths, legends, and sagas of ancient Israel. On the occasion of "the day of Yahweh," Israel looked at her national birth in the context of the creation of the world. The New Year festival was not only the convergence point of her cultic memory, it was also the situation which provided the source of her hope. The celebration of "the day of Yahweh" was both protological and eschatological. Its liturgy called for the recapitulation and the anticipation of Yahweh's triumphs over his enemies—forces of evil in the universe and tyrants in history. Yahweh the creator was also Yahweh the heroic warrior in the past and the ultimate conqueror of all powers of disruption in the future, as well as the judge of all nations.[43]

In the light of this hypothesis, Israel's cultus should not be considered as a merely rhetorical exteriorization of a religious idea. It constitutes a technique by which an event is symbolically, hence actually, repeated, while a hope is enacted in a mimetic form ahead of its fulfillment. Cultus is a sacramental rite for the worshippers who participate in the life and power of the Deity. The worshippers receive a new existence. They are recreated.[44]

Showing in detail the "primitive" character of Hebrew psychology, Johannes Pedersen pointed out many affinities which linked the Hebrew notions of soul, blessing, peace, guilt, curse, sacrifice, atonement, etc., with those of the ancient Semites in general.[45] A few years later in Uppsala, Ivan Engnell applied a similar method to his examination of the place occupied by sacral kingship in the political and cultic life of the Western Semites,[46] especially the proto-Canaanites of Ugarit.[47]

The Scandinavian trends were closely followed or paralleled by a number of British scholars who had been influenced by anthropological studies on archaic mentality and folklore, especially those of William Robertson Smith and Sir James Frazer.[48] In 1933, Samuel H. Hooke edited a collection of essays on *Myth and Ritual*. He maintained that a cultural pattern was common to all the populations of the ancient Near East, thereby implying that the religion of the Hebrews was by no means unique.[49] Further studies in the same direction have included the notable contribution of Aubrey R. Johnson, "The Role of the King in the Jerusalem Cultus."[50] The movement was reaffirmed in Hooke's subsequent collections[51] and other volumes.[52]

The hypothesis of a ritual pattern to which all the cults of Egypt and Asia Anterior conformed for centuries was attacked from several quarters, especially by Henri Frankfort, Martin Noth, and Hans-Joachim Kraus.[53] It seems now clear that the Scandinavian and British schools have erred in stressing the primary and, at times, exclusive importance of the nature myths in Israel's worship. More specifically, the Myth-and-Ritual scholars, fascinated with the examples of cultic syncretism which abound in the biblical record,[54] seem to have paid scant attention to the cultic traditions themselves, which kept alive, not the memory of cyclical myths of nature but the recital of distinct happenings in history.[55]

The Myth-and-Ritual scholars failed to take seriously the problem created by the observable fact that Israel, unlike her Egyptian or Semitic neighbors, has always justified or explained her seasonal feasts by means of historical events, however embellished these may have become through the process of mythologizing the cultic *legenda*.[56]

THE STORY-OF-SALVATION SCHOOL

While traditio-historical exegetes conducted their examination of Semitic syncretism as it manifested itself chiefly during the times of the Judges (thirteenth to eleventh B.C.) and of the Monarchy (eleventh to sixth centuries B.C.), the school of Gunkel went on to investigate the growth of the literary sources of the Pentateuch and the form of the oral traditions which apparently stood behind them.

In 1934, Albrecht Alt analyzed the numerous laws which are now incorporated in the Pentateuch;[57] he distinguished between two types of legal material: casuistic jurisprudence, on the one hand, which grew out of collections of judiciary precedents,[58] and apodictic law, on the other hand, which is clearly independent of trial courts and associated with sanctuary ceremonial.[59] Alt was led to identify the cultic setting of the apodictic law with the seven-year celebration of the feast of the Tabernacles (*Sukkoth*), when "all Israel"—that is, the representatives of all the tribes assembled together—renewed their covenant with Yahweh.[60]

Instead of stressing, with Volz and Mowinckel, the exclusive significance of a hypothetical New Year with the rite of Yahweh's enthronment, form critics of the Alt school, particularly Gerhard von Rad[61] and Martin Noth,[62] conjectured the existence of a national ceremony during which the memories of Israel's origins were ritually reenacted, or at least recited, and were thus transformed into a liturgical present.[63]

According to this view, it was the twelve-tribe league, periodically gathered "in the presence of Yahweh" for the celebration of the feast which provided the situation in life needed for the articulation of the clan sagas into a unified epic.

As von Rad has shown,[64] the liturgy of the harvest thanksgiving in all probability represents the earliest stage of Israel's adaptation to an agrarian culture.[65] This liturgy reveals the

Hebrew concern, not for the mythical fertility of the soil, but for the intervention of Yahweh in history:

> My father was a nomadic Aramaean, exhausted from wandering and ready to perish.[66] And he went down to Egypt and sojourned there. And he became a great nation, powerful and populous. And the Egyptians dealt with us in an evil way, and they afflicted us and laid upon us hard labor. And we cried unto Yahweh, the God of our fathers, and Yahweh heard our voice, and he saw our affliction, and our toil, and our oppression; and Yahweh brought us forth out of Egypt with a mighty hand, and with an outstretched arm, and with great terribleness, and with signs, and with wonders. And he brought us into this place, and gave us this land, a land flowing with milk and honey. And now, behold, I have brought the first fruit of the soil, which thou, O Yahweh, hast given me! (Deut. 26:5–10).

The changes of pronouns in this archaic prayer reveal the most characteristic element of Hebrew cultus. The historical past is made present through the ritual act and its chanted formula (*hieros logos*). In addition, the numinous powers of the soil are not in the slightest way deified (as they were in the Canaanite cult). The motivation of the act of worship is pure gratitude. The Deity is acknowledged as the sovereign Lord of history as well as of nature.[67]

It is possible that this historical credo served as a nucleus for the elaborate "salvation history" (*Heilsgeschichte*) which articulated in consecutive order several clan traditions regarding the *Gesta Dei per Hebraeos* that were recited at various shrines and feasts.[68] While von Rad concluded that the Exodus traditions were originally unrelated to those of the Sinai theophany, studies of the Hittite treaties and other legal documents from the regions of the Upper Euphrates[69] have thrown new light on the Hebraic covenant formulae.[70] They have also led to the conclusion that the Exodus narratives of deliverance from Egypt were not originally separate from the cultic *legenda* of the covenant theophany.[71]

According to recent research, Israel's cultus, unlike that of other nations of the Near East, was both motivated and shaped by the memory of historical events. Mythical motifs, when they appeared at all, were used only as a poetic mode of describing the events and relating their significance to a theological framework of cosmic creation. This seems to have been the case, significantly, in the *legenda* of the Sea of Reeds.[72] The earliest traditions of the Pentateuch did not historicize nature myths. On the contrary, they used—and sparingly—a number of mythical features in describing historical events. From the start, nature was demythologized by a theology of transcendence over the natural elements.[73] The God who gave birth to Israel in history was the same Yahweh who controlled the world. His historical activity could therefore be described in terms of creative activity.[74]

Form-critical exegetes of the Salvation–History school may well have been correct when they concluded that the festival of the covenant was already celebrated during the slow infiltration of the Hebrews through the high valleys of Canaan (thirteenth to twelfth centuries),[75] and that it constituted the primary force in the process of preserving, organizing, and shaping the memories of Israel's origins, beginning with the patriarchal sojourns in the land and concluding with the institution of the twelve-tribe league at Shechem.[76] Such a view implies the historicity of a cultural and cultic disruption in the time of the ancestors, at a given moment of history. It indicates that the fathers renounced, through one act or several acts of decision, the nature rites which prevailed among the Western Semites in the second millenium B.C. It calls for the reasonable assumption that the specifically Hebraic form of a "God-in-history" cultus had a historical beginning.[77] Significantly, the traditions concerning the patriarchs offer a sequence of cultic *legenda* which precisely depict such a cultural disruption and such a cultic innovation. More significantly still, all these cultic *legenda* possess two elements in common: They are anchored in stories of epiphanic visitations to the fathers, and they culminate in the traditions of Moses and of the Sinai theophany.

It would thus appear that the memories of the covenant at Sinai, important as they may have been in developing Israel's sense of historical destiny and in conferring upon her the awareness of being "a holy nation" (Exod. 19:6), were in turn dependent upon a prior reality—the impact of the "perception" of divine presence on the motivation of the fathers.

MODERN TECHNIQUES OF NEW TESTAMENT INTERPRETATION

In several ways, New Testament research has been parallel to that of the Hebrew Bible, since both of them grew out of the concern which Renaissance humanists and Protestant reformers had shown for the authenticity, origin, composition, and meaning of the biblical documents.

Literary criticism of the gospels, however, received its modern impetus chiefly in reaction to the rationalistic caricatures of Jesus.[78] The problem of the Synoptic Gospels had long been known to interpreters, but the matter of their similarities, differences, and contradictions became the object of intensive investigation.[79] Since the middle of the nineteenth century, the majority of literary critics have subscribed to the hypothesis of Mark's anteriority, of an additional common source to both Matthew and Luke and of the specific traditions peculiar to each of them.[80]

As in the case of the Pentateuch, gospel criticism was at first largely confined to the search for sources, but the method of form-critical analysis, introduced fifty years ago by Martin Dibelius[81] and Rudolph Bultmann,[82] has attempted to recapture the oral tradition which linked the life of Jesus to the writing of the documents.[83] Investigation of other New Testament books, especially the Johannine Gospel and the Apocalypse, has shown the determining part which synagogue and church worship has played in the growth not only of the gospels but also of most of the early Christian literature.[84]

Literary criticism, form-critical analysis, and traditio-historical criticism continue to be used jointly, and the revival of interest in redaction criticism points to the continuous need for an articulate interpretation of the growth of theological thinking among the Christians of the New Testament times.

COVENANT AND PRESENCE IN THE HISTORY OF BIBLICAL RELIGION

Religion is far too complex a social and individual phenomenon to be reduced to a single principle of determining forces.[85] It is especially precarious to speak of "biblical religion." On the one hand, many rites and beliefs were inherited, although radically transformed, from the ancient Near East.[86] On the other hand, the "religion" of the Hebrews, the Israelites, the Judahites, the postexilic Jews, and the early Christians evolved significantly in the course of twelve centuries under changing conditions of economics, technology, sociology, politics, and culture in general.[87]

The word "biblical" itself is ambiguous, for, although both Jews and Christians hold a common allegiance to the Hebrew Bible, they do not derive from it the same interpretation of life, of the world, or of religion. Jews have usually read the Torah, the Prophets, and the Hagiographa (*Tanak*) chiefly through the lenses of the Talmud, while Christians have traditionally approached what they call "the Old Testament" in the light of "the New Testament."

The expression "the Old Testament," which represents an abbreviation of the title, "The books of the Old Covenant," has a Christian origin of a relatively late date.[88] It was because

Christians of the first generation, perhaps following the example of the Jewish sectarians of Qumran,[89] thought of themselves as a people waiting for "the new covenant" announced by the prophet Jeremiah[90] that they came to refer to Israel as the people of the old covenant.[91]

While the first-century church, with the possible exception of the author of the epistle to the Hebrews,[92] spoke of the new covenant in eschatological terms,[93] medieval and modern Christendom generally settled down in a mood of "realized eschatology." The expression "the new covenant" lost the sharpness of its futurity and came to designate a *fait accompli*. The era of the new covenant was identified with the Christian dispensation of the divine economy within temporal history.[94] The era of the old covenant was therefore associated with the earlier and obsolete period of divine concern for ancient Israel. This attitude displays a certain amount of Christian presumption which is understandably offensive to modern Judaism.[95]

Recent studies on the importance of the covenant in Hebrew religion have been useful, but there is now an urgent need to go beyond them. Significant as the covenant ritual certainly was for ancient Israel at critical moments in her history and for Judaism at the birth of its hierocratic structure under Ezra in the fourth century B.C., this motif alone cannot provide an adequate principle either for grasping the complexity of Israel's cultus and faith during the centuries of their organic growth or for producing a coherent account of the emergence of Christianity.[96]

1. The diversity of Israel's responses to the sense of her historical destiny from the time of her national origin to the dawn of the church explodes the notion of *the* Hebrew covenant conceived as a single and homogeneous rite or ideology. There are at least two distinct and contradictory theologies of the covenant in Hebrew religion.[97]

First, the Sinai convenant, mediated under Moses,[98] and renewed at Shechem under Joshua,[99] was conditional upon national behavior and was therefore historical and nonmythical. Its validity was dependent upon the cultic and ethical obedience of the people as they moved through history.[100] Its Deuteronomic recasting led to the reform of Josiah in Jerusalem (622 B.C.). It was the Josianic ceremony of covenant renewal (2 Kings 22:1—23:24) which sharpened the conditional character of the covenant and emphasized its historical relativity. The Sinai covenant was endowed with conditionality and historicality.[101]

Secondly, the Davidic covenant, although rooted in the Hebron traditions on Abraham,[102] reflected the Canaanite ideology of divine kingship and the Jebusite myth of the navel of the earth at Jerusalem.[103] In contrast to the Sinai convenant as represented by the early traditions and the great prophets, the Davidic covenant was related to a monarch and his dynasty. It was endowed with a quality of unconditional and eternal validity and was therefore of a suprahistorical and mythical character.[104]

In the exilic age, the Sinai covenant was reinterpreted in the light of the Davidic covenant,[105] and it became in its turn an unconditional, eternal, and mythical reality which extended to the people of Israel as a whole.[106] The self-understanding of Judaism as an eternal people is to be traced less to the Sinai covenant of the early traditions than to the Davidic covenant. It partakes of Canaanite mythology rather than Yahwistic theology.

2. While there are explicit allusions to covenant in the Hebrew Bible and in the writings of the early church, covenant consciousness did not apparently dominate the preoccupations of the religious leaders of Israel, except Joshua in the twelfth century, Josiah in the seventh, and Ezra in the fourth. Outside of Deuteronomy and a few psalms[107] among the many devoted to the Jerusalem cultus and the Davidic monarchy,—the men-

tion of covenant is quite sporadic in the preexilic literature. The word is practically absent from Amos, Isaiah, Micah, Habakkuk, Zephaniah, and Nahum, although it is found in the traditions concerning Elijah and in the poems of Hosea.[108] In spite of the Deuteronomic reform,[109] it plays a relatively minor part in Jeremiah, Ezekiel, and Second Isaiah, except in an eschatological sense.[110]

Though the message of the prophets of the eighth and seventh centuries was predicated on the conviction that the Sinai covenant had been violated, and though many of their speeches reflect the structural patterns of covenant formulation, the thrust of their religious passion and the source of their interpretation of history lay elsewhere. They were grasped by the presence of Yahweh and they were animated by the dynamics of his word.[111]

The sapiential literature assigned no role whatever to the ideology of the covenant. The court officials and other artists in royal wisdom at Jerusalem appeared to have taken the Davidic covenant for granted. Neither covenant thinking nor covenant ceremonial belonged to the realm of their intellectual or spiritual interests.[112]

The Apocrypha and Pseudepigrapha practically ignored the notion.[113] The Dead Sea Scrolls passed it by, although the Damascus Document made limited use of it.[114] The Rabbinical Literature hardly mentioned it.[115] Outside of one saying that found its way into a textual tradition of the Lukan Account of the Last Supper, the covenant is entirely absent from the Synoptic traditions of the teaching of Jesus, and it plays a merely accessorial part in the preaching and writing of the early Christians.[116]

In brief, to explain Israel's religion or the birth of the church in terms of covenant is to ignore (a) its absence from a large part of the Bible, and (b) the pluralism of covenant interpretations in Israel, early Judaism, and even primitive Christianity.

3. To look at covenant as the determining factor of continuity from Hebraism to Christianity is also to confuse the means with the end, for the rite and ideology of covenant are dependent upon the prior reality of presence. The goal of Hebraic worship is to remember and to anticipate the *kairos* of the divine encounter, and the essence of the ancient feasts is to celebrate the *mo'ed* or "moment"—either past or future—of the divine manifestation of proximity. The aim of Hebrew faith is to live now on the strength of the promises made by Yahweh to the fathers and to act in full expectation of the final epiphany. At best, the ritual and legal structure of covenant offers a tool, original and effective as it may be,[117] by which the recollection and the hope of the presence are mediated to the rank and file of the people and transmitted to posterity from generation to generation.

4. Finally, to speak of Israel's religion as that of the old covenant reflects an unconscious adherence to the patristic and medieval bias of theological anti-Semitism. To present the birth of the church as a function of the new covenant is to confuse eschatological hope with real-estate appropriation, promise with earthly possession, and vocation with presumed prerogative. It is to ignore the survival of Judaism for the past nineteen centuries and to brush aside the mystery of Israel in history.

5. To be sure, the significance of the intensive research which has taken place on the covenant motif in recent decades should not in any way be underestimated, for it was indeed in the context of covenant memorial and covenant hope that prophets and psalmists expressed their faith in the purpose of creation and formulated their theology of history.[118] At critical moments of the nation's life, it was through the covenant renewal ceremonies of Joshua, Josiah, and Ezra that Israel, Judah, and early Judaism respectively maintained their sense of continuity. The covenant ritual enabled them to overcome un-

precedented and disruptive situations of political extremity.[119] Nevertheless, the covenant ritual or ideology fails to explain the specificity of Israel's religion among the cults of the ancient Near East or the peculiar quality of the Christian gospel within the religious syncretism of the Mediterranean world at the dawn of the Roman empire. Although the distinctiveness of biblical religion may not be affirmed without qualification, Israel stood obstinately apart from her environment on at least one score: She entertained a unique theology of presence. She knew that her God was always free from the human techniques of ritual or moral manipulation. She conceived the presence of that God to be elusive and unpredictable. Whatever may have been the fascination of the nature cults practiced by her masses and even by her ruling classes in most periods of her history,[120] a spiritual elite in her midst always maintained a standard of faith. It was this standard of faith which distinguished Israel's religion from the religions of her neighbors.

The cults of antiquity offer many close parallels to the religion of Israel, but a basic difference stands out between them. The epiphanies of the gods in the ancient Near East and in classical antiquity imply a deification of the forces of nature, of human desires, of tribal or national needs for economic survival and political stability, and of the dynastic drive for imperial conquest. Such a process appears in Mesopotamia,[121] in Egypt,[122] in Syria-Phoenicia-Canaan,[123] in Iran,[124] and later in Greece and Rome.[125] Cosmogonies were in effect theogonies and therefore suggested the finite character of the godhead. Either the gods and goddesses did not transcend the temporality of the natural forces or else they were identified with a universe viewed as eternal.[126] The pluralism of the deities reveals a fragmentariness of the prevailing world views or appears to have been related to some form of determinism to which the gods themselves were subject.[127]

In Israel, on the contrary, while anthropocentric concerns were not altogether absent, natural space and historical time remained utterly dependent upon a free sovereign, whose transcendence was never divorced from a "pathetic" concern for the welfare of human and even animal life.[128] The knowledge of this free and sovereign God[129] informs Israel's standard of faith. It promotes her ideal of peoplehood and is the main source of her ethics. Such knowledge stems from a single factor: the Hebraic theology of presence.[130]

The religion of the Hebrews, of Israel, of postexilic Judaism, and of the early Christians is permeated by the experience, the cultic recollection, and the proleptically appropriated expectation of the presence of Yahweh among men.[131] At the same time, the Hebraic traditions—and indeed the entire literature of the Bible—portray the Deity as coming to man, not man as commanding the appearance of the Deity.[132] It is Yahweh, in the myth of the Garden, who asks man, "Where art thou?" (Gen. 3:9). Similarly, the legend of Cain and Abel introduces the abrupt question, "Where is thy brother Abel?" (Gen. 4:9). Divine intervention in human affairs is generally, if not exclusively, represented as sudden, unexpected, unwanted, unsettling, and often devastating.[133] The feature of divine disruption is typical of all literary genres in all periods of biblical history. It appears in the primeval *legenda* (e.g., Noah, Gen. 6:13), in the patriarchal saga of epiphanic visitations (e.g., Abraham, Gen. 12:1 ff.), in the national epic of theophanies to Moses (e.g., Exod. 3:1 ff.), in the visions of the great prophets (e.g., Amos, 7:15), in the psalms (e.g., Ps. 139:7), in Job's pleas (e.g., 23:3 ff.), in the Jobian theophany from the whirlwind (Job 38:1 ff.), and in the synoptic traditions on the appearances of the risen Lord (e.g., Mark 16:11 *et par.*). Biblical man is always "surprised by God."

Moreover, for fifteen centuries the recurrent motif of divine nearness is historically limited to a few men. The sense of presence is persistently compounded with an awareness of absence.[134] The prophets, the psalmists, and the poet of Job often allude to their sense of isolation, not only from the community of men but also from the proximity of God. Theophanies of the heroic past are not repeated.[135] Prophetic visions are few and far between. Even within the life span of special men of God, like Abraham, Moses, and the prophets, the immediacy of the Godhead is experienced only for a few fleeting instants. "The presence" as well as "the word" was rare in biblical days.

The record shows that instances of awareness of an immediate encounter with the divine reality not only were extremely brief but also appear to have been the privilege of an extremely restricted elite. What sort of access did the average Israelite or Judahite have to the presence of Deity? As a member of the cultic community, he believed in the real presence of Yahweh at a shrine, he rehearsed the memorial of Yahweh's *magnalia* during the celebration of the seasonal feasts, and he expected—nay, he experienced liturgically and proleptically—the final epiphany of history, when Yahweh would at last bring creation to fulfillment, renew the earth, and unite mankind into a family of nations. A cultic form of presence was sacramentally available. A God who remained historically absent manifested his proximity to the average man through cultic communion.

A similar development took place among the Jews who became the earliest Christians in the first century A.D. The presence of Yahweh—*Adonay, Ho Kyrios, the Lord*—became manifest for them in the person of Jesus of Nazareth, but they would not have been able to formulate this new theology of presence without the shattering impact of their faith in the risen Jesus as "Lord."[136] In the light of the teaching of their master, they radically transformed their expectation of a political messiah. They accomplished this revolution by interpreting the messianic hope in the light of the figure of the Suffering Servant in Second Isaiah. Through the mythopoetic ideology of royal, prophetic, and priestly sonship, they evolved a new concept of messiahship. They emptied the old notion of messiah of its popular connotation as a military and thaumaturgical power, which was held especially by the Zealots, and endowed it with the virtue of universal love.[137] Thus reinterpreted, the name could be applied to the person of the crucified and risen Jesus. The Greek-speaking Jews who accepted the gospel of the living Lord were thus able to speak of "the Christ" not only in terms of their eschatological hope but also in the light of their present experience of divine communion.[138]

Because the visions of the appearances of the living Lord were restricted to a few moments in the lives of a small group of men and women, and eventually ceased altogether,[139] the nascent church survived the initial crisis of divine absence through her apprehension of a new form of presence. Various motifs came into play. Some interpreted that presence in terms of "the indwelling spirit"; others spoke of "being in Christ."[140] Still others borrowed the themes of personified wisdom and personified word.[141] Nevertheless, it was the Hebraic theology of presence which dominated all the interpretations of the person of Jesus, from Mark to Revelation.

The Hebraic theology of presence provides the structure of the Markan gospel,[142] the culmination of Stephen's sermon on the temple,[143] the "self-asseverative formula" ("I am the Lord") in Saul's vision on the Damascus road,[144] Paul's description of the church as the temple of God,[145] the Lukan legenda on the Annunciation,[146] the Johannine prologue on the "word encamped as in a tent",[147] the typology of the epistle to the Hebrews,[148] and the allegory of the new Jerusalem in the book of Revelation.[149] It is the same theology of cultic presence, bringing together in the liturgical present the memory of the magnalia dei and the expectation of the day of Yahweh, which undergirds the eucharistic meal of the early church; for the memory of the last supper is bound to the awaiting of the parousia.[150]

The cultic theophany of ancient Israel was thus reenacted in a new rite which brought together the figure of the historical Jesus and the proleptical experience of the final epiphany. The birth of the church lies not in the reinterpretation of the notion of messiahship but in the appropriation of the temple ideology in the context of the risen Lord.

It is the Hebraic theology of presence, not the covenant ceremonial, that constitutes the field of forces which links— across the biblical centuries—the fathers of Israel, the reforming prophets, the priests of Jerusalem, the psalmists of Zion, the Jobian poet, and the bearers of the gospel. The history of biblical religion hinges upon the growth and transformation of the Hebraic theology of presence.

THE QUEST FOR A BIBLICAL THEOLOGY

In the face of the multiplicity of rituals and beliefs represented in the Bible, many scholars have restricted their endeavors to describing the religious phenomena which have received literary formulation. Recent interpreters have therefore tended to present only the history of the religion of Israel and the history of primitive Christianity. Even writers of an Old Testament theology, like Gerhard von Rad,[151] or of a theology of the New Testament, like Rudolf Bultmann,[152] have stressed the plurality of theological responses within Scripture rather than run the risk of distorting historical complexity through oversimplification.

At the same time, it is not possible to ignore the place the Bible has occupied for centuries—and still occupies today—at the heart of both Judaism and Christianity. The books of the Hebrew Bible for Judaism[153] and of both the Old Testament and the New for Christianity[154] exerted an inward stimulus and a power of restraint on faith long before these writings received recognition of authority by synagogue or church. It was neither the synagogue nor the church which initially decreed that Scripture was to be the rule of faith and order or "the Word of God."[155] Rather, the books of the Hebrew Bible and of the New Testament imposed themselves upon Jews and Christians as the regulating standard of their religious commitment and ethical behavior. *Canon* was originally not a dogmatic structure imposed from without by institutionalized collectivities but an unspoken force which grew from within the nature of Hebrew-Christian religion.[156] The obligations of the Sinai covenant were remembered as the "torah" of Yahweh, a growing collection of instructions which were inserted within the context of the narratives of the Sinai theophany. Thus, the cultic *anamnesis* of the event during which the divine presence disclosed itself to the people through the mediation of Moses prepared and promoted the development of the canon.[157] The idea of the canonicity of a "scripture" was a *fait accompli* when a written document was found in the temple of Jerusalem in 622 B.C. and led to the reform of Josiah and the renewal of the Sinai covenant (2 Kings 22:1 ff.). The "book of the law" (approximately Deut. 12:1—26:19) became the nucleus of "the Bible" (*ta biblia*, "the books") because Huldah the prophetess found it conformed to the living word of the Deity (2 Kings 22:13 ff.) Canonicity went back to the cultic memories of the Sinai-Horeb theophany. It is significant that the final edition of the Deuteronomic law opened with a cultic rehearsal of those memories (Deut. 1:1 ff.) in which the motif of covenant is subordinated to the story of theophanic presence (Deut. 5:2–4).

Likewise, it appears that the letters of Paul, which constituted the original nucleus of the New Testament, were circulated throughout the churches of the Mediterranean world and they were read ceremonially at the paracultic celebrations of nascent Christendom, side by side with the portions of the Law and the Prophets traditionally appointed for the sabbath service and the festivals. Canonicity imposed itself from within, little by little, in the context of the Christian community at worship.

The inwardness of scriptural canonicity and of its growth in the course of several centuries suggests that a certain homogeneity of theological depth binds the biblical books together beneath the heterogeneity of their respective dates, provenances, styles, rhetorical forms, purposes, and contents. The search for the principle of this homogeneity which spanned a considerable period of time points to the dynamic aspect of a continuity of religious aim rather than to a static unity of doctrinal conformity.[158]

As soon as the historian of the Hebrew-Christian religion seeks to determine the nature of this continuity, he goes beyond a merely phenomenological description of rites and beliefs. He does not disregard on that account the historical fluidity of their origin and growth, but he asks the question of the possibility, the legitimacy, and perhaps even the inevitability of biblical theology.

The disrepute in which this discipline is held in some quarters depends on several factors, one of which is the hostile attitude which many biblical theologians of the past century displayed against modern methods of literary and historical criticism. Another of these factors is related to the denominationalism which has colored not a few treatises of biblical theology in which one or another of the scriptural themes was enlisted as the ancillary justification of a dogma peculiar to an individual church, sect, or tradition.

Ironically, the idea of a "biblical theology" originated as a reaction of the Pietists against the scholastic Lutheranism of the eighteenth century.[159] In 1787, in an academic discourse now well-known,[160] Johann-Philip Gabler assigned the "new" discipline with the task of describing in historical sequence the thoughts and feelings of the sacred authors "concerning divine things." Gabler's intention was chiefly to obtain for biblical interpreters a freedom of inquiry from the dogmatic theology of his time. The new discipline, however, fell almost immediately under the spell of the age of the enlightenment. Most treatises published in the nineteenth century under such titles as *Biblical Theology, Old Testament Theology,* and *New Testament Theology* were systematic presentations of the ideas of the Bible on God, man, sin, and salvation.[161]

It is now recognized that such attempts, inherited in part from Platonic conceptual thinking and Aristotelian logic, were bound to translate the *sui generis* thrust of biblical faith into the alien idiom of didactic exposition. Many interpreters have therefore questioned the legitimacy of the discipline of biblical theology.

At the dawn of the twentieth century, the vast majority of scholars restricted themselves to composing essays on the history of the Hebrew religion, the "life" of Jesus, and the "religious experience" of the early church, especially that of Paul. The discipline of biblical theology entered into an eclipse. The concern for *historicism,* on the one hand, and the revival of the Marcionite prejudice against the Hebrew Bible, on the other, introduced the fashion of an atomistic approach to the study of Scripture. Harnack even proposed the "removal" of the Old Testament from the Christian canon.[162]

A new era began during the First World War. In 1920, Rudolf Kittel spoke of the "future of Old Testament science"[163] and urged the rediscovery of the significance of the entire Bible for the religious thinking of modern man. Quite independently of Karl Barth's thunderous proclamation of the Bible as the "Word of God,"[164] a few exegetes who had been trained in the rigors of the critical method slowly assumed a new stance. While they refused to serve the interests of a particular church tradition, and retained intact their respect for the scientific approach, they moved away from a position of analytical compartmentalism and antiquarian remoteness, and they sought to restate in modern terms the meaning of the Bible for contemporary theologians.

In 1926, Johannes Hempel published *God and Man in the Old Testament*, in which he attempted to stress those features of the faith "which came from God and led to God, and which also lead us to God."[165] The same year, Otto Eissfeldt sensed the need to build a new bridge between the religious history of Israel and the theological significance of the Old Testament.[166] In 1929, Walther Eichrodt put squarely the question, "Does the Old Testament theology still have an independent significance within Old Testament studies?"[167] During the following decade, Eichrodt brought out his monumental three-volume *Old Testament Theology,*[168] for which he used the tools of modern research and at the same time sought to discover in the covenant the principle of coherence for the understanding of the Old Testament in its entirety.

Eichrodt's treatment was thorough, incisive, and in many places original. It is still indispensable after a whole generation of further study. Nevertheless, a "pan-covenant" approach to Old Testament theology overlooks the multi-faceted complexity of Hebrew religion.[169] In the ten centuries covered by biblical literature, the importance of the covenant motif was only sporadic. In addition, the wisdom books[170] by and large ignore covenant ideology. This omission is the more remarkable when it is remembered that sapiential circles in Jerusalem during the monarchy were closely related to the royal court and might have been expected to pay strict attention to the theological significance of the Davidic covenant.[171] A covenant-centered interpretation of Old Testament thinking on God and man necessarily underplays the significance of Hebrew wisdom.[172]

In spite of its limitations, Eichrodt's work proved to be the chief incentive for numerous reappraisals of the issues involved in the elaboration of an Old Testament theology.[173] In 1946, H. Wheeler Robinson laid down the principles for a new Old Testament theology which would adequately discover in the historical traditions of Israel the locus of revelation.[174] E. Jacob, Th. C. Vriezen, and G. E. Wright—each in his own style and with his own emphasis—have persuasively presented the dynamic aspect of the self-disclosure of Yahweh in the context of the Hebrew epic traditions.[175]

In 1957, G. von Rad called for an abrupt change of approach. In his two-volume *Old Testament Theology*,[176] he undertook to discern the theological significance of the Hebrew Bible not so much in the sequential continuity of a theological theme in the history of Israel's religion as in the constant revising and reformulating of the creedal confessions in the light of historical change. Although von Rad's achievement remains to this day epoch-making, it cannot justify the title *Old Testament Theology*, for the dichotomy between the theologies of the confessional reinterpretations, on the one hand, and the theologies of the responses of the psalmists, the prophets, and the wisemen, on the other, has not been successfully overcome, nor has a principle of theological homogeneity capable of accounting for the growth of the Hebrew Bible been convincingly elucidated. Neither Eichrodt nor von Rad has discovered within Old Testament religion that organic and specific element which not only points to the gospel of Jesus and the early church but also leads inevitably to the New Testament.[177]

While Eichrodt and von Rad were carrying out this work, intensive research was being undertaken among interpreters on the interrelation between faith and history.[178] G. E. Wright looked for the principle of biblical continuity in the activity of Yahweh as creator, Lord, and warrior;[179] B. S. Childs tended to stress the importance of the community pattern as a vehicle of divine intervention within history.[180] Others have discussed the purposes and methods of Old Testament theology in the light of contemporary trends;[181] G. Fohrer, especially, has proposed that at the center of Old Testament faith lies neither the covenant ideology nor the concept of community but the motif of divine presence, now and on the last day.[182]

The quest for an authentically "biblical" theology is being renewed more actively than ever before,[183] and there are signs that the present generation of New Testament scholarship no longer works in isolation from Old Testament science. Like their Old Testament colleagues, New Testament critics have been interested for many years in history rather than in the theological significance of Scripture. In 1897, W. Wrede reduced the task of "the so-called New Testament Theology" to the historical description of early Christianity.[184] While treatments of a New Testament theology conceived as a system of doctrinal ideas continued to appear,[185] the discipline was no longer the concern of modern exegetes, although a few of them refused to reduce the New Testament either to a series of historical sketches or to a merely didactic exposition.

As early as 1885, A. Schlatter clearly discerned that the thought of Jesus and the apostles was inseparable from their faith and ethics.[186] A generation later, when the impact of the comparative history of religions convinced the students of primitive Christianity that the New Testament documents could not be interpreted in isolation from the sects and the cults of the Mediterranean world, W. Bousset assigned to the ceremonial worship of the Christian communities a major part in the formulation and the transmission of the gospel.[187] In the light of the subsequent discoveries made on the Hellenistic mystery cults, Gnostic groups, and especially the Jewish sectarians of Qumran, many historians of the early church have stressed the need to revise long-standing attitudes concerning the neglected discipline of New Testament theology.[188]

In the meantime, Rudolf Bultmann drew out the theological consequences of his form-critical analysis of the gospel tradition. His *New Testament Theology*,[189] the culmination of many years of exegetical research, is comparable in its field to the masterpieces of Eichrodt and von Rad in the field of Old Testament theology. The considerable achievements of Bultmann are marred by his inability to see the organic affinities which link the faith of Jesus and the early Christians to the theological thrust of Hebraism rather than the speculations of popular Judaism.

With respect to the Old Testament, Bultmann proved to be a neo-Harnackian.[190] In addition, he failed to appreciate the historical foundations of the Christian *muthos*. He did not ask seriously whether the faith in the resurrection of Jesus and later in his virgin birth might not be indissolubly related to, and organically dependent upon, the historical reality of his personality as well as his teaching.[191] He relegated the sayings and the ministry of Jesus to the Jewish background of New Testament theology, as if the faith of the early church had suddenly emerged of itself as a new and particular *gnosis*. While his presentations of Paulinism and Johannism possess qualities of exceptional incisiveness, his theological understanding of the New Testament is largely reduced to anthropological and psychological concerns. Through an exegetical and philosophical *tour de force*, Bultmann has succeeded in eradicating the transcendental dimension of justification by faith.

In a laudable effort to be relevant to the cultural chaos that followed Nazism and the Second World War, Bultmann excessively reacted against the very excesses of historicism, but he undermined and almost negated the historical foundation of New Testament faith. By demythologizing the Christian kerygma, he paradoxically de-historicized the humanity of Jesus and the concreteness of the faith of the early church. Ironically, in transforming New Testament theology into an anthropology of existential self-understanding, he failed to grasp the existential involvement of the church in the political, moral, and cultural realities of history.

A powerful corrective to Bultmann's Marcionic and docetic

tendencies was provided by Oscar Cullmann's insistence on the biblical reality of time.[192] For him Christian faith is centered less on an existential discovery of self-awareness than on a cultic participation in salvation history. He does not deny that faith requires an existential decision, but he maintains that such a decision is always founded upon the certainty that "a divine history" unfolds in the universe and across the generations of men.[193] Christian existence takes place between the "already" and the "not yet" of an eschatological hope which is at once past and future.[194] Cullmann's stress on the interpenetration of *Heilsgeschichte* and eschatological expectation has inspired intensive research concerning faith and history.[195]

In the meantime, biblical theologians have been led to work more closely with the systematic theologians and the philosophers of language in raising the issue of hermeneutics.[196] The distinction between biblical theology, a historical discipline which seeks to elucidate the meaning of the Bible itself, and systematic theology, which attempts to translate biblical dynamics of faith and cultus into the contemporary idiom, needs to be carefully preserved.[197] Biblical theologians are increasingly aware of the relativity of historical research and of the dangers of *historicism*. They recognize the need of becoming critically explicit regarding their epistemological presuppositions, and they constantly remind themselves of their own limitations in attempting to penetrate scriptural meaning and to remain faithful to that meaning while seeking to translate it into the language of the cultural world view of the twentieth century. In addition, they know that to assume their proper responsibility toward the work of systematic theologians, they must perform the "descriptive task" of biblical theology, as it has been called,[198] in a way which goes beyond the mere cataloguing of the mythopoetic formulations of the biblical documents, from the Yahwist epic in the tenth century B.C. to the Johannine Apocalypse at the end of the first century A.D.

By their parallel insistence on *Heilsgeschichte,* biblical theologians like Eichrodt, Vriezen, Jacob, von Rad, Cullmann, and Wright have offered a platform for further research.[199] The warnings of Ebeling on the problematic character of theological coherence within each Testament deserve scrupulous attention,[200] but the arguments that he directed against the unity of the Bible have now lost their sharpness, for contemporary discussion no longer attempts to expound biblical "ideas." It centers on the dynamic continuity of biblical fields of force.[201] Furthermore, general agreement has been reached on Ebeling's plea to understand Scripture in the context of the ancient Near Eastern and Mediterranean cultures, with special emphasis on the extracanonical literature of Judaism in Hellenistic, Hasmonean, and Roman times.[202]

Above all, the very use of the word "theology" in connection with the Bible requires critical scrutiny. Going beyond Ebeling's challenge,[203] the biblical theologian will refuse to apply the word *theo-logia* to the content of the Bible as if it were still overloaded with connotations that are either patristic, medieval, scholastic, or Tridentine on the one hand, or Protestant, modernist, and postexistential on the other. Instead he will seek to discover the biblical meaning of the notion which the Greek term *theo-logia* fails to convey. Plato and Aristotle employed it in the sense of "science of divine things."[204] Quite differently, the Hebraic expression *da'at Elohim,* "knowledge of God," points to a reality which at once includes and transcends intellectual disquisition. It designates the involvement of man's total personality in the presence of Yahweh through the prophetic word, the cultic celebration, and the psychological mode of communion in faith.[205] In the Hebraic sense of "knowledge of God," theology does not mean an objective science of divine things. Although it uses the critical faculties of the mind, it proceeds both from an inner commitment to a faith and from a participation in the destiny of a people which transcends the national and racial particularities of the times.

Theology in this sense implies the dedication of the self, its orientation toward the demands of a specific vocation, and its acceptance of a corresponding mode of living. At its highest level, it aims at promoting a stability of faith independent of the normal fluctuations of the human character, and at facilitating a transmission of that faith to the next generation. It is based on the cultic commemoration of presence and the cultic expectancy of its renewal. It is nurtured by the celebration of presence in the midst of the community of faith which extends from the theophanic past to the epiphanic end of history.[206]

Not on account of an editorial accident of juxtaposition but through a conscious intent which reveals a theological grasp have the Deuteronomists made the *Shema'* ("Hear, O Israel, Yahweh thy God, Yahweh is one") inseparable from the invitation to love God. In the words of Israel's creed (Deut. 6:6 ff.), faith in Yahweh means love of Yahweh, first with the whole of one's mind (*lebh*), second with the whole of one's living being, its instinctual drives and its persistence in selfhood (*nephesh*), and third with the whole of one's potentiality, the abundance or "muchness" (*me'ôd*) of eros, which leads to the extension of the individual into the family, the continuation of the self into the self of one's children and the future generations of man.[207]

It is therefore not on account of a second editorial accident of juxtaposition that Israel's creed was used as a preface for the first textbook on religious education in the history of western culture: "And those words, which I command thee this day, shall remain in thy intellectual consciousness, and thou shalt teach them to thy sons by sing-song rote (*we-shinnànetâ lebhanèkâ*)" (Deut. 6:6 ff. [Heb. 7 ff.]). The pericope concludes with the kerygmatic summary of the *Heilsgeschichte:* "Then, thou shalt say to thy son, "We were Pharaoh's slaves in Egypt. . ."" (Deut. 6:21

[Heb. 20]). Theology is the knowledge of God, but this knowledge is love with the whole of one's mind in the context of a corporate obligation toward the past and the future.[208] Biblical theology as the biblical knowledge of God is indeed the object of science, provided that the biblical theologian is also subject to a personal involvement in the "knowledge" of that God. Biblical theology is thus indissolubly married to biblical spirituality, which in turn remains inseparable from the continuity of the cultic celebration of presence. It is the knowledge of God which provides the clue to the mystery of the people of God, whether Israel or the Church. Such a knowledge points to what has been felicitously called "the sacramental prophetism" of the Bible in its entirety.[209]

Covenant ideology and covenant ceremonial may have played significant roles at critical moments in the history of Israel, and especially in its eschatological form at the birth of the Christian church. Nevertheless, this ideology and ceremonial proved to be chiefly the means of reform in times of corruption or cultural chaos. Covenant making constituted a rite which depended on the prior affirmation of a faith in the intervention of God in a peculiar segment of history. By contrast, the reality of divine presence proved to be the constant element of distinctiveness throughout the centuries of biblical times. It is this reality which produced the power of a "canonical" Scripture, and it is this reality which may renew this power in contemporary Christianity.

Israel maintained her historical existence as a people only in so far as she remembered and expected the manifestation of divine presence. It was the presence which created peoplehood. An individual member of that people partook of the life of the community only in so far as he shared in the presence, either through cultic celebration or by associating himself with the mediators of presence who had experienced its immediacy. When the structure of the covenant exploded, as it did during the exile in Babylon, the people remained conscious of their peoplehood only when they improvised paracultic celebrations of the presence and thereby ritually anticipated the final epiphany.

Because it brings together the divine asseverations, "I am Yahweh," of the Hebraic theophany, and "I am the Lord," of the Christian faith in the resurrection of Jesus, the motif of presence induces a magnetic field of forces which maintains a dynamic tension, in the whole of Scripture, between divine self-disclosure and divine self-concealment.[210] The proximity of God creates a memory and an anticipation of certitude, but it always defies human appropriation. The presence remains elusive.

It is symptomatic of our age that the crisis of contemporary theology is related to the problem of authority in all domains, and that the search for the perennial authority of Scripture requires new tools of semantic interpretation.[211] The problem of responding to the biblical record of the revelation of God from Abraham to Paul moves again to the forefront of the theological enterprise.[212] The Hebraic theology of presence leads to the Christian theology of the eucharistic presence. Because it refuses to accept a separation between cultus and faith and carries at the same time the seed of corporate continuity in history, the biblical theology of presence may provide a prolegomenon to a new biblical theology that in its turn may play a central part in the birth of an authentically ecumenical theology.[213]

Notes

1. On the history of literary criticism, see H.-J. Kraus, *Geschichte der historisch-kritischen Erforschung des Alten Testaments von der Reformation bis zur Gegenwart*, rev. ed. (Neukirchen-Vluyn, 1969); N. C. Habel, *Literary Criticism of the Old Testament* (Philadelphia, 1971).

2. While the name of Wellhausen re-

mains linked with modern literary criticism, it should be remembered that his work, far from having been improvised *de novo*, was painstakingly erected upon the research of many generations of scholars, from Isaac de la Peyrère in 1655, Richard Simon in 1678, and Jean Astruc in 1753, to Eduard Reuss in 1833, Herman Hupfeld in 1853, and especially Karl von Graf in 1866. Scores of other humanists and biblical interpreters deserve to be named.

3. The Yahwist (J, initial of the German name, Jahwist), written in Judah during the ninth century B.C.; the Elohist (E), written in North Israel during the eighth century; the Deuteronomist (D), written in Judah during the seventh century; and the Priestly Code (P), written partly during the Exile in Babylon (sixth century) and partly during the postexilic period, and which gave to the whole Hexateuch its final structure from Genesis to Joshua; see J. Wellhausen, *Prolegomena to the History of Ancient Israel* (Edinburgh, 1885; paperback ed., New York, 1958).

4. A summary of the post-Wellhausenian developments may be found in J. Bright, "Modern Study of Old Testament Literature," *The Bible and the Ancient Near East*, ed. by G. E. Wright (Garden City, N.Y., 1961), pp. 13–31; M. Noth, "P as Narrative and as Literary Framework of the Pentateuch as a Whole," *A History of Pentateuchal Traditions*, tr. by B. W. Anderson (Englewood Cliffs, N.J., 1972), pp. 8–19.

5. See, among others, C. A. Simpson, *The Early Traditions of Israel, A Critical Analysis of the Pre-deuteronomic Narrative of the Hexateuch* (Oxford, 1948).

6. As illustrated by several commentaries of the first part of the twentieth century as well as by the textual apparatus of K. Elliger and W. Rudolph, eds., *Biblia Hebraica Stuttgartensia* (Stuttgart, 1968–).

7. Significantly and ironically, an archaeologist and linguist like William F. Albright, who has been notoriously critical of the Wellhausen school, admits that "although these fundamentalist 'higher critics' are quite wrong in their presuppositions, it does not necessarily follow that the documentary hypothesis is wrong" (*New Horizons in Biblical Research*, London, 1966, pp. 14–15). Albright is justified, however, in adding a word of caution, "But [the documentary hypothesis] does have to be treated with much more critical circumspection than has hitherto been the case" (*ibid.*). Cf. F. M. Cross, *Canaanite Myth and Hebrew Epic, Essays in the History of the Religion of Israel* (Cambridge, Mass., 1973), pp. 3 ff. As is well known, there are still a number of Jewish and Christian scholars who persist in totally ignoring the results of literary criticism.

8. See H. Gressmann, *Altorientalische Texte and Bilder zum Alten Testaments* (Tübingen, 1909).

9. Wellhausen himself had perceived the need to compare Israel's religious practices and beliefs to those of the pre-Islamic Arabs (see *Reste arabischen Heidentums*; Berlin, 1887), but the bulk of his biblical studies had been accomplished before the modern archaeological and comparative data were available in significant number, especially as these affected the literary texts of the ancient Near East.

10. Although Wellhausen was fully aware of the existence of an oral tradition: see *Prolegomena*, pp. 171 ff.

11. See A. Lods, *Le rôle de la tradition orale dans la formation des récits de l'Ancien Testament*," *RHR*, LXXXVII (1923): pp. 31–64; E. Fascher, *Die formgeschichtliche Methode: eine Darstellung und Kritik* (Giessen, 1924).

12. The outstanding contribution of Gunkel has been to show that literary criticism can never be independent of an aesthetic and religious appreciation of the poetic dynamics through which a written document has first come to oral birth. His exceptional sensitivity to the significance of the *Sitz im Leben* of the literature was combined with an awareness

of its relevance for modern Christians. See W. Klatt, *Hermann Gunkel. Zu seiner Theologie der Religionsgeschichte und zur Entstehung der formgeschichtlichen Methode* (Göttingen, 1969). While Gunkel himself was not a biblical theologian, his influence played a major part, quite independently of that of Karl Barth, in reviving among moderns a concern for the theological significance of the Hebrew Bible (see below).

13. See K. Koch, *The Meaning of Form Criticism* (New York, 1967); *id.*, *The Growth of the Biblical Tradition: The Form Critical Method* (London, 1969); M. J. Buss, "The Study of Forms," in J. H. Hayes, ed., *Old Testament Form Criticism* (San Antonio, Texas 1973), pp. 1–56.

14. See E. Werner, "The Psalmodic Forms and their Evolution," *The Sacred Bridge* (Oxford, 1957–58), pp. 128–66. Further work is needed in the area of the cantillation of the rhythmic prose in which the Patriarchal saga and the national epic of the Exodus were preserved; cf. the comparative analysis of folkloric poetry in A. B. Lord, "Singers, Performance and Training," *The Singer of Tales* (New York, 1960), pp. 13–29.

15. R. Knierim, "Old Testament Form Criticism Reconsidered," *In.*, XXVII (1973): pp. 435–68.

16. See K. R. R. Gros Louis et al., eds., *Literary Interpretations of Biblical Narratives* (Nashville and New York, 1974).

17. S. Mowinckel, *Psalmenstudien, I-IV* (Kristiana, 1921–1924), reprinted Amsterdam, 1961); J. Pedersen, "Die Auffassung vom Alten Testament," *ZAW*, XLIX (1931), pp. 161–81; *id.*, *Israel: Its Life and Culture, I-II*, and *III-IV* (London and Copenhagen, 1926–40); I. Engnell, *Studies in Divine Kingship* (Uppsala, 1943).

18. See D. A. Knight, *Rediscovering the Tradition of Israel: The Development of the Traditio-Historical Research of the Old Testament, with Special Consideration of Scandinavian Contributions* (Missoula, Montana, 1973); A. Haldar, "Tradition and History," *Bibli-*

otheca orientalis, XXXI (1974), 26 ff.; R. Rendtorff, *Das überlieferungsgeschichtliche Problem des Pentateuchs* (Berlin and New York, 1977).

19. J. Pedersen, "Passahfest und Passahlegende," *ZAW*, LII (1934), pp. 161–75; *id.*, "The Crossing of the Reed Sea and the Paschal Legend," *Israel, Its Life and Culture, III–IV*, pp. 728–37; P. Laaf, *Die Pascha-Feier Israels. Eine literarkritisch und überlieferungsgeschichtliche Studie* (Bonn, 1970).

20. S. Mowinckel, "L'origine du décalogue," *RHPR*, VI (1926), pp. 409–33, 501–25; J. J. Stamm, *The Ten Commandments in Recent Research* (London, 1967); E. Nielsen, *The Ten Commandments in New Perspective: A Traditio-Historical Approach* (London, 1968).

21. Some traditio-historical critics admit that a number of documents have been written before the Exile. See G. Widengren, "Oral Tradition and Written Literature among the Hebrews in the Light of Arabic Evidence," *AO*, XXIII (1959): 261; G. W. Ahlström, "Oral and Written Transmission," *HTR*, LIX (1966): 69–81.

22. As illustrated in F. F. Hvidberg, *Weeping and Laughter in the Old Testament: A Study of Canaanite-Israelite Religion* (Lund, 1963).

23. The method has nevertheless been applied with notable results in many studies. For example, E. Nielsen, *Shechem: A Traditio-historical Investigation* (Copenhagen, 1955); R. A. Carlson, *David, the Chosen King: A Traditio-historical Approach* (Stockholm, 1964).

24. The impulse of the traditio-historical approach has produced many contributions to the interpretation of the prophets. See W. H. Schmidt, *Zukunftsgewissheit und Gegenwartskritik; Grundzüge prophetischer Verkündigung* (Neukirchen-Vluyn, 1973).

25. See A. H. J. Gunneweg, *Mündliche und schriftliche Tradition der vorexilischen Prophetenbücher als Problem der neueren Prophetenforschung* (Göttingen, 1959); J. G. Williams, "The Social Location of Israel-

ite Prophecy," *JAAR*, XXXVII (1969); 153 –65.

26. S. Mowinckel, "Kultprophetie und prophetische Psalmen," *Psalmenstudien*, III (Kristiana, 1922); F. Hecht, *Eschatologie und Ritus bei den Reformprofeten. Ein Beitrag zur Theologie des Alten Testaments* (Leiden, 1971).

27. See H. E. von Waldow, *Der traditionsgeshichtliche Hintergrund der prophetischen Gerichtsreden* (Berlin, 1963).

28. An important part of the activity of the prophets appears to have been related to a ceremonial which may have included an annual dedication to the covenant (see below). The prophets' intervention in the cultic ritual suggests that the prophets occupied formal offices in the sanctuary. See H. Graf Reventlow, "Propheten Amt und Mittleramt," *ZTK*, LVIII (1961): 269–84; *Das Amt des Propheten bei Amos* (Göttingen, 1962); P. Auvray, "Le prophète comme guetteur," *RB*, LXXI (1964): 191–205; J. Muilenburg, "The Office of the Prophet in Ancient Israel," in *The Bible in Modern Scholarship*, ed. by J. P. Hyatt (Nashville, 1965), pp. 74–97. Even the prophetic condemnation of the cultic abuses reveals intimate participation in the ritual of Israel.

29. See H. Gunkel and J. Begrich, *Einleitung in die Psalmen* (Göttingen, 1933), pp. 397 ff., 415 ff.

30. See A. Weiser, "The Cultic Foundation of the Psalms," *The Psalms* (Philadelphia, 1962), pp. 23–24 and passim.

31. Not all the psalms, however, may be ascribed to a cultic origin. See S. Terrien, "Creation, Cultus and Faith in the Psalter," *Horizons of Theological Education: Essays in Honor of Charles L. Taylor* (Dayton, Ohio, 1966), pp. 124–28; W. Beyerlin, *Die Rettung der Bedrängten in den Feindpsalmen der Einzelnen auf institutionelle Zusammenhänge untersucht* (Göttingen, 1970), pp. 18 ff.

32. See R. North, "The Theology of the Chronicler," *JBL*, LXXXII (1963), 374–

75; F. Michaeli, *Les livres des Chroniques, d'Esdras et de Néhémie* (Neuchâtel, 1967), p. 28; J. D. Newsome, Jr., "Toward a New Understanding of the Chronicler and His Purposes," *JBL*, XCIV (1975), 213.

33. See S. Terrien, *Job, commentaire* (Neuchâtel, 1963), pp. 7–8; *id.*, "Le poème de Job: drame para-rituel du Nouvel-An?" *SVT*, XVII (1969), 220 ff.: *id.*, "The Yahweh Speeches and Job's Responses," *Review and Expositor*, LXVIII (1971), 497 ff.

34. G. Östborn, *Cult and Canon: A Study in the Canonization of the Old Testament* (Uppsala, 1950); K. Schwarzwäller, "Probleme gegenwärtiger Theologie und das Alte Testament," in *Probleme biblischer Theologie* (*Festschrift G. von Rad*), ed., H. W. Wolff (München, 1971), pp. 479–93.

35. J. A. Sanders, "A Call to Canonical Criticism," in *Torah and Canon* (Philadelphia, 1972), pp. ix–xx; "Reopening Old Questions About Scripture," *In.*, XXVIII (1974): 321–33 (on J. Barr, *The Bible and the Modern World*, New York, 1973, esp. ch. 9); "Adaptable for Life: The Nature and Function of the Canon," *Festschrift G. E. Wright* (Garden City, N.Y., 1976), pp. 531 ff; E. Jacob, "Principe canonique et formation de l'Ancien Testament," *SVT*, XXVIII (1975): 101 ff.

36. Before the time of Wellhausen, the work of K. W. C. F. Bähr, *Symbolik des mosaischen Cultus* (Heidelberg, 1837–39) examined Hebrew ritual as symbolic expression of religious ideas. cf. H.-J. Kraus, *Worship in Israel: A Cultic History of the Old Testament* (Richmond, Va., 1962), pp. 1 ff, 4 f. The development of Pentateuchal criticism in general and the Wellhausen's dating of the four documents in particular depended in part on a theory of the development of cultus, the evolution of the character of the festivals and the calendars, the type and nature of the sacrifices, the function of the priests, etc.

37. P. Volz, *Das Neujahrfest Jahwes . . .* (Tübingen, 1912).

38. *Ibid.*, pp. 16–23. While Babylon celebrated the New Year in the spring, Israel held "the day of Yahweh" in the autumn. There were probably in Mesopotamia and elsewhere two critical *rites de passage,* one in the spring and the other in the autumn. In the Fertile Crescent, where the rhythm of vegetation depends less on perennial irrigation than on seasonal rains, the spring festival marked the end of greenness through the onset of the summer heat and drought, and the autumnal fall of the first rains ushered in the rebirth of nature. See also D. J. A. Clines, "The Evidence for an Autumnal New Year in Pre-Exilic Israel Reconsidered," *JBL,* XCIII (1974): 22 ff.

39. S. Mowinckel, *Das Thronbesteigungsfest Jahwäs und der Ursprung der Eschatologie* (Psalmenstudien, II; Kristiana, 1921).

40. H. Zimmern, *Das babylonische Neujahrfest* (Der Alte Orient, XXV, 3; 1926); S. H. Frankfort, *Kingship and the Gods* (Chicago, 1948), pp. 313–33.

41. See J. C. de Moor, *New Year with Canaanites and Israelites* (Kampen, 1972).

42. Mowinckel's rendering of the phrase *Yahweh malak,* traditionally translated "The Lord reigneth" (Pss. 93:1, etc.).

43. A number of scholars maintain that the New Year festival was not adopted until the postexilic period. See Kraus, *Worship in Israel,* pp. 7 ff. 15 ff.

44. S. Mowinckel, *Religion und Cultus...* (*op. cit.*) pp. 115 ff. 127 ff.

45. J. Pedersen, *Israel: Its Life and Culture* (Oxford and Copenhagen, 1926–40), I–II, pp. 99 ff., 411 ff.; III–IV, pp. 299 ff., 376 ff.

46. I. Engnell, *Studies in Divine Kingship,* I (Uppsala, 1943).

47. The Ugaritic texts have produced a considerable literature. In addition to the publication and translation of the texts themselves, see M. Dahood, "Ugaritic Studies and the Bible," *Gregorianum,* XLIII (1962): 55–79; F. M. Cross, "The Ideologies of Kingship in the Era of the Empire: Conditional Covenant and Eter-

nal Decree," in *Canaanite Myth and Hebrew Epic: Essays in the History of the Religion of Israel* (Cambridge, Mass., 1973), pp. 219 ff.

48. W. Robertson Smith, *Lectures on the Religion of the Semites* (Edinburgh, 1889; rev. ed. by S. A. Cook, London and New York, 1927); J. Frazer, *The Golden Bough: A Study in Magic and Religion,* 12 vols. (London, 1910–15); *id. Folklore in the Old Testament: Studies in Comparative Religion, Legend and Law,* 3 vols. (London, 1918–23; abridged ed., New York, 1923); Th. H. Gaster, *Myth, Legend and Custom in the Old Testament* (New York, 1969).

49. S. H. Hooke, ed., *Myth and Ritual: Essays on the Myth and Ritual of the Hebrews in Relation to the Culture Pattern of the Ancient Near East* (London, 1933); S. H. Hooke, *The Origins of Early Semitic Ritual* (London, 1938).

50. S. H. Hooke, ed., *The Labyrinth* (London, 1935), pp. 71–112; cf. A. R. Johnson, *Sacral Kingship in Ancient Israel* (Cardiff, 1955).

51. S. H. Hooke, ed., *Myth, Ritual, and Kingship* (Oxford, 1958); see especially S. G. F. Brandon, "The Myth and Ritual Position Critically Considered," pp. 261–91.

52. E. O. James, *Myth and Ritual in the Ancient Near East* (London, 1958).

53. H. Frankfort, *Kingship and the Gods* (Chicago, 1948), pp. 337–44; *id., The Problem of Similarity in Ancient Near Eastern Religion* (Oxford, 1951); H. and H. Frankfort, "The Emancipation of Thought from Myth," in H. Frankfort et al., *Before Philosophy: The Intellectual Adventure of Ancient Man* (Chicago, 1946; paperback ed., Penguin Books, Baltimore, 1951), pp. 241–48; M. Noth, "God, King, and Nation in the Old Testament," *The Laws in the Pentateuch and Other Essays* (Edinburgh and London, 1966), pp. 145–78; H.-J. Kraus, *Die Königsherrschaft Gottes im Alten Testament* (Tübingen, 1951). Significantly, Engnell himself expressed serious qualifications about the patternistic view in

"Methodological Aspects of Old Testament Study," *SVT*, VII (1960), pp. 19–21.

54. For example, "And the sons of Israel did evil in the sight of Yahweh, and served the Baalim, and they abandoned Yahweh, the Elohim of their fathers, who had brought them out of the land of Egypt, and they followed other gods, among the gods of the peoples that were round about them" (Judg. 2:11–12).

55. G. E. Wright, "Cult and History," *In*, XIV (1962): 3–20. Ironically, it was because they repudiated the method of purely literary criticism that the Scandinavian scholars rejected Wellhausen's conclusions on the written documents of the Hexateuch and developed the method of traditio-historical criticism. Yet, some of them substantially agreed with Wellhausen through their views on the agrarian origin of Hebrew cultus. See Wellhausen, *Prolegomena*, pp. 83–120.

56. While the feast of Passover inherited several features of a pastoral and agrarian celebration of the vernal equinox (new lambs, new ears of barley, etc., cf. Ps. 114), it was directly related to the cultic *legenda* of the Exodus.

57. A. Alt, "The Origins of Israelite Law" (1934), *Essays on Old Testament History and Religion*, tr. by P. A. Wilson (Oxford, 1966), pp. 79–132.

58. That is, related to court decisions and describing judiciary cases in the literary form of the subordinate clause of condition, beginning with the conjunction "if" or such a formula as "whoever, etc." Such legal forms abound in the so-called Book of the Covenant (Exod. 20:22 —23:10) and in the Code of Deuteronomy (chs. 12—26).

59. The apodictic law generally affects the form of a short command or prohibition which is enunciated in the name of the Deity, as in the various decalogues (Exod. 20:1–20; Deut. 5:6–21; cf. Exod. 34:17–26).

60. Deut. 27:11–26, 31:9–13; See Alt, *Israelite Law*, pp. 114 f.

61. Von Rad, *The Problem of the Hexateuch* ... (*op. cit.*), pp. 1 ff.

62. Noth, *The Laws in the Pentateuch*, pp. 28 ff.

63. Cf. the critical comments of A. S. Kapelrud, "Tradition and Worship: The Role of the Cult in Tradition Formation and Transmission," in D. A. Knight, ed., *Tradition and Theology in the Old Testament* (Philadelphia, 1977), p. 106.

64. The cultic formula, "Behold, this day," stressed the actuality of the liturgical recital (Deut. 5:2–3, 26:17, 30:15, etc.). See B. S. Childs, *Memory and Tradition in Israel* (London, 1962), pp. 74 ff.

65. Von Rad, *The Problem of the Hexateuch*, pp. 3 ff. This view has been the object of considerable discussion. See W. Richter, "Beobachtungen zur theologischen Systembildung in der alttestamentlichen Literatur anhand des kleinen geschichtlichen 'Credo'," *Wahrheit und Verkündigung* (Patterborn, 1967), pp. 175–212; C. Carmichael, "A New View of the Origin of the Deuteronomic Credo," *VT*, XIX (1969), 273–289; J. Ph. Hyatt, "Were There an Ancient Historical Credo in Israel and an Independent Sinai Tradition?" *Translating and Understanding the Old Testament* (Festchrift H. G. May), ed. by H. T. Frank and W. L. Reed (Nashville, 1970), pp. 152 ff.

66. Literally, "a perishing Aramaean." The connotations of the two words permit the use of this paraphrase. M. Buber translates, "A straying Aramaean" and believes that the expression referred to Abraham (*The Prophetic Faith*, paperback ed., New York, 1949), p. 32, note 35.

67. The hymns of the Psalter make this point abundantly clear. See S. Terrien, *The Psalms and their Meaning for Today* (Indianapolis, 1952), pp. 26 ff.

68. Jos. 24:2–4; Deut. 6:20–24; cf. I Sam. 12:8; Ps. 78, 105, 136; Neh. 9:13–14. On the part played by the cult in the formulation and the transmission of the traditions, see in addition to the work of G. von Rad and M. Noth, G. E. Wright, "Cult

and History," *In.*, XVI (1962): 3–20; A. S. Kapelrud, "The Role of the Cult in Old Israel," in J. P. Hyatt, ed., *The Bible in Modern Study* (Nashville, New York, 1965), pp. 44–56; S. Herrmann, "Kultreligion und Buchreligion: Kultische Funktionen in Israel und in Ägypten," in *Das ferne und nahe Wort. Festschrift L. Rost* (1967), pp. 94–105.

69. D. D. Luckenhill, "Hittite Treaties and Letters," *AJSLL*, XXXVII (1921–22): 161–211; E. F. Weidner, *Boghazkoï-Studien* (Leipzig, 1933); V. Korošec, *Hethitische Staatsverträge* (Leipzig, 1931); Noth, "Old Testament Covenant-Making in the Light of a Text from Mari" (1955), in *The Laws in the Pentateuch*, pp. 108 ff.

70. G. E. Mendenhall, "Covenant Forms in Israelite Tradition," *BA*, XVII (1954): 50–76; cf. *Law and Covenant in Israel and the Ancient Near East* (Pittsburg, 1955); J. Muilenburg, "The Form and Structure of the Covenantal Formulations," *VT*, IX (1959): 347–65; K. Baltzer, *The Covenant Formulary in Old Testament, Jewish, and Early Writings*, tr. by D. E. Green (Philadelphia, 1970).; D. J. McCarthy, *Old Testament Covenant: A Survey of Current Opinions* (Oxford, 1972).

71. A. Weiser, *The Psalms*, (Philadelphia, 1962), pp. 23 f.; *Das Buch Hiob* (Göttingen, 1951; 5th ed., 1968), p. 11; "Zu Frage nach den Beziehungen der Psalmen zum Kult: Die Darstellung der Theophanie in den Psalmen und im Festkult," *Festschrift A. Bertholet*, ed. by W. Baumgartner et al. (Tübingen, 1950), pp. 513–31, W. Beyerlin, *Origins and History of the Oldest Sinaitic Traditions*, tr. by S. Rudman (Oxford, 1965), pp. 163 f.

72. See notes 19 and 56 above.

73. B. S. Childs, *Myth and Reality in the Old Testament* (London, 1962), pp. 13 ff.; *id., Memory and Tradition*, pp. 74 ff.

74. Terrien, "Creation, Cultus and Faith in the Psalter," pp. 117 f.

75. The picture of the entry of the Hebrew tribes in Canaan remains to this day a matter of debate. See G. Mendenhall, *The Tenth Generation* (Baltimore, 1973),

pp. 19 ff.; S. Yeivin, *The Israelite Conquest of Canaan* (Leiden, 1971); R. de Vaux, *Histoire ancienne d'Israël* (Paris, 1971), pp. 441 –54, 615–20; M. Weippert, *The Settlement of the Israelite Tribes in Palestine* (London, 1971).

76. A discussion on the relative merits of the Myth and Ritual school and the Salvation History school will be found in Kraus, *Worship in Israel*, pp. 16 ff.; G. E. Wright, "Cult and History," *In.*, XVI (1962): 3 ff.; F. M. Cross, "The Divine Warrior in Israel's Early Cult," *Biblical Motifs*, ed. by A. Altmann (Cambridge, Mass., 1966), pp. 11 ff.; *id., Canaanite Myth and Hebrew Epic: Essays in the History of the Religion of Israel* (Cambridge, Mass., 1973), pp. 82–90.

77. See J. Barr, "Story and History in Biblical Theology," *JR*, LV (1975): 348 ff. The Myth and Ritual School fails to face the problem created by this cultural disruption, because it assumes tacitly that Israel in its totality was the prey of Canaanite syncretism until the Babylonian exile and the rise of Judaism. As the biblical record itself admits, agrarian rituals represented a constant threat and became especially virulent after Solomon in the tenth century B.C.

78. Especially those of Samuel Reimarus, *On the Purpose of Jesus and His Disciples —One more Fragment by the Anonymous Writer of Wolfenbüttel* (published by Lessing in 1778); David Friedrich Strauss, *Leben Jesus* (1835); Ernest Renan, *Vie de Jésus* (1863).

79. Cf. G. F. C. Conybeare, *History of New Testament Criticism* (New York, 1910); S. Terrien, "History of the Interpretation of the Bible, III. Modern Period," *IB*, I (1952): 132 f.; G. E. Ladd, *The New Testament and Criticism* (Grand Rapids, 1967).

80. W. G. Kümmel, *Introduction to the New Testament*, 14th rev. ed., tr. by A. J. Mattil Jr. (Nashville and New York, 1966), pp. 33 ff.

81. M. Dibelius, *Die Formgeschichte des Evangeliums* (Tübingen, 1919; etc.), tr. by

B. L. Woolf, *From Tradition to Gospel* (New York, 1935).

82. R. Bultmann, *Die Erforschung der synoptischer Evangelien* (Göttingen, 1925).

83. See E. V. McKnight, *What is Form-criticism?* (Philadelphia, 1969); E. Güttgemanns, *Offene Fragen zur Formgeschichte des Evangeliums* (München, 1970); J. M. Robinson and H. Koester, *Trajectories Through Early Christianity* (Philadelphia, 1971); R. S. Barbour, *Traditio-historical Criticism of the Gospels* (London, 1972).

84. See R. E. Brown, *The Gospel According to John, I–XII* (Garden City, N.Y., 1966), pp. cxi–cxiv and special bibliography on p. cxxvii; D. E. Aune, *The Cultic Setting of Realized Eschatology* (Leiden, 1972).

85. This complexity arises from the difficulty of isolating the religious elements from cultural fluctuations of growth and decay in history. "The *homo religiosus* represents the 'total man'; hence the science of religions must become a total discipline" (M. Eliade, *The Quest: History and Meaning in Religion* [Chicago, 1969], p. 8; cf. pp. 12 ff.; "The History of Religions in Retrospect: 1912–1962," *JBR*, XXXI (1963): 98 ff.). The use of the word "religion" itself is open to misunderstanding, as it refers either to a phenomenological description of practices and beliefs common to a certain ethnic and cultural group over a relatively long period of history or, on the contrary, to the coherent presentation of an attitudinal continuity that is restricted to an elite of spirituality and ethics throughout many generations of ethnic and cultural existence. See I. Troeltsch, "Was heisst 'Wesen des Christentums'?" as quoted by C. J. Bleeker, "The Key-Word Religion," *The Sacred Bridge: Researches into the Nature and Structure of Religion* (Leiden, 1963), p. 37; A. Nygren, *Meaning and Method: Prolegomena to a Scientific Philosophy of Religion and a Scientific Theology*, tr. by Ph. S. Watson (Philadelphia, 1972).

86. See Th. C. Vriezen, "The Study of the Old Testament and the History of

Religion," *SVT*, XVII (1969), pp. 9 f.

87. See J. D. W. Watts, *Basic Patterns in Old Testament Religion*, (New York, 1971); G. Fohrer, *History of Israelite Religion*, tr. by D. E. Green (Nashville and New York, 1972).

88. Early Christians spoke only of "The Scripture" (John 2:22; Acts 8:32; 2 Tim. 3:16; etc.), "The Scriptures" (Mark 12:24; I Cor. 15:3–4; etc.); "The Holy Scripture" (Rom. 1:2); and, like the Jews of the period, "The Book" (neuter in Gal. 3:10; feminine in Mark 12:26). Later Jews spoke commonly of *Miqra'* ("What is Read").

89. See A. Jaubert, *La notion d'alliance dans le judaïsme aux abords de l'ère chrétienne* (Paris, 1963), pp. 269 ff.

90. Jer. 31:3–34; cf. W. Rudolph, *Jeremia* (Tübingen, 1968), pp. 202 ff.

91. The Pauline expression, "reading the Old Covenant" (2 Cor. 3:4) was metonymic, since verse 6 refers to the "New Covenant" and obviously not to the literature of the New Testament. Cf. Rom. 9:4; Gal. 3:15, 17; Gal. 4:24; Eph. 2:12.

92. See O. Michel, *Der Brief an die Hebräer* (Göttingen, 1966), pp. 294 f.; G. W. Buchanan, *To The Hebrews* (Garden City, N.Y., 1972), pp. xxvii ff.

93. See W. Grundmann, *Das Evangelium nach Lukas* (Berlin, 1964), pp. 391–94; E. Käsemann, "The Pauline Doctrine of the Lord's Supper," *Essays on New Testament Themes* (London, 1964), pp. 109 ff.; H. Conzelmann, *Der Erste Brief an die Korinther* (Göttingen, 1969), pp. 235–71.

94. This idea is found as early as the second century A.D. (Irenaeus, *Against Heresies*, III, xi, 8) and has been widely adopted thereafter. It has especially influenced the thought of John Calvin, Johannes Cocceius, and Karl Barth. See H. H. Wolf, "Die Einheit des Bundes," *Beiträge zur Geschichte und Lehre der Reformierten Kirche*, Bd. 10 (Neukirchen, 1958); G. Schrenk, *Gottesreich und Bund im älteren Protestantismus vornehmlich bei Johannes Cocceius* (Gütersloh, 1923; reprint, 1967).

95. In the rabbinical literature, Jews were called "the sons of the covenant." References will be found in W. D. Davies, *Paul and Rabbinical Judaism* (London, 1958), p. 261.

96. The relation between Yahweh and Israel was not expressed simply by a formula which could be traced to the Hittite treaties of vassality. No exact parallelism of form or content has been found so far between the Sinai Covenant and the political contracts of the ancient Near East. See Fohrer, *History of Israelite Religion*, p. 80. At the same time, the primitive notion of the chieftain has clearly molded the religious beliefs of the Hebrews, who viewed themselves as the "kingdom" of Yahweh. A recent survey of the evidence is found in A. E. Glock, "Early Israel as the Kingdom of Yahweh: The Influence of Archaeological Evidence on the Reconstruction of Religion in Early Israel," *Concordia Theological Monthly*, XLI (1970): 558–603. Cf. Mendenhall, "Early Israel as the Kingdom of Yahweh: Thesis and Methods," *The Tenth Generation*, pp. 1 ff.

97. See note 70 above.

98. Exod. 19:2*b*—20:21, 23:20—24:11, etc.

99. Jos. 8:30–35, 24:2–28: cf. Deut. 27:4 ff.; see J. L'Hour, "L'alliance à Sichem," *RB*, LXIX (1962); 5 ff., 161 ff., 350 ff.; Ch. H. Giblin, "Structural Patterns in Jos 24, 1–25," *CBQ*, XXVI (1964): 50 ff.; V. Maag, "Sichembund und Vätergötter," *Hebräische Wortforschung* (Festschrift W. Baumgartner), *SVT*, XVI (1967): 205–18.

100. C. F. Whitley, "Covenant and Commandment in Israel," *JNES*, XXII (1963): 37 ff; D. N. Freedman, "Divine Commitment and Human Obligation," *In.* XVIII (1964): 387–406; E. Gerstenberger, "Covenant and Commandment;" *JBL*, XXIV (1965): 38–51; W. Eichrodt, "Covenant and Law," *In*, XX (1966): 307–21; J. L'Hour, *La morale de l'alliance* (Paris, 1966); E. Kutsch, "Gesetz und Gnade," *ZAW*, LXXIX (1967): 18–35; "Der Begriff

Berit in vordeuteronomischer Zeit," *Das ferne und nahe Wort, Festchrift L. Rost; BZAW*, 105 (Berlin, 1967): 133–43.

101. 2 Kings 22:1–23:24. See R. Kraetschmar, *Die Bundestellung im Alten Testament*, pp. 123 ff.; M. Roberge, *Le sens de l'alliance dans le Deutéronome* (Rome, 1962); M. G. Kline, *Treaty of the Great King: The Covenant Structure of Deuteronomy* (Grand Rapids, 1963); R. Frankena, "The Vassal-Treaties of Esarhaddon and the Dating of Deuteronomy," *Oudtestamentische Studiën*, XIV (1965): 122–54; M. Weinfeld, *Deuteronomy and the Deuteronomic School* (Oxford, 1972).

102. M. Newman, *The People of the Covenant* (New York and Nashville, 1962), pp. 152 ff., 162 ff.; R. E. Clements, *Abraham and David* (London, 1967), pp. 86 f.; cf. *id.*, *God and Temple* (Philadelphia, 1965), pp. 52 f.

103. Terrien, "The Omphalos Myth and Hebrew Religion," pp. 332 f.

104. L. Rost, "Sinaibund und Davidsbund," *TLZ*, LXXII (1947): 129–134; *id.*, "Die Überlieferung von der Thronnachfolge Davids," *Das kleine Credo und andere Studien zum Alten Testament* (Heidelberg, 1965), pp. 160 ff.; G. Widengren, "King and Covenant," *JSS*, II (1957): 1–32; A. H. J. Gunneweg, "Sinaibund und Davidsbund," *VT*, X (1960): 335–41; H. Gese, "Der Davidsbund und die Zionserwählung," *ZTK*, LXI (1964): 10–26; W. Brueggemann, "The Trusted Creature," *CBQ*, XXXI (1969): 484–98; cf. F. C. Prussner, "The Covenant of David and the Problem of Unity in Old Testament Theology," in *Transitions in Biblical Scholarship*, ed. by J. C. Rylaarsdam, (Chicago, 1968), pp. 17–41; M. Weinfeld, "The Covenant of Grant in the Old Testament and in the Ancient Near East," *JAOS*, XC (1970): 184–203; Cross, "The Ideologies of Kingship in the Era of Empire: Conditional Covenant and Eternal Decree," *Canaanite Myth and Hebrew Epic*, pp. 217 ff.

105. W. Eichrodt, *Theology of the Old Testament*, tr. by J. A. Baker (Philadelphia,

1961), I, pp. 61 ff.; O. Eissfeldt, "The Promises of Grace to David in Isa. 55:1–5," in *Israel's Prophetic Heritage*, ed. by W. W. Anderson and W. Harrelson, (London and New York, 1962), pp. 196 ff.; A. Caquot, "Les 'grâces de David'; à propos d'Isaïe, 55/3*b*," *Semitica*, XV (1965): 45–70; Zimmerli, "Sinaibund und Abrahambund," *Gottes Offenbarung* (1963), pp. 205 ff.; Clements, *Abraham and David* (1967), pp. 70 f.
106. Neh. 8:1—10:39; see G. E. Mendenhall, "Covenant," *IDB*, I (1962): 721 f.; J. M. Maier, "Zur Geschichte des Bundesgedankens und zur Rolle der Leviten in der politischen und religiösen Geschichte des alten Israel," *Judaica*, XXV (1969): 222 ff.
107. Pss. 25:10, 14; 44:18; 50:5, 16; 55:20 [Heb. 21]; 74:20; 78:10, 37; 89:4, 29, 35, 40 [Heb. 5, 30, 36, 41]; 103:18; 105:8, 10; 106:45; 111:5, 9; 132:12. In most of these cases, if not in all of them, the psalmists reflect the temple ceremonies in which the Sinai covenant and the Davidic covenant have already been brought into conjunction. Cf. S. Mowinckel, *The Psalms in Israel's Worship*, tr. D. R. Ap-Thomas (Oxford, 1962), I, p. 130.
108. 1 Kings 19:10, 14. The absence is particularly noticeable in Isaiah of Jerusalem (cf. 28:15, 18; 33:8 /?/); See W. Eichrodt, "Prophet and Covenant: Observations on the Exegesis of Isaiah," *Proclamation and Presence: Festschrift G. Henton Davies* (Richmond, 1970), pp. 167 ff. The prophets of the eighth century did not stress the idea of the covenant and may have had little or no knowledge of Israel's covenant with Yahweh, for they conceived the people's relationship to their God as one of a human family. Cf. C. F. Whitley, "Covenant and Commandment in Israel," *JNES*, XXII (1963): 37 ff.; L. Perlitt, *Bundstheologie im Alten Testament* (Neukirchen-Vluyn, 1969), pp. 129 ff.
109. See H. B. Huffmon, "The Covenant Law Suit and the Prophets," *JBL*,

LXXVIII (1959): 286–95; W. Brueggemann, "Amos IV, 4–13 and Israel's Covenant Worship," *VT*, XV (1965): 1–15; R. E. Clements, *Prophecy and Covenant* (London, 1965); F. L. Moriarty, "Prophet and Covenant," *Gregorianum*, XLIV (1965): 817–33; J. Wijngaards, "Death and Resurrection in Covenantal Context (Hos. VI, 2)," *VT*, XVII (1967): 226–39; L. Limburg, "The Root RIB and the prophetic Lawsuit Speeches," *JBL*, LXXXVIII (1969): 291–304; J. D. Martin, "The Forensic Background to Jer. 3:1," *VT*, XIX (1969): 82–92; M. O'R. Boyle, "The Covenant Lawsuit of the Prophet Amos: III 1–IV 13," *VT*, XXI (1971): 338–62; W. Vogels, "Invitation à revenir à l'alliance et universalisme en Amos IX 7," *VT*, XXII (1972): 223–39.
110. See R. E. Clements, "Prophecy and Eschatology," in *Prophecy and Covenant* (London, 1965), pp. 103 ff.; W. Brueggemann, "Isaiah 55 and Deuteronomic Theology," *ZAW*, LXXX (1968), 191 ff.; M. H. Woudstra, "The Everlasting Covenant in Ezekiel 16:59–63," *Calvin Theological Journal*, VI (1971), 22 ff.; M. Weinfeld, "Jeremiah and the Spiritual Metamorphosis of Israel," *ZAW*, LXXXVIII (1976), 17 ff.
111. See below, Chapter IV. The interconnection of presence and word has been described recently in M.-L. Henry, *Prophet und Tradition, Versuch einer Problemstellung*, BZAW, 116 (Berlin, 1969), pp. 19 ff.; D. McCarthy, "God's Presence and the Prophetic Word," in *The Presence of God*, ed. by P. Benoit, R. Murphy, B. van Iersel, *Concilium*, vol. 50 (New York, 1969), pp. 21 ff.
112. The wisdom circles understood the social demands of covenant righteousness, but they viewed it in its cosmic context of world harmony. See Pedersen, *Israel, its Life and Culture*, I–II, (1926), pp. 377 ff.; M. J. Buss, "The Covenant Theme in Historical Perspective," *VT*, XVI (1966): 503.

113. Although it appears more than forty times in 1 Macc. and also in Ps. Sol. 9:18, 10:5, and 17:17.

114. In which it occurs about thirty times. See A. Jaubert, *La notion d'alliance aux abords de l'ère chrétienne* (Paris, 1963), pp. 181 ff.; R. F. Collins, "The Berîth-Notion of the Cairo Damascus Covenant and its Comparison with the NT (*diatheke*)," *ETL*, XXXIX (1967): 555–94.

115. Aboth 3.15; Mekilta Exod. 12.6; Midrash Sifre on Numb. 15.3; Midrash Koh. 2.1; 11.8. Cf. H. L. Strack und P. Billerbeck, *Kommentar zum Neuen Testament aus Talmud und Midrasch* (München, 1922–28), I, p. 243; II, pp. 279 f.; note 1; III, pp. 89 ff., 704, 848; J. Jocz, "The Connections Between the Old and the New Testament," *Judaica*, XVI (1960): 142 ff.

116. In addition to the works listed above, see A. Schreiber, *Der neue Bund im Spätjudentum und Christentum* (Tübingen, 1954–5); W. C. van Unnik, "La conception paulinienne de la Nouvelle Alliance," *NTS*, XXIX (1973): 174–93; R. Deichgräber, *Gotteshymnus und Christushymnus in der früher Christenheit* (Göttingen, 1967), pp. 65 ff.; U. Luz, "Der alte und der neue Bund bei Paulus und im Hebräerbrief," *Ev. Th.*, XXVII (1967): 318–36.

117. The periodicity and character of a covenant festival remains a matter of discussion. See C. F. Whitley, "Covenant and Commandment in Israel," *JNES*, XXII (1963): 37 ff.; G. Fohrer, "Altes Testament—'Amphiktyonie' und 'Bund'," *Studien zur alttestamentlichen Theologie und Geschichte* (1949–66; Berlin, 1969), pp. 84 –119; id., *History of Israelite Religion*, tr. by D. E. Green (Nashville, 1972), pp. 204–5; E. Kutsch, " 'Bund' und Fest. Zu Gegenstand und Terminologie einer Forschungsrichtung," *Theologischer Quartalschrift*, CL (1970): 299–320.

118. R. E. Clements, *Prophecy and Covenant* (London, 1965), pp. 45 ff.; W. Brueggemann, *Tradition in Crisis: A Study*

in Hosea (Richmond, 1968), pp. 13 ff.; C. Westermann, *Basic Forms of Prophetic Speech*, tr. by H. C. White (Philadelphia, 1967), pp. 159 ff.; Zimmerli, *The Law and the Prophets*, pp. 61 ff.

119. Yahweh's covenant with the people was renewed under Joshua (Jos. 24:25), Jehoiada (2 Kings 11:17 = 2 Chron. 23:-3), Hezekiah (2 Chron. 29:10), Josiah (2 Kings 23:3), and Ezra (Ezr. 10:3). The covenant with David and his dynasty is not made "with the people" (2 Sam. 7; Ps. 89:4, 29, 34, 39, 132:12; Jer. 33:21).

120. See bibliography in Terrien, "The Omphalos Myth and Hebrew Religion," p. 326, note 4; Cross, "Ba'l versus Yahweh," in *Canaanite Myth and Hebrew Epic*, pp. 190–94.

121. See E. Dhorme, *Les religions de Babylonie et d'Assyrie* (Paris, 1945), pp. 11–19, 45 ff.; J. Bottéro, "L'idéologie religieuse: la théologie du divin," *La religion babylonienne* (Paris, 1952), pp. 54–68; id., "La théologie de l'univers," pp. 69–87; id., "La théologie de l'homme," pp. 82–107.

122. See S. Morenz, *Egyptian Religion*, tr. by A. E. Keep (London, 1973), pp. 137 ff.; F. Daumas, *Les dieux de l'Egypte* (Paris, 1965); C. J. Bleeker, *Hathor and Thoth: Two Key Figures of the Ancient Egyptian Religion* (Leiden, 1973).

123. See Cross, *Canaanite Myth and Hebrew Epic*; R. du Mesnil du Buisson, *Nouvelles études sur les dieux et mythes de Canaan* (Leiden, 1973).

124. Although serious qualifications apply in this case, see J. Duchesne-Guillemin, *La religion de l'Iran ancien* (Paris, 1962), pp. 170 ff.; G. Gnoli, "Problems and Prospects of the Studies on Persian Religion," in U. Bianchi et al., eds., *Problems and Methods of the History of Religion* (Leiden, 1972), pp. 67 ff.

125. See A. Hus, *Greek and Roman Religion* (New York, 1962), pp. 41 ff., 66 ff., 76 ff., 126 ff., 141 ff.; C. Kerényi, "Peaks of Greek and Roman Religious Experi-

ence," *The Religion of the Greeks and Romans* (London, 1962), pp. 141–62; idem, "The Laughter of the Gods," pp. 192–200. Although W. F. Otto rightly argues against the utilitarian explanation of ancient rites and makes an eloquent plea for sympathetic understanding of ancient rituals by moderns, even he concludes that Greek religion at its best seeks the oneness of god and man and in effect the deification of man (*The Homeric Gods: The Spiritual Significance of Greek Religion*, New York, 1954, p. 236). See also E. des Places, *La religion grecque: dieux, cultes, rites et sentiment religieux* (Paris, 1969); A. D. Nock, "Religious Attitudes of the Ancient Greeks," in *Essays on Religion and the Ancient World* (Cambridge, Mass., 1972), II, pp. 534 ff.

126. See the variety of nature hierophanies described in M. Eliade, *Traité d'histoire des religions* (Paris, 1949), pp. 20–26, 117–25, 114–46, 179–80, 201–03, 213–17, 243–46.

127. See M. David, *Les dieux et le destin en Babylonie* (Paris, 1949), pp. 38 ff.; C. J. Bleeker, "Die Idee des Schicksals in der altägyptischer Religion," *The Sacred Bridge* (Leiden, 1963), pp. 112–29. While B. Albrektson in *History and the Gods* (Lund, 1967) attempted to show ancient Near Eastern parallels to the Hebraic view on divine providence, several scholars have reaffirmed the distinctiveness of Israel regarding this point. See W. G. Lambert, "Destiny and Divine Intervention in Babylon and Israel," in M. A. Beek et al., *The Witness of the Tradition OTS*, xvii, (Leiden, 1972): 65–72.

128. Hebraic theology falls neither into animistic pantheism nor into deistic aloofness. In Israel, nature worship in any of its forms appears to be a violation of Yahwism. In the ancient Near East, on the contrary, cultus aims at the enlisting of the deified environment for the economic and political advantage of a monarch, a dynasty, or a well-defined oligarchy. See H. Frankfort, *Kingship and the Gods: A Study of Ancient Near Eastern Reli-*

gion as the Integration of Society and Nature (Chicago, 1948), pp. 51 ff., 143 ff., 251 ff.; N. C. Habel, *Yahweh Versus Baal: A Conflict of Religious Cultures* (New York, 1964), pp. 51 ff.

129. Th. C. Vriezen, *An Outline of Old Testament Theology* (Oxford, 1970), pp. 180 f.; G. von Rad, *Old Testament Theology*, I, tr. by D. M. G. Stalker (New York, 1962), pp. 136 ff., 227 ff.; R. C. Dentan, *The Knowledge of God in Ancient Israel* (New York, 1968); F. Gaborian, "La connaissance de Dieu dans l'Ancien Testament," *Angelicum*, XLV (1968), 145–83.

130. See especially M. Buber, "Upon Eagles' Wings," *Moses* (London, 1946), reprinted as *Moses: The Revelation and the Covenant* (New York, 1958), pp. 100 ff.; id., "The Silent Question," *At the Turning* (New York, 1952), pp. 43–44; id., "The Dialogue Between Heaven and Earth," ibid., pp. 56–57; id., "The Faith of Judaism," *Mamre: Essays in Religion* (Oxford, 1946), p. 2. See also J. C. Murray, S. J., "The Biblical Problem: The Presence of God," in *The Problem of God* (New Haven, 1964), pp. 10–11.

131. Considerable attention has been devoted to the analysis of this theme: W. W. von Baudissin, "'Gott schauen' in der alttestamentlichen Religion," *Archiv für Religionswissenschaft*, XVIII (1915): 173–239; E. G. Gulin, "Das Antlitz Gottes im Alten Testament," *Annales Academiae Scientiarum Fennicae*, XVII (1923): 21 ff.; J. Hempel, "Die Furcht vor dem nahen Gott," *Gott und Mensch im Alten Testament: Studie zur Geschichte der Frömmigkeit* (Stuttgart, 1926), pp. 6–17; J. Daniélou, *Le signe du temple ou de la présence de Dieu* (Paris, 1942); G. Henton Davies, "The Presence of God in Israel," in *Studies in History and Religion presented to Dr. H. Wheeler Robinson*, ed. by E. A. Payne (London, 1942), pp. 11–29; W. J. Phythian-Adams, *The People and the Presence: A Study of the At-One-Ment* (London: 1942); L. H. Brockington, "The Presence of God, a Study of the Use of the Term 'Glory of Yahweh'," *ET*, LVII

(1945–46): 21–25; A. R. Johnson, "Aspects of the Use of the Term *Pânim* in the Old Testament," *Festschrift O. Eissfeldt,* ed. by J. Fück (Halle a. d. S., 1947), pp. 155–59; H. J. Franken, *The Mystical Communion with JHWH in the Book of Psalms* (Leiden, 1954); Y. M.-J. Congar, *Le mystère du temple* (Paris, 1958); E. Jacob, "Manifestations of God," *Theology of the Old Testament* (New York, 1958), pp. 73–85; G. E. Wright, "God Amidst His People: The Story of the Temple," *The Rule of God* (Garden City, N.Y., 1960), pp. 57–76; G. von Rad, "The Divine Revelation at Sinai," *Old Testament Theology,* vol. I (New York, 1962), pp. 187–279; H. Ringgren, "Manifestations of God," *Israelite Religion* (Philadelphia, 1963), pp. 89–103; R. E. Clements, *God and Temple* (Philadelphia, 1965); W. I. Wolverton, "The Psalmists' Belief in God's Presence," *Canadian Journal of Theology,* IX (1963), pp. 82–94; J. Jeremias, *Theophanie: Die Geschichte einer alttestamentlichen Gattung* (Neukirchen-Vluyn, 1965); H. Renckens, "Not an Exclusive Sense of God's Distance," and "A Full Consciousness Also of God's Nearness," *The Religion of Israel* (New York, 1966), pp. 111–18; W. Eichrodt, "The Forms of God's Self-Manifestation," *Theology of the Old Testament,* vol. II (Philadelphia, 1967), pp. 15–45; J. K. Kuntz, *The Self-Revelation of God* (Philadelphia, 1967); S. Armitham, "To Be Near to and Far Away from Yahweh: The Witness of the Psalms of Lament to the Concept of the Presence of God," *Bangalore Theological Forum,* II (1968): 31–55; B. A. Levine, "On the Presence of God in Biblical Religion," J. Neusner, ed., *Religions in Antiquity: Festschrift E. R. Goodenough* (Leiden, 1968), pp. 71–87; M. Haran, "The Divine Presence in Israelite Cult and the Cultic Institutions" (Review-Article on R. A. Clements, *God and Temple*), *Biblica,* L (1969): 251–67; D. McCarthy, *The Presence of God and the Prophetic Word* (London, 1969); R. de Vaux, "The Presence and Absence of God in

History According to the Old Testament," in P. Benoit et al., eds., *Concilium,* L (1969): 7 ff.; J. I. Durham, "*Shalom* and the Presence of God," in J. I. Durham and J. R. Porter, eds., *Proclamation and Presence: Festschrift H. Henton Davies* (Richmond, Va., 1970), pp. 272 ff.; J. Reindl, *Das Angesicht Gottes im Sprachgebrauch des Alten Testaments* (Leipzig, 1970); Th. C. Vriezen, "The Communion of God with man," *An Outline of Old Testament Theology* (Oxford, 1970), pp. 176–275); P. Grelot, "Présence de Dieu et communion avec Dieu dans l'Ancien Testament," *Lectio Divina,* LXVII (1971): 167–80; H. Mölle, *Das "Erscheinen" Gottes im Pentateuch: Ein literaturwissenschaftlicher Beitrag zur alttestamentlichen Exegese* (Bern-Franfurt/M, 1973); Th. W. Mann, *Divine Presence and Guidance in Israelite Traditions: The Typology of Exaltation* (Baltimore, 1977).

132. The motif of the tree of "absolute knowledge" in the myth of the garden (Gen. 3:5; cf. vs. 22), whatever its origin and the various levels of meaning which it has assumed in the tradition might be, suggests a stringent view of man's inability to know God through his own devices. See J. Coppens, *La connaissance du bien et du mal et le péché du paradis* (Paris, 1948), pp. 73 ff, 118 f; G. W. Buchanan, "The Old Testament Meaning of the Knowledge of Good and Evil," *JBL,* LXXV (1956): 114–20. Likewise, the legendary myth of the tower of Babel may point to a similar interpretation of man's theological limitations: cf., however, A. Parrot, *The Tower of Babel,* tr. by E. Hudson (London, 1955), p. 66 ff.; G. von Rad, *Genesis,* tr. by J. H. Marks, (Philadelphia, 1961), p. 147. Echoes of the myth of religious arrogance are found elsewhere in the literature (Isa. 13:19, 14:13; Jer. 51:6 ff.; Ezek. 28:13; Job 15:7 ff.). A similar thought appears in the sapiential literature. The fragment ascribed to a foreigner, Agur ben Yakeh of Massa, may reflect a satirical attitude toward those religionists who claim direct access to a personal knowl-

edge of God. The poem is presented ironically as a "prophetic oracle (*ne'um*) of a strong man (*gebher*)":

"I have wearied myself about God,
I have wearied myself about God,
and I am exhausted.

Who has ever ascended to the heavens, and come down again?"
(Prov. 30:1, 4.)

The translation, however, is uncertain. See C. C. Torrey, "Proverbs, Chapter 30," *JBL*, LXXIII (1954): 93–96; H. Ringgren und W. Zimmerli, *Sprüche / Prediger* (Göttingen, 1962), pp. 114 f.; G. Sauer, *Die Sprüche Agurs* (Stuttgart, 1963), pp. 97 ff.; E. Lipiński, "Peninna, Iti'el et l'Athlète," *VT*, XVII (1967): 68–75.

133. D. Daube, *The Sudden in Scripture* (Leiden, 1964); Kuntz, *The Self-Revelation of God*, pp. 65 ff.

134. H. Schrade, *Der verborgene Gott: Gottesbild und Gottesvorstellung in Israel und im alten Orient* (Stuttgart, 1949), especially pp. 128 ff., 251 ff.; K. H. Miskotte, *When the Gods are Silent*, tr. by J. W. Doberstein (New York and Evanston, 1967), pp. 24 ff., 257 ff.; L. Perlitt, "Die Verborgenheit Gottes," in H. W. Wolff, ed., *Probleme biblischer Theologie: Festschrift G. von Rad* (München, 1971), pp. 367 ff.

135. The tradition on Elijah at Horeb constitutes a turning point in the history of the religion of Israel as it points out the obsoleteness of the theophanic mode of revelation and opens the age of prophetic vision (1 Kings 19:11 ff.).

136. Among recent studies on the faith in the resurrection of Jesus, see G. Kegel, *Auferstehung Jesu: Auferstehung der Toten. Eine traditionsgeschichtliche Untersuchung zum Neuen Testament* (Gütersloh, 1970); W. Marxsen, *The Resurrection of Jesus of Nazareth* (Philadelphia, 1970); H. C. Snape, "After the Crucifixion of 'The Great Forty Days'," *Numen*, XVII (1970): 188–99; U. Wilckens, *Auferstehung. Das biblische Auferstehungszeugnis historisch unter-*

sucht und erklärt (Stuttgart, 1970); R. H. Fuller, *The Formation of the Resurrection Narratives* (New York, 1971). 137. See S. G. F. Brandon, *Jesus and the Zealots* (New York, 1967); id., "Jesus and the Zealots: Aftermath," *BJRL*, LIV (1971–72): 47–66; O. Cullmann, *Jesus and the Revolutionaries*, tr. by G. Putnam (New York, 1970); M. Hengel, *Victory Over Violence: Jesus and the Revolutionists* (Philadelphia, 1973).

138. O. Cullmann, *The Christology of the New Testament*, tr. by Sh. C. Guthrie and Ch. A. M. Hall (Philadelphia, 1959); E. Fuchs, *Glaube und Erfahrung; Zum christologischen Problem im Neuen Testament* (Tübingen, 1965); R. H. Fuller, *The Foundations of New Testament Christology*, (New York, 1965); J. Knox, *The Humanity and Divinity of Christ; A Study of Pattern in Christology* (Cambridge, 1967); W. Marxsen, *The Beginning of Christology: A Study of Its Problems* (Philadelphia, 1969); H. Boers, "Jesus and Christian Faith: New Testament Christology since Bousset's *Kyrios Christos*," *JBL*, LXXXIX (1970): 450–56; B. Vawter, *This Man Jesus; An Essay Toward a New Testament Christology* (Garden City, N.Y., 1973); N. Perrin, *A Modern Pilgrimage in New Testament Christology* (Philadelphia, 1974).

139. A development which apparently played a part in the formulation of the Lukan narratives on the Ascension. In addition to commentaries on Luke and Acts, in loc., see G. Lohfink, *Die Himmelfahrt Jesu: Untersuchungen zu den Himmelfahrts– und Erhöhungstexten bei Lukas* (München, 1971); F. Hahn, "Die Himmelfahrt Jesu: Ein Gespräch mit Gerhard Lohfink," *Biblica*, LV (1974): 418–26. 140. See R. C. Tannehill, *Dying and Rising with Christ: A Study in Pauline Theology* (Berlin, 1967); J. Coman, "La présence du Christ dans la nouvelle création," *RHPR*, XLVIII (1968): 125–50; J. Galot, *Être né de Dieu, Jean 1, 13* (Rome, 1969); L. B. Smedes, *All Things Made New: A Theology of Man's Union With Christ* (Grand Rapids, Mich., 1970); D. E. Aune, *The Cultic Setting*

of Realized Eschatology in Early Christianity (Leiden, 1972).

141. See B. Botte, "La sagesse et les origines de la Christologie," *RSPT*, XXI (1932): 54–67; A. Feuillet, *Le Christ, Sagesse de Dieu dans les épîtres pauliniennes* (Paris, 1966); W. A. Beardslee, "The Wisdom Tradition and The Synoptic Gospels," *JAAR*, XXXV (1967): 231–40; A. Feuillet, *Le Christ, Sagesse de Dieu* (Paris, 1967); F. Christ, *Jesus Sophia: Die Sophia-Christologie bei den Synoptiker* (Zürich, 1970); J. M. Robinson, "Jesus as *Sophos* and *Sophia*: Wisdom Tradition and the Gospels," in *Aspects of Wisdom in Judaism and Early Christianity* (Notre Dame, Ind., 1975), pp. 1 ff.

142. This structure appears at three turning points of the gospel kerygma: (a) The introduction, which evokes John the Baptist in terms of the prophets' expectation of the final epiphany (Mark 1:2; cf. Mal. 3:1, Isa. 40:3); (b) The transfiguration, which borrows from the theologoumena of the Sinai theophany (Mark 9:2,7; cf. Exod. 19:16, 24:15); and (c) The Passion narrative, which places into prominence the motif of the temple (Mark 13:1–2, 14:58, 15:38).

143. Acts 7:44–50.

144. Acts 9:5.

145. 1 Cor. 3:16.

146. Luke 1:35.

147. John 1:14.

148. Hebrews 7:1—9:28.

149. Rev. 21:2–27. It is significant that the seer of the Apocalypse of John specifically notes, "And I saw no temple therein" (vs. 22*a*).

150. Matt. 26:29; Mark 14:25; Luke 22:18, 30: cf. 1 Cor. 11:26.

151. G. von Rad, *Old Testament Theology*, I–II, tr. by D. M. G. Stalker (New York, 1960–65).

152. R. Bultmann, *Theology of the New Testament*, I–II, tr. by K. Grobel (New York, 1951–55).

153. See J. Weingreen, *From Bible to Mishna. The Continuity of Tradition* (Manchester, 1976).

154. See A. C. Sundberg, Jr., "The 'Old Testament': A Christian Canon," *CBQ*, XXX (1968): 154–55; J. A. Sanders, "Torah and Christ," *In.*, XXIX (1975): 372 ff.; *id.*, "Canon of the NT," *IDB*, *Suppl. Vol.* (1976): 136 ff.

155. The rabbinical college at Jamnia (ca. A.D. 97) did not promulgate the canon of the Hebrew Bible. It decided on the canonicity of marginal or doubtful books. Likewise, it is piquant to observe that the Western church lived for centuries without an official canon of scripture, which was formulated by the Protestant Confessions of the sixteenth century and the decrees of the Council of Trent in response to the Protestant challenge.

156. See G. E. Wright, "The Canon as Theological Problem," *The Old Testament and Theology* (New York, 1969), pp. 166 ff.

157. See above, note 100.

158. See J. Barr, *The Bible in the Modern World* (New York, 1973), p. 181; J. A. Sanders, "Reopening Old Questions About Scripture," *In.*, XXVIII (1974): 322 f.

159. The distinction between "biblical theology" and "scholastic theology" appeared in the *Pia Desideria* of Philip Spener in 1675, although the expression *theologia biblica* was first used by Wolfgang Jacob Christmann in 1624 and Henricus a Diest in 1643. A *Biblische Theologie* was published by Carl Haymann in 1708. A. F. Büsching wrote in 1758 on the "advantages of a biblical theology over a scholastic or dogmatic theology."

160. Cf. R. Smend, "J.-Ph. Gablers Begründung der biblischen Theologie," *Ev. Th.*, (1959), pp. 345 ff.; J. D. Smart, "The Death and Rebirth of Biblical Theology," in *The Interpretation of Scripture* (Philadelphia, 1961), pp. 232 ff.; G. Ebeling, "The Meaning of 'Biblical Theology'," *JTS*, VI (1955), pp. 210–25; *Word and Faith*, tr. by J. W. Leitch (Philadelphia, 1963), pp. 79–97.

161. See the works, among others, of C. F. Ammon (1792), G. L. Bauer (1796), W.

58   *THE ELUSIVE PRESENCE*

M. L. de Wette (1813–16), E. W. Hengstenberg (1829–35); B. Bauer (1838–39); F. C. Baur (1847), J. C. Hoffmann (1840–44), G. F. Oehler (1873), H. Schultz (1869), A. B. Davidson (1904).

162. See A. von Harnack, *Marcion: das Evangelium vom fremden Gott, eine Monographie zur Geschichte der Grundlegung der katholischen Kirche. Neue Studien zu Marcion* (Leipzig, 1924).

163. R. Kittel, *ZAW*, XXXIX (1921): 84; cf. C. Steuernagel, "Alttestamentliche Religionsgeschichte," *ZAW*, XLIII (1925): 266–73; J. D. Smart, "The Death and Rebirth of Biblical Theology," in *The Interpretation of Scripture*, pp. 270 ff.

164. Barth was aware of the sterility of *Historismus*, but he tended to telescope the entire history of Israel into a Christology. Paradoxically, his reaction against the neo-Marcionism of Harnack led him to neglect the historical concreteness and complexity of "the people of God," either in the Hebraic period or at the birth of the church. His influence has generally been felt by systematic theologians rather than by biblical exegetes. One notable exception is that of W. Vischer, who, like Barth and indeed E. W. Hengstenberg (*Christologie des Alten Testaments*, 1829–33), interpreted the Old Testament as "a witness to Christ." Among the many books and articles dealing with Barthian hermeneutics, cf. O. Cullmann, "Les problèmes posés par la méthode exégétique de Karl Barth," *RHPR*, VIII (1928): 70–83; German tr. in *Vorträge und Aufsätze* (Tübingen und Zürich, 1966), pp. 90–101.

165. J. Hempel, *Gott und Mensch im Alten Testament. Studie zur Geschichte der Frömmigkeit* (Stuttgart, 1926; etc.).

166. O. Eissfeldt, "Israelitisch-jüdische Religionsgeschichte und alttestamentliche Theologie," *ZAW*, XLIV (1926): 1–12.

167. W. Eichrodt, "Hat die alttestamentliche Theologie noch selbständige Bedeutung innerhalb der alttestamentli-

chen Wissenschaft?" *ZAW*, XLVII (1929): 83–91.

168. *Theology of the Old Testament* (1933–39), tr. by J. A. Baker from the 6th German ed. (1959), 2 vols. (Philadelphia, 1961–64; etc.).

169. See above, pp. 22–27.

170. See R. E. Murphy, "The Kerygma of the Book of Proverbs," *In.*, XX (1966): 9 ff.; "The Interpretation of the Old Testament Wisdom Literature," *In.*, XXII (1968): 290 ff.; B. L. Mack, "Wisdom Myth and Mythology," *In.*, XXIV (1970): 3 ff.; R. B. Y. Scott, "The Study of the Wisdom Literature," *In*, XXIV (1970): 20 ff.

171. F. C. Prussner, "The Covenant of David and the Problem of Unity in Old Testament Theology," in J. C. Rylaarsdam, ed., *Transitions in Biblical Scholarship* (Chicago, 1968), pp. 17–41.

172. W. Zimmerli, "The Place and Limits of the Wisdom in the Framework of the Old Testament Theology," *SJT*, XVII (1964): 146–58; W. Brueggemann, "Scripture and an ecumenical Life-Style," *In.*, XXIV (1970): 3–19.

173. Cf. W. G. Most, "A Biblical Theology of Redemption in a Covenant Framework," *CBQ*, XXIX (1967): 1–19; J. Jocz, *The Covenant: A Theology of Human Destiny* (Grand Rapids, Mich., 1968); G. W. Buchanan, *The Consequences of the Covenant* (Leiden, 1970); see also note 96 above. Although many essays on biblical theology are still written in the traditional framework of doctrinal ideas, they usually assign a prominent place to the soteriological complex of cultic obedience and faith, even if they present a didactic pattern. See, among others, the works of L. Köhler (1936), P. Heinisch (1940), A. Gelin (1949), P. van Imschoot (1945), and O. Procksch (posthumously published in 1956).

174. H. Wheeler Robinson, *Inspiration and Revelation* (Oxford, 1950).

175. E. Jacob, *Theology of the Old Testament*, tr. by A. W. Heathcote and Ph. J. Allcock (New York, 1958); Th. C. Vriez-

en, *An Outline of Old Testament Theology*, 2nd ed. (Oxford, 1970).

176. See note 151 above.

177. Not more successful has been von Rad's effort to justify mutual complementariness of Old Testament and New Testament. To maintain that the first Christians reinterpreted the creedal confessions of Judaism in a way not unlike that of the Deuteronomists and the Chronicler with regard to the cultic traditions of ancient Israel (cf. von Rad, "The Actualization of the Old Testament in the New" and "The Old Testament's Understanding of the World and Man, and Christianity," in *Old Testament Theology*, vol. II, pp. 319–56) is possible only through the application of a form of typological exegesis which raises serious problems of hermeneutical methodology. Cf. W. Eichrodt, "Typologische Auslegung des Alten Testaments," *Ev. Th.*, XII (1952): 17 ff.; H. Conzelmann, "Fragen an G. von Rad," *Ev. Th.* XXIV (1964): 113 ff., and von Rad's subsequent disquisition *Ev. Th.*, XXIV (1954), pp. 388 ff. See also Eichrodt's comments on von Rad's method and purpose in the revised edition of his *Theology of the Old Testament*, tr. by J. A. Baker (London, 1967) I, p. 34; and those of Vriezen, in "Basis, Task and Method in Old Testament Theology," *An Outline of Old Testament Theology*, pp. 118 ff.

178. See the pioneering essay of A. Weiser on "Faith and History" (1931), reprinted in *Glaube und Geschichte im Alten Testament und andere auswählte Schriften* (Göttingen, 1961); E. Jacob, *La tradition historique en Israël* (Montpellier, 1941); G. Östborn, *Yhwh's Word and Deeds: A Preliminary Study into the Old Testament Presentation of History* (Uppsala, 1951); J. Hempel, *Glaube, Mythos und Geschichte im Alten Testament* (Berlin, 1954); E. Speiser, "The Biblical Idea of History in its Common Near Eastern Setting," *IEJ*, VII (1959): 203; J. Barr, "Revelation Through History in the Old Testament and in Modern Theol-

ogy," *In.*, XVII (1963): 193–205; H. Gese, "The Idea of History in the Ancient Near East and the Old Testament," *JTC*, I (1964): 49–64; E. Osswald, "Geschehene u. geglaubte Geschichte in der alttestamentlichen Theologie," *Wissenschaftliche Zeitschrift der Fried.-Schiller-Universität*, XIV (1965): 705–15; J. J. M. Roberts, "Myth Versus History: Relaying the Comparative Foundations," *CBQ*, XXXVIII (1976): 1 ff.

179. G. E. Wright, *The Old Testament and Theology* (New York, 1969), pp. 70 ff.

180. B. S. Childs, "The God of Israel and the Church," in *Biblical Theology in Crisis* (Philadelphia, 170), pp. 201 ff.

181. J. Barr, "The Problem of Old Testament Theology and the History of Religion," *CJT*, III (1957): 141–49; R. de Vaux, "Peut-on écrire une théologie de l'Ancien Testament?" *Bible et Orient* (Paris, 1967), pp. 59–71; E. Jacob, "La théologie de l'Ancien Testament: Etat présent et perspectives d'avenir," *De Mari à Qumran. Festschrift J. Coppens* (Gembloux et Paris, 1969), pp. 259–71; H.-J. Kraus, "Geschichte als Erziehung. Biblisch-theologische Perspektiven," in *Probleme biblischer Theologie: Festschrift G. von Rad*, ed. H. W. Wolff (München, 1971), pp. 258–74; N. W. Porteous, "Magnalia Dei," *ibid.*, pp. 417–27; G. F. Hasel, *Old Testament Theology: Basic Issues in the Current Debate* (Grand Rapids, Mich., 1972); W. Zimmerli, *Grundriss der alttestamentliche Theologie* (Stuttgart, 1972).

182. G. Fohrer, *Theologische Grundstrukturen des Alten Testaments* (Berlin & New York, 1972), pp. 95 ff. A useful survey of various suggestions for the "central" concept of the Old Testament will be found in G. Hasel, *Old Testament Theology: Basic Issues in the Current Debate* (Grand Rapids, Mich., 1972), pp. 49 ff.

183. See H.-J. Kraus, *Die biblische Theologie: Ihre Geschichte und Problematik* (Neukirchen-Vluyn, 1970), pp. 279 ff.; E. Ladd, "The Search for Perspective," *In.*, XXV (1971): 41–62.

184. W. Wrede, *Über Aufgabe und Methode der sogenanntlichen neutestamentlichen Theologie* (Göttingen, 1897).
185. See the works of P. Feine (1913), F. Büchsel (1935), E. Stouffer (1941), H. Conzelmann (1969), W. G. Kümmel (1969), J. J. Jeremias (1971), G. E. Ladd (1974), E. Lohse (1974), L. Goppelt (1975), H. Clavier (1976).
186. A. Schlatter, *Der Glaube im Neuen Testament* (1885); id., *Theologie des Neuen Testaments* (1909–18); id., *Die Geschichte des Christus* (1921); cf. Kraus, *Die biblische Theologie* (1970), pp. 175 ff. See also the influential book of M. Kähler, *The So-Called Historical Jesus* (2nd. German ed., 1896), tr. by C. E. Braaten (Philadelphia, 1964).
187. W. Bousset, *Kyrios Christos. A History of the Belief in Christ from the Beginnings of Christianity to Irenaeus*, tr. by J. E. Steely (Nashville and New York, 1970; original German edition, 1913).
188. See N. Perrin, "The Challenge of New Testament Theology Today," in Richard Batey, ed., *New Testament Issues* (New York, 1970), pp. 15–34; E. Käsemann, "The Problem of a New Testament Theology," *NTS*, XIX (1972–73): 235–45; W. G. Kümmel, *The Theology of the New Testament According to Its Major Witnesses: Jesus-Paul-John*, tr. by J. E. Steely (Nashville, 1973); H. Conzelmann, *Theologie als Schriftauslegung: Aufsätze zum Neuen Testament* (München, 1975).
189. See note 152 above.
190. R. Bultmann, "The Significance of the Old Testament for Christian Faith," in *The Old Testament and Christian Faith*, ed. by B. W. Anderson (New York, 1963), pp. 8–35. Among the various contributions to this critical appraisal of Bultmann's position, see especially C. Michalson, "Bultmann Against Marcion," pp. 49–63, and E. Voegelin, "History and Gnosis," pp. 64–89. Cf. Bultmann's typical treatment of the Old Testament in his article on "Knowledge" in *TWNT*.
The literature on Bultmann is consider-

able. Among others, see P. Barthel, "Bultmann et l'interprétation du Nouveau Testament," *RHPR*, XXXVII (1957): 257–64; N. J. Young, *History and Existential Theology: The Role of History in the Thought of Rudolf Bultmann* (Philadelphia, 1969).
191. See note 136 above.
192. O. Cullmann, *Christ and Time: The Primitive Christian Conception of Time and History*, rev. ed., tr. by F. V. Filson (London, 1957); *Christology of the New Testament*, tr. by Sh. C. Guthrie and Ch. A. M. Hope (Philadelphia, 1959); id., *Salvation in History*, tr. by S. G. Sowers (New York, 1967): this is in effect a modern treatment of the theology of the New Testament which presupposes the theological significance of the Old Testament for Christians.
193. Cullmann, *Salvation in History*, pp. 313 ff.
194. *Ibid.*, pp. 283 ff., 289 ff.
195. See bibliography in J. M. Robinson, *A New Quest for the Historical Jesus* (London, 1959), pp. 9 ff.; E. Trocmé, "Quelques travaux récents sur le Jésus de l'histoire," *RHPR*, LII (1972): 485–98; Ch. C. Anderson, *The Historical Jesus: A Continuing Quest* (Grand Rapids, Mich., 1972).
196. The problem of the interrelation of exegesis and epistemology has been revived in the past twenty-five years through the development of linguistic analysis and philosophical inquiry concerning the question of objectivity and subjectivity. See F. Bovon, et al., *Analyse structurale et exégèse biblique* (Neuchâtel, 1971); J. A. Sanders, "Hermeneutics," *IDB*, *Suppl. Vol.* (1976), pp. 402 ff.; id., "Adaptable for Life: The Nature and Function of the Canon," *Magnalia Dei: The Mighty Acts of God [In Memoriam G. E. Wright]* (Garden City, N.Y., 1976), pp. 531 ff.
197. In his book, *Biblical Theology in Crisis* (New York, 1969), B. S. Childs referred not to "Biblical Theology" in the historical sense of the word (p. 18, *et passim*), but

to various forms of a neoorthodox theology which appeared on the North American continent in the middle of the twentieth century and was sometimes known as "the Biblical Theology Movement." This misleading expression designates a loose group of heterogeneous trends that have been influenced by Kierkegaard, Dostoievski, Barth, Brunner, Bultmann, Tillich, R. Niebuhr, Sartre, Heidegger, and even Camus. Although several of the representatives of this theological movement have taken seriously the theological significance of the Bible, their work should not in any way be confused with "biblical theology" in the proper sense.
198. See K. Stendahl, "Biblical Theology, Contemporary," *IDB*, I (1962): 429 ff.; cf. "Method in the Study of Biblical Theology," in *The Bible in Modern Scholarship*, ed. by J. Ph. Hyatt (Nashville, 1965), p. 199.
199. See B. Albrektson, *History and the Gods: An Essay on the Idea of Historical Events as Divine Manifestations in the Ancient Near East and in Israel* (Lund, 1967); S. Amsler, "Les deux sources de la théologie de l'histoire dans l'Ancien Testament," *RTP*, XIX (1969): 235–46.
200. G. Ebeling, "The Meaning of Biblical Theology," *JTS*, VI (1955): 210–25; revised and rep. in *Word and Faith* (Philadelphia, 1963), pp. 79–97; see esp. pp. 91 f.
201. See P. R. Ackroyd, *Continuity: A Contribution to the Study of the Old Testament Religious Tradition* (Oxford, 1962). New Testament scholars generally tend to continue presenting theological themes separately, although several of them are trying to bring these themes into a single focus. See H. Thyen, *Studien zur Sündenvergebung im Neuen Testament und seinen alttestamentlichen und jüdischen Voraussetzungen* (Göttingen, 1970).
202. See J. Barr, "Le judaïsme postbiblique et la théologie de l'Ancien Testament," *RTP*, XVIII (1968): 209–17.

203. "What the Bible testifies to and strives after is not theology, but something that happens to man in God's dealings with the world" (Ebeling, *Word and Faith*, p. 93).
204. Plato, *Rep.*, 379a; Aristotle, *Meteor.*, 2, 1–2; *id.*, *Metaph.*, 2, 4, 12; 10, 7, 7; 11, 6, 6; etc. See F. Kattenbusch, "Die Entstehung einer christlichen Theologie. Zur Geschichte der Ausdrücke *theologia, theologos, theologikos.*" *ZTK*, XI (1930): 161 –205; W. W. Jaeger, *Theology of the Early Greek Philosophers* (Oxford, 1947), pp. 4–5.
205. J. Hänel, *Das Erkennen Gottes bei den Schriftpropheten* (Berlin, 1923), pp. 83 ff.; S. Mowinckel, "La connaissance de Dieu chez les prophètes de l'Ancien Testament," *RHPR*, XXII (1942): 69–105; G. J. Botterweck, "*Gott erkennen*" im Sprachgebrauch des Alten Testamentes (Bonn, 1951); J. L. McKenzie, "Knowledge of God in Hosea," *JBL*, LXXIV (1955): 22 ff.; H. W. Wolff, " 'Wissen um Gott' bei Hosea als Urform von Theologie," *Gesammelte Studien zum Alten Testament* (Munich, 1964), pp. 182–205.
206. It is significant that in the revised edition of *An Outline of Old Testament Theology* (Oxford, 1970), Th. C. Vriezen emphasizes the reality of communion between Yahweh and his people above all other factors (see esp. pp. 150, 175).
207. See J. W. McKay, "Man's Love for God in Deuteronomy and the Father/Teacher—Son/Pupil Relationship," *VT*, XXII (1972): 426–35; S. D. McBride, Jr., "The Yoke of the Kingdom: An Exposition of Deuteromony 6:4–5," *In.*, XXVII (1973): 273–306.
208. R. C. Dentan, *The Knowledge of God in Ancient Israel* (New York, 1968), pp. 43 ff.
209. J.-J. von Allmen, *Prophétisme sacramentel; neuf études pour le renouveau et l'unité de l'Eglise* (Neuchâtel, 1964), p. 19; cf. S. Amsler, "Le thème du procès chez les prophètes d'Israël," *RTP*, XXIV (1974); 116–31, esp. p. 130.
210. K. H. Miskotte, *When the Gods are Si-*

lent, tr. J. W. Doberstein (New York, 1967), pp. 257 ff.

211. J. Barr, "The Old Testament and the New Crisis of Biblical Authority," *In.*, XXV (1971): 24 ff. See also R. Rendtorff, "Die Entstehung der israelitischen Religion als religionsgeschichtliches and theologisches Problem," *TLZ*, LXXXVIII (1963), cols. 735–46; *id.*, "The Concept of Revelation in Ancient Israel," in W. Pannenberg, ed., *Revelation as History*, tr. D. Granskou (New York, 1968), pp. 23 ff.; U. Wilckens, "The Understanding of Revelation Within the History of Primitive Christianity," *ibid.*, pp. 55 f.

212. J. Barr, *Old and New in Interpretation* (London, 1966), pp. 149; *id.*, "The Authority of the Bible: A Study Outline," *Ecumenical Review*, XXI (1969), pp. 135–66; *id.*, "The Bible in Theology," in *The Bible in the Modern World* (London, 1973), pp. 89 ff.; *id.*, *ibid.*, "A Basis for Construction," pp. 112 ff. See also the comments of J. A. Sanders on Barr's position in "Reopening Old Questions About Scripture," *In.*, XXVIII (1974), 321–30. For a conservative appraisal of the role of Scripture for Christian thinking, see M. G. Kline, *The Structure of Biblical Authority* (Grand Rapids, 1972).

213. See a pre-Vatican II appraisal by J. K. S. Reid, "Roman Catholicism and the Bible," *In.*, XIII (1959): 71–86; cf. D. R. Jones, *Instrument of Peace: Biblical Principles of Christian Unity* (London, 1965); L. Klein, ed., *The Bible in a New Age* (New York, 1964); J. Lescrauwaet, *The Bible on Christian Unity* (London, 1965); O. Cullmann, *La Bible et le dialogue oecuménique* (Paris, 1967); see also L. J. Swidler, ed., *Scripture and Ecumenism: Protestant, Catholic, Orthodox and Jewish* (Pittsburgh and Louvain, 1965), especially the essays of M. Barth, "Sola Scriptura," pp. 75 ff., and of R. E. Murphy, "The Relevance of Old Testament Studies for Ecumenism," pp. 95 ff.; Concilium, General Secretariat, "Is Scripture Becoming Less Important?" in *The Presence of God*, ed. by P. Benoit et al., (*Concilium*, L [1969]: 157–75); W. Brueggemann, "Scripture and an Ecumenical Life-Style," *In.*, XXIV (1970): 1 ff.; R. E. Murphy, "The Role of the Bible in Roman Catholic Theology," *In.*, XXV (1971): 78–94; H. Cazelles, "Is the Old Testament Relevant to Modern Catholic Theology?" *Theological Soundings, Notre-Dame Seminary Jubilee Studies* (New Orleans, 1973), VI.

2

Epiphanic Visitations to the Patriarchs

In all ages of history, men and women have related memories of moments when they had perceived, with particular intensity, the presence of their gods. The literature of spirituality, be it Jewish, Christian, or Muslim, abounds in stories of divine appearances. In many cases, the "vision" or auditory experience which takes place is described in somewhat ambiguous terms, so that a forceful awareness of numinous proximity is expressed as if the god had "appeared" or "descended" and then "gone away." It is therefore not possible to ascertain from such literature whether a psychological mood, precisely on account of its concreteness, points to an inward emotion of a purely subjective character or to a suprasensorial perception.

In one of his novels, Georges Bernanos writes of a priest who "with an absolute certitude knew" that "the joy he suddenly felt was a presence," and concludes: "The feeling of this mysterious presence was so vivid that he turned his head abruptly, as if to meet the glance of a friend."[1] In similar language, the Hebrew traditions stated long ago, "Yahweh used to speak to Moses face to face, as a man speaks to his friend."[2]

Although the Pentateuch in its final form attributed to Moses the institution of the Hebrew cultus, it also affirmed that the God who revealed himself to the leader of the Hebrew slaves in the desert of Sinai was the same Deity worshipped by their ancestors, and it insisted upon the awareness of theological continuity. Yahweh was "the God of Abraham, the God of Isaac, and the God of Jacob."[3] The northern (E) strand of the cultic *legenda* of Israel maintained that the intimate name of that God, "Yahweh," had not been known before the time of Moses, since it had been revealed only to him at the scene of the Burning Bush.[4] The southern (J) epic, however, maintained that men had already begun "to call upon the name of "Yahweh" in the pre-historic age.[5] Thus the relation between the origins of the Hebrew cultus and the actual events of the distant past remains obscure.[6]

Since most nations allude to the beginning of their ritual ceremonies and religious beliefs in stories of divine self-disclosure to their ancestral heroes, modern historians of Israelite religion have tended to disregard the literal accuracy of the patriarchal traditions. While earlier commentators had exaggerated the influence of the great men and women of the Bible at the expense of corporate forces, twentieth-century scholarship rushed to the opposite extreme. It has been generally believed that the Hebrew cultus gradually emerged as an impersonal and sociological phenomenon in the course of many generations. In recent years, anthropologists and ethnologists have recognized that individual personalities of exceptional stature often play decisive roles in religious reforms and innovations within the collectivities to which they belong. Today, a balanced view of the interaction between individual and society is gaining ground. Attention is again being paid to the intensely personal character of Hebrew faith. It is increasingly recognized that the traits of psychological subtlety that are displayed in the patriarchal stories of divine-human encounter reflect the experiences of concrete individuals endowed with an exceptional stature.

Stress is again being put on the importance of outstanding moments of religious illumination or "epiphany" within the lives of chieftains, poets, musicians, and other tribal leaders. Even when revelation is viewed as history, or rather when history is seen as the locus of revelation,[7] the interpretation of events as media of divine self-disclosure depends upon the consciousness, reflection, and formulation of some gifted individual.[8]

While phenomena of religious perception may involve mass psychology,[9] the comparative history of religions tends to show that collective states are generally related to the activity of influential figures who have had a vision or some form of ecstatic trance.

Biblical Hebrew did not apparently possess an abstract word meaning "presence."[10] The expression "the face of Yahweh" or "the face of Elohim" was sometimes specifically used to designate the innermost being of God, inaccessible even to a man like Moses,[11] but the word *panîm*, "face," was ordinarily used metaphorically in composite prepositions to designate a sense of immediate proximity.[12] More often than not, the storytellers merely said that God "appeared," literally, "showed himself."[13]

One may find it naïve and uncritical to begin a study of the Hebraic theology of presence with a selective analysis of the epiphanic visitations to the patriarchs since literary documentation concerning these visitations is the result of a long process of exchange between cultic celebration and inward faith in later Israel, during the monarchic period. Nevertheless, a limited survey of these narratives constitutes a direct approach to the topic under consideration, for Israel looked at these narratives in her festive ceremonies as models of her own religious stance from generation to generation. As the fathers knew their God, so also the sons could in some way duplicate, imitate, or stimulate in themselves a receptiveness to the renewal of divine entrance into their history. Moreover, the stories of the epiphanic visitations to the patriarchs carried with them promises and warnings for the future.[14] The recital of the appearances of Yahweh to the ancestors of the special people had in effect already assumed the character of a dynamic canon: they were concrete parables of the standards of the faith, they contained the seed of a new life. The coming of God in the past meant more than a simple revelation (*Offenbarung*): its cultic recital promoted an expectation—the hope for fulfillment and the wait for the final manifestation (*Erscheinung*).[15] He who came to the fathers is also *He That Cometh*. From the beginning, Israel's faith was eschatological.

THE PATRIARCHAL TRADITIONS

Archaeological discoveries have shed a great deal of light on the patriarchal age. Data on West-Semitic onomastics,[16] economic and political conditions in Asia Anterior during the Middle Bronze and Late Bronze Ages, ethnic movements, legal customs,[17] and technological advances such as the domestication of the Bactrian camel,[18] have considerably clarified the historical milieu which is presupposed by the early traditions of Genesis regarding the Hebrew fathers.[19] This new climate of knowledge, however, does not permit a demonstration of the literal historicity of the patriarchal saga.[20] There is no evidence that the sequence of the three figures now portrayed as individuals genealogically related—Abraham, Isaac, and Jacob—constitutes a factual account.[21] It is probable that the traditions concerning Abraham and Lot, Isaac and Ishmael, Jacob and Esau, as well as the garland of vignettes about the twelve sons of Jacob, depict less the adventures of individuals than the tribal migrations of patronymic heroes. Nevertheless, contemporary historians have come to exercise a caution which Julius Wellhausen and recent traditio-historical critics have often ignored.

One aspect of this trend toward critical respect for the validity of the tradition concerns the religious experiences of the patriarchs, and this development assumes a particular importance for the study of the origins of the Hebraic theology of presence. Available data interpreted in the light of the history of the ancient Near East during the second millenium B.C. allow the contemporary student to conjecture that the Hebrew ancestors formed not a single family but a group of caravan migrants and herdsmen of the seminomadic type[22] who practiced seasonal commerce and agriculture in limited areas,[23] moved periodically on the highways of the Fertile Crescent,[24] maintained contact with diverse ethnic and political groups, yet remained rigorously distinct from their cultural environment. The distinctiveness of Israel's religion at a later age strongly suggests that a phenomenon of cultic disruption did actually take place at some given time in her past.

This cultic disruption may be considered as either the cause or the symptom of the fathers' cultural aloofness. All the traditions now preserved in Genesis, with one exception,[25] insist on the religious nature of the Hebrews' sociological isolation. From the start of the Yahwist's epic (Gen. 12:1 ff.), the memories of patriarchal travels point to a single motivation: the peculiar summons of a "nomadic" Deity that appears at first to have been completely independent of a localized shrine or priesthood.[26] This feature is the more remarkable when it is remembered that the narratives, whatever may have been their initial modes of formulation, were preserved for posterity through the festive celebrations of Israel in the sanctuaries of Canaan after the Hebrew tribes settled in the land. At the same time, one of the factors which played a decisive part in the growth of the oral tradition was related to the process of "Hebraicization" of the Canaanite shrines. The stories of the epiphanic visitations of Yahweh to Abraham, Isaac, and Jacob may well have had their roots in the remote past, perhaps in the first half of the second millenium B.C., but they belong, at least in their present form, to the cultic etiology of a later age. They almost invariably tell how the ancestors built altars to commemorate and sacralize the places where they heard the summons of a strange deity, Yahweh. In the time of the Judges and the Kings, toward the end of the second millenium B.C., these places became the chief sanctuaries of Israel—Shechem, Mamre, Beersheba, Bethel, Penuel, and so on.

The patriarchs may have worshipped a number of sky or mountain deities, like El Elyon, El Shadday, El Roy, El Bethel, and El Olam.[27] In addition, they possibly held allegiance to their clan gods, like "the Shield of Abraham" (Gen. 15:1), "the Fear (or Kinsman) of Isaac" (Gen. 31:42, 53), "the Champion of Jacob" (Gen. 49:24).[28] All these gods were in the course of time identified with Yahweh, the God of Moses (Exod. 3:13 ff.). At the present stage of Old Testament science, it is not possible to know with certainty whether or not Yahweh was worshipped by Abraham and the other patriarchal figures.[29] Nevertheless, the epiphanic visitations to the patriarchs are now presented in a Yahwistic context, and this points to a significant aspect of the Hebraic theology of presence.

THEOPHANY AND EPIPHANIC VISITATIONS

The use of the expression "epiphanic visitations" is here proposed rather than the traditional, "theophany," because the latter is in several respects inadequate. The etymology of the word[30] and its early usage[31] betray some of the characteristics of the Greek myths, in which the gods and goddesses are "seen" by human eyes.[32] There is reason to believe that such a vocabulary depended, as in many other instances, upon semantic habits inherited from the Northwest Semites in proto-

Hebraic times. The "Hebrew" tongue, after all, had in all probability reached a status of philological distinctiveness within the West-Semitic languages before it became a tool for a new and specifically Hebraic formulation of religious faith.[33] Moreover, the Hebrew stories of "theophany" make use of visual features in such a way that the deity is not really seen by man. Either there is too much light, in which case the storytellers emphasize the blinding quality of the experience, or there is too little light—the experience occurs in the gloom of night or in a cloud of total darkness—and the storytellers pile up synonyms for obscurity in order to stress divine invisibility. In a Hebrew "theophany," Yahweh is not really "seen" by man, but only "heard," although there are visible signs of his presence.

The word "theophany" is also inadequate when one interprets it in the context of the patriarchal narratives, because it conveys not only the features of light and darkness but also a variety of wonders such as whirlwinds, hurricanes, storms, rain, hail, flashes of fire (especially bolts of lightning), claps of thunder, smoke, and earthquakes. These elements abound in the mythical material of the ancient Near East,[34] as well as in that of Greece and Rome at a later age. They also appear in the many poetical allusions to "theophanies" which are found in the hymns of the Psalter and in the prophetic literature.[35] Some of these are present in the various traditions concerning the Sinai theophany,[36] but they are lacking in the narratives of divine-human encounters in the patriarchal period.[37] Quite clearly, these narratives do not belong to the same literary *Gattung* or *genre* as those of the Sinai-Horeb theophanies.[38] Moreover, the many poetic allusions to the coming of Yahweh in the beginning or at the end of Israel's history, especially those in the hymns of praise for the warrior God,[39] and which are usually described as a literary form of theophany, likewise differ both from the Sinai-Horeb type and from the patriarchal *Gattung*. Form-critical analysis shows that they belong either to the cultic hymn or to the cultic-prophetic oracle which liturgically enacts Yahweh's final epiphany.[40]

On the one hand, a "theophany" insists on the visibility of the natural phenomena which accompany the divine appearances, but this visibility is subordinated to their *hieroi logoi,* the sacred words of revelation and command. A "theophany" also concerns an individual, but this individual is a mediator, like Moses or Elijah. The theophanic intervention, as reenacted or proleptically acted in the cultus, addresses itself to a community at worship. It subordinates the visibility of the natural wonders to the *hieros logos* ("holy word"), and the *hieros logos* to the *Heilsgeschichte* ("History of Salvation").

On the other hand, the patriarchal narratives should not be called "theophanies," for they form a *sui generis* type of divine manifestation. They concern themselves exclusively with individuals of the distant past; they are free from the display of natural *mirabilia;* and they are couched in the style of simple meetings, naively and concretely described as the sudden encounter of two strangers who were going their separate ways.[41] These meetings are succinctly described, with a minimum of visual elements, and they center on a dramatic dialogue between God and man. They are suddenly begun and swiftly terminated. They are presented as normal happenings of daily existence, although they always succeed in preserving, by the use of some rhetorical or semantic device, the mystery of divine transcendence. They differ from the Sinai-Horeb theophanies,[42] the visions of the prophets,[43] the "whirlwind theophany" in Job,[44] the theophanic pictures of the Psalms and other victory hymns, and the prophetic oracles on the final epiphany of history. By contrast, the patriarchal stories deal with what may be called "epiphanic visitations."[45]

Form-critical analysis of the speeches of Deity which constitute the climax of these stories[46] shows that the traditions underwent a long process of development and stylization before they acquired their present form of literary expression. Several motifs of the epiphanic discourses belong to the cultic style of Mesopotamian, Egyptian, Ugaritic, and Israelite oracles.[47]

1. The opening formula of self-asseveration, "I am Yahweh," links the patriarchal stories of epiphanic visitation[48] with the theophanies of the Mosaic age: "I am Yahweh, the god of thy fathers" (Exod. 3:6). The recital of this sort of divine self-identification during the act of worship evoked at once in the mind of the community the whole history of salvation—"I am Yahweh, thy God, who brought thee out of the land of Egypt" (Exod. 20:2)—which in turn led to the formulation of the confessional response: "My father was an exhausted Aramaean nomad" (Deut. 26:5).[49] Likewise, the Egyptian god Harmakhis said to Thut-mose IV (1421–1413 B.C.), "I am thy father, Harmakhis-Khepri-Atum. I shall give thee my kingdom upon earth at the head of the living."[50] In the same manner, the Mesopotamian goddess declared to Essarhaddon of Assyria (680–669 B.C.), "I am the goddess Ishtar of Arbela, who will destroy your enemies from before your feet."[51]

2. The entreaty of reassurance, "Fear not,"[52] points to the language of the *Heilsorakel* (Salvation-oracle), which was pronounced, probably at an early age, in the sanctuaries of Israel.[53] It finds an echo, side by side with the opening motif of self-asseveration, in the oracular proclamations of the ancient Near Eastern temples.[54]

3. The promise of continuing companionship, "I will be with thee" (Gen. 26:24), provides a link with the Mosaic theophanies (Exod. 3:12, etc.). It implies a distinction between the experience of divine presence, quasi-sensorial and limited in time, and the awareness of psychological communion, which lasts beyond the brevity of the epiphanic visitation. The archaic feature of approval for the legendary Enoch, who "walked with Elohim" (Gen. 5:22), has become the cardinal element of Israel's faith.[55] Not only the patriarchs and Moses but also the prophets and the psalmists of a later age expressed a similar

awareness (e.g., Jer. 1:8, Ps. 73:23), and the liturgical motto of
the nation's eschatological hope was "Immanuel," "El-with-us"
(Isa. 7:14; cf. Ps. 46:7, 11 [Heb. 8, 12]).

From the start of Israel's history, during the early days of
Moses, Joshua, the judges, and the first kings, cultus and faith
were inseparable. In the ceremonial commemoration of the
epiphanic visitations to the patriarchs, the nation learned the
purpose of her *modus vivendi* and the meaning of her *modus
orandi*. Under the promise of posterity and land, which provided the unifying structure of all the patriarchal stories of
epiphanic visitation, one may discern a deeper and wholly inter-
nal theme of a strictly theological character. The promise of
seed and real estate, important as these may be, is subordinated
to the search for identity in the context of universal meaning.[56]
In ceremonially rehearsing the stories of Yahweh's manifestations to Abraham, Isaac, and Jacob, the nation was, in effect,
asking about her own place among the nations of the earth and
her own purpose in the history of man. Posterity and land are
conditions of historical existence, but they should not be confused with ends in themselves. Israel was animated by the vision
of unity for "all the families of the earth," and she transmitted
that vision in the festive recitals of the first narrative of patriarchal obedience to a call. From the start, the Hebraic theology
of presence was organically bound to the Hebraic theology of
history.

THE CALL OF ABRAHAM (*Gen. 12:1–6*)

The Yahwist epic places the call of Abraham at the head of the
history of salvation. The narrative contrasts sharply with the
picture of international chaos which immediately precedes it.[57]

No less than three times in the tradition on the Tower of Babel (Gen. 11:1–9) the expression appears, "scattered abroad over the face of the entire earth" (11:4*b*, 8*a*, 9*b*). Man's attempt to obtain security in territorial terms has failed. The figure of Abraham is introduced as the embodiment of a new form of society which deliberately severs its bonds with a static past in order to experiment in time. The nomadic motif of movement through space emerges as a symbol of openness to the future. Israel has sensed that history is not merely historiography—the recording of the past. Israel treasures cultically her epic memory on account of her will to understand and to prepare her future.

The form-critical analysis of the pericope of Abraham's call is the fruition of many scholars' work,[58] but E. Speiser appears to have succeeded in discovering the poetic structure of the epiphanic speech:[59]

12:1. And Yahweh said to Abram:
  "Get thee out of thy country, and of thy clan,
    Even away from thy father's home,
    To the land I will show thee.

  2. I will make thee a great nation,
    Bless thee and make thy name great:
    Be thou a blessing!

  3. I will bless them who bless thee
    And curse him who curses thee:
    In thee shall bless one another
    All the families of the earth!"
  4. And Abram went as Yahweh told him.

The scene is tersely staged. There is no hint of a visual setting. The pericope begins without introduction. The words "epiphany" and "theophany" are not fitting, for the Deity is not even said to appear. One uncovers here the features of the literary *Gattung* which is later used by the eighth- and seventh-

century prophets in the narratives of their calls. The epiphanic
speech is couched in metrical and strophic structure: two *tricola*
culminating in a rare *quadricolon*, with rhythmic stress falling on
the last words, "all the families of the earth."[60] In every generation, the people of the covenant are asked to decide, and the
decision is painful and thrilling. It is painful for it is first a
renunciation: "Get thee out!" The imperative *lekh-leka* is constructed with the formerly misnamed *dativus ethicus*,[61] a seemingly pleonastic pronominal suffix, reading literally, "Go for
thyself," which emphasizes the tense, complex, and definitive
character of the act in question; hesitation is legitimate, but
when the decision is taken, there is no return. Like Abraham,
Israel is uprooted,[62] and her alienation from the historical past
of mankind results directly from her theology of presence.

The threefold progression moves from larger to narrower
sociological allegiance—country, clan, home—and it stresses
the cruel aspect of the renunciation. At the same time, the
decision also has a radiant ring, for it leads to the expectation
of a blessing. The word *berakah* designates far more than the
pseudomagical virtue of material wealth, physiological fertility,
and immediate success. It evokes well-being in a corporate
sense, and it implies social responsibility.[63] It conveys, to be
sure, the connotation of sexual potency and procreative lar-
gesse, but always in the sense of loyalty to the future generations. Blessing is that power which transforms an individual
man of the static past into the historical man, *homo historicus.*
While the builders of the Tower of Babel attempted vainly to
make a name for themselves (Gen. 11:4), Abraham received a
blessing, and therefore his name was to become great. More
than this, he himself is called to become a blessing.

The imperative phrase "be a blessing!" is indeed unusual,
but the Masoretic pointing is well established, and there is no
valid reason to correct it (Gen. 12:2c). This is the mission of
Abraham and of Israel: "Be a blessing!" Such a rhetorical inno-

vation fits the revolutionary character of the thought. In a time of self-satisfied nationalism, when David and perhaps also Solomon (if the Yahwist first proclaimed the ancient tradition during Solomon's reign, in the middle of the tenth century B.C.) have indeed conquered the land of Canaan but have also been insidiously corrupted by the Canaanite culture, the cultic ceremonial of Israel reminds the community of faith of its theological vocation and its existential predicament. In the Yahwist epic, God says to man, "Dust thou art!" (Gen. 3:19), and to the father of the nation, "Be a blessing!" (Gen. 12:2c).

The mission of Israel in history was to effect a reconciliation among all the families of the earth.[64] The vision of a united mankind was far too modern for ancient times, and the theme disappeared from general notice in the centuries which followed. It remained in the ceremonial of Jerusalem, however, as the hymn for the celebration of the autumn festival, perhaps even the New Year, clearly testifies:

"The princes of the earth are assembled
   as the people of the God of Abraham" (Ps. 47:9 [Heb. 10]).

Second Isaiah, at the depth of the exile in Babylon, remembered that Israel, the seed of Abraham (Isa. 40:8), was called to be "a light unto the nations" (42:6, etc.). The intensity of Israel's search for her identity has led her to express, for the first time in history, an ideal of universalism, for which she assumed the burden of responsibility.[65]

The form of the epiphanic speech in which the nation gave literary form to the sense of her mission was borrowed from her cultic life. The "blessing" of Abraham and the "blessing" which Abraham is called upon to become are the blossoming of a moment of divine proximity, and the response to the epiphanic speech constitutes the Hebraic stance of faith. All the other stories of epiphanic visitation to the patriarchs introduce the theme of the testing of that faith. Because the fulfilment of the blessing is delayed and the self-disclosure of Yahweh remains limited to short instants of visitation, the Hebraic theology of presence at once acquires the elements of absence or at least hiddenness. From the start of the tradition regarding the history of salvation, cultus and faith are inextricably bound.

THE COVENANT WITH ABRAHAM (Gen. 15:1–21)

The present chapter of Genesis, which describes the covenant between Yahweh and Abraham (15:1–12, 17–21), combines several strands of ancient traditions, both Elohistic and Yahwistic,[66] with a priestly reinterpretation (vss. 13–16).[67] As Abraham had no heir, and the promise of his vocation lost all meaning, a second epiphanic visitation appears in the narrative: "After these things, the word of Yahweh came unto Abram in a vision," (Gen. 15:1a). This is the language of the prophetic *Gattung* of a later age. It will be observed that the word "vision" suggests the realm of sight, but no visual perception is recorded. On the contrary, it is the theologoumenon of the word which claims the audience's attention. The presence of the divine manifests itself in auditory rather than in visual ways even when the "word" comes in a "vision."[68] Once again, the religious encounter is dominated by an epiphanic speech:

"Fear not, Abram!
   I will be thy shield
   and thy exceedingly great reward!"

(Gen. 15:1b).

Quite naturally, the recipient of this assurance protested, since he continued to be childless (vs. 2), and the storyteller insisted:

"Behold, the word of Yahweh was to him, saying,
   ... He that shall come forth out of thy own loins
   shall be thy heir."   (Gen. 15:4).

Presumably still in the course of the same vision, Yahweh "brought him outside" to show him the stars in the night sky as the symbol of his innumerable offspring (vs. 5). The conclusion followed: "[Abraham] had faith on Yahweh, who imputed it to him for righteousness" (Gen. 15:6).

The verb *he'emîn*, "to have faith," is used in a theological context.[69] The semantic connotations of the root suggest solidity and firmness not only in the realm of space but also in that of time; hence it indicates durability, reliability, and endurance. Abraham took Yahweh at his word. He believed the truth of the promise made to him. He placed his entire trust in the epiphanic speech. He responded with the entirety of his being to the articulated thrust of the divine presence. He had no tangible or visible evidence; indeed, fragments of other ancient traditions woven into the final form of the narrative indicate that although his faith never wavered he made repeated attempts to receive a confirmation of his certitude. Nevertheless, he firmly maintained his acceptance of the word. This is not an intellectual assent to a propositional truth. It is the insertion of the wholeness of one's personality into a relation of total openness toward the reality of God. Yahweh had pledged his honor in promising Abraham a son, and Abraham "had faith upon Yahweh."

The attitude which is thus described is precisely akin to that of "righteousness," in the Hebrew sense of the word *tsedaqah*.[70] The history of this word is long and tortuous, but the Yahwist, followed by the great prophets and the psalmists, used it to indicate a dynamic and harmonious relationship between two human beings, between social groups, or again between God and man.[71] The word originally had little—if anything—to do with forensic justice, although in late Judaism it came to designate "deeds of piety," hence, "meritorious acts" and "merits."[72] The idea of righteousness in the context of legal judgment (cf. the Vulgate *justitia*) represents a distortion of the ancient Hebraic view of ongoing communion between God and man. It is against this distortion that Paul laboriously developed the formulation of what became a widely misunderstood "doctrine," that of "justification by faith" (Rom. 4:3–22, Gal. 3:6, etc.).[73]

Abraham had no law to obey.[74] In such a context, his righteousness was not viewed as a reward for obedience. The text points to the inwardness of his attitude and to the totality of his devotion. Jesus, Paul, and the Protestant Reformers keenly sensed the importance of this Hebraic notion as an intrinsic part of a theology of presence. It is significant that both the word *faith* and the word *righteousness* became perverted as soon as they were divorced from the temporally unstable and psychologically elusive apprehension of divine presence. Faith generally became mistaken for "mere belief" as soon as righteousness was held as an abusive synonym for "merit." The context of this narrative of epiphanic visitation shows that for the Yahwist, righteousness is not a quality or a virtue which Abraham earned by his achievement. Rather it is a way to describe man's living under God, or, in the favorite metaphor of the Hebrew religious semantics, man's "walking with God." The term suggests the continuity and the duration in time of the existential trust.

The final editor of the Pentateuch has interwoven in the narrative some archaic memories concerning the rite of covenant (Gen. 15:7–12, 17–21). Significantly, the divine self-asseveration again constitutes the initial element of this epiphanic sequence: "I am Yahweh who brought thee out of Ur of the Chaldeans" (vs. 7). Abraham's reaction to the holy was so traumatic that, just before sunset, a trancelike, hypnotic, or mantic sleep (*tardēmah*) seized him: "and behold, a dread, something like a great darkness, kept falling upon him" (vs. 12). As in the parallel tradition (vs. 1), the clear consciousness of the patriarch has been altered by the revelatory process. The "vision" (*maḥazeh*) took place, we are now told, in a peculiar form of "dream" which emerges in turn from a peculiar form of sleep.[75]

It should be noted that the narrative includes the rite of the covenant, but that such a motif is subordinated to that of the epiphanic presence.

THE STRANGERS BY THE OAKS OF MAMRE
(Gen. 18:1–16)

A masterpiece of the folkloric art, this story again represents the skillful interweaving of Yahwist and Elohist strands of oral tradition.[76] Its anthropomorphic character appears more clearly than that of the other stories of epiphanic visitation, for the three strangers who stood in front of Abraham as he sat at the opening of his tent in the heat of the day (vs. 1) soon became identified directly with the Deity (vs. 13). Yet, these men accepted Abraham's hospitality and ate as he stood by them under the trees (vs. 8). Afterward, in accordance with nomads' etiquette, the host accompanied them on the path to set them on their way. Accounts of visits by divine beings disguised as casual strangers are found everywhere in the legends of primitive societies.[77] In some earlier stage of the tradition,[78] the motif of the terebinths or oak trees of Mamre may have assumed an animistic meaning, but the Yahwist epic has absorbed it within the theme of epiphanic visitation.

The appearance of Yahweh in the guise of three men and later in the course of the tale in the guise of one of two angels or messengers[79] did not raise any difficulty with the Hebraic mentality. It indicates the realism with which the ancient mind believed in the actuality of divine rapport with men and its directness.[80]

18: 1. And Yahweh appeared to him
        by the terebinths of Mamre,
    As he sat at the door of his tent
        in the heat of the day.
2. He lifted up his eyes and looked,
        and behold! three men stood in front of him.
    When he saw them, he ran from the tent door to meet
        them,
        and bowed himself toward the earth and said,

3. "My lord, if I have found favor in thy sight,
        do not pass by thy servant.
4. Let a little water be brought, and wash your feet,
        and rest yourselves under the tree,
5. While I fetch a morsel of bread
        that you may refresh yourselves,
    And after that you may pass on—
        since you have come to your servant."

6. And they said, "Do thus as thou hast spoken."

All commentators have noted the exquisite artistry with which this scene is portrayed.[81] Its mythical feature of the hero who entertains gods unaware cannot detract from the specific quality of this Hebraic narrative of epiphanic visitation. The storyteller insists on the natural simplicity of the encounter between God and men of faith. At the same time, he subtly intimates the undefinable but unmistakable dimension of the holy.

At first, Abraham addressed only one of the visitors,[82] although his expression of welcome embraced all three.[83] The well-known dialogue on the announcement of the birth of a son and on Sarah's laughter (vss. 9–15) introduces Yahweh alone as the divine interlocutor (vss. 10, 13). The plural reappears as the men depart (vss. 16, 22). After Yahweh's soliloquy (vss. 17–19) and Abraham's intercession on the behalf of Sodom (vss. 20–31), the story suddenly refers to "the two messengers" or "angels" (19:1). Apparently, several strands of independent traditions have been woven together. The initial tale of the guests of Mamre, couched in rhythmic prose, is now followed by a divine monologue and a divine-human dialogue, the form and style of which point to a different milieu and perhaps another age.[84]

By such a work of juxtaposition, the Yahwist theologian deliberately inserted the promise of Abraham's posterity within the universal vision of the *Heilsgeschichte*. The nation of Abraham is viewed, once again, for the sake of "all the nations of the earth," as a tool for the divine completion of the created universe. Promise and election may never be separated from the salvation of the entire world. Centuries before the Second Isaiah, in the Babylonian exile, Hebrew theologians discerned the religious origin of an ethic of international peace and at the same time the ethical responsibility of the religious experience. In placing the narrative of epiphanic visitation "by the terebinths of Mamre" together with a divine soliloquy on the purpose of election, the Yahwist was warning Israel, much before the time of Amos and the other great prophets, of the universal responsibility of her mission: "I have known him, so that he may teach his sons and his household after him to keep the way of Yahweh in doing righteousness and justice" (vs. 19). In all probability, the festival ceremonies, during which such a narrative was recited, aimed in part at challenging the nascent nationalism of the kingdom under David and Solomon.

THE TEST OF ABRAHAM'S FAITH (*Gen. 22:1-19*)

This independent *novella* originated with the northern traditions of the Elohist stratum.[85] It is known in Judaism as the *Akedah* or "Binding," that is, the "tying-on" of Isaac for the sacrifice. Several features of the story exhibit a keenness of psychological introspection—the father's silence, the lad's bewilderment and fear, etc.—but they should not be allowed to detract from the theological crux of the tale. Psychology in the Hebrew epic is the intelligent handmaid of theology. The sacrifice of Isaac is simply the occasion of an epiphanic visitation.

While the narrator warns explicitly that "Elohim tested Abraham" (Gen. 22:1), he builds dramatic tension not only by stirring sympathy for the heroes, father and son, but also by eliciting from his audience a suspicion concerning the character of the Godhead. What kind of a deity is it who addresses man, his servant, indeed "his friend," and commands: "Take thy son, thy only son, him whom thou lovest, Isaac, and go to the land of Moriyyah and offer him there as a fiery sacrifice upon one of the hills I shall tell thee" (vs. 2)?

Abraham is precisely the man who had faith in God. This faith was acknowledged as the outward evidence of his inward devotion, the engagement of his total personality. Clearly the narrator wished to insist on the cruel aspect of the command, since he piled on four direct objects: "thy son, thy only son, him whom thou lovest, Isaac." He felt the pathos of the situation as deeply as the modern reader does, if not more, since memories of the horrors of child sacrifice probably lurked at the origin of the tradition and in any case haunted the mind of an ancient audience.

Whatever the cultural environment of the tale may have been, the Elohist rehearsed it in the sequence of other stories in order to convey far more than a polemic against Canaanite or Northwest-Semitic practices.[86] Like the Yahwist, he aimed at portraying the meaning of faith in the framework of an epiphanic visitation. For him, too, the command of Elohim was shocking and passed human comprehension. Not only was Isaac the child of Abraham's old age, his only son, the one whom he loved,[87] but he also represented for him and for the audience the only sign of the trustworthiness of God.

Abraham's faith was put to the test in two ways. First, the command crushed the heart of a father, and second, it shattered in one instant the entire edifice of his hope and the whole meaning of his existence. The basis of his decision to live for the future of mankind by participating in the time of God was annihilated. As Luther observed, his prospect was his own eternal death as well as the death of his son.[88]

The story insists also on the simplicity of Abraham's faith. It never vacillates. Not only did the father make himself available and receptive in his initial response, *Hinneni*, "here am I,"[89] but he also persisted in his determination. The manifold signs of his concern for his son's well-being confer on the dramatic situation an added touch of irony. As the denouement releases the emotion, the theologian has implicitly made his point. The second "here am I" (vs. 11) introduces the final word of the epiphanic speech: "Now I know that thou fearest Elohim" (vs. 12). The fear of God in the language of Hebrew religion meant supreme devotion.[90] The sign of the purity of faith was love at any cost for a God who conceals his Godhead in appearances of hostility.[91]

Israel rose to a sublimity of theological perception because she understood the paradox of presence in absence. She knew that God hidden is still God. She served a God who forsook her and even stood up against her as an enemy in order to teach her the selflessness of devotion.[92] Grace in God means gratuitous love in man.[93] Intimacy between God and Israel is secure. The word *Akedah* means not only the binding of Isaac for the sacrifice but also the binding of Yahweh to his people. The willingness to accept an order which pushes beyond the limits of practicality—that is, to the *ab-surdum*—the mystery and the freedom of the Godhead or the devotion of man annuls the validity of all archaic forms of religion. In the context of the Hebraic theology of presence, with the absurdity of its demands, religion no longer means the ritual exchange of sacrality with a static cosmos through which man attunes himself to the life of nature but, on the contrary, the courage to face the abyss of being, even the abyss of the being of God, and to affirm, at the risk of assuming all risks, the will to gamble away not only one's ego but even one's hope in the future of mankind.

The story of the *Akedah*, crowning as it does the narratives of epiphanic visitations to Abraham, celebrates the tempering of Hebraic faith. The fear of God is now exhibited in a man. The willingness to sacrifice one's son, that is to say, one's love, one's hope, and one's faith, has made all the static hierophanies of sun, moon, water, earth, fertility, and sexuality obsolete.[94]

JACOB'S DREAM OF THE HEAVENLY STAIRWAY (*Gen. 28:10–22*)

Traditions concerning Jacob differ markedly from those concerning Abraham and Isaac, for they picture Jacob, the eponymic father of Israel, with an unrelieved realism sometimes tinged with sarcastic humor. The name "Jacob" is explained as "supplanter" or "heel-kicker" (Gen. 25:22–26). The hero's character emerges from a series of loosely connected anecdotes as that of an unscrupulous trickster.

Like her eponymic ancestor, however, Israel remains the bearer of a unique vocation. In spite of her blemishes and even crimes, she is still summoned to assume the honor and the burden of a special mission in history. Two narratives of epiphanic visitation express the theological ambiguity of Israel's mystery: Jacob's dream at Bethel and Jacob's fight at Penuel.

The story of Jacob's dream at Bethel (Gen. 28:10–22) provides far more than the foundation *legenda* of a famous shrine.[95] It reasserts the role of one nation toward all other nations. Once again, the concept of faith with its dynamic outreach is inserted at the center of cultus. The temple of Bethel is "the gate of heavens" (vs. 17). The God who is worshipped there is the master architect who has devised a plan for the future of man, and he has chosen Israel to fulfil it. Whatever the secondary elements of the narrative may be, such as its reminiscences of cultic architecture from Mesopotamia[96] and possibly Egypt,[97] the epiphanic speech reaffirms the double theme of offspring and land, but it does so in the light of a teleological concern which is almost identical with that of Abraham's call (Gen. 12:1-3):

> "By thee, and by thy descendants,
>   shall bless one another all the families of the earth"
>   (Gen. 28:14).

The setting of this epiphanic speech is that of a dream, but when the hero awakens he does not need any sensorial perception to know the reality of presence, for he says: "Surely, Yahweh is in this place!" (vs. 16). Once again, the elements which characterize the other stories of epiphanic visitation appear in the formal sequence of the *Gattung:* on the one hand, a revelatory experience, limited in time, localized in space, and aiming at the distant future; on the other, the awareness of divine proximity without any mediating intrusion—an awareness both linked to a shrine and transcending the spatial and temporal limitations of cultus.

JACOB'S FIGHT AT THE JABBOK FORD
(*Gen. 32:22-32*)

This tale appears to be one of the etiological *legenda* preserved at the sanctuary of Penuel,[98] but it aims at explaining through the Hebraic theology of presence the name of the covenant people, Israel.[99] With its implications concerning the stringency of the faith, the thematic thrust of this pericope is similar to that of the *Akedah*. In some ways, it may even go beyond the latter's disquisition on the folly of loving God, for it introduces the theological motif of the *agon*, not just by implication of divine hostility, as in the Akedah, but by explicit use of the motif of divine aggressivity.

Once again, the Yahwist narrator has borrowed anecdotal strands from tribal memories of pre-Hebraic times. The story may well have originally sought to explain the name of the torrent "Jabbok" through the meaning of the verb 'abhaq, "to struggle." At the earliest layer of the tradition, one may uncover the motif—common to all folklore—of the daimon or numen of a ford, especially in mountain streams.[100] The spirit of the ford jealously guards the sanctity of a remote and desolate place through which travelers are compelled to pass on account of the nature of the terrain.

Jacob, the Hebrew Hercules,[101] was endowed with legendary strength. People said that he could single-handedly roll away the stone which covered the lid of a cistern,[102] while the feat ordinarily required the combined efforts of several shepherds. Why was the torrent called "*Yabboq*"? Because our ancestor Jacob "fought" (*'abhaq*) there. It may be that at some archaic stage of the growth of the tradition, it was the numen of the ford which could not overcome Jacob, for the syntax of the passage leaves the identity of the antagonists quite uncertain. Jacob, the eponymic father of Israel, was endowed with such supernatural force that he could even overcome ford daimons. The core of the tale presents itself in the form of three strophes: one tricolon and two sets of bicola:

32:24[Heb. 32:25]. And Jacob was left alone,
       and there wrestled with him a man
       until the lifting of dawn.
[26]. When he saw that he prevailed not against him,
       he hit the hollow of his thigh,
     And the hollow of Jacob's thigh was torn
       as he wrestled with him.
[27]. And he said, "Let me go,
       for dawn is lifting!"
[28]. But he said, "I shall not let thee go
       except thou bless me!"

The night daimon apparently could not remain after daybreak, for his sacrality required invisibility.[103] Yet, Jacob was still holding on to him: a suprahuman exploit, especially since a foul blow had injured Jacob's vital parts.[104]

The Yahwist discerned at this point the theological import of the etiological tale. He transformed a bit of animistic folklore into a catechetic parable. He retold the anecdote by inserting it within the context of Jacob's biographical sequence of turpitude. At the climax of a recital of crafty behavior, unscrupulous ambition, disloyalty, deceit, and treachery, the story reaches a pitch of unbearable suspense. Jacob, the supplanter, has come to his existential moment.

Twenty years previously, his cowardice had prompted him to flee the avenging anger of his twin, Esau, whom he had fraudulently deprived of their father's blessing. Now he again faced the same brother, and he was overpowered by fear. His clan, his herds, his baggage, his wives, and his children descended the steep track which wound its way down the canyon of the Jabbok (now called the *Nahr ez-Zerqa*). He let the caravan pass the ford ahead of him, and he remained alone at the bottom of the gorge. High above him on the Transjordan plateau, his family encamped under the windswept sky. From where he was, that same sky looked like a narrow band sharply cut by two somber cliffs. Around him, the subtropical jungle of oleanders and creeping vines crawled with unpleasant animals, with mountain lions and snakes coming to the water's edge. "And Jacob was left alone." Did he choose to remain behind at the ford—surely a place already charged with sacrality for aeons—in order to meditate on himself and on the uncertainties of the morrow? The tale is terse. It simply sketches his being pounced upon by a stranger in the darkness and the interlocking of the two figures in mortal combat throughout the night.

For the Yahwist, the physical fight was inseparable from the psychological struggle and the spiritual transformation of the hero. In his enemy, Jacob discovered a quality of the holy other than the animistic sacredness of a *topos*. Because he needed a renewal of his being in order to face the ordeal of the next day, he said to the mysterious foe: "I shall not let thee go except thou bless me."[105] The supplanter has to be made into a new man. Passing through a death of the self, he wishes for a new personality and he obtains its inception in the form of a new name.[106] Jacob becomes "Israel."

The Yahwist was thinking, no doubt, of the prophetic description of the nation. Like a prince (*sar*), Israel perseveres in striving, in struggling (*yisreh*), even with her God. To be sure, the etymology of the word "Israel" is uncertain,[107] but folkloric habits of suggesting semantic undertones play on assonantal associations. The Yahwist uses the device of popular etymology in order to proclaim a message. The intent of the narrator appears in the words of the invisible assailant, now transformed into a prophetic revealer, a mediator, and an agent of blessing:

"Thy name shall no longer be Jacob but Israel,
    for thou hast striven with God and men, and prevailed!"
    (Gen. 32:28[Heb. 29]).

The man who kicked his twin in the womb and supplanted him in his youth is indeed a fighter with God and men, but his titanic presumption is not altogether condemned. Israel is a princely fighter in history, as well as a supplanter. This is why his victory with God and men is always ambivalent. He is wounded at the seat of his vitality. He bears thereafter the mark of his conceit, his endurance, and his courage, and also of his defeat and renunciation. Jacob fought, and he only half-conceded the fight in begging for a benediction. The one who prevailed is also the loser: "As the sun rose upon him, he passed over a place called "The-face-of-God," but he was halting on his thigh" (Gen. 32:31[Heb. 32]). The conqueror is blessed but maimed. He struggled against his rebirth and had to surrender to the maker of his new being. But the struggle left a scar in his flesh. Here again the tradition has adapted an archaic motif from an earlier version of the tale. The word *thigh* was a euphemism for the seat of procreation, and the muscles of the thigh played a part in several sacrifical rites. The Yahwist hinted at the ambiguity of the blessing, which not only implies a reaffirmation of the promise of progeny but also carries a mysterious impediment and the curse of perennial pain.

The "man" (*'ish*) who fought with Jacob at the ford is never identified explicitly with Yahweh, but the implication of the context is unmistakable. Above and beyond the objective projection of his own fears of Esau, the supplanter discerns the presence of the Godhead. His numinous assailant cannot be reduced to a depth-psychology personification of nemesis or the objectifying of guilt. To be sure, depth-psychology provides a valuable tool at the threshold of the exegetical analysis by revealing the mechanism of guilt repression which the tale dramatically portrays. Nevertheless, an authentically theological—versus a merely humanistic—frame of reference, views moral conscience as an adjunct, not as the agent, of self-discovery. The *corps-à-corps* which is evoked in the night of the psyche is not just a hand-to-hand struggle between two halves of a divided self. It is the *agon* of guilty finiteness with supramoral infinity.

Jacob is not merely struggling with the recognition of his misdeed. He is engaged in a death struggle with the giver of life who transcends his self-interest. He thought that "God would be with him," but he did not know that the presence of the divine may be the revelation of judgment. From the protecting god of human religions to the sovereign Lord of Hebraic faith there is no easy crossing. Jacob becomes Israel only when he perceives the presence of the Godhead. The Yahwist narrator uses the psychology of individual fear and remorse in order to provide a historical setting for his theological philosophy of Israel's mission in the world. He transfers the folkloric tale from its animistic milieu to a diagnosis of sin through self-aggrandizement, and in turn he presents his hero as the patronymic Israel. The prehistoric, proto-Hebraic *numen* of the stream becomes a Yahwistic *theologoumenon*. Existential birth for the chosen people requires an existential death. With cultic hindsight, as the story is recited at the shrines of the land after Israel has entered Canaan, the nation spells out her birth as an epiphanic combat: "I have seen God face to face."

Jacob asked for the name of his unknown antagonist. Just as the name of a man signifies his character and his destiny, so also the name of a god reveals that god's intention.[108] The request is denied, for the presence is elusive. The proximity of the divine is never made available at the expense of transcendence. But Jacob receives a blessing, that is to say, the vitality of his patriarchal manhood. And it is in the instant of the reception of that blessing that he learns the divine identity of that "man," his antagonist. He had striven with Elohim (vs. 29), and he had concluded exultantly and not without a mixture of awe and relief: "I saw Elohim face to face" (vs. 31).

The narrator insists upon the concreteness of Jacob's sensorial perception by using an anthropomorphic formula. At the same time, his language needs to be understood in the context of the story, The "sighting" of Elohim took place at night, at the bottom of a dark gorge. The physical implications of this "sighting" are immediately cancelled out by the total obscurity of the environment. Moreover, the expression "face to face" (*panîm 'el-panîm*), which probably belonged to the etiological *legenda* of the sanctuary of *Penuel* ("the face of El"), should not be construed as referring literally to visual perception. It is an idiom, often used with verbs of auditive rather than visual perception,[109] and it refers simply to the direct, nonmediated (i.e., immediate) character of a manifestation of presence. It describes a "person-to-person" encounter, without the help or hindrance of an intermediary.[110]

In all probability, the story of Jacob at the Jabbok survived orally in various forms as late as the eighth century B.C.,[111] for the prophet Hosea (ca. 745–725 B.C.) quoted fragments of a hymnic poem which presented Jacob as the ambiguous symbol of the nation, always arrogant with its God and always ready to repent:

> "In the womb he kicked his brother with the heel;
> in his manhood he wrestled with Elohim.
> He wrestled with the angel and prevailed;
> he wept and implored him for mercy" (Hos. 12:4).

This quotation made by a prophet in later times suggests that the tradition of the Yahwist which was preserved in Genesis reveals the processes of theological reinterpretation of proto-Hebraic memories. Here again, the narrator proved himself to be an analyst of Israel's faith, anchored as it was in the Hebraic theology of presence. He detected in that faith the endurance of the will to wait, an awareness of the risk of committing lese majesty in a life of intimacy with God, and the ability to triumph over despair by the assurance that, in the end, a God who is resisted and fought against will reaffirm life.[112] The wrestling with God is inseparable from the inner struggle of Israel over her national guilt, and from her obstinate prayer for mercy.[113]

The eponymic ancestor is viewed without illusion and without shame, since the cultic celebrations rehearsed the manifold aspects of the national life and presented the national self as bearing a blessing in darkness. Israel was able to look at the presence of Yahweh as the source of her vocation to greatness, and therefore also as the indirect occasion of her pride: the constant threat of her sinfulness, the mirage of her self-sufficiency.

Renewed in the story of Jacob's fight at the Jabbok, the blessing of Abraham is interpreted in the cultic recital with a sense of elation and agony. Through the *anamnesis* of her feasts, Israel remembered that she "prevailed" over God; but she also remembered that this triumph was a sign both of her grandeur and of her misery.

The changing of the hero's name shows clearly that the Yahwist understood the story of epiphanic visitation as a parabolic presentation of the cultic community of Israel. Drawing upon the themes already suggested by the narrator, Charles Wesley composed a hymn, now well-known, which interprets the pericope as a poetic statement on the ambivalence of man's attitude toward the presence of God:

> Come, O thou, traveller unknown,
>   whom still I hold but cannot see!
> My company before is gone,
>   and I am left alone with thee;
>
> With thee all night I mean to stay,
>   and wrestle till the break of day.
>   . . .
> My prayer hath power with God. His grace
>   unspeakable I now receive;
> Through faith I see thee face to face—
>   I see thee face to face, and live!

More than an example of spirituality which bears the influence of eighteenth-century pietism, this poem constitutes an exegesis of the biblical story. In spite of its tone of religious individualism, it points to the secret life of man at the genesis of his faith. Like the *Akedah*, the story of Jacob's fight at the Jabbok delineates, within the Hebraic theology of presence, the contradictory aspect of divine communion which inspires man, caught in the labor of his growth, with both love and hate for the Deity. "God the friend" is never far away from "God the enemy."[114]

The patriarchal stories of epiphanic visitation reveal the unique character of the Hebraic theology of presence. Although these stories were told at the shrines of Israel during the cultic celebrations of the seasonal feasts, they are not concerned with the details of the cultus. To be sure, an epiphanic disclosure led ordinarily to the erection of a commemorating altar,[115] which later traditions inevitably associated with the great sanctuaries like Shechem, Beersheba, Hebron (Mamre), Bethel, Penuel, and so on,[116] but the narrators of the ancient traditions, unlike the priestly reinterpreters of the exilic time,[117] never used their material for the justification of some rite. Long before the great prophets, they were the catechists of the theology of presence. They were interested in the experience of divine immediacy as it elicited the attitude of faith.[118]

Archaeological excavations and topographical surveys have shown that the sites of the Palestinian sanctuaries were occupied for centuries before the arrival of the Hebrews in the land of Canaan during the Late Bronze Age.[119] The stories of the patriarchal encounter with Yahweh enabled the Israelite theologians to place a distinctly Yahwistic stamp on the Canaanite shrines which they appropriated. Similar processes of cultic transfer of holy places have been widely observed by historians of religions. At the same time, the festive liturgists of Israel also pursued a theological intention when they chose to preface the recital of the *Gesta Dei per Hebraeos* with the stories of epiphanic visitation to the patriarchs. In effect, they transcended the spatial limitation of cultic topography by means of the motif of nomadism interpreted theologically.

While the Canaanite city-states worshipped deities attached to a *hieros topos* (sacred place), the patriarchs were pictured as nomads who worshipped a traveling God. Yahweh did not *dwell* in shrines but he preceded the patriarchs from site to site and *spoke* to them of the future of the nation.

The content of the epiphanic speeches found in the ancient traditions of Genesis conferred upon the Hebraic theology of presence a unique character. To be sure, the style of divine self-asseveration, as Eduard Norden has shown,[120] is common to all the cultures of the ancient Near East and the Mediterranean world. Obviously, the formulators of these narratives were the heirs of a long-established pattern of epiphanic style.[121] Nevertheless, they adapted this rhetorical form of discourse to what appears to be genuine memories of ecstatic experiences.[122] The *hieros logos* of the Hebraic stories is couched in a language which is conditioned by the cultures of Mesopotamia, Phoenicia, and Egypt, but it differs strikingly at many points from the environment out of which it emerged. The chief difference is its suggestion of elusiveness in a context of sequential persistence from generation to generation, and articulated upon a teleological anticipation of a united mankind. Such language reveals a concern for the mystery of being.[123]

The *hieros logos* of the Hebraic stories is addressed to individuals—Abraham, Isaac, and Jacob—for the divine-human encounter occurs at the most intimate level, of human consciousness, which is necessarily that of isolation from society; but it is without exception oriented toward the destiny of Israel in the midst of all the nations (Gen. 12:1–3). The Hebraic theology of presence preserves the freedom of the Deity from human manipulation. Its teleological thrust is without parallel in the ancient world.

The various epiphanic speeches are consequently linked together, not by the requirement of cultus, sacerdotal college, or ritual act related to sacred space, but by the principle of continuity in historical time.[124] The God who manifests his presence to Abraham, Isaac, and Jacob is the same God who summons Moses at Sinai.[125]

It was the epiphanic mode of presence which promoted in Israel—and later in the Christian church—the psychological mode of communion. "I am girded like Abraham to go. I know not where," said Martin Luther, "but sure of this, that God is everywhere."[126] This knowledge, however, has remained to this day charged with ambivalence. For Israel and for the church, there has always been

"a great wind of light blowing, and sore pain."

At the same time, the epiphanic mode of presence helped Israel and the Christian church develop and refine the notion of faith as the central theme in their interpretation of life, for they saw that their trust in a God whose presence is elusive demands, without fail, a response to a word. And they believed that this word, even when no longer heard, is to be remembered and to be expected again. The word may be hard to bear, but in the end the word *is* life. As Luther retold the story of the sacrifice of Isaac, he concluded: "See how divine majesty is at hand in the hour of death. We say, 'In the midst of life we die.' God answers, 'Nay, in the midst of death we live.' "

The *anamnesis* or liturgical rehearsal of the word became the distinctive factor of Hebrew cultus. Faith was so closely related to the cultic community's obedience to the word that it could survive both cultic disruption and divine hiddenness, as the exile in Babylon showed in the sixth century B.C. Faith and cultus, however, could not have found the dynamics of their interaction without the impact of the Exodus and the Sinai theophany.

Notes

1. G. Bernanos, *Sous le soleil de Satan* (Paris, 1926), p. 104.

2. Exod. 33:11.

3. Exod. 3:15; cf, Deut. 26:7, etc.

4. Exod. 3:13 ff., 6:13 ff.

5. Gen. 4:26.

6. Cf. G. E. Wright, "Cult and History," *In.*, XVI (1962): 11 ff.; B. S. Childs, *Memory and tradition in Israel* (London, 1962), pp. 81 ff.; H.-J. Kraus, *Worship in Israel. A Cultic History of the Old Testament*, tr. by G. Buswell (Richmond, Va., 1965), p. 24; M. Noth, *A History of Pentateuchal Traditions*, tr. by B. W. Anderson (Englewood Cliffs, N. J., 1972), pp. 136 ff., 156 ff., 252 ff.

7. W. Pannenberg, et al., *Revelation as History*, tr. by D. Granskou (New York, 1968), p. 8; cf. J. Barr, "Revelation Through History in the Old Testament and in Modern Theology," *In.*, XVII (1963): 197;

8. G. Fohrer, "The Personal Structure of Biblical Faith," *Fourth World Congress of Jewish Studies, Papers, I* (1967), pp. 161–66; R. Rendtorff, *Men of the Old Testament*, tr. by F. Clarke (Philadelphia, 1963); M.-L. Henry, "Individuelle Gottesbeziehung als Problem der Tradition," *Prophet und Tradition* (Berlin, 1969), pp. 5–10.

9. The traditions concerning the Exodus (14:31) and the Sinai theophany (Exod. 19:8; etc.) bring in the people as witnesses of the divine intervention in history. A Midrash of the Roman times insisted that "even the lowliest maidservant at the Red Sea saw what Isaiah, Ezekiel, and all the other prophets never saw" (*Melikta de-Rabbi Ishamel*, ed. by J. Z. Lauterbach [Philadelphia, 1949], 24 ff., as quoted in E. L. Fackenheim, *God's Presence in History: Jewish Affirmations and Philosophical Reflections* [New York, 1970; paperback ed., 1972], p. 4).

10. Even the Greek word *parousia*, "presence," was found chiefly in secular contexts. (AEschylus, *Persians*, 169; Sophocles, *Electra*, 948; *Ajax*, 540: Euripides, *Alcestis*, 606). It occurs most sparingly in Septuagintal Greek, although it becomes the well-known *terminus technicus* of Christian belief in the Second Coming of the Lord in glory.

11. Cf. two distinct meanings of the word *panîm:* in Exod. 33:14 ("presence") and in verse 23 ("face").

12. Cf. the Greek *prosôpon*, "face," sometimes the equivalent of *prosopeion*, "mask." The Hebrew composite prepositions *liphnê*, "in the presence of," and *mippenê*, "away from the presence of," are used hundreds of times in biblical Hebrew.

13. On the metaphorical use of the names of parts of the human body and the anthropomorphic language of the stories, see J. Boehmer, "Gottes Angesicht," *BFChTh*, XII (1908): 323–47; E. Dhorme, "L'emploi métaphorique des noms des parties du corps en hébreu et en akkadien, III. Le visage," *RB*, XXX (1921): 374–99; E. G. Gulin, *Das Antlitz Jahwes im Alten Testament* (Helsinki, 1923); F. Nötscher, "*Das Angesicht Gottes schauen" nach biblischer und babylonischer Auffassung* (Würzburg, 1924); J. Hempel, "Die Grenzen des Anthropomorphismus Jawes im Alten Testament," *ZAW*, LVII (1939): 75 ff.; A. R. Johnson, "Aspects of the Use of the Term PANIM in the Old Testament," *Festschrift O. Eissfeldt* (Halle, 1947); 155–59; Th. Boman, *Hebrew Thought Compared With Greek*, tr. by J. L. Moreau (London, 1960), pp. 106 ff.; J. Reindl, *Das Angesicht Gottes im Sprachgebrauch des Alten Testaments* (Leipzig, 1969); H. Mölle, *Das "Erscheinen" Gottes im Pentateuch. Ein literaturwissenschaftlicher Beitrag zur alttestamentlichen Exegese* (Bern & Frankfurt, 1973); Th. W. Mann, *Divine Presence and Guidance in Israelite Traditions: The Typology of Exaltation* (Baltimore, 1977), pp. 252 ff.

14. W. Pannenberg, "Appearance as the Arrival of the Future," tr. by D. Griffin, *JAAR*, XXXV (1967): 107–18. "The futurity of the Reign of God became a power determining the present" (p. 112).

15. H. Mottu, "Trace de Dieu: la manifestation," *Bulletin du Centre Protestant d'Etudes*, V (1973), no. 4–5 (Septembre), p. 47.

16. M. Noth, "Mari and Israel, eine Personnamenstudie," in *Geschichte und Altes Testament* (A. Alt Festschrift, Tübingen, 1953), pp. 127–52; "Remarks on the Sixth Volume of the Mari Texts," *JSS*, I (1956); 322–33.

17. See R. de Vaux, "Les patriarches et le milieu oriental," *Histoire ancienne d'Israël: Des origines à l'installation en Canaan* (Paris, 1971), p. 213 ff.; G. E. Mendenhall, *The Tenth Generation: The Origins of the Biblical Tradition* (Baltimore and London, 1973), pp. 10 ff., 156 ff., 174 ff.; Th. L. Thompson, *The Historicity of the Patriarchal Narratives: The Quest for the Historical Abraham* (1973); J. van Seters, *Abraham in History and Tradition* (New Haven, 1975), pp. 5 ff.

18. In addition to extensive bibliography in S. Terrien, *Job* (Neuchâtel, 1963), p. 56, note 3, see C. H. Gordon, "Hebrew Origins in the Light of Recent Discoveries," in A. Altmann, ed., *Biblical and Other Studies* (Cambridge, Mass., 1963), p. 10.

19. See de Vaux, (*Histoire ancienne d'Israël*, pp. 85 ff., 123 ff.

20. A number of scholars have made broad claims for the historicity of the patriarchal narratives merely because these narratives fit the Near Eastern world of the second millenium B.C. See G. E. Wright, "History and the Patriarchs," *ET*, LXXI (1959–60): 292–96; de Vaux, "Les traditions patriarcales et l'histoire," *Histoire ancienne d'Israël*, pp. 182 ff.

21. See the vigorous rejoinders of G. von Rad, "History and the Patriarchs," *ET*, LXXII (1960–61): 213–16; M. Noth, "Der Beitrag der Archäologie zur Geschichte Israels," *Congress Volume, Oxford, 1959, SVT*, VII (Leiden, 1960): pp. 262–82.

22. Although arguing at length against the "pure nomadism" of the Hebrew fathers, N. K. Gottwald admits their nomadic migrations. See "Were the Early Israelites Pastoral Nomads?" in J. J. Jackson and M. Kessler, ed., *Rhetorical Criticism* (Pittsburgh, 1974), pp. 223 ff.; van Seters, *Abraham in History*, pp. 13 ff.

23. In the traditions of Genesis, however, there is no direct evidence, that the patriarchs were more than shepherds—at first pure nomads and later seminomads in the transitional process of sedentarization.

24. Comparison has been made with some of the modern Bedouin tribes which sometimes migrate in search of new pastures under divine inspiration; see V. Maag, "Der Hirte Israels. Eine Skizze von Wesen und Bedeutung der Väterreligion," *STU*, XXVIII (1958): 2 ff.; "Malkûth JHWH," *Congress Volume, Oxford, 1959, SVT* VII (Leiden, 1960), p. 138, notes 1; cf. "Das Gottesverständnis des Alten Testaments," *NTT*, XXI (1967): 161–207.

25. Gen. 14, a late midrash—possibly containing early traditions—in which Abraham is described as a warrior. See bibliography in S. Terrien, "The Omphalos Myth and Hebrew Religion," *VT*, XX (1970): 318, note 5; J. A. Emerton, "The Riddle of Genesis XIV," *VT*, XXI (1971): 403–39; J. G. Gammie, "Loci of the Melchizedek Tradition of Genesis 14:18–20," *JBL*, XC (1971): 385–96; de Vaux, *Histoire ancienne d'Israël*, pp. 208 ff., 336 ff.; W. Schatz, *Genesis 14: Eine Untersuchung* (Bern, 1972); F. L. Horton, *The Melchizedek Tradition: A Critical Examination of the Sources to the Fifth Century A. D. and in the Epistle to The Hebrews* (Cambridge, 1976), pp. 13 ff.

26. H. Gunkel, *The Legends of Genesis*, tr. by W. H. Carruth (New York, 1901); reprinted New York, 1964), pp. 88 ff.; J. Lindblom, "Theophanies in Holy Places in Hebrew Religion," *Hebrew Union College Annual*, XXXII (1964): 91–106.

27. Gen. 14:18–22, 16:13, 17:1, 31:13; etc; see M. Haran, "The Religion of the Patriarchs. An Attempt at a Synthesis," *ASTI*, IV (1965): 30–55; H. Ringgren, *Israelite Religion*, tr. by D. E. Green (Philadelphia, 1966), pp. 21 ff. K. Koch, "Šaddaj," *VT*, XXVI (1976), 299 ff.

28. See A. Alt, "The God of the Fathers," in *Essays on Old Testament History and Religion*, tr. by R. A. Wilson (Garden City, N. Y., 1968), pp. 32 ff.; D. Hillers, *"Paḥad Yiṣḥaq," JBL*, XCI (1972): 90 ff.

29. F. M. Cross, "Yahweh and the God of the Patriarchs," *HTR*, LV (1962): 225–59.

30. From the Greek, *theos*, "god," and *phanein*, "To shine, to appear, or to bring into light."

31. A *theophaneia* is the visual appearance of a god; the word is used by Herodotus (1.51) to designate the climactic moment in the festival at Delphi, during which the statues of Apollo and other deities were shown to the worshippers. At the feast of *ta theophania* (plural neuter), statues of the gods were "monstrated" publicly. An *epiphaneia* usually designates the sudden manifestation of a divine power or even a visual appearance of a deity (Plutarch, *Themistocles*, 30; Diodorus of Sicily, 1, 25). There are many stories of divine appearances in the ancient Near East and in classical antiquity. In most cases, the vision of the gods is restricted to special individuals. For example, "Not unto every one doth Apollo appear, but unto him that is good," says Callimachus, quoted by C. Kerényi, "Apollo Epiphanies," *Spirit and Nature: Papers from the Eranos Yearbooks* (Bollingen Series, XXX.I, New York, 1954), p. 60.

32. The phrase *wayyera' Yahweh* (verb "to see" in the niph'al voice) means "And Yahweh appeared," literally, "was seen" or "showed himself" (Gen. 12:7; etc.). See Mölle, *Das "Erscheinen" Gottes im Pentateuch*, pp. 5 ff.

33. W. L. Moran, "The Hebrew Language in its Northwest Semitic Background," in *The Bible and the Ancient Near East*, ed. by G. E. Wright (Garden City, N. Y., 1961), pp. 54–72.

34. See list of parallel features in J. Jeremias, *Theophanie: Die Geschichte einer alttestamentliche Gattung* (Neukirchen-Vluyn, 1965), pp. 88 f.

35. *Ibid.*, pp. 16 ff.

36. *Ibid.*, pp. 100 ff.

37. Not even excepting the Yahwist account of covenant-making with Abraham in Gen. 15:1–21, although its conclusion introduces the motif of nature *mirabilia:* "And just as the sun had set, there was a blazing flame (LXX), and behold! a fiercely burning furnace with smoke and a flash of fire which passed by between the two-pieces [of the covenant sacrificial animal]" (vs. 17). It will be observed, however, that Abraham saw this strange fire just a few moments after "a deep trance had fallen upon him" (vs. 12). Moreover, the whole pericope breaks the formal pattern of epiphanic encounter not only in Genesis but in the Pentateuch generally, for it borrows elements from the *Gattung* of the prophetic vision. "The word of Yahweh came to Abraham in a vision" (vs. 11). This formula indicates contamination from the preprophetic style, ca. the end of the second millenium B.C.

38. One may therefore understand why J. Jeremias did not include the patriarchal narratives in his study on *Theophanie*, although one should add that he failed to distinguish between the genuinely theophanic form of the Sinai-Horeb type and the hymnic allusions to epiphanic intervention in the past and in the future. P. D. Hanson's methodological remarks on Jeremias' search for a theophany-*Gattung* in Zechariah 9 apply to other parts of this otherwise extremely valuable study. See P. D. Hanson, "Zechariah 9 and the Recapitulation of an Ancient Ritual Pattern," *JBL*, XCII (1973): 52, note 45.

39. For example, Deut. 33; Judg. 5:4–5; Isa. 30:27–33, 59:15b–20; 63:1–6; Mic. 1:3–4; Nah. 1:3b–6; Hab. 3:3–15; Zech. 8:14; Pss. 18:7–15 [Heb. 8–16], 50:1–3, 68:7–33 [Heb. 8–34], 77:16–19, 97:2–7. Cf. P. C. Craigie, "Yahweh is a Man of War," *SJT*, XXII (1969): 185 ff.; F. M. Cross, "The Divine Warrior in Israel's Early Cult," *Biblical Motifs*, ed. by A. Altmann (Cam-

bridge, Mass., 1969), pp. 14 ff.; P. D. Miller, *The Divine Warrior in Early Israel* (Cambridge, Mass., 1973).

40. C. Westermann, "The Epiphany of God," *The Praise of God in the Psalms*, tr. by K. R. Crim (Richmond, Va., 1961), pp. 93 ff.; cf. A. Weiser, "Zur Frage nach den Beziehungen der Psalmen zum Kult: Die Darstellung der Theophanie in den Psalmen und im Festkult," *Festschrift A. Bertholet* (Tübingen, 1950), pp. 513–31; *The Psalms*, tr. by H. Hartwell (Philadelphia, 1962), p. 38, note 2; H.-P. Müller, "Die kultische Darstellung der Theophanie," VI, XIV (1964): 183 ff.

41. See the form-critical analysis of the *Gattung* in J. K. Kuntz, *The Self-Revelation of God* (Philadelphia, 1967), pp. 52 ff.; however, this uncovering of the theophanic form depends exclusively on the patriarchal narratives and must be altered if it is applied to the Sinai pericopes.

42. The theophany of Elijah on Mt. Horeb (1 Kings 19:9–18) provides a transition between the Mosaic type of revelation and the era of prophetic inspiration (see below, chapter III).

43. The "theophanic" elements in the vision of Ezekiel point to the priestly understanding of cultic presence (Ezek. 1:1—3:15).

44. J. L. McKenzie, "God and Nature in the Old Testament," *CBQ*, XIV (1952), pp. 18–39, 124–45; W. Lillie, "The Religious Significance of the Theophany in the Book of Job," *ET*, LXVIII (1956–57): 355–58; S. Terrien, *Job* (Neuchâtel, 1963), p. 45, note 2, and pp. 246 ff.

45. See note 31 above. It appears that the word "epiphany," unlike its cognate "theophany," was first applied to the appearances of Greek deities, such as Apollo, Asclepius, or Dionysus. See L. Weniger, "Theophanien, altgriechische Götteradvente," *ARW*, XII (1923–24): 16 ff.; W. F. Otto, "The Myths of His Epiphany" in *Dionysus: Myth and Cult* (Bloomington, Ind., 1965), pp. 74 ff. The expression "epiphanic visitation" seems to be more fitting than "theophany" to describe the patriarchal experiences, for it suggests the concreteness, simplicity, and swiftness of the divine appearance. Cf. H. Schmid, "Gottesbild, Gottesschau und Theophanie," *Judaica*, XXXIII (1967): 241–54.

46. J. Muilenburg, "The Speech of Theophany," *Harvard Divinity School Bulletin*, XXVIII, 2 (Jan. 1964): 35–47; Kuntz, *The Self-Revelation of God*, pp. 104 ff.

47. The speeches of the gods constitute a literary genre in Egypt. See C. Kayatz, *Studien zu Proverbien 1—9* (Neukirchen-Vluyn, 1966), pp. 15 ff. Mann, "Motifs of Divine Presence in the Ancient Near East," *Divine Presence*, pp. 27 ff.

48. See the intentional lengthening of the formula from Gen. 15:7 to 26:24, 28:-13, etc. W. Zimmerli, "Ich bin Jahve," *Geschichte und Altes Testament. Festschrift A. Alt* (Tübingen, 1953), pp. 179–209; K. Elliger, "Ich bin der Herr—Gott," *Festschrift K. Heim* (Hamburg, 1954), pp. 9–34; "Das Wort des göttlichen Selbsterweises (Erweiswort), eine prophetische Gattung," *Festschrift A. Robert* (Paris, 1957), pp. 155–64; R. Rendtorff, " 'Offenbarung' im Alten Testament," *TLZ*, LXXXV (1960), cols. 833–38.

49. The nucleus of the early traditions was constituted by the creed of Deut. 26:5 ff. and the covenant ceremony at Shechem (Jos. 24). It is probable, however, that the traditions concerning the patriarchal epiphanic visitations originated from heterogeneous groups. Cf. von Rad, *The Problem of the Hexateuch*, pp. 8 ff., 54 f.; id., *Old Testament Theology*, I, pp. 166, 170.

50. The "Sphinx Stela," tr. by J. A. Wilson, "Egyptian Oracles and Prophecies," *ANET*, p. 449.

51. "Akkadian Oracles and Prophecies," tr. by R. H. Pfeiffer, *ANET*, p. 449. See other Near Eastern parallels in S. Mowinckel, "The Name of the God of Moses," *HUCA*, XXXII (1961): 123.

52. Gen. 15:1, 21:17, 26:23–24, 28:13

(LXX), 46:1–4; cf. Isa. 44:8, etc.; also Luke 1:13.

53. See H. Gressmann, "Die literarische Analyse Deuterojesajas," *ZAW, XXXIV (1914)*: 254–97; L. Köhler, "*Die Offenbarungsformel 'Fürchte dich nicht' im Alten Testament,*" *Schweizerische Theologische Zeitschrift,* XXXVI (1919): 33–39; J. Begrich, "Das priestliche Heilsorakel," *ZAW, LII (1934)*: 81–92; J. Becker, *Gottesfurcht im Alten Testament* (Roma, 1965), pp. 50–55; H. M. Dion, "The Patriarchal Traditions and the Literary Form of the 'Oracle of Salvation'," *CBQ,* XXIX (1967): 198 ff.

54. "King of Assyria, fear not!" in "Oracles Concerning Esarhaddon," *ANET,* p. 450; "Fear not, O Ashurbanipal!" in "Oracle of Ninlil Concerning Ashurbanipal," *ANET,* p. 451. Cf. J. Hempel, "Die Furcht vor dem nahen Gott," *Gott und Mensch im Alten Testament* (Stuttgart, 1936), pp. 8 ff.; N. Krist, *Formkritische Untersuchung zum Zuspruch "Fürchte dich nicht!" im Alten Testament* (Dissert., Hamburg, 1968), pp. 125 ff.

55. A sense of communion between God and man dominates the religion of the Yahwist. See Th. C. Vriezen, *An Outline of Old Testament Theology,* 2nd ed. (Oxford, 1970), p. 313.

56. M. Noth, "Das Thema 'Verheissung an die Erzväter'," *Überlieferungsgeschichte,* pp. 58 f.; cf. von Rad, *Old Testament Theology,* p. 168.

57. G. von Rad, *Genesis, A Commentary,* tr. by J. H. Marks (Philadelphia, 1961), pp. 154 f.; Speiser, *Genesis,* pp. XLVIII f., 87 f.; B. Gemser, "Questions Concerning the Religion of the Patriarchs," *Adhuc Loquitur* (Leiden, 1968), pp. 56 ff.; see also R. Kilian, *Die vorpriesterlichen Abrahams Überlieferungen* (Bonn, 1966), pp. 10 ff.

58. Cf. N. C. Habel, "The Form and Significance of the Call Narratives," *ZAW,* LXXVII (1965): 297 ff.; esp. 321 f.

59. The poetic structure here reproduced is that of Speiser, *Genesis,* p. 85, but the translation is that of the author.

60. See J. Muilenburg, "Abraham and the Nations: Blessing and World History," *In.,* XIX (1965): 387–98; cf. Gunkel, *Genesis,* p. 164; von Rad, *Genesis,* pp. 154 f.; Speiser, *Genesis,* p. 86. The theological outlook of this epiphanic speech differs from that of the other patriarchal traditions, for it emphasizes the universalism of Israel's mission in the history of mankind rather than the exclusivism of the promise of the land. Significantly, the ambivalence of the word *'ereṣ,* "land," or "earth," is used by the Yahwist with special intent. Having placed the story of the call of Abraham against the picture of an "earth-wide" chaos produced by the erection of the Tower of Babel (Gen. 11:- 9), the Yahwist proceeds to show that Abram has to leave his "country" (12:1) and go to a "land" for the eventual sake of all the nations of the "earth" (vs. 3). This feature is not always brought out clearly by the commentators.

61. E. Kautzsch, *Gesenius' Hebrew Grammar,* tr. by A. E. Cowley (Oxford, 1910), p. 381; C. Brockelmann, *Hebräische Syntax* (Neukirchen, 1956), pp. 100 f.; H.-P. Müller, "Imperativ und Verheissung im Alten Testament," *Ev. Th.,* XXVIII (1968): 558.

62. The awareness of being a people "dwelling alone . . . among the nations" (Nu. 23:9) follows Israel throughout her historical existence. It is basic to the theology of the Mosaic covenant (Exod. 19:- 5). Even on her land, she herself to be only a people of "strangers and sojourners," but these strangers and sojourners are "with Yahweh" (Lev. 25:23; Ps. 39:12 [Heb. 13]). See von Rad, *Genesis,* p. 154; Gemser, "The Religion of the Patriarchs," p. 58.

63. See C. Westermann, *Der Segen in der Bibel und im Handeln der Kirche* (München, 1954), p. 54; G. Wehmeier, *Der Segen im Alten Testament* (Basel, 1970); J. Helfmeyer, "Segen und Erwählung," *BZ,* XVIII (1974): 208 ff.

64. The translation of verse 3c is uncer-

tain. The niph'al voice, *nibhrekhu*, is understood by some commentators as passive (LXX; cf. Sir. 44:21, Acts 3:25, Gal. 3:8), "will be blessed," and by others as reflexive, "will bless themselves" (cf. Gen. 18:18, 28:14). With this verb, however, the idea of the passive is commonly expressed by the pu'al, while the niph'al, like the hithpa'el (cf. Gen. 22:18, 26:4) signifies the reflexive (cf. Gen. 48:20, Jer. 29:22, etc.). In the plural, however, the niph'al and the hithpa'el may convey the idea of the reciprocal. According to this interpretation, the climactic line of the speech does not suggest that mankind "will bless itself" or "acquire blessing" (cf. J. Schreiner, "Segen für die Völker in der Verheissung an die Väter," *BZ*, N.F. VI (1962): 4 ff.; and Wolff, "The Kerygma," p. 137) by imitating Abraham or by praising, pleasing, or supporting his descendants. It rather intimates that all the nations will exchange effective signs of peace, prosperity, and growth through their mysterious association with Abraham and his descendants. It is not clear, according to several exegetes, whether the Yahwist incorporated this epiphanic speech in his Hebrew epic in order to enhance the upsurging nationalism of David and Solomon or to elicit among his contemporaries a sober emulation of the Abrahamic obedience to the vision of a united mankind. The theology of the Yahwist, however, beginning with the myth of the garden, favors the latter interpretation.

65. B. Gemser, "God in Genesis," *OTS*, XII (1958): 21; P. Altmann, *Erwählungstheologie und Universalismus im Alten Testament* (Berlin, 1964), pp. 9 ff.; R. Martin-Achard, *Israël et les nations. La perspective missionnaire de l'Ancien Testament* (Neuchâtel, 1959), pp. 32 ff.; id., *Actualité d'Abraham*, pp. 71 f.

66. See A. Caquot, "L'alliance avec Abraham," *Semitica*, XII (1962): 51 ff.; H. Cazelles, "Connexions et structure de Gen. XV," *RB*, LXIX (1962): 321–49; H.

Seebas, "Zu Genesis 15," in *Wort und Dienst*, VII (1965): 132–49; cf. "Gen. 15.2*b*," *ZAW*, LXXV (1963): 317–19; Clements, *Abraham and David*, pp. 19 ff.; N. Lohfink, *Die Landverheissung als Eid*, Stuttgarter Bibelstudien, 28 (1967), pp. 85 ff.; J. Dus, "Der Jakobbund, Gen. 15.8 ff." *ZAW*, LXXX (1968): 35–38 (who conjectures that the narrative was originally told of Jacob).

67. The second story of the covenant with Abraham (Gen. 17:1–21) represents a slow development of the tradition among the priestly circles of Jerusalem. Its purpose is to relate to the patriarchal promise the origin of the rite of circumcision. See bibliography in W. Zimmerli, "Sinaibund und Abrahambund. Ein Beitrag zum Verständnis der Priesterschrift," *TZ*, XVI (1960): 268–86; repr. in id., *Gottes-Offenbarung. Gesammelte Aufsätze* (München, 1963), pp. 205–16; S. R. Külling, *Zur Datierung der 'Genesis-P-Stücke'*, *namentlich des Kapitels Genesis XVII*, (1964).

68. The word *mahᵃzeh*, "vision," is a cognate of the word *hozeh*, "seer," "man of visions," which the priest of the temple of Bethel hurled at Amos (7:12).

69. It comes from the root *'mn*, related to the word *amen*, the noun *'emunah*, "faith," and its doublet, *'emeth*, "truth." On the growth of the notion of faith in Hebrew religion, see P. Michalon, "La foi, rencontre de Dieu et engagement envers Dieu dans l'Ancien Testament," *NRT*, LXXV (1953): 587 ff.; H. Pfeiffer, "Glauben im Alten Testament," *ZAW*, LXXI (1959): 158 ff.; cf. the warnings of J. Barr, " 'Faith' and 'Truth'—An Examination of Some Linguistic Arguments," in *The Semantics of Biblical Language* (London, 1961), pp. 161 ff.; See also Gemser, "The Religion of the Patriarchs," p. 60; M. G. Kline, "Abram's Amen," *WTJ*, XXXI (1968): 1 ff.

70. A. Jepsen, "[Ṣedeq] und [Ṣedaqah] im Alten Testament," in *Gotteswort und Gottes Land, H-W. Hertzberg Festschrift*, ed. by H.

Graf Reventlow (Göttingen, 1964), pp. 78 -89.

71. See von Rad, *Old Testament Theology*, I, p. 155; *id.*, "Faith Reckoned as Righteousness," *The Problem of the Hexateuch*, pp. 125–30; F. Hahn, "Genesis 15, 6 im Neuen Testament," in H.-W. Wolff, ed., *Probleme biblischer Theologie. Festschrift G. von Rad* (München, 1971), pp. 91 f.

72. E. A. Speiser renders this phrase in the light of rabbinic theology, "He put his trust in Yahweh who accounted it to his merit" (*Genesis*, p. 110).

73. A. Heschel, in an otherwise perceptive essay, 'Man's Quest for God (New York, 1954), pp. 107 f., misunderstands the Pauline thought because he ignores the Hebraic notion of faith. See also M. Buber, *Two Types of Faith* (New York, 1951), pp. 44 ff.; cf. J. A. Ziesler, *The Meaning of Righteousness in Paul: A Linguistic and Theological Enquiry* (Cambridge, 1972).

74. This is clear from the early JE traditions. The Priestly traditions, however, elaborated upon the early narratives at the time of the exile in order to support etiologically a number of ritual practices which became central to postexilic Judaism, especially the law of circumcision (Gen. 17:1–14).

75. See E. L. Ehrlich, *Der Traum im Alten Testament* (Berlin, 1953), pp. 35 f.; A. L. Oppenheim, *The Interpretation of Dreams in the Ancient Near East* (Philadelphia, 1956), pp. 184 ff.; A. Reach, *Der Traum im Heilsplan Gottes* (Freiburg i. B., 1964), pp. 57 ff.;

The appearance of the Deity after sunset (vs. 17) introduces into the patriarchal narratives of epiphanic visitation the element of fire, which is usually typical of the Mosaic theophanies. See G. Ch. Aalders, "The Theophanies of the Old Testament," *Free University Quarterly*, VIII (1962): 13.

76. See H. Gunkel, *Genesis*, pp. 193 f.

77. E.g., *Odyssey*, xvii, 485–87; see von Rad, *Genesis*, p. 200.

78. Sir James G. Frazer, *Folklore in the Old Testament*, abridged ed. (New York, 1923), pp. 333 ff.

79. F. Stier, *Gott und sein Engel im Alten Testament* (Münster, 1934), p. 5, note 12; A. Caquot, "Anges et démons dans l'Ancien Testament," *RHR*, CLXVII (1965): 117–19.

80. J. Barr, "Theophany and Anthropomorphism in the Old Testament," *Congress Volume, Oxford, 1959, SVT*, VII (Leiden, 1960), pp. 33 ff.

81. See Gunkel, *Genesis*, pp. 163 ff.; C. Westermann, "Verheissungserzählungen. Arten der Erzählung in der *Genesis*," *Forschung am Alten Testament* (München, 1964), pp. 28, 58 ff.

82. Read *Adony*, "my lord," rather than the Masoretic anachronism, *Adonay*, "The Lord," a later euphemism for the tetragrammaton.

83. The fluctuation between singular and plural may well reflect the Hebraic theology of transcendence. Cf. A. R. Johnson, *The One and the Many in the Israelite Conception of God* (Cardiff, 1961).

84. The anthropomorphism of the detail which depicts Yahweh as waiting for man appeared too gross for Judaism in the Hellenistic age. "And the men turned away from there, and went to Sodom, but Yahweh still tarried, standing in the presence of Abraham" (vs. 22). The two names are exchanged in the Masoretic text which now reads, through one of the eighteen *Tiqqune Sopherim* ("corrections of the Scribes"), "And Abraham still tarried, standing in the presence of Yahweh" (cf. LXX).

85. See R. Kilian, "Die vorpriesterlichen Abrahams Überlieferungen," *Bonner biblische Beiträge*, XXIV (1966): 263–78; *id.*, *Isaaks Opferung. Zur Überlieferungsgeschichte von Gen 22* (Stuttgart, 1970); H. Graf Reventlow, *Opfere deinen Sohn. Eine Auslegung von Genesis 22* (Neukirchen-Vluyn, 1968), esp. pp. 32 f.; G. W. Coats, "Abraham's Sacrifice of Faith," *In.*, XXVII (1973): 389 ff.; J. Crenshaw, "Journey Into Oblivion: A Structural Analysis of Gen. 22:1–19," *Soundings*, LVIII (1975): 243 ff.; R.

Lack, "Le sacrifice d'Isaac—Analyse structurale de la couche élohiste dans Gn 22," *Biblica*, LVI (1975): 1 ff.

86. See 2 Kings 3:27, 16:3, 17:31, 21:6; cf. Jer. 7:31, 19:5; Ezek. 16:20–21, 33:37; Isa. 57:5. The polemic against child sacrifice is present in the tradition, but it remains secondary. See R. de Vaux, *Les institutions de l'Ancien Testament*, II (Paris, 1960), pp. 328 f.

87. The triple stress aims at offending the feelings of the audience beyond the limits of endurance. The use of the so-called *dativus ethicus* with the imperative "go!" (vs. 2)—exactly as in the initial command of Gen. 12:1—indicates the enormity of the decision which is hereby requested.

88. M. Luther, *Lectures on Genesis, IV (chapters 21—25)*, tr. by J. Pelikan (St. Louis, 1964), pp. 91–117. See also, "The father raised his knife; the boy did not wince. The angel cried, 'Abraham, Abraham!' See how divine majesty is at hand in the hour of death. We say, 'In the midst of life we die.' God answers, 'Nay, in the midst of death we live'." (*Weimar Ausgabe*. XLIII, 220 ff.; tr. and quoted by R. H. Bainton, *Here I Stand: A Life of Martin Luther* (New York and Nashville, 1950), p. 370.

89. A typical formula in the dialogue form between God and man in all periods of Israel's religion.

90. See B. Olivier, *La crainte de Dieu, valeur religieuse de l'Ancien Testament* (Bruxelles, 1960); S. Terrien, "Fear," In *IDB*, II (1962): 260; S. Plath, *Furcht Gottes, der Begriff YR' im Alten Testament* (Stuttgart, 1963), p. 46 ff.; J. Becker, *Gottesfurcht im Alten Testament* (Roma, 1965), p. 193 f.

91. Auerbach, *Mimesis*, pp. 6 f.

92. Von Rad, *Old Testament Theology*, I, p. 174; *id., Genesis*, pp. 233 f.

93. The story of the testing of Abraham's faith has inspired a rich harvest of haggadic and other interpretative essays in Judaism, Christianity, and Islam. Cf. the extensive bibliography in R. Martin-Achard, *Actualité d'Abraham* (1969), p. 75, note 57, and pp. 185–93. See also H.

Westman, "The Akedah," in *The Springs of Creativity* (New York, 1961), pp. 108–12.

94. M. Eliade, *Cosmos and History: The Myth of the Eternal Return*, paperback ed. (New York, 1959), p. 109, note 6.

95. Von Rad, *Genesis*, pp. 278 f.; Speiser, *Genesis*, p. 219. By rehearsing at a time of religious apostasy and moral corruption the tales concerning Jacob, the Elohist narrators were in effect saying to the people at worship, "You are like Jacob!" Cf. T. E. Fretheim, "The Jacob Traditions: Theology and Hermeneutic," *In.*, XXVI (1972): 419–36, esp. p. 435. Likewise, in the eighth century the prophet Hosea used the hymnic sequences on Jacob-Israel, most likely a part of the liturgical celebration of the Autumn Feast at Bethel, in order to sharpen the incisiveness of Yahweh's judgment and at the same time the wonder of the divine grace. Cf. E. M. Good, "Hosea and the Jacob Tradition," *VT*, XVI (1966): 137–51.

96. J. Delorme, "A propos du songe de Jacob," *A la rencontre de Dieu: Mémorial A. Gelin* (Le Puy, 1961), pp. 47–54, esp. p. 48; A. de Pury, *Promesse divine et légende cultuelle dans le cycle de Jacob: Genèse 28 et les traditions patriarcales*, 2 vols. (Paris, 1976).

97. J. Gwyn Griffiths, "The Celestial Ladder and the Gate of Heaven (Genesis xxviii.12 and 17)," *ET*, LXXVI (1964–65): 229 f.; C. Houtmann, "What Did Jacob See in His Dream at Bethel? (Some Remarks on Genesis xxviii 10–22)," *VT*, XXVII (1977): 336 ff.

98. See Gunkel, *Genesis*, p. 359.

99. See H. Eysing, *Formgeschichtliche Untersuchung zur Jakobserzählung der Genesis* (Emsdetter, 1939), pp. 118–37; F. van Trigt, "La signification de la lutte de Jacob près du Yabboq: Gen. xxxii 23–33," *OTS*, XII (Leiden, 1958): 280–309; J. L. McKenzie, "Jacob at Peniel: Gn. 32, 24–32," *CBQ*, XXV (1963): 71–76; R. Martin-Achard, "L'analyse structurale d'un texte de l'Ancien Testament," in R. Barthes et al., *Analyse structurale et exégèse biblique* (Neuchâtel, 1971), pp. 41–62; R.

Barthes, "La lutte avec l'ange; analyse textuelle de Genèse 32.23–33," *ibid.*, pp. 27–39; H.-J. Hermisson, "Jakobs Kampf am Jabbok (Gen. 32, 23–33)," *ZTK*, LXXI (1974): 239–61.

100. Sir James G. Frazer, *Folklore in the Old Testament*, abridged ed. (New York, 1923), pp. 251–58; N. Schmidt, "The Numen of Penuel," *JBL*, XLV (1926): 269.

101. J. Bewer shows how the primitive tale was incorporated into the theological epic. See his "Progressive Interpretation, *ATR*, XXIV (1942), 89 ff.

102. Gen. 29:10.

103. Gunkel, *Genesis*, p. 364.

104. There is no need to suggest, as some exegetes have done, that at some early stage of the tradition it was Jacob who used a wrestler's trick and mutilated his assailant. Some have assumed that, at a later period, when the spirit of the ford came to be identified with Yahweh, the sexual undertone of the motif was thought to be theologically unseemly. Against this view, it should be observed that the memory of Jacob's lameness was apparently ancient (see vs. 31), and that it was clearly connected with the detail of an injury inflicted on him. The etiological motif of the legal prohibition on the eating of the sciatic nerve (vs. 32), however, may well have originally been independent (see MacKenzie, "Jacob at Peniel," p. 72).

105. See Eissfeldt, "*Non Dimittam Te, Nisi Benedixeris Mihi,*" *Mélanges bibliques . . . A. Robert* (Paris, 1957), p. 78.

106. In ancient religions, the name possessed a numinous quality which carried with it an objective power. See, among others, Pedersen, *Israel, Its Life and Culture*, I–II, pp. 245 ff.; J. Sainte-Fare Garnot, "Les fonctions, les pouvoirs et la nature du nom propre dans l'ancienne Egypte," *Journal de Psychologie*, XLI (1948): 463–72.

107. G. A. Danell, *Studies in the Name of Israel in the Old Testament* (Uppsala, 1946), R. Coote, "The Meaning of the Name Is-

rael," *HTR*, LXV (1972): 137–46.

108. D. Piccard, "Genèse, 32/23–33: 'Dis-moi, quel est ton nom?' " *Hommage à Wilhelm Vischer* (Montpellier, 1960), pp. 187 f.

109. "Yahweh spoke to Moses face to face" (Exod. 33:11; cf. Deut. 5:4; 3 John, 14). In one instance, Moses is credited with the phrase, "Thou, Yahweh, art seen face to face" (Num. 14:14), but the context shows that he is referring to the presence of the Godhead "in the midst of the people" through the theologoumenon of "the cloud."

110. P. Dhorme, "L'emploi métaphorique des noms de parties du corps en hébreu et en akkadien," *RB*, XXX (1921): 374–99; A. R. Johnson, "Aspects of the Use of the Term PNYM in the Old Testament," *Festschrift Otto Eissfeldt*, ed. by H. J. Fück (Halle an der Saale, 1947), pp. 155–59.

111. Th. C. Vriezen, "La tradition de Jacob dans Osée xii," *OTS*, I (1942): 64–78; A Bentzen, "The Weeping of Jacob, Hos. xii 5a," *VT*, I (1951): 59; H. L. Ginsberg, "Hosea's Ephraim: More Fool than Knave. A New Interpretation of Hosea 12:1–14," *JBL*, LXXX (1961): 339–47; P. R. Ackroyd, "Hosea and Jacob," *VT*, XIII (1963): 245–59; E. M. Good, "Hosea and the Jacob Tradition," *VT*, XVI (1966): 137–51.

112. Von Rad, *Genesis*, p. 320. E. A. Speiser, who rightly warns against trying to spell out the details which the narrator himself only "glimpsed as if through a haze" (*Genesis*, p. 256), admits that Jacob was now a changed man.

113. Hosea understood the tale of Jacob at the Jabbok through a theology of grace since the hymnic fragment which he quoted stressed the hero's weeping and "begging for mercy" (*wayyithhannen lô*, 12:4). See K. Elliger, "Der Jakobskampf am Jabboq, Gen. 32, 23 ss., als hermeneutisches Problem," *ZTK*, XLVIII (1951), 29.

114. S. H. Blank, "Men Against God:

The Promethean Element in Biblical Prayer," *JBL*, LXXII (1953): 1–13; *id.*, "Some Observations Concerning Biblical Prayer," *HUCA*, XXXII (1961): 75–90.

115. Gen. 12:7, 13:18, 26:25, 46:1.

116. J. Lindblom, "Theophanies in Holy Places in Hebrew Religion," *HUCA*, XXXII (1964): 91.

117. Von Rad, *Old Testament Theology*, I p. 175.

118. "There can be no doubt that, though the key-word 'faith' occurs only once . . ., it is the problem of faith which lies at the back of these stories . . ." (ibid., p. 171).

119. See bibliography in G. E. Wright, "The Archaeology of Palestine," in *The Bible and the Ancient Near East* (Garden City, N. Y., 1961), pp. 101 ff.

120. E. Norden, *Agnostos Theos. Untersuchungen zur Formengeschichte religiöser Rede* (Leipzig/Berlin, 1913), pp. 77 ff., 207 ff.

121. M. J. Buss, "The Language of the Divine 'I'," *JBR*, XXIX (1961): 102 ff.

122. Against the opinion of J. Lindblom, "Theophanies in Holy Places," p. 106. See the observation of Kuntz, *The Self-Revelation of God*, p. 32, note 19.

123. P. Tillich, "The Word of God," in *Language: An Inquiry Into Its Meaning and Function*, ed. by R. N. Anshen (New York, 1957), p. 123; cf. M. Heidegger, *An Introduction to Metaphysics*, tr. by R. Manheim (New Haven, 1959), pp. 98 ff., 132 ff.

124. Muilenburg, "The Speech of Theophany," p. 37.

125. Gen. 26:24, 28:13, 31:13, 46:3; cf. Exod. 3:6, etc.

126. Quoted by R. Bainton, *Here I Stand: A Life of Martin Luther* (Nashville, 1950), p. 100.

127. *Ibid.*, p. 370.

3

The Sinai Theophanies

Traditions which are now embedded in the Pentateuch contain a great deal of information about Moses, but they do not constitute the equivalent of historiographic archives. As cultic *legenda* they were couched in rhythmic prose, for they were recited musically at the celebration of the seasonal feasts at the shrines of Yahweh in the land of Canaan or among the communities of the first Jews during the exile in Babylon. The image of Moses as the great lawgiver does not belong to the earliest strata of these traditions. Although the decalogue (in its lapidary form of ten short words) may be attributed to him,[1] the historical Moses was primarily a military leader of a charismatic character.[2]

In or about 1275 B.C., at the height of the reign of Ramses II (1290–1224 B.C.),[3] a Hebrew bearing the Egyptian name of *Mosheh* (Moses) fomented an insurrection among the labor camps of the northeastern delta of the Nile and led a group of Hebrew slaves out of Egypt across the flat marshes of the Isthmus of Suez in the vicinity of the Bitter Lakes.[4] In the name of "the god of [their] fathers," Moses guided these men and women, an amorphous mass of refugees, toward the Sinai wilderness, and molded them into an organic community through the ritual of a covenant with Yahweh. Before his death, he brought their sons and daughters within sight of the land of Canaan, on the Plateau of Moab, east of the Dead Sea. The conquest of the land remained the task of his successors—Joshua, the Judges, and even David and Solomon—2-1/2 centuries later.[5] Within this historical framework, however, little is known about the man. Yet, the traditions are unanimous in ascribing his exceptional eminence to a complexity of religious factors: Moses was remembered as a man who "spoke face to face" with the Deity, and such "happenings" were described in spatial and temporal terms.

At a certain place, on a certain day, Moses was brought into the immediate proximity of the holy in the midst of a scene of nature in wonder (the Burning Bush) or of nature in tumult (Mount Horeb or Mount Sinai). Such experiences were told and preserved in a certain literary form which may be called "theophany."[6] As has been noted above, the early traditions concerning Moses present several affinities with the patriarchal narratives of epiphanic visitation. Both of the scenes just mentioned stress the immediacy of the presence, the abruptness of the way in which this presence manifests itself or vanishes, the subordination of each scene to a dialogical speech, and the specific relatedness of such a speech to the decision for man to act in history.

The Mosaic narratives, however, differ from the patriarchal stories in several aspects:

1. The patriarchal stories concern a multiplicity of places, like Shechem, Mamre, Beersheba, Moriah, Bethel, Penuel, and so on. The Mosaic traditions, on the contrary, ascribe the theophanies to a single place, the *har elohim* or "mountain of God," and its immediate vicinity.[7]

2. The patriarchal stories tell of altars which the patriarchs

built in order to commemorate the various sites of the epiphanic visitations, and these sites were venerated at a later age as shrines of Yahweh in the land of Canaan.[8] Moses, however, erected no topographically fixed shrine in the wilderness of Sinai,[9] and there is no evidence of Hebrew, Israelite, or Jewish pilgrimages to "the mountain of God" during the biblical period.[10] The stories of the Mosaic theophanies became the literary anchor for the clustering of most of the legislation of Israel, so much so that the final form of the Pentateuch came to be known as the *Torah*, or "Law," and its entire composition became ascribed to Moses by fundamentalist Jews and Christians.

3. The patriarchal stories, like the narratives of prophetic vision in the age of the great prophets,[11] were articulated within the setting of an ordinary landscape and normal conditions of nature. Whenever the storytellers included a motif of a supernatural character, like that of the fire in the Yahwistic story of the covenant with Abraham (Gen. 15:17) or of the celestial ladder in the scene of Jacob asleep at Bethel (Gen. 28:12), they were careful to suggest by contextual juxtaposition that such elements of *mirabilia naturae* belonged to the realm of psychic vision (Gen. 15:1) or of dream (Gen. 15:12, 28:12). Such was not the case with the Sinai theophanies. Indeed, the element which sets these modes of presence apart from both the patriarchal stories of epiphanic visitation and the prophetic confessions of psychic experience is just that of natural wonder.

4. The ancient traditions concerning the Sinai theophanies differ from the modes both of epiphanic visitation to the patriarchs and of prophetic vision because they are concerned with *the theologoumenon of the name.* The first story of Sinai theophany discloses the name to Moses (Exod. 3:1—4:14); the second expounds the historical significance of that name for the people in the context of the covenant (Exod. 19:1—24:11); the third establishes a dramatic contrast between the theologoume-

non of the name and the theologoumenon of the glory (Exod. 33:12–23).

THE DISCLOSURE OF THE NAME (*Exod. 3:1—4:17*)

The scene is identified with the wilderness of the mountain of Elohim, "westward toward Horeb" (3:1). The geographical designation ("Horeb" rather than "Sinai") is a mark of the northern (E) stratum of the traditions. The name "Horeb" is used in the directional form, *Horebah*, which implies that Moses went toward the mountain. There is no reason to believe that he ascended to its top. On the contrary, two features of the story suggest that the setting was at the foot of the rocky mass, presumably near a spring. Moses was keeping flocks of sheep and goats, and the sort of vegetation suitable for grazing animals grows in valleys and not on mountain peaks. Moreover, the presence of "a bush" indicates the proximity of water and points to a relatively low level of land.[12] In any case, the storytellers place the site in the immediate vicinity of the mountain (3:12).

The core of the narrative grew between the twelfth and the ninth centuries B.C. in the northern sanctuaries of Israel (the Elohistic strand of tradition) and may have influenced the shaping of a new literary genre, that of the "prophetic vision of calling."[13] This is not surprising, since Moses was remembered as the prophet par excellence, the authentic mouthpiece of Yahweh.[14]

The Setting of the Theophany (*Exod. 3:1–6*)

As in some stories of epiphanic visitation to the patriarchs, the Godhead first "appeared,"[15] literally, "was seen," or perhaps "showed itself" in the anthropomorphic guise of the "messenger" (*mal'akh*, "angel") of Yahweh. The feature, however, should not be taken literally since this mysterious figure is enveloped in a flame of fire and soon evanesces from the scene:

> The messenger of Yahweh appeared to him in a fiery flame out of the midst of the bush; and he looked, and behold, the bush was burning with fire; yet, the bush was not consumed. And Moses said. "I must indeed turn around it, and see this great sight, why the bush does not burn itself out!" (vss. 2–4).

In the sequence of the narrative, the "messenger" makes room for "the God" (*ha-Elohim*), later called *Yahweh*. The presence of the Deity is signified to man by a kind of fire which does not correspond to empirical verification. Fire is a symbol of prompt becoming. It suggests the desire to change, to hasten time, to bring life to its beyondness. In the entire history of religions, the contemplation of fire amplifies human destiny; it relates the minor to the major, the burning bush to the life of the world, and the desire for change to the vision of renewal.[16]

The theophany differs from the epiphanic visitation on the one hand and from the prophetic vision on the other because it uses an element of nature in the context of tumult or of wonder as a starting point for an experience of the divine.

Moses is visually aware of the presence, but he perceives no fixed shape or form. The fire, which does not consume itself, is an eternal becoming. Formless but lasting, the visual feature is soon absorbed by the spoken word. The Hebraic theophany is more heard than seen. Divine-human dialogue, with questions and answers, objections and counter-statements, give-and-take, interacting tension between Godhead and manhood, is the primary characteristic of the speech of theophany. The scenic setting disappears at the expense of the pressing question, "Moses, Moses!" (vs. 4), which in turn elicits the reponse of self-availability and potential readiness, "Here am I!" At the same time, the theophanic dialogue cannot proceed without a warning of the risk involved in the nearness of the presence. The storytellers, unable to manipulate the abstraction of philosophical discourse, are stunningly competent in conveying the ambivalence of "the holy."

> "Do not come hither!
> Remove thy shoes from thy feet,
> For the place (*maqôm*) wherein thou standest
> is holy ground (*'adhmath qodhesh*)" (vs. 5).

As the guardians of northern sanctuaries, especially those of Bethel and Shechem, the Elohist theologians told that story in the context of a cultic ceremonial. The expression "holy ground," literally, "soil of holiness," reflects the language of the shrine in an agrarian society for which the earth acquires its special significance as the living "soil" of fertility. It is difficult to think of *'adhamah* on the rocky slopes of Mt. Sinai.

Affinity is here insinuated between "the numinous" of religious experience, which contains the portentous horror of the unknown, and "the sacred," which is contained and delimited within the precincts of a temple esplanade. However, the context indicates that the motif of the "holy place" (*maqôm qadhôsh*), which perhaps was echoed in Jacob's dream at Bethel (Gen. 28:17) and which was common to most religions (cf. the *hieros topos* of the Greeks) was here limited radically in duration: "the holy" obtains its significance not from geography but from the intervention of the Deity, and it is reduced to the temporal dimensions of the theophany. There is no indication that the "holy ground" remains holy after the termination of the divine appearance. The "holy" is not a permanent quality attached to topography, as at Bethel, Shechem, or Mt. Zion. It is in response to the speech of theophany that Hebrew man experiences the *mysterium tremendum* not just as the indefinite power of an animistic nature but as the manifestation of a nature-transcending Godhead. "When Yahweh saw that [Moses] turned aside to see, He called him from the midst of the fire" (vs. 4a). Moses is compelled to elevate both the numinous aspect of the fire and the sacredness of a cultic structure—both common to archaic systems of worship—to the level of a personal, a-topographic "holiness." "He veiled his face for he was afraid to look upon God" (vs. 6). His desire for the sight of the divine, which is the characteristic of all forms of mysticism, is arrested by self-masking. Biblical faith does not belong to the class of mystical religions.

As in the epiphanic visitations to the patriarchs, the vision of God is prevented at the last instant by respect for the holy. Hebraic response to holiness preserves a distinction between the divine and the human realms. Finiteness is never identified with infinity. Presence is real but unseen. The invisibility of a God who yet speaks remains the cardinal tenet of a Hebraic theology of presence. For the northern theologians of the Elohist tradition, the visual faculty of man, the symbol of his sensorial and rational ability to know, is enlisted only in a preliminary way. Sight is submitted to hearing. Man never sees God, but the word is heard. The eye is closed but the ear is opened. Hebraism is a religion not of the eye but of the ear.

The Mission and the Promise of Communion (3:7-12)

Yahweh's intervention in history is motivated by his emotion of sympathy for the oppressed. He has seen the suffering of the Hebrews in Egypt. He shares the misery of his people (vss. 7, 9). Therefore, his intention is not only to deliver them from oppression but also to bring them to a land flowing with milk and honey (vs. 8). Moses is summoned "to bring forth [God's] people . . . out of Egypt" (vs. 10).

Man always shrinks from the prophetic calling. "Who am I" for such a task? The initial reaction of Moses is a refusal dictated by humility and perhaps a lack of courage. Therefore, the summons lead directly to a promise of support:

I shall be with thee (*'eheyeh 'immakh*),
And this will be for thee the sign
That it is I, indeed, that sent thee
To bring forth [my] people out of Egypt,
So that [all of] you will serve God on this mountain (vs. 12).

This passage presents a number of grammatical and exegetical difficulties which explain the variety of renderings and interpretations.[17] There is no syntactical objection to understanding the demonstrative pronoun ("and *this* will be the sign") as referring to the preceding clause. Hence the meaning seems to be that the promise of continuing presence will constitute the "sign" of the authenticity of the mission.

An important development arises from this promise. The Godhead offers Moses a spiritual reality—divine companionship and help—that will outlast the temporal limits of the "appearance" at the Burning Bush. We witness a shift from one mode of presence to another. The psychological mode of presence, as distinguished from the specific experience of encounter, was already hinted at when the Yahwistic tradition said of the antediluvian hero, "Enoch walked with God" (Gen. 4:22).

It will be noted that the promise of enduring communion uses the verbal form *'eheyeh*, "I shall be," (vs. 12*a*), an expression which is also found in the patriarchal narratives of epiphanic visitation[18] and which constitutes the key to the understanding of the next episode in the theophany, the disclosure of the divine name (3:13–15).

The Meaning of the Name of God (3:13–15)

As the theophanic scene becomes exclusively dominated by the dialogical speech, the dynamics of the narrative articulate the unfolding of God's self-asseveration as a gradual response to the objections advanced by the would-be but reluctant prophet.

Apparently, an inward and spiritual promise of a lasting presence is not deemed to be sufficient: Moses projects the image of his "political" anxiety:

> And Moses said to the Elohim,
> "Behold, when I come to the sons of Israel and I say to them,
> The Elohim of your fathers has sent me toward you,
> And if they say, What is his name?
> What shall I say unto them?" (3:13)

The request for the disclosure of the divine name is not made by man on his own behalf, as in the narrative of the epiphanic visitation to Jacob at the Jabbok (Gen. 32:29), but is explicitly related to the historical activity which has been outlined by the divine command. The revelation of the name is justified by a concern for a theology of history. Moses makes his request on the ground of his commission and for the sake of its success. Nevertheless, the storyteller may have been hinting at some inner conflict within his hero, for the reply of God is bewildering:

> 3:14 And Elohim said to Moses,
> " '*Eheyeh 'asher 'eheyeh.*"
> And he said, "Thus wilt thou say to the sons of Israel,
> '*Eheyeh* has sent me to you."
> 3:15 And Elohim said again to Moses,
> "Thus wilt thou say to the sons of Israel,
> *Yahweh,* the Elohim of your fathers,
> the Elohim of Abraham,
> the Elohim of Isaac, and
> the Elohim of Jacob,
> Has sent me to you.
> This is my name forever,
> And this is my memorial for generation of generation."

The text bristles with exegetical problems.[19]

1. The "name" (shem) is placed parallel to the "memorial" (zeker) in the context of the mission of Israel. This feature alone indicates the cultic use of the passage in the shrines at a later time. The English word "memorial" is in some respects unfortunate, for it fails to convey the sacramental aspect of the original Hebrew word, which refers to memory in worship.[20] The zeker does not merely signify a recall of the past. It designates a ceremonial commemoration which summons the people to take a stand for action in view of Yahweh's purpose in history. The climactic statement of the pericope relates the name of God to the future generations. The "memorial" corresponds in effect to an eschatological memorandum, a token of the not-yet which is sure to come. The name of Israel's God, Yahweh, is thus presented not as a tool of cultic invocation, as in the religious folklore of mankind, but as a kerygma of hope, an affirmation of certainty in the power of the divine intention toward its fulfillment.[21]

2. The oral conflator or final redactor of the traditions here preserved places the name Yahweh (vs. 15)[22] in parallel sequence to the word 'Eheyeh (vs. 14b), which in turn appears immediately after, and is indeed a repeated part of, the mysterious phrase 'eheyeh 'asher 'eheyeh, traditionally rendered "I am that I am" (vs. 14a). Clearly, the narrator intends to illuminate the meaning of the divine name with the help of this initial statement.

3. Although the phrase in question is known to us only through its written form in the present Masoretic text, and therefore reflects the phonetic use which prevailed among the synagogue singers of the first millenium A.D., traditio-historical criticism shows that it was originally part of a cultic recital of the national epic in Israel's formative centuries—the period of the

Judges and of the United Monarchy (thirteenth to tenth centuries B.C.).

4. If it could be demonstrated that, in its oral stage, the phrase *'eheyeh 'asher 'eheyeh* came from the time of Moses, namely, the Late Bronze Age, one would be in the position to conclude with a remarkable degree of certainty that it was not pronounced in this way. Comparative Northwest Semitics shows that the verb *hayah,* "to be," was primitively *hawah.* Consequently, the phrase of verse 14*a* might be restored, in keeping with the peculiarities of the verbal conjugation of such verbs (which belong to the doubly laryngeal type, as well as " *'ayin-yod,"* primitively " *'ayin-waw"*) as *'ahweh 'asher 'ahweh.* It will be observed at once that the verbal form *'ahweh,* first person singular masculine imperfect-future of the verb *hawah,* "to be," used in verse 14*a* twice and repeated in verse 14*b* as a proper name, is phonetically and morphologically very close to the tetragrammaton *Yahweh,* the third person masculine of the same verb. According to this restoration, the unexpected discrepancy in the sounds of *'eheyeh* (vs. 14 *a* and *b*) and *Yahweh* (vs. 15) disappears. Moreover, the verbal form *'ahweh,* first person singular, or *yahweh,* third person singular, is grammatically ambiguous, for it may be understood as belonging to the *Qal* voice (simple active) or to the *Hiph'il* voice (causative-factitive). It follows that the translation of verse 14*a* might be either "I am who I am" (possibly in the future, "I shall be who I shall be") or "I cause to be whatever I cause to be." Consequently, the name *Yahweh* might be interpreted, according to the Elohistic narrative of the Burning Bush, as either "He is" or "He causes to be."

5. The "causative-factitive" interpretation of the phrase in verse 14*a* and of the tetragrammaton *Yahweh* in verse 15 is possible and attractive[23] but not probable.

(a) The meaning of *Yahweh* as "the Creating One," or "He who causes to be," fits the contextual sequence admirably.

When Moses offers a fourth objection to the acceptance of his prophetic task by pleading that he is not eloquent (4:10), Yahweh replies most pointedly, "Who has *made* man's mouth? . . . Is it not I, *Yahweh*?"

(b) The wide use of the tetragrammaton throughout the Hebraic literature of the entire biblical period gives semantic support to the interpretation of the divine name in the sense of creative activity.

(c) Many parallels in ancient Near Eastern onomastics (Sumerian, Egyptian, Akkadian, Amorite, and more specifically proto-Canaanite; compare also the Sinaitic inscriptions) tend to indicate that theophoric names included the idea of causative creativity, although this was never the case with the verb *hawah*, "to be" (or its Semitic cognates and equivalents). To be sure, the form *Yahwi* is found in the formation of Amorite personal names, but there is no way of discovering whether it was understood as active or as causative-factitive.

(d) The fact remains that the Hebraic literature has never understood the tetragrammaton in the creative sense.[24] Indeed, as early as the eighth century B.C.—at a time when the Elohistic epic tradition was probably still in oral form—the prophet Hosea appeared to allude to the dialogical speech of the Burning Bush theophany when he used the verb *'eheyeh* exactly as it is found in the present Hebrew text of Exodus 3:14*a* and *b*. Speaking to unfaithful Israel, *Lô-'Ammi*, "Not-My-People," Yahweh says, through the mouth of his prophet,

"You are not-my-people (*Lô-'Ammi*),
    and I, for you, *I-am-not* (*Lô-'Eheyeh*)" (Hos. 1:8).

The sapiential circles also used the verb *hayah* intransitively.[25] It is not impossible that the idea of being and nonbeing, in a proto-ontological form of speculation, was familiar to the theologians of northern Israel. The tellers of the story of the

Burning Bush suggested that the God who manifested his active presence to Moses was not to be associated with derivative forces but represented beingness par excellence.

While the most accurate translation of Exod. 3:13–15 must remain a matter of uncertainty, the foregoing discussion shows that the traditional rendering, which was already reflected in Hellenistic times by the translation of the Septuagint,[26] is probably correct.[27]

6. The meaning of the tetragrammaton, however, requires further discussion. Was the verb *hayah-hawah* understood by the ancient Hebrews in the simple meaning of "being"?[28] The dynamics of the entire narrative indicate that the phrase of 3:14–15 should not be divorced from the context in which it is found. The exegete will recall that the promise of a lasting communion (vs. 12) was strikingly expressed in the words *'eheyeh 'immakh,* "I shall be with thee." Likewise, after Moses' repeated attempts to escape the responsibility of the mission given to him, Yahweh insisted, *we-'anokhi 'eheyeh 'im pîkha,* "And I, even I, shall be with thy mouth" (4:12; cf. vs. 15). By employing the method of contextual juxtaposition, the storytellers have framed the phrase of 3:14 within the offer of divine presence[29]

Whatever the etymology and original meaning of the name *Yahweh* may have been, the storytellers wished to promote their own interpretation of it. To the vacillating Moses, Yahweh first gave assurance by affirming, "I shall be with thee" (3:12). When Moses persisted by conjecturing that the sons of Israel might well demand a precise identification of the God of their fathers, he was in effect asking indirectly, on his own behalf, for a clarification of his own knowledge of the divine. He was attempting to expand the limits of that knowledge. More than intellectual curiosity was implied, for he betrayed a doubt as to the validity of his own experience.

In the light of the other strata of this ancient tradition (Exod. 4:1–17), in which Moses objected three times to his prophetic calling, one may surmise that the request for the disclosure of the name (vs. 13) was both a symptom of man's reluctance to obey and the manifestation of a legitimate move toward theological certainty. Prophetic revelation and prophetic summons are inextricably bound in Hebraic faith. As Moses was still delaying his response, God replied, "I shall be whoever I shall be" (vs. 14). Such a reply may well represent a qualification of the promise to offer supportive presence (vs. 12). In the present redaction of the story, it sharpens the dynamics of the theophanic interchange and anticipates the divine anger which brings the dialogue to its climax (4:14).

According to this interpretation, the name indeed carries the connotation of divine presence, but it also confers upon this presence a quality of elusiveness. The God of biblical faith, even in the midst of a theophany, is at once *Deus revelatus atque absconditus*. He is known as unknown.[31] The semantics of the phrase "I shall be whoever I shall be" prepares the syntactically similar saying of the third Sinai theophany, "I shall grace whomever I shall grace and I shall be merciful with whomever I shall be merciful" (Exod. 33:19).

Moses expressed his own anxiety, for he wrongly thought that the people would be reluctant to trust him readily and at once. This anxiety was not only of a psychological, sociological, and political nature ("Will they believe what I say?") but was also and primarily the result of a theological *Angst*. He wanted religious certainty. He wished to see with his own power of perception. He intended to comprehend. Yahweh's disclosure of his name was both an answer and the denial of a request.[32] Such an ambivalence was to remain "forever" (vs. 15*b*) the mark of the Hebraic theology of presence.

The Covenant Theophany *(Exod. 19:1—24:18)*

Few pages in the literature of mankind compare to this awesome description of an encounter between God and man. Yet, mountains have played a significant part in most religions. Men have seen them

> in clusters swelling
>> mighty, and pure, and fit to make
>> the ramparts of a Godhead's dwelling.[33]

Homer sang of Titans who piled Mount Pelion and Mount Ossa on the top of Mount Olympus in a vain attempt to scale the dwelling of the gods.[34] For centuries, the proto-Canaanites of Ugarit had evoked in their liturgies the storm theophany and the mountain of the north,[35] in strains which have inspired Hebrew poets in a later age.[36] There is no reason, however, for assimilating the Sinai traditions to the mythologies of ancient Near Eastern or classical antiquities. A historical event stood at the base of the Hebraic *legenda*. All available evidence leads to the conclusion that Moses and the refugees who had fled the Egyptian labor camps pitched their tents at the foot of a mountainous massif, not far from the Sea of Reeds. There, some weeks after the spring equinox, a seasonally late thunderstorm was the setting of a collective experience of the holy which became the norm of Hebrew religion.

The cluster of heterogeneous traditions, narratives, and laws, which is now found at the heart of the book of Exodus (19:1—24:18), represents the only story of "theophany" in the strict sense of the word, for it contains two elements not found elsewhere in the biblical literature: first, the constantly reiterated feature of nature in tumult; second, the participation of the people standing as a witness to a solitary man of God. In other narratives of a similar character, as in the epiphanic visitations to the patriarchs or the visions of the great prophets, nature is absent or offers only a neutral background. In the other two stories of theophany which are told of Moses (Exod. 3 and 33), where some element of scenic wonder is called into play, the people is absent.

Substantial disagreement lingers among scholars concerning the exact delineation of the ancient strata of the traditions which have been woven into the present text,[37] but one may reasonably maintain that two different sets of stories can be discerned behind the various repetitions, stylistic changes, and lexicographic discrepancies of the present text. In one, the Elohist theologians of northern Israel, who lived near the shrines of Shechem and Bethel in the First Iron Age during the conquest and the early monarchy (twelfth to ninth centuries B.C.), stressed the element of hearing sounds and voices and or obeying words. They were followed by the Deuteronomists (ninth to seventh centuries), who interpreted the same traditions in a similar way (Deut. 4:33 ff., etc.). In the other, the Yahwist theologians, from Judah, told their own versions in the sanctuaries of Hebron and Jerusalem and insisted on the vision of the divine glory.

More clearly than in the scene of the Burning Bush, the present text of the covenant theophany points to a tension between two different religious stances. The first thinks of divine presence according to the theologoumenon of the name, and the second conceives it in terms of visibility. The conflict between the ear and the eye persisted throughout the centuries of Hebrew religion in biblical times and appears in modified forms both in Judaism and Christianity.

The Elohist Proclamation of the Name

Northerners remembered the Horeb theophany as an event which concerned *all the people,* not just a hierarchy. The covenant played a significant part in this event, but it was initiated by the prior reality of presence. The covenant appears to be a ritual act of mutual obligation which is precisely intended to prolong in a modified form the most extraordinary, indeed a unique, perception of the holy: the self-manifestation of the creator of the universe, the possessor of the whole earth, the ruler of nature and the liberator who is able to overcome the most powerful army in history. The covenant aims therefore at transcending the ravages of time, preventing the erosion of ancestral memories, and bringing to life for the children yet unborn the fathers' "ancient rapture." It attempts to bridge the gap between generations. It is directed toward the future actuality of a past which risks inevitable oblivion. It constitutes a deed of truly "historical" significance, for its purpose is far more embracing than the aims of imperial archives or historiography. It is to mold the Israel of tomorrow into the pattern of living with God as "a holy nation."

The following pericopes may be identified as fragments of the Elohist tradition which have been preserved in the present redaction of the Pentateuchal story:

Summons to Moses (19:2b–3)

19:2b And Israel encamped there in front of the mountain.
3   And Moses went up to [the mountain of] Elohim (LXX)
   And Yahweh called him from the mountain and said,
      Thus shalt thou say to the house of Jacob
      And reveal to the sons of Israel.

This introduction to the theophany proper is phrased in an unspectacular style. It is reminiscent of the conversational tone used in the epiphanic visitations to the patriarchs and anticipates the simple intimacy with which the great prophets in a later age received divine orders. The message is directed to "the house of Jacob," a designation of Israel that is typical of the Northern theologians.

Message to the People (19:4–6)

19:4 You, yourselves (*'attem*), you have seen
   What I have done to the Egyptians

And how I carried you on wings of eagles
And I brought you to myself.

5 And now (*we 'attah*), if you will obey my voice indeed
And keep my covenant,
You will be for me, out of all peoples, a peculiar treasure,
For the whole earth is mine.

6 And you, yourselves (*we 'attem*), you will be for me
A priestly realm and a holy nation.

These are the words which thou shalt speak to the sons of
Israel.

The strophic structure of the poem is enhanced by the strategic location of key words which create assonance, although they are not cognates: *we 'attem*, "and you," *we 'attah*, "and now." The literary genre of the call narratives which may be discerned in this pericope indicates a long history of prophetic spirituality. Moses is the mouthpiece of the Deity. He does not act on his own behalf. He is the ambassador of the Great King.

The divine speech opens with a recital of the *Magnalia Dei*. The manifestation of Yahweh's presence on Mount Horeb is prefaced by the manifestation of Yahweh's indirect presence at the Crossing of the Sea. According to a late midrash, "even the lowliest maidservant at the Red Sea *saw* what Isaiah, Ezekiel, and all the other prophets never saw."[38] The dialogical speech announcing the Mount Horeb theophany already played upon the human faculty of sight: "You, yourselves, you have *seen!*" This statement clearly intimates that divine presence can manifest itself in various ways. The Exodus and the Crossing of the Sea, however, are only the preludes to a far more significant event, the appearance of God himself on the mountain. The purpose of the Exodus is indeed the liberation from slavery, but the liberation from slavery has no meaning unless it leads to God: "I brought you toward myself!" Geography has become the *topos* for the pilgrimage of the spirit. Israel has seen the acts of God. Now, Israel will see her own destiny as the act of God.

Presence is that which creates a people. Presence is the reality to which man must attune himself if he is to live at all, for there is no solitary life. The family and the tribe grow into a welded society. The Hebraic notion of "peoplehood" represents a new reality in the history of mankind. The technological societies of the ancient world—Mesopotamia, Egypt or the city-states of the Fertile Crescent—are hierarchic structures in which the many work for the few. As they move through an economic wilderness, the liberated slaves cannot develop into a coherent community unless they are converted into priestly agents for the sovereign of history. The Horeb theophany is to transform the uncouth mass of slaves into a united people of free men and women. Presence, after the fire is extinct and the thunders are silent, will transmute its shattering but momentary impact into a sociological cement which will create a sacerdotal realm, hence a holy nation.

Collective homogeneity means social solidarity, which in turn implies a standard of ethical behavior. The validity of the covenant depends upon the *hearing* of a voice, that is to say, the obeying of a formulated word. The covenant has to be kept, observed, preserved, maintained. It is conditional. Initiated by presence, it leads to presence. Out of all peoples, the new people will become Yahweh's "special treasure" (*segullah*).[39] Israel, the covenant people, is bound to a God whose sway embraces nothing less than the entire earth. The separation of Israel from all other peoples points to the idea of election, although the word is not yet used. To be the object of a unique love means "to be chosen." Election is predicated on the emotional awareness of "predilection." Israel, however, is not loved in a historical vacuum. Yahweh is not a dilettante. Israel is loved so as to become Yahweh's priestly kingdom in the history of the world. The expression "kingdom of priests," obscure as it may be since it has no parallel in the biblical literature,[40] shows that the northern theologians have meditated in a revolutionary way upon the institution of sacerdotal mediation. The notion of priesthood, which goes back to the prehistoric shrines or at least to centuries of ancient Near Eastern life in holy places,[41] is lifted out of its institutional functionalism. Priests are specialized servants of the gods in sanctuaries. Their function is to administer the sacred acts in sacred places at sacred times. They are therefore sacred persons. In the view of the theology of northern Israel, Israel in its entirety becomes "a holy nation," because Israel's vocation is to become the priest of the King of history. Israel, the covenant people, is to mediate the presence of Yahweh to the world. The theme is not essentially different from that of the Abrahamic call: "In thee all the nations of the earth shall be blessed and bless one another" (Gen. 12:3).

The Elohist theology of presence promotes a religion of suprasacerdotalism, in which the traditional function of priesthood is collectivized and sublimated. Consequently there can be within the exercise of this religion no distinction between clergy and laity.

The People's Commitment (19:7–8)

19:7 And Moses came and summoned the elders of the people,
        And he placed before them all these words
        Which Yahweh had commanded him.
    8 And all the people answered together and said,
        All that Yahweh has spoken, we will do.
        And Moses reported to Yahweh the words of the people.

The terms of the covenantal conditions are transmitted to "all the people" by their elders. In nomadic societies, elders do not represent a political structure of external authority but emerge from within the informal nuclei of the community: family, clan,

and tribe.[42] Stress is also laid on the unanimity of the assent:
all the people "answered *together*."

The People's Readiness to Meet God (19:10–11a, 14)

19:10 And Elohim said to Moses, Go the people
          And consecrate them today and tomorrow,
          And let them wash their garments,
  11a   And let them be ready on the third day.
  14 And Moses went down from the mountain to the people,
          And he consecrated the people,
          And they washed their garments.

The people are bidden to prepare for the divine encounter. The
proximity of the holy calls for special acts of a symbolic and,
indeed, sacramental significance. Just as Moses was asked to
remove his shoes at the scene of the Burning Bush, so also
Moses is invited to perform a series of acts of "sanctification"
which are not otherwise described. The washing of garments
does not represent a specifically cultic act of ritual significance,
for it is universally observed in anticipation of a solemn event.
To be sure, the theophany is told within the temporal framework of cultic reenactment, but the ritual features are merely
hinted at. The series of gestures or deeds which are implied by
the verb "to consecrate" appear to be entirely compatible with
the nomadic destitution of the wilderness.

The Storm Theophany (19:16–17, 19)

19:16 On the morning of the third day
          There were thunders and flashes of lightning,
        And a heavy cloud upon the mountain,
          And the sound of the *shophar* was exceedingly strong,
          And all the people who were in the camp trembled.
  17 And Moses brought the people out to meet Elohim,
          And they stood beneath the slope of the mountain.

19 And as the sound of the *shophar* went on,
   Growing exceedingly strong,
   Moses spoke,
   And Elohim asnwered him in thunder.

The day has come. The visual features include a heavy cloud (
'anan kabhed), which presumably masked the top of the mountain, and flashes of lightning, but the Deity was not seen—in any
shape or in any mode. The auditive elements dominate: the
thunders and the sound of the *shophar*. It is not possible to
determine whether the allusion to the ram's horn is metaphorical or points to a cultic detail of the reenacted ceremonial.
Likewise, the meaning of the word *qôl* (vs. 19*b*), used for the
answer of God, is uncertain: it may refer to a thunderstroke or
to an articulated voice.

The People's Refusal to Meet God (20:18–21)

20:18 And all the people saw the thunders and the lightnings
      And the sound of the *shophar* and the mountain smoke,
      And the people were afraid and they trembled
      And they stood afar off.
   19 And they said to Moses, Speak thou with us and we will
      hear,
      But let not Elohim speak with us lest we die.
   20 And Moses said to the people, Fear not
      For it is to test you that Elohim has come
      And that the fear of him may be before you
      So that you may not sin.
   21 And the people stood afar off,
      And Moses drew near to the thickdarkness where
      Elohim was.

The verb "to see" is again used, but some of the objects of this
"sight" are thunders and the sound of the *shophar*. Clearly, the
storytellers suggest the general faculty of perception through
the senses. Smoke now envelops the mountain but does not

constitute a volcanic sign, since brush fires are generally ignit-
ed on the slopes of mountain ranges during subtropical thunderstorms.[43] The people, in any case, do not see God. They
even fear to hear him. Moses, far from being the appointed
intercessor who stands forever between God and man, is here
an *ad hoc* delegate. He represents the people because they cannot muster the courage to face the holy. The nature of the divine
"test" or of the human "sin" is not defined.[44] In contrast to the
cowardice of the people, Moses dared "to draw near the thickdarkness (*'araphel*) where Elohim was" (vs. 21*b*).

This detail appears to constitute the climax of the theophany.[45] Apparently, the northern storytellers did not hesitate
to localize the presence of the Godhead, but they selected a
most peculiar word for designating the place of this divine
spatialization. Although the word *'araphel* points to the mythology of the storm god,[46] it designates, more specifically than
the thunderhead (which is, to be sure, at the origin of this
theological term) a total darkness which is the symbol both of
divine presence and of divine hiddenness.[47] Unlike the other
Hebrew words for obscurity, such as those which refer to night
or to the gloom of the underworld, the word *'araphel* is at once
a portent of menace and a promise. It may be that, originally,
the image of the thundercloud indicated destruction through
lightning and life through the rain which followed. At any rate,
it was a symbol of divine power in both its danger and its
blessing,[48] and it came to designate the complete blackness of
the innermost room in the Jerusalem sanctuary.[49]

Moses dared to approach that which the people recoiled
from: with eloquent succinctness, the narrator merely said,
"Moses drew near the thickdarkness, where Elohim was." The
word "theophany," with its connotation of shining brightness,
is totally inadequate. Moses came into the immediate presence
of the Godhead, but he, like the people, saw nothing other than
"the mask of Yahweh."[50]

The Divine Recital of the Name (20:1–2)

20:1 And Elohim spoke all these words, saying:
  2   I am Yahweh thy God who brought thee out of the land
      of Egypt,
    From the house of slaves.

The scene of the Burning Bush was dominated by the self-disclosure of the name. The Elohist tradition of the theophany on Mt. Horeb culminates in the divine recital of the meaning of the name.[51] In both narratives, the name is linked to a theological interpretation of history. Yahweh is intervening in the life of the nations for the sake of a particular purpose. His name stands for his will to reach that purpose. It has a relational meaning and a teleological function. In effect, therefore, the recital of the name is the rehearsal of God's acts. It celebrates the presence of God in history. When Yahweh proclaims his name, he recites *ipso facto* his historical deeds, but he does so in view of the future, not of the past. The *Magnalia Dei* receive their significance from God's ultimate intention. Israel is brought out of slavery because Israel is elected to bear the responsibility of God's presence in history. Therefore, the proclamation of the name leads to the formulation of God's will for his chosen instrument of presence in history.[52]

The Exodus is the prelude to the historical life of Israel, and the first manifestation of the name of God. Israel cannot become a priestly realm and a holy nation without hearing God's words and behaving according to his will. What are these words? The proclamation of the name becomes the prologue of the Ten Words. Presence is the root of *peoplehood* and the source of the *Torah*.

The Ten Words (20:3–4, 7a, 8, 12–17a)

20: 3 I. Thou shalt have no other gods in my presence.
  4 II. Thou shalt not make for thyself any graven image.

7a III. Thou shalt not invoke the name of Yahweh thy
     Elohim in vain.

8 IV. Remember the sabbath day to make it holy.

12 V. Honor thy father and thy mother.

13 IV. Thou shalt not murder.

14 VII. Thou shalt not commit adultery.

15 VIII. Thou shalt not steal.

16 IX. Thou shalt not bear false witness against thy
     neighbor.

17a X. Thou shalt not covet.

The sobriety of the demands fits the life-situation of a people during their formative stage. No objection may be validly raised today against the antiquity of the Ten Words, although the traditional view of a Mosaic "authorship" or "transmitting action" is not, of course, susceptible of historical demonstration.[53] When it is pruned of its catechetic accretions which clearly point to a later age,[54] the ethical decalogue[55] contains not a single element that might reveal an agrarian and mercantile mode of civilization. In its pithy form, the decalogue provides a key to the Hebraic understanding of the theological basis of ethics. The call for the exclusive worship of Yahweh is explicitly made in terms of the overwhelming experience of his presence.[56] The accent is that not of the legal mind but of the prophetic attunement to a living power which surrounds and penetrates the wholeness of human existence. The equally revolutionary requirement of aniconism in worship[57] indicates a bold and original thrust of theologians who know that the God of Israel transcends all forces of nature and history and yet dare to oppose the whole burden of cultic devotion which has flourished among the religionists of the Near East ever since the prehistoric age. The prohibition of idolatry is the inevitable consequence of the theological radicalism which characterizes the Elohist version of the Mount Horeb theophany. The northern theology of presence, which stresses the hearing of the divine will, is suspicious of any finite representation of infinity. The ear, once again, prevails over the eye.

The Oath and the Covenant (24:3–6, 8)

24:3 Moses came and told the people all the words of Yahweh
[. . .]58
And all the people answered with one voice and said,
All the words which Yahweh has spoken we will do.
4 And Moses wrote all the words of Yahweh,
And he rose early in the morning,
And he built an altar beneath the slope of the mountain,
And twelve pillars, according to the twelve tribes of Israel,
5 And sent youths of the sons of Israel to offer burnt offerings
And to sacrifice communion sacrifices to Yahweh
[. . .]59
6 And Moses took half the blood and put it in basins,
And half the blood and threw it against the altar.
7 And Moses took the blood [from the basins] and threw it on the people,
And he said, Behold, the blood of the covenant
Which Yahweh has made with you in accordance with all these words.

This fragment of the Elohist tradition concludes the Mount Horeb theophany. Analysis of the present text has revealed that it bears traces of amplification, probably because it deals with a rite that had been reenacted many times in the shrines of Israel after the conquest. It is no longer possible to ascertain with any degree of historical confidence whether the ceremonial of the covenant-making here described goes back to Moses himself. What must be noted, however, is that no new vision of the Godhead is hinted at by the northern narrators. Contrasts with the details of the southern recital are notable.

The Southern Vision of the Glory

Instead of stressing the motif of obedience by "all the

people," the southern narrators are concerned with the eternal status of Moses as the intermediary between God and man. They also play up the spatial elements of sacredness, the cultic topography, and the visual aspects of the theophany.

The Appointment of the Covenant Intercessor (19:9a)

19:9a And Yahweh said to Moses,
    Behold, I am coming to thee in the thickness of the cloud,[60]
    That the people may hear when I speak with thee
    And may believe thee for ever.

The Elohist version had presented Moses as an *ad hoc* representative of the people who were afraid to approach the realm of the holy. There, Moses had been delegated by "all the people." Here, on the contrary, we discover that Moses was appointed by God himself to the status of mediator, a status that would last "forever." This status is probably akin to the notion of an eternal priesthood, which was nurtured in the Jerusalem temple.[61]

The Rite of Preparation (19:11b–13)

19:11b [. . .] On the third day, Yahweh will come down upon Mount Sinai
    In the sight of all the people.
12 And thou shalt set territorial lines for the people all around,
    Saying, Take heed that you do not go up to the mountain
    Or touch the edge of it.
    Whoever touches the mountain shall be put to death.
13   No hand shall touch him,
    But he shall be either stoned or shot,
        Whether beast or man, he shall not live.
    [At the sound of the ram's horn, they shall come up to the mountain.][62]

Mount Sinai is the site of Yahweh's descent from heaven. The descent will be "in the sight of all the people." The mountain is to be prepared as a holy place, according to the traditional customs of the Semitic shrines. Boundary lines must be carefully marked, so that no man or beast shall trespass. Unlike the mountain of the northern versions ("Mount Horeb"), which received its quality of *mysterium tremendum* through the event for which it was a temporary setting, Mount Sinai possesses an intrinsic "substance" of sacredness. Here again, the exegete must observe that the Yahwist tradition contains the seed of the sacerdotal notion of topographic holiness which the priestly writers in the Babylonian exile applied to the site of Zion.

The Smoke and Fire Theophany (19:18, 20–25)

19:18 And Mount Sinai, all of it, [was covered] with smoke
    On account of the fact that Yahweh descended upon it in fire,
  And its smoke was like the smoke of a kiln,
  And the whole mountain quaked exceedingly,
20 And Yahweh descended upon Mount Sinai, to the top of the mountain,
    And Yahweh called to Moses to the top of the mountain,
    And Moses went up.
21 And Yahweh said to Moses, Go down and warn the people
    Lest they crash through toward Yahweh
    And many of them fall [dead].
22 And even the priests, those who draw near to Yahweh,
    Let them sanctify themselves
    Lest Yahweh burst out in their midst.
23 And Moses said to Yahweh, The people cannot come up to Mount Sinai,
    Since, thou, thyself, hast warned us, saying,
    Set territorial lines to the mountain and make it sacred!
24 And Yahweh said to him, Go down and come back,
    Thou, and Aaron with thee, and the priests,

> But let not the people crash through to go up toward
> Yahweh
> Lest he burst out in their midst.
> 25a And Yahweh went down to the people.

Whereas the motif of the storm theophany was used at the
beginning of the narrative (vs. 9a), the Yahwist narrators centered their attention on the features of smoke, fire, and earthquake. Nevertheless, one cannot conclude from this that the
southern tradition has been colored by reminiscences of volcanic eruptions, for the fire descends from heaven with Yahweh
rather than rises from the mountain. Earthquakes, moreover,
commonly occur in Asia Anterior and are not directly related
to volcanic eruptions. Once again the commentator will observe that the Yahwist emphasized the element of sacredness in
the spatial sense of a sacred precinct, and the rites of purification that are proper for priestly personnel. A distinction between a sacerdotal caste, headed by Aaron, and the common
people, is typical of the priestly traditions of the Pentateuch,
which in turn reflect the Jerusalem temple tradition in exilic
times. More than the northern story of the Mt. Horeb theophany, the southern narrative of the Mt. Sinai theophany shows the
signs of a long development at the hands of a "clergy" distinct
from a "laity."[63]

The Vision of God (24:1–2, 9–11)

> 24:1 And he said to Moses, Come up to Yahweh,
> Thou, and Aaron, Nadab and Abihu,
> And seventy of the elders of Israel, and worship afar off.
> 2 Moses alone shall come near to Yahweh,
> But the others shall not come near,
> And the people shall not come up with him.
> 9 And Moses went up, and Aaron, Nadab and Abihu,
> And seventy of the elders of Israel.
> 10 And they saw the God of Israel,
> And there was under his feet, as it were,

A pavement of sapphire stone,
Like the very heaven in purity.
11 And upon the nobles of the sons of Israel he did not lay
his hand,
And they beheld Elohim, and they ate and drank.

Such a story is without parallel in the Hebrew tradition. Hellenistic Jews must have found it shocking, since the Septuagint version added, "God is not seen, only the place were he stood" (vs. 10), and the phrase "they beheld God" was rendered "they appeared in the place of God" (vs. 11b). To be sure, after his fight with a mysterious assailant at the ford of the Jabbok, Jacob was made to say, "I have seen God face to face and yet my life is preserved" (Gen. 32:30), but this phrase was apparently inspired by the need to explain the name Peniel, "the face of El," and, in any case, the encounter had taken place in the darkness of the night. Jacob had not really "seen" the Godhead.

Again, both the prophet Micayah ben Yimlah and the prophet Isaiah, in the ninth and eighth centuries respectively, were reported to have said in almost identical terms, "I saw Yahweh sitting on his throne" (1 Kings 22:19) and "I saw Yahweh sitting on a throne" (Isa. 6:1). However, these first-person accounts make it evident that the two prophets believed themselves to have been the recipients of ecstatic experiences that did not involve the sensorial perception of their bodily eyes. The same is obvious of the confession of the prophet Ezekiel who used the phrase "I saw visions of God" (mar'oth Elohim; Ezek. 1:1), although he also made it clear that "the heavens were opened."

In this narrative, on the contrary, the setting is topographically concrete, the human witnesses are many, and the visual perception of the Godhead, twice affirmed (vss. 10 and 11), is made even more explicitly sensorial by its sequential climax: "they ate and drank" (Exod. 24:11b).

Scholars are divided concerning the unity and the authorship or provenance of this passage.[64] That it belongs to the southern tradition is doubtful, for it bears close affinities with the story of Jethro, priest of Midian (Gen. 18:1 ff.), most of which is not related to a peculiar stratum of the Jahwist tradition. Nevertheless, this narrative of the vision of God appears to have been preserved in the priestly circles of the Jerusalem temple, for it bears all the marks of their peculiar concerns: Moses is surrounded by a sacerdotal group, made up of Aaron, Nadab and Abihu;[65] the elders of the people are not simply the tribal chieftains through whom Moses communicates with the sons of Israel, as in the Elohist tradition (cf. 19:7), but they constitute a privileged class with a religious status akin to that of the priests;[66] clerical status becomes linked with the notion of territorial sacredness, as in the shrines of the ancient Near East—a prelude to the topography of worship in the Second Temple, with its various courts reserved for various groups of worshippers;[67] finally, and in a language which is more explicit than elsewhere, the theophany is presented in terms of sensorial sight.[68]

To be sure, what these men saw was blurred by the dazzling light (vs. 10). Nevertheless, instead of stressing the darkness of the storm cloud, or the total obscurity of the 'araphel (cf. 20:21), the narrators prefer the theologoumenon of blinding luminescence that is typical of the ancient Near Eastern mythology of the divine splendor.[69]

It was probably not through mere coincidence that the visio dei in dazzling light received more and more attention among the Jerusalem priestly circles, and especially from Ezekiel, who was the son of a Jerusalem priest.[70] It appears that a continuity of thought and formulation led from the southern tradition of the Yahwist, from Hebron and Jerusalem, to the exilic priestly circles that prepared the Second Temple. The theology of presence through visual experience led from Judah to Restoration Judaism.

The Priestly Vision of the Glory (24:15–18)

24:15 And Moses went up to the mountain,
              And the cloud covered the mountain.
  16 The glory of Yahweh settled on Mount Sinai,
              And the cloud covered it for six days,
              And on the seventh he called Moses out of the cloud.
  17 And the appearance of the glory of Yahweh was like a
              devouring fire
                  On the top of the mountain, in the sight of the sons of
                  Israel,
  18 And Moses entered into the midst of the cloud and went
              up the mountain.
              And Moses was on the mountain forty days and forty
              nights.

Scholarly consensus ascribes the concluding passage to the priestly tradition. It is included in this analysis of the ancient Yahwist tradition because it spells out in explicit terms the implicit and yet obvious orientation of the southern theologians, who had plainly stated that Moses and the favored group of priests and elders with him "saw" the Deity. The priestly tradition of exilic times went a step farther by stating that "the sons of Israel saw the appearance of the glory of Yahweh." Again, the affinities of this narrative with the style of the prophet Ezekiel are evident.[71] The terminology of the "cloud" was maintained (vss. 15–16), but a hitherto unknown motif was introduced, the theologoumenon of the glory (vs. 17). Once again, the storytellers are attempting to qualify the boldness of their formulation, for they carefully say "the appearance of the glory" rather than merely "the glory." Nevertheless, a new language was tried out. A study of the story of the third theophany granted to Moses at Horeb-Sinai reveals that northerners and southerners were separated by far more than a quarrel of words. They interpreted their theological approach to the divine in two radically divergent ways: while the northerners interpreted divine presence through the theologoumenon of the name, the southerners eventually adopted an interpretation of divine revelation through the theologoumenon of the glory. "Israel," properly speaking, led to the theology of the great prophets, while Judah, with its Yahwist fountainhead in Hebron and Jerusalem, prepared Restoration Judaism and the Second Temple.

THE NAME AND NOT THE GLORY
(*Exod. 33:1a, 12–23*)

Several stories about the departure of Moses from Mt. Sinai-Horeb have been pieced together in the latter part of the book of Exodus. Commentators are almost unanimous in pointing out that these stories were originally independent. The link which connects them is the theme of "God's presence endangered."[72] Although the narrative concerning the "tent of meeting" (33:7–11) also deals in part with this theme, it belongs geographically and thematically to another phase in the saga of the sons of Israel in the wilderness.[73] The remaining pericopes of chapter 33 (vss. 1–3, 46, 12–17, and 18–23), however, are somewhat unified, and the rhetorical structure which the Pentateuchal redactors have preserved suggests a liturgical situation. The material was probably recited at the occasion of a seasonal feast.[74] Analysis further reveals that the various pericopes belonged to the northern tradition,[75] which was preserved at the sanctuary of Shechem.

Moses is pictured in conversation with God, presumably on Mount Horeb-Sinai, and he makes three requests, each one more insistent and demanding than the preceding one. The divine answers remain wholly ambiguous. God's presence is defined in terms of the theologoumenon of the name but not of the glory.

The First Request (33:12-14)

The Plea for the Knowledge of God (vss. 12-13)

33:12 And Moses said to Yahweh:
> Look! Thou art saying to me, Lead forth this people!
> Yet, thou, thyself, hast not let me know
> Whom thou wilt send with me,
> But thou, thyself, hast said,
> I know thee by name, and even thou hast found favor in my eyes.
13 But now, if I have truly found favor in thy eyes,
> Please! let me know thy ways, in order that I may know thee,
> That I may [indeed] find favor in thy eyes.
> And look! [I say this] because this nation is thy people.

The Divine Answer to the First Plea (vs. 14)

33:14 And [God] said: My presence will go,
> And I will give thee rest.

The plea of Moses is provoked by the order from Yahweh to depart from the mountain (33:1a). Moses replies with an earnestness which reveals the intensity of his feeling.[76] The repeated use of imperatives ("Look!", vss. 12b and 13d) and of personal pronouns of address ("Thou!", vss. 12b, c, d), the adverb "now" (vs. 13a), and the precative particle ("Please!" vs. 13c) lead to the expostulation, "because this nation (goy; cf. 19:6) is thy people!" (Vs. 13d). Such a story is told by someone who has personally experienced the horror and fear of sensing divine separation, the drought of spiritual loneliness, and the anxiety of Godless living. Like lovers about to part, mystics are profoundly perturbed when they become aware of the end of ecstasy. Moses is less upset by the prospect of leading a people through the wilderness—although this prospect plays a part in the dynamics of this anxiety—than by the urge to know God with a deeper certainty than the assurance which he has hitherto received: "Please, let me know thy ways in order that I may know thee."

Presence and the risk of losing its comfort combine within the human spirit to create the need for religious knowledge. Presence is the begetter of theology. The all-demanding desire of Moses is "to know" God.[77]

By asking to know God's *ways* in order to know *God himself*, the human contender speaks as a theologian of the name. The ways of God are the signs of his purpose. They represent his creative will. They manifest his name. At this moment of the encounter, Moses discerns that the only knowledge of God that is accessible to his human finiteness is an acquaintance with divine presence in history. The inner core of the divine reality, precisely because it is divine, forever escapes man's grasp. Yet, the very fact that Moses asks to know God's ways implies that he has in mind a further dimension of knowledge. He wishes passionately to go beyond what he has already learned.

As the theme of continuing presence is abruptly grafted upon the theme of knowledge, Moses senses that God ignores his request and in effect rebukes the claims of finitude. God promises not an absolute gnosis, but rather his presence and the soothing power thereof: "My presence will go and I shall make you restful." The word *panîm*, literally, "face" or "countenance," is the anthropomorphic symbol of presence.[78] The Sinai-Horeb site of special revelation will be left behind, but God's presence will be on the move. A mode of psychological communion is thereby implied, for the phrase carries no hint of the later priestly motif of the column of fire or of the cloud which journeyed in the wilderness ahead of the people (Exod. 13:21 f., etc.). The era of theophanies may have come to an end. A new form of presence will keep Israel in the vicinity of her God wherever the people may be.[79] Temporality overcomes spatiality.

The phrase "And I will give thee rest" (vs. 14*b*) literally means "I will cause thee to be transformed from a fretful to a secure person." The verb *nûᵃḥ* is used here in the causative voice, and not the noun *menûḥah*, which designates "arrest from movement," and therefore "a resting place."[80]

The Second Request (33:15-17)

The Plea for the Continuing Presence (vss. 15-16)

33:15   And [Moses] said to him:
     If thy presence will not go,
      Do not lead us forth from here!
  16 For in what way will it ever be known
      That I have found favor in thy eyes, I and thy people?
     Is it not in thy going with us
      That we may be different, I and thy people,
      From every people on the face of the earth?

The Divine Answer (vs. 17)

33:17 And Yahweh said to Moses:
     This very word which thou hast spoken I will do,
      For thou hast found favor in my eyes
      And I know thee by name.

Apparently, the discussion is leading nowhere. Moses shows by his insistence that God's promise is not sufficient to eradicate his fear of the unknown future. How can he be certain that the promise will be fulfilled? Man again requires a confirmation. It is possible that the doubt of Moses is related to his lingering belief that the mountain of God is the only place of divine presence. A polemical intent against the cultic mode of presence in a sanctuary may have been detected by the audiences of a later age when this narrative was recited to them. Because worshippers went to a temple in order "to see Yahweh's face," some radical theologians of the name remembered the lingering belief of Moses when they attacked the special virtue of a sacred place (Deut. 4:37; Isa. 63:9).[81]

Once again, the expression of personal uncertainty summons to mind the thought of the future of God's people. Moses develops in the second plea, therefore, what was implied in the first (cf. vs. 13d): "Is it not in thy going with us that we may be set apart, I and thy people, from every people on the face of the soil?" (Vs. 16c–e). The distinctiveness of Israel, the mark which sets the people apart from other nations is strictly theological. Israel has no ethnic meaning unless the presence of Yahweh remains with the people. The peoplehood of Israel, in contrast to all other peoples, lies in this unique relationship, failing which it vanishes.

Once more, the Godhead appears to ignore the concern of Moses for the historical purpose of Israel. The commitment which Yahweh emphatically repeats is not the promise of the land, but the comforting power of his companionship to Moses personally.[82] Religion begins and maintains itself at the level of the lonely spirit of man, even—and especially—when it aims at social coherence and embraces vast movements in history.

The second answer does more than confirm and reiterate. It adds a significant element. The theme of the knowledge of God, which was evoked in the first request is still at the threshold of man's consciousness. Moses wants to know God in a way which surpasses his previous experience, and now God turns the relationship around. "To know God" is an anthropocentric exercise. What Moses is now learning is that he is known by God: "For thou hast found favor in my eyes, and I know thee by name."

Man's knowledge of God depends upon man's knowledge of being known by God. "I know thee by name" is the reply to the man who begs "Let me know thee, O God!" To be known by God is to be transformed into a new man. Theology is not the science of a divine object, but the knowledge of self-transformation by a divine subject. Moses discovers unwillingly that theology is not to know God but to be aware of being grasped and called to do the will of God in history.[83] The thought is too momentous for him to conceive. His anxiety is not quelled. A third request is necessary.

The Third Request (33:18–22)

The Plea for the Vision of Glory (vs. 18)

33:18 And he said, Let me see, I pray, thy glory.

The Divine Refusal (vss. 19–20)

33:19 And he said, I, myself, will make all my goodness pass in
          thy presence,
          And I will proclaim the name of Yahweh in thy
          presence,
        And I will be gracious to whom I will be gracious,
          And I will show mercy to whom I will show mercy.
   20 And he said, Thou canst not see my face,
          For no man shall see me and live.

The Divine Concession (vss. 21–23)

33:21 And Yahweh said, Behold [there is] a place by me
          Where thou shalt stand, upon the rock,
   22 And it shall be that, as my glory passes by,
          I will place thee in a cleft of the rock,
        And I will cover thee with the palm of my hand until I
        have passed by.
   23   Then I will take away the palm of my hand,
          And thou shalt see my back.
          But my face shall not be seen.

This passage may have originally been independent, for the dialogical form differs from the preceding context. At the same time, it may be that the climactic aspect of the theme demanded a hastening of the pace on the part of Moses, and a slowing down of the reply on the part of God. The first two formulas, "And he said" (vss. 19*a*, 20*a*), deal with the divine refusal, whereas the last one, "And Yahweh said" (vs. 21), introduces the partial compromise of the Deity. Moses makes a third request, but, in contrast with the first two, it is as concise as possible: "Let me see, I pray, thy glory." There is no circumlocution of language. The man of God, already standing at the edge of the infinite realm, attempts to tilt the mystery. He yields to the lure of infinity.

Prepared by the implications of the first two quests, the audience is attuned to the expectation of this heroic demand. Moses is prey to *libido theologica*, the lust for absolute knowledge. He refuses to accept historical relativity. God's ways may be discerned, but not with certainty, and they refer in any case to the periphery of his reality. Now, the challenger of divine privacy abandons his indirect approach. He no longer asks for help in his historical task. He wants more than the assurance of God's presence for the sake of Israel's distinctiveness in fulfilling her historical destiny. He goes right to the point of his egocentric desire. Bluntly comes the sharp, unadorned, indeed, arrogant, directness of the prayer: "Show me, please, thy glory!"

As often occurs in Hebrew rhetorics, the divine speech proceeds by a juxtaposition of terms in order to connote their meanings through equivalence with other meanings which are not at first sight their synonyms. God equates his glory with his face (vs. 20), just as he relates, by implication, the passing by of his goodness with the proclamation of his name (vs. 19). The anthropomorphic contrast between his face and his back (vs. 22), crude as it may sound to modern ears, is a powerful symbol of the distinction between his glory and his name. Within the framework of a theophany, the northern theologians endorsed and even exalted the theologoumenon of presence through the name, whereas they unambiguously repudiated the theologoumenon of presence through the glory.

The symbol of *kabhod* ("glory"), and its synonyms, especially *tiph'ereth* ("splendor") and *hôd* and *hadhar* ("majesty"), are regularly translated in Septuagintal Greek by the word *doxa;* hence, the Vulgate rendering *gloria* and the traditional versions of the Western world. It appears, however, that the semantics of the term are quite complex and that the connotations of the idea differ according to literary school, writer, and century. The etymological cognation with the idea of heaviness (*kabhed*, "heavy" and "liver") does not seem to have played a part in the theological language, unless a comparison was made between the Deity and the royal or military figures. Applied to God, the word suggests not heaviness by human standards but the effulgence of light.[84] The two ideas may have originally been related in the proto-Hebraic stages of Northwest Semitic dialectal evolution through the cultic use, on feast days, of gold masks on the statues of the gods to reflect sunlight, or through the sacerdotal persons of kings.[85]

While many studies have been devoted to the motif of divine glory in Hebrew religion,[86] it is not generally pointed out that the ancient traditions of Israel practically ignored the notion. The northern narratives and the Deuteronomists stress other symbols, such as the name. Because the southerners and the majority of the psalmists have evolved in the shadow of the Davidic monarchy and around the mythology of Zion, it was they who emphasized the significance of the term.[87] The Jerusalem priests and their descendants saw no conflict between the theologoumenon of presence through the name and the theologoumenon of presence through the glory.[88] The two terms became interchangeable in nascent Judaism during the Babylonian exile and the Persian period.

In the third theophany on Mt. Horeb, however, which has

been preserved chiefly according to the northern tradition, *glory* is made dramatically distinct from *name,* for it remains, as the inner characteristic of the transcendent Godhead, beyond the reach of even a man of God like Moses.

The pericope on the tent of meeting (Exod. 33:7–11), which now precedes the requests of Moses but editorially intrudes upon the scene of the theophany on Mt. Horeb,[89] points to the exceptional aspect of the familiarity with which the Godhead conversed with Moses: "Thus Yahweh used to speak to Moses face to face" (vs. 11). The idiom *panîm el panîm,* "face to face," should not be taken literally, especially when it is used with a verb of speaking and hearing.[90] It means "directly" and "without intermediary."

In the third request, Moses is denied the vision of the face, for the term is here equated with glory, the innermost secret of divinity. Moses, a hero but a mortal man, becomes at this juncture a Hebraic figure of tragedy, for he is "being halted upon a metaphysical threshold."[91]

The divine denial, however, is not complete. The narrators attempt to portray the exact limit of human exposure to the openness of God, and again they favor the psychological symbol of the ear over that of the eye, even when they picture Yahweh making a sublime concession in granting his servant "the vision" of his work in history. This appears to be the most probable interpretation of an enigmatic detail which has baffled the imagination of exegetes for centuries. His eyes masked by the palm of the divine hand as the divine face passes by, Moses is permitted, from the cleft of the rock, to glimpse the divine back. This startling anthropomorphism should be plainly distinguished from the mythical representations of deities in the ancient Near Eastern or Greco-Roman pantheons. No confusion is possible between a narrative which uses a part of the human anatomy to suggest the divine ordination of historical events and the iconographic or literary representations of an

Apollo Musagetes or of an Aphrodite Kallipyge, which aim at inspiring—legitimate and even noble as this may be—aesthetic sensuousness.

When the northern theologians venture to depict Yahweh, they must do so in human terms, but they are careful, through contextual juxtaposition, to prevent any misunderstanding. The sovereign Lord of heaven and earth transcends nature, man, and sexuality. Within the context of the three requests, the back of God can have only one meaning: just as the face is identified with the glory, so also the back corresponds to the goodness which passes by and therefore also to the proclamation of the name and the unfolding of the divine ways.

The dual word 'aḥorayim, traditionally rendered "back parts," was used in a manner parallel to that of the plural word panîm, "face" or "glory," Just as "face" is the other side of "back," so also "glory" is the other side of "goodness." The ideas are not antonymic, but they are distinct. Glory is the face which may not be seen. Goodness, as the back of God, can be in no way identified with glory.[92]

To the ears of an Oriental listener, attuned to etymological assonances, the word 'aḥorayim, "back," suggested its cognates 'aḥᵃrith, "end," and 'aḥᵃrôn, "last." Expressions of time, in Hebrew as well as in most languages, are borrowed from the thought-forms of space. Both "goodness" and "back parts" pass by, and Moses is allowed to sight them. They signify the *Magnalia Dei*, past and future. This interpretation is in no way allegorical. It seeks to derive the meaning of an admittedly obscure phrase from its contextual wholeness.

Ṭôbhah, "goodness," has acquired a wide range of meanings in the course of the twelve or more centuries of its biblical usage, but "the goodness of Yahweh" clearly alludes to the true benefits of his promise, the fruit of his blessing, and the consequence of fidelity to his covenant.[93] When the prophet Hosea evokes the renewal of the bond between Yahweh and his unfaithful bride, he announces that the people "shall come in fear to Yahweh and to his goodness in the latter days" (Hos. 3:5). The Jeremianic school, during the exile in Babylon, expects that at the last "they shall be radiant with joy over the goodness of Yahweh" (Jer. 31:12), and Yahweh himself declares, "My people will be satisfied with my goodness" (Jer. 31:14). To see "the goodness of Yahweh in the land of the living" (Ps. 27:13) is the hope of those who have been taught "the way" of Yahweh (Ps. 27:11). "Goodness" is the manifestation of his providence toward the people of his predilection. In the passing by of the divine goodness, Moses is offered a spiritual vision of the centuries to come.[94]

The northern narrative of the third theophany links the ec-static, time-limited reality of a direct encounter with God to the knowledge of his name. By so doing, it confers on the word *panîm* a meaning which corresponds to the idea of psychological presence. When used with a verb of visual perception, the word means "face" and designates the inner being of God, or his "glory." When used with a verb of movement, as in the phrase "My *panîm* will go with thee," it points to an awareness of communion. The northern narrative also introduces the pro-phetic notion of *the word:* "And Yahweh said to Moses, This very word which thou hast spoken I will do, for thou hast found favor in my eyes, And I know thee by name" (33:17). The fulfilment of Yahweh's word is linked with the proclamation of his name in the context of lasting communion.[95]

The geographical milieu to which all the traditions of Israel have ascribed the origin of their bond with Yahweh is the moun-tain of Horeb-Sinai. They viewed this origin through the dra-matic mode of *theophany*. The modern historian or theologian is no longer able to ascertain the precise character of these experiences. Is it possible, as many commentators have specu-lated, that the landscape itself provided the shape—and perhaps also the occasion—of these experiences? Possibly influenced by the storm-theophany traditions of the Northwest Semitic nations, the theologians of the Israel shrines could not have invented *ex nihilo* such a conglomerate of stories. In contrast to the mythic poets of the neighboring cultures, they were always able to point to the transcendence of their God. Natural forces were mobilized only to manifest his presence. Or do these traditions constitute an instance of mass psychology, combining the witnessing of a mountain storm with the fresh memories of recent events—the totally unexpected deliverance from Egyptian oppression and annihilation—and the contemporary endurance of economic destitution in a wilderness? According to Martin Buber,

> ... The representatives of Israel come to see [YHVH] on the heights of Sinai. They have presumably wandered through clinging, hanging mist before dawn; and at the very moment they reach their goal, the swaying darkness tears asunder (as I myself happened to witness once) and dissolves except for one cloud already transparent with the hue of the still unrisen sun. The sapphire proximity of the heavens overwhelms the aged shepherds of the Delta, who have never before tasted, who have never been given the slightest idea, of what is shown in the play of early light over the summits of the mountains. And this precisely is perceived by the representatives of the liberated tribes as that which lies under the feet of their enthroned *Melek* [king].[96]

Of course, many migrating tribes—hungry, thirsty, and collectively insecure—have witnessed mountain storms before sunrise without seeing any deity. Whatever may have been the precise nature of the event as it was preserved in the memory of Israel, it is significant that the northern and southern interpretations thereof, while they corresponded broadly and sometimes minutely, differed markedly in ways which announced fateful developments in the history of Israel and Judah during the monarchy.

Both Elohist and Yahwist circles have preserved the motif of the divine name as the unifying theme of the three Horeb-Sinai theophanies.[97]

It was the disclosure of the meaning of the name at the Burning Bush that transformed a runaway shepherd into a leader of people. It was on the mountain with fire and storm that the name was proclaimed. A folkloric symbol or archetypal origin has been used as the setting for a wholly unexpected calling into existence of a new form of society.

Fire feeds man's unconscious urge to think in terms of "prompt becoming." When fire does not consume its own fuel and survives its own death, it suggests the slow and sustained becoming of historical transformation:

> Fire is the ultra-living reality. Fire is intimate and it is universal. It lives in our heart. It lives in the sky. It ascends from the depths of substance and offers itself like love. It descends again in matter and conceals itself, latent, self-contained, like hate or revenge. Among all phenomena, it is truly the one which may receive clearly two contrary valorizations: good and evil. It shines in Paradise. It burns in Hell. It is sweetness and torture. It is cuisine and apocalypse. It is pleasure for the child who wisely sits near the hearth; it punishes however any disobedience if one plays too closely with its flames. It is well-being and it is respect. It is a tutelary and terrible god, benevolent and mean. It can contradict itself. It is therefore one of the principles of universal explanation.[98]

Most appropriately, the secret of the name is revealed from the midst of a fire which renews itself. And it is in the word-defying grandeur of a display of fire upon the mountain that the word is given to man to live by. Fire plays a part in the sociological chemistry which transforms Hebrew man into *homo historicus.* Babylonians, Egyptians, and Canaanites are servants of dynasties or of shrines. Hebrews, whenever they hear the word and bear the honor of the name, are the servants of the Lord of history. History implies a unified view of mankind and a purpose for created nature. The God of history persists while he changes his modes of activity with seasons and times. The people of the presence is bid to take the name in earnest, not to take the name in vain—that is to say, "in the pursuit of nothingness."[99]

The name of Yahweh is not an empty sound. It bears the presence of infinity within the finite,[100] but it is at once revelatory and reticent. It is revelatory, because it links the presence to the peoplehood of Israel and its mission in the history of man. It is reticent because it preserves the freedom of the divine. Ultimately, it is ineffable, for it stands for the reality of a faith which cannot be pinned down, the security of a hope which cannot be demonstrated with pragmatic evidence, the sobriety of a dedication which finds its delights beyond the sensuality of agrarian luxuriousness.

T. E. Lawrence was not devoid of utopian imagination when he wrote, perhaps with starry eyes, of the Semite discovering true life in the desert. His judgment, however, may apply to Hebrew man, if the Hebrew man has been seized by the power of the name:

> In his life he had air and winds, sun and light, open spaces and a great emptiness. There was no human effort, no fecundity in nature: just the heaven above, and the unspotted earth beneath. There unconsciously he came near God. God was with him not anthropomorphic, not tangible, not moral or ethical ... [Man] could not look for God within him: he was too sure he was within God.[101]

Perhaps Buber was partially right, after all, when he expatiated on the rugged landscape of the Sinai mountain as the stage for the Mosaic theophanies. The desert and its vastness and the poverty of its resources—after the onions, the leeks, and the fleshpots of even a jaillike Egypt—predisposes man to listen to the speech which comes from beyond man's self-centeredness.

In Hebraic religion, the name plays the theological role which other religions ascribe to divine images and cultic representations.[102] The dynamic and worldwide demands of the name, however, bring a unique power to Hebraic religion. The hearing of such a name and the bearing of its implications require a response different from that inherent in the contemplation of an image. The name demands active participation in the totality of life. The seeing of an image—or the cultic symbol of the glory—tends to lull the worshippers into the delights of passive spirituality and the loss of social responsibility.[103]

The study of the cultic mode of presence in Israel will bring out historical developments which tend to illustrate the validity of this analysis.

Notes

1. It is also significant that Martin Buber, who explicitly claimed to repudiate most of the results of modern literary, form-critical, and traditio-historical criticism, actually used the ancient J and E traditions and not the sacerdotal reinterpretation (P) of the Jerusalem priests in exile when he wrote his essay, *Moses: The Revelation and the Covenant* (Oxford, 1946; rev. ed., New York, 1958).

2. The extreme caution which prevailed at the beginning of the twentieth century concerning the historicity of Moses and his work has given place to a balanced attitude of critical moderation. Cf. G. Widengren, "What Do We Know About Moses?" in *Proclamation and Presence. Festschrift G. Henton Davies* (Richmond, Va., 1970), pp. 21 ff.; R. de Vaux, "La mission de Moïse," *Histoire ancienne d'Israël* (Paris, 1971), pp. 305–440; E. F. Campbell, Jr., "Moses and the Foundations of Israel," *In.*, XXIX (1975), 141–54; E. Auerbach, *Moses*, tr. by R. A. Barclay, and I. D. Lehman (Detroit, 1975); Th. W. Mann, *Divine Presence and Guidance in Israelite Traditions: The Typology of Exaltation* (Baltimore, 1977).

3. The chronology of the Exodus has

been the object of protracted discussion. A few scholars favor a late-thirteenth century date (ca. 1230 B.C.); see H. H. Rowley, *From Joseph to Joshua: Biblical Traditions in the Light of Archaeology* (London, 1950), pp. 109 ff., 164. Others argue for the first part of the thirteenth century. Cf. E. Drioton, "La date de l'Exode," *RHPR*, XXXV (1955): 36–49; K. A. Kitchen, *Ancient Orient and Old Testament* (Chicago, 1966), pp. 57–75.

4. Exod. 14:21. The location of the Sea of Reeds (traditionally, Red Sea) is not certain. Modern historians do not appear to have paid sufficient attention to the topographical and geological survey of the region conducted by a technician of the Suez Canal administration. See C. Bourdon, "La route de l'Exode de la terre de Gessé à Mara," *RB*, XLI (1932): 370–92, 539–49.

5. The conquest of the land of Canaan was not completed until after David's capture of the Jebusite fortress of Jerusalem (2 Sam. 5:6 ff.) and even the Pharaoh's transfer of the Canaanite city of Gezer to Solomon in the tenth century B.C. (1 Kings 3:1, 9:16).

6. See Jörg Jeremias, *Theophanie: Die Ge-*

schichte einer alttestamentlichen Gattung
(Neukirchen-Vluyn, 1965), pp. 7 ff.
7. Exod. 3:1–22, 19:1—24:8, 33:12–23.
The location of Mt. Sinai-Horeb has been
a matter of considerable debate. The traditional location of Djebel Musa, which
did not appear before the Byzantine age
(fourth century A.D.) fits the topography
of the JE traditions concerning the wan-
dering of the *Benê Israel* after the crossing
of the Sea. Modern attempts to localize
the sacred mount among the extinct vol-
canoes of the northwestern Arabian
Peninsula, southeast of the Gulf of
Aqaba, are based on a misinterpretation
of the narratives of Exod. 19:1 ff. and
24:1 ff. The theologoumena of fire,
smoke, cloud, and darkness are entirely
compatible with the phenomena of the
thunderstorm and the lightning-induced
fires in underbrush and low forest. The
references to "shaking" and "quaking"
do not necessarily refer to seismic trem-
ors, since it is well known that thunder-
claps, especially in mountainous and
desertic regions, give the illusion of earth
quaking. Moreover, (a) there is in the
narratives concerning Sinai-Horeb
neither lava nor projection of fiery
stones; (b) Moses could not be represented as standing on the top of a volcano in eruption; (c) the flames were not
depicted as going up, but on the contrary
as "coming down"; (d) the motif of vol-
canoes in eruption has never become a
feature of the Hebrew mythopoetic formulations of the historical theophanies
or of the eschatological epiphany (cf.
Deut. 4:11, Judg. 5:4, 2 Sam. 22:8–14 =
Ps. 18:8–14; cf. Hab. 3:3–15, etc.). Nor
does the volcano motif appear, several
commentators to the contrary, in the final strophe of the hymn on creative providence (Ps. 104:31–32). The traditions
which are preserved in Exodus 19:1 ff. do
not permit a precise identification of the
site. See a survey of the various views in
de Vaux, *Histoire ancienne*, pp. 398–410.
The north-Arabian volcano hypothesis,

defended long ago by Eduard Meyer,
("Die Mosesagen und die Lewiten," in
Die Israeliten und ihre Nachstämme [Halle a.
S., 1906], pp. 67 ff.) has been laboriously
revived by J. Koenig, "Les itinéraires
sinaïtiques en Arabie," *RHR*, CLXVI
(1964): 121 ff.; "Le Sinaï, montagne de
feu dans un désert de ténèbres," *RHR*,
CLXVII (1966): 129–55; "Aux origines
des théophanies iahvistes," *RHR*, CLIX
(1966): 1 ff.
8. Josh. 24:1 ff.; Judg. 9:6, 20:18 ff.; 1
Sam. 7:16, 8:2; 2 Sam. 2:1 ff.; 1 Kings
2:11, 12:1, 26; 1 Chron. 3:1 ff.; 2 Chron.
13:8 f.; Amos 8:14; etc.
9. The cultic objects ascribed to Moses
(the ark, the tent of meeting and/or the
tabernacle) were of course portable. This
matter will be discussed below in Chapter
IV. It is not clear, from the early strata of
the tradition, whether Mt. Sinai-Horeb
was originally viewed as the topographic
"abode" of Yahweh. Allusions are found
in the early poetry of Israel to Yahweh's
"holy encampment," "mountain,"
"abode," or "sanctuary," and these were
probably interpreted during the monarchic period as referring either to Mt.
Garizim (northerners) or to Mt. Zion
(southerners). Some scholars believe
that these allusions originally applied to
Mt. Sinai (Exod. 15:13, 17; Ps. 78:54;
etc.). The memory of Yahweh's sojourn
in Sinai has persisted for many generations (Judg. 5:4–5, Deut. 33:2, Hab. 3:3–
6) but this fact does not necessarily prove
that the theologians of Israel believed in
the myth of a permanent dwelling of Yahweh on the rocky top mentioned in the
Mosaic theophanies. There are significant differences between the poetic language of the Hebrews and the
proto-Canaanite (Ugaritic) descriptions
of "the mountain of El." See an analysis
of the parallels in F. M. Cross, *Canaanite
Myth and Hebrew Epic* (Cambridge, Mass.,
1973), pp. 112–44; R. J. Clifford, *The Cosmic Mountain in Canaan and in the Old Testament* (Cambridge, Mass., 1972); cf. S.

Terrien's review of this work in *Biblica*, LV (1974): 443 f.

10. The tradition on Elijah's flight to Horeb in the ninth century B.C. (1 Kings; 19:4 ff.) is no exception, since the prophet was rebuked in his undertaking, and the so-called Horeb theophany of Elijah actually forms a transition between the Mosaic mode of divine disclosure and the prophetic type of presence through vision. See below, in Chapter V.

11. See below, in Chapter V.

12. The word *seneh*, "bush," or "thorn," was associated at a later date with the name *Sinai*, which the southern tradition (J) favored (Exod. 16:1). The *Blessing of Moses*, which contains archaic fragments of poetry, speaks of the God "who sojourned in the bush" (Deut. 33:16), but the Exodus narratives make it clear that Yahweh's appearance was related to "the flame out of the midst of the bush" and not to the bush itself (Exod. 3:2). Moreover, it will be noted that the Deity declares explicitly, "I have come down" (vs. 8). See E. J. Young, "The Call of Moses," *WTJ*, XXIX (1967): 117–35; XXX (1968): 1–23; H. D. Preuss, " '. . . ich will mit dir sein'," *ZAW*, LXXX (1968): 139–73; D. N. Freedman, "The Burning Bush," *Biblica*, L (1969): 245 f.; B. S. Childs, *The Book of Exodus* (Philadelphia, 1974), pp. 47 ff.

13. See J. Hempel, "Berufung und Bekehrung," *Festschrift G. Beer* (Stuttgart, 1935), pp. 41 ff.; W. Zimmerli, "Zur Form-und Traditionsgeschichte der prophetischen Berufungsgeschichte der prophetischen Berufungserzählungen," in *Ezechiel*, vol. I (Neukirchen, 1955), pp. 16 ff.; L. Rost, "Die Gottesverehrung der Patriarchen im Lichte der Pentateuchquellen," *SVT*, VII (1960): 346–59; N. Habel, "The Form and Significance of the Call Narratives," *ZAW*, LXXVII (1965): 297 ff.; R. Kilian, "Die prophetischen Berufungsberichte," *Theologie im Wandel* (München, 1967), pp. 356; W. Richter, *Die sogenannten vorprophetischen Berufungsberichte* (Göttingen, 1970); W.

Vogels, "Les récits de vocation des prophètes," *NRT*, XCV (1973): 3–24.

14. Deut. 34:10; see K. Baltzer, "Considerations Regarding the Office and Calling of the Prophet," *HTR*, LXI (1968): 567 ff.

15. Exod. 3:2; cf. Gen. 16:7, 9–11, 15; etc. On the expression "appeared," see F. Schutenhaus, "Das Kommen und Erscheinen Gottes im Alten Testament," *ZAW*, LXXVI (1964): 10 ff.

16. See G. Bachelard, *La psychanalyse du feu* (Paris, 1947; reprinted, 1949), p. 35.

17. See a summary of the discussion in Childs, *The Book of Exodus*, pp. 56 ff.

18. Gen. 26:3 (Isaac), 31:3 (Jacob), 39:2 (Joseph, with the preposition *'eth*, "with"); cf. Jos. 1:5 (Joshua), Judg. 6:16*a* (Gideon).

19. The number of critical studies on the name "Yahweh" is too extensive for a listing. It will be observed that the matter under consideration is not that of the proto-Hebraic roots of the Yahweh cult, nor that of the possibly foreign origin of the word "Yahweh" (a liturgical shout associated with awe, hard breathing, storm wind, etc.), but rather that of the theological understanding which is proposed by the Elohistic tradition in telling the story of Moses within the context of the theophany of the Burning Bush. See R. Mayer, "Der Gottesname Jahwe im Lichte der neuesten Forschung" (with bibliography), *BZ*, NF II (1958), 26–53; Childs, *The Book of Exodus* pp. 47–89; W. H. Brownlee, "The Ineffable Name of God," *BASOR*, no. 226 (April, 1977): 39 ff.

20. See Hos. 12:6, 14:8; Isa. 26:8; Ps. 135:13; Prov. 10:7; Eccl. 9:5, Cf. B. S. Childs, *Memory and Tradition in Israel* (Naperville, Ill., 1962), p. 9 (note 3), 11 f. P. A. H. de Boer, *Gedenken und Gedächtnis in der Welt des Alten Testaments* (Stuttgart, 1962); W. Schottroff, " 'Gedenken' " *im alten Orient und im Alten Testament; die Wurzel* zakar *im semitischen Sprachkreis* (Neukirchen-Vluyn, 1964); R. Martin-Achard, "Souvenir et mémorial selon l'Ancien

Testament," *RTP*, XCVIII (1965): 302–10.

21. "He who does not himself *remember* that God led *him* out of Egypt . . . is no longer a Jew," M. Buber, quoted (italics added) in W. Herberg, ed., *The Writings of Martin Buber* (New York, 1956), p. 31. Cf. the religious usage of "memory" in classical Greece, where man did not attempt to grasp the past as much as to obtain a divine and everlasting truth. See J. P. Vernant, *Mythe et pensée chez les Grecs; études de psychologie historique* (Paris, 1965), pp. 51–78; cf. N. A. Dahl, "*Anamnesis;* mémoire et commémoration dans le christianisme primitif," *Studia theologica*, I (1947): 69–95.

22. The name *Yahweh* is never found in the Masoretic Text. The tetragrammaton (four sacred consonants) is written therein with the vowels of the word *Adonay*, "my Lord," (sometimes of the word *Elohim*, "God"), hence, the misreading, "Jehovah," which was introduced by Galatinus in 1520. All available evidence (Hebrew theophoric names, Amorite onomastics, Greek transliterations in the magical papyri of the Greco-Roman period, testimony of the Church Fathers, especially Clement of Alexandria) points to an original pronunciation of "Yahweh."

23. It was apparently first proposed by P. Haupt, "Der Name Jahweh," *OLZ*, (1909), cols. 211–14; cf. D. N. Freedman, "The Name of the God of Moses," *JBL*, LXXIX (1960): 151 ff.; Cross, *Canaanite Myth and Hebrew Epic*, pp. 68 ff.

24. The effort to explain the expression *Yahweh Sebaoth* (1 Sam. 4:4, 2 Sam. 6:2, etc.) as "He Who Creates the [Heavenly] Armies" requires further demonstration. See Cross, *Canaanite Myth and Hebrew Epic*, p. 69.

25. Job 6:21, 7:21, etc. See S. Terrien, *Job, Poet of Existence* (Indianapolis, 1957), pp. 50 ff.; *id., Job: Commentaire* (Neuchâtel, 1963), pp. 81 ff., 92.

26. LXX, *Egô eimi ho ôn*, "I am the Being One,"; cf. Vulgate, *Ego sum qui sum*.

27. See Th. C. Vriezen, "'ehje 'ašer 'ehje." *Festschrift A. Bertholet* (Tübingen, 1950), pp. 598 ff.; de Vaux, *Histoire ancienne d'Israël*, pp. 329 ff. De Vaux, however, should have been careful not to use the verb "to exist" for the Deity, for *existere* implies dependence and derivativeness.

28. See C. H. Ratschow, *Werden und Wirken: eine Untersuchung des Wortes hajah als Beitrag zur Wirklichkeitserfassung des Alten Testaments* (Berlin, 1941); Th. Boman, *Hebrew Thought Compared With Greek*, tr. by J. L. Moreau (London, 1960), pp. 38 ff.

29. This is not to say that the translation of *Eheyeh* should be "I shall be there" (*contra*, Vriezen, Buber, et al. Cf. von Rad, *Old Testament Theology*, I p. 182; B. S. Childs, *The Book of Exodus*, p. 69.

30. The present inquiry will not concern itself with the many conjectures which have been proposed on such problems, nor will it review the proposals concerning the proto-Hebraic worship of Yahweh in the ancient Near East, the so-called Kenite hypothesis, etc.

31. See J.-H. Nicolas, *Dieu connu comme inconnu: essai d'une critique de la connaissance théologique* (Paris, 1966), pp. 185 ff., 366 ff.

32. Contrast Childs, *The Book of Exodus*, p. 69 and p. 76.

33. Th. Moore, *Rhymes on the Road*, i, 26.

34. *Odyssey*, xi, 315 f.

35. Cross, "The Storm Theophany," and "The Revelation at Sinai," in *Canaanite Myth and Hebrew Epic*, pp. 147 ff.

36. Ps. 29, Deut. 33:2 ff., Isa. 35:1–10, etc.

37. Considerable work has been done on this passage. See J. Jeremias, *Theophanie* (Neukirchen-Vluyn, 1965), pp. 100 ff.; O. Eissfeldt, *Die Komposition der Sinai Erzählung, Exodus 19–34* (Berlin, 1966); H.-J. Kraus, *Worship in Israel*, tr. by G. Buswell (Richmond, 1966), pp. 93 ff., 179 ff.; J. K. Kuntz, *The Self-Revelation of God*

(Philadelphia, 1967), pp. 72 ff; K. Baltzer, *The Covenant Formulary in Old Testament, Jewish, and Early Christian Writings*, Tr. by D. E. Green (Philadelphia, 1970); R. de Vaux, *Histoire ancienne d'Israël* (Paris, 1971), pp. 410 ff.; E. Zenger, *Die Sinaitheophanie* (Würzburg, 1971); Childs, *The Book of Exodus*, pp. 340.

38. See E. L. Fackenheim, *God's Presence in History* (New York, 1970), p. 4.

39. See M. Greenberg, "Hebrew *Segullah:* Akkadian *Sikiltu*," *JAOS*, LXXI (1951): 172 ff.; M. Dahood on the Ugaritic *sglt* in *Biblica*, XLVI (1965): 313; XLVII (1966): 26; L (1969): 341.

40. See W. Caspari, "Das priestliche Königreich," *Theologische Blätter*, VIII (1929): 105–10; R. B. Y. Scott, " 'A Kingdom of Priests,' Ex xix,6," *OST*, VIII (1950): 213–19; J. B. Bauer, "Könige und Priester, ein heiliges Volk (Ex. 19,6)," *BZ*, II (1959): 283–6; W. L. Moran, "A Kingdom of Priests," in J. L. McKenzie, ed., *The Bible in Current Catholic Thought; Festschrift M. J. Gruenthaner (New York, 1962), pp. 7–20;* G. Fohrer, " 'Priesterliches Königtum', Ex. 19,6," *TZ*, XIX (1963): 359–62, also published in *Studien zur alttestamentliche Theologie und Geschichte* (Berlin, 1969), pp. 149–53; R. Martin-Achard, "Israel, peuple sacerdotal," *Verbum Caro*, XVIII (1964): 11–28; J. H. Elliott, *The Elect and the Holy. An Exegetical Examination of I Peter 2:4–10 and the Phrase* basileion hierateuma (Leiden, 1966); A. E. Glock, "Early Israel as the Kingdom of Yahweh," *Concordia Theological Monthly*, XLI (1970): 558 ff.

41. See H. Kees, *Das Priestertum in ägyptischen Staat vom neuen Reich bis zur Spätzeit* (Leiden, 1953); E. O. James, *The Nature and Function of Priesthood: A Comparative and Anthropological Study* (London, 1955); L. Sabourin, *Priesthood: A Comparative Study* (Leiden, 1973).

42. See J. Pedersen, *Israel, Its Life and Culture, I–II* (London and Copenhagen, 1926), pp. 36 ff.; J. van der Ploeg, "Les anciens dans l'Ancien Testament," (Lex

Tua Veritas [*Festschrift H. Junker*] (Trier, 1961), pp. 175–92.

43. *Contra* Koenig, pp. 213 ff.; etc.; Cf. Jeremias, pp. 7 ff.

44. See M. Greenberg, *NSH* in Exodus 20:20 and the Purpose of the Sinaitic Theophany," *JBL*, LXXIX (1960): 273 ff.

45. Most commentators agree that the pericope of 20:18–21 was displaced by the Pentateuchal redactors, who had to link the decalogue to the so-called Code of the Covenant.

46. Cf. 2 Sam. 22:10 = Ps. 18:9[Heb.10] and the Ugaritic *'rpt;* Ezek. 34:12; Zeph. 1:15. See Cross, *Canaanite Myth and Hebrew Epic*, pp. 164–5. Northwest Semitic cognates suggest either "covering" or "dripping" (of dew, etc.).

47. The LXX translated *gnophos*, "thick-darkness."

48. Cf. Deut. 4:11, 5:19; Ps. 97:2; Job 22:13. Yet see Job 38:9.

49. 1 Kings 8:12, 2 Chron. 6:1.

50. G. E. Mendenhall, unfortunately, omitted the examination of this word in his chapter, "The Mask of Yahweh," *The Tenth Generation* (Baltimore, 1973), p. 62.

51. W. Zimmerli, " 'Ich bin Jahwe'," *Geschichte und Altes Testament* (Tübingen, 1953), pp. 179 ff.; H. Graf Reventlow, *Gebot und Predigt im Dekalog* (Gütersloh, 1962), pp. 25 ff.; K. Elliger, " 'Ich bin der Herr, euer Gott'," *Kleine Schriften zum Alten Testament* (München, 1966), pp. 211 ff.; cf. similar and different examples of formulae of divine self-asseveration in Hellenistic religions in J. Bergman, *Ich bin Isis. Studien zum memphitische Hintergrund der griechischen Isisaretalogien* (Uppsala, 1968), p. 29; cf. K. Baeschlin, *Moses, der Verkündiger des "Ich bin"* (Bern, 1962); R. Knierim, "Das Erste Gebot," *ZAW*, LXXVII (1965): 20 ff.

52. "In the speaking of the name Yahweh makes himself present, present in a way that no alternative way of speaking could perform. He is near when the name is heard and spoken. In this word his transcendence is turned to immanence, He is

'now' for Israel. So the name makes meeting possible, Yahweh is meeting his people in this unique way. In the personal address he becomes present. Israel may now belong to this God, and there can never be for her an ultimate isolation. . . . The name is historical. The self becomes historical in receiving a name. The self now enters into the community with a name." (J. Muilenburg, "The Speech of Theophany," *Harvard Divinity Bulletin,* XXVIII, 2 [January 1964]: 40).

53. Discussion of the origin and authorship of the ethical decalogue has been lively for the past fifty years. See H. Gese, "Der Dekalog als Ganzheit betrachtet," *ZTK,* LXIV (1967): 21 ff.; A. Jepsen, "Beiträge zur Auslegung und Geschichte des Dekalogs," *ZAW,* LXXIX (1967): 277 ff.; E. Nielsen, *The Ten Commandments in New Perspective: A Traditio-Historical Approach* (London, 1968); E. Zengler, "Eine Wende in der Dekalogsforschung?" *Theologische Revue,* III (1968): 189 ff.; H. Caxelles, "Les origines du décalogue," *Eretz Israel,* IX (1969): 14ff.; G. Fohrer, "Das sogenannte apodiktisch formulierte Recht und der Dekalog," *Studien zur alttestamentlichen Theologie und Kirche* (Berlin, 1969): 120 ff.; A. Phillips, *Ancient Israel's Criminal Law; A New Approach to the Decalogue* (Oxford, 1970); W. H. Schmidt, "Überlieferungsgeschichtliche Erwägungen zur Komposition des Dekalogs," *SVT,* XXII (1970): 201–220; M. Lestienne, "Les dix 'paroles' et le décalogue," *RB,* LXXIX (1972): 484 ff.; B. Reicke, *Die zehn Worte in Geschichte und Gegenwart* (Tübingen, 1973); H. Haag, "Das Buch des Bundes (Ex 24 7," in *Wort Gottes in der Zeit* (Düsseldorf, 1973), pp. 22 ff.; Childs, *The Book of Exodus,* pp. 385 ff.

54. The present form reveals catechetic accretions from the Jerusalem priestly circles and other sources. For example, the observance of the sabbath is justified as an act of sacramental celebration in participation with the Creator of the universe (Exod. 20:11); the words and the ideas are closely akin to those of the priestly story of creation and of the cosmic sabbath in Gen. 1:1—2:4a. The text which has been preserved in northern and Deuteronomic circles (Deut. 5:6—21), however, presents the sabbath in terms of human, not divine, rest. It appeals to the feeling of humaneness toward workers and even toward toiling animals, and it recalls the memory of the Egyptian slavery.

55. It is only by way of contrast with the "cultic" or "ritual" decalogue of the Yahwist tradition (Exod. 34:10 ff.) that the Ten Words of the Elohist school have been called "ethical." They constitute in fact a code of religious as well as moral behavior for a society which acknowledges the central importance of the individual character in the maintenance of communal solidarity and at the same time knows that integrity of character depends on a theocentric orientation.

56. The text of verse 2 literally states, "Thou shalt not have (or "there shall not be for thee") other gods besides (or "upon" or "against") my face."

57. See J. Ouellette, "Le deuxième commandement et le rôle de l'image dans la symbolique religieuse de l'Ancien Testament: Essai d'interprétation," *RB,* LXXIV (1967): 504 ff.; de Vaux, "L'interdiction des images," *Histoire ancienne d'Israël,* pp. 433 ff.; cf. W. H. Schmidt, *Alttestamentlicher Glaube und seine Umwelt* (Neukirchen-Vluyn, 1968), pp. 68 ff.

58. The redactor added "and all the ordinances" as a link with the text of the Code of the Covenant which is now immediately preceding (Exod., chs. 21—23).

59. The mention of "bulls" is anachronistic since herds of heavy cattle could not have survived in the rocky wilderness of Sinai, or for that matter could hardly have been taken away from the land of Goshen across the Sea of Reeds.

60. The use of the expression *'abh he'anan,* "the mass of the dark cloud," is different from that of *'anan kabhed,* "a heavy

cloud," in the Elohist tradition (vs. 16).

61. Cf. Ps. 110:4.

62. This detail may reflect a later rite in the celebration of a feast. The *yobhel*, "ram's horn," instead of the *shophar* of the Elohist tradition, suggests a practice which led to the priestly legislation of the Jubilee (Lev. 25:13, etc.; cf. Jos. 6:4, etc.).

63. It is generally admitted that the southern narrative came to include in the course of its growth a "decalogue" or "dodecalogue" of commands and prohibitions, which the Pentateuchal redactors have placed amid the chaotic cluster of material dealing with the breaking of the first set of stones and the granting of the second set (Exod. 34:10–26b). The Yahwist "dodecalogue" is essentially ritual and nonethical.

64. See C. Westermann, "Die Herrlichkeit Gottes in der Priesterschrift," *Wort—Gebot—Glaube* [*Festschrift W. Eichrodt*] (Zürich, 1970), pp. 227 ff.; Th. C. Vriezen, "The Exegesis of Exodus XXIV 9–11," *Oudt. St.*, XVII (1972): 100 ff.; E. W. Nicholson, "The Interpretation of Exodus XXIV 9–11," *VT*, XXIV (1974): 77 ff. *id.*, "The Antiquity of the Tradition in Exodus XXIV 9–11," *VT*, XXV (1975): 69 ff. *id.*, "The Origin of the Tradition in Exodus XXIV 9–11," *VT*, XXVI (1976): 148 ff.

65. The mention of Aaron's sons, Nadab and Abihu, indicates that this tradition was anterior to that which describes the events of Lev. 10:1–3. Late *midrashim* speculated that it was the vision of God which was eventually the cause of the death of these men.

66. The strange expression "seventy from the elders of Israel" suggests the initial phase in the development of the institution of "the seventy."

67. Cf. W. F. Stinespring, "Temple, Jerusalem," *IDB*, IV, p. 556, Plate 34.

68. The juxtaposition of the verbs *ra'ah*, "to see" (vs. 10a) and *ḥazah*, "to gaze at" (vs. 11b) can hardly indicate an ecstatic

trance, since the text immediately adds, "and they ate and drank" (vs. 11b).

69. See E. Cassin, *La splendeur divine. Introduction à l'étude de la mentalité mésopotamienne* (Paris, 1968), especially pp. 23 ff.

70. "The priest Ezekiel, son of Buzi" (Ezek. 1:3).

71. Cf. the expression, "the appearance of the glory of Yahweh" (vs. 17) with Ezek. 1:16, 26, 27, 28, etc.

72. According to the felicitous phrase of Childs, *The Book of Exodus*, p. 582.

73. This pericope will be studied in the next chapter, on the cultic mode of presence.

74. See Noth, *Exodus*, pp. 253 ff.; W. Beyerlin, *Origins and History of the Oldest Sinaitic Traditions*, tr. by S. Rudman (Oxford, 1961), pp. 22 ff., 98 ff.; J. Muilenburg, "The Intercession of the Covenant Mediator (Exodus 33:1a, 12–17)," *Words and Message* [*Festschrift D. Winton Thomas*] (Cambridge, 1969), pp. 159 ff. The form identified by Muilenburg in verses 12–17 is modified in verses 18–23 but belongs basically to the same pattern and theme. See also A. Laurentin, "Weᵉattah—Kai nun. Formule caractéristique des textes juridiques et liturgiques (à propos de Jean 17,5)," *Biblica*, XLV (1964): 168 ff.; especially 174 f., 184.

75. The list of the nations which occupy the land of the promise (vss. 2–3) and the stylistic features ("stiff-necked people," "consume," etc.) point to the Elohist-Deuteronomic circles.

76. See Muilenburg's rhetorical analysis in "The Covenant Mediator," p. 161 f., 171 f.

77. Traditional and modern exegetes agree in finding in this narrative a warning against metaphysical speculation on divine essence as well as against the claims of mystical perception. For a convenient survey of the history of interpretation, see Childs, *The Book of Exodus*, pp. 598 f. Paul Ricoeur has well described the dialectic of name and ethics in "Nommer

Dieu," *Etudes théologiques et religieuses*, LII (1977): 489 ff.

78. See W. von Baudissin, " 'Gott schauen' in der alttestamentlichen Religion," *Archiv für Religionswissenschaft*, XVIII (1915): 173 ff.; G. Gulin, "Das Antlitz Jahwes im Alten Testament," *Annales Academicae Scientiarum Fennicae*, XVII (1923); F. Nötscher, *"Das Angesicht Gottes schauen" nach biblischer und babylonischer Auffassung* (Würzburg, 1924); A. R. Johnson, "Aspects of the Use of the Term PNYM in the Old Testament," *Festchrift O. Eissfeldt* (Halle, 1947), pp. 155 ff.; J. Reindl, *Das Angesicht Gottes im Sprachgebrauch des Alten Testament* (Leipzig, 1970); see also above, Chapter I, note 131.

79. See W. Beyerlin, *Origins and History of the Oldest Sinaitic Traditions*, pp. 90 ff., 101 f., 161 f.

80. However, see Deut. 3:20, 12:10, etc; cf. Ps. 132:14.

81. See Noth, *Exodus*, p. 257; R. E. Clements, *God and Temple. The Idea of Divine Presence in Israel* (Oxford, 1965), p. 27.

82. "He is offered the comfort of God" (Childs, *The Book of Exodus*, p. 594).

83. See Muilenburg, "The Covenant Mediator," p. 177, note 1, who quotes E. Baumann, 'YD' und seine Derivate im Hebräischen," *ZAW*, XXVIII (1908): 30 f.; see also above, chapter I, note 205.

84. See J. Hempel, "Die Lichtsymbolik im Alten Testament," *Studium generale*, XIII (1960): 352 ff.; P. Humbert, "Le thème vétéro-testamentaire de la lumière," *RTP*, XVI (1966): 1 ff.

85. See F. Daumas, "La fonction symbolique de l'or chez les Egyptiens," *RHR*, CXLIX (1956): 1 ff; Cassin, *La splendeur divine: Introduction à l'étude de la mentalité mésopotamienne* (Paris, 1968), pp. 83 ff., 103 ff.; Mendenhall, "The Mask of Yahweh," in *The Tenth Generation* (1973), p. 59. The storm cloud was called once *ʿanan kabhed*, "the heavy cloud" (Exod. 19:-16), and the thundering deity in the Ugaritically inspired poem is introduced as *ʿel kabhod*, "the god of glory" (Ps. 29:-

3). It is probable, however, that the term originated with the royal ideology. Cf. Cross, *Canaanite Myth* (1973), p. 153 (note 30), pp. 164 ff.

86. See W. Caspari, *Die Bedeutung der Wortsippe k-b-d in Hebräischer* (Leipzig, 1908); A. H. Foster, "The Meaning of *doxa* in the Greek Bible," *ATR*, XII (1929–30): 311 ff.; G. R. Berry, "The Glory of Yahweh and the Temple," *JBL*, LVI (1937): 115 ff.; H. G. May, "The Departure of the Glory of Yahweh," *JBL*, LVI (1937): 309 ff.; B. Stein, *Der Begriff Kebod Yahweh und seine Bedeutung für die alttestamentliche Gotteserkenntnis* (Emsdetten i. W., 1939); L. H. Brockington, "The Presence of God: A Study of the Use of the Term 'Glory of Yahweh'," *ET*, LVII (1945–46): 21 ff.; "The Septuagintal Background to the New Testament use of *Doxa*," in D. E. Nineham, ed., *Studies in the Gospels* [*Festschrift R. H. Lightfoot*] (Oxford, 1955), pp. 2 ff.; E. Jacob, *Theology of the Old Testament*, tr. by A. W. Heathcotte and Ph. J. Allcock (New York, 1955), pp. 79 ff.; von Rad, *Old Testament Theology*, I (1962), pp. 234 ff.; G. Henton Davies, "Glory," *IDB*, II, pp. 401 ff.; J. Morgenstern, *The Fire Upon the Altar* (Chicago, 1963), pp. 90 ff.; W. Eichrodt, *Theology of the Old Testament*, tr. by J. A. Baker, Vol. II (Philadelphia, 1967), pp. 29 ff.; R. Rendtorff, "The Concept of Revelation in Ancient Israel," in W. Pannenberg, ed., *Revelation as History*, tr. by D. Granskou (New York, 1968), pp. 39 ff.

87. See Exod. 16:7, 10; 24:16 f.; 40:34 f.; etc.

88. The priestly thinking was not moving in the direction of perceptibility versus invisibility but was influenced by the problem of sin and atonement. See J. Barr, "Theophany and Anthropomorphism," *VTS*, VII (1960): 35. See below, chapter IV.

89. This section will be analyzed in the following chapter, as it deals with the cultic mode of presence and the origin of sanctuaries.

90. See also Deut. 34:10, "And there has not arisen since in Israel a prophet like Moses, whom Yahweh *knew* face to face."

91. H. Barzel, "Moses: Tragedy and Sublimity," in K. R. R. Gros Louis et al., eds., *Literary Interpretations of Biblical Narratives* (Nashville & New York, 1974), p. 128.

92. See H. H. Rowley, "The Good Life," in *The Faith of Israel* (London, 1955), pp. 124 ff.; J. Hempel, "Good," *IDB*, II, pp. 440 f.

93. *Contra* many commentators who maintain that Moses saw in the "goodness" a weak "reflection of the glory of the Lord" (J. Lindblom, "Theophanies in Holy Places in Hebrew Religion," *HUCA*, XXXII [1964]: 107).

94. It is significant that in the Yahwist tradition which is parallel to this narrative (Exod. 34:1–35), the proclamation of Yahweh's name (vs. 5) is used as a preface to the dodecalogue (vss. 14–26). At the same time, the southern theologians, in conformity with the "quasi-spatial" notion of holiness, represent Moses with a shining halo after his descent from Mt. Sinai (a feature which was misunderstood by translators as "horns") This motif is absent from the northern tradition. See J. Morgenstern, "Moses with the Shining Face," *HUCA*, II (1925): 1 ff.; J. de Fraine, "Moses 'cornuta facies' (Ex. 34, 29–35)," *Bijdragen, Tijdscrift voor filosophie en theologie*, XX (1959): 28 ff.; F. Dumermuth, "Moses strahlendes Gesicht," *TZ*, XVII (1961): 241 ff.; E. G. Suhr, "The Horned Moses [Ex 34,25–35 . . .]," *Folklore* LXXIV (63): 387 ff.

95. O. Grether, *Name und Wort Gottes im Alten Testament* (Giessen, 1934), pp. 20, 163 ff.

96. M. Buber, *Moses: The Revelation and the Covenant*, paperback ed. (New York, 1958), p. 117.

97. On the meaning of the name in Hebrew religion, see G. von Rad, "Deuteronomy's 'Name' Theology and the Priestly Documents' 'Kabod' Theology," *Studies in Deuteronomy*, tr. by D. Stalker (Chicago, 1953), pp. 37 ff.; *idem.*, *Old Testament Theology*, I, pp. 179 ff.; E. Jacob, "The Name of God," *Theology of the Old Testament* (1958), pp. 82 ff.; R. Abba, "Name," *IDB*, III, pp. 500 ff.; J. Murtagh, "The Name in Egypt and in Israel," *Bible Today*, XXXVII (1968): 2585 ff.

98. G. Bachelard, *La psychanalyse du feu* (Paris, 1937; paperback ed., 1949), pp. 19 f.

99. The Hebrew word *shawᵉ'* means "emptiness, chasm, void, nothing." Cf. Ps. 89:47 [Heb., 48], "What is the nothingness for which thou hast created the sons of man?"

100. P. Tillich, "The Divine Name," *Christianity and Crisis*, XXI (1960–61): 55.

101. T. E. Lawrence, *Seven Pillars of Wisdom* (Garden City, N. Y., 1936), p. 40.

102. R. Tournay, "Le Psaume VIII et la doctrine biblique du nom," *RB*, LXXVIII (1971): p. 19.

103. See C. J. Bleeker, "L'oeil et l'oreille," *The Sacred Bridge: Suppl. to Numen*, VII (Leiden, 1963), pp. 52 ff.

4

Presence in the Temple

Most religions have erected temples. The notion of sacred space, which goes back to prehistoric times, is manifest in the entire ancient Near East, where the ruins of sanctuaries testify to the spread of the belief that gods and goddesses, whatever their special realms of being might be, also dwell in holy places. They are present in their own palaces, built by men—often on heavenly models.[1]

Modern culture tends to dismiss hastily the notion of sacred space, and it may thereby miss a reality of religious psychology which is deeply anchored in the human psyche. Some might ask, with Siegfried Sassoon, and like him answer:

What is Stonehenge? It is a roofless past;
Man's ruinous myth; his uninterred adoring
Of the unknown in sunrise cold and red;
His quest of stars that arch his doomed exploring.[2]

One may be inclined to range the temple of Solomon on Mt. Zion with the glories of Nineveh and Tyre or to think of the Hebraic awareness of cultic presence as "man's ruinous myth." Ancient Israel herself was not of one mind on this burning issue. A grievous tension between two cultic views of the divine presence appears in the literature of Israel and Judah during the fateful centuries of the Divided Monarchy (922–722 B.C.), of the surviving kingdom of Judah (722–586 B.C.), and of the infancy of Judaism (586–397 B.C.). Here again it will be useful to distinguish between a theologoumenon of presence through space and a theologoumenon of presence through time. Such a distinction is supported by documentary evidence. It will lead to a more accurate representation of the difference, already observed in the ancient traditions, between a theology of the name and a theology of glory.

During the nomadic stage of their historical existence, the Hebrews knew of no fixed abode for Yahweh, not even Mt. Horeb-Sinai.[3] At the same time, the early strata of the epic memories of Israel mentioned two cultic objects, "the ark of Yahweh" and "the tent of meeting," both related in widely different ways to a belief in the intermittent recurrence of Yahweh's presence. In addition, the priestly writers of the Babylonian exile, reflecting a long-held tradition of the Jerusalem temple, described in detail, under the name "tabernacle," their idealized picture of the sanctuary during the desert wanderings.

The ark provided a link between the memories of Moses and the erection of the temple of Solomon in Jerusalem, some three hundred years after the Exodus.[4]

THE ARK OF YAHWEH

We are accustomed to speak of "the ark of the covenant," and we generally imagine it to have contained the tables of the law. This time-honored opinion, however, represents an anachronistic telescoping of the early traditions concerning Moses with the later theological interpretations which arose among the

Deuteronomists (Deut. 10:1 ff.) and the Deuteronomistic editors of the books of Samuel and Kings (1 Kings 8:9, etc.).[5] In ancient times, the ark was called "the ark of Yahweh" or "the ark of Elohim."[6] The epic traditions, both in the North and in the South, are silent about its construction, its size, its shape, and its function.[7]

The Ark in Mosaic Times

From only two references in the early sources of the Pentateuch, it may be inferred that such a sacred object was a military emblem, symbol, or token of the nearness of Yahweh in battle. It belonged originally to the ideology of the Holy War.[8]

Theophanies never last long. Moses had to descend from the mountain of God. The sons of Israel—at least those tribal groups which had escaped from Egyptian slavery—had to move away, sooner or later, from the site of their national birth. Although there is no direct evidence from the text, one may surmise that the prohibition of images—a custom without real parallel in the ancient Near East—created a problem for the worshippers of Yahweh. In the absence of representations of the Deity, the sense of divine nearness could hardly survive among the people at large. The idea of the omnipresence of God is too diffuse and vague for effective awareness in daily existence, in the midst of all sorts of conditions and temperaments. The psychological experience of divine communion— let alone the ecstatic vision—may not be accessible to a large number of men and women, certainly not at all times. This is shown by the testimony of the eighth- and seventh-century prophets, as well as of the mystics of several religions.

How could the presence of Yahweh be made manifest to the rank-and-file populace that surrounded Moses? What was he to do, especially in time of existential crisis, such as warfare, when man needs particularly to be reassured of divine protection?

One has the right to speculate that Moses himself was a theologian of sacramental presence, but such a speculation is fragile, for the ancient traditions do not report that he ordered the manufacture of the ark. He may well have received it from Jethro and the Kenites (Exod. 18:1 ff.).

Moses himself might have been satisfied with the theophanic promise, "My presence shall go with thee" (Exod. 33:14). For tribal soldiers in the hour of combat, however, this promise had to be translated into a concrete center of sensorial attention.

The Hebrew word 'arôn, "ark," designated a small chest,[9] like that in which the bones of Joseph were preserved (Gen. 50:26), or an offering box, such as the one which was placed at later times in the entrance to the temple of Jerusalem (2 Kings 12:10; cf. 2 Chron. 24:8). It is not impossible that the ark was originally a tribal *palladium*, similar to the 'utfah, the *merkab*, or the 'abu-Dhûr, which various Arabs, until modern times, used to bring to battle on camel back, and which was attended by a chief's daughter or a beautiful maiden. In the early centuries of the Christian era, and perhaps even before, pre-Islamic Arabs had a *qubbah* or tent of red leather which contained the stone gods of a tribe.[10] In biblical times, the Egyptians maintained processional boats on which were displayed sacred boxes.[11] The Hebraic ark, however, was not conceived in the desert days as a permanent container or shelter of the divine presence. It was rather a sort of pedestal or stool from which Yahweh, so it was believed, ascended before a battle or to which he descended after a victory.

According to an archaic poem which may well have been quoted from the *Scroll of the Wars of Yahweh*, now lost but mentioned elsewhere,[12] the ark was carried forward at the beginning of military engagements while Moses used to sing,

"Rise up, O Yahweh! And let thine enemies be scattered!
And let them that hate thee flee before thee!" (Num. 10:35).

Likewise, when the ark was put to rest, Moses used to say,

> "Return, O Yahweh! Unto the many thousands of Israel!"
> (Vs. 36.)

The expression "many thousands of Israel" may be archaic and hyperbolic, although it may also indicate that the Song of the Ark, in spite of its present context, belongs to the time of the Judges and the conquest.

If this poem is ancient, it would seem to identify, in the mind of Moses and his warriors, the movements of Yahweh with the motions of the ark. One should not conclude from this observation, however, that Moses is presented as addressing the ark itself as Yahweh. In the preceding context, which appears to belong, like the probable quotation from the *Scroll of the Wars of Yahweh*, to the Yahwistic tradition, the narrator depicts the carrying of the ark ahead of the tribes as they finally depart from the holy mountain, but he significantly adds, "the cloud of Yahweh was over them by day" (Numb. 10:33–34). An ambiguous tension is maintained between the sacred object and the para-theophanic manifestation of the presence through the cloud.

To be sure, the popular mind would easily tend to look at the ark as the bearer of real presence at all times, but the fragments of the tradition which have been preserved insist on the transitory character of this presence, since it was limited to periods of migration and times of battle. These two periods were of course likely to be identical, or at least overlapping, since migration into an unknown and alien area would intensify the risk of defensive attacks on the part of other nomads.[13]

The Ark During the Conquest

Under Joshua and the Judges, and during the youth of Samuel (ca. 1230–1050 B.C.), the descendents of the desert wanderers gradually settled in the mountain range of Canaan. While the ark may have played a part in the crossing of the Jordan at Gilgal (Josh. 3:17, etc.) and at the fall of Jericho (Josh. 6:9 ff.), it is difficult to ascertain the reliability of the nucleus of ancient memories which is now embedded in the text.[14]

The narratives on the youth of Samuel (eleventh century B.C.) were written in later times and edited by the Deuteronomistic school, but they include an incidental note on the ark, which bears the mark of authenticity.

The ark was apparently kept in the temple of Shiloh, in the central mountain range of Ephraim,[15] but there is no indication that it played any significant part in the life of the nation. The narrative merely states: "The lamp of Elohim had not yet gone out, and Samuel was lying down in the temple of Yahweh, where the ark of Elohim was. . ." (1 Sam. 3:3). The text does not suggest that the cultic object was considered as the visible sign of the permanent presence of Yahweh in the shrine. On the contrary, the recital of the vision in which Samuel was called to a prophetic mission clearly implies that the divine manifestation was distinct from the ark: "And Yahweh came, and he stood forth, calling, Samuel! Samuel!" (vs. 10).[16]

Some scholars maintain that it was in the temple of Shiloh that the ark came to be understood as the footstool or the empty throne of Yahweh and that it was surrounded by carved objects known as the cherubim. The liturgical formula "Yahweh of Hosts who is enthroned upon the cherubim" is found for the first time in the stories of Samuel at Shiloh.[17] There is no evidence, however, that the cherubim, twin objects of the temple of Solomon in Jerusalem, belonged to the Yahwistic iconography of the Shiloh sanctuary.[18] In an early psalm of thanksgiving, the core of which may well be Davidic, Yahweh is described as going to war "riding upon a cherub"[19] or on the storm cloud in fury. In all likelihood, it was the mythopoetic language of the Holy War which influenced the liturgists of Shiloh during the days of the conquest. A few generations later,

Solomon's architects from Tyre introduced carved cherubim, overlaid in gold, to the temple of Jerusalem.[20]

During the Philistine invasions of the eleventh century B.C., the military commanders of Israel summoned the ark to battle. As the soldiers were being routed at Aphek, the elders said, "Let us bring the ark of [our God][21] here from Shiloh, so that he will come among us and save us from the power of our enemies" (1 Sam. 4:3). The dramatic discomfiture which followed this cultic attempt to influence divine decision was complete. The ark was captured by the enemy. In the course of the years during which these sorry events were committed to the national memory, stories were told in order to show half humorously the residual power of the cultic object in spite of its shameful failure during the battle of Aphek (1 Sam. 6:1 ff.). At last, the ancient trophy came to rest in the town of Kiriath-Jearim, where it remained in obscurity for some twenty years (1 Sam. 7:2).

The Ark in Jerusalem.

The renaissance of interest in the ark under David (ca. 1000 B.C.) was the prelude to a most important development in the Hebraic theology of presence. It contributed to the astounding development of the myth of Zion.

With the magnetism of his complex personality, David of Bethlehem in Judah succeeded in uniting the tribes of Israel. He not only expelled the Philistines from the mountain range of "Palestine" (Philistina), but he also restored on a broader basis the kingdom which Saul of Benjamin had vainly initiated a few years previously in the heart of Ephraim. His accession to the throne of a united monarchy, however, resulted in a dramatic shift of influence in the political, cultural, and religious history of the nation. Little by little, in the course of two centuries, the catalytic center of Hebraic faith moved from Israel properly speaking to the ethnically heterogeneous tribe of Judah and thus prepared the birth of Judaism in the sixth century B.C.

The fortress of Jebus (Jerusalem), strategically located in a Canaanite enclave between Israel and Judah for nearly 2½ centuries of Hebraic infiltration in the land of Canaan, finally yielded to the military skill of David and the bravery of his warriors (2 Sam. 5:1 ff.). The triumphant king made Jerusalem his capital. This move proved to be a stroke of political genius, for it enabled him to offer a rallying point to both North and South on a neutral ground—a distant anticipation of the American "District of Columbia."

In an effort to put the stamp of Hebraic Yahwism on Canaanite Jerusalem, David sought out the ark in its half-forgotten retreat at Kiriath-Jearim and with great pomp brought it inside the fortress of Jebus.[22] The narrative of the transfer of the ark to Jerusalem is adorned with anecdotes which suggest that it was originally part of a cultic ceremonial in which the *legenda* of the ark were chanted and even enacted many times after David's reign during the festive occasions of the Davidic monarchy.[23] Apparently, the disgrace of the Philistine episodes could safely be erased from the national memory. Far from being merely a politician's ploy, David's decision was inspired by an authentic devotion to Yahweh. The presence of the ark near a stronghold which had been until then a center of Canaanite worship could be viewed not only as a symbol of Yahweh's triumph over the deities of the land but also as a link with the faith of the fathers in the wilderness. The notorious scene in which the king danced ecstatically "in the presence of Yahweh" (2 Sam. 6:13) testifies to the passionate character of his attachment to the God who had delivered him from all his enemies.[24]

The military and nomadic characteristics of the ark in Mosaic times were profoundly altered by its transfer to Jerusalem. From its sporadic significance on the day of battle, the ark acquired the status of permanent visibility. It moved from the realm of historical time to that of cultic space. Above all other considerations, David was probably motivated by his concern for keeping alive the old tribal confederation of Israel. The ark embodied the memories of the triumphs of Yahweh during the early days of the conquest. In Shechem (Jos. 8:30–35), possibly Bethel (Judg. 20:26 f.; cf. vs. 18 and 21:2), and finally Shiloh (1 Sam. 3:3, etc.), the ark conferred its cultic concreteness upon both dimensions of the Mosaic covenant: vertical, since it exhibited the bond which united Yahweh to Israel; and horizontal, since it cemented the solidarity of heterogeneous tribes under their common allegiance. The ark of Yahweh became known as "the ark of the covenant."[25] By moving it to Jerusalem, David was in effect signifying to the whole nation that its religious as well as its political center had been transferred from Shechem to Jerusalem.[26]

The nomadic aspect of the ark was not forgotten, however, for its original connection with the ideology of the Holy War and the sojourn in the wilderness was reenacted in the ceremonies of its procession in later times.[27] The fact that David sheltered it in a tent, which he had especially pitched for it, suggests that he was fully aware of its desert origin and of the nomadic implications of the theology which it represented. Nevertheless, the king's attempt to erect "a house of cedar" for the permanent residence of the ark (2 Sam. 7:1 ff.) reveals his ambivalence and possibly his spiritual confusion.

Significantly, the story of this attempt is embedded in a narrative which articulates the nomadic theology of the ark with a sequence of dynastic oracles.[28] These dynastic oracles (2 Sam. 7:8–29) seek to replace the conditional, ethical, and historically contingent character of the Mosaic covenant (Exod. 19:5–6) with an unconditioned, permanent—indeed, eternal, hence suprahistorical and mythical—covenant, binding the God of Israel "forever" to the Davidic dynasty (vs. 16). The juxtaposition of the reference to the ark with the promise of an eternal covenant suggests that a radical change was proposed—although temporarily rejected—in the theology of presence, and that this radical change entailed political consequences of a revolutionary nature. The notion of a divinely ordained and hereditary kingship was alien to the theology of a conditional covenant.[29] For early Israel, Yahweh was the only King.[30] Now, David wished to imitate the kings of all the nations.

Consulted on David's projects in sacred architecture, the prophet Nathan, answering at first on his own behalf as a court adviser, expressed his agreement (2 Sam. 7:3). Yet nocturnal vision compelled him to reverse his judgment. The oracle he had to communicate to David implies a theology of presence which is strictly compatible with the nomadic character of the ark:

> Thus says Yahweh: Wouldst thou build for me a house to sit in? I have not sat in a house since the days I brought up the people of Israel from Egypt to this day, but I have been walking about in a tent and in an encampment.[31] In all the places where I have walked about with all the people of Israel, did I speak a word with any of the judges[32] of Israel whom I commanded to shepherd my people Israel, saying, Why have you not built for me a house of cedar? (2 Sam. 7:5-8.)

This prophetic oracle constitutes one of the most important statements of the Hebraic literature on the modes of presence, hence on the tensions between two conflicting theological interpretations of history. Under the seemingly naive anthropomorphism of the image of a sitting or walking Godhead, the text indicates a polemic against the notion of a static Deity, attached to a temple built by man, and therefore subjected to the limitations of human worship. Nathan's prophetic word defends the freedom of Yahweh.

God is near, but his presence remains elusive. He is "a walking God."

A theology of time is endorsed at the expense of a theology

of sacred space which confines "a sitting God" and subjects him to anthropocentric manipulation. The thrust of the oracle is aimed at institutional shrines which perform rituals destined to influence, curb, and in effect enslave the Deity. Nathan's prophetic insight is a forerunner of the violent attacks which the eighth- and seventh-century prophets delivered against the national temple of Israel at Bethel (Amos and Hosea) and the national temple of Judah at Jerusalem (First Isaiah, Micah, Jeremiah).[33]

The sojourn of Yahweh in a tent was compatible with his walking about in the midst of his people. His sitting in a house of cedar, built by man, was open to the clerical institutionalism common to all the religions which enlist the deified forces of nature for the benefit of a privileged class, dynasty, people, or church. In Mosaic Yahwism, divine power transcends nature and history.

It is therefore no accident that the Nathan oracle juxtaposes a nomadic view of the ark in a tent with a reference to judges who shepherd the nation. Such a nomadic view of the ark is interconnected with an elective and charismatic doctrine of national leadership that is alien to the Semitic ideology of divine kingship and hereditary monarchy. The several layers of dynastic oracles on the Davidic covenant which have agglutinated over Nathan's message and which contradict the implications of the Mosaic covenant testify indirectly to the eventual victory of the royalist theologians who surrounded the Jerusalem monarchy.

The theologoumenon of presence through the name was being displaced by the theologumenon of presence through the glory; such a displacement carried with it ominous consequences in the realm of political ethics.

The Ark and the Theologoumenon of Glory.

Brought to Jerusalem, the ark became a suitable vehicle for an interpretation of Yahweh's visible presence through the theologoumenon of glory. It will be recalled that the Yahwistic stories of the Sinai theophanies stressed the visual aspect of the divine manifestation at the expense of the hearing of the word. At the end of the monarchy and after the destruction of the temple of Jerusalem, the priestly circles retold the Sinai theophany in terms of a vision of glory (Exod. 24:15–18). The appropriation of the ark by the cultic institutions of David and Solomon marked an intermediary stage in this development.

Already in Shiloh, during the Philistine invasions, the ark had been talked about in the context of the glory of God. Upon hearing that the ark had fallen into the hands of the enemy, the daughter-in-law of Eli (the priest of Shiloh during the youth of Samuel) gave birth to a son whom she called *Ichabod*, "No glory" or "Alas-for-the-glory!"—for, she said, "the glory" (*kabod*) "has departed from Israel, because the ark of Elohim has been captured" (1 Sam. 4:20–22).

Alluding to this event, a Jerusalem hymnodist belonging to the musical guild of Asaph[34] explained that God

> ". . . had delivered his power (*'oz*) into captivity,
>   his splendor (*tiph'ereth*) into the hand of the foe"
>
> (Ps. 78:61).

The association of the notion of divine power (*'oz*) with the idea of divine splendor (*tiph'ereth*) and its synonyms, "glory" (*kabod*), "honor" or "majesty" (*hadar*), "magnificence" (*'addereth*), and several others[35] appears in psalms which were sung at the autumn festival, when the Lord of nature is hailed in the storm epiphany that marks the renewal of the year. Psalm 29, "the Hymn of the Seven Thunders" (cf. Rev. 10:3), betrays the influence of the proto-Canaanite mythology of Ugarit.[36] It invites "the sons of the gods" to ascribe "glory and power" to Yahweh at the occasion of the "epiphany of [his] holiness."[37] This event should probably be identified as the autumn feast, when the death of nature through the drought of summer is at last ended by the return of the rain through the first thunderstorm of a new agricultural year. In their syncretistic embracing of the myth-opoetic language of the ancient Near East, the Jerusalem hymnodists went so far as to attempt a reconciliation between the theologoumenon of the name and the theologoumenon of the glory, for they asked the heavenly beings to "ascribe to Yahweh the glory of his name" (vs. 2*a*). At any rate, the poem may be described as a distant antecedent of the *Gloria in Excelsis* which culminates with a *Pax in Terris* (vss. 1 and 10), since it begs for the blessing of Yahweh's people with the fertility of the autumnal rain.

Some scholars conjecture that this poem brings together the ambivalence of the thunderstorm—potentially both destructive and portentous of new life—with the "monstrance" of the ark as it is borne processionally out of the temple. As mountains, cedars, and animals are stunned with dread, worshippers sing the praise of the Lord of nature:[38]

> The roaring of Yahweh causes the desert to writhe,
>   Yahweh causes the desert of Kadesh to writhe in agony!
> The roaring of Yahweh makes the hinds bring forth,
>   And he strips bare the forests,
>   But in his temple, all say, Glory! (Vss. 8–9).

The ark and the glory are explicitly related in another hymn which hails the entrance of the ark in the sanctuary, perhaps at the conclusion of the processional rite:

> Lift up your heads, O ye gates,
>   And be ye lifted up, ye everlasting doors,
>   That the King of glory may come in!
> Who is the King of glory?
>   Yahweh, strong and mighty,
>   Yahweh, mighty in battle![39]

Lift up your heads, O ye gates,
  And be ye lifted up, ye everlasting doors,
  That the King of glory may come in!
Who is *this* King of glory?
  Yahweh of Hosts,
  He is the King of glory! (Ps. 24:7–10).

Even if the ritual phrase "Lift up your heads, O ye gates" is not an echo of the command "Lift up your heads, O ye gods," which the *Ba'al* of the Ugaritic poetry shouts at the members of the divine council as they bow down in dread of Yam, "the Sea," there is no doubt that Psalm 24 organically articulates the ritual of the ark, as emblem of the Holy War, with the myth of creation (vss. 1–2). The cultic object is inseparable from the belief in Yahweh, the Hero of Battle, triumphant over cosmic as well as historical enemies.[40]

The story of the erection of the Jerusalem temple by Solomon culminates with the scene of the ark's entrance into the innermost room of the edifice: "A cloud filled the house of Yahweh, so that the priests could not stand to minister on account of it; for the glory of Yahweh filled the house of Yahweh" (1 Kings 8:10 ff.). The pattern is well established. The ark is henceforth associated with the theologoumenon of glory.

It may have been the opposition of the North to the Jerusalem temple which brought about, at least in part, the Deuteronomic reinterpretation of the ark as the container of the tables of the law (Deut. 10:1 ff.).[41] In any case, the Jerusalem priests, at least as early as the seventh century, identified the cultic object with the throne of Yahweh on earth. Soon after the destruction of the temple—and presumably of the ark also—Jeremiah spoke of the new Jerusalem in the suprahistorical times to come:

"In those days, says Yahweh, they shall say no more,
  The ark of the covenant of Yahweh!
It shall not come to mind, or be remembered, or missed.
  It shall not be made again!" (Jer. 3:16).

Significantly, this expression of antagonism to the ark (*ca.* 587 B.C.) is prefaced by an implied criticism of the Davidic dynasty:

> "And I will give you [says Yahweh] shepherds after my
> own heart who will feed you with knowledge and
> understanding" (vs. 15).

Moreover, Jeremiah is clearly condemning the Jerusalem interpretation of the ark, not the theology of presence as such, for he concludes:

> "At that time, Jerusalem shall be called the throne of
> Yahweh, and all nations shall gather to it, in the
> presence of Yahweh in Jerusalem" (vs. 17).

As in the Nathan oracle against David's intention to build a house of cedar to shelter the ark permanently, the motif of the humble and elected shepherd is juxtaposed with the theology of nomadic presence. The ark has become totally incompatible with the Mosaic notion of covenantal peoplehood, with its classless ideal of corporate solidarity. The political implications of the theologoumenon of glory are irreconcilable with those of the theologoumenon of the name.

THE TENT OF MEETING

Entirely different from the ark of Yahweh, which conveyed associations of the Holy War and possessed affinities with the theologoumenon of the glory, was another cultic object, "the tent of meeting," which was originally related to the prophetic aspect of Yahwism and contained the seed of the theologoumenon of presence through the divine name.

The Tent in the Wilderness

While nothing is known of its appearance, form, or dimensions, one may assume that the *'ohel mo'ed*, "tent of meeting" or "tent of reunion,"[42] looked like any other shelter of canvas which desert nomads wove out of goat hair until modern times. The Hebrew words suggest the rendering "tent of tryst," for *mo'ed* is a date even more than an appointed place for meeting. It later designates a festive season.[43]

The tent was neither a military symbol nor a manufactured token of the permanence of divine nearness. Rather, it constituted a spatial vehicle for oracular communication. The tent was an empty shelter which at times could be filled with the presence, but only the presence of a God in dialogue with man. It was not in any way the container of diffuse sanctity, a sort of sacramental enclosure that is common to most religions. Rather, it sought to answer the human quest for the disclosure of the divine will on specific occasions.

More especially, the tent of meeting provided Moses with the solitariness, privacy, and isolation which have always been the mark of the encounter between God and man. The tent concealed in its darkness those moments of intimate immediacy when Yahweh and Moses, in the bold anthropomorphism of the storytellers, "spoke together face to face" (Exod. 33:11) or even "mouth to mouth" (Num. 12:8)—that is, without obstacle, distance, or intermediary.

"Face to Face" (Exod. 33:7-11). The first reference to the tent is now found out of context in the sequence of episodes during which Moses, still at the foot of Mt. Sinai-Horeb, but about to depart with the sons and daughters of Israel toward the promised land, prayed for the continuation of the gift of presence as a *vade mecum* and even begged to see the glory (vss. 12-23).[44]

> Now Moses would take the tent and pitch it outside the camp, far away from the camp, and he called it "tent of meeting" because it was outside the camp. Anyone who sought Yahweh would go out of the camp to the tent of meeting. And it came to pass that whenever Moses would go out, the entire people would rise and

present themselves, each man at the entrance of his own tent, and their eyes would intently follow Moses until he had entered the tent.

And it came to pass, as Moses entered the tent, that the pillar of cloud would descend and stand at the entrance of the tent while [Yahweh] spoke with Moses. And when the entire people would see the pillar of cloud at the entrance of the tent, the entire people would rise and worship, each man at the entrance of his own tent. And Yahweh would speak with Moses face to face as a man speaks with his neighbor.

When he would return to the camp, his attendant, Joshua the son of Nun, a lad, would not walk away from the inside of the tent (Exod. 33:7–11).

Among the many strange features of this narrative, only a few salient ones need be mentioned here:

1. Moses pitched the tent "outside the camp." The repeated emphasis on the word "tent" indicates in all probability the narrator's intention to differentiate this cultic object from the ark,[45] and possibly even from the "tabernacle" (*mishkan*) with which the later Jerusalem priestly tradition confused it.[46]

2. The tent was not a portable sanctuary which provided an abode or a permanent residence for the divine, but a spatial setting, geographically unattached, to which both Yahweh and Moses would "go" in order to "meet."

3. The keeper of the tent was not a priest, but a mere youth who had not even reached puberty (*na'ar*), and who served as the personal attendant of Moses.

4. Although the tent had been erected for anyone who wished to seek Yahweh,[47] the tradition tells us that the only human being who penetrated into its shadow for an oracular purpose was Moses himself.[48]

5. To those who stood outside, the presence of God was made manifest by the descent of the pillar of cloud, but without the attending elements of a spectacular display of nature in

tumult as in the theophanies of Mt. Sinai-Horeb. Commentators apparently err when they associate the tent of meeting with the theologoumenon of the glory, for it is precisely in the cluster of the traditions which now surround this pericope that Moses is denied the vision of the face of Yahweh.[49] Through contextual juxtaposition, the divine face is identified with the divine glory. (vs. 18).

6. The pillar of cloud "would stand at the entrance of the tent," namely, outside. However, it was inside the tent that Yahweh would speak with Moses "face to face" as a man speaks with his neighbor (vs. 11). There is no contradiction between the denial of the vision of the face and the speaking "face to face," for this expression is clearly idiomatic and signifies "without intermediary." The distinction lies in the difference between seeing and speaking. The narrator insists on the homely character of the dialogical exchange. The tone is devoid of the dramatic frills of an apotheosis or the emotional thrills of an ecstasy. The idea of a simple conversation, conducted in the form of a "chat," places this peculiarly Mosaic mode of presence in the lineage of the stories of epiphanic visitations to the patriarchs and prepares the literary genre of the prophetic vision, as illustrated especially by Amos (ch. 7) and Jeremiah (ch. 1). The frequentative form of the verbs indicates that Moses would occasionally, and perhaps even often, go out of the camp to the tent of meeting in his search for the disclosure of God's intentions.

7. Whenever Moses went to the tent, all the people would stand, each man outside of the entrance to his own tent. In this mediated mode of presence, they would rise and worship in ritual prostration. Moses is thus depicted as the prophet *par excellence,* mediator of the Godhead to man, a human bridge between Yahweh and the entire community of Israel, but not in any way the giver of the law, with its minute regulations on purity and impurity or licit and illicit relations and the like, nor

again as the priest before an altar, engaged in the performance of sacerdotal ceremony.

In short, while the tent must be viewed as a cultic object, since the people's response is that of a ritual of adoration in the presence of the holy, one may not construe it as the prefiguration of a shrine in which sacred acts are performed by sacred persons at sacred times. On the contrary, one should interpret the manufacture, use, and function of the tent of meeting as pointing to a nexus of religious activity and thinking which distantly anticipates the psychological mode of presence through the inward processes of communion.

The oracular purpose of this nomadic shelter of goat hair in which God and man spoke "face to face" prepares the spiritual interiority unwittingly exhibited by the great prophets, the psalmists, and the poet of Job. Since the tent, however, was a material edifice of canvas which belonged to the realm of spatiality, it related such a spiritual interiority to a concrete environment of the physical world. Its mobility, at once, kept it detached from a static *topos* and permitted the potential character of human universality. It could not be restricted to a holy land, even less to a sacred cave, spring, tree, or hilltop. It owned the whole earth.

Without reducing the complexity of historical change to a simplistic schematization, one might say that the tent of meeting favored a theology of presence that was compatible, not with the worship of Yahweh in a single temple, but with a type of cult which promoted the *beth tephillah,* "the house of intercessory prayer." In Persian times, the late sixth century B.C., an anonymous prophet of nascent Judaism categorically opposed this mode of presence to the ideology of a priestly sanctuary (Isa. 56:7). In still later times, the fourth or third centuries B.C., Hellenistic Judaism called the *beth tephillah* by the Greek word *synagôgê,* "synagogue."

"Mouth to Mouth" (Num. 12:1-9). The tent of meeting belongs so clearly to the theology of elusive presence that it plays a significant part in another tradition of ancient origin, in which the religious phenomenon of a temporally limited disclosure of the divine will is explicitly associated with the mystery of prophetic revelation.[50] This narrative refers to Miriam's and Aaron's claim to have access to divine speech, in competition with Moses:

> And Miriam and Aaron spoke against Moses on account of the Cushite woman whom he had taken. And they said, Has Yahweh indeed spoken only through Moses? Has he not spoken also with us? And Yahweh heard it.
>
> Now, the man Moses was very meek, above all the men who were upon the face of the earth. And Yahweh spoke suddenly to Moses, and to Aaron, and to Miriam, Come out [of the camp], the three of you, to the tent of meeting. And the three of them came out. And Yahweh came down in a pillar of cloud, and he stood at the entrance of the tent. And he called Aaron and Miriam, and both of them came out [of the tent].
>
> And he said, Hear now my words:
> > If there be a prophet among you,
> >   I, Yahweh, shall make myself known to him in a vision;
> > In a dream shall I speak with him.
> >   Not so with my servant Moses!
>
> > [Alone] in all my household, he is a man of faith:
> >   Mouth to mouth shall I speak with him,
> > In clear language[51] and not in riddles,[52]
> >   And the form of Yahweh will he behold.
>
> > Now, therefore, why were you not afraid
> >   To speak against my servant Moses? (Num. 12:1-8.)

This is a unique story, which confirms the oracular use of the tent in the wilderness. Although of archaic origin, as shown by the poetic rhythm and strophic structure of Yahweh's speech, it was probably recited in the prophetic circles during the conquest and the early monarchy (eleventh to fifth centuries B.C.), when discussions arose on the nature of prophetic inspiration.

Moses was remembered as the model of the true prophet. A criterion was sorely needed to distinguish between the Canaanite bands of raving ecstatics (1 Sam. 10:5, etc.) that had been more or less "Yahwehicized" and the authentic servants of the Hebraic faith. The story also set the status of Moses apart from that of those professional diviners who functioned at the sanctuaries of Yahweh in the land of Canaan. The mode of revelation through "vision" and "dream" was not repudiated, but four characteristics of the prophet *par excellence* were put forth—significantly, in the context of the tent of meeting.

First, Moses is the peculiar "servant" or "slave" of Yahweh, the head of a long line of messengers of the Deity who speak in his name, to whom Amos referred in the eighth century when he asked rhetorically:

> Do two walk together,
>   Unless they have made an appointment?[53]
> The lion has roared,
>   Who will not fear?
> The Lord Yahweh has spoken;
>   Who can but prophesy? (Amos 3:3, 8.)

At the core of this poem, Amos said,

> Surely, the Lord Yahweh will do nothing
>   Without revealing his secret
>   To his servants the prophets (vs. 7).

Like Moses in the tent of meeting, the true prophets are the slaves of the Deity, who speaks with them confidentially.

Second, the true prophet, like Moses, is different from "the entire household of Yahweh," for he is a man of faith, therefore a faithful man who may, without reservation, be trusted with the sovereign's secret. In him, as in Abraham, Yahweh has faith (Gen. 15:6), just as the man of faith trusts Yahweh.

Third, the true prophet converses with the Godhead in the most intimate manner, "mouth to mouth," and the divine will is made known to him in clear language, without ambiguity.

Fourth, Moses alone, however, is allowed "to examine, to look intently, to observe," the "form" or image of Yahweh (*temunah*). To be sure, the form is not the face (*panîm*), which Moses was not permitted to see (Exod. 33:23 *b*). It is therefore remarkable that the northern storytellers, who meditated on the theological significance of the Mt. Horeb-Sinai theophany and specifically stated that Israel "heard the voice of the words, but . . . saw no form (*temunah*)" (Deut. 4:12), would grant Moses this unique privilege. While their intention may not be determined with certainty, it is probable that they sought an intermediate way of expressing visual perception. On the one hand, their phrase was commensurate with the directness of the auditive immediacy suggested by the anthropomorphism of "mouth to mouth." On the other hand, their statement was capable of safeguarding the invisibility of Yahweh's face, namely, his glory —the manifestation of his inner being (cf. Exod. 33:23*a*).

Finally, it should be noted that Aaron and Miriam were commanded to come out of the tent. Yahweh refused to offer them oracular words within the private retreat reserved for Moses alone. Intimacy of confidential presence is different from the abruptness of rebuke.[54] The tent of meeting seems to have been a locus of privileged setting, appropriate for divine converse with the true servant of Yahweh. Moses is presented by implication as the spiritual ancestor of the prophetic lineage.

The Commission of Joshua (*Deut. 31:14–23*). The third reference to the tent of meeting that appears in the ancient traditions regarding the wilderness confirms the interpretation that this cultic object belongs to the prophetic theology of the word. Like the other two, it favors the ear over the eye, the theologoumenon of the name rather than the theologoumenon of the glory.

Describing the last days of Moses before his death on the plateau of Moab, the editors of the book of Deuteronomy reproduced an ancient narrative which told how the responsibility of leadership was conferred upon Joshua, son of Nun (Deut. 31:14 –23). The youth who had attended to the tent of meeting in its early days (Exod. 33:11) was now a mature adult. It was in the same tent of meeting that he received his commission (vss. 14, 23).

The event did not involve a ritual of priestly or royal anointing. It included neither blessing nor laying-on of hands. It consisted of hearing the prophetic word. The divine speech was at once reminiscent of the patriarchal summons and anticipatory of the prophetic calls. The tent of meeting was the locus, not of an institutional ceremony for the transmission of power from one generation to another, but of a divine intervention into the inner life of a man who was "commanded" to act:

And [Yahweh] commanded Joshua, the son of Nun, and said,
  Be strong and of good courage,
    For thou wilt indeed bring the sons of Israel
    Into the land I swore to them.
And I will indeed be with thee (vs. 23).

The Hebrew original stressed the I-Thou relationship, for it used emphatic pronouns: "it will be *thou* who ... and I, *even I,* etc." The charge of Joshua was a commission by command, with a promise of communion. It linked vocation to obedience and surrounded both with the psychological mode of presence. It had nothing to do with sacerdotal consecration. It prefigured prophetic ordination.

The tent of meeting in the days of the wilderness was not associated with the ark of Elohim.[55] It provided a setting for the awesome introduction of Moses and Joshua into "the goodly fellowship of the prophets."

The Tent in the Land of Canaan.

Whether the sacred object which Moses erected in the wilderness actually survived the damage of time and the wars of the conquest cannot be known. It may have been replaced or it may have been preserved with utmost care by the chieftains of the clans related most closely to the centers of the tribal confederation, first in Shechem and later in Shiloh. In any case, its original function appears to have been blurred in the course of two hundred years of Hebrew contact with Canaanite culture. The traditions regarding Samuel's youth incidentally told of the misbehavior exhibited by the sons of Eli, the priest of the house of Yahweh at Shiloh (1 Sam. 1:7): they "lay with the women who served at the entrance of the tent of meeting" (1 Sam. 2:22).

Since the sanctuary was described as "a house" and "a temple" (1 Sam. 1:7, 3:3), it was manifestly an architectural edifice. Hence we must assume that the tent of meeting stood outside of it, within its sacral terrace or precinct. Whether Eli's sons followed the Canaanite practice of hierogamy or indulged in sexual license cannot be ascertained.

The ark of Elohim, on the contrary, was kept within the edifice (1 Sam. 3:3). The ark and the tent were thus separated as late as the eleventh century B.C.

Was the tent of meeting ever transferred to Jerusalem? The answer to this question seems to be negative. When David, a generation later than Samuel, brought the ark to his new capital, he pitched "a tent" for it (2 Sam. 6:17). Likewise, when he spoke to the prophet Nathan of his intention to build a temple for Yahweh in Jerusalem, David said, "The ark of Elohim dwells in the midst of 'a spread of canvas' (yeri'ah; 2 Sam. 7:2), and Nathan's oracle stated that Yahweh had always been "walking about in a tent ('ohel) and in a sojourning encampment" (mishkan). The expression "tent of meeting" was not used.

It is likely that the tent of meeting was saved from destruction when the temple of Shiloh perished during the Philistine invasions and that it was removed to safety to the high place at Gibeon, a few miles to the south. The editor of the Book of Chronicles, during the Persian period (fourth century B.C.), states that Solomon went to Gibeon "because the tent of meeting of Elohim, which Moses the servant of Yahweh had made in the wilderness, was there" (2 Chron. 1:3; cf. 1 Chron. 21:29 f.).

If this detail is based on reliable memories, the tent of meeting was still associated, at the time of Solomon (tenth century B.C.), with oracular divination. The editors of the Book of Kings (ca. 610 B.C.) preserved the account of the pilgrimage which the young sovereign made to the ancient shrine of Gibeon at the time of his accession to the throne. Solomon spent the night there for a specific purpose: he conformed to the practice of oniric incubation (1 Kings 3:4).

During the centuries of the monarchy in Jerusalem (ca. 1000–587 B.C.), some of the psalmists who composed hymns for the ceremonies of Solomon's temple sometimes used the word "tent" when they in fact were referring to the Zion sanctuary. In so doing, they kept alive the old interpretation of the tent of meeting in the wilderness. For example, a psalm of introit apparently destined to be sung in a ritual of entrance to the shrine would ask a ritual question:

"Yahweh, who will sojourn (*gûr*) in thy tent?
Who will encamp (*shaken*) on thy holy mountain?

(Ps. 15:1).

The answer to this question, however, did not deal with ritual matters like sacrificial offerings, cleansing acts, or purification techniques but exclusively with standards of ethical behavior—inner integrity and social compassion (vss. 2–5).[56]

In the time of the exile in Babylon (sixth century B.C.), the descendants of the Jerusalem priests, eager to offer a model for the reconstruction of the temple, retold the story of the tent, which they confused with the tabernacle (*mishkan*). Whether a tabernacle, in addition to the ark and the tent of meeting had existed in the wilderness remains a moot question.[57] There is no doubt, however, that the theology of presence represented by the priestly stories of the tabernacle had nothing in common with that which the early traditions ascribed to the tent. The priestly tabernacle was entirely dominated by an obsessive concern for propitiation and atonement.

Originally, both the ark and the tent pointed to an intermittent and elusive presence of the Godhead.[58] They reflected a theology which respected the freedom of Yahweh and preserved it from sacerdotal manipulation. With the settlement in the land of Canaan, the appropriation of Canaanite shrines, and especially the erection of Solomon's temple, the myth of the *hagios topos* radically transformed the ancient faith. Hebraism was a nomadic religion which sacralized time. The religion of Judah, which eventually gave birth to Judaism, mythicized space by promoting the belief in the permanent presence of God in Zion.

THE TEMPLE OF SOLOMON

Of the manifold aspects of the irrational in religion, that of the holy place is one of the most enigmatic. Certain sites have become sacred for reasons which are now lost to history, reasons which were not recorded in the tribal memories or in the archives of a shrine. Some sites have been endowed with a peculiar "numinosity" on account of an awesome feature of the landscape—a mountain peak, an island, a promontory, a sea cliff, a spring, a cascade, a canyon, a rock, or a tree.[59] Others have emerged from hagiography: they are remembered as sacred because they commemorate heroic deeds, epic battles, tragic events, or the religious visions of innovators.

To Oedipus at Colonus, Antigone said,

"This place is holy, to all appearance,
luxuriant with laurel, olive, and vine,"[60]

but the secret of this holiness is buried in the distant past. In modern times, Maurice Barrès viewed the hill of Sion-Vaudé-mont in Lorraine as "one of the places where breathes the spirit ... places which are elected from eternity to be the seat of religious emotion."[61] Many spots in both East and West have become hallowed ground for poets and religionists.

Sacred topography generally survives ethnic and cultural changes. It was not through mere coincidence that the Hebrews localized their stories of epiphanic visitation to the patriarchs in the vicinity of ancient sanctuaries like Shechem, Bethel, Hebron, or Beer-sheba, the sacredness of which antedated by centuries Israel's military occupation of the land.[62] The search for the presence of Yahweh led the descendants to worship the God of Moses in spatial identification with their ancestors in Canaan. Territorial familiarity provided a potential for a sacramental participation in "the ancient rapture."

The site of Jerusalem was different. Its pre-Davidic sacrality, which originated in the Northwest Semitic belief in the omphalos of the earth, provoked a radical transformation of Yahwistic theology. The elusiveness of presence, which had been until then the cardinal foundation of Hebraic faith, slowly gave way to the myth of Zion. The universal potentiality of a theology that had been unfettered to a sacred place was now going to face the challenge of cultic Zionism.

The Pre-Davidic Sacrality of Zion

Although postexilic Judaism equated Jerusalem with Moriah in an apparent effort to relate it to the sacrifice of Isaac (2

Chron. 3:1 ff.; cf. Gen. 22:2), the early traditions preserved in the books of Joshua, Judges, and Samuel ignore this patriarchal association. Until its capture by David, the Jebusite fortress had remained in Canaanite hands.[63] In all likelihood, David selected it as his capital not only for strategic and political reasons but also because he was not unaware of the unique sacrality of Zion.

In all periods of history, the motivations of conquerors and kings have usually been mixed with religious concerns, whether sincere or expedient. On the one hand, David was eager to move the seat of his government to a geographically central and historically neutral ground. Jerusalem had until then belonged neither to Israel nor to Judah. It was thus susceptible of rallying the allegiance of both northerners and southerners. On the other hand, the religious significance of Canaanite Jebus could hardly have escaped the king's attention. There is valid reason to conjecture that he was eager not only to bring Israel and Judah together but also to reconcile the surviving Canaanites with the Hebrew invaders.[64]

The identification of Yahweh with El Elyon, traditionally known in English as "God Most High" (Gen. 14:18, 22), reflected the desire to discover a *modus vivendi* for Israelites and Canaanites. It led to the telling of the story of Melchizedek, king of Salem, who conferred a blessing upon Abraham (Gen. 14:-19).[65] The Davidic dynasty maintained its ideology of a priestly kingship "after the order of Melchizedek" (Ps. 110:4). The god Zedek belonged to the cultic pantheon of both Melchizedek, king of Salem (Gen. 14:18) and Adonizedek, king of Jerusalem (Judg. 1:5–7),[66] while the priest of David and Solomon, Zadok, bore a name suggestive of the same cultic tradition and was probably of Jebusite origin.[67] It is not impossible that Salem was historically related to the Canaanite city of Jerusalem, and that the psalmist of a later age was preserving an authentic memory when he sang of Yahweh's hut in Salem and residence in Zion (Ps. 76:2 [Heb., 3]).

Obviously, Yahwistic theology and Canaanite mythology met halfway when Yahweh became identified with El Elyon, "the begetter of heaven and earth" (Gen. 14:19).[68] Although Canaanite culture and religion had had an influence on the Hebrew settlers long before the era of David, in the patriarchal times and during the two centuries of the conquest of Canaan,[69] it was David's appropriation of Jerusalem as the new capital of the united kingdom which accelerated the syncretistic trend. This act of collusion with Northwest Semitic paganism profoundly affected the Hebraic theology of presence.

Just as the god El of the proto-Canaanite cult of Ugarit was thought to reside on the mythical Mt. Zaphon,[70] so also Yahweh came to dwell on Mt. Zion. Indeed, Mt. Zion and Mt. Zaphon became poetically identified (Ps. 48:2 [Heb., 3]). The presence of Yahweh among his people was no longer elusive, confined to moments of human-divine encounter. It arose from the *hagios topos*. The original nucleus of Nathan's oracle which opposed David's plan to erect a temple—Yahweh walks but does not sit down (2 Sam. 7:6)—was absorbed within a dynastic oracle on David's election and his posterity forever in Jerusalem (2 Sam. 7:8–29). The choice of Zion as the permanent residence of Yahweh on earth, as well as the divine election of David and of his dynasty in Jerusalem, became indissolubly linked in ritual and narrative alike.[71] Sang the Jerusalem musicians of a later age, possibly during a ceremonial procession of the ark:

Yahweh swore to David a truthful oath
    from which he will not repent:
"One from the fruit of thy loins
    I shall install upon thy throne.
If thy sons keep my covenant,
    and my testimonies which I shall teach them,
Their sons also forever
    shall sit upon thy throne."
For Yahweh has elected Zion,
    he has desired it for his residence:

"This is my resting place forever,
   Here shall I dwell, for I have desired it" (Ps. 132:11-14).

The second oracle quoted in this psalm, "Here I shall dwell,"
literally, "I shall sit down" (vs. 14), contradicts the theology of
Nathan's oracle opposing David's intention to build "a house
of cedar" for Yahweh (2 Sam. 7:1 ff.; cf. vs. 6). The Jerusalem
priesthood has insidiously overcome the ancient theology of
presence.[72]

David himself could hardly have been ignorant of the religious character of his political decision to make the Canaanite
fortress of Jebus the seat of his government: when he brought
the ark of Elohim to Jerusalem and danced before it, he was
girded in a linen ephod and he exposed his nudity to the crowd
(2 Sam. 6:14, 16, 20 ff.). From available evidence, it appears that
such an attire and such a display betrayed the king's submission
to the Canaanite ritual of Jebus.[73] No doubt, he was a sincere
devotee of Yahweh, but he failed to understand the specificity
of the Hebraic faith. A politician usually refrains from engaging
in the theological scrutiny of his religion. Some twenty-five
centuries later, Henry of Navarre, king of France, echoed such
an attitude when he tried to overcome, in different but not
altogether dissimilar circumstances, the opposition of fanatic
religionists; he said, "Paris vaut bien une messe!"

Still more ominous was David's purchase, from Araunah "the
Jebusite," of a high rocky terrace which dominated the city to
the north (2 Sam. 24:18). He could not have been innocent of
the cultic function of a Canaanite threshing floor. Like many
other agrarian cultures, the Northwest Semites sacralized all
the activities of farming, from ploughing and sowing to harvest-
ing and threshing.[74] The purpose of David's transaction was
precisely to "erect an altar to Yahweh on the threshing floor of
Araunah the Jebusite" (2 Samuel 24:18).

Inasmuch as the rocky hill became the site of Solomon's

temple a few years later, it may be inferred that David's earlier attempt to build for Yahweh "a house of cedar" remained in the back of his mind (cf. 2 Sam. 24:16–25 with 1 Chron. 21:15—22:1). Moreover, the sacrality of the rock probably proved irresistibly attractive in a unique way, for it was assimilated to the cosmic mountain—that is to say, to the navel of the earth. The examination of this particular aspect of the Jebusite myth, which explains the persistence of the magnetism of Zion for later Judaism, must await a brief analysis of the building of the temple of Solomon.

The Building of the Temple.

Modern historians of Israel's religion hold more sober views of Solomon's achievements than ancient readers have held. Milton's praise for the son of David who,

> ... for wealth and wisdom
> Famed, the clouded ark of God,
> Till then in tents wandering, shall
> In a glorious temple enshrine,[75]

has been superseded by a somewhat critical appraisal of the monarch's apparent motivation. In postexilic Judaism, stories were told about how, like his royal colleagues of the ancient Near East and elsewhere, Solomon obeyed a vision which revealed to him the celestial prototype of the edifice to be erected on earth.[76] Early sources are silent on this score. The fact that Solomon commissioned a Phoenician architect, Hiram of Tyre (1 Kings 7:13 f.), is sufficient to indicate the derivative and alien character of the edifice.

The sites and designs of temples have always contributed to the alteration of theological consciousness.[77] Instead of planning a sanctuary that might have expressed in visual and functional form the Hebraic theology of presence, with its peculiarity of elusive transcendence, Solomon's appointee followed the pattern of sacred architecture that was common to Palestine and Syria at the end of the second millenium B.C.[78] In any case, how could he devise a specifically Yahwistic shrine, since the Yahwistic opposition to the building of "a house of cedar," as manifested by Nathan's oracle to David (2 Sam. 7:1 ff.), most probably persisted two decades later?[79]

This is not the place for a detailed description of Solomon's temple.[80] While several aspects are still uncertain, analysis of the available data shows that its plan consisted of three rooms *en enfilade*,[81] precisely oriented toward sunrise at the equinox.[82] The innermost room rested upon the sacred rock of Araunah's threshing floor—the top of which is still visible under the dome of the Mosque of the Rock, although it was cut off irregularly in the course of the centuries. It was originally called the *Debir* (not yet "the Holy of Holies" of the postexilic temple), a word probably meaning "the Oracle," and related to chthonian divination.[83] The decoration and ornamentation were suggestive of the Canaanite forms of the fertility cult: sculpted cherubim of gigantic size standing in the innermost room,[84] pomegranates, lions, palms, and cherubim carved in ronde-bosse on the walls of the middle room "like male and female in embrace" (1 Kings 7:36c),[85] three-storied balconies for side-chambers with beds.[86]

The significance and function of the free-standing columns, Jachin and Boaz, which were placed on either sides of the entrance, remain to this day enigmatic,[87] but the Bronze Sea, resting in the temple court on twelve statues of bulls beside the main altar, clearly carried a cosmic symbolism.[88] All these features converge toward the same conclusion: David selected Araunah's threshing floor and Solomon built upon its rock a sanctuary for Yahweh because the Jebusites had for centuries looked at this site as the world center, the navel of the earth. This myth, which is common to many cultures, generally entails a number of recurrent practices, such as the cult of the Earth

Mother, male prostitution, ophiolatry, and sun worship.[89] It so happens that these practices, in spite of intermittent reforms,[90] persisted in the temple of Jerusalem until its destruction by the Babylonians in 587 B.C. A question must have arisen in the minds of many: was the temple erected by Solomon's Phoenician architect intended for the worship of Yahweh or for the worship of the sun-god?

The Consecration of the Temple.

That a state of confusion had been created in the popular mind by the ambiguities of the edifice may be inferred from the wording of the formula of consecration. At the end of the seventh century B.C., the Deuteronomic editors of the Book of Kings rewrote the details of the ceremony from the point of view which prevailed in their time, but they cited a poetic phrase which seems to be archaic:[91]

> And Solomon said:
>> [The sun! Yahweh has set in the heavens;][92]
>> He promised that he would sojourn in the thickdarkness.
>> Therefore, I have built for thee an exalted house,
>> A place for thee to dwell in forever (1 Kings 8:12–13).

In view of the historically explosive atmosphere in which the ceremony must have taken place, one should consider the choice and order of the words. In this formula, Solomon or his advisers sought to avoid the charge of syncretistic conformism, but in fact they hastened the process by which the ancient theology of elusive presence became transformed into a theology of mythicized topography.

The sun! Such was no doubt the thought which stirred the imagination of the bystanders. In line with the agrarian mysticism of Canaan, which enabled farmers to commune in the

most profound sense with the Earth Mother, it was the deified
sun, from Egypt to Mesopotamia, that exercised a truly enduring and wide-spread attraction upon the religious emotions of
the populace. The new edifice presented many of the characteristics of sun worship. At once, Solomon attempted to dis-
pel any misunderstanding.[93] He established a radical
distinction between Yahweh and the sun, which was thereby
reduced—however appreciated and even revered—to the status
of a heavenly body.[94] Without implying any particular form of
the creation myths, the phrase affirms that the sun—the most
manifestly resplendent force of nature—is utterly dependent on
Yahweh. The Hebrew Deity is the master of nature and may
never be identified with it.

Thickdarkness. The syntactic sequence between the first colon
and the second colon is not clear, as no conjunction binds the
two phrases. Should the interpreter consider the second clause
as a developing or as a corrective addition to the first? The
English term "thickdarkness" represents an approximate way
of rendering a difficult Hebrew word, *'araphel,* which designates
total and ominous obscurity, a portent of danger but also a
harbinger of life.[95] It appears in one of the narratives of the
Sinai-Horeb theophany. One of the narrators spoke of lightning and of the thick cloud which attended the descent of Yahweh upon the top of the mount. He also mentioned the *'araphel*
"where Elohim was" and which Moses dared to approach (Exod. 20:21). The term admirably fitted the ambiguity of the Hebraic theology of presence, for the meaning which it carried,
gloom, also conveyed the symbol of the hiddenness of God at
the exact moment of his proximity.

Solomon appears to have been well advised to quote this
ancient line (vs. 12) in the ceremony of consecration, for the
term could not fail to stress, at the very place which was obviously reminiscent of alien worship, the historical roots of Yahwism, and to bind Jerusalem to Sinai. On the one hand, the

motif of the *'araphel* preserved the sense of the numinous which was inherent in the holiness of Yahweh. On the other hand, it also suggested the promise of prosperity for the nation and the renewal of vegetation at the first thunderstorm in the autumn.

One should remember that the death of nature in the climate of the Canaan mountain range occurred during the summer drought, and that the new year began with the rebirth of greenness in the autumn. The festival of *'asiph,* "ingathering" or "harvest," later combined with *Sukkoth,* "tabernacles," proffered the cultic moment when an agrarian population would beg the divine master of nature to manifest his presence through the gift of rain.[96] The motif of the *'araphel* provided the symbol of a double grace: that of the election of Israel as a holy nation (Exod. 19:5 ff.) and that of the yearly miracle of vegetation, when pluvial fertilization of the soil was popularly understood as the divine insemination of the earth. Indeed, it was during the autumn festival that Solomon consecrated the temple of Yahweh (1 Kings 8:1–2).

Sojourn and Dwelling. According to the second colon of the first poetic verse of the dedication formula (vs. 12), the promise of Yahweh to sojourn in the *'araphel* is not to be construed as a commitment to dwell forever in a holy place. On the contrary, the use of the nomadic term *shaken,* originally meaning "to alight for the night," "to encamp for a time," "to sojourn," reiterates the traditional stance of Yahwism on the transience of divine manifestations.[97] Moreover, the verb *yashabh,* "to dwell," literally, "to sit down," which is used in the second verse of the poem (vs. 13*b*), is precisely that which Nathan's oracle to David emphatically placed in the negative when it stated that Yahweh walks about but does not sit down (2 Sam. 7:6). It appears that Solomon purposely attempted to link the two phrases by the adverb "therefore" in order to promote a shift of meaning toward the synonymity of the two verbs. The relation of cause and effect between Yahweh's promise and the erection of the new edifice inevitably tended to identify the 'araphel of intermittent presence with the total obscurity of the innermost room in the temple which was being consecrated. Through contextual juxtaposition, the power of innuendo was capable of transforming the notion of a nomadic transitoriness of presence into that of a cultic permanence of proximity. Yahweh dwelt in his temple. His inaccessibility to human eyes was preserved, but the worshippers' secure feeling of his residence on the rock of Zion could not fail to be a welcome one. In the course of the following centuries, the verb "to sojourn" became synonymous with the verb "to dwell" and acquired the meaning of abiding presence.[98] The temple of Jerusalem was henceforth the residence of Yahweh on earth.

By yielding to pre-Hebraic beliefs that were deeply buried in ancestral memories, Solomon was truly completing the conquest of the land.[99] Compared with the shrines of Egypt and Mesopotamia, the Jerusalem temple was a modest achievement in size and wealth, but it could not fail to appeal to the population as well as to the princes. The Jebusite belief in the pre-Davidic sacrality of Zion exercised its power of fascination in such a thorough way that it was soon incorporated within the theology of election. Yahweh had chosen the city of Jerusalem for his residence "out of all the tribes of Israel" (1 Kings 11:32) just as he had chosen "his servant David."

During the centuries which followed, the hymnists of the temple ceremonial never tired of proclaiming their belief that Zion was Yahweh's residence:

> Great is Yahweh and excellently to be praised,
>   In the city of our God, his holy mountain,
> Fair in its height, the joy of the whole earth,
>   Mount Zion, the extremities of Zaphon,
>   The citadel of the Great King! (Ps. 48:1–2 [Heb. 2–4]).[100]

To the edifice erected by Solomon, Melville's oft-quoted quatrain applies:

> Not magnitude, not lavishness,
> But form, the site;
> Not innovating wilfulness
> But reverence for the archetype.[101]

From the perspective of Yahwistic faith, the new theology of
presence which the temple of Jerusalem displayed and taught to
the Judahites, ancestors of the postexilic Jews, was "innovating
wilfulness." In fact, however, it was extremely ancient, for it
reverted to the mythic pattern of Neolithic and Bronze Age
cultus.

The Name or the Glory?

The story of the consecration of the temple reflects a long
development of theological meditation on the meaning of presence. Unlike the archaic formula of dedication (1 Kings 8:12–
13), Solomon's long prayer (vss. 22–53) incorporates the seventh-century views of the Deuteronomistic historians who edited the Book of Kings.[102]

The narrative of the introit of the ark had culminated with a
note of concreteness which appealed to the senses of the worshippers and implied the notion of God's lasting residence in
the *hagios topos:* "A cloud filled the house of Yahweh so that the
priests could not stand to minister on account of the cloud, for
the glory of Yahweh filled the house of Yahweh" (vss. 10–11).
Yet, Solomon's long prayer asked pointedly, "But will God indeed dwell on earth?" (Vs. 27). The prayer insists repeatedly
that heaven is Yahweh's dwelling place (vss. 34, 36, 39, 43, 49).
It even proclaims emphatically, "Behold, heaven and the highest heaven cannot contain thee: how much less this house!" (vs.
27b.)[103]

Once again, we witness a profound tension between two opposite views of presence: the story of the introit of the ark objectifies the psychological awareness of presence and localizes it in a man-made structure. It seeks religious certainty by attempting to revitalize the neolithic and Bronze Age myth of sacred space. Solomon's long prayer, on the contrary, attempts to safeguard a theology of spatial transcendence: it even demythicizes "heaven" as the spatial container of divinity. At the same time it accommodates to the needs of man the belief in the elusiveness of presence and recognizes within the sacred edifice a reality which justifies its construction:

> Turn to the prayer of thy servant and to his supplication, O Yahweh, my God, listening to the cry and to the prayer which thy servant prays before thee this day, that thy eyes may be open night and day toward this house, the place of which thou hast said, My name shall be there! (vss. 28–29).

Solomon does not consider "this house" as the residence of Yahweh. On the contrary, he describes it as a house for Yahweh's name. By using the theology of the name, long favored by the northern tradition, the theologians who formulated this document reflect the thinking of the Deuteronomists.[104]

Shechem and the Theology of the Name. After the death of Solomon (922 B.C.), the tribal elders of the old confederation of Israel gathered at Shechem, in the heart of Ephraim, and revolted against the rule of the Davidic dynasty (1 Kings 12:1 ff.). Rehoboam, the son of Solomon, had to journey from Jerusalem to Shechem in order to be confirmed or even "elected" there as monarch of the United Kingdom.[105]

It was at Shechem that the oak tree of the Moreh ("The Teacher" or "The Diviner") marked the "place" where, according to tradition, Abraham had first worshipped Yahweh in the land of Canaan (Gen. 12:6–7). It was at Shechem that Joshua, at the end of the thirteenth century, had celebrated a covenant ceremonial which bound various ethnic and tribal groups to Yahweh, and created in effect the Israelite League (John. 24:1 ff.). It was at Shechem that Joshua erected, in witness to this covenant, a large stone "under the oak tree which is in the sanctuary of Yahweh" (vs. 26). It was at Shechem that the bones of Joseph were buried (vs. 32).[106] It was at Shechem during the twelfth century that Abimelech made an ill-fated attempt to establish a hereditary monarchy over Israel (Judg. 9:6). It was most likely at Shechem that the early law of covenant ceremonial, now preserved in the Code of Deuteronomy (Deut. 12:1 ff.), provided for the national cult; it did so in terms of a theology of the name:[107] "You will seek the place which Yahweh your Elohim has chosen from all your tribes to set his name and make it sojourn there" (Deut. 12:5). It is no accident that the Code of Deuteronomy intimately links the worship of Yahweh to a theology of the name: The cultic perception of divine presence is inseparable from the hearing of his word, which is obedience to stipulated standards of individual and social behavior, aimed at promoting the growth of the covenant people.

As is now recognized, the Book of Deuteronomy has preserved cultic, civil, and criminal legislation which originated in the old confederation of the tribes during the days of the Judges, or at least in the kingdom of Israel which Jeroboam I created in 922 after the secession from Judah.[108] The northern and relatively ancient provenance of this body of jurisprudence, together with the absence of any mention of Jerusalem or even any implicit reference to the capital of Judah and to its temple, in addition to many other considerations—such as the concern of Deuteronomy for Sechem and Mt. Garizim, and the affinities of its legal tradition with the Elohistic traditions—converges to suggest that the theology of the name was nurtured in the old cultic center of Shechem.

It will be remembered that the Code of the Covenant, probably promulgated at Shechem, had conceived the presence as "coming" to any place where Yahweh "caused his name to be remembered" (Exod. 20:24).[109] This archaic law of the altar implied an understanding of communion between God and man in which the offering of a sacrifice in the context of prayer was independent from the archetypal myth of space. At the same time, the Code of the Covenant also included a law concerning the seasonal feasts, which prescribed that every Israelite male had to go up three times a year "to appear in the presence of Yahweh" (Exod. 23:17). Such a prescription implies the existence of a central shrine, perhaps an exclusive sanctuary, at an early date.

Within the same tradition of worship, the Deuteronomic law unambiguously demanded that the nation gather at a single, unnamed site, "the place which Yahweh chooses to set his name there for its sojourn" (Deut. 12:5).[110] It thus appears that, in the North as well as in the South religionists developed a notion of cultic presence that was charged with a quality of permanence and which was also spatially limited. In the North, however, the presence of the Deity was not conceived as if it were inescapably and intrinsically bound to the realm of geographical location. It depended on the divine decision to send the divine name in such a place "for its sojourn" (vs. 5). The name stood for a religious phenomenon of considerable complexity, which blended divine initiative and human response: the word "name" appears to have been a device for designating Yahweh's will to create a holy people within the history of mankind and at the same time Israel's acceptance of this election.[111] It is therefore not correct to state that the divine name "verges closely upon an hypostasis,"[112] for the reality which the word designates implies the cultic congress and the participation of man in the perspective of time. To speak of a place where the name of Yahweh sojourns is to refer to the ceremonial of a congregation at worship. The name cannot be divorced from the divine purpose in history nor can it be separated from the interaction which is wrought in the participants by the acts of their adoration: sacrificial meals and offerings, prayers, hymns, and recitals of the *Opus Dei*. Such an interaction also involves the renewal of the worshippers' commitment to obey the words of the covenant in their secular existence. A theology of the name implies a presence which transcends the *hagios topos*, for it involves the prolongation of the cult in a particular mode of behavior outside the shrine.

It was in full agreement with the implications of this understanding of cultic presence that the Deuteronomists gave a meaning to the ark that differed dramatically from that of the Holy War tradition.[113] They called the ancient palladium "the ark of the covenant," and they conceived it as a container for the tablets of the Ten Words (Deut. 10:1–5).[114] Such a view was entirely congruent with their theology of the name, which required both hearing and obedience to a standard of ethical behavior in the secular world. It stressed the ear rather than the eye, for it promoted a faith in which man sought to translate his love for God into his own conduct as a member of society.

In Deuteronomy, the dedication of the self is immediately linked with the proclamation of the name. As the name is heard, so man loves. This at least is one of the meanings of the *Shema'*:

"Hear, O Israel, Yahweh, our Elohim, Yahweh is One,
 And thou shalt love Yahweh thy Elohim with thy whole mind,
 and with thy whole drive for self-preservation,
 and with the "muchness" of thy whole being" (Deut. 6:4–5).[115]

It is also on account of their theology of the name that the Deuteronomists reinterpreted the northern traditions concerning the theophany of Yahweh at Mt. Horeb. In reciting the national epic, they took great care to reserve the use of the sense of sight for the witnessing of historical events, which in turn constituted manifestations of Yahweh's presence in history.[116] At the same time, they deliberately denied that Moses— and a fortiori, the people—had ever been granted a vision of God himself.

It is impossible to miss the intention of the narrator when he recalls, on the one hand, "Your eyes have seen what Yahweh did at Baal-Peor" (Deut. 4:3) and when he evokes, on the other hand, the "spectacular" yet invisible descent of Yahweh upon the summit of the mountain:

> You came near and you stood at the foot of the mountain while the mountain was burning with fire to the heart of heaven, yet wrapped in the darkness, in the cloud, and in the thickdarkness (*'araphel*). Then Yahweh spoke to you, out of the midst of the fire; you heard the sound of words, but you saw no form. There was only a voice. And he proclaimed to you his covenant, which he commanded you to perform, that is, the ten words (Deut. 4:11– 13).

The theology of the name affirms the sense of hearing at the expense of the sense of seeing. When the inquiring mind confronted the problem of revelation, the Deuteronomists offered him a cultic *anamnesis* which brought into the liturgical present the historical moment of the national birth. They said that God discloses his will for man but remains inaccessible to his sight. In so far as the human faculty of cognitive reason was associated with the sense of sight, the theologians of the name affirmed that God stands close to, but not within, the grasp of man. For man, communion with God cannot mean the possibility of exercising, at will, his own power against the divine power. According to the theology of the name, man receives sufficient knowledge of God when he hears the word which he is bidden to obey in his daily life.

Such an interpretation of presence led to ethical consciousness and responsibility. The laws of Deuteronomy were prefaced with the hearing of the name. In the words of Paul Tillich, "the presence of the divine in the name demands a shy and trembling heart." The name "is never an empty sound; it is a bearer of power; it gives Spiritual Presence to the unseen."[118]

Jerusalem and the Theology of Glory. Josiah's Reform of the cult of Yahweh in the temple of Jerusalem under the influence of the Deuteronomic theology of the name was short lived.[119] A long-ingrained theology of glory in Zion had prevailed ever since the foundation of the temple. The consecration ceremony had clearly promoted the notion of indwelling presence.[120] Even though the archaic formula of dedication (1 Kings 8:12–13) had affirmed the nomadic concept of sojourn, it had slanted this concept by assimilating it to that of sedentary inhabitation: Yahweh was invited to "sit forever in an exalted house."[121]

In the eighth century the prophet Amos, who had worked for a while among the shepherds from Teqoa in the far south, or at least the prophetic circles of Judah which preserved his poems, took it for granted that, on the last day of history,

"Yahweh [would] roar from Zion,
    from Jerusalem he [would] sound his voice" (Amos 1:2).[122]

It was in the temple of Jerusalem a few years later that the prophet Isaiah had a vision which summoned him to a special calling (Isa. 6:1–13), but his position toward the temple was ambivalent. He exploded the priestly notion of a divine glory that dwelled within the sacred space, for he heard the seraphim sing, in the presence of Yahweh:

"The whole of the earth is filled with his glory" (vs. 3).[123]

Furthermore, he demythicized the sacrality of the Rock. By

coining the metaphor of the living corner stone, Isaiah interiorized the notion of sacred space. Nevertheless, Zion remained important, for it was the place—the geographical location—in which God would raise the new community of the faithful:

> Therefore, thus says Adonay Elohim:
>   Behold: I am about to lay[124] in Zion a stone,
>   A tested stone, the corner-stone of the splendid glory,[125]
>   As a foundation that is solidly based:
>   He who has faith shall not be anxious (Isa. 28:16).

The quality of the faith in Yahweh—the dynamic attitude of trust which was inherited from the old Yahwistic tradition concerning the epiphanic visitation to Abraham (Gen. 15:6)—was reinterpreted as the constitutive element of a new society: the seat of divine presence is man.[126]

At the same time, the prophet conformed to the language of his time and perhaps even maintained the ancient belief when he referred to

"Yahweh of Hosts, who dwells on Mt. Zion" (Isa. 8:18).[127]

Isaiah's hope, however, is otherworldly. He expected that, at the end of time,—beyond the historical economy of human existence—a new Jerusalem would be the rallying point for all the nations of the earth (2:2 ff. etc.).[128]

The theology of real presence in the sanctuary continued to flourish in Jerusalem. According to a tradition of the Isaianic school, King Hezekiah, having received a threatening letter from the Assyrian emperor, Sennhacherib, "went up to the temple [in order to] spread it *before Yahweh*" (2 Kings 19:14).

The New Jerusalem and the Theology of the Name. At the end of the seventh century, the prophet Jeremiah was compelled by his prophetic mission to announce the destruction of the temple

(Jer. 7:1 ff., 26:6 ff.), but he apparently was torn between the demands of his oracular vocation and his devotion to the temple ideology of permanent presence. The collection of his poems includes a communal lament in which he seemed to espouse the people's beliefs:

"Hast thou utterly rejected Judah?
    Does thy very being loathe Zion? . . .
Do not despise us, for the sake of thy name,
    do not dishonor the throne of thy glory!" (Jer. 14:19a, 21.)[129]

It is unlikely that this psalm of complaint would have been composed by the prophet, for it isolates from any ethical consideration the ideology of "the throne" of the divine "glory," a language that is typical of the Jerusalem priesthood. The prophet's condemnation of the temple was not only couched in the style of the Deuteronomic theology of the name but also revealed the moral sensitivity which was characteristic of his entire interpretation of life outside as well as inside the sanctuary:

"Has this house, in which my name is invoked,
    become a den of robbers in your eyes?
Behold, I myself have seen it, says Yahweh" (Jer. 7:11).[130]

The choice of words in the exordium of the temple sermon implies a sarcastic reversal of the notion of presence:

"Thus says Yahweh of Hosts, the Elohim of Israel,
Improve your ways and your actions,
    and I shall let you dwell in this place!" (Jer. 7:3.)

The question was no longer whether Yahweh would continue to dwell (shaken) in the hagios topos, but rather whether he would allow worshippers who are devoid of morality to remain there. Even if this document had been composed by the Deuteronomistic editors of the book of Jeremiah, the thought expressed corresponds to the theological sharpness of the prophet's mind and bears the formal marks of his language. Like Isaiah a century before him, Jeremiah displaced the myth of Zion from the belief in the sacrality of a rock to the belief in the holiness of presence among men. He demythologized space for the sake of time. He raised the status of sanctuary from the level of the para-magical to that of the religious. He did not deny the importance of the holy place as a stage for promoting the temporal possibility of a divine-human encounter, but he attacked the people's trust because it was misdirected to the house. He polemized not against the institution of the temple as such but against the people's confusion of the relative and the absolute. He thus contributed to the refinement of the meaning of faith, which resists man's ancestral quest for crude certainty through territorial possessiveness, sensual perception, or in other times and cultures, the finite power of reason.

Jeremiah's interpretation of presence—which finds the temple useful but not indispensable—enabled the Judahites to survive the disruption caused by the Babylonian exile and especially the trauma produced by the destruction of the temple in 587 B.C. Jeremiah was the unwitting creator of Diaspora Judaism.

After the first surrender of Jerusalem to Nebuchadnezzar in 597 B.C., the elite of the population was exiled to Lower Mesopotamia, but Jeremiah was left behind with the working classes under King Zedekiah's government, which was submissive to Babylon.[131]

The prophet sent a letter to those first exiles in which he advised them to settle down in the foreign and impure land.[132] More extraordinarily still, he wrote them, in the name of Yahweh: "Seek the welfare of the city where I sent you into exile, and pray to Yahweh on its behalf . . . " (29:7a). A thousand miles from Jerusalem, Jeremiah proclaimed the thesis of the accessibility of Yahweh to prayer. He proposed the formula of a religious community living and prospering in a totally alien environment (vss. 4-6). By so doing, he implicitly initiated a mode of divine presence which was independent of the temple and eventually came to fruition in the synagogue. Judaism was born. The Judahites in exile had become the Jews.

To be sure, the prophet also predicted the eventual return to Jerusalem of these first exiles: "For thus says Yahweh: When seventy years are completed in Babylon, I will visit you and fulfil my promise to you and bring you back to this place . . . to give you a future and a hope" (29:10). It is clear from the context that the role of "this place" will be subjected to a prior reality: the immediacy of presence: "Then you will call on me, come and pray to me, and I will hear you. You will seek me and find me; when you seek me with the whole of your heart, I will be found of you, says Yahweh" (vss. 13-14a).

At an earlier time, Jeremiah had so clearly anticipated the annihilation of the temple that he had referred without apparent qualm to the total disappearance of the ark—that ancient palladium of the theologoumenon of glory: "In those days, says Yahweh, they shall no more say, 'The ark of the covenant of Yahweh!' It shall not come to mind, or be remembered, or missed; it shall not be made again" (3:16bc). This oracle shows that the prophet's interpretation of the new mode of presence exploded the confines of an edifice to include the wholly human reality of a new society: "At that time, Jerusalem shall be called 'The Throne of Yahweh,' and all the nations shall gather to it, *to the name of Yahweh, to Jerusalem*" (3:17).[133] A number of commentators render the last phrase, "to the *presence* of Yahweh in Jerusalem."

In any case, after the final catastrophe of 587 B.C., Jeremiah apparently did not announce the rebuilding of the temple, even in a suprahistorical and otherworldly economy of existence. At the end of his life, he did contemplate in the oracle of the new covenant the prospect of a radical transformation of human nature, but he remained silent about a new temple.[134]

> Behold, the days are coming, says Yahweh, when I will make a new covenant with the house of Israel and the house of Judah, . . . I will place my law within them and I will write it upon their hearts; and I will be their God and they shall be my people. And no longer shall every man teach his neighbor, every man his brother, saying, Know Yahweh! For they shall all know me, from the least of them to the greatest, says Yahweh (31:31, 33–34).

The new mode of existence implied by this prediction made all the agencies of cult superfluous. The will of Yahweh was to be imprinted upon the will of men. Presence and covenant were to coalesce in a new creation that would transcend the disobedience, disease of the will, and guilt of the historical covenant people. To know Yahweh was to mean to live in his presence—immediate, continuous, and common to all members of the new society. In the subsequent oracle on the rebuilding of the city (31:38–40), if indeed it is Jeremianic, the prophet described, within the concreteness of "this earth", the advent of the kingdom of God upon "a new earth." The new Jerusalem was to belong to a new nature.

The New Jerusalem and the Theology of Glory. The language and the thought of Ezekiel, Jeremiah's younger contemporary, were different. A temple priest (Ezek. 1:1), he had been deported to Babylon with the first exiles of 597 B.C., but he received the prophetic vocation to minister to his fellow exiles in 592 B.C., five years before the destruction of Jerusalem (587 B.C.). On the one hand, Ezekiel belonged to the tradition of the great prophets, from Amos to Jeremiah, for he courageously asserted that a corrupt nation would not survive. On the other hand, he spoke as a temple priest, and he was apparently more concerned with pagan syncretism and cultic impurity than with moral abuses or social injustice. Significantly, he thought of presence in terms of a theology of glory.

Far from Zion, the prophet saw in a trance the acts of idolatrous worship performed in the Jerusalem temple. He told of "the altar of the image of pleasure," in all likelihood a phallic object (8:5),[135] of the ophiolatric rites (8:9–10),[136] of the ceremonial weeping for Tammuz (8:14),[137] and of the ceremonial of adoration for the sun-god (8:16).[138] He knew that "the glory of the Elohim of Israel was there" still (8:4), but he understood that "these great abominations" would soon drive away that glory from a profaned sanctuary (8:6). Thereupon, he was granted a preview of "the departure of the glory of Yahweh."[139]

The stylistic and thematic features of the account were similar to those of the narrative on the introit of the ark in the temple of Solomon (1 Kings 8:10–11). However, the word cherubim referred no longer to cultic statues standing in the innermost room. The cherubim appeared in Ezekiel as mythical beings with wings.[140] They carried the glory in its ascent away from the shrine. First they hovered for a moment over the east gate of the temple court, as if hesitating to leave, and then they flew eastward in the direction of the Mount of Olives (10:3 ff.)— where, it will be recalled, Christian folklore, centuries later, placed the ascension of the living Lord (Acts 1:12).

Like Jeremiah, but from a divergent perspective, Ezekiel recognized that geographical distance from Zion did not necessarily mean absence from Yahweh. Nevertheless, he was unable to speak of divine presence in a foreign land except by using a metaphorical language derived from the institution of the temple: "Thus says Adonay Yahweh, although I removed them far away among the nations, . . . yet have I been, for a little while, a sanctuary to them in the countries where they have gone" (11:16). For the priest-prophet, communing with the Deity was in effect identical with adoring Yahweh in his temple.[141] If no sanctuary was available, the psychological mode of presence was expressed in terms of a spiritualized shrine.

The dominant trait of Ezekiel's temperament and cultural makeup was so inescapably cultic that the promise of hope which he proclaimed to his fellow exiles culminated in the vision of a new temple (40:1—48:35). His description was so minute and elaborate that architects have been able to make models of this ideal edifice that was never built.

The people of the new presence were to be delivered from the vicissitudes of historical relativity. Ezekiel's eschatology remained in the realm of otherworldly myth, for it looked forward to a stage of human existence which would stand beyond nature as well as beyond history. The waters of grace, reminiscent of the rivers flowing from Paradise, would burst forth out of the entrance of the new temple court, cause the desert of Judah to bloom, and purify the salty sterility of the Dead Sea (47:9). The prophet himself said that the new land would be "like the garden of Eden" (36:35).

In terms that are in some ways similar to those of the Jeremianic understanding of the new covenant (Jer. 31:31 ff.), Ezekiel discerned that the inner nature of man would need to be radically transformed. He proposed a novel principle for the correlation of divine presence with human volition by juxtaposing his prediction of God's tabernacle in the midst of men with the doctrine of the indwelling spirit of God.[142]

On the one hand, Ezekiel spoke of an everlasting presence which would be concomitant with an everlasting covenant of peace:

> I will make a covenant of peace with them: it shall be an everlasting covenant with them and I will make gifts to them and multiply them, and I will set my sanctuary in the midst of them forever. My tabernacle (*mishkan*) shall be in the midst of them forever. And I will be their God and they shall be my people, and the nations shall

know that I, Yahweh, will make Israel holy when my sanctuary shall
be in the midst of them forever (37:26–28).

On the other hand, he spiritualized the presence without rendering the temple superfluous:

> A new heart also will I give you and a new spirit will I put within
> you; and I will take away the heart of stone out of your flesh, and
> I will put my spirit within you, and cause you to walk in my statutes
> (*ḥuqqîm*) and to be careful to observe my ordinances (*mishpaṭim*).
> You shall dwell in the land which I gave to your fathers, and you
> shall be my people, and I will be your God (36:26–28).

The ethical element may not have been absent from the
prophet's thought, but it was not spelled out. Moreover, the
ambiguous words "statutes" and "ordinances" were likely to
receive only a ritual interpretation since the announcement of
the gift of the divine spirit was embedded within the promise
of a lustral purification: "I will sprinkle water of purity over you
and cleanse you from all your impurities" (36:25; cf. 36:29).
Through a prophet of the Jeremianic type, Yahweh would have
said, "I will forgive you all your iniquities" (cf. Jer. 31:34). While
Jeremiah spoke of a presence through which men would
"know" Yahweh, thus promoting the genuine *theologia* of Hosea
(*daʿat Elohim*), Ezekiel spoke of a presence through which Israel
would be made holy.

It was not by coincidence that his vision of the new presence
continued to be permeated with the theologoumenon of glory:
"And behold, the glory of the Elohim of Israel came from the
east, and the sound of his coming was like that of mighty waters,
and the earth shone with his glory" (43:2). Ezekiel apparently
meant that the full reality of the Godhead would inhabit the new
temple. Allusions to the primeval waters[143] and to the shining
brightness of the glory[144] show affinities with the priestly myth

of creation in Genesis (1:2–3). The motif of the effulgence which will illumine the earth may also have been associated with the shining face of Moses in the priestly narrative of his conversation with Elohim (Exod. 34:30).[145]

At the same time, Ezekiel's insistence in comparing the vision of the return of the glory (43:3) not only with the previous vision of its departure (9:1 ff.) but also with his inaugural vision of the heavenly chariot supporting "a likeness as it were of a human form" (1:26) reinforces the thesis of his kinship with the Jerusalem priesthood.[146] Furthermore, he revived the mythology of the Holy War with which the theologoumenon of glory through the ark was originally connected and he adapted it to the situation of his time. How could he prevent his contemporary Judahites, decimated, buffeted, and humiliated, from falling prey to heathenish conformism?

Looking backward, the Deuteronomists in the seventh century had summoned the mythology of the Holy War to express their fears of cultic and cultural disintegration: had the populations of the land been exterminated, Israel would have been protected from their pagan superstitions.[147] Looking forward, Ezekiel in the sixth century summoned the mythology of the Holy War to buttress his hope that the recreated people would be forever safe from the risk of cultic and cultural contamination.

As a preface to the rebuilding of the temple—rather, to the building of an entirely new temple—Ezekiel sketched the lurid scenario of a cosmic battle against Gog, king of Magog (38:1 ff.), at the culmination of which Yahweh "would set [his] glory among the nations" (39:21).[148] It is in this eschatological context that one may discern an underground link in Ezekiel's thinking which united *glory* and *apartness*. He overreacted to the syncretism of Solomon's temple cultus and to the temptations of the Babylonian environment. His understanding of sin led him to stress the fear of physical contacts with sources of ritual impurity—especially corpses and foreigners—at the expense of ethical sensitivity to social injustice and inhumanity to man.[149] His persistent concern—not to say his obsessiveness—with the ritual uncleanness of blood and sexual secretions played a part in the cultic degradation of womanhood in Judaism.[150] It was most likely in the school of Ezekiel that the descendants of the Jerusalem priests in exile edited and formalized the traditions of the Holiness Code (Lev. 17:1 ff.)[151] as well as the priestly stories concerning the desert tabernacle—the dwelling place of glory.[152]

In divergent ways, Jeremiah and Ezekiel were able to convince the deportees that, although Yahweh had left his temple desolate, his presence had not abandoned them. Hebrew faith, at the dawn of Judaism, was evolving a new theology of presence. Other factors played a part in this religious development. The confessions and sermons of the great prophets were being written and published; the songs of the temple musicians were being collected and sung; the poem of Job was being chanted as a paracultic drama for the New Year festival. Judaism in its infancy was discovering a new dimension of presence: the prophetic vision, the psalmodic communion, and the sapiential reflection.

Notes

1. See W. Andrae, *Das Gotteshaus und die Urformen des Bauens im Alten Orient* (Berlin, 1930); H. H. Nelson et al., "The Significance of the Temples in the Ancient Near East," *BA*, VII (1944); 41 ff.; = *The Biblical Archaeological Reader* (Garden City, N.Y., 1961), pp. 145 ff.; R. E. Clements, "Sacred Mountains, Temples and the Presence of God," *God and Temple* (1965), pp. 1 ff.; G. Barrois, "Temples," *IDB*, IV, 560 ff.;

2. Siegfried Sassoon, "The Heart's Journey, IX," *Collected Poems* (London, 1947), p. 179.
3. Some scholars have maintained that Mt. Sinai was to be viewed as the permanent abode of Yahweh. It is true that the poetic memory of Israel, for several centuries, alluded to the coming of Yahweh from the deep South (Judg. 5:4–5; cf. Ps. 68:8, 17 [Heb. 9, 18], Deut. 33:2, Hab. 3:3). At the same time, one has no right

to correct the Hebrew text in Deut. 33:16 to read, "The one who inhabited Sinai" (*sinay*) instead of "the bush" (*seneh*, an allusion to Exod. 3:2). Moreover, the Mt. Horeb theophany narrative plainly states that Yahweh "came" and "descended" upon the mountain (Exod. 19:18, 20).

4. The ark has been the object of intensive discussion. See J. Gutmann, "The History of the Ark," *ZAW*, LXX (1971): 22 ff.; J. Jeremias, "Lade und Zion. Zur Entstehung der Zion-tradition," in H.-W. Wolff, ed., *Probleme biblischer Theologie* [*Festschrift G. von Rad*] (München, 1971); R. Schmitt, *Zelt und Lade als Thema alttestamentlicher Theologie* (Gütersloh, 1972).

5. The Deuteronomic attempt to associate the ark with the covenant and especially with the stones of the Ten Words radically transformed the military character of the ark in ancient times. Some commentators maintain that the Deuteronomic interpretation may be faithful to an ancient practice. It is pointed out, for example, that ancient Near Eastern sanctuaries contained receptacles for the preservation of documents. In Egypt, the sixty-fourth chapter of *The Book of the Dead* was supposedly found on a slab of alabaster under the feet of the god Thot, while a letter of Ramses II states that his treaty with a Hittite king was placed under the feet of the god Ra (See R. de Vaux, *Les institutions de l'Ancien Testament*, II [Paris, 1960], p. 132). Similar customs have been observed elsewhere. They may help to explain the origin of the Deuteronomic interpretation, but they do not demonstrate in any way the antiquity of the Deuteronomic tradition.

6. 1 Sam. 3:3, 6:1; 2 Sam. 6:2; 1 Kings 19:15; etc.

7. The Priestly writers may have preserved a kernel of accuracy when they described the ark's dimensions (54 x 27 x 27 inches) and material (accacia wood).

8. See G. von Rad, *Der heilige Krieg im alten Israel* (Zürich, 1951); P. C. Craigie, "Yahweh Is a Man of War," *SJT*, XXII (1967):

185 ff.; F. M. Cross, "The Divine Warrior in Israel's Early Cult," in A. Altmann, ed., *Biblical Motifs* (Cambridge, Mass., 1969), pp. 14 ff.; *id.*, *Canaanite Myth and Hebrew Epic* (Cambridge, Mass., 1973), pp. 105 f.; 226 ff.; R. Smend, *Yahweh War & Tribal Confederation*, tr. by M. G. Rogers (Nashville, 1970), pp. 27 ff.; F. Stolz, *Jahwes und Israels Kriege: Kriegs Theorien und Kriegserfahrungen im Glauben des alten Israel* (Zürich, 1972); P. D. Miller, *The Divine Warrior in Early Israel* (Cambridge, Mass., 1973).

9. Psychoanalytical research has shown that chests, caskets, coffins, and other boxes are to be interpreted as portable substitutes for sacred caves, or at least as indicative of the craving for the protection of the maternal womb. See A. B. Ulanov, *The Feminine in Jungian Psychology and in Christian Theology* (Evanston, Ill., 1971), pp. 157 f., and the works quoted in notes 25 and 26. Whether the ark of Yahweh was originally related to the archetypal unconscious of the chthonian feminine principle escapes present demonstration but deserves further investigation. In later times, the ark became associated in Solomon's temple with various objects and rites that suggest the worship of *Terra Mater*. See S. Terrien, "The Omphalos Myth and Hebrew Religion," *VT*, XX (1970): 315 ff.

10. See A. Musil, *The Manners and Customs of the Rwala Bedouins* (New York, 1928), pp. 521 ff.; H. Lammens, *L'Arabie occidentale avant l'Hégire* (Beyrouth, 1928), Pp. 100 ff.; J. Morgenstern, "The Ark, the Ephod and the Tent," *HUCA*, XVII (1942 –43): 207 ff.; R. de Vaux, *Les institutions de l'Ancien Testament*, II, pp. 125 ff.; cf. Hebr. *qubbah*, generally rendered "domed tent," used once as a synonym for the *'ohel mo'ed* by the priestly writers (Num. 25:8).

11. The Egyptian god Amun, personification of the wind, was probably represented at times by an empty container, symbol of captured wind or air. See K.

Sethe, *Amun und die acht Urgötter von Hermopolis* (Berlin, 1929), pp. 60, 98 f., etc.

12. In connection with quotations of short songs which are probably as ancient as the Song of the Ark (Num. 21:14–15; cf. vss. 17–17, 27–30).

13. The only other reference to the ark in the ancient traditions of the Pentateuch (Num. 14:14) also belongs to a military context. Moses had opposed an attempt to invade the hill country against the Amalekites and the Canaanites, saying, "Yahweh will not be in your midst" (vs. 42) or "with you" (vs. 43). The text adds that neither the ark nor Moses departed from the camp on that occasion.

14. Some reliable elements of tradition have been identified within the late redaction of Joshua, chs. 3—6. See F. Langlamet, *Gilgal et les récits de la traversée du Jourdain, Jos. III–IV* (Paris, 1969), pp. 16 ff., 86 ff., 104 ff.; J. Maier, *Das altisraelitische Ladeheiligtum* (Berlin, 1965), pp. 4 ff.; J. A. Soggin, *Le livre de Josué* (Neuchâtel, 1970), pp. 45 ff.

15. See S. Holm-Nielsen, "Shiloh in the Old Testament," in M.-L. Buhl et al., *The Danish Excavations at Tall Sailun* (Copenhagen, 1969), pp. 56–59, especially note 289.; cf. H. Kjaer, *The Excavations of Shilo, the Place of Eli and Samuel* (Jerusalem, 1930).

16. G. von Rad ignores the verb in the expression, "And Yahweh came." See "The Tent and the Ark," *The Problem of the Hexateuch and Other Essays,* tr. by E. W. Trueman Dicken (Edinburgh and London, 1965), p. 108.

17. 1 Sam. 3:3, 10; 4:4, 7; 2 Sam. 6:2; 2 Kings 19:14–15; cf. Jer. 3:16–17; Ezek. 43:7.

18. *Contra* Cross, *Canaanite Myth*, p. 69.

19. 2 Sam. 22:11–12 = Ps. 18:10–11 [Heb., 11–12].

20. 1 Kings 6:23 ff, 8:6 f.; See M. Haran, "The Ark and the Cherubim: Their Cultic Significance in Biblical Ritual," *IEJ*, IX (1959): 32 ff.; cf. W. McKane, "The Earlier History of the Ark," *Glasgow University Oriental Society Transactions*, XXI (1965–66): 68 ff.; R. E. Clements, *God and Temple,* pp. 30–36: cf. H. Gressmann, "Die Kerube im Tempel Salomos überhaupt," *Die Lade Jahves* (Stuttgart, 1920), pp. 47 ff.

21. According to the reading of LXX[B] (*Vaticanus*); the Masoretic text reflects the anachronistic terminology of a later age, "The ark of the covenant of Yahweh."

22. 2 Sam. 6:1 ff. David apparently respected the nomadic origin of the ark for "he set it in its place, inside the tent which David had pitched for it" (2 Sam. 6:17).

23. This hypothesis is strengthened by the presence of several allusions to processional outings of the ark during the four centuries of the monarchy (ca. 950–587 B.C.). See A. Bentzen, "The Cultic Use of the Story of the Ark in Samuel," *JBL*, LVII (1948): 317 ff.; D. R. Hillers, "Ritual Procession of the Ark and Ps. 132," *CBQ* XXX (1968): 48 ff.; Cross, *Canaanite Myth*, pp. 96 ff.; 242 ff.; cf. R. A. Carlson, *David, the Chosen King: A Traditio-Historical Approach to the Second Book of Samuel* (Stockholm, 1964), pp. 62 ff.; 77 ff.; 85 ff.; E. F. Campbell, *The Ark Narrative (1 Sam. 4—6, 2 Sam. 6): A Form-Critical and Traditio-Historical Study* (Missoula, Mont., 1975), p. 117 ff.

24. David's dancing before the ark may well have been also due to his political flair, for he must have known the significance of ritual dance for the Canaanites of Jebus. See J. Pedersen, *Israel, Its Life and Culture, III–IV* (Oxford and Copenhagen, 1940), p. 759; C. H. Gordon, "David the Dancer," *Y. Kaufmann Jubilee Volume* (Jerusalem, 1960), pp. 46 ff.; G. Ahlström, *Aspects of Syncretism in Israelite Religion* (Lund, 1963), pp. 34 ff.; J. H. Eaton, "Dancing in the Old Testament," *ET*, LXXXVI (1974–75): 1369 ff.

25. The expression, "the ark of the covenant," is never found in the early traditions. It becomes common usage only in the seventh century B.C. with the Deuteronomists (Deut. 10:8; 31:9, 25; Josh. 4:7; 6:8; 1 Sam. 4:4; etc.).

26. The king was of course aware of the central significance of the Shechem sanctuary for the tribal confederation of Israel, but he probably exploited the Jebusite myth of Zion in an attempt to make of Jerusalem the rallying point between Israel proper and the southern tribe of Judah. See S. Terrien, "The Omphalos Myth and Hebrew Religion," *VT*, XX (1970): 316 ff.

27. See W. Beyerlin, *Origins and History of the Oldest Sinaitic Traditions*, tr. by S. Rudman (Oxford, 1965), pp. 31 ff.; cf. M. Newman, *The People of the Covenant* (New York & Nashville, 1962), pp. 60 ff.; D. R. Hillers, "Ritual Procession of the Ark and Ps 132," *CBQ*, XXX (1968): 48 ff.; Cross, *Canaanite Myth*, pp. 94 ff.

28. See L. Rost, *Die Überlieferung von der Thronnachfolge* (Stuttgart, 1926), pp. 47 ff. M. Simon, "La prophétie de Nathan et le temple (Remarques sur II Sam. 7)," *RHPR*, XXXII (1952): 41 ff.; M. Noth, "David und Israel in II Sam. 7," *Mélanges bibliques A. Robert* (Paris, 1957), pp. 122 ff. = "David and Israel in II Samuel VII," in *The Laws in the Pentateuch and Other Studies*, tr. by D. R. Ap-Thomas (Edinburgh and London, 1966), pp. 250 ff.; G. W. Ahlström, "Der Prophet Nathan und der Tempelbau," *VT*, XI (1961): 8 ff.; H. W. Hertzberg, "House of God and House of David," *I&II Samuel: A Commentary*, tr. by J. S. Bowder (Philadelphia, 1964), pp. 281 ff.; A. Weiser, "Die Tempelbaukrise unter David," *ZAW*, LXXVII (1965): 153 ff.; cf. H. van den Bussche, "Le texte de la prophétie de Nathan sur la dynastie davidique," *ALBO*, II, 7 (1948); A Caquot, "La prophétie de Nathan et ses échos lyriques," *SVT*, IX (1962): 213 ff.

29. G. Widengren, "King and Covenant," *JSS*, II (1957): 1 ff.; A. H. J. Gunneweg, "Sinaibund und Davidsbund," *VT*, X (1960): 335 ff.; M. Tsevat, "Studies in the Book of Samuel, III. The Steadfast House: What was David Promised in II Sam. 7: 11b–16?" *HUCA*, XXXIV (1963): 71 ff.; H. Gese, "Der Davidsbund

und die Zionserwählung," *ZTK*, LXI (1964): 10 ff.; Clements, *God and Temple* pp. 40 ff.; *id.*, *Prophecy and Covenant* (London, 1965), pp. 153 ff. J. A. Soggin, *Das Königtum in Israel* (Berlin, 1967), pp. 73, 123.

30. See O. Eissfeldt, "Jahwe als König," *ZAW*, XLVI (1928): 81 ff.; G. E. Mendenhall, "Early Israel as the Kingdom of Yahweh," *The Tenth Generation: The Origins of the Biblical Tradition* (Baltimore, 1973), pp. 29 f.

31. Lit., "in a tent" ('*ohel*) "and in a sojourning camp" (*mishkan*). The latter word was used by the priestly writers to designate the "tabernacle," the model of the desert shrine as they conceived it during the Babylonian exile (possibly earlier). They knew the archaic distinction between *yashabh*, "to sit" or "to dwell," and *shaken*, "to sojourn" (hence, the synonymity of *mishkan* and '*ohel* in ancient times, "tent"). Cf. A. Weiser, "Die Tempelbaukrise," p. 159, note 19; F. M. Cross, *Canaanite Myth*, pp. 245 f.

32. MT, *shibhṭê*, "tribes"; cf. 1 Chron. 17:6, *shôphᵉṭê*, "judges." However, see Ph. de Robert, "Juges ou tribus en 2 Samuel VII 7?" *VT*, XXI (1971): 116–18.

33. See below, chapter V: The Hebrew invaders built altars at many places in the land of Canaan, and the legislation of the time of the conquest reflects their awareness of Yahweh's presence in their midst at the moment of worship (Exod. 20:24; cf. J. J. Stamm, "Zum Altargesetz im Bundesbuch," *TZ*, I (1945): 304–06). Nevertheless, the idea of erecting a new edifice for Yahweh's abode represented a radical departure with the past. At the same time, the appropriation of the house of Baalberith in Shechem (Judg. 9:4) and of the Canaanite shrine at Shiloh—later remembered as "the temple of Yahweh" (1 Sam. 1:9) and even "the house of Yahweh" (1 Sam. 3:15; cf. Jer. 26:6)—points to a process of pagan corruption in which David participated, perhaps unconsciously.

34. M. J. Buss, "The Psalms of Asaph and Korah," *JBL*, LXXXII (1963): p. 385.

35. Cf. Pss. 71:8, 89:18, 96:8, etc.

36. See F. M. Cross, "Notes on a Canaanite Psalm in the Old Testament," *BASOR*, no. 117 (1950): 19 ff.; yet cf. B. Margulis, "The Canaanite Origin of Psalm 29 Reconsidered," *Biblica*, LI (1970): 332 ff.

37. Traditionally rendered, "in the beauty of holiness"; cf. P. R. Ackroyd, "Some Notes on the Psalms," *JTS*, XVI (1966): 392 ff.

38. See S. Terrien, *The Psalms and their Meaning for Today* (Indianapolis, 1952), pp. 41 ff.; A. Weiser, *The Psalms* (Philadelphia, 1959), pp. 263 ff.; H.-J. Kraus, *Psalmen* (Neukirchen, 1959–60), pp. 238 ff.

39. Lit., "the man of war," "the war hero."

40. See Cross, *Canaanite Myth*, pp. 98 ff.

41. See T. E. Fretheim, "The Ark in Deuteronomy," *CBQ*, XXX (1968): 1 ff. It is not known whether this interpretation of the ark was ever translated into reality. Some scholars conjecture that there were several arks in the course of the centuries and that the ark containing the tables of the law was introduced in the temple of Jerusalem by King Josiah in 621 B.C. See J. Gutmann, "The History of the Ark," *ZAW*, LX (1971): 22 ff.

42. In addition to the titles on the ark, which generally deal also with the Tent of Meeting, see F. Nötscher, '*Das Angesicht Gottes schauen' nach biblischer und babylonischer Auffassung* (Würzburg, 1924); M. H. Segal, "The Tent of Meeting" (Heb., with Eng. sum.), *Tarbiz*, XXV (1955–56): 231 ff.; M. Haran, "The Nature of the ʾOhel Moʿedh in Pentateuchal Sources," *JSS*, V (1960): 50–65; R. J. Clifford, "The Tent of El and the Israelite Tent of Meeting," *CBQ*, XXXIII (1971): 221–27; R. Schmitt, *Zelt und Lade als Thema alttestamentlicher Wissenschaft* (Gütersloh, 1972); O. Eissfeldt, "Kultzelt und Temple," *Wort und Geschichte: Festschrift K. El-*

liger (Neukirchen-Vluyn, 1973), pp. 51–56; Childs, *The Book of Exodus*, pp. 582 ff.

43. From the verb *yaʿad*, "to appoint," hence, *ʿedah*, "assembly," "congregation," and *moʿed*, "season," "seasonal feast" (Hos. 9:2, etc.). The *ʾohel moʿed* cannot be understood as "the tent of the assembly" either of the gods or of the tribes from the few references in the early traditions. The fact that the word *moʿed* may also apply to the divine assembly (Ps. 74:4) or to the mythical assembly of the gods (Isa. 14:13), like its proto-Canaanite cognate in the Ugaritic texts (fourteenth to thirteenth centuries B.C.), is not sufficient for supporting the conjecture that the Mosaic tent of meeting was borrowed from the Northwest Semitic mythology of the "tent of El," which shelters this god permanently. For a contrary view, see F. M. Cross, "The Tabernacle: A Study from an Archaeological and Historical Approach," *BA*, X (1947): 65; *Canaanite Myth*, p. 231, note 2; R. J. Clifford, "The Tent of El and the Israelite Tent of Meeting," *CBQ*, XXXIII (1971): 221–26.

44. See above, pp. 141 ff.

45. The ark stood "in the midst of the camp" (Num. 14:44). There is no valid reason for supposing that the phrase *naṭah-lô*, "[Moses] pitched for himself" (the tent) should be rendered "he pitched (the tent) for it" (Exod. 33:7), i.e., "for the ark." Yet, many scholars, following Wellhausen (*Die Composition des Hexateuchs* [Berlin, 1885], p. 93), maintain that the tent of meeting contained the ark. See O. Eissfeldt, "Lade und Stierbild," *ZAW*, LVIII (1940–41): 191; A. Alt, "Zelte und Hütten," *Festschrift F. Nötscher* (1950), p. 24, note 41; Cf. the contrary opinion of R. Hartmann, "Zelt und Lade," *ZAW*, XXXVII (1917–18): 213.

46. The priestly writers used the expression "tent of meeting"—more than a hundred times—synonymously with the word "tabernacle," sometimes even the conflated designation, "tabernacle of the

tent of meeting" (Exod. 39:32, etc.).

For the priestly view of the tabernacle, see Haran, "The Nature of the "Ohel Mo'edh' in Pentateuchal Sources," *JSS, V* (1960): pp. 63 ff.; "The Complex of Ritual Acts Performed Inside the Tabernacle," *Scripta Hierosolymita*, VIII (1961): 272 ff.; "Shiloh and Jerusalem: The Origin of the Priestly Tradition in the Pentateuch," *JBL,* LXXXI (1962): 14 ff.; "The Tabernacle: A Graded Taboo of Holiness" [in Hebrew], *Festschrift M. H. Segal* (Jerusalem, 1964), pp. 33 ff.; "The Priestly Image of the Tabernacle," *HUCA,* XXXVI (1965): 191 ff.; A. Levine, "The Descriptive Tabernacle Texts of the Pentateuch," *JAOS,* LXXXV (1965): 312 ff.; V. W. Rabe, "The Identity of the Priestly Tabernacle," *JNES,* XXV (1966): 132–134.

47. The verb *biqqesh,* "to seek," was used especially for the quest of the presence of God (cf. 2 Sam. 12:16, 21:1; Hos. 3:5, 5:6, 5:15, 7:10; etc.).

48. Yet, cf. Num. 11:16.

49. Even M. Haran, who has correctly characterized the tent of meeting as "a prophetic-nabhi'ic institution—not a cultic (priestly) one" (see "The Nature of the "Ohel Mo'edh'", pp. 56 f.)—introduced an element of confusion by referring constantly to "the Cloud of Glory," although the word "glory" is absent from the early traditions.

50. Another fragment of tradition refers to the tent of meeting. It may go back to the remote past, although it is now embedded in material which bears some of the marks of the priestly writers in the exile of Babylon (sixth century B.C.). Yahweh addressed Moses as follows: "Gather for me seventy men of the elders of Israel, whom you know to be the elders of the people and their officers (*shôterim*), and bring them to the tent of meeting, and let them take their stand there with thee. And I will come down and speak with thee there. I will lay aside in reserve (*'aṣal*) some of the spirit which is on you and place it on them, and they will bear with

thee some of the burden of the people, so that thou wilt not, by thyself, bear it alone" (Num. 11:16–17). Although the notion of "the spirit" to be divided (note the use of the partitive), as well as several other features, point to the rehearsing style of a later period, the allusion to the tent of meeting as the place where such a transfer occurs confirms the association of the sacred object with prophetic "inspiration." Let it be added that the seventy elders quite obviously could not have been crowded inside the tent and must have stood outside. Moses alone was allowed to go inside the tent. The sequence of the narrative (Num. 11:24–25) deals with Eldad and Medad, two men who had remained in the camp and yet "were prophesying in the camp" (vss. 26–27). The report led Moses to exclaim, "Would that all the people of Yahweh were prophets, that Yahweh would place his spirit upon them!" (Vs. 29.)

51. MT reads "and a vision"; LXX and Syriac, now confirmed by two Dead Sea Scroll fragments (4QNum[a] and [b]) have preserved the reading "in plain visibility." See Cross, *Canaanite Myth,* p. 204.

52. "Riddles" or "dark utterances" (*ḥidhôth*) were elliptical poems, usually ditties or quatrains, especially in the sapiential genre, which required considerable efforts of interpretation (Judg. 14:14, 1 Kings 10:1; cf. Hab. 2:6, Prov. 1:6, Ezek. 17:2). The complexity of divination hermeneutics (common to the ancient Near East in general and to Greece as well, as shown especially by the Delphic oracles) was superfluous with the great prophets of Israel, who were bluntly explicit in the formulation of their attacks on the society of their times.

53. From the verb *ya'ad,* which provides the root of the noun *mo'ed* in the expression "tent of meeting" (see note 43 above). The exegete will refrain, however, from suggesting that Amos was consciously aware of the etymological and semantic relations of the word.

54. It was also at the entrance of the tent of meeting that, according to a story of obscure origin, "the sons of Israel . . . cried" after one of them had brought a Midianite woman (Num. 25:6).

55. The tent of meeting and the ark became associated in later times, when various tents were identified with the Mosaic structure: the tent of the Shiloh sanctuary (1 Sam. 2:22), perhaps the tent which David pitched for the ark in Jerusalem (2 Sam. 6:17; cf. 1 Kgs. 2:28 and 2 Chron. 1:4), the tent of the Gihon shrine where Solomon was anointed (1 Kgs. 1:39), and even the tent of the Gibeon high-place, where Solomon endured his ordeal of royal initiation (2 Chron. 1:3). See M. Görg, *Das Zelt der Begegnung* (Bonn, 1967), pp. 80 ff., and cf. Cross *Canaanite Myth and Hebrew Epic*, p. 243.

56. See also Pss. 27:5, 61:4 (Heb. 5); cf. Ps. 78:60, 91:1.

57. See note 45 above.

58. See W. Eichrodt, *Theology of the Old Testament*, tr. J. A. Baker (Philadelphia, 1961), I, p. 110. Eichrodt offers a perceptive analysis of the tension between the ark and the tent, "not an irreconcilable opposition" (p. 109).

59. Cf. V. Scully, "Landscape and Sanctuary," *The Earth, the Temple, and the Gods: Greek Sacred Architecture*, rev. ed. (New York, 1969), pp. 1 ff.; for a modern, psychoanalytical interpretation, see R. L. Rubenstein, "The Cave, the Rock and the Tent: The Meaning of Place in Contemporary America," *Morality and Eros* (New York, 1970), pp. 164 ff.; cf. W. Jansen, "Geography of Faith: A Christian Perspective on the Meaning of Places," *Studies in Religion—Sciences religieuses*, III (1973–74): 166 ff. Cf. Clements, "Sacred Mountains, Temples and the Presence of God," *God and Temple*, pp. 1 ff.

60. Sophocles, *Oedipus at Colonus*, 16.

61. M. Barrès, *La colline inspirée* (Paris, 1913), p. 2.

62. R. Brinker, *The Influence of the Sanctuaries in Early Israel* (Manchester, 1946).

63. In spite of the defeat of Adonizedek, king of Jerusalem (Jos. 10:1, 3; cf. Judg. 1:5–7; also Jos. 18:16, 28; Judg. 19:10–11). See Noth, "Jerusalem and the Israelite Tradition," *The Laws in the Pentateuch*, pp. 132–33. The city of *Urusalim* (Akkadian approximation of the Northwest Semitic name which was later Hebraicized into *Yerushalayim*, "Jerusalem") is mentioned in the Tell el-Amarna Letters (fourteenth century B.C.).

64. See, among others, M. Haran, "The Gibeonites, the Nethinim and the Sons of Solomon's Servants," *VT*, XI (1961): 159 ff.; cf. J. J. M. Roberts, "The Davidic Origin of the Zion Tradition," *JBL*, XCII (1973): 329 ff.; K. Rupprecht, *Der Tempel von Jerusalem: Gründung Salomos oder jebusitischer Erbe?* (Berlin and New York, 1976).

65. See above, chapter III, note 25; see also L. R. Fisher, "Abraham and His Priest King," *JBL*, LXXXI (1962): pp. 264 ff.

66. MT, "Adonibezek."

67. A. Bentzen, "Zur Geschichte der Ṣadokiten," *ZAW*, LI (1933): 175 ff.; H. H. Rowley, "Zadok and Nehushtan," *JBL*, LVIII (1939): 134 ff.; "Melchizedek and Zadok (Gen. 14 and Psalm 110)," *Festschrift A. Bertholet* (Tübingen, 1950), pp. 461–72; C. E. Hauer, "Who Was Zadok?" *JBL*, LXXXII (1963): 89–94. Some scholars disagree but not on solid ground; See de Vaux, *Ancient Israel*, pp. 114, 374; Cross, (*Canaanite Myth*, pp. 207 ff.) judges that "many of the arguments for the hypothesis [of Zadok's Jebusite origin] are painfully weak" (p. 209), but the arguments he advances in defense of Zadok's Hebronite and Aaronide ancestry are even weaker.

68. See P. Humbert, "*Qânâ* en hébreu biblique," *Festschrift A. Bertholet* (Tübingen, 1950), pp. 259 ff.; cf. N. C. Habel, "Yahweh, Maker of Heaven and Earth": A Study in Tradition Criticism," *JBL*, XCI (1972): 321 ff.

69. See G. W. Ahlström, *Aspects of Syncretism in Israelite Religion* (Lund, 1963); J. A.

Soggin, "Der offiziell gefördete Syn-cretismus in Israel während des 10. Jahr-hunderts," *ZAW*, LXXVIII (1966): 179 ff.; S. Segert, "Surviving of Canaanite Ele-ments in Israelite Religion," *Festschrift P. G. Rinaldi* (Genova, 1967), pp. 155 ff. "The fact remains: the Abrahamic tradi-tion became socially functional only after the incorporation of the old Canaanite cities into the empire of David, and . . . the result was a thorough paganization of the state and culture" (G. E. Mendenhall, *The Tenth Generation: The Origins of the Bibli-cal Tradition*, Baltimore and London, 1973, p. 180).

70. See extensive bibliography in S. Ter-rien, "The Omphalos Myth and Hebrew Religion," *VT*, XX (1970): 317, note 5; see also H. Schmid, "Jahwe und die Kult-traditionen von Jerusalem," *ZAW*, LXVI (1955): 168 ff.; G. Wanke, *Die Ziontheologie der Korachiten in ihrem traditionsgeschichtli-chen Zusammenhang* (Berlin, 1966); J. H. Hayes, "The Tradition of Zion's Inviola-bility," *JBL*, LXXXII (1963): 419 ff.; F. Stolz, *Strukturen und Figuren im Kult von Jerusalem: Studien zur altorientalischen vor-und frühisraelitischen Religion* (Berlin, 1970); E. A. S. Butterworth, *The Tree at the Navel of the Earth* (Berlin, 1970). R. de Vaux argues against the Jebusite theory in "Jerusalem et les prophètes, *RB*, LXXIII (1966): 495 ff.; see also J. J. M. Roberts, "The Davidic Origin of the Zion Tradition," *JBL*, XCII (1973): 329 ff.

71. The widely discussed hypothesis of a yearly ceremony of the Enthronement of Yahweh in Jerusalem is not directly rele-vant to this aspect of our study.

72. See J. R. Porter, "The Interpretation of II Sam. 6 and Psalm 132," *JTS*, V (1954): 161 ff.; T. E. Fretheim, "Psalm 132: A Form-Critical Study," *JBL*, LXXXVI (1967): 289 ff.; D. R. Hillers, "Ritual Procession of the Ark and Ps 132," *CBQ*, XXX (1968): 48 ff.; Cross, *Ca-naanite Myth*, pp. 94 ff., 232 ff.; J. Schrein-er, *Sion-Jerusalem: Jahwes Königssitz* (München, 1963), pp. 103ff.

73. Porter, "The Interpretation of II Sam. 6," p. 165; N. L. Tidwell, "The Linen Ephod: 1 Sam. II 18 and 2 Sam. VI 14," *VT*, XXIV (1974): 505 ff.

74. See S. Smith, "The Threshing Floor at the City Gate," *Palestine Exploration Quarterly*, LXXVIII (1946); 5 ff.; G. Ahl-ström, "Nathan und der Tempelbau," *VT*, XI (1961): 115 ff.

75. *Paradise Lost*, XII, 340.

76. 1 Chron. 28:19 ff., amplified by oral traditions preserved in the rabbinical lit-erature. See R. Patai, *Man and Temple* (London, 1947), pp. 130 ff.; cf. A. S. Kapelrud, "Temple Building: A Task for Gods and Kings," *Orientalia*, XXXII (1963): 56 ff.

77. V. Scully, *The Earth, the Temple and the Gods* (New Haven, 1962), pp. 214 ff.

78. See W. Andrae, *Das Gotteshaus und die Urformen des Bauens im alten Orient* (Berlin, 1930); G. E. Wright et al., "The Signifi-cance of the Temple in the Ancient Near East," *BA*, VII (1944): 41 ff.; Th. H. Bu-sink, "Les origines du temple de Salo-mon, *Jaarbericht Ex Oriente Lux*, XVII (1963): 165–92; A. Kuschke, "Der Tem-pel Salomos und der 'syrische Tempel-typus'," *Festschrift L. Rost* (Berlin, 1967); pp. 124 ff.; H. Mayer, "Das Bauholz des Tempels Salomos," *BZ*, XI (1967): 53–66; Y. Aharoni, "Arad: Its Inscriptions and Temple," *BA*, XXXI (1968): 2 ff.; yet see J. Brand, "Remarks on the Temple of Solomon," *Tarbiz*, XXXIV (1964–65): 323 ff.; the author claims that the edifice constituted a genuinely Israelite creation.

79. See V. W. Rabe, "Israelite Opposi-tion to the Temple," *CBQ*, XXIX (1967): 227 ff.

80. See K. Möhlenbrink, *Der Tempel Salo-mos: Eine Untersuchung seiner Stellung in der Sakralarchitektur des alten Orients, BWANT*, IV 7 (1932); G. E. Wright, "Solomon's Temple Resurrected," *BA*, IV (1941): 17–31; *Biblical Archaeology* (Philadelphia, 1957), pp. 136–42; L. H. Vincent, *Jérusa-lem de l'Ancien Testament*, II–III (Paris, 1956), pp. 373–431; *id.*, "Le caractère du

temple salomonien," *Festschrift A. Robert* (Paris, 1957), pp. 137–48; Th. A. Busink, *Der Tempel Salomos (Der Tempel von Jerusalem*, I), (Leiden, 1970); J. Gray, *I & II Kings: A Commentary*, rev. ed. (Philadelphia, 1970), pp. 149–212; H. Schmidt, "Der Tempelbau Salomos in religionsgeschichtlicher Sicht," *Festschrift K. Galling* (Tübingen, 1970), pp. 241 ff. H. Bardtke, "Der Temple von Jerusalem," *TLZ*, XCVII (1972): 801–10 (critical review of Busink, *Der Tempel Salomos*, 1970); Y. Aharoni, "The Solomonic Temple, the Tabernacle, and the Arad Sanctuary," *Alter Orient und Altes Testament*, XXII (1973), 1 ff.; K. Rupprecht, *Der Tempel von Jerusalem: Gründung Salomos oder jebusitisches Erbe?* (Berlin and New York, 1976).

81. Like most temples of the ancient Near East.

82. L. A. Snijders, "L'orientation du temple de Jérusalem," *Oudt. St.*, XIV (1965): 214–34.

83. H. Schult, "Der Debir im solomonischen Tempel," *ZDPV*, LXXX (1964): 46–54; J. Ouellette, "The Solomonic DeBÎR According to the Hebrew Text of I Kings 6," *JBL*, LXXXIX (1970): 338–43.

84. See bibliography in Terrien, "The Omphalos Myth," p. 328, note 3.

85. Hbr., kᵉma'ar 'îsh wᵉloyôth, following Rashi's interpretation based on *Yoma* 54a.

86. See J. Ouellette, "The yāṣia' and the ṣᵉlā'ot: Two Mysterious Structures in Solomon's Temple," *JNES*, XXXI (1972): 187 ff.

87. See R. B. Y. Scott, "The Pillars of Jachin and Boaz," *JBL*, LVIII (1939): 143 ff.; W. F. Albright, "Two Cressets from Marisa and the Pillars of Jachin and Boaz," *BASOR*, No. 85 (1942): 18 ff.; H. G. May, "The Two Pillars Before the Temple of Solomon," *BASOR*, No. 88 (1942): 19 ff.; W. Kornfeld, "Der Symbolismus der Tempelsäulen," *ZAW*, LXXIV (1962): 50 ff. However, J. Ouellette maintains that the columns were not freestanding: see "Le vestibule du temple de Salomon était-il un *bît* Hilâni?" *RB*, LXXVI (1969): 365 ff.

88. See A. R. Johnson, "The Rôle of the King," in *The Labyrinth*, p. 87; C. C. Wylie, "On King Solomon's Molten Sea," *BA*, XII (1949): 86 ff.; G. Bagnai, "The Molten Sea of Solomon's Temple," in *Festschrift T. J. Meek* (Toronto, 1964), pp. 114 ff.

89. See E. A. S. Butterworth, *The Tree as the Navel of the Earth* (Berlin & New York), 1970; A. Fitzgerald, "The Mythological Background of Jerusalem as a Queen and False Worship as Adultery in the Old Testament," *CBQ*, XXXIV (1972): 403 ff.; R. J. Clifford, *The Cosmic Mountain in Canaan and the Old Testament* (Cambridge, Mass. 1972).

90. Especially those of Asa (913–873 B.C.; 1 Kings 15:12), Hezekiah (ca. 715–687 B.C.; 2 Kings 18:4) and Josiah (ca. 640–609 B.C.; 2 Kings 23:1 ff.).

91. See F. J. Hollis, "The Sun-Cult and the Temple of Jerusalem," in S. H. Hooke, ed., *Myth and Ritual* (London, 1933), pp. 89 ff.; J. A. Montgomery and H. Gehman, *The Book of Kings* (I.C.C., Edinburgh, 1951), pp. 189 ff.; W. F. Albright, *Yahweh and the Gods of Canaan* (Garden City, N.Y., 1968), p. 231; cf. E. Würthwein, *Die Bücher der Könige.1 Könige 1–16* (Göttingen, 1977), pp. 87 ff.

92. MT does not include the first colon, which is here rendered from the LXX of verse 53. It is not certain whether the verb *egnôrisen* ("recognized"), reflected the Hebrew *hikkîr* ("observed"), *hēkîn* ("set") or even *hôphîᵃ'* ("caused to shine"), but its general meaning is sufficiently indicative of the contextual thought. The LXX added that the formula "was written in the Book of the Song" (*Sepher hash-Shir*), a probable error for the *Book of Yashar* (*Sepher hay-Yashar*), which is also quoted in Josh. 10:13 and 2 Sam. 1:18. See Noth, *Könige*, (Neukirchen, 1965–) pp. 172, 181 f; A. van der Born, "Zum Tempelweihespruch (I K viii 12 f)," *Oudt. St.*, XIV (1965): 235 f.

93. Although Solomon's successors failed to prevent sun worship in later years: King Josiah expelled "the horses of the sun" in 622 B.C. (2 Kings 23:11) and heliolatric rites were performed in the temple a few years later (Ezek. 9:16 ff.). See H. G. May, "Some Aspects of Solar Worship at Jerusalem," *ZAW*, LV (1937): 269 ff.

94. Cf. Ps. 104:19, where the sun is treated as an obedient slave who knows when to get off the stage.

95. Cf. Deut. 4:14, 5:19, etc.; see above, p. 190.

96. See H.-J. Kraus, *Worship in Israel: A Cultic History of the Old Testament*, tr. G. Buswell (Richmond, Va., 1962), pp. 61 ff.; G. Fohrer, *History of Israelite Religion*, tr. D. E. Green (Nashville, 1972), pp. 202 ff.

97. See G. J. Thierry, "Remarks on Various Passages of the Psalms," *Oudt. St.*, IX (1951): 4, 5; Clements, *God and Temple*, 92, note 2; Noth, *Könige*, pp. 181 f.

98. Cf. Isa. 8:18; Joel 4:17, 21; Ps. 68:16 [Heb. 17], 19, 135:21; etc.

99. See W. D. Davies, *The Gospel and the Land: Early Christianity and Jewish Territorial Doctrine* (Berkeley, Cal., 1974), pp. 5 ff., 132 ff.

100. The poetic juxtaposition of Mount Zion with the extremities of Ṣaphôn indicates how much the Yahwists of Jerusalem had absorbed the Canaanite mythology. See A. Robinson, "Zion and Ṣaphôn in Psalm XLVIII 3," *VT*, XXIV (1974): 118 ff.

101. *Complete Works*, XVI (London, 1924), p. 287.

102. See L. Rost, "Sinaibund und Davidsbund," *TlZ*, LXXIV (1947): 129 ff.; J. Gray, *I&II Kings* (Philadelphia, 1970), pp. 212, also pp. 6 ff.

103. See W. Eichrodt, "Yahweh's Dwelling-Place in Heaven," *Theology of the Old Testament*, II (Philadelphia, 1967), pp. 186 ff.

104. See G. von Rad, "Deuteronomy's 'Name' Theology and the Priestly Document's 'Kabod' Theology," *Studies in Deuteronomy*, tr. D. Stalker (London and Chicago, 1953), pp. 37 ff. Following the view of W. Andrae (*Das Gotthaus und die Urformen des Bauens im Alten Orient*, Berlin, 1930, pp. 14 ff.), von Rad maintains that "the temple was Yahweh's dwelling place, yet it was so because in its worship [God] 'came' to manifest his presence there" (*Old Testament Theology*, I, p. 63). Cf. R. Hentschke, *Die Stellung der vorexilischen Schriftpropheten zum Kultus* (Berlin, 1957), pp. 47 ff.

105. Like Jebus, Shechem had been a shrine before the Hebraic conquest, but it became "Hebraicized" two or more centuries before Jebus. It may have been considered by its early inhabitants as the navel of the earth. See Terrien, "The Omphalos myth," p. 331, and note 4; also G. R. H. Wright, "The Mythology of Pre-Israelite Shechem," *VT*, XX (1970): 75 ff.

106. See G. R. H. Wright, "Joseph's Grave Under the Tree by the Omphalos at Shechem," *VT*, XXII (1972): 476 ff.

107. R. de Vaux maintains that Deuteronomy contains no theology of the name. See "Le lieu que Yahvé a choisi pour y établir son nom," *Festschrift L. Rost* (Berlin , 1967), pp. 219 ff. His arguments are not convincing. See M. Weinfeld, "The Concept of God and the Divine Abode," *Deuteronomy and the Deuteronomic School* (Oxford, 1972), pp. 194 ff.

108. See A. Alt, "Die Heimat des Deuteronomiums," *Kleine Schriften*, II pp. 250 ff.; G. von Rad, "The Provenance of Deuteronomy," *Studies in Deuteronomy*, pp. 60 ff.; E. W. Nicholson, *Deuteronomy and Tradition* (Oxford, 1967), pp. 58 ff.; cf. F. Dumermuth, "Zur deuteronomischen Kulttheologie und ihre Voraussetzungen," *ZAW*, LXX (1958): 59 ff., who attempts to show that Bethel, rather than Shechem, was the cultic center of the Confederation.

109. See Childs, *Memory and Tradition*, pp. 12 ff.; *id.*, *Exodus*, pp. 447, 466. There is no valid reason for correcting the MT in order to read, "see the face of Yah-

weh" (Clements, *God and Temple*,) p. 77, note 5.

110. Cf. Deut. 12:11, 21; 14:23 f.; 16:2, 6, 11; etc.

111. The complex interaction of a theology of election with the awareness of divine presence through the name has not received the attention it deserves, although considerable research has been done on both subjects. See O. Grether, *Name und Wort Gottes im Alten Testament* (Giessen, 1934), pp. 159 ff.; E. Jacob, *Théologie de l'Ancien Testament* (Neuchâtel, 1955), pp. 66 ff.; F. Dumermuth, "Zur deuteronomischen Kulttheologie," pp. 69 ff.; R. E. Clements, *God's Chosen People: A Theological Interpretation of the Book of Deuteronomy* (Valley Forge, Pa., 1969), pp. 45 ff., 74 ff.; Th. C. Vriezen, *An Outline of Old Testament Theology* (Oxford, 1970), pp. 208 ff.

112. See von Rad, "Deuteronomy's 'Name' Theology," p. 38.

113. See von Rad, "Deuteronomy and the Holy War," *Studies in Deuteronomy*, pp. 45 ff.; N. K. Gottwald, " 'Holy War' in Deuteronomy: Analysis and Critique," *Review and Expositor*, LXI (1964): 296 ff.

114. See T. E. Fretheim, "The Ark in Deuteronomy," *CBQ*, XXX (1968): 1 ff.

115. The words *lebhabh*, *nephesh*, and *me'odh*, traditionally rendered by "heart," "soul," and "might" respectively, designate aspects of the human person which do not correspond exactly to English notions. They refer in turn to the intellectual faculties, to the desire to persist in being, and to the corporate personality with its responsibility toward present and future communities. On the *Shema'* and the love of man for God, see W. L. Moran, "The Ancient Near Eastern Background of the Love of God in Deuteronomy," *CBQ*, XXV (1963): 77 ff.; N. Lohfink, *Das Hauptgebot: Eine Untersuchung literarischer Einleitungsfragen zum Deuteronomium 5–11*, Rome, 1963; *Höre, Israel!* (Düsseldorff, 1965); D. J. McCarthy, "Notes on the Love of God in Deuteronomy and the Father-Son Relationship Between Yahweh and Israel," *CBQ*, XXVII (1965): 144 ff.; Clements, "The Worship of the Heart," *God's Chosen People*, pp. 82 ff.; S. D. McBride, Jr., "The Yoke of the Kingdom: An Exposition of Deuteronomy 6:4–5," *Int.*, XXVII (1973): 273 ff.

116. E. L. Fackenheim, in *God's Presence in History* (New York, 1970), pp. 3 f., recalls the Midrash according to which the Israelites saw God and recognized him when they passed through the Red Sea. The Midrash states that they saw what Isaiah, Ezekiel, and all the other prophets never saw (Melikta de-Rabbi Ishmael, J. Z. Lauterbach, ed. [Philadelphia, 1949], II. pp. 24 ff.; as quoted by Fackenheim, *God's Presence*, p. 31, note 1). The Midrash uses the verb "to see" in the sense of "to discern the intervention of" God in historical events, not in the sense of psychological vision.

117. See von Rad, "Endeavours to Restore the Past," *Old Testament Theology*, I, pp. 69 ff.

118. P. Tillich, "The Divine Name," *Christianity and Crisis*, XX (1960–61): 55.

119. The exact date of the reform is still in question: cf. 2 Kings 22:1 ff. with 2 Chron. 34:3. It is probable that the princes of Judah undertook cultic reforms during the minority of Josiah, five years before the discovery of "the book of the law."

120. See above, pp. 152 ff.

121. The *beth zebhul*, "exalted house," may well mean "a royal edifice," "a house fit for a king." See M. Held, "The Root ZBI/SBI in Akkadian, Ugaritic and Biblical Hebrew," *JAOS*, LXXXVIII (1968): 90.

122. Most commentators miss the eschatological character of this poetic introduction to the sermons of Amos. The roaring of Yahweh from Zion will be a part of the events of the last day, "the day of Yahweh" (Amos 5:18).

123. Such an interpretation is confirmed

by the motif of the shaking of the threshold foundations: divine reality cannot be contained within a man-made structure (Isa. 6:4).

124. MT reads perfect tense, "he has laid," but either of the two Qumran readings (QIsa[a,b]) may be correct, for a participle denoting an imminent future is demanded by the idiom *hinneni*, "Behold, I...."

125. The corner-stone is that of the *yiqrat*, a word related to *yaqar*, "precious," "splendid." Cf. the "glorious full moon" in Job 31:26, and the Arabic cognate *waqara*, "to be in glory."

126. This interpretation fits the contextual sequence of the entire poem, in which the prophet polemizes against both Zion and its leaders. "Yahweh of Hosts himself," he predicts, "will be a crown of beauty and a diadem of splendor" [rather than the temple] "for the remnant of his people" (Isa. 28:5). On this controversial passage, see N. Rhodokanakis, "Omphalos und *Eben Shetiia,*" *Wörter und Sachen*, V (1913): 198 ff.; K. Fullerton, "The Stone of the Foundation," *AJSL*, XXXVII (1920–21): 1 ff.; L. Lindblom, "Der Eckstein in Jes. 28, 16," *Festschrift S. Mowinckel* (Oslo, 1955), pp. 123 ff.; O. Kaiser, *Isaiah 13—39: A Commentary*, tr. by R. A. Wilson (Philadelphia, 1974), pp. 252 f.

127. It may be presumed that by the eighth century the verb *shaken*, originally "to sojourn," had become synonymous with the verb *yashabh*, "to dwell," precisely on account of the priestly theology of the Jerusalem temple (see above, p. 195).

128. R. de Vaux fails to distinguish between the prophets' allusions to the historical Jerusalem and their prediction of the new Jerusalem after the earth will have been recreated. See "Jérusalem et les prophètes," *RB*, LXXIII (1966): 481 ff.

129. Cf. 8:19, in which Jeremiah knows that the people cry, "Is Yahweh not in Zion?" Another communal lament, or fragment thereof, has been preserved in 17:12, where the sanctuary is called "the throne of glory, set on high from the beginning (*merishôn*)," possibly an allusion to the myth of the earth navel.

130. The Jeremianic phrase, "in which my name is invoked," differs from the Deuteronomic formula, "in which I shall cause my name to sojourn" (Deut. 12:11, etc.). The prophet stressed more clearly than Deuteronomy the factor of the invocation of the name in prayer, sacrifice, and other acts of worship. He may have been more aware than the Deuteronomists of the mystery of a presence which involves the moral quality of the worshippers. A house in which Yahweh's name was invoked by worshippers who were robbers was a contradiction in terms (7:8 –9). "The temple, he says in effect, is not what men call it or imagine to be, but what by their actions they make it. It might have been the place where Yahweh's gracious presence was experienced if they had hallowed His name by lives lived in piety and righteousness" (J. Skinner, *Prophecy and Religion* [Cambridge, 1940], p. 175). Cf. A. Strobel, "Jeremias, Priester ohne Gottesdienst? Zu Jer 7, 21," *BZ*, I (1957): 214 ff.; W. Eichrodt, "A Study of Jeremiah 7:1–15," *Theology Today*, VII (1950): 15 ff.; Ph. Reymond, "Sacrifice et 'spiritualité', ou sacrifice et alliance? Jér. 7, 22–24," *TZ*, XXI (1965): 314 ff.; H. Graf von Reventlow, "Gattung und Überlieferung in der 'Tempelrede Jeremias', Jer 7 und 26," *ZAW*, LXXXI (1969): 315 ff.

131. See P. R. Ackroyd, "The Historical Situation in the Exilic Age," *Exile and Restoration* (London, 1968), pp. 17 ff.; G. Fohrer, *History of Israelite Religion*, tr. by D. E. Green (Nashville and New York, 1972), pp. 307 ff.

132. See A. Robert, "La lettre de Jérémie," *DBS*, IV (1948): 849 ff.

133. The words, "to the name of Yahweh, to Jerusalem," are textually uncertain. It is possible that the entire passage

came from the Jeremianic school after 587 B.C. but its contents are consonant with the prophet's theology of the name. Cf. M. Weinfeld, "Jeremiah and the Spiritual Metamorphosis of Israel," *ZAW*, LXXXVIII (1976): 19 f.

134. See H. Ortmann, *Der alte und der neue Bund bei Jeremias* (Berlin, 1940); W. Lemp, *Bund und Bundeserneuerung bei Jeremias* (Tübingen, 1954–55); R. Martin-Achard, "La nouvelle alliance selon Jérémie," *RTP*, XII (1962): 82 ff.; J. Coppens, "La nouvelle alliance en Jér. 31, 31–34," *CBQ*, XXV (1963): 12 ff.; P. Buis, "La nouvelle alliance" *VT*, XVIII (1968): 1 ff,; J. Swetnam, "Why was Jeremiah's New Covenant New?" *SVT*, XXVI (1974): 111 ff.; cf. F. Hecht, *Eschatologie und Ritus bei den 'Reformpropheten': Ein Beitrage zur Theologie des Alten Testaments* (Leiden, 1971), pp. 29 ff., 104 ff.

135. The word *qin'ah*, traditionally rendered "jealousy," means "zeal" in the sense of "passionate love" and refers here to the cult of the Earth Mother. Cf. 2 Kings 21:7 with 2 Chron. 33:7; see also 2 Kings 23:6.

136. Snake worship, which had been temporarily eradicated by King Hezekiah in the eighth century B.C. (2 Kings 18:4), had apparently been reintroduced at a later date. Its occurrence has been observed together with the cult of the *Terra Mater*, male prostitution, and heliolatry in relation to the belief in the myth of the earth navel. See S. Terrien, "The Omphalos Myth," p. 320; K. R. Joines, "The Bronze Serpent in the Israelite Cult," *JBI*, LXXXVII (1968): 245 ff.; id., *Serpent Symbolism in the Old Testament* (Haddonfield, N.J., 1974).

137. Cf. Isa. 1:29 ff., 10:4, 17:1. In Laments for *Dumuzi*, (Tammuz), Mesopotamian poets mourned the abasement of the sun over the horizon after the summer solstice. See J. B. Pritchard, ed., *Ancient Near Eastern Texts Relating to the Old Testament* (Princeton, 1955), p. 109.; Th. Jacobsen, *Toward the Image of Tammuz*

(Cambridge, Mass., 1970); "Religious Drama in Ancient Mesopotamia," H. Goedicke & J. J. M. Roberts, ed., *Unity and Diversity: Essays in the History, Literature, and Religion of the Ancient Near East* (Baltimore, 1975), pp. 65 ff.

138. See Ezek. 8:17, in which sun worship appears to have been related to male cultic homosexuality. A. Bertholet, *Das Buch Hesekiel* (Freiburg i. B., 1897), p. 50; W. Zimmerli, *Ezechiel* (Neukirchen, 1956), pp. 222 f.; *contra* W. Eichrodt, *Ezekiel: A Commentary*, tr. by C. Quin (Philadelphia, 1970), pp. 127 ff.

139. See the hypothesis of H. G. May, "The Departure of the Glory of Yahweh," *JBL*, LVI (1937): 309 ff. Ezekiel's formulation of the divine abandon of the temple may have been influenced by the liturgy of Tammuz.

140. The prophet has kept alive the mythopoetic thinking of the theophany in which several features are bound together, such as the storm cloud (2 Sam. 22: 11 = Ps. 18:10 [Heb., 11]), and the winged mask. See H. Frankfort, *Cylinder Seals* (London, 1939), pp. 208 ff.; B. Stein, *Der Begriff K^ebod Yahweh und seine Bedeutung für die alttestamentliche Gotteserkenntnis* (Emsdetten i. W., 1939), pp. 272 f., 276 ff. G. Mendenhall, "The Mask of Yahweh," in *The Tenth Generation: The Origins of the Biblical Tradition* (Baltimore and London, 1973), pp. 54 ff. See also D. Baltzer, *Ezechiel und Deuterojesaia* (Berlin, 1971), pp. 51 ff.

141. Although the expression "a sanctuary for a little while" could hardly have referred to the first synagogue (cf. A. Menès, "Tempel und Synagoge," *ZAW*, L [1932]: 268 ff.), the idea of a new form of religious assembly at worship arose among the deportees in the sixth century. See H. H. Rowley, *Worship in Ancient Israel* (Philadelphia, 1967), pp. 213 ff.; cf. Baltzer, *Ezechiel und Deuterojesaja*, pp. 34 f.

142. See Eichrodt, "The Basis and Aim of the New Divine Creation," *Ezekiel*, pp. 494 ff.

143. See H. G. May, "Some Cosmic Connotations of MAYIM RABBIM, 'Many Waters'," *JBL,* LXXIV (1955): 9 ff.

144. See H. G. May, "The Creation of Light in Genesis 1, 3–5," *JBL,* LVIII (1939): 209 ff.

145. See J. Morgenstern, "Moses with the Shining Face," *HUCA,* II (1925): 1 ff.; J. de Fraine, "Moses 'cornuta facies' (Ex. 34, 39–35)," *Bijdragen: Tijdschrift voor filosophie en theologie,* XX (1959): 28 ff.; F. Dumermuth, "Moses *strahlendes Gesicht,*" *TZ,* XVII (1961): 240 ff.; also, for the observations of luminosity or "aura" among mystics of other cultures, see H. Thurston, *The Physical Phenomena of Mysticism* (Chicago, 1952), pp. 162 ff.; E. G. Suhr, "The Horned Moses," Folklore, LXXIV (1963): 387 ff.

146. M. Weinfeld points out the relationship between the Ezekielian imagery and the motif of the *imago Dei* in Gen. 1:26–27; see "The Concept of God and the Divine Abode," *Deuteronomy and the Deuteronomic School,* pp. 200 ff.

147. See von Rad, "Deuteronomy and the Holy War," *Studies in Deuteronomy,* p. 54; C. H. Jones, " 'Holy War' or 'Yahweh War'?" *VT,* XXV (1975): 642 ff., esp. 655 f.

148. See B. Erling, "Ezekiel 38—39 and the Origins of Jewish Apocalyptic," *Ex Orbe Religionum: Festschrift Geo. Widengren* (Leiden, 1972), II pp. 104 ff.

149. Ezek. 43: 7 ff.; 44: 4 ff.; etc.

150. See Terrien, "The Omphalos Myth," p. 337; "Toward a Biblical Theology of Womanhood," *Religion in Life,* XLII (1973–74): 330.

151. See Patai, "Sins and Calamities," *Man and Temple,* pp. 140 ff.; cf. W. Gispen, "The Distinction Between Clean and Unclean," *OST,* V (1948): 190 ff.; K. Elliger, "Das Gesetz Leviticus 18," *ZAW,* LXVII (1955): 1 ff. and especially p. 23; L. E. Elliott-Binns, "Some Problems in the Holiness Code," *ZAW,* LXVII (1955): 26 ff.; H. Graf Reventlow, *Das Heiligkeitsgesetz* (Berlin, 1964), pp. 192 ff.; J. G. Vink, "The Date and Origins of the Priestly Code in the Old Testament," *OST,* XV (1969): 1 ff.; J. Neusner, "The Idea of Purity in Ancient Judaism," *JAAR,* XLIII (1975): 16; cf. K. Koch, "Sühne und Sündenvergebung um die Wende von der exilischen zur nachexilischen Zeit," *Ev. Theol.* XXVI (1966): 217 ff.

152. See note 46 above.

5

The Prophetic Vision

Prophets are usually mistaken for predictors. The prophets of Israel unveiled not the future but the absolute.

Traditionally, the prophets of Israel have been viewed as the announcers of the Messiah. In fact, however, very few of their utterances were concerned with messianic hope, even when they hailed the advent of God upon a new earth.

For the past hundred years, the prophets of Israel have been presented chiefly as social reformers. In fact, however, they expected history soon to crash in a cosmic doom, after which, they hoped, God would create a new earth and a new humanity.

Recently, the prophets of Israel have come into their own as the poets of divine presence, even when they prayed to a *Deus absconditus.*

All true poets have received

... the prophet's vision,
The exultation, the divine
Insanity of noble minds.[1]

The prophets of Israel were true poets. They not only cultivated all forms of rhetorical beauty and possessed a respect for the word that provokes thinking, but they also lived in the exultation of their vision. As its burden became unbearable, they entered a kind of insanity which attuned their minds to the demands of urgency in human society. It was a divine insanity—the awful consequence of the presence—but it was an insanity which conferred upon their minds the ecstasy and the horror of nobility. In the presence, they understood that nobility is the freedom to differ, the courage to condemn, and the folly to hope. Noble minds are those who accept with diffidence and alacrity their election to speak. The prophets of Israel were the poets of an electing presence.

The Greek version of the Septuagint, which reflects the translating usage of the Alexandrian and other Hellenistic synagogues in the third and second centuries B.C., used the word *prophêtês*, "prophet," for the Hebrew word *nabi'*. Now, the Greek *prophêtês*, like the Hebrew *nabi'*, designated a wide variety of religious functionaries, from technical soothsayers and ecstatic diviners to the poetic interpreters of glossolalic oracles.[2] In early Israel, dancing and raving "bands of prophets" roamed the countryside (1 Sam. 10:5), individual seers (1 Sam. 9:9) occasionally rose to positions of national leadership (1 Sam. 7:3 ff.), special prophets acted as royal advisers (2 Sam. 7:2, etc.), circles of court prophets were maintained by some kings as official consultants to the government (1 Kings 22:6), Moses himself was remembered as the prophet *par excellence* (Deut. 34:10); and then, there were a few others—whether cultic officials[3] or secularly employed laymen, shepherds or farmers—who obeyed a prophetic vocation and are remembered as the great prophets of Israel.[4]

Such a wide range of functions and identities lends itself to terminological confusion. The word *nabi'* was at times a synonym of *ro'eh*, "seer," or "*hozeh*, "extra-lucid," but never of the various designations of astrologers and magicians. When

Amos was rebuked by the priest of the royal sanctuary of Bethel in 751 B.C. for being a *hozeh*, "a man with visions," he objected, "I am not a *nabi'*, nor a member of the prophetic guild" (Amos 7:14). Nevertheless, he used the verb "to prophesy" (*hinnabe'*) to describe his activity (vs. 15).

Professionals of divination abounded in the ancient Near East, and many parallels have been pointed out between them and the Hebrew prophets.[5] No Semitic equivalent to the Hebrew word, however, has yet been discovered in the extant literature. In all probability, the term *nabi'* meant "one called [of God]."[6] If this conjecture is correct, it is understandable that the few men who have remained known to posterity as "the great prophets" would have composed the narratives of their call to prophesy with a rhetorical artistry of exceptional sophistication.[7] While their experiences may have been of an ecstatic nature,[8] the great prophets practiced a rigid discipline of literary expression. They recalled their emotional incandescence in intellectual tranquillity.[9]

The epiphanic visitations to the Patriarchs and the Mosaic theophanies were recounted in the epic style of community ceremonial. The visions of the great prophets, while following to a certain degree the rhetorical pattern of the epiphanic and theophanic narratives, acquired a form of their own, for they were narrated autobiographically. Moreover, they no longer invoked "nature in tumult" but echoed "the tempests of the soul." The theophany was a happening of wonder. The prophetic vision was a confession of psychological solitariness.

The tradition of Elijah on Mt. Horeb (1 Kings 19) offers a dramatic turning point in the Hebraic theology of presence, for it closed the era of theophany and relegated it to the realm of an unrepeatable past. At the same time, it opened the era of prophetic vision, where miracles of nature became miracles of character.

FROM THEOPHANY TO VISION

The editors of the Book of Kings prefaced the scene of Elijah on Mount Horeb by the concatenation of narratives on the fire at Mount Carmel and the slaughter of the prophets of Baal (1 Kings 18:1 ff.).[10]

Elijah's Flight and Despair (1 Kings 19:1–8)

The story of the fire on Mount Carmel showed a Deity who used nature in a thaumaturgical way and who was also fiercely exclusive and even vindictive. As the fire came down from heaven and consumed not only the burnt offering and the wood but also the stones and the dust, even licking the water that was in the trench, all the people saw the wonder, fell on their faces, and cried, "Yahweh, he is God! Yahweh, he is God!" (vs. 39). The prophet immediately said to them, "Seize the prophets of Baal; let no one of them escape!" (vs. 40).

The figure of Elijah is portrayed as suprahuman. The rain falls at his command. Endowed with the physical strength of a demigod, he runs about seventeen miles ahead of the king's chariot to Jezreel. Yahweh's victory may have thrilled the imagination of the masses, but the agency of Elijah the thaumaturgist is in the end hollow. The king and the queen are not converted to a new style of conduct. Elijah, the superman, runs away for his life and flees to the Negeb, the southern wilderness. After a day's journey, he throws himself under a shrub and prays for death: "It is enough, now, O Yahweh, take away my life, for I am not better than my fathers" (1 Kings 1:1–4). The superman is merely a man.

Is it that the narrative wishes to show in parabolic form that miracles of a cosmic nature, even of the magnitude of that which elicited collective enthusiasm and conviction on Mt. Carmel for a day, do not truly transform human nature? In the end, there are only the wonders of the human person. Like Moses in the

tradition of the manna (Num. 11:10–15), the man of God is
ready to give up. Why then does he sojourn at Mt. Horeb
(1 Kings 19:8)? The context implies that for Elijah, in the ninth
century b.c., the site of the "mount of Elohim" stands for the
historical moment of two related events: the theophanic encounter between Yahweh and Moses, and the offer of the covenant to the people. The narrative which follows interweaves
intimately the two motifs.[11]

The Entrance of the Cave (1 Kings 19:9–18)

It has been noted for a long time that a certain amount of
repetition overloads the theophanic speech, since the opening
of the dialogue is found twice (vss. 8b, 9abc; vss. 13bcd). So is
also the opening confessional statement of the prophet (vss. 10
and 14). Coming after the first description of Yahweh's silence
(vss. 11–12), the prophet's reiteration of his confessional statement suggests a dramatic recital of a liturgical character. Elijah's disciples and the schools of the prophets were exposed to
the incoherence of man's reaction to the display of divine silence after the display of divine violence through natural elements.

The story involves two distinct phases: first, the prophet is
commanded to stand on the mountain before Yahweh, literally,
"in the presence of Yahweh" (vs. 11). The narrator adds, in the
language of the Mosaic theophany which opposed the motif of
the name to the motif of the glory (Exod. 33:19), "And behold!
Yahweh passed by" (1 Kings 19:11b). Three times, the negative
statement dissociates the presence from the natural elements of
nature in tumult, the wind, the earthquake, and the fire. It is that
very force, the fire, which comes in a climactic position and
inevitably recalls the victory on Mt. Carmel.

The threefold repetition, "And Yahweh was not in the wind,"
"And Yahweh was not in the earthquake," "And Yahweh was
not in the fire," constitutes a repudiation not only of the mode

of divine intervention on Mt. Carmel but also of the possibility that the Mosaic theophany on Mt. Horeb could occur again in later history. The era of theophany is now closed, and its validity is consigned to the hoary glamour of distant ages.

After three negative phrases, the positive statement provides the key to the understanding of the whole narrative: "And after the fire, the sound of utmost silence" (vs. 12b).[12] After the display of nature in violent motion, there comes the stillness which, by dramatic antithesis, may indeed be heard. It is a silence which may—so to speak—be "cut with a knife." It has nothing to do with "the still small voice" of conscience so dear to Immanuel Kant and the Protestant moralists of the nineteenth and twentieth centuries. Nor is it related to the notion of *nada*, characteristic of certain Spanish mystics, nor to the idea of nothingness, promoted by existential philosophers, both ancient and modern. It designates a reality that is proximate and provisional, subsequent to cosmic noise and preparatory to the awareness of presence.

The phrase which follows assumes a special function in the articulation of the story: "And when Elijah heard it [namely, the sound of utmost stillness], he wrapped his face in his mantle and he went forth and stood at the mouth of the cave" (vs. 13a). In the dynamics of this parabolic tale, this pivotal phrase binds together the two phases of the scene. Man conceals his face and especially his eyes, so as not to gaze on the Deity. The gesture is an acknowledgement of the inward certainty of the presence and, at the same time, the recognition of the *mysterium tremendum* of holiness: a theological assent of Elijah to the Mosaic acceptance of not seeing the glory (Exod. 33:23).

The *second* phase continues the theophanic speech but only after an entirely different mood has been established. Once again, "Behold, there came a voice to him, saying, 'What art thou doing here, Elijah?'" (vs. 13b.) The prophet repeats his previous stand (cf. vs. 10 with vs. 14). He shows a passionate concern for Yahweh and the covenant people, but his zeal is tinged with a hint of self-pity (vs. 14). In an attempt to justify his extraordinary journey, aiming at rediscovering the creative moment of the national life, is he tempted also to become a second Moses? More specifically, does Elijah wish to recapture not only the past but also a mode of presence which might overcome his doubt concerning the future of Yahweh's experiment with Israel?

Thus, the voice of Yahweh, plain and articulate, pronounces the word of prophetic mission. The presence, from the epiphanic visitations to the patriarchs and from the Mosaic theophany to the prophetic vision of call and commission, causes the recipient of the word to become a *poète engagé*. He must act in history through other men.

First, Elijah receives a threefold command: to anoint Hazael as king of Damascus, as a retributive agent of the Lord Judge of history who summons even foreigners into his service against his own people; to anoint Jehu as king of Israel and to foment a *coup d'état* with a change of dynasty for the sake of religious reform; and to anoint Elisha as his own successor, thereby ensuring the goodly succession of faithful men across the generations.

Second, the solitary man of God receives an announcement of extraordinary significance for the later development of Hebraic faith: the seven thousand who have not bent the knee before the Baals constitute a new sociological entity which needs to be distinguished from the traditional reality of national religion. The expression "I have caused to remain [seven thousand]" (vs. 18) germinated in the following centuries into the notion of the "remnant,"[13] a community of the faithful which could survive the destruction of the state and the annihilation of cultus, and which could potentially explode the restrictiveness of an ethnic community. Here we witness the birth of the idea of *ecclesia*, an assembly of those who trust their God rather than submit to the tyranny of political or institutional conformism.

The Point of No Return

The story of Elijah on Mt. Horeb presents itself chronologically and thematically as a transition between the *legenda* of the presence in historical events and the historical sobriety of the records of the great prophets, for whom presence is individualized, interiorized, and often curtailed or adumbrated. Three points of theological significance arise:

1. The nature of the encounter between God and the prophet is that of a passing by or an approach.[14] The nomadic metaphor is renewed in a situation of agrarian and technological civilization. The deities of the ancient Near East are not comparable to Yahweh. Even the cultic ideology of a temple must be submitted to the critique of prophetic experience. Yahweh is not to be closely associated with a given context, a sanctuary ritual, or a stable and localized institution. He is a God on the march. He never ceases from going and coming. In a manner of speaking, his absence is never far from his presence, and silence precedes the hearing of his word. Yahweh is neither manifest in the violent displays of nature nor present in the silence. When silence comes, however, and when man truly hears it and enters into the proper attitude of theocentric worship, God speaks.

2. The God who is coming is altogether different from the one that man expects. He is not the God whom memory, reason, or imagination anticipates, however marvelous and comforting the traditions may have been, and however satisfying the anticipation of a visionary presence might be. By journeying forty days and forty nights to Mt. Horeb, the site of the Mosaic theophanies, Elijah attempts to receive a testimony of theological persuasiveness, but when he witnesses the elements of thaumaturgical "evidence," he learns inwardly that Yahweh is

absent. The narrative invites a modern audience to reflect on the illusory character of man's attempts to return to an archaic past (as in biblical fundamentalism), to rely on proofs of God's existence (as in theological rationalism), or to seek sensorial perceptions of the divine (as in most forms of mysticism).

Religiously initiated and educated man is completely deceived. The unexpected comes at the core of the expected. Yet Yahweh gives a sign which does not deceive. The presence is elusive but real. Elijah receives a form of certainty which transcends his natural faculties. God preserves his incognito while making his ways known. He does not reveal his being, his inner self, or—to use the language of the Mosaic theophany—his glory (Exod. 33:18, 20), but he discloses parabolically an intention of momentous consequences for mankind. Presence does not alter nature but it changes history through the character of men.

3. The encounter between God and man does not operate in a historical vacuum. In the presence of the Hebraic God, man is not separated from his cultural context. Indeed, Elijah is dramatically rebuked for his deliberate flight from the world. Yahweh's order, "Go, return on thy journey" (vs. 15), seems to echo his twice-made query, "What art thou doing here, Elijah?" (Vss. 9, 13).[15] God is not standing aloof in heaven, away from the affairs of this world. He is not involved, however, in the interests of single groups—even the special people of the covenant—without, at the same time, raising for himself in Damascus, as well as in Samaria, agents of his historical purpose. By keeping a nascent "remnant" for the sake of the purity of faith, this God stands above all political structures. The manifestation of divine presence to Elijah on Mt. Horeb links the Abrahamic ideology of "all the families of the earth" (Gen. 12:3) to the theology of Israel, the suffering servant of Yahweh chosen to be "a light to the nations" (Isa. 42:6, etc.).

The last theophany renders "old-time religion" obsolete. It

ushers in a new mode of presence, which involves men in the
influence of character. When Elijah heard the silence which
followed the display of the absence of God, "he wrapped his
face in his mantle and went out and stood at the entrance of the
cave" (vs. 13). Though he recognized the presence, he did not
see God. He only heard a voice, and it was the voice of commission. Elijah was not a new Moses. He became the forerunner
of Amos.

THE VISIONS OF THE CALL

When Amos, Hosea, Isaiah, Jeremiah, and Ezekiel described
their visions, their purpose was always to proclaim their prophetic commissions. Diviners and mystics search for God and
believe that they can find him.[16] They depend on some institutional or technical mode of presence. Not the great prophets.
Like the patriarchs, Moses, and the Judges, they were the bearers of an unexpected and generally disruptive call.[17] They did
not initiate: they responded.

Form-critical analysis has shown in modern times that the
stories of the prophets' calling were composed according to a
literary genre closely akin to that of the epiphanic visitations to
the Patriarchs or to that of the Mosaic theophanies.[18] The *Gattung* of the prophetic calling may also have been influenced by
the Egyptian literary genre of the installation of the grand vizier
at the Pharaonic courts.[19] Like the lord chamberlain of the Pharaoh, the prophet was "ordained" to become the mouthpiece of
the Deity.[20] Such a formal stylization of literary expression,
however, does not in any way preclude the genuineness of the
prophetic vision.

Amos and his successors were confronted with the sudden
discovery of a presence. "Yahweh kidnapped me from behind

my flock," exclaimed Amos, as if he had in mind the memory of some lamb seized by a mountain lion (Amos 7:15). Unprepared and unaware, the prophets faced the abrupt knowledge of a reality which did not spring out of cultic space or cultic time. With the possible exception of Isaiah,[21] they received their call in a secular place and apparently not in some sacred season or during the celebration of a festival, although it was in such circumstances and surroundings that they publicly recounted the salient aspects of their experiences.

Amos of Teqoa (751 B.C.)

The prophet's recounting of his own visions (7:1–9, 8:1–3, 9:1–4) was interrupted by his expulsion from the royal sanctuary of Bethel (7:10–17). The reason for the surprising sequence of the present text seems to be clear. The prophet's message of doom for the kingdom of Israel provoked a challenge to his authority. It was not willingly or boastfully that he recounted the moments of intimacy which created a new consciousness in him. It was the only way he could justify the enormity and the scandalous character of his message.[22]

It has long been observed that the visions of Amos do not correspond to the pattern of those of the other great prophets.[23] Amos may well have received his initial summons (7:1–15) in a previous experience which has not been recorded for posterity, but the five visions which are preserved offer a unique insight into the slow maturation process which presided over the growth of his consciousness as a prophet of doom.[24] These visions were apparently spread over several months, from spring to autumn.[25] This lapse of time may reveal the evolution of the prophet's mind under the impact of divine prodding and the progressive acceptance of his detestable mission. The shattering effect of repeated encounters with the Deity gradually molds man's acquiescence to the incredible prospect of national disaster.

The First Vision: The Locusts (7:1-3). April-May is the season which separates the two growths of grass in the pastures. The first growth belongs to the royal government, since fodder is needed for the king's horses. If locusts devour the second growth, cattle will starve during the summer drought.

> 7:1. Here is what my Master Yahweh caused me to see:
> He was busy creating locusts,
> When fresh green grass grows again in springtime
> After the king's mowing.
> 2. As they finished eating up the herb of the earth,
> I said, Forgive, I pray thee, my Master Yahweh!
> How could Jacob rise again? He is so small!
> 3. Yahweh grieved deeply[26] over this:
> It shall not be, said Yahweh.

The prophet intercedes. Man's prayer stirs God's pathos. The vision concerns only natural objects, but the presence confers upon this banality a prophetic significance. Man's freedom and God's compassion are held in tense equilibrium.[27]

The Second Vision: The Great Abyss (7:4-6). The meaning of the trial of the great abyss by fire is not clear. In the sequence of the visions which precede and follow, the occasion for the second was likely the dog days which usually follow the summer solstice in July. During a heat wave, the bottom of the lowest canyon on earth—nearly a mile below Teqoa—the Dead Sea looks like a boiling caldron. The fear of cosmic annihilation prompts the prophet to step up the tone of his intercession. Instead of praying, "forgive," he expostulates, "desist!" Solidarity with the poor of Jacob leads the intercessor to challenge the Deity. Presence intensifies freedom.

The Third Vision: The Plumbline (7:7-9). The form of the third vision is radically different. No longer witnessing an event in nature and its mythical environment, the prophet penetrates the realm of history. Yahweh will place a plumbline in the midst of his people Israel and no longer pass them by (vs. 8). Since walls are rebuilt every summer around orchards and vineyards in an effort to protect maturing fruits from animal and human marauders, the seasonal setting for the third vision is July-August. The exact image of the plumbline is a matter of scholarly discussion,[28] but the general meaning of the symbol is clear enough. From the picture of a cosmic ordeal, the prophet's attention is steered toward the corruption of the covenant people. The prophet no longer intercedes on the behalf of the small nation: the wall crumbles from within. Presence, which cultic rite summons, maintains, or renews, has turned into the power of judgment.

The Fourth Vision: The Basket of Fruits (8:1-2). The use of a paronomasia tightens the rhetorical crispness, and the finality of the verdict emerges from the assonance as well as from the semantic association: a basket of fruits (qayiṣ) signifies that the end (qêyṣ) has come. The season is August-September. While olives, pomegranates, almonds, and grapes overload their branches, "ripeness is all." Maturity ushers in the finality of putrescence. The prophet no longer interferes. He assents. A picture of chaos follows (vss. 3-14).

The Fifth Vision: "Strike the Altar!" (9:1-6). Yahweh himself is standing on the altar and orders Amos to strike its cornice. God intends to pursue all with divine fury, even to the mythical extremities of the universe. Commentators generally agree that this scene was suggested by the celebration of the autumn festival in September-October. The form of high stylization, with repetitions and significant variations, indicates once again that the power of the ecstatic image stimulates rather than impedes intellectual reflection. Vision and word are inseparable.

Presence appears at once to burst forth climactically from a long acquaintance of intimacy with the divine and to crystallize an inwardly appropriated inheritance of Yahwistic faith.[29] The last two visions, particularly, indicate that Amos stood squarely within the tradition of the Mosaic theophany[30] as it was cultically concretized through the covenant celebration of the yearly feast.[31] Amos reversed the popular eschatology which this tradition had produced. He expected the day of Yahweh to be a day of judgment.[32] At the same time, the sapiential "humanism" to which Amos had been exposed broadened spectacularly his historical horizon.[33] The sweep of the divine concern for mankind included all nations and all races, the distant and different Ethiopians, even the most hated enemies of Israel—the Philistines and the Syrians (9:7).

The five visions seem to have come after years of protracted and sustained meditation upon society and the world in a peculiarly prophetic mode of presence: day-in and day-out intimacy with a traveling companion, a God-man companionship comparable to the lasting familiarity of two men walking in the wilderness together (3:2–7). They share secrets (vs. 7).[34] Vision and word are inseparable because vision follows communion. Far from reducing the prophet's volition to passivity, or producing aphasia, inaction, and social withdrawal, the power of ecstasy[35] enhances his passion to intervene actively within the life of the nation and increases the inner strength which enables him to face social opprobrium and threats to his safety. The prophetic brand of response to presence is not through an "ecstasy of absorption" but through an "ecstasy of concentration" which heightens the faculties of critical analysis as well as the emotional drive to involve the self deliberately and perhaps wrecklessly in the historical situation.[36]

Response to the stimulus of presence becomes the mold of theology. Ideas follow images, as "irrational" vision slowly brings forth "rational" certainty. The recital of the last visions flows into the formulation of discourses (8:4–14), and discourses in turn exteriorize and explain action (9:1–6).[37] Such a phenomenon is not the mark of mystical quietism. The visions move from emotion to thought and from thought to deed. The

ardor of Yahweh the Judge reaches a climax with the frenzy of
Yahweh the Executioner, and the prophet himself is bidden to
act as the Executioner's assistant (9:1). The prophet is a true
poet, in the etymological sense of the Greek word *poiêtês*. Presence calls him to be a speaker and an actor with God, almost an
actor for God. The last vision introduces the "prophetic act,"
by which the presence is so intense that the prophet becomes
the impersonator and the living incarnator of divinity.[38]

It is not by chance that the action of the prophet (9:1) is
summoned in the context of an attack upon the localized, con-
centrated mode of presence in the cultus. The sword stroke
upon the cornice of the altar initiates the universal broadening
of the scope of presence in judgment. In a flight of rhetorical
imagination, the prophet expresses as never before the cosmic
sweep of the presence. He depicts Yahweh reaching out into the
underworld—a motif unexpressed elsewhere in Hebraic
thought, except in wisdom poetry.[39] He even places the myth of
the sea serpent within the compass of divine omnipotence.

Hosea of Benjamin (ca. 743)

The Book of Hosea contains no story of prophetic vision nor
does it record any dialogue of prophetic vocation. However, the
biographical narrative of his marriage (1:2–9) and the autobiographical confession of his remarriage (3:1–5) offer data on the
most peculiar form of human response to divine presence that
may be found in the religious literature of ancient Israel.[40]

Outwardly, these stories describe a series of prophetic acts[41]
similar to those which are told in the books of Isaiah, Jeremiah,
and Ezekiel. In a scandalously startling manner, which was
bound to compel attention, Hosea was attempting effectively to
convey Yahweh's message. He married a whore "because the
land had prostituted itself by abandoning Yahweh" (1:2). Inwardly, these stories throw light on the hidden process of near

identification with the divine reality by which a prophet enters into "the knowledge of God" (6:6).

The Biographical Narrative (1:2-9). There is no compelling reason for rejecting the plain meaning of the text. Hosea was already conscious of his vocation when he was told to take for himself "a handsome and promiscuous woman"[42] as a living symbol of Israel. At the same time, one should admit that a proleptical telescoping of memory may have led the prophet years after the event to interpret his fascination for the woman he married as part of his prophetic mission.

Be that as it may, the first child of the couple was legitimate, for the text pointedly states, "and she conceived and she bore him a son" (vs. 3). Hosea named him "Jizreel" ("God sows the seed"; cf. 2:22–23 [Heb. 24–25]). The symbolism of the name was related explicitly to Jehu's coup d'etat and bloodshed, a portent of the nation's corruption (vs. 4). The second and third children were illegitimate, for the text omits the pronoun "to him" when it states that the woman conceived again and bore a daughter (vs. 6) and, later on, conceived once more and bore a son (vs. 8). The names of these infants reflect the prophetic consciousness of their legal father: Lo-ruhamah, "One-who-does-not-receive-motherly-love," and Lo-ammi, "Not-my-people." They also seem to suggest that Hosea knew the children were illegitimate. The way he spoke elsewhere of the love of Yahweh for Israel may even indicate that Hosea acted at times as a substitute mother for these bastard children, teaching them how to walk, taking them up in his arms, caressing them against his cheek,[43] and feeding them when they were hungry (cf. 11:3–4). The concreteness of the language unmistakably reveals personal experience.

Hosea thus endured public shame and dishonor in order to portray not only an unfaithful Israel but also a dishonored and shamed Deity. Through the performance of prophetic acts, presence became "incarnational." Representing God, the prophet suffered in his own life the agony of God.[44] The style of the divorce proceeding (2:1–13 [Heb. 4–15]) cannot conceal the pain of an emasculated ego. In a fit of erotic jealousy, the prophet projected his own turmoil into the divine realm. An accent of emotional authenticity permeates every line of the poem. The reader is no longer able to discern whether the rage with which the deceived husband promises himself to strip the woman naked and expose her lewdness to the world (2:3 [Heb. 5]) applies to the injured God of a covenant that has been violated or to Hosea himself, caught in the depth of his being by the very cruelty of a love which finds no response.

The Autobiographical Confession (3:1–5). The text unambiguously says, as it does in the biographical narrative of the marriage (1:2), that the prophet received and obeyed orders:

And Yahweh said to me again, Go, love [the] woman[45] who is loved of a lover and is an adulteress, even as Yahweh loves the people of Israel, though they turn to other gods and love raisin cakes.[46] So I bought her for fifteen shekels of silver and a homer and a lethech of barley. And I said to her, Thou wilt dwell as mine for many days; thou wilt not play the harlot or belong to any man; so will I also be to thee (3:1–4).

The style of personal address and confession probably indicates that the prophet told this story within the intimate circle of his followers. Is it that gratuitous love—human or divine—requires the reticence of privacy? The dynamics of obedience are so enmeshed with the dynamics of experience that one cannot speculate on the anteriority of psychological introspection over theological revelation, or vice-versa.

The transition from the decision to repudiate to the intention to save is unexpected, unless one sees the autobiographical confession in the light of the poetry of a new betrothal (2:14–23 [Heb. 16–25]). It may be that the poet's bruised *erôs* was the laboratory for the discovery of Yahweh's *agapê*. The startling order to love the adulterous woman, as Yahweh loves unfaithful Israel, implies a notion of self-giving love (*agapê*) rather than the egocentric, self-seeking "love" (*erôs*) of natural anthropology. The Greek-speaking Jews of Alexandria in the Hellenistic period did not miss the nuance, as shown by the Septuagint translation of this passage.[47] The distinction does not oppose spiritual to sexual love, as has often been maintained on the assumption of a dualistic anthropology, for the denial of sexual intimacy is only part of a temporary trial, a symbol of political, cultic, and economic restraint in the national return to "the wilderness" (vs. 5). Once again, the language intermingles the prophet's own experience and the theological word. The prophetic consciousness is inseparable from the lover's introspection.

The prophet Amos, before Hosea, had considered the faint possibility of divine grace for a remnant, but explicitly and unambiguously he tied this possibility to the previous fulfillment of several radical conditions: national repentance, the hate of evil, the love of good, and the establishment of justice in the civil and judiciary branches of the government (Amos 5:15). He apparently did not expect that such a conversion would take place, and his eschatology was one of unrelieved doom.

On the contrary, Hosea discerned in self-giving love a power of educational persuasiveness which would make repentance possible, both at the level of the man-woman relationship and in the realm of the covenant renewal:

"Therefore, behold, I will allure her,
    and bring her into the wilderness,
    and speak tenderly to her" (2:14 [Heb. 16]).

The psychological complexity of the prophetic act continues to penetrate the formulation of the theological hope:

"In that day, says Yahweh, thou wilt call me My Husband (*'ish*) and no longer wilt thou call me My Master" (*ba'al;* 2:16 [Heb. 18]).

The expectation of a national crisis is not, as in Amos, colored by the finality of a cosmic annihilation.[48] It is predicated upon a philosophy of suffering which unites psychology and theology and discerns in the experience of pain a process of character transformation (Hos. 3:4–5). That the prophet used his own faculties of subjective reflectiveness in order to give rhetorical shape to his theological word[49] and therefore to find in his own emotional upheaval the mirror of divine pathos is implied by many of his poetic sayings.[50] None of these is more eloquent than his oft-quoted strophe on the *agon* of hesitation which comes from the depths of his prophetic consciousness and bears at the same time the mark of a lover's passionate quandary:

How can I give thee up, Ephraim?
How can I hand thee over, Israel?

My own heart recoils against me,
My grief and my compassion[51] are kindled together:
I will not execute the rage of my wrath,
I will not return to destroy Ephraim!
For I am God and not man,
The Holy One in the midst of thee,
And I will not come in anger[52] (Hos. 11:8–9).

Repentance is the response to gratuitous love, not its condition. The new marriage will be founded not only upon respect for justice and right but also upon the more subtle realities of fidelity and mercy, and its aim will be the immediacy of knowledge between God and man:

I will betroth thee to me forever,
  I will betroth thee to me in justice and in right,
  In loyalty and in tender compassion,
I will betroth thee to me in faith,
And thou wilt know Yahweh

                                    (Hos. 2:19-20 [Heb. 20-21]).

The response "My God" (2:23 [Heb. 25]) will seal the renewal of the covenant relationship.[53]

The prophet has been invaded and permeated by the presence of Yahweh in such a way that he has become a living monstrance of the divine reality. Yet one should not understand this near-identification of God and man as a fusion, either mystical or mythical, for the tension between transcendence and immanence is never abrogated. Yahweh may be "in the midst of" Israel as he manifests his being "within" Hosea, but he is also the Holy One. The use of the name *Haq-qadosh,* "the Holy One," shows that for Hosea the Godhead remains charged with the terror of the "wholly other." Yahweh is God and not man. This is precisely why, unlike man, he is moved by the self-giving quality of a love that is centered upon the good of its object. Hosea learns from the Holy One that a certain kind of love possesses the virtue of healing, saving, and life-renewing. *Da'at Elohim,* "the knowledge of God" (Hos. 6:6),[54] discloses to the prophet that *agapê* constitutes the core of holiness.

Isaiah of Jerusalem (ca. 742-683 B.C.)

The paradox of holiness which Hosea perceived in the power of love also dominated the thinking of his southern disciple, Isaiah of Jerusalem; but it produced a different form of hope, since it reduced the salvation of the people to a converted remnant.

The Vision in the Temple (Isa. 6:1-13). Isaiah was probably a cultic prophet attached to the temple of Jerusalem.[55] He presumably received a vision while prostrate in the middle room (*hêkal*) of the edifice. Nevertheless, presence did not mean for him the inviolability of Zion.[56] Analysis of the narrative shows that "the house" which elsewhere always designates an earthly sanctuary, was only the setting of a suprasensorial perception of the heavenly temple.[57]

1. The divine manifestation.

In the year of King Uzziah's death, I saw Adonay sitting on an exalted throne and his royal robes filled the middle room of the sanctuary. Seraphim stood above him. Each of them had six wings, two for covering their faces, two for covering their feet,[58] and two for flying. And they alternated their acclamations, saying,
 Holy, holy, holy, Yahweh of Hosts,
  the whole earth is filled with his glory.
The hinges of the doors vibrated at the voice of those who made the acclamations, and the house was filled with smoke.

2. The prophet's reaction

And I said,
 Woe is me! I am utterly lost,
  for I am a man of impure lips,
  and I dwell in the midst of a people of impure lips,
  yet my eyes have seen the King, Yahweh of Hosts!

3. The purification

And one of the seraphim flew toward me. He had in his hand
a burning coal that he had taken with tongs from the altar.
And he touched my mouth, saying,
 Behold, this has touched thy lips,
  thy guilt is removed, and thy sin atoned for.

4. The vocation

And I heard the voice of Adonay saying,
 Whom shall I send and who will go for us?

And I said,
  Here am I, send me.

5. *The commission*

And he said,
  Go and say to this people,
    Hear continually, but do not understand,
    See and go on seeing, but do not know . . .
  Lest they see with their eyes, and hear with their ears,
    and turn and be healed.

6. *The question*

Then I said,
  How long, Adonay?

7. *The reply*

And he said,
Until the cities lie in waste without inhabitants,
  and houses without men,
And the land is utterly desolate . . .
Although a tenth still remain,
  it will be burnt,
Like a terebinth or an oak,
  of which only a stump remains when it is felled;
  this trunk is the seed of the Holy One.[59]

This majestic scene, told with solemnity and stylistic restraint, has received innumerable commentaries over the centuries. Historians of comparative religions have pointed out
cultic and mythic features which Isaiah appears to have borrowed from the ancient Near East. Form-critical and traditio-
historical exegetes have shown the affinities which link this
narrative with the literary *Gattungen* of the epiphanic visitation
to the patriarchs (especially the Abrahamic dialogue), the Mosaic theophany (especially the scene of the Burning Bush), and the
council of Yahweh (especially the vision of Micayah ben Yim-

lah).[60] Nevertheless, an Isaian distinctiveness sharply delineates itself within the traditional pattern:

1. The royal majesty of God stands above historical kingship: "In the year of the death of King Uzziah . . . my eyes have seen the King."[61]

2. The holiness of Yahweh transcends cultic edifices, for his glory fills the earth in its entirety instead of being confined to a sanctuary.[62]

3. The prophet's guilt-consciousness arises both from his sense of social solidarity as member of a corrupt people and from his vision of the holy God. The quality of the presence is so overwhelming that the prophet, certainly not a moral or legal delinquent, feels by contrast the guilt of his finiteness. Yet, awareness of sin comes only to those who stand at the verge of reconciliation. Despair over the self grows from a sense of unworthiness, but it cannot annihilate the personality of the prophet. Within holiness, the disciple of Hosea discerns the healing quality of love: he is purified and accepted.

4. Purification and atonement are cultic rites, but they are performed by the seraphim, heavenly beings of the flame, who belong to the realm of divine holiness. The prophet's vision transcends the sacerdotal system, for it is God who initiates and fulfils the institutional deed.

5. The prophet's surrender to the holy presence precedes and prepares the readiness of his answer to the call. Form-critical analysts are compelled to recognize that the pattern of human hesitation, refusal, or even revolt is here broken. When Isaiah becomes aware of Yahweh's summons and of his search for a messenger at a given moment of history, he knows only one response, direct, unswerving, unqualified, unhesitating: "Here am I, send me."

6. The negative character of the commission does not prevent the prophet's decision to obey the call. Prospects of prag-

matic success or failure do not affect Isaiah's motivation. The question "How long, Adonay?" should not be interpreted as part of the form-critical structure of "objection," nor should the divine reply be construed as the traditional motif of "reassurance."[63] Rather, the plaintive interjection of the ancient Near Eastern prayer of supplication indicates that he stood for a moment, like Amos, as an intercessor on behalf of the doomed people.[64] Thereupon, as a diplomatic attaché, loyal to the Great King, he stood by his orders.[65] There was no hope for the kingdom of Judah, but a remnant, a seed of the Holy One, would eventually usher in the era of peace.

The Deus Absconditus (8:16–18). The moment before God is swiftly spent, even for a prophet, and it may never return. Isaiah appears to have lived most of his adult years on the strength of his initial appointment as a prophet. Soon after his unsuccessful intervention with King Ahaz, during the Syro-Ephraimitic War (735–734 B.C.) and his prediction of the birth of the mysterious Immanuel (7:14), he announced before witnesses the birth of his own son, Maher-shalal-hash-baz (8:1–4). Thereupon, he seems to have retired from public life, perhaps in imitation of God's own withdrawal from the history of the covenant people. For many years, he apparently confined his energies to the training of "prophetic seminarians," preparing for the next generation.

Such is probably the significance of a somewhat enigmatic statement, now inserted in the series of the Immanuel oracles (7:1—9:7 [Heb. 6]):

> Bind up the testimony,
>   Seal the teaching among my disciples:
> I will wait for Yahweh
>   who hides[66] his face from the house of Jacob,
>   And I will hope in him.

Behold, I and the children whom Yahweh has given me
are signs and portents in Israel,
from Yahweh who dwells on Mount Zion.[67]

(Isa. 8:16–18)

This short passage brings together in a surprising way a number of motifs which are not apparently related: the establishment of a prophetic school, the silent testimony of the prophet and of his children endowed with symbolic names, and the declaration of hope in the *Deus absconditus*.

As is well known, the latter theme was destined to become exceptionally popular among religious thinkers of Judaism and Christianity. The passive latinity of the expression *Deus absconditus*, "the hidden God," may fail to convey the meaning of active and sustained determination which the Hebrew original carries.[68] For the prophet, there is no doubt that the God who hides his face is very much alive. During the eclipse of God, the man of faith formulates a theology of hope; and he is able to wait creatively,[69] for he remembers the power of his prophetic vision. The presence which conceals itself is not an absence.[70]

In his inner being, the prophet nurtured the awareness of a presence which was anchored both in the past and the future. He remembered and he waited. In the meantine, his own children became signs and portents. Like the offspring of the Hosea household, Isaiah's children carried names which proclaimed insistently and even stridently the word he received during the vision of his call, not only Maher-shalal-hash-baz, "Hurry-to-the-spoil-hasten-to-loot," but also Shear-yashub, "A-Remnant-shall-be-converted." Even the name of the wonder-child, Immanuel, who may or may not have been his own,[71] carried a prophetic warning regarding the ambiguity of the divine nearness, "God-with-us," an ambiguity which was similar to that of Hosea's oracle on the Holy One in the midst of Israel.[72]

Both the children and the disciples of Isaiah may represent

his participation in the remnant—a historical link or bridge destined to connect the doomed economy of historical existence with the reign of universal peace at the advent of the Prince of peace.[73] Like his predecessors, Amos and Hosea, the prophet who saw Yahweh dwelling on Mount Zion no longer believed in the historical continuity of political and cultic institutions. The knowledge of the dynamic power of holiness which he received in his prophetic vision prompted him to discern the ambivalence of the holy place. It was no accident that his enigmatic statement on the *Deus absconditus* is now prefaced by an appeal to transcend the sanctuary:

> Yahweh of Hosts, him shall you hold as holy!
>   Let him be your fear, and even your terror,
>   And he will become a sanctuary,
> And a stone of offense, and a rock of stumbling . . .
>   A trap and a snare . . .
>
> (Isa. 8:13–14)

The prophet has become a theologian of the unfettered, uncontrollable holy. What Rudolf Otto wrote of Martin Luther may be applied to the Hebrew prophet who first grasped the rapport between holiness and self-concealing presence: "That before which his soul quails again and again in awe is not merely the stern Judge demanding righteousness . . . but rather at the same time God in his 'unrevealedness,' in the aweful majesty of his very Godhead: He before whom trembles not simply the transgressor of the law, but the creature, as such, in his 'uncovered' creaturehood."[74]

Between the memory of his vision of holiness and the waiting for Yahweh, the prophet lived by faith. It was apparently he who revived the Abrahamic motif of *'emunah,* "faith,"[75] and gave it theological currency. He had experienced the staying power of the *Amen:* "No faith, no staith," was perhaps his motto.[76] His faith was the ground of his hope.

Jeremiah of Anathoth (ca. 626–580 B.C.)

The prophet Jeremiah belonged to a sacerdotal family living in Anathoth, a few miles north of Jerusalem, in the old territory of Benjamin (Jer. 1:1). It was there that Solomon, in the tenth century B.C., had banished Abiathar, the priest of David, who had opposed Solomon's illegal seizure of the throne (1 Kings 2:26–27). Jeremiah may therefore have been brought up in a family tradition of opposition to the Solomonic style of kingship and especially to the Zadokite priesthood of Jerusalem.

The story of Jeremiah's vision and call is told in three parts, each one presented as a distinctive coming of Yahweh's word to him.[77] In fact, however, it records neither a vision nor, strictly speaking, a call. To be sure, it contains traditional elements, such as the prophetic protest of the Mosaic type, or the seeing of trivial objects as in Amos.[78] Nevertheless, the structure of the scene is original and defies the ingenuity of form-critical analysis.[79] Most significantly, Jeremiah was not invited to become a prophet. Rather Yahweh informed him in a unique way that he had been brought into being specifically to be a prophet.[80]

Born to Be a Prophet (1:4–10). Amos had thought that—one day in time—Yahweh had seized him from behind his flock (7:14–15); Hosea had received the order—one day in time—to marry a promiscuous woman (1:2); and Isaiah had seen—one day in time—the royal splendor of Yahweh (6:1 ff.). All three, like Moses, could remember the exact day they had become prophets. In a similar way, Jeremiah could remember the day he had experienced an immediate encounter with the Godhead. Unlike his predecessors, however, Jeremiah was not made a prophet by that day in time. Instead, it disclosed to him a most peculiar conviction—he had come into being for the purpose of proclaiming the prophetic word:

"Before I formed thee in the womb I knew thee;
And before thou camest forth I made thee holy;
A prophet to the nations I ordained thee" (vs. 5).

Commentators who discern here a notion of divine foreknowledge or of predestination—doctrines of a later age which
are generally mistaken for a form of philosophical determinism
—seem to miss the warmth of the self-awareness which the
prophet experienced at the moment of this disclosure. He
learned that he was surrounded spatially and temporally by the
divine mind. He discovered that he himself had been created
for a divinely defined purpose. Poets of the Jeremianic school
have applied to new situations the prophet's sense of creatureliness.[81]

The prophetic consciousness of Jeremiah was inseparable
from his ontological awareness. He was not a man called to
prophethood. He had been born to be a prophet. His existential
selfhood belonged to the *telos* of the Creator. Presence preceded his being brought into existence. His finiteness was shored
up by the intention of God.

Jeremiah also learned that Yahweh had not only known and
appointed him but had also "consecrated" him, literally, made
him "holy." This is an unexpected and in fact unique claim for
a great prophet of Israel. Translators and commentators are
apparently so surprised by the expression that they soften or
even ignore its importance. Many render the Hebrew verb *hiq-
dashtika*, "I have made thee holy," by the rather neutral and
secular phrase "I have set thee apart." The notion of holiness,
however, did not apply to objects or to persons other than
divine, except among priestly circles.[82] Jeremiah thought of
himself as entirely "devoted" to Yahweh by Yahweh himself,
and he therefore shared in some mythopoetic fashion in the
holiness of Yahweh. Presence of the holy threw Isaiah into the
terror of self-hate and self-destruction. Presence of the holy

embraced Jeremiah and drew him into an awesome involvement with the divine. "A priest is holy to his God" (Lev. 21:7) was the motto of the sacerdotal collegium which survived the exile from Jerusalem. A theological gulf, however, separated the priests from Jeremiah. To them the Holiness Code admonished, "Consecrate yourselves, and be ye holy, for I am Yahweh your God" (Lev. 20:7). Ritual manipulated the holy. To Jeremiah, Yahweh himself said, "I have consecrated thee." Presence of the holy made him holy.

The theocentricity of Jeremiah's introspective insight into his own identity—even if this insight emerged from a shattering moment of trance—left him with no freedom to refuse. He was not invited to answer a call. He was informed that he was born to be a prophet. Nevertheless, he dared to respond, not with a protest of refusal, but with a plea for mercy that was based on his youth and his inability to speak (vs. 6). Yahweh promised him the assurance of a continuous presence, according to the Mosaic pattern of vocation:

"I shall be with thee to succor thee" (vs. 8).

Jeremiah heard no seraphic *Sanctus*. He shared in the "apartness" of the holy. He was not overwhelmed by a sense of guilt. He did not need a purification of the lips. Instead, he received the visual, tactile, and auditory sensation of Yahweh's hand touching his mouth and of the divine voice saying,

"Behold, I have put my words in thy mouth" (vs. 9).[83]

The prophet understood that he was more than a bearer of the word[84] who faithfully repeated a message. He had been transformed into the mouthpiece of the Deity. Mythopoetic thinking even led him in later years to develop his own interpretation of the presence of the word in the startlingly concrete terms of a quasi-sacramental absorption. He said to his God in a prayer: "As soon as thy words came to me, I ate them, and thy word was for me cheerfulness and joy" (15:16).[85] The process of prophetic revelation was fully interiorized. The word had been "inwardly digested." As is well known, this image appealed to the imagination of Jewish and Christian mystics and became especially popular with Protestant divines after the Reformation.

For Jeremiah, presence of the holy produced a sense of participation in the word which was akin to physical nourishment.

Wakeful Over the Word (1:11–12). As the first "vision" climaxed with the ingestion of the divine word, the second followed hard upon it:

> And the word of Yahweh came to me, saying:
>   What seest thou, Jeremiah?
> And I said, I see a branch of almond-tree in blossom;
>   And Yahweh said to me, Thou hast well seen,
>   For I am wakeful over my word to fulfill it.

The consonantal alliteration of "almond-tree" (*shaqed*) and "wakeful" (*shoqed*) stressed through playful etymology the urgency of speaking the divine word.[86] On the hillside below Anathoth, the almond trees bloom ahead of other trees. Their white and rose flowers, with fragile stems, are soon blown away by the January winds. Etymological association suggests wakefulness at the earliest season and ephemerality under duress, thereby justifying inner strength as well as hard determination. Yahweh watches over his word as he watches over the life of nature. The prophet of the word is implicitly invited to enter into the *imitatio Dei.*

The Heated Crucible (1:13–19). The third part of the "vision" of the call, like the second, interprets the sighting of a seemingly neutral object. A crucible heated on a fire that has been "blown upon" (*naphûᵃḥ*) by the wind[87] is tilted away from the north: a marvellously ambivalent image which ushers in both an oracle of judgment and a promise of reassurance:

"From the north disaster shall flare up[88]
   against all the inhabitants of the land,
For, behold! I am about to summon all the nations
   and all the kingdoms of the north, said Yahweh" (vs. 14).

The art of metallurgy, which is evoked by the sight of the heated crucible, is lifted out of its original connotation of the military-industrial complex and is now used to introduce the motif of presence which makes strength:[89]

"But thou! Tighten thy champion's girdle!

Behold! I make thee this day a fortified city,
   a pillar of iron, a battlement of bronze
Against the whole land, the kings and princes of Judah,
   the priests and the common people:
They will wage war against thee but not prevail,
   for I am with thee to succour thee, Oracle of Yahweh!"
                                                    (vss. 17–19).

The presence of Yahweh had revealed to Jeremiah that he was born to be a prophet to the nations (vs. 4). The sight of almond blossoms invited him to watch with Yahweh over the word. The sight of a heated crucible brought to his mind the signal of his conversion from irresponsible timidity to stalwart adulthood. Although later in life he found himself prey to mockery, persecution, mistreatment, and the dread of death, he was able to endure. He knew the tortures of ostracism and solitary confinement, but he outlived five kings as well as the kingdom. Presence had turned a weakling into a metal-girded fortress.

Ezekiel of Tel-Aviv (ca. 593 B.C.)

Strikingly different from the narratives of his predecessors was the story of Ezekiel's vocation (1:1—3:15).[90] The son of a Jerusalem priest, Ezekiel presumably belonged to the Zadokite family. After the first siege of Jerusalem (597 B.C.), he was deported with the elite of the city to the marshes of southern Mesopotamia. Four years later, in the torrid torpidity of a summer day, as he sat amid the giant reeds near the water-edge of the "river Chebar,"[91] he "saw visions of Elohim" (1:1). The bizarre description of his experience has colored the accounts of many apocalypticists and mystics ever since.[92]

The Fiery Chariot (1:4-21). No prophet before Ezekiel had claimed that "the heavens were opened" for him. This specific aspect of his ecstasy may have been inspired by his sacerdotal upbringing. As the member of a priestly family, the young deportee had doubtless believed that Yahweh dwelt in Zion. He could not expect that Yahweh would manifest his presence in a remote and totally alien land except through some shattering of the cosmic order.

The prolixity of the style of this account contrasts sharply with the elliptical crispness of Amos or with the stateliness of Isaiah's picture of the holy. Later in his career, however, Ezekiel used parables, dirges, and satires, which reveal his mastery of many poetic idioms. If he told the story of his call with lexicographic and syntactic ponderousness, he may have been obeying a valid impulse: the visions were ineffable. How could he convey in spatial and necessarily static terms the dynamic motility and the fluid effulgence of the divine glory? Thus he relied on strange comparisons which risked misunderstanding and required qualifying correction. By a repetitive accumulation of synonyms, he sought to guard against the betrayal of similes.

Through such impossible incongruities as wheels with eyes, Ezekiel discerned and conveyed his perception of divine omniscience. The four living beings in the midst of fire evoked the four corners of the universe, but they were not immersed in nature. Their anthropomorphic and zoomorphic features would not permit a confusion with the human or animal realm, for he presented them only as an adumbration of the corporateness of the divine personality. The alternation of feminine and masculine genders for the pronouns referring to these beings merely stressed the beyondness of the Godhead over the finitude of human sexuality.[93] God was distinct, and at the same time near.

The Likeness of the Glory (1:22-28). As the record of the visions proceeded to penetrate closer to the core of mystery, the accumulation of mutually exclusive elements helped to build up the awareness of transcendence. Sound and sight were intermingled. The "awesome crystal" evoked the ice of the mythical north (cf. Job 37:22). The blue sapphire designated not the firmament but its likeness (cf. Exod. 24:10). Sounds were compared in rapid succession to the rush of primal waters, the thunder of the Mosaic theophany, and the tumult of marching hosts. Noises piled up and canceled one another out. There was light, brightness, flame, and dazzling effulgence. "Seated above the likeness of a throne was a likeness as it were of a human form" (vs. 26). Did then the prophet perceive the fullness of the divine reality? Not at all. He saw only "the appearance of the likeness of the glory of Yahweh" (vs. 28). Clearly, this theologian of "the mystical vision" was most careful in his use of words.

While considerably emphasized, the visual elements did not amount to an accurate photograph of the Deity. Perhaps one might say in all seriousness that Ezekiel's film was overexposed. Unlike Jacob in the midnight gloom at the bottom of the Jabbok canyon or Isaiah prostrate in the latticed dimness of a temple hall filled with smoke, Ezekiel saw God in a blinding light—as effective a mask of the Deity as darkness. The *essentia* of God eluded him, just as it had eluded Moses. Only the fleeting presence of a moment was granted to his prophetic humanity.

The Prophetic Send-Off (2:1—3:11). Traditional features of the literary genre of "commission," such as a message to the people and a promise of reassurance, appear in the balance of the narrative, but they are couched in a novel form:

> And [God] said to me: Son of man, stand up on thy feet, that I may speak to thee. Then the Spirit entered into me when he spoke to me. And he said to me, Son of man, I will send thee to the house of Israel, to the rebellious people.... Be not afraid of them! ... [even] if you must live among scorpions (vss. 1-6).

As the vision is about to fade, presence continues to impart its power to man under the mode of "the Spirit." From Amos to Jeremiah, the great prophets had avoided the use of this motif,[94] but Ezekiel favored it above all other means of indicating the force which at once compelled him and confirmed him as the Deity's envoy.[95] The spirit of Yahweh was held as the initiator and the sustainer of life.[96] It did not designate a divine attribute but pointed to the transmission of bio-energy, the persistence of being, and the fight against death. Applied to the psychic process of "prophetic inspiration," the word was related to the psychic motion through which the will of the Deity was learned by man.

Likewise, borrowing another expression, which this time had been used by some of the prophets, Ezekiel thought that the hand of Yahweh had fallen upon him.[97] Quasi-physically he perceived on himself the sign of an outside intervention, which he interpreted not only as divine mastery but also as appointment and trust.

So concrete was his consciousness of having received a message which he was commanded to deliver that he remembered having eaten a scroll that bore "words of laments, sighs, and woes" (2:10) on both sides. His revulsion against speaking such words was overcome by the sublimity of his vision of glory. The scroll tasted as sweet as honey (3:1–2).[98] It is not possible to infer from the text whether Ezekiel was recounting as best he could the memory of a trancelike state or was using the language of mystical metaphor.[99] He believed, in any case, that his entire personality had been altered by his vision of the fiery chariot. God himself, on the marshy banks of the river Chebar, had summoned him to the prophetic task. Ezekiel's commission was confirmed by the hand of Yahweh and empowered by the spirit of Yahweh. In addition, the prophet had "incorporated" the word of Yahweh. The "bad taste" of pronouncing oracles of horror to people who feverishly clung to their illusions was now sublimated into a "good taste." With "a forehead as hard as diamond" (3:8), he could henceforth dare to confront in Tel-aviv the hostility, unbelief, and rebelliousness of his fellow deportees.

In modern times, students of the great prophets have tended to look sociologically at these few giants of the faith, as if they had been chiefly, if not exclusively, the product of an institutional office.[100] To be sure, the poems of Amos and his successors show the influence of festal liturgies, and the accounts of their visions may well follow the structure of the installation ceremonies for cultic officials. At the same time, the diversity of these accounts and their accent of personal emotion point to the genuineness of the experience. Amos, Hosea, Isaiah, Jeremiah, and Ezekiel were prophets of the presence. Their visions are alive with shattering memories of glimpses of infinity, while the aesthetic quality of their individual styles points to the interpenetrative process by which poetic expression was initiated and sustained.[101] The burden of the great prophets' "office" was the burden of the word which had privately been forced upon them. They subordinated their entire lives to the intrusion of the presence.[102]

FROM VISION TO FAITH

Elijah understood that the era of theophany was closed. His successors, the great prophets, knew their God in secret moments of ecstasy, the prophetic vision.[103] The precise nature of such an encounter may not be susceptible of analysis by modern psychology,[104] but the relationship between the prophets' specific experiences of divine nearness and their knowledge of God's purpose for history can hardly be doubted. Kierkegaard rejected as pagan the claims of mystical vision,[105] but his outburst represented an extreme reaction to the sensualism of religious sentimentalism. The great prophets were not pagan when they testified to their own awareness of divine immediacy in particular instances of encounter with the holy. This very obedience to the prophetic vision went against their national allegiance and their religious upbringing. It enabled the nation to survive the state.

Presence in Judgment.

The cultic rehearsal of Yahweh's saving acts in history had conditioned the covenant people to such an extent that political disaster was bound to entail religious disintegration. After the fall of Jerusalem in 587 B.C., it would have been useless to maintain that "even the lowliest maidservant at the Red Sea saw what Isaiah, Ezekiel, and all the prophets never saw."[106] It was the prophetic vision, not the belief in the presence of Yahweh in history or in a shrine, which explains the birth of Judaism. After the Babylonian "holocaust," the surviving Judahites became the Jews instead of assimilating themselves to their pagan environment, because Jeremiah and Ezekiel "saw" in the catastrophe, not the sign of Yahweh's absence, but, on the contrary, the manifestation of his presence in judgment. This interpretation was the direct outgrowth of their knowledge of God (*da'at Elohim*). In turn, this knowledge encompassed a far more inclusive realm than that of intellectual information. Not only Jeremiah, but all the great prophets, were aware of being "known" by Yahweh (Jer. 1:5). Their knowledge of God was one aspect of an intrinsic experience of mutuality. It was crystallized and deepened by the prophetic vision, but it exceeded the temporal limits of a chronological memory. It affected the psychological mode of a presence which amounted to a revelatory discipline.

Epistemological Communion.

Moments of rapture never last. The prophetic vision always fades. After the unexpected ascent to the inward summit, the prophets descended, no doubt sensing a loss of the kind which prompted countless mystical poets after them to confide:

Ah, now it fades! it fades! and I must pine
Again for that dread country crystalline,
Where the blank field and the still-standing tree
Were bright and fearful presences to me.[107]

The prophets, however, did not seek to renew or to prolong those times of "bright and fearful presences," for they shared, before and after, what might be called "a traveling mateship" with the Godhead. The ancient ideal of "walking with God," associated with the antediluvian figure of Enoch (Gen. 4:24), was revived by Amos: "Will two men walk together [in the wilderness] unless they have agreed to do so?" (3:3.) The textual alternative, "unless they know one another," which represents the reading of Greek-speaking Jewry in the Hellenistic period,[108] provides an insight into the inner workings of a daily spirituality inseparable from the function and possibility of theology. Because God and prophet were comparable to traveling companions in the desert, Amos and Jeremiah mythopoetically believed they shared in the secret of the divine council.[109] In addition to the prophetic vision, day-in and day-out communion was the milieu of their theological epistemology.[110]

Long-sustained acquaintance with this companionship, however, never deteriorated into casual familiarity. The God-prophet relation could not become a mere "fellowship," as if the Deity were reduced to the finite status of a "fellow being." The psychological mode of presence never cancels out the element of awe and even terror which is inherent in the proximity of holiness. Yet, the "diplomatic attaché" of Yahweh did not find holiness repellent. Its *mysterium tremendum* was transformed into a delight, for selfhood was appointed to greatness although never absorbed into infinity. The prophetic vision and the prophetic communion were compatible with happiness.

Jonathan Edwards, belying his reputation for one-sidedness in his presentation of a fearful God, was able to write in a mood which reflected the spiritual pleasure of the prophets: "Holiness . . . appeared to me to be of a sweet, pleasant, charming, serene, calm nature, which brought an inexpressible purity, brightness, peacefulness, and ravishment to the soul . . . , like a field or garden of God, with all manner of pleasant flowers."[111] In a way similar to that of prophetic vision, prophetic communion itself could and did fade, and the prophet would then experience the void of spiritual isolation. In moments of urgency, he would call out, petition, or even challenge, but to no avail. Prophetic prayer took the form of an act of defiance (Jer. 32:16–25), the question of a doubter (Jer. 12:1–2), or even the bitter reproach of a deceived lover (Jer. 15:17 f. 20:7). When Yahweh was silent, the prophet prayed but he could never compel. Here lies the central element which distinguishes prophetic faith from anthropocentric religion.[112]

The elusiveness of presence gave birth to the prophetic prayer and the poetry of spiritual agony.[113]

Divine Self-Abasement

The prophets interpreted Yahweh's absence from history as the sign of his presence in judgment. It may well be that their experience of Yahweh's absence from their own lives in moments of need led them to understand a new dimension of divinity: the self-abasement of God. Communion had been for them an epistemological channel through which they had learned the obligation of divine righteousness: Yahweh must convict his own people. Alienation revealed to the prophets an even deeper dimension of divinity: the creator of the universe and the soveriegn of the nations humbles himself for the sake of his own people. He suffers as he convicts. He wounds himself as he destroys. The kenotic theology of a later age[114] may well find its roots in the prophetic sense of the divine absence.

The elusiveness of presence thus fulfilled a double function. It not only pointed to the transcendence of God's freedom over nature and man, but it also became a symbol of God's self-imposed weakness as a model for human power.

When in the eleventh century B.C. the ark had been captured by the Philistines (1 Sam. 4:11), the sacramental monstrance of presence appeared lost, but a prophetic poet of the presence discerned in the event the evidence of Yahweh's judgment: God rejected the people who had first rejected him:

When Elohim heard, he was enraged,
   And he utterly rejected Israel.
He forsook his tabernacle in Shiloh,
   The tent where he had sojourned among men,
And he delivered his power to captivity,
   His magnificence into the hand of the foe.

                        (Ps. 78:59–61)

Presence in judgment meant absence in history, but the divine decision meant a divine humiliation. Yahweh surrendered his sovereignty to the shame of alien imprisonment. He voluntarily relinquished his royal magnificence (*tiph'ereth*) to the power of the enemy. The prophetic singer of the *Magnalia Dei* celebrated the reduction of divine magnitude to divine servitude.[115]

The motif of the self-abasing God reappeared in the eighth century B.C., when the prophet Hosea acted out in his own life God's self-exposure to the mockery of man. The symbolic representation of Israel as a whore entailed the blasphemous implication that Yahweh had to be compared to a betrayed husband, whose honor had been impugned. As the lover of unfaithful Israel, however, Yahweh was represented not as yielding to the dishonorable weakness of laissez-faire tolerance but as assuming the inner form of an affirmation whose aim was to rehabilitate rather than to annihilate.[116]

A few years later, in the prophetic underground which kept alive the teachings of Amos, Hosea, and Isaiah, during the days of Manasseh's capitulation to the Assyrian forces, the prophet Micah or a disciple inverted the liturgy of the covenant lawsuit (Mic. 6:1–8).[117] As modern form-critical analysis has shown, in all probability the autumn festival included a ceremony of covenant renewal. In the course of the ritual, a cultic prophet pronounced in the name of Yahweh a series of invectives against the people (Deut. 32:1 ff., Isa. 1:2, etc.).[118] In this reversal of the traditional pattern, Yahweh was no longer the accuser but the defendant:

> "O my people, what have I done to thee?
> In what have I wearied thee? Answer me!"
>
> (Mic. 6:3.)

The questions were those of a wistful partner, eager to find out in what area of his conduct he might have failed. The review of the history of "the saving acts of Yahweh" (vs. 5) became in effect a pathetic appeal to recognize the patience, the open grace, and the humility of God. Yahweh is the incomparable

Deity who "bears (*nasa'*) the guilt and passes over the transgression, on the behalf of the remnant of his inheritance" (Mic. 7:18).

At the beginning of the sixth century B.C., the end came. Did the prophet Ezekiel go a step further in delineating a kenotic theology? The answer may be inferred from one of the most dramatic enactments of prophetic symbolism ever performed. Analysis of the Song of the Sword (Ezek. 21:8–17 [Heb. 14–22]) indicates that the prophet acted out a sword dance at the same time as he sang the words of a poem:[119]

> "Let the sword double over! Let it [fall] a third time!
>   It is the sword of the slain,
>   The sword of the great one who is pierced,
>   [the sword] which will cut around them . . ." (vs. 14 [Heb. 19]).

The dance of the sword involved a mimetic portrayal of the Deity. The choreographic stance interpreted visually and kinesthetically the prophetic oracle couched in the first person singular: God himself was dancing through the prophet. Ezekiel acted as a stand-in for the divine Actor. Sword dances always involve the perilous art of juggling with a blade. They regularly include the self-inflicting of body wounds, and sometimes end with the artful faking of self-emasculation.[120]

As the Deity and the prophet entered into a rapport of mystical empathy through the emotional intensity of the singing, dancing, and self-mutilating, the dance of death revealed that Yahweh, the executioner of his own people, was also taking upon himself the risk of self-immolation.

The word *theonomy* has been used to indicate the theocentricity of the prophets' worldview. Israel could not live, they believed, apart from its center. Humanistic autonomy is a manifestation of self-destructive heteronomy. Prophetic theonomy, on the contrary, points to the distinctiveness of Hebraic faith, which radically alters the anthropocentric concerns both of the ancient Semitic rituals and of modern religiosity. Even when hidden, the presence enters into the human predicament. Beyond a theology of pathos, so well outlined by Abraham Heschel,[121] one should speak of a theology of self-immolation. The prophets understood the language of the divine "I"[122] less as demand than as gift. Their theology was a divine anthropology.[123]

When the presence left the temple and the prophetic vision faded, Jeremiah and Ezekiel lived with a new intensity through the inwardness of their faith. They extolled the presence in its mode of prophetic vision, but they could survive the awareness of absence for they knew how to wait for the final epiphany. "The day of the Lord" was more important to them than "the house of the Lord."[124] Thanks to them, the sabbath, sacrality in time, could be observed as a substitute for the temple, sacrality in space. The celebration of the sabbath, a sacramental participation in the first day (Exod. 20:11), could become a sacramental anticipation of the last day. Once again, the ear prevailed over the eye, since the survivors' faith could renounce space for the sake of time.

The prophetic vision was short-lived, but there may have been in its loss a grace in disguise. "Les contacts de l'éternel dans le temps sont affreusement éphémères."[125] Mystical poets have often noted that human beings are unable to bear the burden of prolonged rapports with "visible" presence.[126] Periods of spiritual wilderness in the absence of presence may be a disguised freedom from the joy and terror of revelation.

Like the prophets deprived of vision, the temple musicians bereft of the temple reached a *modus orandi et adorandi*. The presence, which in the end eluded them, modified itself in such a way that they could clothe their faith in aesthetic splendor: they mediated to new generations their own brand of presence as they composed the Psalms.

Notes

1. H. W. Longfellow, *Kéramos* (Boston, 1878), p. 9.

2. See K. Köhler, *Der Prophet der Hebräer und die Mantik der Griechen in ihrem gegenseitigen Verhältnis* (Darmstadt, 1860); E. Fascher, *PROPHETES. Eine sprach- und religionsgeschichtliche Untersuchung* (Giessen, 1927), pp. 4 ff.

3. See A. R. Johnson, *The Cultic Prophet in Ancient Israel* (Cardiff, 1944); J. Jeremias, *Kultprophetie und Gerichtsverkündigung in der späten Königszeit Israels* (Neukirchen-Vluyn, 1970). Even if some of the great prophets have been cultic officials (for example, Isaiah of Jerusalem), they polemized fiercely against the duplicity of the ceremonial performed by immoralists. See G. W. Ahlström, "Some Remarks on Prophets and Cult," in C. J. Rylaarsdam, ed., *Transitions in Biblical Scholarship* (Chicago, 1968), pp. 113 ff.; M. Sekine, "Das Problem der Kultpolemik bei den Propheten," *Ev. Th.*, XXVIII (1968): 605 ff.

4. It will be remembered that the few great prophets were among the so-called literary prophets. This expression, however, refers not to writers but to poets whose words have been preserved orally by disciples and later on recorded in manuscripts. The prophets themselves, with the possible exception of the Second Isaiah and the First and the Second Zechariah (Zech., chs. 1—8; 9—14), were not writers. The traditional distinction between "major" and "minor" prophets referred to the relative length of the books which bear their names.

5. See A. Lods, "Quelques remarques sur les poèmes mythologiques de Ras-Shamra et leurs rapports avec l'Ancien Testament," *RHPR*, XVI (1936): 122 ff. W. I. Moran, "New Evidence from Mari on the History of Prophecy," *Biblica*, I (1969): 15 ff.; J.-C. Heintz, "Oracles prophétiques et 'guerre sainte' selon les archives royales de Mari et l'Ancien Testament," *SVT*, XVII (1970): 112 ff.; J. S. Holladay, Jr., "Assyrian Statecraft and the Prophets of Israel," *HTR*, LXIII (1970): 29 ff.; J. F. Ross, "Prophecy in Hamath, Israel, and Mari," *HTR*, LXIII (1970): 1 ff.; S. D. Walters, "Prophecy in Mari and Israel," *JBL*, LXXXIX (1970): 78 ff.; J. G. Heintz, "Prophetie in Mari und Israel" (review article of F. Ellermeier's book)," *Biblica*, III (1971): 543 ff.; J. F. Craghan, "Mari and its Prophets," *Biblical Theology Bulletin*, V (1975): 32 ff.

6. Proposed by H. Torczyner (Tur-Sinai); see W. F. Albright, *Yahweh and the Gods of Canaan* (Garden City, N.Y., 1968), pp. 208 ff.

7. They followed literary forms but they adapted them to their particular needs in highly original ways. See H. J. Boeker, "Anklagereden und Verteidigungsreden im Alten Testament," *Ev. Th.*, XX (1960): 398 ff.; J. Blenkinsopp, "The Prophetic Reproach," *JBL*, XC (1971): 267 ff.; C. Westermann, *Basic Forms of Prophetic Speech*, tr. by H. C. White (Philadelphia, 1967). G. Fohrer has pointed out the freedom with which the prophets used rhetorical patterns to suit their inspiration: See "Tradition und Interpretation im Alten Testament," *ZAW*, LXXIII (1961): 1 ff.; "Remarks on Modern Interpretation of the Prophets," *JBL*, LXXX (1961): 313.

8. See S. Mowinckel, "Ecstatic Experience and Rational Elaboration in Old Testament Prophecy," *Acta Orientalia*, XIII (1935): 264 ff.; J. Lindblom, *Prophecy in Ancient Israel* (Oxford, 1962), pp. 47 ff.; D. R. Hillers, "A Convention in Hebrew Literature: The Reaction to Bad News," *ZAW*, LXXVII (1965): 86 ff.

9. A. Heschel, *The Prophets* (New York, 1962), p. 389.

10. See J. Gray, *I & II Kings: A Commentary* (Philadelphia, 1970), pp. 405 ff.

11. See G. Fohrer, *Elia* (Zürich, 1957), pp. 48 f., 87 ff.; R. M. Frank, "A Note on

I Kings 19.10, 14," *CBQ*, XXV (1963): 410 ff.; J. Jeremias, *Theophanie. Die Geschichte eine alttestamentlichen Gattung* (Neukirchen, 1965), pp. 113 ff.; J. J. Stamm, "Elia am Horeb," *Festschrift Th. C. Vriezen* (Wageningen, 1966), pp. 327 ff.; O. H. Steck, *Überlieferung und Zeitgeschichte in den Elia-Erzählungen* (Neukirchen-Vluyn, 1968), pp. 20 ff., 90 ff, especially 109–125; R. A. Carlson, "Elie à l'Horeb," *VT*, XIX (1969): 416 ff.; E. Würthwein, "Elijah at Horeb—Reflections on I Kings 19.9–18," *Festschrift G. Henton Davies* (Richmond, Va., 1970), pp. 152 ff.; K. Seybold, "Elia am Gottesberg," *Ev. Th.*, XXXIII (1973): 13 ff.

12. The phrase *qôl demamah daqqah* has been traditionally rendered "a still small voice." The word *qôl* means voice, noise, or sound, depending on the context. Thus, it may designate human or divine speech, but also the cry of animals, the bleeting of sheep, the neighing of horses, the roaring of lions, the lowing of cattle. It applies to the voice of Yahweh in the immediate context (vs. 13), just as elsewhere to the voice of angels, or to the cries of the seraphim in Isaiah's vision (Isa. 6:4). It refers to the timbre of musical instruments; the peal of thunder; the stamping of hooves; the sound of the steps of runners, of wheels, of the sea, of whips, of the thump of a fall; the deep rumbling of an earthquake; the din of war or of multitudes; the rustling of wings; the roar of flames; the crackling of thorns; the grinding of millstones; etc. It seems that the idea of voice is not inevitable. When the word is followed by the word *demamah* (from the root *d.m.m.*, "to be silent"; cf. Job 4:16, Ps. 107:29) and especially with the qualifying epithet *daqqah* (from the root *d.q.q.*, "to crush," "to pulverize," or "to be thin"), the phrase evokes the utter quiet and even the audible vacuity which may be perceived after the ear-splitting forces of nature which have been unleashed. See G. G. Mollegen, *Elijah on Mount Horeb: A Form-critical*

and Exegetical Study of I Kings 19.8b–19a (typescript, Columbia University, New York, 1968), pp. 98 ff. Cf. J. Lust, "A Gentle Breeze or a Roaring Thunderous Sound? Elijah at Horeb: I Kings 19:12," *VT*, XXV (1975): 110 ff. Lust proposes "a crushing *and* roaring sound" but ignores the absence of the repetition, "And Yahweh was not in [it]." Cf. R. Davidson, "Some Aspects of the Theological Significance of Doubt in the Old Testament," *ASTI*, VII (1970): 48.

13. The noun *shᵉʿar*, "remnant," derives from the verb *sha'ar*, "to remain." On the development of this theological motif, see B. F. Meyer, "Jesus and the Remnant of Israel," *JBL*, LXXXIV (1965): 123 ff.; G. F. Hasel, *The Remnant Idea from Genesis to Isaiah* (Berrien Springs, Mich., 1972).

14. Cf. the expression "And behold, Yahweh passed by" (I Kings 19:11) with the characteristic feature of the Mosaic theophany concerning the name and the glory, "I will make my goodness pass before thee" (Exod. 33:19), and "When my glory passes by ... until I have passed by" (vs. 22).

15. See Johnson, *The Cultic Prophet*, p. 27.

16. A. Neher, *L'essence du prophétisme* (Paris, 1955), p. 98.

17. See H. Graf Reventlow, *Liturgie und prophetisches Ich bei Jeremia* (Gütersloh, 1963), pp. 24 ff., 77 ff.; N. C. Habel, "The Form and Significance of the Call Narratives," *ZAW*, LXXVII (1965): 297 ff.; R. Kilian, "Die prophetischen Berufungsberichte," *Theologie im Wandel, Tübinger theologische Reihe*, I (München, 1967): 356 ff.; B. O. Long, "Prophetic Call Traditions and Reports of Visions," *ZAW*, LXXXIV (1972): 494 ff.; W. Vogels, "Les récits de vocation des prophètes," *NRT*, XCV (1973): 3 ff.

18. See Habel, "The Form and Significance," pp. 320 ff.

19. See K. Baltzer, "Considerations Regarding the Office and Calling of the Prophet," *HTR*, LXI (1968): 567 ff.

20. See J. F. Ross, "The Prophet as Yahweh's Messenger," in *Israel's Prophetic Heritage [Festschrift J. Muilenburg]* (New York, 1964), pp. 98 ff.; S. H. Blank, " 'Of a Truth the Lord Hath Sent Me': An Inquiry into the Sources of the Prophet's Authority," *Interpreting the Prophetic Tradition* (Cincinnati, 1969), pp. 1 ff.

21. It is not certain whether the temple of which Isaiah spoke was the edifice of worship in Jerusalem, built by Solomon, or "the heavenly temple" to which the prophet was permitted to have visionary access. The theme of the "Council of Yahweh" which influenced a northern prophet like Micayah ben Imlah (1 Kings 22:19–23) also appears in Isaiah's vision. See M. M. Kaplan, "Isaiah 6.1–11," *JBL*, XIV (1926): 251 ff.; I. Engnell, *The Call of Isaiah. An Exegetical and Comparative Study* (Uppsala, 1949), pp. 28 ff. See also H. Wheeler Robinson, "The Council of Yahweh," *JTS*, XLV (1944): 151 ff.; F. M. Cross, "The Council of Yahweh in Second Isaiah," *JNES*, XII (1953): 274 ff.; *id.*, *Canaanite Myth and the Hebrew Epic* (Cambridge, Mass., 1973), pp. 186 ff.; E. C. Kingsbury, "The Prophets and the Council of Yahweh," *JBL*, LXXXIII (1964): 279 ff.

22. Cf. von Rad, *Old Testament Theology*, II, p. 55. It is probably that the first three visions were recounted at the sanctuary, while the last two, which followed the prophet's expulsion, may have been spoken confidentially to his followers, among whom may well have been Hosea and the young Isaiah.

23. On the basis of form-critical analysis, N. Habel maintains that these visions do not constitute narratives of the call ("The Form and Significance," pp. 305 f.). Diversity among prophets prevails over conformity, however, and there are at least four types of such narratives. Cf. Vogels, "Les récits de vocation," pp. 6 ff.

24. See H. W. Wolff, *Dodekapropheton II: Joel-Amos* (Neukirchen-Vluyn, 1969), pp. 337 ff.; G. M. Tucker, "Prophetic Authenticity: A Form-Critical Study of Amos 7:10–17," *In.*, XXVII (1973): 423 ff.

25. See S. Talmon, "The Gezer Calendar and Seasonal Cycle of Ancient Canaan," *JAOS*, LXXXIII (1963): 184.

26. The verb *niḥam* means "to be afflicted," "to suffer grief," "to have compassion," as in Jer. 15:6, Ps. 90:13; cf. Job 42:6, etc. It is the verb *shûbh*, which means "to return," "to repent."

27. See A. Heschel, "The Theology of Pathos," *The Prophets* (New York, 1962), pp. 221 ff.; von Rad, *Old Testament Theology*, II, pp. 70 ff.

28. For a different interpretation, see G. Brunet, "La vision de l'étain," *VT*, XVI (1966): 387 ff.

29. This trait appears throughout the discourses, and especially in the quotations from ancient psalmodic expressions of praise. See J. D. Watts, "An Old Hymn Preserved in the Book of Amos," *Vision and Prophecy in Amos* (Grand Rapids, Mich., 1958), pp. 51 ff.; cf. R. Vuilleumier-Bessard, "La présence actuelle de Dieu," *La tradition cultuelle d'Israël dans la prophétie d'Amos et d'Osée* (Neuchâtel, 1960), pp. 16 ff.

30. J. L. Crenshaw, "Amos and the Theophanic Tradition," *ZAW*, LXXX (1968): 203 ff.

31. C. van Leeuven, "The Prophecy of the YOM YHWH in Amos V 18–20," *OTS*, XIX (1974): pp. 113 ff.; cf. Vuilleumier-Bessard, "Les manifestations de Dieu dans l'avenir," *La tradition cultuelle*, pp. 22 ff.

32. W. Brueggemann, "Amos IV 4–13 and Israel's Covenant Worship," *VT*, XV (1965): 1 ff.; W. Vogels, "Invitation à revenir à l'alliance en Amos IX 7," *VT*, XXII (1972): 223 ff.

33. S. Terrien, "Amos and Wisdom," *Israel's Prophetic Heritage (Festschrift J. Muilenburg,* New York, 1962), pp. 108 ff.; H. W. Wolff, *Amos the Prophet: The Man and His Background*, tr. by F. R. McCurley (Philadelphia, 1973), pp. 6 ff., 88 ff.; contra J. L. Crenshaw, "The Influence of the

Wise upon Amos. The 'Doxologies of Amos' and Job 5, 9–16; 9:5–10," *ZAW*, LXXIX (1967): 42 ff.

34. On the word *sôdh*, "secret" and "secret council," cf. Amos 3:7; Prov. 11:13, 20:19, 25:9 with Jer. 23:18, 22; Ps. 35:14, 89:8.

35. See note 17 above. After years of a rational emphasis on the psychology of the prophets, modern psycho-analytical study and comparative history of religion have revived interest in the study of the phenomena of ecstasy in conjunction with the source of the prophets' message. See C. W. Williams, Ecstaticism in Hebrew Prophecy and Christian Glossolalia," *Studies in Religion/Sciences religieuses*, III (1973–74): 320 ff.

36. Cf. L.-P. Horst, "L'extase chez les prophètes d'Israël d'après les travaux de Hölscher et de Gunkel," *RHPR*, II (1922): 337 ff.; H.-W. Hertzberg, *Propheten und Gott* (Gütersloh, 1928); J. Lindblom, "Die Religion der Propheten und die Mystik," *ZAW*, XLII (1939): 54 f.; *id.*, "Einige Grundfragen der alttestamentlicher Wissenschaft," *Festschrift A. Bertholet* (Tübingen, 1950): 325 ff.; *id.*, *Prophecy in Ancient Israel* (Oxford, 1962), pp. 122 ff.

37. Neher, *Amos*, pp. 133 ff., 137 ff.

38. Since the text does not state that the order to strike was carried out, the fifth vision constitutes only an anticipation of the symbolic act which prophets later than Amos performed in obedience to divine command.

39. Amos 9:2; see Ps. 139:8; cf. Prov. 15:-11, Job 26:6.

40. See A. Allwohn, *Die Ehe des Propheten Hosea in psycho-analytischer Beleuchtung* (Berlin, 1926); F. S. North, "Solution of Hosea's Marital Problems by Critical Analysis," *JNES*, XVI (1957): 128 ff.; J. M. Ward, *Hosea: A Theological Commentary* (New York, 1966), pp. 3 ff.; J. L. Mays, *Hosea: A Commentary* (Philadelphia, 1969), pp. 22 ff.; H. W. Wolff, *Hosea: A Commentary on the Book of Hosea*, tr. by G. Stansell (Philadelphia, 1974), pp. 8 ff., 56 ff., 67 f.

41. G. Fohrer, "Die Gattung der Berichte über symbolische Handlungen der Propheten," *Studien zur alttestamentlichen Prophetie (1949–63)* (Berlin, 1967), pp. 92 ff.; E. R. Fraser, "Symbolic Acts of the Prophets," *Studia biblica et theologica*, IV (1974): 45 ff.

42. The expression *bath diblayim* is usually translated "daughter of Diblayim," although such a proper name is not known elsewhere and the last word affects the dual form. One Arabic cognate means "large goblet" or "mouthful of delight," and appears in erotic poetry. It may have designated "two fig cakes" used in Canaanite ritual (cf. *debhâlah*, "lump of pressed figs," and *dibhlathayim*, geographical name; cf. also *'ashishê 'anabhîm*, "raisin cakes" (Hos. 3:1). The words *'esheth zenunim*," literally, "a woman of prostitutions," probably designate not "a prostitute," but "a woman prone to prostitution." Cf. similar uses of the word "woman of" constructed with abstractions (Prov. 6:24, 9:13, etc.).

43. Vocalizing the Hebrew Consonantal text *'ul*, "infant," instead of *'ol*, "yoke" (vs. 4). The traditional reading, "lifting a yoke from the jaw [of a heifer]," abruptly changes the imagery of the child. Moreover, a yoke is never lifted from the jaw or cheek of an animal. It is raised from the nape of its neck.

44. See Heschel, *The Prophets*, pp. 47 ff.

45. The absence of the definite article does not impose the traditional rendering, "a woman." On the contrary, it may indicate a stress on the person or object in question. Cf. 2 Sam. 6:2, Amos 5:17, Isa. 10:6, etc.

46. Probable allusion to hierogamic rites (cf. Song of Sol., 2:5), or the worship of the Mother goddess (cf. the *kawwanim*, "cakes" in Jer. 7:18, 44:19). This indictment of Israel does not necessarily imply that the woman was a cultic prostitute or a temple slave. She may have fallen into secular prostitution or slavery. Hence the need to "purchase" her for a price which

may be computed as that of a slave (cf. Exod. 21:32, Zech. 11:13).

47. The phonetic distinction between the active and the stative conjugation of the verb "to love" (*'ahabh* and *'ahebh*, respectively) was not possible in all forms, but it appears here. The Masoretic Text reads *'ehabh* (stative) rather than *'ahobh* (active imperative). The LXX translated the active use of the verb in 1 Kings 11:1 ("King Solomon loved [active] many foreign women") by the noun *philogunês*, "a womanizer," whereas they rendered the command to Hosea (stative) by using the verb *agapaô*, "to love unselfishly and devotedly." Cf. other uses of the stative conjugation in Hos. 11:1, 14:5; Pss. 4:2 [Heb., 3], 119:167; Prov. 1:22, 3:12, 4:6, 8:17; Mal. 1:2; etc.

48. The last verses of the book of Amos (9:9c–15) belong to the canonical growth of the prophetic literature.

49. See W. Brueggemann, "Hosea as Bearer of the Word," *Tradition in Crisis: A Study in Hosea* (Richmond, Va., 1968), p. 106.

50. See J. L. McKenzie, "Divine Passion in Osee," *CBQ*, XVII (1955): 167 ff.

51. The plural noun *niḥûmîm*, "grief," "sorrow," and "compassion," is derived from the verb *niḥam*, "to be afflicted" (see note 26 above). As used in the present context, the noun indicates a violent struggle between conflicting emotions and should therefore be rendered by two different English nouns, placed in contradicting juxtaposition.

52. The obscure *bᵉ'îr*, "in a city" or "in [the] city," probably conceals a word derived from the root *'îr* or *'ûr*, "to excite," "to arouse." Cf. Jer. 15:8, where the word *'îr* probably means "anguish," "terror."

53. See O. Eissfeldt, " 'Mein Gott' im Alten Testament," *ZAW*, LX (1945): 8.

54. See H. W. Wolff, " 'Wissen um Gott' bei Hosea als Urform von Theologie," *Ev. Th.*, XII (19:52): 533 ff.; *id.*, "Erkenntnis Gottes im Alten Testament," XV

(1955): 426 ff.; J. L. McKenzie, "Knowledge of God in Hosea," *JBL*, LXXIV (1955): 22 ff.; E. Baumann, " 'Wissen um Gott' bei Hosea als Urform der Theologie?" *Ev. Th.*, XV (1955): 416 ff.; W. Eichrodt, "The Holy One in Your Midst: The Theology of Hosea," *In.*, XV (1961): 259 ff.; cf. F. Buck, *Die Liebe Gottes beim Propheten Osee* (Rome, 1953).

55. Cf. M. Schmidt, *Prophet und Tempel* (Zürich, 1948), pp. 32 ff.; and A. H. J. Gunneweg, *Mündliche und schriftliche Tradition der vorexilischen Prophetenbücher* (Göttingen, 1959), p. 103.

56. See above, pp. 196 f.

57. Cf. Ps. 11:4, 18:6 [Heb., 7]; Mic. 1:2; Hab. 2:20; etc. See note 21 above.

58. Euphemism for *genitalia* (cf. Isa. 7:20; Exod. 4:25; etc.). The seraphim are mentioned only here. They seem to be celestial beings akin to the cherubim who serve as attendants to the Deity. They veil themselves in the presence of holiness. See E. Lacheman, "The Seraphim of Isaiah 6," *JQR*, LVIII (1967–8): 71 f.; S. Terrien, "The Omphalos Myth . . . " (*op. cit.*): 328 f.

59. Text uncertain. Probably read *haqqadosh*, "the holy one," with the definite article (see the Qumran variant).

60. See M. M. Kaplan, "Isaiah 6 1–11," *JBL*, XLV (1926): 251 ff.; A. Vaccari, "Visio Isaiae (6)," *VD*, X (1930): 100 ff.; V. Herntrich, "Die Berufung des Jesajas," *MPT*, XXV (1939): 158 ff.; I. Engnell, *The Call of Isaiah* (Uppsala, 1949); E. Jenni, "Jesajas Berufung in der neueren Forschung," *TZ*, XV (1959): 321 ff.; H. Wildberger, "Theophanie und Sendungsauftrag (6 1–13)," *Jesaja* (Neukirchen-Vluyn, 1968), pp. 230 ff.

61. See O. Eissfeldt, "Yahweh als König," *ZAW*, (1928): 81 ff.

62. See above, chapter IV, note 123.

63. *Contra* Habel, "The Form and Significance," p. 312.

64. See S. Blank, "Traces of Prophetic Agony in Isaiah," *HUCA*, XXVII (1956): 81 ff.

65. See Baltzer, "Considerations Regarding the Office," p. 575.

66. When it is applied to Yahweh, the expression means not only "to withdraw favor from" but also "to conceal marks and manifestations of presence from." Cf. Jer. 33:5 with Ps. 13:1 [Heb., 2], etc. The suggestion to understand the hiph'il *histir* (from the stem *s.t.r.*), "to hide," as a Ugaritic fixed t-form derived from the stem *sûr*, "to turn away from" is not likely, since the verb *histir*, "to hide," occurs many times with the direct object *panîm*, "face," but without an indirect object. Cf. Deut. 3:18, Job 3:24, etc. Contra J. A. Thompson, "A Proposed Translation of Isaiah 8 17," *ET*, LXXXIII (1971–72): 376.

67. See above, chapter IV, note 127.

68. See Mic. 3:4, where Yahweh's decision to hide his face arises from his refusal to answer the cry of those who do evil deeds. Cf. Deut. 31:17, 32:20, etc.

69. The intensive voice (*pi'el*) of the verb *hikkah*, "to wait," refers to an active attitude of looking for the future with a passionate longing, desire, or aspiration. Cf. Isa. 30:18, 64:3; Hab. 2:3; Zeph. 3:8; Ps. 33:20. The synonym *qiwwah*, "to hope," also in the intensive voice, carries the image of twisting or stretching into tension, as in the making of a rope.

70. See E. L. Fackenheim, *God's Presence in History: Jewish Affirmations and Philosophical Reflections* (New York, 1970), p. 29.

71. The problem of the birth of Immanuel has been the object of considerable discussion from which no consensus has emerged, for the uncertainty and the obscurity of the text has led to contradictory interpretations. See, among others, E. Hammershaimb, "The Immanuel Sign," *Studia theologica*, III (1949): 124 ff.; N. Gottwald, "Immanuel as the Prophet's Son," *VT*, VIII (1958): 36 ff.; R. Kilian, *Die Verheissung Immanuels, Jes. 7.14* (1968); J. Lust, *The Immanuel Figure. A Charismatic Judge-Leader* (Leiden, 1971); H. W. Wolff, "A Solution to the Immanuel Prophecy in

Isaiah 7 14—8 22," *JBL*, XCI (1972): 449 ff.

72. Cf. Hos. 11:9 with Isa. 8:8, 10.

73. See Hasel, *The Remnant*, pp. 282 ff.

74. R. Otto, *The Idea of the Holy*, tr. by J. W. Harvey (London, 1928), p. 98.

75. See above, p. 77. In his warning to Ahaz and the princes, the young prophet had played on the two meanings of the verb *amen*: "If you do not have faith (*ta'amînû*), surely you will not endure (*te'amenû*, Isa. 7:9).

76. See H. Blank, "The Meanings of Faith" in *Prophetic Faith in Isaiah* (New York, 1958), pp. 34 ff.; cf. A. Weiser, "The Old Testament Concept [of Faith]." G. Friedrich, ed., *Theological Dictionary of the New Testament*, tr. by G. W. Bromley, VI, pp. 182 ff.

77. Literally, "the word of Yahweh 'was' (*hayah*) toward him" (vss. 4, 11, 13). See C. H. Ratschow, *Werden und Wirken. Eine Untersuchung des Wortes* hajah *als Beitrag zur Wirklichkeitserfassung des Alten Testaments* (Berlin, 1941), p. 34 ff.

78. See F. Horst, "Die Visionsschilderungen der alttestamentlichen Propheten," *Ev. Theol.*, XX (1960): 200 f.

79. See Habel, "The Form and Significance," pp. 297 ff.; cf. J. MacL. Berridge, *Prophet, People, and the Word of Yahweh: An Examination of Form and Content in the Proclamation of the Prophet Jeremiah* (Zürich, 1970), pp. 26 ff.

80. See J. S. Skinner, "Predestination and Vocation," in *Prophecy and Religion: Studies in the Life of Jeremiah* (Cambridge, 1922), pp. 18 ff.; M. Gilula, "An Egyptian Parallel to Jeremiah I 4–5," *VT*, XVII (1976): 114; W. Rudolph, *Jeremia* (Tübingen, 1968), pp. 4 ff.; Berridge, *Prophet*, pp. 26 ff.

81. Cf. Job 10:8 ff., Ps. 139:13.

82. See Exod. 28:28; Lev. 22:2, etc.; Num. 3:13; etc. Cf. Th. J. Meek, "Was Jeremiah a Priest?" *The Expositor*, XXV (1923): 215 ff.

83. See Lindblom, *Prophecy*, pp. 14 ff., 111 ff., 190; K. Gouders, " 'Siehe, ich lege

meine Worte in deinen Mund'. Die Berufung des Propheten Jeremia (Jer. 1 4–10)," *Bibel und Leben*, XII (1971): 162 ff.

84. See F. L. Moriarty, "The Prophets: Bearers of the Word," *The Bridge*, III (New York, 1958), pp. 54 ff.; cf. H. W. Hertzberg, "Jeremias Stellung zum 'Wort'," in *Prophet und Gott: Eine Studie zur Religiosität des vorexilischen Prophetums* (Gütersloh, 1923), pp. 83 ff.

85. Cf. Ezek. 3:1–3.

86. See note 76 above; see also P. S. Wood, "Jeremiah's Figure of the Almond Rod," *JBL*, LXI (1942): 199 ff.

87. For other interpretations, see W. A. Irwin, "The Face of the Pot, Jeremiah 1:13b," *AJSL*, XLVII (1931): 288 ff.; H. Graf Reventlow, *Liturgie und prophetisches Ich bei Jeremia* (Gütersloh, 1963), pp. 210 ff.; H. Lamparter, *Prophet wider Willen, der Prophet Jeremia* (Stuttgart, 1964), p. 155.

88. Read *tuppaḥ*, from *naphaḥ*, "to blow upon," instead of *tippathaḥ*, "it will be opened." Graphically, the two Hebrew words are almost identical.

89. See H.-W. Jüngling, "Ich mache dich zu einer ehernen Mauer: Literarische Überlegungen zum Verhältnis von Jer 1, 18–19 zu Jer 15, 20–21," *Biblica*, LIV (1973): 1 ff. The traditional rendering, "a boiling pot" or "a seething cauldron," is not impossible, for the word *sîr* designates a container such as a jar for liquids (water, oil, wine, etc.; see 2 Kings 4:38, Exod. 27:3, etc.). However, the qualifying passive participle *naphûªḥ*, "blown upon," indicates the idea of forced and excessive heat, of the kind needed by a smith for melting metals (cf. Akkadian *napaḥu*, "to set on fire," and *nappaḥu*, "smith"; cf. Ezek. 22:20, Job 20:26, and see "a furnace blown upon" in Sir. 43:4). The rendering "a heated crucible" reveals the rhetorical movement from the oracle of judgment to the oracle of reassurance as it prepares the comparison of Jeremiah's newly endowed steadfastness to "a pillar of iron, a battlement of bronze" (vs. 18).

90. See L. Dürr, *Ezechiel's Vision der Erscheinung Gottes [Ez. c. 1 u. 10] im Lichte der vorderasiatischen Altertumskunde* (Münster i. W., 1917), pp. 8 ff.; G. A. Cooke, *A Critical and Exegetical Commentary on the Book of Ezekiel* (Edinburg, 1936), p. 3 ff.; G. Fohrer, *Ezekiel* (Tübingen, 1955), pp. 5 ff.; W. Zimmerli, *Ezekiel*, tr. by C. Quin (Philadelphia, 1970), pp. 51 ff.

91. See P. A. Ackroyd, *Exile and Restoration* (London, 1968), pp. 31 ff.; for a modern description of the region, see W. Thesiger, *The Marsh Arabs* (London, 1964), pp. 5 ff., 58 ff.

92. Cf. 3 Macc. 6:18; Test. of Levi 2–3; Matt. 3:16 ff.; Mark 1:10 f; Luke 3:22 f.; John 1:51; Acts 7:56, 10:10–16; Rev. 4:1, 19:11.

93. *Contra* E. Höhne, *Die Thronwagenvision Hezekiels* (Dissertation, Erlangen, 1953–54), pp. 80 f.

94. The *rûªḥ*, "breath" or "spirit," of the Deity was, according to the ancient storytellers, the source of the power and wisdom of the exceptional heroes (see Gen. 41:38; Num. 11:29, 24:2; Judg. 13:25; etc.). The word also helped to describe the prophetic bands at the time of the Canaanite syncretism (1 Sam. 10:6; cf. 16:14 f.). Hosea probably reflected the language of his enemies when he said, "The prophet is a fool, the man of the spirit is mad" (Hos. 9:7). Isaiah reserved the term for designating God (Isa. 31:3) or the virtues of his agent at the end of time (Isa. 11:2, etc.). Micah may have applied the term to his own experience (Mic. 3:8; cf. Isa. 30:1).

95. See D. Lys, *Rûach: Le souffle dans l'Ancien Testament: Enquête anthropologique à travers l'histoire théologique d'Israël* (Paris, 1962), p. 121 f.; Lindblom, *Prophecy*, pp. 176 ff.; K. W. Curley, *Ezekiel Among the Prophets: A Study of Ezekiel's Place in Prophetic Tradition* (London, 1975), pp. 23 ff.

96. See Ps. 104:30; cf. Gen. 1:2.

97. See Ezek. 1:3, 3:14, 3:22, etc., cf. Isa. 8:11, Jer. 15:17.

98. See Lindblom, *Prophecy*, p. 111; Eichrodt, *Ezekiel*, pp. 64 f.

99. For similar experiences among mystics of other cultures, see G. Widengren, *Literary and Psychological Aspects of the Hebrew Prophets* (Uppsala, 1948), pp. 100 ff.

100. See K. Baltzer, "Considerations Regarding the Office and Calling of the Prophet," *HTR*, LXI (1968): 567 ff.; H. Graf Reventlow, *Wächter über Israel: Ezechiel und seine Tradition* (Berlin, 1962); *id.*, *Das Amt des Propheten Amos* (Göttingen, 1962); *id.*, *Liturgie und prophetisches Ich bei Jeremia* (Gütersloh, 1963); E. Gerstenberger, "Jeremiah's Complaints: Observations on Jer. 15.10–21," *JBL*, LXXXII (1963): 393 ff.; Cf. W. L. Holladay, "The Background of Jeremiah's Self-Understanding: Moses, Samuel, and Psalm 22," *JBL*, LXXXIII (1964): 153 ff.

101. See Brueggemann, *Tradition in Crisis*, p. 107; J. Bright, "Jeremiah's Complaints: Liturgy, or Expressions of Personal Distress?" in *Proclamation and Presence* (*Festschrift G. Henton Davies*, Richmond, Va., 1970), pp. 189 ff.; Berridge, *Prophet*, pp. 26 ff.; Curley, *Ezekiel Among the Prophets*, pp. 74 ff., 86 (note 27).

102. W. Zimmerli, "The Special Form and Traditio-Historical Character of Ezekiel's Prophecy," *VT*, XV (1965): 516; cf. *id.*, *Ezechiel*, p. 31; also, *id.*, *Ezechiel: Gestalt und Botschaft* (Neukirchen-Vluyn, 1972), pp. 22 ff.

103. "The prophets *have* a secret . . ., a certain inward experience which cannot be understood by the uninitiated observer," in H. Gunkel, "The Secret Experiences of the Prophets," *The Expositor*, I (1924): 356; cf. E. Benz, *Die Vision. Erfahrungsformen und Bilderwelt* (Stuttgart, 1969), pp. 143 f.

104. See notes 35 and 36 above.

105. See comments of R. G. Smith, *Secular Christianity* (New York, 1966), p. 63. It is clear that the Hebrew prophets, in spite of the immediacy of their experiences of encounter with the divine, were not mystics in the absorption-type of identification with infinity common to various forms of pantheism. See F. Heiler, "General Characteristics of Mysticism and Prophetic Religion," in *Prayer: A Study in the History and Psychology of Religion*, tr. by S. McComb (London, 1932), pp. 135 ff.; cf. S. Mowinckel, "Ecstatic Experience and Rational Elaboration in Old Testament Prophecy," *Acta Orientalia*, XII (1934): 264 ff.

106. "R. Eliezer says: Whence can you say that a maidservant saw at the [Red] sea what Isaiah, Ezekiel, and all the prophets never saw?" J. Z. Lauterbach, ed., *Mekilta de-Rabbi Ishmael*, II (Philadelphia, 1933), p. 24 (*Tractate Shirata*, III, 30); paraphrased by E. L. Fackenheim, *God's Presence in History* (New York, 1970), pp. 4 ff.

107. Edwin Muir, "Horses," *Collected Poems 1921–1951* (New York, 1957), p. 19.

108. MT: *nô'adû*, "they have agreed; LXX implies metathetic reading of *nôda'û*, "they know one another" (Amos 3:3).

109. Amos 3:17, Jer. 23:22.

110. "The fundamental conviction common to them all is, that their thoughts are from God himself. The prophet did not find them. 'They were found' (Jer. 23:16)," in H. Gunkel, "The Secret Experiences of the Prophets," *The Expositor*, II (1924): 29. Cf. S. Mowinckel, *Die Erkenntnis Gottes bei den alttestamentlichen Propheten* (Oslo, 1941), pp. 6 f., 54 ff.

111. Jonathan Edwards, "Extracts from his Private Writings," *Works*, I (London, 1817), pp. 33–34.

112. Sacerdotal rites and diviners' techniques, of course, were not granted total credence in the ancient Near Eastern cults. Cf. J. J. M. Roberts, "Divine Freedom and Cultic Manipulation in Israel and Mesopotamia," in H. Goedicke and J. J. M. Roberts, eds., *Unity and Diversity: Essays in the History, Literature, and Religion of the Ancient Near East* (Baltimore and London, 1975), pp. 181 ff.

113. See H. Blank, "The Confessions of Jeremiah and the Meaning of Prayer,"

HUCA, XXI (1948): 331 ff.; *id.*, "Men Against God: The Promethean Element in Biblical Prayer," *JBL*, LXXII (1953): 1 ff.; *id.*, "Some Observations Concerning Biblical Prayer," *HUCA*, XXXII (1961): 75 ff.; *id.*, "The Prophet as Paradigm," *Festschrift J. Ph. Hyatt* (New York, 1974), pp. 111 ff.1 R. Bach, *Die Aufforderungen zur Flucht und zum Kampf in alttestamentlichen Prophetenspruch* (Neukirchen, 1962); H. J. Stoebe, "Seelsorge and Mitleiden bei Jeremia," *Wort und Dienst*, IV (1955): 116 ff.; *id.*, "Jeremiah, Prophet und Seelsorger," *TZ*, XX (1964): 385 ff., especially 401 ff.

114. Paul described as a *kenosis*, "self-emptying," the mystery of the incarnation of Jesus (Phil. 2:7): see D. G. Dawe, *The Form of a Servant: A Historical Analysis of the Kenotic Motif* (Philadelphia, 1963); J. Coppens, "Phil., II, 7 et Is., LIII,12. le problème de la 'Kénose', " *ALBO*, IV (1965), No. 21; R. P. Martin, *Carmen Christi: Philippians ii. 5–11 in Recent Interpretation and in the Setting of Early Christian Worship* (Cambridge, 1967), pp. 165 ff.

115. However, see above, chapter IV, p. 167. Cf. Deut. 32:19–20, 23 ff., 29 f. See A. F. Campbell, *The Ark Narrative (1 Sam 4–5; 2 Sam 6): A Form-Critical and Traditio-Historical Study* (Missoula, Montana, 1975), p. 210.

116. See above, pp. 242 ff.

117. G. W. Anderson, "A Study of Micah 6:1–8," *SJT*, IV (1951): 193 ff.; Th. Lescow, "Redaktionsgeschichtliche Analyse von Micha 6–7," *ZAW*, LXXXIV (1972): 182 ff.

118. See M. Delcor, "Les attaches littéraires, l'origine et la signification de l'expression biblique 'Prendre à témoin le ciel et la terre'," *VT*, XVI (1966): 8–25.

119. See Cooke, "The Sword of Yahweh," *The Book of Ezekiel*, pp. 226 ff.; O. Eissfeldt, "Schwerter Schlagene bei

Hesekiel," *Studies in Old Testament Prophecy [Festschrift Th. H. Robinson]* (Edinburgh, 1950), pp. 73 ff.; W. Zimmerli, "Das Schwert," *Ezechiel*, pp. 469 ff. A. van der Born (*Ezechiël*, Roermond en Maaseik, 1954, pp. 134 ff.) has pointed out that the words of the Sword-Song implied an actual dance. J. Steinman (*Le prophète Ezéchiel* [Paris, 1953], p. 46) noted that this barbarous poem was meant to be danced, and he called it "La danse de la mort," Cf. Eichrodt, *Ezekiel*, p. 293.

120. Compare the prophets of Baal on Mt. Carmel who not only skipped but also "cried and cut themselves after their custom with swords and lances, until the blood gushed out upon them" (1 Kings, 18:28), and the eighty men from Shechem, Shiloh, and Samaria who came with "their bodies gashed" (Jer. 41:4); cf. Zech. 13:6?

121. See *The Prophets*, pp. 221 ff. Heschel might have strenghtened his analysis of pathos had he not omitted Ezekiel from his formal treatment (although he included a number of isolated quotations and references).

122. See M. J. Buss, "The Language of the Divine 'I'," *JBR*, XXIX (1961): 102 ff.

123. In a slightly different sense, but with similar implications, a Jewish philosopher like Rabbi Heschel could write: "The Bible is not man's theology, but God's anthropology" (*Man is Not Alone*, New York, 1951, p. 129).

124. See A. Heschel, *The Sabbath* (New York, 1951), p. 79.

125. "Contacts with eternity within time are woefully ephemeral." G. Thibon, in Simone Weil, *La pesanteur et la grâce* (Paris, 1948), p. vi.

126. M. Hamburger, commenting on Hölderlin's *Patmos* and *Der Rhein*, in *Reason and Energy: Studies in German Literature* (New York, 1957), p. 57.

6

The Psalmody of Presence

Modern study has shown that the Psalter reached its final form after several centuries of editing and compiling. The temple musicians who composed most of the 150 psalms now found in the canonical collection lived between the time of David in the tenth century B.C. and the Persian restoration in the fifth and perhaps even fourth centuries.[1]

Preserving as it does a selection of 700 years of psalmody, such an anthology is bound to reflect a wide diversity of styles and attitudes. This diversity helps to explain why the Psalms are the only book of spirituality that has remained common to the entire spectrum of Jewry and Christendom, from Hassidic rabbis and Mt. Athos monks to American Quakers and the Salvation Army. At the same time, the Psalms constitute far more than a manual of devotion. Like the poetic discourses of the great prophets, they represent theological thinking at its keenest and deepest. They mirror both the uniqueness and the universality of the Hebraic theology of presence. They produce fields of force which maintain on the one hand the tension and the ease of an equilibrium between emotional contemplation within the confines of cultic space, and ethical passion for the world outside, on the other. Such an equilibrium led the psalmists to transcend racial and ritual particularity in spite of the fact that the shelter of a shrine, the enjoyment of a closed brotherhood, and the delights of liturgical aesthetics might have led them to indulge in a socially irresponsible pietism.

For the psalmists, Yahweh's presence was not only made manifest in Zion. It reached men and women over the entire earth. It was this conviction which stirred them to face risks anywhere and to welcome the future anytime. Not restricted to sacred space or to a political structure, the sense of Yahweh's presence survived the annihilation of the temple and the fall of the state in 587 B.C.[2] Elusive but real, it feared no geographical uprooting and no historical disruption.

Most of the early hymnists belonged to the musical guilds of David and Solomon. Commissioned choristers and instrumentalists of the ceremonial, they extolled the nearness of God in Zion. Their successors, however, betrayed a certain ambivalence toward the cultus, alert to its corruptibility. Some of them developed a mode of presence which transcended the myth of the divine residence in a shrine. In interaction with the prophets, they conferred upon Hebraic faith its quality of inwardness and breadth, which saved Yahwism from the obsoleteness of temporality and territoriality.[3] Away from Jerusalem, they still lived in the proximity of God. Poets of the interior quest, they were not satisfied with mere intimations of the ultimate, but they never committed the clerical sin of reducing the ultimate to the proximate. Having faced the void in history and in their personal lives, they knew the absence of God even within the temple esplanade and festivities. The inwardness of their spirituality, bred by the temple, rendered the temple superfluous. In the end they became the theologians of the ear, not of the eye. They sang the name while expecting the glory. Functionaries of the cultus, they sensed the supracultic dimension of the presence. Artists nurtured in the sanctuary, they could demythologize Zion by lending substance to the vision of a heavenly Jerusalem. The myth of time enabled them to renounce the myth of space. Landless, they

> ... looked at that prophetic land
> Where, manifested by their powers,
> *Presences perfected* stand
> Whom night and day no more command
> Within shine and shadow of earthly hours.[4]

Although the guilds of the temple musicians were trained in the formal patterns of ancient Near Eastern hymnody,[5] many of the psalmists displayed a theological originality which set them apart from the religious poets of Egypt, Canaan, and Mesopotamia.[6] By sensing the relativity of cultic ceremonial and by experiencing spiritual alienation, they affirmed in effect the freedom of Yahweh from the techniques of ritual and the resources of institutionalized religion.[7] Even the *Royal Psalms*,[8] composed by kings or for their use, revealed the religious paradox which characterizes, *par excellence*, the ancient Hebrews: intimacy with the Godhead tempered by the dread of divine abandon.

ROYAL COMMUNION

The story of David testifies at once to the grandeur and the misery of the warrior king. The Court Diary which is now embedded in the Second Book of Samuel does not conceal the contradictions and conflicts which wrenched the character of this extraordinary man.[9] Shepherd and musician, David was physically brave and aesthetically sensitive. Guerrilla leader, he elicited uncommon loyalties but he would on occasion deal treacherously with his most devoted servants. Astute diplomat, he reconciled factions, secured alliances, and conquered an empire, but he did not foresee the deleterious effects of military conquest and colonial expansion. Consummate politician, he served the nation more than himself and he was ridiculously weak with his own family. At once magnanimous and cruel, he resorted to murder for *raison d'état* or if driven by erotic passion, but he also preserved a keen sense of social justice. Above all, he exhibited in his own life the ambiguities of religion.

It has often been suggested that David's decision to bring the ark to Jerusalem in the presence of "all the elite warriors of Israel" (2 Sam. 6:1) indicates the acuity of his political flair. To be sure, the king probably saw in the cultic object of the ancient tribal confederation a rallying force that was attractive to both northerners and southerners. Beyond its Philistine fiasco, the ark summoned to the popular mind the memories of the Holy Warrior in Sinai and Edom as well as the *Magnalia Dei* in the conquest of Canaan.[10] David's act was probably meant to unite under Yahweh the tribesmen of Israel properly speaking with the brash young heroes of Judah as well as the keepers of the Yahwist tradition in the southern shrine of Hebron. There is no evidence, however, that his move was solely dictated by political opportunism.

The notorious scene of the procession of the ark to Jerusalem, in which the king danced ecstatically "in the presence of Yahweh" (2 Sam. 6:13), reveals the overpowering nature of his fervor. It is not legitimate to infer from the story that he exposed himself deliberately in conformity with a Canaanite ceremonial which involved ritual nudity. Rather, his carefree deportment seems to indicate the abandon of a soldier to his piety.[11] Captains and politicians sometimes conceal within the intensity of their religion an urge to search for the plenitude of their being. This is one of the reasons religion partakes of the more ambiguous elements of the human psyche and may be thoroughly self-deceiving. Dancing before the ark in neglect of decorum perhaps indicated the frustration of a genius whose deeper cravings remained unfulfilled by military prowess and political achievement.

David's devotion to Yahweh appears elsewhere in the record. It was in all likelihood on account of his faith that he had on occasion freed himself from the dread of ritual breach. At the shrine of Nob he had violated the sacrality of the "Bread of Presence" by demanding its requisition for the use of his famished companions.[12] He knew that humaneness prevailed over legal prohibition. He may have dimly sensed that divine presence in battle was more precious than sacramental presence at an altar.

The purity of David's faith assumed a quality of elegance which has often gone unnoticed in modern times. When his son Absalom revolted against his rule, the aging monarch was compelled to flee Jerusalem. As the cultic personnel carried the ark out to follow him in his exile, David said to Zadok the priest:

> Take the ark back to the city: if I find grace in the eyes of Yahweh, he will bring me again and he will show me the ark and its abode, but if he says, "I take no delight in thee," behold! Let him do to me as it seems good in his eyes! (2 Sam. 15:25–26).

It was on the ascent to the Mount of Olives that the king revealed his faith with such candor. Ten centuries later, in the garden of Gethsemane, on the slopes of the same Mount of Olives, Jesus similarly pinned his trust upon the will of his God, even when he knew that it demanded rather than delivered (Mark 14:36 *et par.*). He waited there for his arrest instead of attempting an easy escape "over the hill" at the edge of the desert.

David anticipated by a whole millenium the prayer of Jesus. He refrained from ascertaining the good or the evil of his situation. He did not claim right for his own cause. He prefigured implicitly the psalmists' concern for the *summun bonum*.[13] "He found it sufficient to identify goodness with the will of God, even at mortal risk: *Deo non pareo,* said Seneca, *assentior.* "God I do not obey—I acquiesce."[14] The immediacy of presence attuned the human ego to the divine purpose and therefore took precedence over the sacramental ideology of presence associated with the ark. There is little doubt that the king was endowed with a theological perspicuity that placed him in the lineage of Moses and Samuel.

If one considers, in addition, that his spiritual alertness was matched by a most unusual talent for turning a poetic verse with exquisite diction and also vigor,[15] one can easily accept the validity of a tradition which saw in the Bethlehem shepherd who attained the crown a poet and a musician who initiated the psalmody of Zion.

Presence as "The Rock"

In early Israel, as in most young nations, chieftains usually came to the limelight through military exploit. It was generally thought that physical prowess and the magnetism of command were related to a psychic quality of a religious nature. Captains were deemed to have been endowed with the power of the numinous. The "Judges" of the conquest of Canaan were charismatic in the sense that most of them had been the favored recipients of special hierophanies. They were changed into new beings by the rushing of the spirit of Yahweh upon them. One tradition presented Saul's rise to kingship as the result of his being anointed by Samuel and grasped by the spirit (1 Sam. 10:1, 6); another as the result of his victory over foreign invaders (1 Sam. 11:15). David's ascent from a shepherd's hut to a king's mansion passed through many an outlaw's cave. The crown fell upon him after he had lived many deaths in many battles. It was a soldier's sense of divine presence in the midst of peril which inspired his *Psalm of Thanksgiving* (2 Sam. 22 = Ps. 18).[16]

This poem shows various marks of amplification, for it was

probably used by David's successors when they ascended the throne of Judah in Jerusalem or when they celebrated their own victories.[17] There is no valid argument, however, for doubting the Davidic authorship of the psalm in an original form,[18] or the accuracy of its introductory note: "Then David spoke to Yahweh the words of this song on the day when Yahweh delivered him from the hand of all his enemies, and from the hand of Saul" (vs. 1). The opening strophe is couched in a wild language which betrays the accent of a fighter who has survived mortal engagements and who knows presence as protection:

Ps. 18:1 [Heb. 2]   I am in love with thee, Yahweh, my strength!
2 [3]   Yahweh, my rock, my fortress, my rescuer!
          My God, my cliff, to whom I make my escape!
          My shield, the horn of my deliverance, my
              retreat on the heights!
3 [4]   Praised be he! I will cry out to Yahweh, my
              stronghold!
          I have been saved from my enemies!

The verbal expostulation which starts the song is unique in Hebrew literature. The verb *rachem,* "to love," of which the noun *rechem,* "uterus," or "womb," is a derivative, evokes the visceral passion of a mother for her child.[19] That a military hero like David would use such a word has surprised many commentators, both Jewish and Christian.[20] Elsewhere in the religious poetry of ancient Israel, this verb is applied directly to the love of Yahweh for human beings,[21] never to the love of human beings for Yahweh.[22] It is not impossible, however, that a seasoned guerrilla leader would have quite naturally formulated his explosion of gratitude with vernacular force, however coarse a connotation the word might have evoked in some ears.[23]

The importance of this psalm for the study of the Hebraic theology of presence is manifest. It brings into convergence three aspects of Yahwistic faith: the elemental experience of divine nearness, the liturgical anamnesis of the Sinai theophany, and the behavioral implications of loyalty to the presence.

The Elemental Experience of Divine Nearness. God had stood at the side of David through a thousand deaths. Again and again, the hovering presence had preceded him to safety. A crag or a precipitous bluff had become for him the very symbol of the Godhead. Even if the term "Rock" was traditionally used as an appellation of Yahweh,[24] the warrior poet renewed the live imagery through the juxtaposition of half a dozen other allusions to defensive warfare in mountainous terrain. As a battle-scarred veteran, he would know the full impact of comparing divine protection to natural shelters. His deliverance from mortal peril was associated with a mode of presence that he was not likely to forget. In breathless sequence, he piled up as many as nine metaphors which pinpointed his memory of having "effleuré l'abîme," and been saved by "his" most personal God.[25]

Long before the modern aphorism "There's no atheist in a foxhole," soldiers had been aware of a sudden armor screening them from finality. When it overcomes man's dread of imminent death, presence is grasped and recollected with the total simplicity of awe. The memory of communion in distress is recalled with a quality of naïveté which is the mark of ultimate knowledge. Pure religion, as distinguished from magic or any ritual that verges on the manipulation of the holy, begins with the raw emotion of thankfulness.

Hebraic faith was the response, *par excellence,* of relief from the terror of annihilation. Countless times, David had been saved *in extremis.* Safety was for him inseparable from presence. When at last he was delivered from his enemies, he sang a psalm of gratitude to Yahweh, the ever-present Deity. This man had therefore penetrated to the center of being. Presence meant for him the power of life over death, and it produced in him the power of love. Overpowered by this love, he cried out, "I am in love with thee, Yahweh, my strength!" He told it "like it is," with a touch of semantic vulgarity.

The Liturgical Anamnesis of the Sinai Theophany. After this outburst of personal witness to the most intimate "science" of divine nearness independent from sacred space and time, the psalmist continued his eulogy of the ever-present God in the language of the *Heilsgeschichte:*

> "[Yahweh] bent the heavens and he came down,
>   and thickdarkness was under his feet" (Ps. 18:9 [Heb. 10]).

The word *'araphel,* "thickdarkness," summoned to mind the motif of invisible presence in the thunderstorm (Exod. 20:21; cf. 1 Kings 8:12).[26] Instead of continuing to develop the theme of royal communion as in the first strophe, the poet borrowed the liturgical form of the theophany from the national epic of the Exodus and of Sinai. In the language of Canaanite mythology, he pictured Yahweh coming down to fight for him on the clouds of the storm.[27] A man of war, he knew the Holy Warrior.[28] Like many other psalms thereafter,[29] David's *Song of Thanksgiving* celebrated the advent of Yahweh in the midst of his people at worship. Even in the early days, this ceremonial act had most likely taken place during the autumn festival, the highest moment of the sacred calendar.

As Yahweh "bent the heavens and descended," not only did his "anointed one" (*mashîªh,* royal messiah) escape death, but he did so as the result of a divine intervention similar to the Sinai theophany. The people did not die but lived. David did not die but lived. The king became the cultic incarnation of Israel. The recipient of the presence as an individual, he was the single focus and justification of God's descent upon earth: the king was poetically and ritually associated with the covenant people.

The Behavioral Implication of Loyalty to the Presence. Because David linked his own apprehension of the presence as a refuge (vss. 1–5 [Heb. 2–6]) with the recital of a theophany patterned on the anamnesis of the national epic (vss. 6–19 [Heb. 7–20]), he provided insight into the interaction between the elusiveness of presence and the conditional character of the Sinai covenant.

Brought up on the Yahwism of Judah in Bethlehem and Hebron, David was later exposed to the "catechism" of covenant loyalty to Yahweh. His "righteousness" (vs. 24 [Heb. 25]), however, should not be interpreted as the self-righteousness acquired by legal scrupulousness as a technique of merit. As is well known, obedience to the law in a later age could be interpreted as an attempt to force the divine favor and thereby to limit the freedom of God. In the context of the psalm, the word "righteousness" alludes to the dynamic harmony which flows from the habit of living in the presence. The key to the understanding of the so-called—and misnamed—profession of moral purity (vss. 20 ff. [Heb. 21 ff.]) is to be found in the final word of the theophany:

"He rescued me because he delighted in me" (vs. 19*b* [Heb. 20*b*]).

The verb "to delight in" (*chaphes*) and its cognates mean "to be eagerly mindful" and "to desire to give protection."[30] David sensed that the safety he had enjoyed in war was the perceptible facet of God's pleasure toward him. He wanted to respond in all aspects of his behavior to this mark of divine delight in him. He was a *chasid* in the early sense of the word: the leal lover of God. In all circumstances, he remained "intensely loyal" to the God who cultivated "with" him such an "intense loyalty" (vs. 25*a* [Heb. 26*a*]).[31] Likewise, as a "man of noble stature" who was completely and undividedly "devoted to Yahweh," he received the grace of wholeheartedness:[32]

"With the man of soundness and integrity,
thou showest and conferrest soundness and integrity"

(vs. 25*b* [Heb. 26*b*]).

Response to presence in the awareness of love is the foundation of ethics. Behavior is not motivated by obedience to "ordinances" and "statutes." Rather, it is the response to presence which determines this obedience (vs. 22 [Heb. 23]).[33] The will to behave is conditioned by the desire to love.

Man's loyalty to God's loyalty not only effects an ethical style, it also entails psychosomatic consequences. Homer's Greek adage generally known in its Latin form, *mens sana in corpore sano,* as well as the word "psycho-somatic," betrays an anthropological dualism which was foreign to ancient Hebraic thinking. David's integrity manifested itself in a form of moral conduct which was inseparable from his superb physique.[34]

"For it is thou, O Yahweh, who gives light to my lamp,
thou, O my God, who illumines my darkness.
For by thee I can outrun an armed band
and by my God I can leap over a wall!"

(vss. 28–29 [Heb. 29–30].)

The athlete might have boasted of his own discipline in training, but he ascribed the origin of his muscular prowess to Yahweh's delight in him. The three motifs of the psalm are thus blended in a strophic reprise: Yahweh's presence, the warrior's *askesis,* and the chasid's fidelity:

For who is God, except Yahweh?
And who is "the Rock," except our God?
The God who girded me with strength
and gave me the wholeness of my way,
Who made my feet as swift as hinds' feet
and enabled me to stand upon the heights,[35]

Who trained my hands for war
and my arms to bend a bow of bronze.[36]

(Vss. 33–35 [Heb. 34–36])[36]

David knew presence as *the Rock*. Yahweh wields supreme power
in the universe. At the same time, the young king may have
grasped a theological truth which captured the attention of
prophets in later centuries: the self-imposed abasement of the
omnipotent Deity for the sake of man:

"Thy right hand supported me
and thy humility made me great" (vs. 35 [Heb. 36]).

The spatial imagery of God's "descent" in the theophany (vs.
9 [Heb. 10]) underscores the specific character of Hebraic
theology. The presence of the transcendent Being means his
willingness to accept self-limitation. The verse does not formulate a logical antithesis between divine lowliness and human
greatness. It seeks to express in anthropomorphic language the
power of love which wears the appearance of weakness. If the
traditional Hebrew text is correct,[37] David's *Song of Thanksgiving*
contains one of the most startling examples of the preprophetic
understanding of divine pathos.[38]

To the self-abasement of Yahweh, the king responds with a
liturgical acclamation which may well have unconsciously
echoed the proto-Canaanite liturgy of the dying and rising god
of vegetation:[39]

"May Yahweh live![40] Blessed be my Rock!
May he rise, the God of my deliverance!"

(vs. 46 [Heb. 47].)

To say "May Yahweh live!" in the context of the theme of the
divine self-abasement and immediately before the wish "May he

rise!" indicates perhaps an attempt to stress once more through poetic analogy the cost of the divine "descent."

A soldier who sings the presence with such intensity of feeling and radiates his borrowed strength with such magnetic power of leadership becomes in effect a mediator of the holy. David unwittingly promoted a quasi-incarnational mode of presence, which did not totally contradict the Near Eastern mythology of the divine king and which was ritually carried on by his descendants on the throne of Judah.[41] Like Moses and Samuel, he became at once a priestly and a prophetic figure.[42] The traditional triad of Priest-Prophet-King which later Judaism and Christianity associated with the eschatological "Messiah" found its roots in the awareness of divine presence which permeated the character and the achievements of the Bethlehem shepherd.

It will be noted that nothing of this *Song of Thanksgiving* indicates that David himself was aware of a so-called Davidic covenant. He had been brought up in the Sinai covenant tradition and knew its conditional character. Not only was he conscious of Yahweh's "ordinances" and "statutes,"[43] but he also hailed the harmonious reciprocity—which bound him in intimate communion with his God—as an elusive reality which could be ruptured.[44] After him, his dynasty dreamed of a covenant which would last forever.[45] Instead of a covenant which was historical and relative because it depended in part upon man's response, the Davidic dynasty promoted a covenant which was supposed to transcend the vicissitudes and corruption of man. The so-called Davidic covenant was viewed as eternal, and therefore as suprahistorical and mythical. For David himself, however, presence conceived as deliverance respected the freedom of God and thus remained in the theology of the Sinai covenant. For David's successors, presence was conceived as an adoption into divine sonship, and it became institutional. Instead of "presence as the Rock," the mode of royal communion which eventually prevailed must be called "presence as the Crown."

Presence as "The Crown"

The awe produced by the military prowess and apparent immunity from danger which set David apart from ordinary mortals was not necessarily transferable to his progeny. The principle of hereditary monarchy had to entail some ritual through which the new monarch received the power of sacrality. Dynastic princes who ascended the throne by right of birth, unlike charismatic "Judges" and prophets, participated in the holy through a series of sacral acts: the ceremonies of anointing, enthronement, and coronation. The mythical ideology of the ancient Near East concerning divine kingship penetrated the mentality of the Davidic dynasty, albeit in a limited and somewhat modified form.[46]

The Farewell Psalm of David (2 Sam. 23:1–7), generally known as *The Last Words of David* or his *Hymnic Testament*,[47] probably originated with the coronation feast of his successors. With high lyricism, the poet expatiates on the oracular function of the king as Yahweh's prophetic mediator:

"The oracle of David, the son of Jesse,
    the oracle of the man who was raised on high,[48]
The anointed of the God of Jacob
    and the darling of the singers of Israel"

(vs. 1).[49]

Through the device of juxtaposition, the psalmist hints that a theological bond unites prophetic oracularity and the aesthetics of sacred music. For him, David's artistic inspiration was correlated with his prophetic inspiration. He composed and he modulated while speaking on behalf of the Deity. The musician, the poet, and the prophet were one.

In the four strophes which follow the introduction, the ideal monarch is indirectly portrayed. The word "anointed" is on the way to acquiring the connotation of finality which was centuries later attached to the word "Messiah" as a *terminus technicus.*

I

23:2 The spirit of Yahweh speaks by me,
and his word is upon my tongue.
3 The God of Jacob has spoken,
the Rock of Israel has said to me:

II

"When one rules justly over men,
ruling in the fear of God,
4 He is like the morning light at sunrise,
like the dawn of a cloudless day.
[Shining with] brightness after the autumn rain
the new grass will sprout from the earth."

III

5 Is not thus my house in communion with God?
For he has set for me an eternal covenant,
well-ordered in all things, and well-kept.
Thus he is my whole salvation and my whole delight:
will he not make my descendants spring forth?

IV

6 As for men of nought, they are wind-tossed thorns.
One cannot take them by hand.
The man who will smite them
arms himself with iron
and the staff of a spear.
They will be burnt by fire,
utterly consumed in flames.

The coming of Yahweh's spirit to the sovereign marks him as the mediator of presence for the nation and for the land. First, he speaks the divine word (vss. 2–3*ab*). Second, royal communion manifests itself in a just rule of government (vs. 3*cd*).

Third, the immediate consequence of the king's intimacy with his God is the fertility of nature at the renewal of the year, when grass "sparkles" under the autumn rains (vs. 4). Finally, royal communion is not confined to the individual founder of the dynasty. It continues to unite forever the house of David with Yahweh through "an eternal covenant" (vs. 5).

In contrast with the conditional covenant of the early Sinai traditions,[50] the Zion-Davidic theology of presence introduced into Hebrew religion a factor which vitiated the concept of divine freedom. Moreover, a suprahistorical myth of unconditioned protection for the kings of Judah inevitably undermined the ethical demands of official Yahwism. To be sure, the epithets which qualified this eternal covenant as "well ordered in all things and well kept" implied a critical concern for the moral character of the monarch and the social fairness of his administration, but the exact sense of these words remained ambiguous (vs. 5). If the fulmination of the last strophe against "men of nought" (vs. 6) refers to corrupt kings, one may conclude that this "eternal covenant" was after all only temporal and the expression should be ascribed to court language with the hyperbolic overtones of New Year's wishes. It seems, however, that the expression "men of nought" designates the enemies of the kings rather than the sons of David themselves.

In effect, the *Coronation Hymn* (now preserved as Ps. 2) stresses even more than the *Last Words of David* the sacrality of the ruler.[51] It implies a royal intimacy with God in terms of filial adoption:[52]

"[Yahweh] said to me, Thou art my son!
This day, I have begotten thee!"

(Ps. 2:7.)

The idea expressed in this verse went beyond the similar notion which court prophets developed after David's reign within the framework of Nathan's oracle.[53] In that theological charter of the Judahite monarchy, on the day when a new king was enthroned, Yahweh was made to declare, "I shall be a father to him, and he will be to me a son" (2 Sam. 7:14). Here, the language is more graphic. While the statement of God's begetting did not refer to an act of biological procreation either through the rite of hierogamy or through a mythical belief in supranatural conception,[54] it was nevertheless something other than a simple metaphor.

The ancient Near Eastern mentality concerning divine kingship inevitably insinuated itself into the royal circles of Jerusalem. The survival of the Jebusites, on the one hand, and the presence of foreign queens and diplomats, on the other, promoted the habit of ambiguous adulation for "the chief of state" —a collective delusion which has persisted throughout the history of mankind, including the Western democracies of today. As the unbroken line of Davidic succession lengthened over several generations in spite of wars and domestic upheavals,[55] the aura of legend which surrounded the founder of the dynasty was bound to reflect upon the sons. A coronation hymn which included the oracle "Today, I have begotten thee" tended to separate the anointed monarch from other human beings not only socially but also ontologically. The notion of sacred sonship, even viewed as the result of a ritual adoption, tended to blur the sharp distinction which Mosaic Yahwism had maintained between the human and divine realms. A "mystical bond" was deemed to unite Yahweh and the incumbent of David's throne. As the adopted son of the Godhead, the king could do no wrong, and autocratic caprice easily trespassed the limits of Yahwistic ethics. Presence as royal adoption represented a deterioration of the Hebraic theology of presence. It was corrupted by the notion of a "hierarchy," or "sacred rule," especially as it became associated with the myth of Zion. Such an association appears not only in Psalm 132,[56] but also

and especially in another coronation hymn now preserved in
Psalm 110.[57]

This poem provides a further example of the ambivalence
which some court circles entertained vis-à-vis the majesty of the
royal person. While it does not erase the Hebraic distinction
between divinity and humanity, it ascribes to the sovereign a
number of attributes which definitely set him apart from the
rest of humanity as one living in the presence, in the intimacy,
and by the power of Yahweh. The psalm presents itself in the
form of an oracle of God himself addressed to the king as "my
Lord" (*Adonî*). One can easily imagine why Psalm 110 received
sustained attention among the first Christians of the New Testament.[58]

Ps. 110:1 Oracle of Yahweh to my Lord:
           Sit down at my right hand
               till I make thy enemies thy footstool.
       2   Let Yahweh stretch forth from Zion the scepter of
               thy power:
           Rule in the midst of thy enemies!
       3   Thy people will offer themselves freely
               on the day of thy battle.[59]
           Through the splendor of holiness,[60] from the womb
               of dawn,
           to thee [belongs] the dew of thy young men.[61]
       4   Yahweh has sworn and will not repent:
           Thou art priest for ever
           According to the order of Melchisedek!"

The above translation attempts to respect the Masoretic text
but must remain highly tentative. In spite of several uncertainties and obscurities of meaning, four elements appear to be
relatively clear. First, on the day of his coronation the new king
was ritually introduced to the heavenly council as one of the
sons of God. It is not obvious from the text that the new monarch was officially enthroned in the Jerusalem sanctuary, at the
right side (south) of the ark. If the original wording of the

poem, now lost in the Masoretic text, is correctly preserved in the Greek version of the Septuagint,[62] divine sonship lay in the mind of the psalmist as he expressed poetically the myth of the king's procreation by the Deity. Even the allusions to "womb," "dawn," and "dew," which appear in the textual tradition of the medieval synagogue, call to mind the myth of a cosmic procreation, not unlike that of the personified figure of wisdom (Prov. 8:22 ff.).

Second, the new monarch received the promise of military allegiance in words which summon to memory the prowess of David and the selfless sacrifice of his young heroes.

Third, this pledge of a supreme freewill-offering in death was consecrated by the temple ideology. The divine Lord of Zion himself handled the king's scepter. Secular power represents a manifestation of the cultic presence of Yahweh in the sanctuary.

Fourth, the new monarch was endowed "forever" with a priestly status and function related to the legendary figure of Melchisedek, priest of El Elyon and king of Salem (Gen. 14:18–20).[63] An effort may be discerned here to bind the Davidic House not only to an institutionalized presence related to the Zion mythology—through the implied identification of Jerusalem with Salem—but also to the Abrahamic promises and the Heilsgeschichte of the national epic.

Thus, in fourfold fashion—as the adopted son of God, as the recipient of a freewill sacrifice in war, as the regent of the Lord of Zion, and as the Melchisedekian type of eternal Priest-King—the Judahite monarchs became, at least in the minds of members of their entourage, the instruments of Yahweh in all spheres of human existence, including the destiny of peoples spread over the "widest earth."[64]

When confined to David, presence as "the Rock" was viewed as the gift of grace. When linked by ritual to the Davidic dynasty, presence as "the Crown" became a mythic ideology of cultic nationalism which attempted to ignore the relativity of history, with its human vicissitudes and even royal criminality. The former respected the freedom of Yahweh. The latter tended to enlist divine power into "the texture of time." The former let God be God. The latter was on its way to making a god in man's image.

Presence as "The Scepter"

Biblical records themselves have mercilessly depicted the sorry deeds of the Judahite kings—not only the many interlopers, treacherous captains, and other murderers who ruled the Northern Kingdom of Israel proper (922–722 B.C.) but also those princes who belonged to the hallowed line of David. With the exception of a few reformers among them,[65] the kings of Judah followed the example of worldly tolerance which Solomon had set. David's immediate successor, it will be remembered, had tolerated within the palace grounds the foreign worship familiar to his queens, and the Phoenician architecture of his temple courted the mysterious attractiveness of the nature cults.

Direct and indirect evidence indicates that in most of the decades over a period of four centuries (975–587 B.C.), the worship of Yahweh was dubiously and laboriously maintained in rival accommodation to that of the Earth-Mother goddess, with such religious practices as idolatry in various forms, necromancy, witchcraft, hierogamy, male prostitution, heliolatry, ophiolatry, and—at least during the reigns of Manasseh and Amon in the seventh century—the worship of the official pantheon of Assyria.[66]

It is difficult to reconcile the relative loftiness of the psalmists' theology with this polytheistic syncretism, unless one conjectures, as most scholars do, that the psalmody of the first temple was effectively censored through the process of oblivion. It is probable that objectionable hymns and laments were merely dropped from the hymnals of the Second Temple.

A lack of documentation on the inner life of the kings[67] makes it precarious to speculate on their response to the mode of presence which was ceremonially imparted to them at their coronation. Nevertheless, Psalm 89 provides at least one exception to this literary dearth.

In this complex poem,[68] probably composed for a national day of mourning and fast, the king is fully aware of the status of divine sonship. He is compelled to recognize, however, that the presence of Yahweh through ritual adoption has failed to provide him with divine protection. Presence as "the Crown" has become Presence as "the Scepter of Judgment."

Intricately knit within a strophic structure which shows its unity of form and thought in spite of the diversity of its poetic genres,[69] Psalm 89 consists of three parts framed by a liturgical invocation and a thematic *inclusio*. The invocation (vss. 1–4 [Heb. 2–5]) recalls the "loyal deeds of Yahweh," equating his faithfulness as the creator of a harmonious cosmos with his faithfulness as the protector of the Davidic throne. The first part (vss. 5–18 [Heb. 6–19]) is a *hymn* developing the first theme of the invocation. It exalts Yahweh's power over the arrogance of the Sea and his triumph against Rahab, the mythical monster of chaos.[70] The second part (vss. 19–37 [Heb. 20–38]) is an *oracle* which expounds the second theme of the invocation: it recalls two sets of Yahweh's promises, those to David (vss. 19–27 [Heb. 20–28]) and those to his posterity (vss. 28–37 [Heb. 29–38]). The third part is a *lament* (vss. 38–51 [Heb. 39–52]), lexicographically and thematically related to the first two.

Yahweh spoke once in a vision to David. He promised to make him—"a stripling"—into "a hero" (*gibbôr*), his "first-born son," "the highest of the kings of the earth." In gratitude, David replied, "Thou art my Father, my God, my Rock, my Savior" (vss. 19–27 [Heb. 20–28]). Furthermore, Yahweh swore that David's seed would endure forever and that his throne would be "as the days of heaven" (vss. 29 [Heb. 30]). The promise, however, was qualified. If some of David's sons violated Yahweh's "law," "ordinances," "statutes," and "commandments," their transgressions would be punished "with the rod" and their guilt "with stripes" (vss. 30–32 [Heb. 31–33]). No ancient singer of the psalm could have missed the irony: the word for "rod" (*shébhet*) is the same as the word for "royal scepter," now turned against its holder. The very symbol of kingship has become the symbol of judgment.

The oracle concluded in reiterating the promise. The throne of David would remain forever, "like the sun and the moon, a faithful witness in the heavens" (vss. 33–37 [Heb. 34–38]). The theology of the Davidic covenant has been incorporated into the theology of creation. In the midst of the Fertile Crescent, where dynasties rose and fell, the throne of Judah was secure, for it drew the same divine concern as the natural order. At the same time, the rigorous attention which Yahwism had always paid to social justice, communal ethics, and integrity in government could not allow the immorality or the political and religious irresponsibility of individual monarchs to go unchecked. Royal status meant divine sonship but not immunity against punishment for lawlessness. The king's scepter may be hurled against him as the rod of retribution.

As a criterion for the understanding of history, and as a ground for hope in the future of the nation, the David *legenda* gained admittance in the religion of Yahweh. More than Nathan's oracle (2 Sam. 7) or the Psalm of the Ark (Ps. 132), however, the oracle of Psalm 89 shows that safeguards have been erected against the oriental myth of the divinity of kings. Even as an adopted son of God, the chief of state is not above the law. The lamenter in Psalm 89 ignored the stipulation of the oracle. He protested his misfortunes as if Yahweh himself had violated his own covenant:

> Yet, thou! Thou hast spurned and rejected thy anointed,
>   Thou hast become enraged against him,
> Thou hast denounced thy covenant with thy servant,
>   Thou hast profaned his crown in the dust,
>
> Thou hast brought his luster to an end,
>   Thou hast hurled his throne to the ground!
>
> (vss. 38–44 [Heb. 39–45])

True to the Hebraic style of brusqueness in prayer, the remonstrance goes so far as to accuse Yahweh. The oracle had unambiguously stated that the covenant with David and his seed did not exclude moral retribution for individual occupants of the throne, but the language of the complaint shows no sign of penitence, not even an awareness of wrongdoing. Indeed, the tone suggests the mentality of a prince who has "inhaled" for too long the adulation of his courtiers. In the face of adversity, he merely felt betrayed by his God. He did not deny God's presence. He charged that the presence had become a scourge —without cause.

By providing a clause for the punishment of individual kings, the oracle had in effect undermined the ancient notion of collective personality.[71] The lamenter attempted to seek shelter under the Davidic dynasty, which he conceived as a sacrosanct corporateness transcending time and generations.

Tyrants are notorious for their fear of treason. They tend to misconstrue expressions of dissent as acts of lese majesty. If they believe in the myth of their divine right, they may find a solace for their anxieties:

> "There's such divinity doth hedge a king
>   That treason can but peep to what it would,
>   Acts little of his will."[72]

But if they interpret adversity as a sign that God himself conspires against them, what becomes of the myth of their near-divinity?

As if he had sensed the force of this irony, the psalmist altered his stance. No longer arrogant he begged:

> "How long, O Yahweh, wilt thou hide thyself forever?
> Will thy wrath continue to burn like a fire?"
>
> (vs. 46 [Heb. 47].)

The poets and the prophets of Mosaic Yahwism had said that God averted his face and concealed himself from human crimes.[73] The motif of the *Deus absconditus* may have hinted in the psalm at an ethical dimension, but the explicit confession of wrongdoing is missing. Still, hidden presence is not absence, and the king's faith, though shaken, was not shattered. His plea to Yahweh persisted, more urgent than before:

> "Remember! [Here] I [am], . . . What is a life-span?[74]
>   For what kind of emptiness hast thou created the sons of man?
> What man of stature shall live and not see death?
> Will he escape the power of Sheol?"
>
> (vss. 47–48 [Heb. 48–49].)

The rhetorical movement is theologically significant: no longer defiant, the king has become human. He has asked the existential question. He has discovered his solidarity with the human race.

The thought of mortality, far more than the experience of national calamity, has pierced the royal illusion of superhumanity. The son of David, after all, was less the adopted son of God than the created son of man. The word for "man," *Adam*, may have been pointedly chosen as a veiled allusion to the myth of the garden. Even for a "man of noble stature" (*gebher*) destined to royal splendor, the end is death. Perpetuation of the self in the underworld was viewed as under the image of sleep or at best as a semiexistence, bleak and impassive, which was contrary to life,[75] and whose goal could be described only through the image of vacuity, an emptiness devoid of substance or meaning.

What is the purpose of creation? Is there at the origin or in the sustenance of the cosmos the evidence of an intelligent and benevolent Doer? Why should man praise the Lord of nature and the creator of universal harmonies if the *telos* of life is death? What is the meaning of an existence whose ultimate destiny is nothingness? These questions were asked by the inquiring minds of the wisdom movement. The sapiential world transcended frontiers, dynasties, languages, cultic rites, and nationalities. Diplomats, officers of the foreign services of the oriental courts, multilingual public servants, and "the wise" all faced philosophical issues. They anticipated the flowering of classical philosophy. The royal hymnist of Psalm 89, who turned royal plaintiff, eventually spoke as if he belonged to the circles of royal wisdom. His intellectual voyage reflected the itinerary of his spiritual travail. His query showed that he still responded to a presence, now veiled as a great Unknown.

Deprived of martial success, he never experienced the presence as "the Rock." Heir to a noble lineage and ritually hallowed, he felt the presence not as "the Crown" but as "the Rod of Judgment." Unaware of presence as rescue, he hoped that presence as adoption would mean victory and happiness. It proved to be presence as censure. In the end, God remained near him, hiding behind an impenetrable mask. Yet from it he learned the humility and universality of the human condition. He also acquired a thirst for ultimate knowledge.

Whether Psalm 89 was composed for an enthronement ceremony or a New Year festival that included a rite of royal abasement and restoration cannot be ascertained in the light of present research. What is important for the study of the Hebraic theology of presence, however, is the fact that such a complex piece of psalmody found its way into the hymnal of the temple. With its critique of the monarchy, this poem prepared the nation to maintain the Yahwist ideal of justice through tribal solidarity in the context of divine presence.

Searching for a principle of political stability, the prophetic circles of Judah, no doubt in concert with the sapiential circles of the court, never dismissed the Davidic monarchy, although they condemned the Davidic kings. The dynastic oracles and the coronation hymns became perhaps the most important factors in the shaping of the messianic hope.

Backing away from the weak and corrupt princelings who sat on the throne of David, the prophet Isaiah postponed till the end of time his hope for a righteous ruler. In a programmatic poem (Isa. 11:1–5), which may be called a manifesto for sane government, he envisaged the growth of "a shoot from the [cut-off] tree of Jesse"—thereby expecting historical discontinuity from the dynasty but ideological continuity from the Davidic model—upon whom "the spirit of Yahweh" would "alight like a bird"—thereby stressing the element of theological disruption and wonder. The prophet understood that living in the intimacy of Yahweh was the *sine qua non* of integrity and wisdom in government.[76] In another age, he might have insisted on the principle of separation between church and state, but, in any case, he would have wanted the chief of state to be a genuine man of God. In addition, by linking the sevenfold spirit to seven aspects of the art of kingship, he intimated that familiarity with the presence was less a virtue of military valor than a skill of administration.

Isaiah's attempt to integrate the concepts of wisdom and presence into a viable formula for political leadership was influential in bringing about the expectation of the eschatological Messiah.

Whatever may have been the specific occasions for which they were composed or used, the royal psalms were poems on the mystery of royal communion. During the four centuries of the monarchy, these poems evolved from the evocation of a soldier's amazement at protection from peril to the frustration of a crowned functionary whose mystical status was no longer believable but whose questioning faith remained so dynamic that he faced the enigma of life and death without renouncing hope. His last word was therefore the request of a common man, even if he still begged for relief from shame as Yahweh's anointed (Ps. 89:51 [Heb. 52]).[77]

Because they showed individuals in prosperity and distress, the royal psalms, by their form and content, influenced the psalmody of many temple musicians.

As members of the liturgical guilds, most of the psalmists learned from the royal psalms how to express in melody and verse their own enjoyment or deprivation of the divine presence. The hymnology of the First Temple was on the whole a psalmody of presence. The spiritual longings which it exhibited remained in many ways unfulfilled. For this reason, much of the psalmody of presence deserves to be called a psalmody of the mystical quest.

MYSTICAL QUEST

It has been maintained that the Hebraic spirit was not "mystical." The word "mysticism" usually describes the religious attitude which loses subject-object awareness, overcomes the differences between the human and the divine, negates the boundary between finiteness and infinity, claims to reach in trance or in ecstasy an awareness of identification with the Godhead, and fuses the proximate with the ultimate. As a consequence of such an attitude, the human self is absorbed into divinity. Defined along these lines, the word "mysticism" is not appropriate for describing Hebraic faith in general or the inner life of the psalmists in particular.[78]

The insistence of Mosaic faith on making a radical distinction between God and man reflected a reaction against the fascination which the ancient Near Eastern cults exercised on Israel. The storytellers of the epic age and the great prophets during the monarchy waged an uncompromising polemic against practices which tended to promote a mystical union with the numinous forces of nature. Canaanite syncretism sought to attune human beings to the feminine principle of the deified earth. The sacerdotal status of the queens of Judah, snake and sun worship, the recurring presence of male prostitutes in the Jerusalem temple, and several other data[79] indicate that a religious eroticism related to agrarian and animal fertility was constantly alluring court and masses alike. Through the extreme stimulation of all their senses, worshippers attained that marginal twilight between life and death which appears to transcend time and space. Such states of awareness have been described in the language of spiritualized sexuality by mystics of many cultures.[80]

When some scholars speak of the mysticism of the prophets[81] and of the psalmists,[82] they refer not to the *unio mystica* reached in a sexual or sublimated form but to a sense of elusive communion with Yahweh. Communion does not lead to the fusion of divine and human identities. Whenever the psalmists used poetic metaphors to evoke the immediacy of communion, they also referred, contextually, to its relativity. Even when they used a vocabulary which was later appropriated by Jewish and Christian mystics, they alluded, in effect, to spiritual longings which remained unfulfilled. The psalmists were not mystics, although some of them may have engaged in a mystical quest.

Guests of the Sanctuary

Since most of the psalmists belonged to the musical guilds of the Jerusalem temple, they participated in the celebration of the feasts and in the national services of thanksgiving. For these public ceremonies, they composed and sang hymns of praise for the sovereign of nature and history.[83] That the Lord of heaven and earth manifested his presence in the sanctuary during such cultic events was the basic assumption of the hymnology. More especially, it is probable that the culmination of the festive ceremonial was marked by a symbolic and, in effect, "sacramental" theophany—the anticipation of the victory of Yahweh at the end of history.[84]

The details of the cultic theophany are not known. While the theophany did not include the "monstrance" of a statue of the Deity, as in Egypt and Mesopotamia or later in Greece, a number of inferences in the Psalter and elsewhere suggest that, at the highest moment of worship, a dramatic apotheosis was made perceptible to the senses of the worshipers through a convergence of liturgical devices:

> "Elohim has ascended at the ritual shout!
>   Yahweh, with the sound of the *shophar!*
>   Play ye the harps for Elohim, play ye the harps!
>   Play ye the harps for our King, play ye the harps!"[85]

The symbolic event—which corresponded in the believers' minds not to a mere sign but to a sensuous token of reality—has survived, through modified forms, in the synagogue as the bringing out of the Torah scrolls and in the church as the consecration of the eucharistic elements.

The psalmists believed so thoroughly in the concreteness of the cultic advent as the effective prefiguration of the final epiphany that they expatiated on the theme of universal harmony, when "the princes of the peoples are gathered as the people of Abraham."[86] It was the ideology of the cultic advent in the temple of Jerusalem which prepared in large measure the rise of Jewish and Christian eschatology, with the beliefs in the last judgment and the fulfillment of creation.[87]

"Out of Zion, the perfection of beauty,
   Elohim is shining forth.
Our Elohim will come, he will not keep silent."[88]

The psalmists were so thoroughly inspired by the realism of the cultic advent of Yahweh during the act of ceremonial worship that for them, also, divine presence lingered in the temple, even without the conjunction of sacerdotal and congregational activity. In Zion, the psalmists were at home as the guests of Yahweh. It is therefore to be expected that an overwhelming sense of divine nearness permeated their personal prayers.

Some of the individual laments were probably commissioned by temple officials for the use of private worshippers who sought pastoral comfort, ritual cleansing, and judiciary asylum in the sacred precincts. Special psalms were sung when individuals were indicted for crimes, impaired by disease, pursued by enemies, or otherwise buffeted by adversity. It is even possible, although not demonstrated, that a few of these poems were chanted in rites of exorcism or of protection from witchcraft.[89] Others may have been recited during legal procedures, not merely as protests of innocence but also as ritual devices for the testing of veracity.[90]

In any case, the poets who composed the individual laments showed a depth of theological perceptiveness which points to the authenticity of their encounter with the divine. Nowhere in the collection of personal prayers is the complexity of the interaction between the theology of Zion and the inwardness of faith more graphically expressed than in Psalm 27.

Some exegetes in modern times have missed the purpose of the poet by failing to recognize the literary homogeneity of the psalm.[91] Observing a change of rhythm and of mood between verses 1–6 and verses 7–14, they have hastily concluded that it represents an editorial conflation of two independent pieces. On the contrary, an analysis of the structure and of the articulation of the key words with the themes suggests a unity of composition.

In the *first* strophe (vss. 1–3), the psalmist links his certitude of deliverance to his ability to overcome fear:

> Ps. 27:1. My light is Yahweh, and also my safety!
> whom shall I fear?
> The fortress of my life:
> of whom shall I be in dread?
> 2. When evildoers close in on me
> to devour my flesh,
> My foes and my enemies themselves
> will stumble and fall.
> 3. Though a whole army would encamp against me,
> my heart will not fear,
> Even if a whole battle were waged against me,
> at that very moment I shall trust.

This creedal confession does not smooth over the gravity of the crisis. The sense of trust is itself prompted by the urgency of the situation. Reminiscences of David's *Song of Thanksgiving*[92] suggest that temple musicians were the spiritual as well as artistic heirs to the legendary warrior king. Like David, they were pursued by enemies, and their perils only intensified their conviction of God's nearness. Like David, they compared Yahweh to a fortress, to a lamp, or to light. Unlike David, however, a temple musician could avail himself of the institutional means of sacramental grace. Yahweh was present in his sanctuary.

In the *second* strophe (vss. 4–6), therefore, the psalmist expressed his religious desire on two levels at once. He sought in the sacred precinct an asylum from secular harassment and also a locus for engaging in a mystical quest:

> Ps. 27:4. A single wish I ask of Yahweh,
> this alone I earnestly seek,
> To dwell in the house of Yahweh
> all the days of my life
> That I may see the beauty of Yahweh
> and have a vision in the sanctuary.

May the Souls of all the faithful departed, through the mercy of God, rest in peace. Amen.

IN LOVING MEMORY OF

Rev. Paul Barrett, O.P.
Dec. 23, 1919
Apr. 25, 1993

May the angels lead you into Paradise, may the martyrs come to welcome you and take you to the holy city, the new and eternal Jerusalem. May the choir of angels welcome you. Where Lazarus is poor no longer, may you have eternal rest. Amen.

SCHOEN FUNERAL HOMES

5. He will indeed conceal me in his canopy
    on the evil day.
    He will shelter me in the shelter of his tent,
    he will set me on high upon a rock.
6. Soon he will raise my head
    above my enemies on every side
    And I shall share in his tent
    communion meals with shouts of joy.

A single wish monopolized this man's psyche. It eliminated all his other aspirations. His only desire was to become a permanent resident in the temple. This request contained a deeper craving. He wanted, in a trance, to behold the beauty of Yahweh. Such a strange expression (vs. 4c) may have been inherited from the cultic language of Egypt, where, on feast days, priests would unveil the statue of the god and present it for the adoration of the worshippers.[93] The Hebrew psalmist referred not to a cultic object, however, but to a psychological experience of inner sight.[94] The word *no'am*, inadequately rendered as "beauty," implies a response of wonder akin to the delights of love[95] and possibly even a relational exchange between the "seer" and the "seen." Cognates of the same word apply to physical charm, erotic and aesthetic enjoyment, the various emotions of friendship,[96] the thrill of learning, and the holy pleasure of liturgical singing.[97] Because the two *cola* of the poetic line are synonymously parallel, "to see the beauty of Yahweh" means "to have a vision in the sanctuary" (vs. 4c).[98] Dwelling in the temple of Zion provides the opportunity for a flight into the divine realm of being. Sacramental presence is a means for ecstasy.

The "canopy" and the "tent" call to mind the mythic world of the cultic theophany.[99] Sacrifices will be offered in the sanctuary, but they are transfigured into communion meals in the heavenly home of God. The beauty of Yahweh is not only seen but also tasted and "inwardly digested." Nevertheless, the entire prospect belongs only to the poet's imagination. He did not say that his cravings were fulfilled. On the contrary, he continued his appeal in a *third* strophe (vss. 7–10), which introduced a different mood:

> Ps. 27:7. Hear, O Yahweh, my voice! I cry!
> Be gracious unto me and answer me!
> 8. My heart remembers thy word:[100]
> "Seek ye my face!"
> Thy face, O Yahweh, I seek.
> 9. Hide not thy face from me,
> Repel not in anger thy servant:
> Thou hast always been my help.[101]
> Reject me not, abandon me not,
> God of my safety![102]
> 10. If my father and mother were to abandon me,
> Yahweh would gather me up [unto himself].

A prayer for grace conceals an appeal to the maternal side of divinity.[103] It does not necessarily imply a sense of guilt. Rather it arises from the renunciation of all claims, right, or merit. It represents a determination to act in a *situation-limite*, "where no helper is." The petitioner persists in asking for a vision of Yahweh, for he remembers the liturgical invitation which was extended repeatedly in the cultic ceremonial: "Seek ye my face!" (Vs. 8.)[104] Deprived of a *prima facie* ecstasy, this religious sensualist at last surrenders to his existential finitude.

In post-Kantian philosophy, no cogent evidence of God's being satisfies the thinker. *Mutatis mutandis*, in Hebraic theology, no sensual perception of the Godhead gratifies the worshipper.

Will the psalmist transfer his expectation to the moment of his death? The final certitude, "Yahweh will gather me [unto himself]" (vs. 10*b*), might be understood as an allusion to eternal bliss, but the exceptional use of the verb "to gather up" does not permit exegetical opinion.[105]

Ambiguity remains attached to the metaphor of the divine face. Presence is an absence and even an abandon when it is hidden, but this absence has the power to bring forth the most peculiar ingredient of Hebraic theology: faith as an instrument of knowledge as well as a *modus vivendi.*

Hölderlin's paradox may illustrate the unexpected aftermath of mystical deprivation. "It is no longer the presence of God," he wrote, "but his absence that reassures man." The psalmist's position of strength argues against the validity of modern theologies of experience and feeling. In his determination to hold firm to his faith, the psalmist closed as he began. He reaffirmed his trust in the God of his safety (vss. 1, 3*b*, 9*b*). This reaffirmation, however, was offered in a new context. With a quasi-serene obstinacy, he simply stated that divine love never fails (vs. 10). The ground of man's fidelity is God's fidelity. Hidden from the mystical quest, Yahweh will yet protect. Parental love provides a completely inadequate comparison.

An unquenched desire has promoted a new stance. The psalmist continued to sing in the temple. He still believed in the cultic mode of presence, but he "experienced" God by absence and want, as one who knows water by thirst. His unquenched desire was also the source of a hitherto undetected self-awareness. Some reality was lacking in his own character. Hence a *fourth* and final strophe (vss. 11–14):

Ps. 27:11 Teach me, O Yahweh, thy way
and lead me on the even path
on account of my adversaries.
12 Give me not up to the lust of my foes!
False witnesses have risen against me
and they breathe violence.
13 I believe[106] I shall see the goodness of Yahweh
in the land of the living.
14 Wait in hope for Yahweh, be brave,
and he will strengthen thy heart.
Wait in hope for Yahweh!

Literary critics who fail to discern the unity of the composition of Psalm 27 miss the poet's purpose, which was to translate abroad the power of communion. The mystical quest had come to a dead end. The search for a mode of behavior in the midst of a hostile society became the petitioner's primary concern. He no longer hoped "to see the beauty of Yahweh," but he still waited to be taught "the way of Yahweh." Hebraic spirituality is never divorced from ethics, and ethics can have no other root than divine nurture. The comparison of Yahweh to a teacher reflects a newly gained humility on the psalmist's part. He wants to be nursed, as a plant is, to his maturity.[107] When a man asks his God, "teach me" and "lead me," he shows that his passion for ecstasy has been replaced by a passion for the art of living within the vicissitudes of history.

Like Moses, who was denied the vision of the face but had seen the goodness of Yahweh pass by (Exod. 33:19 f.),[108] the poet of Psalm 27 was satisfied "to see the goodness of Yahweh in the land of the living" (vs. 13).[109] Once again, the theology of the name has overcome the theology of the glory. The prophet Isaiah waited with his disciples for the God who veiled his face (Isa. 8:17).[110] In the same vein, the psalmist concluded his prayer of supplication with an exhortation to "wait in hope for Yahweh" (vs. 14).[111] Hope is the edge of trust which begets inward power and conquers time.

The Superfluity of Zion

It can hardly be doubted that the psalmists obtained their spiritual acuity from their Zion-centered theology. The temple musicians received all the benefits of institutional worship. The *askesis* of the cultic calendar, with its rhythm of feasts and fasts, molded and refined their sense of divine nearness. Participation in the rites of the ceremonial assemblies, the brotherly congeniality of the musical guilds, the catechetic power of the chants, and above all the awesome certainty that Yahweh had permitted his presence to reside in the darkness of the edifice—all these factors combined to maintain a greenhouse form of environment conducive to exceptional fervor and exceptional perceptivity. Cultus as an institution could serve as a ferment for revelational knowledge. The psalmists learned theological subtleties through a constant intimacy with the holy that never seemed to erode into secular callousness. Even when they appropriated the ritual inwardly, it was primarily on account of the myth of Zion that they felt "at home" with Yahweh.

At the same time, it is not generally recognized that the psalmody of presence, born of cultus, could in effect transcend it. Away from the holy hill—perhaps exiled and detained, certainly uprooted and "excommunicated" from congregational worship since they were unable to go to Jerusalem—psalmists like the poet of Psalm 84 sang their cultic nostalgia and discovered unwittingly that in their cultic homelessness they were still in communion with their God.[112]

The key to understanding Psalm 84 is in the sequence of three refrains which articulate the strophes (vss. 4, 5, 12) and mark a progression of theological thinking. Not surprisingly, these three refrains are "beatitudes" or rather "macarisms," exclamations of wishes for happiness which have apparently risen among wisdom circles[113] and differ markedly from the priestly blessings.[114]

First, a man of religious passion, whose "whole being longs, yes, faints for the courts of Yahweh" (vs. 2 [Heb. 3]), pities his homelessness and is so much overcome by emotion at the memory of Zion that he cries out, unsyntactically, "Thy altars! . . . O Yahweh of Hosts, my king and my God!" (vs. 3 [Heb. 4]). Of course, he extols the happiness of the temple residents who can continually praise the Lord of Zion (vs. 4 [Heb. 5]). The first macarism hails the cultic mode of presence.

The second macarism immediately follows the first, since it opens rather than closes the second strophe (vs. 5 [Heb. 6]).

The psalmist is now introducing an element of movement. No longer does his attention center upon those who dwell in Zion. His imagination pictures those who are on the way to Zion (vss. 6–9 [Heb. 7–10]), and his poetic mind shifts toward a new concern. He now wishes happiness for the men whose inner strength is in Yahweh (vs. 5 [Heb. 6]).

In the climactic strophe, the psalmist contrasts "uneasy tenseness at the threshold of the house of [his] God"[115] with the "indolent and secure lounging"[116] that he may have indulged in as he sojourned "in the tents of the wicked" (vss. 10–11 [Heb. 11–12]). A new theme has been ushered in. Although the poet still prefers critical uncertainty at the edge of his spiritual home to comfortable insouciance achieved at the price of ethical compromise in the secular world, his concern is no longer the joy which emerges from an idealistic memory of the temple community but the realistic suspicion that life at the sanctuary presents problems. The horizon of the poet has broadened to include the open spaces. The *hagios topos* has been replaced by the wide world. This homeless worshiper is now interested in the enlightenment and protection which Yahweh offers to those "who walk in integrity" (vs. 12 [Heb. 13]). It is as if this man had left the sacristy for the market place. The realm of moral conduct takes precedence over the aesthetics of the sacred. Yahweh is "a sun" and "a shield" for those who behave with wholeness from day to day; that is to say, he provides a light and a guideline in the ethics of decision. Even the strictly theological reality of "glory," hitherto confined to the inaccessible core of the divine Being, has become, with "grace," a gift from above by which man can see "goodness," the virtue of social coherence:

> "For Yahweh is a sun and a shield:
> he will give grace and glory;
> Goodness Yahweh will not withhold
> from them that walk in integrity
>
> (vs. 11 [Heb. 12])."

The final macarism transforms a cloistered cultist into a man of the street whose trust in God enables him to overcome the pain of topographical distance and perhaps even institutional excommunication. The refrain is no longer "Happy the ceremonialist" or even "the pilgrim," but

> "Happy is the man who places his confidence in thee"
> (vs. 12 [Heb. 13])."

A temple musician who was cultically homeless could still be with his God. The man who walked tête-à-tête with Yahweh learned to celebrate life away from the *hagios topos*. He has been liberated from a theology of space. He received through Zion a faith which taught him the superfluity of Zion.

Of course, when a sacramentalist is deprived of the "real presence," he runs the risk of spiritual sloth and of accommodation to what Alice Meynell, taunting Protestants, called "real absence." On the other side, the peril that is built into the structures of institutional worship leads to the smugness of self-comfort. "Faith that does not perpetually expose itself to the possibility of unfaith is no faith but merely a convenience."[117]

Not unlike the poet of Psalms 42 and 43, who was apparently banished to northern Galilee at the high waters of the Jordan, the singer of Psalm 84 was an uprooted alien, whose heart was pulsing beyond the fear of nothingness. He gave up the lure of sight to accept the hazard of faith.

For the would-be mystics of Zion, faith was "the earnest of things unseen." They nursed a divine truth which clamored to be fleshed in a human personality.

Beyond Death

Form-critical analysis has failed objectively to identify literary criteria for the genre of "the sapiential psalm." Nevertheless, exegetes admit that many laments and didactic poems of the psalter show close affinities with the wisdom circles.[118] It appears that temple musicians were acquainted with the intelligentsia of the court. In all probability, they discussed problems of human existence with princes, public officials, and foreign diplomats in a para-philosophical way. Intellectuality met with spirituality, and it is significant that one of these musicians—the poet of Psalm 73—began a song on the issue of theodicy and ended it as a credo on the eternal presence.[119]

The psalmist did not offer any intellectual solution to the problem of evil, but it was the intellectual consideration of this problem which stirred his religious consciousness and led him to receive the dispensation of a new truth. Nothing can separate him—not even death—from the divine embrace.

The bold thinker must have entertained some heterodox or even outrageously blasphemous doubts on divine justice, but his faith prevented him from publishing them abroad.

> If I had said, I will speak thus and so,
>   behold! I would have betrayed the assembly of thy sons.[120]
> And when I considered the best way to grasp this matter,
>   it was too hard for me
> Until I went to the sanctuary of God[121]
>   and imagined the eventual destiny [of the wicked].
>
> (Vss. 15–17)

An inquisitive essay has become a prayer. The skeptic, who pondered intellectual answers to difficult questions, suddenly addressed the Deity as "Thou." He inserted his doubt into the context of his adoration. His dutiful reaffirmation of the traditional dogma of retribution à retardement did not suffice to remove the stumbling block (vss. 18–20). Therefore, he no longer pursued his trend of thinking within the confines of his autonomous self, but pursued it instead in the presence of the Godhead. At once, the poet became aware of his existential

finitude. Yet the discovery of his intellectual limitations did not
push him either to revolt or to despair:

> "Thus, my mind was embittered,
>   but I continued to pine inwardly;[122]
> I was like a brute, unable to know,
>   really a monstrous beast[123] in thy presence"
>
> (vss. 21–22).

At the very core of his *Anfechtung*, the thinker found out that his
cosmic solitude was an illusion. He was not alone. All along,
though without knowing it, he had been in the immediate com-
pany of Yahweh. Perhaps he stressed the *I-with-Thee* formula
(vss. 22*b*, 23*a*, 25*a*) to show that his egocentric endeavor had
been unwittingly oriented Godward.[124] In any case, he was now
raised to a new level of knowledge. He received the epistemology of faith:

> "Nevertheless, I am continually with thee,
>   thou holdest me by my right hand,
> Thou guidest me by thy purpose,
>   and afterwards thou wilt take me to glory"
>
> (vss. 23–24).

The horrors of human existence, with its painful collection of
cosmic, biological, and psychological riddles, may continue to
torment the questioner, but his future is no longer comparable
to an isolated groping in obscurity. This man knows that an
intelligent and benevolent transcendence is guiding his steps.
The boulders remain ahead of him, but they are no longer
skandala, "rocks of stumbling." His right hand is held by another hand which directs him to his goal while his mind remains
in a state of agnostic suspense. He has not, however, settled
into a state of unrelieved ignorance, for the purpose of his life
is sure.

God's "purpose" (*'eṣah*) is also his "counsel," analogous to the expert opinion of government advisers who collect the evidence needed for eventually reaching a decision.[125] Divine companionship is divine guidance, but divine guidance respects a man's freedom of choice. The holding of man's right hand means manacling him with flowers, not with irons. The man of faith is eager to accept "by touch" the sense of his orientation.

Death itself becomes a mode of access to a new form of being, when *unio mystica* will at last be consummated:

> "And afterwards thou wilt take me to glory"
>
> (vs. 24*b*).

The meaning of this phrase has been the object of much disputation.[126] The force of the expression "thou wilt take me" should not be underestimated, for it reminded the poet's audience of the legend of Enoch, who "walked with God and he was not, for God took him" (Gen. 5:24), or of the legend of Elijah, who was "taken away" in a chariot of fire (2 Kings 2:3, 5). These reminiscences, however, did not suggest that the psalmist expected a metaphysical "translation" of his body into heaven. Rather, he was properly reticent about the mode of his ultimate destiny. He merely affirmed that death was neither extinction nor alienation from divinity, as the traditional expressions of "sleeping with one's ancestors" or "descending into Sheol" implied.[127] Presence gained the intensity of an eternal dimension.

Furthermore, the psalmist did not espouse the foreign myth of the resurrection of the flesh, which later forms of Judaism bequeathed to Christianity. Even less did his statement prefigure the Hellenistic idea of the immortality of the soul, with its implication of an arrogant claim to eternal life by virtue of a natural birthright. He was merely convinced that nothing could interrupt his present intimacy with God. The startling character of the psalmist's discovery lay in his glimpse of a new theology of presence: no longer *elusive* as it now seemed to be, it would some day surround him and hold him forever. The menace of

> "Life's profound disorder,
> Ephemerality,"[128]

has already retreated from his horizon. The perpetuality of presence prompts him to think of death not as a descent but as an ascent. "Afterwards," God will "abduct him into glory." The image subsumed by this phrase belonged, of course, to the realm of mythopoetic thinking, but the myth it summoned was free from egomaniac presumptuousness.

In this phrase, the word "glory" continues to designate the inner being of divinity, inaccessible to finite creatures. At the end of his mortal existence, the psalmist expected to be taken into the very realm of divinity. Such an eschatological perspective necessarily involved a transformation of human nature.

Later poets and prophets depicted this transformation under the figure of a new creation. This figure did not mean what the vagabond Vladimir calls, in Samuel Beckett's *Waiting for Godot,*

> "Astride of a grave and a difficult birth."

The psalmist did not evoke the laborious rites on moralistic deeds which religionists of all cultures have performed in order to earn, merit, or *achieve* immortality. He did not believe that

> "Down in
> the hole, lingeringly, the grave-digger puts on the
> forceps,"[129]

as if the birth of the new being was "worked out" by human technology, cultic or secular. With enormous simplicity he held to the conviction that God himself would take him to glory.

His contemporaries may have sought to assuage their fear of extinction by worshipping *Môt*, "deified death," the Canaanite god who moved down into the underworld and rose up with his own minions.[130] His faith in Yahweh monopolized all his concerns, desires, and ambitions. He rested content to wait with nonchalance for the divine rapture:

> "Whom have I in heaven but thee?
> 　There is none upon earth I desire beside thee.
> My flesh and my heart may fail:
> 　God is the rock of my heart and my lot forever"
> 　　　　　　　　　　　　　　　　　　　　　　(vss. 26–27).

The rock, image of military defense, has been interiorized, and so also the earthly "plot" or "portion," the territorial dream of any nomad. As a musician of the temple, the psalmist was in all probability a Levite, therefore landless. His religious wealth delivered him from the greed of real estate. His "lot" was neither earthly nor heavenly, for it did not belong to the category of space. God himself had become for him an eternal acre.

The mystical quest had been blocked by the existential boundaries of creatureliness. Identification between finite creature and infinite Creator could only be a mocking fancy, but the mystical quest persisted among all the hymnologists of presence. They transferred it beyond their own death.

PRESENCE IN ABSENCE

As the kingdom of David crumbled from within and eventually fell to Babylonian imperialism, the temple psalmodists continued to praise Yahweh as the lord of Zion, the sovereign of nature, and the judge of history. With candor, they also confessed their own agonies. Although they sometimes borrowed hackneyed formulas which went back to Sumerian laments, they also gave poetic shape to their original insights into the crucible of religious discovery. As lyrical poets of sickness, harassment, doubt, and guilt, a few became channels of divine revelation. Some of the psalmodic theologians labored under the plight of their spiritual isolation. They sang the hidden God. Others were tortured by an obsession for God. They sang the hauntingness of presence. A few reached a plateau of confident serenity. They sang the sufficient grace.

The Hidden God

When the prophet Isaiah of Jerusalem observed that "Yahweh concealed his face" (Isa. 8:17) or the Second Isaiah in Exile mourned the absence of Yahweh from the fate of his own people, saying,

"Verily, verily, thou art a God that hidest thyself"

(Isa. 45:15),

their complaint amounted in effect to a confession of faith. To be aware of divine hiddenness is to remember a presence and to yearn for its return. The presence of an absence denies its negativity.

The poet who composed Psalm 22 was a theologian of dereliction.[131] His cry, "My God, my God, why hast thou forsaken me?", has been echoed by legions who have been tormented by cosmic solitude. In a sense, the psalmist showed that he had been a poet of cultic presence, but he ignored the myth of holy space. He substituted for the category of the sanctuary the living reality of the act of praise offered by the whole community—past, present, and future—of the people of God:

"... Thou art holy,
    enthroned upon the praises of Israel"

(vs. 3 [Heb. 4]).

It is only through exegetical legerdemain that commentators discern in this phrase an allusion to the ark upon which Yahweh of Hosts was believed by some to have been ceremonially seated. The psalmist used a spatial verb with an auditive object that belonged to the realm of humanity. The ear triumphed over the eye. The mystery of divine nearness depended less on the *hagios topos* than upon the social reality of adoration.

Now, the lamenter has been cut off from the source of his life. Not only has he been deprived of the protection he expected from the Lord of history, but he has also been dispossessed of his divine filiality.

> "... Thou art he who took me from my mother's womb,
>   Thou caused me to feel safe on my mother's breasts,
>   Upon thee was I cast from my mother's womb,
>   And from my mother's belly thou hast been my God!"
>
> (vss. 9–10 [Heb. 10–11].)

These ritual gestures of paternal adoption may indicate that the lament was intended to be intoned by the king at the ceremonial of the New Year, if indeed such a drama of royal humiliation, torture, and execution did take place at any time in the temple of Jerusalem (vss. 19–21 [Heb. 20–22]).[132] Unfortunately, the Hebrew text of the critical lines is obscure and probably corrupt. In any case, in mid-course the lament becomes a hymn of praise, as if the hero has been raised from symbolic death to a new life (vss. 22–30 [Heb. 23–31]).

From dereliction, the perspective of the psalmist broadened its scope to include "all the families of the nations." In a reminiscence of the Abrahamic promise (Gen. 12:1–3), the reborn hero hailed Yahweh's kingdom "to the extremities of the earth." His horizon has now transcended the categories of time. Both the dead and the generations yet to be born are invited either to eat at the heavenly banquet or to hear the good news of the *Opus Dei*.[133]

Inasmuch as the motif of divine hiddenness in Psalm 22 was unrelated to any sense of sin—a most unusual omission in Near Eastern and Hebraic laments—and on account of the universalism of its eschatology, the early Christians appropriated this extraordinary poem of presence lost and regained to describe the passion of Jesus, his death in forsakenness, and his triumph over mortality and time in the life of his followers.[134]

Psalm 22 constitutes an exception in the psalmody of presence. Other laments which complained of the veiling of the Deity were confessions of sin. In Hebraic theology, Yahweh concealed his face from human criminality. If the hero of the poem was not a king but a single member of the community, his plight must have been the more intolerable, for he had no answer to the question "why" and he found neither justification nor meaning in his spiritual, as well as physical, agony. After his ordeal, however, he was ushered into the future. Looking back, he understood that absence was presence deferred. His dereliction had been the prelude to what Kierkegaard many centuries later called "the moment before God." The cruelty of his trial proved to be as disproportionate as the magnitude of his eventual mission.[135]

The appeal from dereliction to communion is heard in the psalter especially when laments are confessions of sins. When a guilty man asks for forgiveness and rehabilitation, he begs at the same time for the renewal of presence. The penitential psalm *par excellence*, known as the *Miserere* or Psalm 51, exhibits the intricacy of the theological transition which links the request for mercy with the request for presence.[136]

In an unexpected way, the psalmist at first used the motif of hiddenness in a reversed form. He begged the Deity to hide from his sins:

"Hide thy face from my sins
  and blot out my guilt!"

(vs. 9 [Heb. 11].)

The exact nature of the petitioner's lawlessness is unknown. Since the worshippers of the Second Temple during the Persian centuries ascribed some thirteen psalms to specific events in the life of David, it is quite understandable that this poignant confession of criminality would have been related to the king's notorious murder of Uriah, Bathsheba's husband (Ps. 51:1; cf. 2 Sam. 12:14 ff.). The horror of the deed and the total incapacity of its perpetrator to make amends led the poet to ask in effect for the death of his inward self and for his rebirth under the mythical trope of a cosmic creation:

> Create in me a pure heart, O God,
>   and make new within me a steadfast spirit,
> Cast me not away from thy presence,
>   and take not the spirit of thy holiness away from me.
> Restore unto me the mirth of thy rescue
>   and let the spirit of nobility uphold me
>
> (Vss. 10–11 [Heb. 12–14]).

God comes only to those who are pure of heart, but how can the heart of man be pure? God alone is able to cleanse an enormous guilt ('awônôth, a superlative). No ritual will suffice,[137] for man is utterly depraved.[138] More than ceremonial ablutions or characterial amelioration are needed. Nothing less than a radical innovation is required. The psalmist borrowed the verb bara', "to create," from the cosmogonies of the sapiential circles,[139] and he dared to apply it to his own, minuscule, situation. As God creates a world, so also can he create a man.

The idea of the new being was articulated within the theology of presence. The poet reflected on his estrangement, no longer in terms of God's hiddenness, but according to the image of his own expulsion: "Cast me not away from thy presence!" He also developed his hope of communion through the triple use of the word "spirit." First, the newly created being needs the power of survival, or the gift of self-maintenance. He therefore must be able to resist temptation and to overcome self-doubt: "Make new within me a steady, firmly attached, coherent spring of moral behavior!" Second, estrangement must be enduringly bridged. The power which will permanently heal the poet's alienation from God will be so penetrating that holiness itself will flow from God to him. "Do not take away from me the spirit of thy holiness!"[140]

Since the ancient notion of holiness connoted the dread of "the wholly other," the psalmist's prayer was unprecedented. He viewed the holy no longer as the *mysterium fascinans atque tremendum,* forever exterior to man as the numinous force which attracts and repels him at the same time, but as the source of vitality which sharpens conscience, activates the will to shun evil, and stirs the imagination to do the good. A world is aborning also within man. Creation may be microcosmic as well as macrocosmic. Presence and spirit coalesce to animate the new being.

Third, the slave of egocentricity discovers freedom from the self. "Let the spirit of nobility uphold me!" A noble man is one who assumes his obligation of social responsibility. A knight is not a knave. He helps and respects others with the ease, elegance, and style of a prince. The new being is a moral aristocrat, not of birth but of service. Freedom to be oneself implies the power to serve willingly. A fresh innocence will obliterate the murderous past. The poet has joined those

"who were so dark of heart they might not speak,
a little innocence will make them sing."[141]

The psalmists exhibited theological maturity because they were forced to a recognition of their true selves vis-à-vis their God, even when that God was hiding from their plight. By evading their pleas, that God became more and more manifest to them, even when he seemed to

> ". . . adjourn, adjourn . . .
> To that farther side of the skies."[142]

It was that very hiding which disclosed to them not only the meaning of their existence but also the intrinsic quality of divinity. The God of the psalmists made them live in this world, and they lived without using him. It is when man tries to grasp him that God veils himself. The *Deus revelatus* is the *Deus absconditus*.

The Haunting God

Some of the psalmists were constantly begging for God's presence. Others tried to flee from it. The laments and supplications of the psalter include prayers of search and prayers of escape. Taken together, however, they do not constitute a thematic antithesis, but they point to the theological specificity of Hebraism, in which the relationship between God and man remains ambiguous. Even starved for transcendence, most of the pious were in dread of divine nearness. Even begging for a respite, they were in fact asking for a deeper communion. Psalm 139 is a case in point.[143] It is in appearance both a praise of presence and an expression of its dread, but the poetic *inclusio* which frames the whole piece (vss. 1 and 23-24) reveals the poet's unexpressed concern. He fears God's love, but he asks for more.

It may be that Psalm 139 was composed for a particular situation of ritual jurisprudence as a protest of innocence to be intoned by a defendant indicted for idol worship. Some exegetes believe that the poet asks his God to test him in order to demonstrate to the congregation of the faithful that he is not guilty of any apostasy. The ramifications of the psalm, however, extend far beyond the limits of a juridical ordeal.

Strophe I

Ps. 139:1 O Yahweh, thou searchest me and thou knowest.
2 Thou knowest my sitting down and my rising;
  Thou comprehendest my secret thoughts from afar;
3 Thou winnowest my path and my lying down
  and art acquainted with all my ways.
4 There is not a word on my tongue
  but lo, O Yahweh, thou knowest it altogether.

5 Thou hast beset me behind and before
  and laid the palm of thy hand upon me.
6 Such knowledge is too much of a wonder for me;
  it is far too high, I cannot attain it.

The link which ties this man to his God is intimate and somewhat painful. The verb *haqar*, "to search," "to examine," means literally "to dig," as if one looked in the earth for a treasure or probed in the depths. God's testing of man is not an easy or pleasant adventure. Like Job, the poet knows that he is being tried by God himself far more than by men.[144] He does not suffer from spiritual vacuity or cosmic solitude. On the contrary, he feels that God is too much with him. He is the victim of a divine attention which he cannot endure. A scalpel probes his innermost being. God knows him in his existential totality.

The text does not say: "Thou knowest me." Rather, the object of the verb is left purposely unspoken: "Thou knowest." God knows the poet's character as well as every instant of his waking life. He also watches him from evening to morning: on the one hand probing his dreams, on the other watching him during insomnia, at the very threshold of consciousness. Before one of the psalmist's secret thoughts can find articulation, God seizes it in its entirety.

The verb *zarah*, "to winnow," means "to cut to pieces," "to dissect," "to hack away." God "winnows" the poet's "path" and his "couch," just as a nomad investigates tracks in the sand to reconstruct in astonishing detail the behavior of those who have passed there. Again, like Job (3:11), the poet is fenced in as if he were a beast or a criminal. The image suggests less the embrace of love and the enclosure of protection than the stockade of detention. Not just God's hand but 'the palm" of God's hand lies upon him. Haunted by presence, man experiences *la pesanteur de la grâce.* No wonder he wants to escape.

Strophe II

Ps. 139:7 Whither shall I go from thy spirit,
            or whither shall I flee from thy presence?
        8 If I ascend into heaven, thou art there;
            if I make my bed in Sheol, behold, thou!
        9 If I take the wings of the dawn
            and sojourn at the uttermost parts of the sea,
        10 Even there shall thy hand lead me,
            and thy right hand shall hold me.

        11 If I say, surely, darkness shall cover me
            and night shall encompass me about,
        12 Even darkness darkens not from thee
            but the night shines as the day:
            darkness and light are both alike to thee.

Why should any pious Yahwist wish to go away from the spirit of Yahweh? Although this is not a penitential prayer and the poet does not display any sense of guilt, the implication of his attempts to establish a cosmic distance between that presence and himself suggests that he is afraid of the all-seeing eye. Like "the man" in the myth of the garden who hid himself in the thickest thicket "from the presence of Yahweh Elohim" (Gen. 3:8), the psalmist must have had a reason when he fancifully thought of fleeing to inaccessible places.[145]

His attitude toward the haunting God, nevertheless, is not altogether one of dread. An undertone of admiration and perhaps a hint of praise are audible in the strains of his complaint. The wonder of divine knowledge at the end of the first strophe (vs. 6) is echoed by the discovery at the end of the second (vs. 12) of divine creativity. The lamenter becomes a hymnist as he almost intones a doxology.[146] The God who owns darkness and light has also created him.

Strophe III

Ps. 139:13 Yes, it is thou who hast made my innermost being!
Thou didst weave me in my mother's womb.
14 I will praise thee for I was made in awesome wonder!
Marvellous are thy works,
and my very self knows it right well.
15 My bones were not hid from thee
when I was fashioned in secret,
embroidered in the depths of the earth.
16 Thy eyes did see my embryo,
and in thy book all my days were written
when as yet there was none of them.

17 How precious, for me, are thy secret thoughts, O God!
How great is the sum of them!
18 If I should count them, they are more numerous than
the sand!
When I awake, I am still with thee!

Like Job again (10:8–12), the poet turns from the theme of his frustration at being cornered to the moment of exhilaration over the miracle of his embryological growth. His body is an *objet d'art* fashioned before his birth by the master artist. The sense of aesthetic appreciation is blended with a scientific curiosity concerning embryology which points to the sapiential circles. From the mood of wonder, the poet soon passes to the consideration of God's foreknowledge of his own days. The

word "predestination" has often been used to describe the
notion of the divine transcendence of time, but it is misleading,
for the psalmist never accepted the ancient Near Eastern idea
of fate or destiny. Through the contemplation of his origin, his
coming forth out of the hands of his maker, he slowly reconciles
his previous apprehensiveness with the welcome of Yahweh's
surrounding presence.

While the text is obscure and the translation of several words
is hypothetical, it appears that the psalmist at last awakens from
either a trancelike meditation or the depths of religious rêverie,
only to find out—apparently with relief—that the companionship of his creator had never been interrupted.

Strophe IV

Ps. 139:19   Surely, thou wilt slay the wicked, O God!
        Depart from me, therefore, you, murderers!
  20   (For they speak against thee in malicious tone,
        and thy enemies take thy name in vain.)
  21   Do I not hate them, O Yahweh, that hate thee?
        Am I not grieved with those that rise up against thee?
  22   I hate them with perfect hatred,
        and I count them as my own enemies.

  23   Search me, O God, and know my heart,
        test me and know my doubts,
  24   And see if there is any idolatrous way in me,
        and lead me in the everlasting way!

The modern mind is easily repelled by such an expression of
religious hatred. It will be observed, however, that the words
may have belonged to a ritual of self-defense in a trial for apostasy. Suspected of cultural compromise, the defendant bowed
to the prescribed text in order to protest his innocence. It is
also possible that he was actually threatened by a murderous
plot. In addition, as a member of the sapiential circles he was
perturbed by the scandal of historical evil. The intellectual

problem of theodicy was for him aggravated by his experience of divine presence in its universality and its individuality.

The actual situation in which the poet lived remains unknown. In the end, he appeared to question the validity of his attitude as he begged for a continuation of the trial to which God had submitted him. He had already been tested (vs. 1). Now, he willingly sought further testing (vs. 23a). He even asked the ever-present sovereign of his life to know his "doubts" (vs. 23b).[147] For a man of cosmopolitan culture, "the way of idolatry" (vs. 24) was not a simple matter of clear-cut refusal. Anyone who maintained social contacts with foreign officials was bound to discern the relativity of national beliefs and cultic practices. The exclusive demands of Yahwism placed a unique burden on the Hebraic man of the world. A subtle compromise in his allegiance to Yahweh reflected temptations from which he may not have been entirely free. He was candid enough to admit his doubts before the awesome majesty of his God.

Presence, hitherto unendurable, at last became the opening of "the way" which transcended temporality and perhaps even mortality. By attempting to fly away from the spirit of Yahweh, the psalmist learned that he was also wasting his own selfhood. The mention of his "doubts" may have been an elliptical allusion to his fear of extinction, in a mood not entirely dissimilar to that expressed by Aeschylus:

> ... Whither can I fly?
> In all this Apian land is there no lair
>   Hid deep from every eye?
> I'd be a wisp of smoke, up-curled
> To the soft clouds above the world,
>   Up, without wings, in the bright day,
> Like dust, in dying streamers whirled
>   To pass in nothingness away.[148]

No longer anguished by the divine pursuit, the psalmist was ready to welcome the presence which is sufficient.

The Sufficient God

Among the many psalms which arose from situations of extremity, a few stand out in which a state of spiritual equilibrium and of satisfaction without smugness points to the unwavering, unruffled steadiness of complete trust. In no other song does the sense of the sufficient God,[149] who neither hides nor haunts, appear with better simplicity in form or thought than in Psalm 23.[150]

Like most hymns and laments composed for the worship of Yahweh in the temple, Psalm 23 reflects the tradition of Zion, but it has internalized and universalized "the house of faith."[151] This best-known of all psalms is built with an economy of words and a sophistication of rhythm on a pyramidal structure of three strophes. Each strophe contains an increasing number of double or triple lines (two, three, and four *bicola* or *tricola*) with a corresponding growth of amplitude (from two to six metrical stresses). The effect is a crescendo in breadth which brings forth an increasing elation as the theme of never-failing presence reaches its climactic moment.

I

Ps. 23:1 My shepherd is Yahweh.
　　　　I shall not want.
　　2 In green pastures he gives me rest.
　　　　To pools of tranquility he leads me.
　　3　He revives my inner self.

II

　　　　He leads me on reliable paths
　　　　　for the sake of his name.
　　4 Even if I walk in glens of mortal gloom,
　　　　I fear no evil
　　　　　for thou art with me.
　　　　Thy rod and thy staff,
　　　　　it is they that comfort me.

III

5 Thou preparest ahead of me the pasture
   against my adversaries;
   Thou anointest my head with oil;
   my cup is inebriating.
6 Only goodness and love will pursue me
   all the days of my life,
   And I shall reside in the house of Yahweh
   for the length of [my] days.

This is a testimony of religious completeness and humility. The comparison of Yahweh to a skillful and conscientious shepherd[152] implies that man is an irresponsible and guileless being, for the sheep is that "most silly and foolish animal" (Aristotle). A confession of solidarity in human sin is also implied by the admission of a need for discipline which lingers behind the expression of total confidence in Yahweh, the provider, leader, and protector. A shepherd carries a rod for defense against mountain lions and other wild animals; he also leans over his crook as he patiently moves along with the grazing sheep. Occasionally, he will use both rod and crook against the wayward members of the flock who stay behind or stray from the right path. Thus, the psalmist is probably conscious of the ambiguity of the image. He is comforted by the symbols of divine protection *and* correction. He indulges in no illusion concerning the frailty of human nature.

The harsh realities of the outside world are not ignored. Travel through valleys of deep darkness in which death always lurks[153] cannot be avoided, but Yahweh's presence overrules fear. The poet's memory of narrow escapes sharpens the intensity of his emotion so acutely that he passes without transition from the third-person style of meditation about God to the second-person form of address in prayer: "Thou art with me." It is the "Thou-with-me" rather than the "I-Thou" formula which characterizes the language of theocentric Yahwism.

As traditionally rendered, the text of verse 5 imposes an abrupt change of imagery, from shepherd to host of human travelers. Aesthetic canons of poetic unity, in Near Eastern as well as in western rhetorics, would suggest a compositional flaw, especially for such a short piece as Psalm 23. How else could one explain the table in the presence of enemies, or the overflowing cup of sociability, or again the anointing of the head with oil? The difficulty vanishes when it is remembered that words acquire new meanings in new environments, especially when a language passes from a nomadic to a sedentary mode of culture.

Half a century ago, Lebanese and Syrian shepherds still used the Arabic equivalent of the Hebrew expression 'arakh shulḥan, "to set a table," when they described their task of surveying the pasture ahead of their flock. They would uproot thorns and poisonous weeds, pour hot fat in scorpions' nests and vipers' holes, and generally make sure that the sheep's natural enemies, vegetal or animal, would for a while be neutralized. In spite of the shepherd's preventive care, accidents would still happen. Every traveler to sheep-grazing regions has witnessed the evening ritual of the "rodding" of the sheep, when the shepherd singles out each animal with his rod as the flock rushes to enter the fold. He shoves aside the wounded, which will be later anointed with oil (cf. Luke 10:34), and the exhausted, which will later receive the lift of a medicinal cocktail in a wooden cup.[154] Thus, Psalm 23 maintains the image of the shepherd throughout.

Yahweh is compared to a shepherd because his presence embraces all facets of existence. He is the feeder, the guide, the protector, and the physician. The psalmist assures himself, in still another comparison to the plight of the sheep, that divine "goodness and love"—not ravenous beasts—will pursue him all the rest of his life, and that he will reside[155] in the house of Yahweh for the length of his days.[156]

Critics do not agree concerning the date and milieu in which this song originated, although they generally recognize that it breaks literary precedents and has its own, unique style. The poet's hope of spending old age in "the house of Yahweh" has prompted many scholars to stress the cultic and more particularly the Zionistic flavor of the poem. Some have even related its imagery to the ceremony of the royal coronation, but such interpretations are far fetched. The comparison of Yahweh to a shepherd entails a view of human life spent within the theater of secular history.

As for other prayers which reveal the spirituality of temple musicians and depict an exquisite sense of communion on a day-by-day basis away from the sanctuary, one should readily admit that the theology of presence which is here disclosed makes ritual worship secondary. It is even probable that the poet refers in the last line, not to the temple as the receptacle of presence, since divine nearness and care accompany him everywhere, but to the household of faith.[157]

Like Moses, who "could be trusted anywhere within [Yahweh's] household" (Num. 12:7), the psalmist appears to have used figurative language throughout the poem. When he alludes to the theology of the name (vs. 3b), he refers to far more than a shepherd's honor and reputation, for "the name" summons to the mind of his audience the Hebraic notion of God's activity in history—from the call of Israel to the healing of the nations. The shepherd is the shepherd of Israel,[158] a people uniquely entrusted to fulfill a universal mission. Psalm 23 does not deal with an easy return to the sacramental womb, nor does it support pietistic individualism. It spiritualizes and interiorizes presence for the sake of the *Opus Dei* across the centuries.

The psalmody of presence has evolved from royal communion to the inner life of the common man. To be sure, the Yahwism of Moses had already promoted the universality of prophethood (Num. 11:29), but the rise of the monarchy, the erection of Solomon's temple, and the concomitant growth of a ruling class in the religious as well as in the secular realm threatened democratic access to Yahweh. The cultic musicians shared their faith with everyone. They shifted the stress of religion from the ritual acts to the humanity of the worshippers. "The house of Yahweh" became in effect "the household of God's children."

At the same time, the psalmists did not promote an esoteric club of mystics who would escape from worldly concerns by fusion with an infinite reality. They remained attentive to the problems of society. Their response to presence became the springboard of their ethics. Like the great prophets, they interiorized the cultus and helped to prepare the birth of Judaism after the destruction of the temple in 587 B.C.

During the cultic vacuum of the exile in Babylon, the surviving Judahites became the first Jews when they celebrated the feasts in some paracultic form and discovered the proximity of Yahweh in a foreign land. Destitute and displaced, they could still sing:

> How precious is thy steadfast love, O God!
>   The children of men take refuge in the shadow of thy wings.
> They feast on the abundance of thy house;
>   Thou givest them drink from the rivers of thy delights;
> For with thee is the fountain of life,
>   in thy light do we see light"
>
> (Ps. 36:7-9 [Heb. 8-10]).

Each of these words implies a theology of holy pleasure. The "rivers of thy delights" brings immediately to the poetic mind the streams of the garden of Eden.[159] The enjoyment of Yahweh's presence telescopes into the existential moment nostalgia for an ideal humanhood and the expectation of a new creation. Protology meets eschatology in the sublimated hedonism of communion.

By expressing their faith through poetic idiom, the psalmists conferred upon the theological enterprise an intrinsic quality which conventional Judaism and institutional Christendom in a later age have generally ignored. A creed is to be sung as a doxology, not signed as a didactic or legal document.[160] The professional artists of the Zion ceremonies were authentic theologians, for they refused to separate the sense of wonder from their intellectual reflection. They adored their God with the aesthetics of the rational and the emotion of the mind.[161] They were therefore able to bring together a belief in the purpose of life in the world and their trust in a personal creator. The link between the Yahweh of their cosmogony and the Yahweh of their self-integration resulted directly from their theology of presence. Their savior was their creator. Trust empowered them to articulate their curiosity for truth together with their sense of well-being. They understood that "faith is the state of being grasped by the Spiritual Presence and opened to the transcendent unity of unambiguous life."[162]

The psalmists' refusal to divorce their intellect from their spirituality, as well as their determination to contemplate the elusiveness of presence with artistic creativity, made them, along with the prophets, the instruments of revelation. In addition, the more daring among them showed evidence of an affinity with the sapiential circles.[163] Beyond a dissimilarity of function, "the psalmody of presence" was theologically bound to "the play of wisdom."

Notes

1. On the literary *genres* of the Psalms, their cultic origin and setting, the problems of their authorship, date, compilation, textual preservation, etc., see, among others, S. Mowinckel, *Psalmenstudien, I–VI* (Oslo, 1921–24); H.-J. Kraus,

Psalmen, I (Neukirchen, 1960), pp. xxxvii ff.

2. In addition to the titles mentioned in note 1 above, see A. C. Welch, *The Psalter in Life, Worship and History* (Oxford, 1926); H. Gunkel, "The Religion of the Psalms," in *What Remains of the Old Testament and Other Essays*, tr. by A. K. Dallas (London, 1938), pp. 69 ff.; S. Terrien, *The Psalms and their Meaning for Today* (Indianapolis & New York, 1952); P. E. Bonnard, *Le Psautier selon Jérémie: influence littéraire et sprituelle de Jérémie sur trente-trois psaumes* (Paris, 1960); H. Ringgren, *The Faith of the Psalmists* (Philadelphia, 1963); W. I. Wolverton, "The Psalmists' Belief in God's Presence," *Canadian Journal of Theology*, IX (1963): 82 ff.; J. Thévenet, *La confiance en Dieu dans les Psaumes* (Paris, 1965); H. H. Guthrie, *Israel's Sacred Songs: a Study of Dominant Themes* (New York, 1966); L. Jacquet, *Les Psaumes et le coeur de l'homme*, I (n. p., 1975); E. Gerstenberger, "Zur Interpretation der Psalmen," *Verkündigung und Forschung*, XIX (1974): 22 ff.

3. Cf. Terrien, *The Psalms*, pp. xii ff.

4. Siegfried Sassoon, "Presences Perfected," in *Modern British Poetry*, ed. by L. Untermeyer (New York, 1950), p. 318.

5. See R. T. Callaghan, "Echoes of Canaanite Literature in the Psalms," *VT*, IV (1954): 164 ff.; A. Barucq, *L'expression de la louange divine et de la prière dans la Bible et en Egypte* (Le Caire, 1962). M. Dahood has produced a highly original translation of the Psalms by dividing and repointing many Hebrew words of the Masoretic Text on the basis of Ugaritic (*Psalms*, I–III [Garden City, N.Y., 1966–70]). While his suggestions are sometimes valid, his contribution to the understanding of the Psalter remains conjectural. See S. Terrien, in *Union Seminary Quarterly Review*, XXIII (1967–68): 389 ff.; *ibid.*, XXVI (1970–71): 431 ff.; C. Brekelmans, "Some Considerations on the Translation of the Psalms, I, by M. Dahood," *Ugarit Forschung*, I (1969): 5 ff.; J. Greenfield, in

JAOS, LXXXIX (1969): 174 ff.; cf. H. Donner, "Ugaritismen in der Psalmenforschung," *ZAW*, LXXXIX (1967): 322 ff.; P. H. J. Houwink ten Cate, "Hittite Royal Prayers," *Numen*, XVI (1969): 81 ff.

6. See S. Mowinckel, "Traditionalism and Personality in the Psalms," *HUCA*, XXII (1950–51): 205 ff.; cf. *id.*, *The Psalms in Israel's Worship*, tr. by D. R. Ap-Thomas, 2 vols. (New York and Nashville, 1962), pp. 216 ff.

7. They did so in a way which defies exact parallel in the ancient Near East. Cf. the attempts of several historians of comparative religion who deny the specificity of Hebraism: B. Albrektson, *History and the Gods: An Essay on the Idea of Historical Events as Divine Manifestations in the Ancient Near East and in Israel* (Lund, 1967), pp. 11 ff.; J. J. M. Roberts, "Divine Freedom and Cultic Manipulation in Israel and Mesopotamia," in H. Goedicke and J. J. M. Roberts, eds., *Unity and Diversity* (Baltimore, 1975), pp. 181 ff.; "Myth Versus History: Relaying the Comparative Foundations," *CBQ*, XXXVIII (1976): 1 ff.

8. H. Gunkel classified under this rubric a number of heterogeneous poems which do not actually present a single literary form but generally deal with the king, the events of his life, and his cultic as well as national functions (Pss. 2, 18, 20–21, 45, 72, 101, 110, 132, 144). There are both direct and indirect allusions to the monarch in other psalms. See G. B. Gray, "The References to the 'King' in the Psalter, in their Bearing on Questions of Date and Messianic Beliefs," *JQR*, VII (1894): 658 ff.; K. R. Crim, *The Royal Psalms* (Richmond, Va., 1962); S. Mowinckel, "What are 'Royal Psalms'?" *The Psalms in Israel's Worship*, pp. 46 ff.; N. Poulssen, *"Die Königspsalmen (Ps 2 und 110)," König und Tempel im Glaubenszeugnis des Alten Testamentes* (Stuttgart, 1967), pp. 55 ff.

9. See L. Rost, *Die Überlieferung von der Thronnachfolge Davids* (Stuttgart, 1926); cf. R. A. Carlson, *David, the Chosen King: A Traditio-Historical Approach to the Second*

Book of Samuel, tr. by I. J. Sharpe and S. Rudman (Stockholm, 1964), especially pp. 131 ff.; J. A. Soggin, "David—König von Juda," *Das Königtum in Israel* (Berlin, 1967), pp. 63 ff.; J. W. Flanagan, "Court History or Succession Document? A Study of 2 Samuel 9–20 and 1 Kings 1–2," *JBL*, XCI (1972): 172 ff.; G. E. Mendenhall, "The Monarchy," *In.*, XXIX (1975): 155 ff.; R. N. Whybray, *The Succession Narrative: A Study of II Samuel 9–20; I Kings 1–2* (London, 1968); but cf. D. M. Gunn, "Traditional Composition in the 'Succession Narrative'," *VT*, XXVI (1976): 214 ff.

10. See above, chapter IV, pp. 164 ff.

11. The king's attitude was compatible with a priestly function, as shown by his wearing "a linen ephod" (cf. 1 Sam. 2:18, 22:18). It will be observed that at that early date in the history of the religion of Israel, five centuries before the birth of Judaism, priests were hardly more than sanctuary keepers and formed no sacerdotal class. There was no distinction between "clergy" and "laity" as in the Second Temple restoration. On the incident of David's dance before the ark, see W. O. E. Oesterley, *The Sacred Dance: A Study in Comparative Folklore* (Cambridge, 1923), p. 36; G. W. Ahlström, *Aspects of Syncretism in Israelite Religion* (Lund, 1963), pp. 34 ff.; C. H. Gordon, "David the Dancer," *Festschrift Y. Kaufmann* (Jerusalem, 1960), pp. 46 ff.; S. Amsler, *David, roi et messie* (Neuchâtel, 1963), pp. 22 ff.; H. W. Hertzberg, *I & II Samuel: A Commentary*, tr. by J. S. Bowden (Philadelphia, 1974), pp. 280 ff.; A. Phillips, "David's Linen Ephod," *VT*, XIX (1969): 485 ff.; cf. N. L. Tidwell, "The Linen Ephod: 1 Sam. II 18 and 2 Sam. VI 14," *VT*, XXIV (1974): 505 ff.

12. 2 Sam. 21:1–6 (Heb. vss. 2–7). While the exact nature of the ritual violation is not known (cf. Mark 2:25 ff. *et par.*), David clearly brushed aside the distinction between the sacred and the profane. See Hertzberg, *I & II Samuel* (1964), p. 180;

cf. P. A. H. de Boer, "An Aspect of Sacrifice. I. Divine Bread: Some Remarks on the Meaning of LḤM HPPNYM," *SVT*, XXVIII (Leiden, 1972): 29.

13. See Ps. 73:28.

14. Cited by J.-P. Bonnes, *David et les Psaumes* (Paris, 1957), p. 69.

15. As shown by *The Dirge Over the Death of Saul and Jonathan*, also known as *The Song of the Bow* (2 Sam. 1:19–27); see S. Gevirtz, "David's Lament over Saul and Jonathan," *Early Poetry of Israel* (Chicago, 1963), pp. 72 ff.; Cross, *Canaanite Myth and Hebrew Epic*, pp. 122 ff.; W. H. Shea, "David's Lament," *BASOR*, no. 221 (February, 1976), pp. 141 ff.

16. See E. Baumann, "Struktur-Untersuchungen im Psalter I," *ZAW*, LXI (1945–48): 131 ff.; F. M. Cross and D. N. Freedman, "A Royal Song of Thanksgiving," *JBL*, LXXII (1953): 16 ff.; cf. *id.*, *Studies in Ancient Yahwistic Poetry* (Missoula, Mont., 1959), pp. 136 ff.; H.-L. Kraus, *Psalmen*, I (Neukirchen, 1960), pp. 136 ff.; Hertzberg, *I & II Samuel*, pp. 388 ff.; Carlson, *David the Chosen King*, pp. 246 ff.; F. Crüsemann, *Studien zur Formgeschichte von Hymnus und Danklied in Israel* (Neukirchen-Vluyn, 1969), pp. 254 ff.; G. Schmuttermayr, *Psalm 18 und 2 Samuel 22: Studien zu einem Doppeltext* (München, 1971); D. Eichhorn, *Gott als Fels, Burg und Zuflucht: Eine Untersuchung zum Gebet des Mittlers in den Psalmen* (Bern und Frankfurt, 1971).

17. Cross and Freedman, "A Royal Song," p. 125.

18. The MT vocalizes sha'ûl, "Saul," but the reading shᵉ'ôl, "the Underworld," is possible in view of the references to death in vss. 4–7. See M. Dahood, *Psalms* I, p. 104.

19. See S. Terrien, "Toward a Biblical Theology of Womanhood," *Religion in Life*, XLII (1973–74): 328.

20. Instead of the powerful reading in the MT 'erchamᵉka, "I am in love with thee," these commentators and translators gratuitously emend it to read the tame and rather hackneyed verb which is

found in some liturgical prayers of thanksgiving, *ᵃrimᵉka* or *ᵃrēmᵉka*, "I exalt thee." The *hiph'il* of this verb, however, is used of Yahweh as subject. (cf. 1 Kings, 14:7; Pss. 75:7 [Heb. 8], 89:19 [Heb. 20]). It is the *po'el* that is required (cf. Pss. 30:1 [Heb. 2], 145:1; Isa. 25:1), but this correction would entail further consonantal alteration. If the verb "to exalt" had been original, why should it have disappeared from the text of Ps. 18:2 as well as from the LXX of both 2 Sam. 22 and Ps. 18? Moreover, how could one explain the scribal intrusion of the *lectio difficilior*, "I am in love with thee"?

21. Cf. the name of Hosea's daughter, the prophetic symbol of Israel: *Lô-Ruchamah*, "Not-loved" (Hos. 1:6). Also, the plural of majesty of the noun for "womb," *rachmim*, "motherly compassion," "tender mercies" (Ps. 51:1 [Heb. 3], etc.).

22. See "I love Yahweh" (Ps. 116:1), in which the common verb *'ahebh* (LXX, *agapaô*) is used. David might have consciously avoided this word because it had a connotation of covenantal obligation, loyalty, service, and obedience. See W. L. Moran, "The Ancient Near Eastern Background of the Love of God in Deuteronomy," *CBQ*, XXV (1963): 82 f. Such a connotation would not have been appropriate for expressing an extemporaneous paroxysm of religious passion.

23. The semantic overtones of the verb varied widely. It is difficult to ascertain its exact meaning in tenth-century Hebrew. Cf. G. Schmuttermayr, "*RḤM*—Eine lexikalische Studie," *Biblica*, LI (1970): 501 f. and note 3 (bibliography).

24. See H. Franken, *The Mystical Communion With JHWH in the Book of Psalms* (Leiden, 1954), p. 26; cf. D. Eichhorn, *Gott als Fels, Burg und Zuflucht. Eine Untersuchung zum Gebet des Mittlers in den Psalmen* (Frankfurt, 1971).

25. One will notice the repetition of the personal pronoun "of me" (rendered in English by the possessive adjective "my"), especially in the expression "my El." See O. Eissfeldt, "'Mein Gott' im Alten Testament," *ZAW*, LXI (1945–48): 3 ff.; H. Cazelles, "El et le dieu personnel," in "Le pouvoir de la divinité à Ugarit et en Israël," *Ugaritica*, VI (Paris, 1969): 36 ff.; H. Vorländer, *Mein Gott. Die Vorstellungen vom persönlichen Gott im alten Orient und im Alten Testament* (Kevelav, 1975).

26. See above, chapter III, pp. 128, 136, and chapter IV, p. 194.

27. See Cross, *Canaanite Myth and Hebrew Epic*, pp. 158 ff.

28. See above, chapter IV, pp. 164 f.

29. Many other psalms (see especially Pss. 29, 50, and 97) have been composed as hymns for the celebration of the yearly feast of the Autumn; they contain evocations of the theophany. See J. Jeremias, *Theophanie* (Neukirchen-Vluyn, 1965), pp. 101, 105 ff.; A. Weiser, "Zur Frage nach den Beziehungen der Psalmen zum Kult: Die Darstellung der Theophanie in den Psalmen und im Festkult," *Festschrift A. Bertholet* (Tübingen, 1950), pp. 513 ff.; H.-P. Müller, "Die kultische Darstellung der Theophanie," *VT*, XIV (1964): 183 ff.

30. Cf. the Arabic *ḥafiza*, "to be attentive to," "to keep," "to protect."

31. The Hebrew phrase defies English translation, since the verb and the noun represent the same root: "He *loyals* the loyal one." The preposition *'im*, "with," implies immediate and sustained communion, as in the phrase which miniatured the Yahwistic ideal of living, "Enoch walked *with* God" (Gen. 5:24).

32. The expression *'im gebhar tamin tittammam*, "he completes the man of completeness," employs the verb in the *hithpa'el* voice (a *hapax legomenon*) probably to indicate the complex mutuality of total devotion between Yahweh and his chosen servant. The Hebraic notion of "integrity" (*tummah* and cognates) implies social and psychological "integration" as well as ethical honesty and unimpaired soundness. See J. Pedersen,

Israel: Its Life and Culture, I–II (London & Copenhagen, 1926), pp. 336 f.

33. It has often been maintained that this profession of moral integrity indicates the later hand of the seventh-century Deuteronomists. This view is superfluous, for neither the vocabulary nor the ideology of this passage is other than that of the ancient traditions of the national epic. What is strikingly pre-Deuteronomic and true to the northern theology of the name is the stress on the devotion of man's entire personality, without duplicity and compromise. Obedience to Yahweh's "ordinances" (*mishpaṭim*) and "statutes" (*ḥuqqîm*) was a condition of the Sinai covenant (vs. 22 [Heb. 23]; cf. Exod. 15:25, Jos. 24:25).

34. The word *gebher,* "man," used in vs. 25 (Heb. 26), designates the superior male, sexually vigorous, socially responsible, religiously dedicated, and potentially a hero (*gibbôr*). Cf. the name of the angel "Gabriel." See H. Kosmala, "The Term *Geber* in the Old Testament and in the Scrolls," *SVT,* XVII (1969): 159 ff.; S. Terrien, "Le poème de Job: drame pararituel du Nouvel-An?" *Ibid.,* p. 226.

35. Allusions to foot fighting, the scaling of cliffs, and other feats of physical stamina (vss. 29, 33, 37 [Heb. 30, 34, 38]) point to a date which is earlier than the reigns of Solomon and his successors who fought in horse-drawn chariots. The traits mentioned here appear to be strictly Davidic.

36. This detail is found in the legends and myths of several cultures in the ancient Near East and classical Greece. For example, it was the god Seth who taught the Pharaoh to use a bow. See H. Gunkel, *Die Psalmen* (Tübingen, 1926), p. 65; cf. B. Couroyer, "L'arc d'airain," *RB,* LXXII (1965): 508 ff. The poet may well have alluded to his own experience.

37. The word *'anawah,* "humility," "poverty," "affliction," "weakness" (cf. the *'anawim* among the psalmists of a later time) is nowhere else applied to God in the Hebraic literature (cf. Zeph. 2:3, Prov. 15:33, etc.). The Samuel recension of Ps. 18 reads *'anoth⁰kha,* "thy answer" (from *'anah I;* cf. *"Dein Zuspruch,"* favored by H.-J. Kraus, *Die Psalmen . . .,* p. 139). The LXX rendered "thy discipline" (cf. Vulg. *disciplina tua*). Traditional English versions have respected the *lectio difficilior* of the MT but have also softened the meaning of the Hebrew word into "gentleness," "meekness," etc. Several emendations are implied by most modern translations. A. Weiser has well seen the paradoxical character of the thought suggested by the MT: "The king owes his rise to greatness to the 'condescension' of God, a statement which is unique in the language of the Old Testament" (*The Psalms,* tr. by H. Hartwell [Philadelphia, 1962], p. 195).

38. See above, chapter V, pp. 245, 268.

39. In a Ugaritic liturgy of the spring festival, the celebrant repeats: "I know that he lives (*ḥy*) the powerful Ba'al" (I AB, III, 3, 8, 20). See C. H. Gordon, *Ugaritic Handbook* (Rome, 1947), p. 138; H. L. Ginsberg, "Ugaritic Myths, Epics and Legends," *ANET,* p. 140. Cf. Job 19:25, where the affirmation "he lives" is coupled with the "he will rise" (*yaqûm*), as in Ps. 18:46 (Heb. 47).

40. M. Dahood correctly endorses Ewald's interpretation of this phrase "as an archaic formula of precative type" (*Psalms I,* p. 118; citing H. Ewald, *Ausführliches Lehrbuch der hebräischen Sprache,* 6th ed. [Leipzig, 1855], p. 501). Cf. E. Rosenstock-Huessy, *"Vivit Deus,"* In *Memoriam Ernst Lohmeyer* (Stuttgart, 1951), pp. 178 ff.; G. Widengren, *Sakrales Königtum im Alten Testament und in Judentum* (Stuttgart, 1955), p. 69.

41. A comparison with a late Royal Hymn of Victory (Ps. 144:1–15) shows at once the difference between original and derivative poetry. Psalm 144 clearly depends on Ps. 18.

42. See the cultic aspect of the mon-

arch's office from the time of Solomon onward (1 Kings 8:1 ff., etc.).

43. Vs. 22 (Heb. 23); See above, p. 129.

44. Vss. 26 f. (Heb. 27 f.).

45. The idea appears in the last line of Ps. 18 (vs. 50 [Heb. 51]), which, according to modern consensus, reflects its liturgical use by the David dynasty and is not a part of the original poem. It will be noted that David is here referred to in the third person. Considerable attention has been given to the complex relation between the Sinai and the Davidic covenants. See L. Rost, "Sinaibund Davidsbund," *TLZ*, LXXII (1947): 129 ff.; G. Widengren, "King and Covenant," *JSS*, II (1957): 17 ff.; A. H. J. Gunneweg, "Sinaibund und Davidsbund," *VT*, X (1960): 335 ff.; W. Zimmerli, "Sinaibund und Davidsbund," *TZ*, XVI (1960): 268 ff.; H. Gese, "Der Davidsbund und die Zionserwählung," *ZTK*, LXI (1964): 10 ff.; A. D. Mayer, "The Covenant on Sinai and the Covenant with David," *Hermathena*, LX (1970): 37 ff.; M. Weinfeld, "The Covenant of Grant in the Old Testament and in the Ancient Near East," *JAOS*, XC (1970): 184 ff.; R. de Vaux, *Histoire ancienne d'Israël* (Paris, 1971), pp. 389 ff.

46. Extensive research has been undertaken on this controversial issue over the past several decades. See a summary of the discussion in J. Gray, "Sacral Kingship in Ugarit," *Ugaritica*, VI (1969): 289 ff.

47. See O. Procksch, "Die letzten Worte Davids," *Festschrift R. Kittel* (Leipzig, 1913), pp. 113 ff.; S. Mowinckel, "Die letzten Worte Davids," *ZAW*, XLV (1927): 30 ff.; P. A. H. de Boer, "Texte et traduction des paroles attribuées à David en 2 Samuel xxiii 1–7," *SVT*, IV (1957): 47 ff.; H. W. Hertzberg, *I & II Samuel*, pp. 398 ff.; H. N. Richardson, "The Last Words of David: Some Notes on II Samuel 23:1–7," *JBL*, XC (1971): 257 ff.; cf. D. N. Freedman, "II Samuel 23:4," ibid., pp. 329 ff.

48. The wording (*ne'um hag-gebher*, "ora-

cle of the he-man") is similar to that of the oracle of Balaam (Num. 24:4) and of the sayings of Agur (Prov. 30:1 ff.).

49. Meaning uncertain. Literally, "[Most] delightful [with respect to] the songs of Israel."

50. Exod. 19:5; See above, pp. 119 ff., 129 f.

51. See J. A. Soggin, "Zum zweiter Psalm," *Festschrift W. Eichrodt* (Zürich, 1970): 191 ff.; H. J. Boecker, "Anmerkungen zur Adoption im Alten Testament," *ZAW*, LXXXVI (1974): 86 ff.

52. See G. Cooke, "The Israelite King as Son of God," *ZAW*, LXXIII (1961): 202 ff.; J. H. Eaton, "The King as God's Witness," *ASTI*, VII (1970): 27.

53. 2 Sam. 7:4–17, followed by a prayer of David (vss. 18–29). See L. Rost, *Die Überlieferung von der Thronnachfolge Davids* (1926), pp. 47 ff. (= *Die kleine Credo und andere Studien zum Alten Testament* (Heidelberg, 1965), pp. 160 ff.

54. See the cautious attitude of M. Noth, "God, King, and Nation in the Old Testament," *The Laws in the Pentateuch and Other Studies*, tr. by D. R. Ap-Thomas (Edinburgh and London, 1966), p. 173.

55. Although Queen Athaliah usurped the throne for a short time in the ninth century, the young Davidic prince Joash was duly anointed king by the people at the time of her downfall (2 Kings, 11:12).

56. See above, p. 294.

57. See K. Homburg, "Psalm 110, im Rahmen des judäischen Krönungs zeremoniells," *ZAW*, LXXXIV (1972): 243 ff.

58. See D. M. Hay, *Glory at the Right Hand: Psalm 110 in Early Christianity* (Nashville, 1973).

59. The LXX reads, "With thee [is] the government in the day of thy power."

60. Or, "[Thou art clothed] with holy majesty from the day of thy birth." See A. Caquot, "*In splendoribus sanctorum*," *Syria*, XXXIII (1956): 36 ff.; "Remarques sur le Psaume CX," *Semitica*, VI (1956): 33 ff. The LXX reads, "In the splendor of the holy ones from the womb."

61. The "dew," "night mist," or "light rain," was the mythical symbol of fertility. It is not impossible that this royal psalm was used in connection with the seasonal cycle of feasts, especially after the autumnal rains had failed. See J. G. Gammie, "A New Setting for Psalm 110," *ATR*, LI (1969): 4 ff. The word *yalduth*, "childhood," "youth," may also refer to "young men" collectively. The traditional rendering, "To thee belongs the dew of thy youth," yields a circular meaning. The LXX reads, "Before the day star I have begotten thee."

62. See note 61 above.

63. See above, chapter II, note 25.

64. Vs. 6, *'ereṣ rabbah.*

65. Especially Asa, Hezekiah, and Josiah. See 1 Kings 15:3; 22:46; 2 Kings 18:4, 23:7 ff.

66. See discussion and extensive bibliography in S. Terrien, "The Omphalos Myth and Hebrew Religion," *VT*, XX (1970): 315 ff.; R. J. Clifford, S.J., *The Cosmic Mountain in Canaan and the Old Testament* (Cambridge, Mass., 1972); cf. E. A. S. Butterworth, *The Tree at the Navel of the Earth* (Berlin-New York, 1970); F. Stolz, *Strukturen und Figuren im Kult von Jerusalem: Studien zur altorientalischen vor- und frühisraelitischen Religion* (Berlin, 1970), pp. 226 ff.

67. Notable exceptions are the prophetic *legenda* of the Isaianic school concerning Hezekiah (2 Kings, 18:13 ff.; cf. Isa. 36:1 ff.) and the Deuteronomic account of Josiah's Reformation (2 Kings 22:1 ff.).

68. See J. M. Ward, "The Literary Form and Liturgical Background of Psalm LXXXIX," *VT*, XI (1961): 321 ff.; G. W. Ahlström, *Psalm 89. Eine Liturgie aus dem Ritual des leidenden Königs* (Lund, 1959); J. Neusner, "The 89th Psalm: Paradigm of Israel's Faith," *Judaism*, VIII (1959): 226 ff.; L. Dequeker, "Les *qᵉdôšîm* du Psaume 89 à la lumière des croyances sémitiques," *ETL*, XXXIX (1963): 469 ff.; N. M. Sarna, "Psalm 89: A Study of Inner Biblical Exegesis," in *Biblical and Other Studies*, ed. by A. Altmann (*Studies and*

Texts, I, Cambridge, Mass., 1963), pp. 29 ff.; O. Eissfeldt, "Psalm 80 und Psalm 89," *Die Welt des Orients*, III (Göttingen, 1964), 27 ff.; J. T. Milik, "Fragment d'une source du Psautier (4Q Ps89)," *RB*, LXXIII (1966): 94 ff.; E. Lipiński, *Le poème royal du Psaume LXXXIX 1–5. 20–38* (Paris, 1967); J.-B. Dumortier, "Un rituel d'intronisation: Le Psaume LXXXIX 2–38," *VT*, XXII (1972): 176 ff.

69. As cogently demonstrated by Ward, "The Literary Form," pp. 321 ff.; supported in part by Dumortier, "Un rituel d'intronisation," pp. 176 ff. The problem of unity of structure has been rendered even more complex by the discovery of a scroll fragment from Qumran which contains vss. 1–5 and 20–38. See J. T. Milik, "Fragments d'une source du psautier (4QPs89) et fragments des Jubilés, du Document de Damas, d'un phylactère dans la grotte 4 de Qumran," *RB*, LXXIII (1966): 94 ff. Unfortunately, Dumortier did not concern himself with vss. 39–52.

70. Cf. Job 9:13, Isa. 51:9.

71. See H. Wheeler Robinson, "The Hebrew Conception of Corporate Personality," *Werden und Wesen des Alten Testaments*, ed. by P. Volz, F. Stummer u. J. Hempel (Berlin, 1936), pp. 49 ff.; A. R. Johnson, *The Vitality of the Individual in the Thought of Ancient Israel* (Cardiff, 1949); J. de Fraine, "Individu et société dans la religion de l'Ancien Testament," *Biblica*, XXXIII (1952): 324 ff., 445 ff.; G. E. Mendenhall, "The Relation of the Individual to Political Society in Ancient Israel," *Festschrift H. C. Alleman* (Locust Valley, N.Y., 1960), pp. 108 ff.; H. G. May, "Individual Responsibility and Retribution," *HUCA*, XXXII (1961): 105 ff.

72. Shakespeare, *Hamlet*, IV, v. 122–4.

73. Deut. 31:17, 32:20; Isa. 8:17; Mic. 3:4; Pss. 13:2; etc. See above, pp. 251 ff.

74. The word *ḥeledh* means "limited duration." Cf. Ps. 17:14, Job 11:17, etc.

75. See C. Barth, *Die Errettung vom Tode in den individuellen Klage- und Dankliedern des Alten Testaments* (Zollikon, 1947); L.

Wächter, *Der Tod im Alten Testament* (Stuttgart, 1967). N. J. Tromp, in *Primitive Conceptions of Death and the Netherworld in the Old Testament* (Rome, 1969) has unsuccessfully attempted to revise the traditional view of Sheol; cf. *RHR*, CLXXVIII (1970): 206 ff.; and *RB*, LXVIII (1971): 292 f.

76. Isa. 11:1–5. See R. Koch, "La théologie de l'esprit de Yahvé dans le livre d'Isaïe," *Sacra pagina* (Gembloux, 1959), I, 419 ff.; H. Wildberger, *Jesaja 1–12* (Neukirchen, 1972), pp. 436 ff.

77. The benediction of vs. 52 [Heb. 53] is not a part of Ps. 89 but marks the end of one of the "books" which now constitute the Psalter.

78. See L. Köhler, *Theology of the Old Testament*, tr. by A. S. Todd (Philadelphia, 1957), pp. 115, 125, 183; W. Eichrodt, *Theology of the Old Testament*, tr. by J. A. Baker (Philadelphia, 1961–67), I, p. 312 (note 4), pp. 317 f., 365 f., II, pp. 48 f., 64 f., 79 ff., 354 f.; H. Ringgren, *The Faith of the Psalmists* (Philadelphia, 1963), pp. 56 ff.; *Israelite Religion*, tr. by D. E. Green (Philadelphia, 1966), p. 130.

79. See Terrien, "The Omphalos Myth," pp. 328, 330.

80. See A. Neher, *L'essence du prophétisme* (Paris, 1955), pp. 71, 99 f.

81. See J. Tyciak, *Prophetie und Mystik. Eine Deutung des Propheten Isaias* (Düsseldorf, 1953); U. Simon, "The Mysticism of Jeremiah," *Church Quarterly Review*, CLXI (1960): 270 ff.; cf. R. Kittel, *Die hellenistische Mysterienreligion und das Alte Testament* (Stuttgart, 1924), pp. 64 ff.

82. See C. G. Montefiore, "Mystic Passages in the Psalms," *JQR*, I (1889): 143 ff.; F. Heiler, "Die Kontemplation in der christlichen Mystik," *Eranos-Jahrbuch*, I (1933): 249 ff.; H. J. Franken, *Die Mystical Communion with JHWH in the Book of Psalms* (Leiden, 1954), p. 70; M. Smith, *An Introduction to the History of Mysticism from the Oldest Elements in the Old Testament* (Amsterdam, 1973), pp. 13 ff. It will be observed that E. Müller introduces the

History of Jewish Mysticism (Oxford, 1946) with a chapter on "Mystical Aspects of the Bible" (pp. 13 ff.), but he traces the first manifestations of actual mysticism in the postbiblical period (pp. 27 ff.). See also G. G. Scholem, *Major Trends in Jewish Mysticism* (New York, 1954), pp. 40 ff.

83. See C. Westerman, *The Praise of God in the Psalms*, tr. by K. R. Crim (Richmond, Va., 1961); F. Crüsemann, *Studien zur Formgeschichte von Hymnus und Danklied in Israel* (Neukirchen-Vluyn, 1969); J. Becker, *Wege der Psalmenexegese* (Stuttgart, 1975).

84. See Mowinckel, *The Psalms in Israel's Praise*, I, pp. 94 ff., 109 ff., 118 ff.; Weiser, *The Psalms*, pp. 23 ff.; J. K. Kuntz, "Theophany and the Book of Psalms," *The Self-Revelation of God* (Philadelphia, 1967), pp. 169 ff.

85. Ps. 47:5 f. (Heb. 6 f.). See J. Muilenburg, "Psalm 47," *JBL*, LXIII (1944): 235 ff.; A. Caquot, "Le psaume 47 et la royauté de Yahvé," *RHPR*, XXXIX (1959): 311 ff.; J. H. Kroeze, *Psalm 47* (The Hague, 1966); J. J. M. Roberts, "The Religio-Political Setting of Psalm 47," *BASOR*, no. 221 (Feb. 1976): 129 ff.

86. Ps. 47:9 (Heb. 10). The proposed reading of the MT *'am*, "people," as *'im*, "to," "toward," on the basis of the Ugaritic (see Roberts, "Psalm 47": 131, note 12) is ingenious but not probable since such a meaning of the preposition *'im* is not attested elsewhere in biblical Hebrew and the *lectio difficilior* of the MT remains to be explained.

87. See H.-P. Müller, *Ursprünge und Strukturen alttestamentlicher Eschatologie* (Berlin, 1969).

88. Ps. 50:2 f. See E. Beaucamp, "La théophanie du Psaume 50 (49)," *NRT*, LXXXI (1959): 897 ff.; N. H. Ridderbos, "Die Theophanie in Ps. 1 1–6," *OTS*, XV (1969): 213 ff.; J. Schreiner, *Sion-Jerusalem: Jahwes Königssitz* (München, 1963), pp. 288 ff.

89. According to the widely discussed hypothesis of S. Mowinckel on the phrase

po ʿolê 'awen, traditionally rendered "the workers of iniquity" (see *'Awän und die individuellen Klagpsalmen. Psalmenstudien I*).

90. On the *Sitz im Leben* of the individual psalms and on the discussion concerning their judiciary use, see H. Schmidt, *Das Gebet der Angeklagten im Alten Testament* (Giessen, 1928); W. Beyerlin, "Die *tôda* der Heilsvergegenwärtigung in den Klageliedern des Einzelnen," *ZAW*, LXXXIX (1967): 208 ff.; L. Delekat, *Asylie und Schultzorakel am Zionsheiligtum: Eine Untersuchung zu den privaten Feindpsalmen* (Leiden, 1967), pp. 270 ff.; cf. W. Beyerlin, *Die Rettung der Bedrängten der Einzelnen auf institutionelle Zusammenhänge untersucht* (Göttingen, 1970), esp. pp. 43 ff., 139 ff.

91. See H.-J. Kraus, *Psalmen*, I (Neukirchen, 1949), pp. 220 ff.; Weiser, *The Psalms*, pp. 244 ff.; Delekat, *Asylie*, pp. 194 ff.; W. Beyerlin, *Die Rettung*, pp. 122 ff.; A. H. van Zyl, "The Unity of Psalm 27," *Festschrift A. van Selms* (Leiden, 1971), pp. 233 ff.; cf. D. J. McCarthy, "An Installation Genre?" *JBL*, XC (1971): pp. 40 f.

92. Ps. 18 = 2 Sam. 22; See above, pp. 283 f.

93. S. Morenz, *Egyptian Religion*, tr. by A. E. Keep (Ithaca, N.Y., 1973), pp. 88 ff.; cf. A. Moret, *Le rituel du culte divin journalier en Egypte* (Paris, 1902), esp. p. 7.

94. The verb *ḥazah* means "to gaze in a vision" (*ḥazon*) analogous to that of a "seer" (*ḥozeh*) who practiced psychic divination.

95. See Song of Sol. 7:7, Prov. 9:17. The syntactic construction, with a proposition, implies intensity of beholding and a participatory exchange between the beholder and the "beheld." Cf. Mic. 4:11, Job 36:25, Isa. 47:13, Song 7:1.

96. Cf. 2 Sam. 1:26 (used by David to describe Jonathan's love), Song of Sol. 1:16, Ezek. 32:19.

97. Prov. 2:10, 2 Sam. 23:1, Ps. 135:3, etc.

98. 2 Kings 16:15. Cf. the Arabic *baqara*, "to see in depth," "to probe," and *baqqara*, "to rise up early at dawn." Dahood

renders the verb here, "awaking each dawn" (*Psalms*, I, p. 167). The notion may have been associated with the ritual of incubation and oniromancy.

99. Cf. Ps. 18:11 (Heb. 12), Job 36:29.

100. Literally, "My heart [used of the intellectual process of memory] said to thee [quoting God's own saying?]." Ancient versions reflect the exegetical difficulty.

101. The exceptional emphasis introduced by the verb *hayitha*, "thou art" or "thou hast been," implies the completeness and the constancy of the divine help.

102. Same word as in the opening statement (vs. 1).

103. Literally, "grace me," "let the compassions of thy womb be moved toward me."

104. See Ps. 105:4.

105. The verb appears in the expression "to gather [someone] to one's fathers." Cf. 2 Kings 22:20.

106. The MT *lu le'i* is uncertain. Literally, "*If* I did not believe . . ." The phrase may be elliptical, with the apodosis left unexpressed. Cf. Exod. 32:32, etc.

107. The verb *horah*, "to teach" is a cognate of *moreh*, "teacher," or "autumn rain."

108. The poet may well allude consciously to the Mosaic theophany.

109. "The land of the living" always refers to a this-worldly economy of historical existence. Cf. Isa. 38:11, 53:8; Ps. 52:5 (Heb. 7); Job 28:13; etc. *Contra* M. Dahood, *Psalms*, I, p. 170.

110. The psalmist appears to be aware of the theme of the *Deus absconditus*.

111. The motif of hope in the psalmody of presence, which connotes the image of stretching and tensity, is often related to the theme of the way. Cf. Ps. 25:3, etc.

112. See E. Lipiński, "Le psaume 84. La visite au Seigneur dans sa maison," *Assemblées du Seigneur*, LIV (Bruges, 1966), 16 ff.; Delekat, *Asylie und Schutzorakel am Zionheiligtum*, pp. 241 ff.

113. See E. Lipiński, "Macarismes et

psaumes de congratulation," *RB*, LXXV (1968): 321 ff.; W. Janzen, "'AŠRÊ in the Old Testament," *HTR*, LVIII (1965): 215 ff.; J. Dupont, "'Béatitudes' égyptiennes," *Biblica*, XLVII (1966): 155 ff.; W. Käser, "Beobachtungen zum alttestamentlichen Makarismus," *ZAW*, LXXXII (1970): 225 ff.; C. Westermann, "Der Gebrauch von 'SHRY im Alten Testament," *Forschung im Alten Testament*, II (München, 1974), 197 ff.

114. The Latinity of the word "beatitude" is appropriate for the static quality of the sacerdotal blessing, since "*beatus,*" "blessed," corresponds to a passive participle, *barukh.* On the contrary, the dynamic sense of the exclamation *'ashrê*, "O the ongoingness of . . . ," defies English rendering, with connotations of "stepping ahead along the way toward a goal."

115. The word *histopheph* is usually translated "to be a doorkeeper." The construct infinitive of a verb in the *hithpo'lel* voice which is apparently related to the noun *saph*, "threshold," this *hapax legomenon* does not designate a profession. With its connotation of oscillation, or back-and-forth movement, it probably suggests uncertainty and tenseness at the entrance.

116. The verb *dûr*, "to dwell" (cf. Arabic *da'ra*), originally meant "to move in a circle" [of tents which were pitched together in an encampment for security reasons]. Cf. the Akkadian *dûru*, "fortress."

117. M. Heidegger, *Introduction to Metaphysics*, tr. by R. Manheim (New Haven, 1959), p. 7.

118. See P. A. Munch, "Die jüdischen 'Weisheits-Psalmen' und ihre Platz im Leben," *Acta orientalia*, XV (1937): 112 ff.; S. Mowinckel, "Psalms and Wisdom," *VTS*, III (1955): 205 ff.; R. Murphy, "A Consideration of the Classification 'Wisdom Psalms'," *VTS*, IX (1963): 156 ff.; J. K. Kuntz, "The Canonical Wisdom Psalms: Their Rhetorical, Thematic and

Formal Dimensions," in J. J. Jackson and M. Kessler, eds., *Rhetorical Criticism* (Pittsburgh, 1974), pp. 186 ff.

119. See A. Caquot, "Le psaume LXXIII," *Semitica*, XXI (1971): 29 ff.; M. Mannati, "Sur le quadruple *avec toi* de Ps. LXXIII 21-26," *VT*, XXI (1971): 59 ff.; *id.*, "Les adorateurs de Môt dans le Psaume LXXIII," *VT*, XXII (1972): 420 ff.; A. Schmitt, *Entrückung-Aufnahme-Himmelfahrt* (Stuttgart, 1973).

120. The word *dôr*, "generation," originally meant "community," "assembly," and may have referred to the heavenly council. See F. Neuberg, "An Unrecognized Meaning of Hebrew *Dôr*," *JNES*, IX (1950): 216.

121. Literally, "until I went to the sacred places of El." On the basis of the late text of Wisd. of Sol. 2:22, many translate, "until I entered the mysteries of God," but the word *miqdash*, "sanctuary," may be used in the plural, probably referring to the terraces, esplanades, and open courts of the sacred edifice. Cf. Jer. 51:51.

122. Literally "I was pricked in my reins [the seat of desire and fear]."

123. Literally, "Behemoth," mythological animal, counterpart of Leviathan. Cf. Job 40:15 ff.

124. See Mannati, "'Avec toi' de Ps. LXXIII 21-26," p. 63.

125. See P. A. H. de Boer, "The Counsellori" *SVT*, III (Leiden, 1955): 42 ff.

126. The syntactic construction is not as difficult as many claim. The verb *laqah*, "to take," is used with two objects, the pronoun "me" and the noun "toward glory" (without the need of a Hebrew preposition, in the sense of a directional goal). Some prefer to take the word *'ahar* as a preposition introducing the word *kabhod*, "glory," and translate it, "behind glory" (cf. Zech. 2:12; see H. Ringgren, "Einige Bemerkungen zum 73.Psalms," *VT*, III [1953]: 270), but the meaning remains obscure.

127. See G. W. Coats, "Death and Dy-

ing in Old Testament Tradition," *Lexington Theological Quarterly*, I (1975): 9 ff.

128. K. S. Alling, *Kingdom of Diagonals* (Bloomington, Ind., 1954), p. 19.

129. Samuel Beckett, *Waiting for Godot: A Tragicomedy in Two Acts* (New York, 1954), p. 58.

130. See M. Mannati, "Les adorateurs de Môt," pp. 420 ff.

131. See R. Martin-Achard, "Notes bibliques: Remarques sur le Psaume 22," *Verbum Caro*, XVII (1963): 119 ff.; N. H. Ridderbos, "The Psalms: Style, Figures, and Structures . . . ," *OTS*, XIII (Leiden, 1963): 43 ff.; L. R. Fisher, "Betrayed by Friends. An Expository Study of Psalm 22," *In.*, XVIII (1964): 20 ff.; R. Kilian, "Ps 22 und das priesterliche Heilsorakel," *BZ*, XII (1968): 172 ff.; H. Schmid, "Mein Gott, mein Gott, warum hast du mich verlassen?" *Wort und Dienst*, NF, XI (1971): 119 ff.

132. See discussion in G. Fohrer, *History of Israelite Religion*, tr. by D. E. Green (Nashville and New York, 1972), pp. 142 ff.

133. See C. Krahmalkov, "Psalm 22, 28–32," *Biblica*, L (1969): 389 ff.; E. Lipiński, "L'hymne à Yahwé Roi au Psaume 22, 28–32," *Biblica*, L (1969): 153 ff.; O. Keel-Leu, "Nochmals Psalm 22, 28–32," *Biblica*, LI (1970): 405 ff.

134. See A. Rose, "L'influence des Psaumes sur les annonces et les récits de la Passion et les récits de la Résurrection dans les Evangiles," in R. de Langhe, ed., *Le Psautier* (1962), pp. 297 ff.; H. Gese, "Psalm 22 und das Neue Testament," *ZTK*, LXV (1968): 1 ff.; H. D. Lange, "The Relation Between Psalm 22 and the Passion Narrative," *Concordia Theological Monthly*, XLIII (1972): 610 ff.; J. A. Soggin, "Notes for Christian Exegesis of the First Part of Psalm 22," in *Old Testament and Oriental Studies* (Rome, 1975), pp. 152 ff.; J. H. P. Reumann, "Psalm 22 at the Cross: Lament and Thanksgiving for Jesus Christ," *In.*, XXVIII (1974): 39 ff.

135. The MT merely reads, "that Yahweh did" (vs. 30b). Modern translators err when they supply the pronoun "it" as a direct object. The verb is used intransitively in an absolute sense. The psalm ends on the evocation of the act of God in the history of the world.

136. Among the many monographs on Ps. 51, see especially those which deal with vss. 10–12 (Heb., 12–14): R. Press, "Die eschatologische Ausrichtung des 51.Psalms," *TZ*, XI (1955): 241 ff.; P. Bonnard, "Le psaume de pénitence d'un disciple de Jérémie," *Bible et vie chrétienne*, XVII (1957): 59 ff.; id., "Le vocabulaire du Miserere," *Festschrift A. Gelin* (Paris, 1961): 145 ff.; E. R. Dalglish, *Psalm Fifty-One in the Light of Ancient Near Eastern Patternism* (Leiden, 1962); L. Neve, "Realized Eschatology in Ps 51," *ET*, LXXX (1968–69): 264 ff.; P. Auffret, "Note sur la structure littéraire de Ps LI 1–19," *VT*, XXVI (1976): 142.

137. Cf. A. Caquot, "Ablution et sacrifice selon le Ps 51," *Proceedings of the XIth International Congress of History of Religion*, II (Leiden, 1968), pp. 75 ff.

138. Cf. Job 14:1 with Ps. 51:7 [Heb. 9]. See J. K. Zink, "Uncleanness and Sin. A Study of Job XIV and Psalm LI 7," *VT*, XVII (1967): 354 ff. The statement of Ps. 51:7 (Heb. 9) does not refer to the sinfulness of sexuality but implies the universality of sin and the solidarity of the human race from generation to generation.

139. The story of creation in Gen. 1:1—2:4a represents ancient traditions which have affinities with wisdom poetry. See G. M. Landes, "Creation Tradition in Proverbs 8:22–31 and Genesis 1," *Festschrift J. M. Myers* (Philadelphia, 1974), pp. 279 ff.

140. The traditional rendering, "thy holy spirit," risks anachronistic connotations with the Jewish and Christian hypostasis. Moreover, the context shows that the word *ruªḥ* is used three times in the sense of "virtue" as energy. Although it is unlikely, the psalmist may have referred to

"the angel of the presence," an expression which appeared after the Babylonian exile in parallel with the spirit of God's holiness (Isa. 63:9; cf. vss. 10–11).
141. e. e. cummings, *XAIPE*, no. 51, in *Poems 1923–1954* (New York, 1954), p. 456.
142. Peter Viereck, "Incantation at Assisi," *The First Morning: New Poems* (New York, 1952), p. 39.
143. See R. Kilian, "In Gott geborgen. Eine Auslegung des Psalms 139," *Bibel und Kirche*, XXVI (1971): 97 ff.; R. Lapointe, "La nuit est ma lumière," *CBQ*, XXXIII (1971): 397 ff.; M. Mannati, "Psaume 139 14–16," *ZAW*, LXXXIII (1971): 257 ff.; H. Schüngel-Strautmann, "Zur Gattung und Theologie des 139.Psalms," *BZ*, XVII (1973): 39 ff.
144. Thematic, stylistic, and linguistic affinities between Ps. 139 and the wisdom literature are numerous. More especially, a dozen words or expressions appear only in this psalm and in the poem of Job. For a long time it has been suggested that both literary pieces derive from the same poet or at least the same poetic school. See M. Buttenwieser, *The Psalms* (Chicago, 1938), pp. 541 ff.
145. Allusions to cosmic travel seem to be rhetorical devices of the poetic imagination. Hyperbole stresses the inescapability of the presence. It is not impossible, however, that vss. 7–10 allude to the parapsychological experiences of initiates in mystery cults. See T. H. Gaster, "A Canaanite Ritual Drama," *JAOS*, LXVI (1949): 69 ff.; H.-J. Kraus, *Psalmen II*, p. 919.
146. Cf. Amos 5:8, 4:13; Job 9:8 ff.; etc.
147. This seems to be the meaning of the word *sar'appim* (also spelled *sa'appim;* cf. Ps. 94:19; Job 4:13, 20:2; and the cognate "doubters" in Ps. 119:13). The root of the word means "to cleave," "to divide," "to branch out." Elijah used another word of the same family when he asked the people of Israel, "How long will you

go on limping on two divided opinions?" (*se'ippim;* 1 Kings 18:21.)
148. Aeschylus, *Suppliant Women,* (tr. Gilbert Murray, London, 1930), 781 ff.
149. Although the phrase "a sufficient God" is not found in the Hebrew Bible, the Greek-speaking Jews of the Hellenistic times translated the divine name "Shadday" as *Ho Hikanos,* "The Sufficient One" (Job 21:15, 31:2, 39:32; Ruth 2:20, 21). The apostle Paul may have echoed this usage when he wrote, "Our sufficiency comes from God" (2 Cor. 3:5).
150. See A. L. Merrill, "Psalm XXIII and the Jerusalem Tradition," *VT*, XV (1965): 354 ff.; O. Eissfeldt, "Bleiben im Hause Jahwes [Ps 23 . . .]," *Festschrift P. Altheim* (Berlin, 1969), pp. 76 ff.; G. Schwartz, ". . . 'Einen Tisch angesichts meiner Feinde'? Eine Emendation [zu Ps 23,5 . . .]," *VT*, XX (1970): 118 ff.; A. von Rohr Sauer, "Fact and Image in the Shepherd Psalm," *Concordia Theological Monthly*, XLII (1971): 488 ff.; R. von Ungern-Sternberg, "Das 'Wohnen in Hause Gottes', Eine terminologische Psalmen-Studie," *Kerygma u. Dogma*, XVII (1971): 209 ff.; D. N. Freedman, "The Twenty-third Psalm," *Michigan Oriental Studies: Festschrift G. G. Cameron* (Ann Arbor, Mich., 1976), pp. 139 ff.
151. A. R. Johnson, "Psalm 23 and the Household of Faith," in *Festschrift G. Henton Davies* (Richmond, Va., 1970), pp. 255 ff.; cf. P. Milne, "Ps. 23: Echoes of the Exodus," *Studies in Religion/Sciences religieuses*, IV (1974–75): 237 ff.
152. The motif of the divine shepherd was not necessarily borrowed from the figure of the shepherd king of the Egyptian eschatology, for the image is common to the ancient Near Eastern literature in general. The designation of Yahweh as the "shepherd" or "feeder" of Israel had appeared in archaic poetry and later became traditional. See Gen. 49:24; Ps. 28:9, 79:13, 80:1 [Heb. 2]; Hos. 4:16; 1 Kings 22:17; Ezek. 34:11 ff.; Isa. 40:11,

49:9, 63:14; cf. John 10:15. On the theological implications of the expression, see Ph. de Robert, *Le berger d'Israël. Essai sur le thème pastoral dans l'Ancien Testament* (Neuchâtel, 1968); cf. J. G. S. S. Thomson, "The Shepherd-Ruler Concept in the Old Testament and its Applications in the New Testament," *SJT*, VIII (1955): 406 ff.; O. Kiefer, *Die Hirtenrede. Analyse und Deutung von Joh 10.1–18* (Stuttgart, 1967); A. J. Simonis, *Die Hirtenrede im Johannes Evangelium* (Rome, 1967).

153. The MT reads two words *ṣal maweth*, "the shadow of death," instead of the single word *ṣalmuth*, "deep shadow." The semantic overtone of the idea of death was obvious, since narrow gorges shelter potential enemies, animal or human.

154. The word *rewayah* does not mean "overflows," although its cognates may refer to the saturation of well-irrigated fields. The meaning is that of "intoxication" either by drinking (Isa. 34:5) or through sexual passion (Prov. 5:19, 7:18). Therapeutic potions given to ailing sheep in the Middle East are generally made of fermented hemp or barley with medicinal herbs and honey.

155. The MT reads *shabhti*, "return," but the LXX reads *shibhti*, "reside," which seems to be correct in view of the element of circumstantial duration implied by the expression "for the length of [my] days."

156. A formula which refers to old age (Job 12:12; cf. Deut. 30:20; Prov. 3:2, 16).

157. See A. R. Johnson, "Ps. 23," pp. 264 ff.

158. See note 152 above.

159. Gen. 2:10 ff. Cf. "Eden" (sing.) and "delights" (ʿadhanim, pl.), two forms of the same word in biblical Hebrew, although they may have originally come from two different Semitic roots.

160. See G. W. Anderson, "Israel's Creed: Sung, Not Signed," *SJT*, XVI (1963): 21 ff.

161. See F. Stoop, "Le sens de Dieu dans les Psaumes," *Schweizerische Zeitschrift für Geschichte*, XIX (1969): 32 ff.

162. P. Tillich, "The Spiritual Presence," *Systematic Theology*, III (Chicago, 1963), p. 131. On the meaning of life and fulfillment in the Psalms, see von Rad, " 'Righteous' and 'Life' in the Cultic Language of the Psalms," *The Problem of the Hexateuch and Other Essays*, tr. by E. W. Trueman Dicken (Edinburgh and London, 1966), pp. 253 ff.; J. I. Durham, "Shalom and the Presence of God," *Festchrift G. Henton Davies* (Richmond, Va., 1970), pp. 281 ff.

163. See S. Mowinckel, *The Psalms in Israel's Worship*, II, pp. 104 ff.; *id.*, "Psalms and Wisdom," *VTS*, III (1955): pp. 205 ff.

7

The Play of Wisdom

In the Sistine capella fresco of the creation of man, Michelangelo has painted the figure of a hauntingly beautiful woman. Half-hidden among the angels in the mantle of God, she stares with astonishment at the birth of human life.[1] Her enlarged eyes reveal her anxiety. Wisdom, who had played in the presence of Yahweh at the creation of the world (Prov. 8:30), now looks at nascent humanity with foreboding. Can it be that her "delights" are now with the sons of men (vs. 30c)? The play of Wisdom includes a tragic tinge. "Brooding over the mysteries of Being,"[2] Wisdom at play is deadly serious, for play "pre-empts the future."[3]

DAUGHTER OF GOD—LOVER OF MEN

The meaning of "wisdom" in ancient Israel is open to scholarly debate.[4] No objective criterion from literary form or content has been agreed upon as determinative of the *Gattung* that is traditionally known as "sapiential." The books of Job, Proverbs, and Qoheleth (Ecclesiastes) in the Hebrew Bible, along with the Wisdom of Jesus ben Sirach (Ecclesiasticus) and the Wisdom of Solomon in the Apocrypha, are ranged in the category of wisdom literature, but the word *ḥokmah*, "wisdom," escapes precise definition, for it covers a wide range of usages.[5] It designates not just the virtue of sagacity but also an aesthetic reflection on human life,[6] and it attempts to express this reflection in the epigrammatic succinctness of proverbs, in teasing riddles, or in enigmatic fables and parables. As a rhetorical mode, wisdom is a playful form of social exchange which borders on aesthetic entertainment. As a personified figure, wisdom belongs to the realm of divinity.

Wisdom Personified

The origins of wisdom in Israel are obscure, for the sapiential tradition remained oral for centuries. Some of it has a folk flavor and partakes of the egalitarianism of Mosaic faith, with its stress on social justice.[7] It is chiefly this kind of wisdom which influenced the legislators, prophets, and psalmists.[8] A large number of proverbs, however, deal with kingship and the art of government. These proverbs reflect a littérateur's flair as well as a cosmopolite's culture. They probably emerged from the international intelligentsia with which the royal courts of Israel and Judah came in contact from the time of Solomon and especially Hezekiah.[9] Devoid of cultic and national particularism, Hebrew wisdom displayed a broad view of human nature and society. It generally affirmed the success of a prudential savoir-faire, but its hopeful humanism was also colored by a touch of skepticism and toned down by a note of pessimism.[10]

Canaanite, Mesopotamian, and Egyptian wisdom left deep marks on the sapiential circles of the Jerusalem court.[11] Extensive sections of the *Instruction of Amen-em-Ope*—a second-millenium Pharaonic scribe—were quoted indirectly in the book of Proverbs.[12] It was most likely under foreign influences that the Jerusalem sages came to think of wisdom not only as a human virtue but also as a divine quality and perhaps even as a semiautonomous attribute.

The Hebraic figure of personified wisdom may have originated in Canaanite mythology, which included a goddess of wisdom,[13] but its literary formulation presents verbal affinities with the Egyptian goddess Isis[14] and also with the Egyptian goddess Maat, "Truth-as-cosmic-and-social-order." Maat was represented as a divine child who was caressed and kissed by her father, the sun-god of the Heliopolis pantheon.[15] In addition, the erotic overtones of Wisdom's delights with both God and men echoed the liturgies of Ishtar, Queen of Heaven, the Mesopotamian goddess of love and wisdom.[16]

The hymns on wisdom which have been preserved from various ages[17] are couched in ambiguous language. Was their feminine personification of wisdom a prosopopeia or a hypostasis? Scholars are divided on this question, which may never be answered satisfactorily.[18] The imagination of poets and philosophers is able to view an abstraction as concretely as a living being. The mythopoetic mind does not need to choose between a figure of speech and reality, especially when the object of its concern is the enigma of the cosmos and the ultimate meaning of life. More important than a precise interpretation of these hymns is the light which they throw upon the nature of faith among the sages.[19]

Unlike the prophets, prone to vision, or the psalmists, bent on the mystical quest, the wise reflected by themselves and among themselves. This does not necessarily mean that their humanism was strictly anthropocentric. In comparing wisdom to a woman, they expressed in their own way their theology of presence.

Elusive Wisdom (*Job 28:1–28*)

The Book of Job includes in its finished form a hymn on wisdom which was probably intended as a musical interlude—

similar to the Greek chorus—between the poetic discussion (3:1—27:23) and the hero's peroration (29:1—31:40). This hymn was probably quoted from an oral tradition of ancient origin.[20] Its refrain wistfully affirms that neither *homo faber*, with his superb technique (vss. 1–11), nor *homo religiosus*, with his lavish rites (vss. 14–19), knows the path to wisdom. Human knowledge and human power are astounding,

> "But where shall Wisdom be found,
>   and where is the lode of intelligence?
> Mortal man is ignorant of her way:
>   she is not to be found in the land of the living"
>
> (vss. 12–13).[21]

While the Abyss (*Tehom*) and the Sea (*Yam*) deny that Wisdom resides among them (vs. 14), Utter Depths (*Abaddôn*) and Death (*Môth*) admit that they heard of her fame (vs. 22). The point of this distinction is now lost. In any case, the hymn proclaims that

> "God alone is aware of her way;
>   It is he who knows the place of her dwelling"
>
> (vs. 23).

The poet does not say that God created her. Yet, the third strophe implies that the creator and the sustainer of nature would not act without her presence. Significantly, the cosmic elements that are mentioned—wind, watery deep, rain, and flashes of lightning—suggest the autumn storms, which announce the renewal of fertility. As the divine sovereign presides over the initiation of a new year, he activates or restrains the powers of life and destruction. Without transition, the hymn concludes:

> "Then, he sees [Wisdom] and measures her,
>   he sets her up and he sounds her out"
>
> (vs. 27).

The meaning of this climactic line is by no means certain. The ambiguity of its verbs may well have been understood, in the context of the autumn feast, in an erotic sense:

> "Then, he sees her and he celebrates her,
>   he embraces her and he penetrates her."[22]

If this is the case, the imagery may have evoked a cosmogonic myth which pictured the creation of the world as a divine act of love play. A radical difference, however, would separate the theology of this hymn from that of the agrarian cults. No sexual rite of hierogamy, involving the fertilization of the earth-goddess, would be implied. Wisdom, sublimated lover of the Creator, transcends the created order.[23]

The incorporation of this hymn into the poem of Job shows particular insight into the theology of presence. The last verse of the chapter (vs. 28) provides a contextual link which indicates the raison d'être of the hymn at the end of the poetic discussion and before the hero's protest of innocence:

> "Then [God] said to man,
>   Behold, the fear of Adonay is wisdom,
>   to shun evil, this is intelligence."

Commentators generally dismiss this line as an editorial addition, but if the Jobian poet himself quoted the hymn on wisdom, he may well have introduced this poetic transition in order to obtain a specific effect on the audience which heard the chanting of the entire poem. Through the device of impressionistic juxtaposition, he ascribed to wisdom a new fluidity of meaning and function. Man cannot acquire nor possess wisdom through effort. Job is the lonely, abandoned sufferer. God and man are estranged. Yet the hero will be surprised by the voice from the whirlwind (chs. 38 ff.). In anticipation of this moment, as well as an "interlude" between "acts," the poet may well have directed that a chorus should sing the hymn on wisdom, with its affirmation of the greatness of the creator, the wonder of wisdom, and the need for man to recognize his own finitude.

While divine wisdom remains elusive to the natural faculties of *homo faber*, *homo religiosus*, and *homo moralis*, she makes herself available to Job under the mode of "the fear of the Lord."[24] Wisdom assumes, in effect, the role of the mediatrix of presence.

Wisdom's Delight (Prov. 8:22–31)

The function of Wisdom as the instrument of rapprochement between God and man is delineated more sharply in another hymn (Prov. 8:22–31),[25] which contains a lyrical self-appraisal of Wisdom playing in the divine presence:

I

8:22. It was Yahweh who begot me,[26] first fruit of his power,[27]
       prelude of his masterpieces of old.
   23. From all times I was consecrated,[28]
       from the beginning, from the first days of the earth.

II

   24. I was conceived when the abysses were not yet,
       even before the fountains of the deep came to exist.[29]
   25. Before the mountains had been planted in their bases,
       ahead of the hills, I was brought forth.
   26. [It was] at a time when he had not yet made the earth or space,
       or even the first of the cosmic dust.[30]

III

   27. I was there when he prepared the heavens,
       When he drew a circle on the face of the abyss,
   28. When he condensed the clouds for the waters of above,
       and the springs of the abyss gushed forth,

29. When he assigned an engraved limit to the sea
    that its waters should not trespass [the word of] his
    mouth,
    and when he traced the foundations of the earth.[31]

IV

30. Then I was at his side, [his] darling child![32]
    Then I was [his] delight day after day,
31. Playing and dancing[33] in the whole span of the earth!
    And [now] my delight is with the sons of men!"[34]
32. Thus, my sons, listen to me!
    Happy are those who keep my ways!

Centuries before the christological speculations of the
Church Fathers, the Jerusalem wise men boldly asserted that
Wisdom was "begotten, not made."[35] In addition to the temporal prepositions and other syntactic devices which indicate the
preexistence of Wisdom to the created world, the poet has
placed a threefold stress on the mode by which Wisdom, unlike
nature, came into being. Wisdom sings: "Yahweh begot me"
(vs. 22*a*), "I was conceived" (vs. 24*a*), and "I was brought forth"
(vs. 25*b*). Wisdom is a member of the family of God. Like the
psalmists and the prophets, who freely alluded to the sons of El
and the council of Yahweh, the wise men did not find in their
theology any objection to using a mythopoetic language in order to convey their ideas concerning the many-sided corporateness of divinity.

The context of Proverbs 1—9, in which Wisdom appears on
earth as hostess, entertainer, and educator,[36] does not in any
way jar with the implications of the hymn on the transcendence
of Wisdom. On the contrary, the structural finale of the poem
points to her dual role. She is at once the delight of the creator
and the companion of human beings. Her own delight is "with
the sons of men" (vs. 31*b*). Unlike the Jobian hymn, in which
wisdom was viewed solely as a reality of the divine realm (Job

28:1–27) and received its anthropological orientation through the impressionistic device of contextual juxtaposition (vs. 28), this poem builds up suspense by expatiating on the heavenly playfulness of Wisdom, only to throw in, at the last instant, the unexpected climax:

"And [now] my delight is with the sons of men!"

(vs. 31b.)

The delight which Wisdom induces in the Deity (vs 30b) is akin to the delight she experiences in the society of mankind (vs. 31b). The objective delight of Wisdom with God becomes the subjective delight of Wisdom with men. The delight she gives the creator is the delight she receives from the creature. Playful Wisdom is the mediatrix of presence.

Not unlike the psalmist who ridiculed the dread of cosmic evil by saying that Yahweh made "*that* Leviathan . . . to play with him" (Ps. 104:26), the Jobian hymnist exalted the goodness of creation by evoking the play of Wisdom in the presence of the Creator, thereby offering a rare glimpse of "pleasure in heaven" (cf. Luke 15:7). Pictured on the model of human corporateness, God enjoyed "en famille" the wonders of universal harmonies

"when the morning stars sang together[37]
and the sons of El shouted for joy"

(Job 38:7).

It is Wisdom, at once divine and human, who reveals to man the meaning of the universe, with its origin and its end. One should not speak of the "self-revelation of creation."[38] By using the figure of personified wisdom, at once the entertainer of divinity and the educator of humanity, the hymnist hinted at a similarity, perhaps an actual kinship, between the human thirst for knowledge and the childlike freedom of the Godhead. Science, philosophy, art, and the knowledge of God are united in the celebration of play.[39]

The Embrace of Wisdom

While the prophets compared the life of communion between Yahweh and Israel to a marriage of love, and while the psalmists discovered a mode of presence which depended on cultus and also went beyond its public ceremonial, the sapiential circles spoke of access to presence through the love of wisdom. They meant in appearance a man-initiated enterprise but in depth a human response to a transcendental call.

Men are enjoined to seek Wisdom and "to acquire" her, only because Wisdom herself waits for them and invites them to come toward her (Prov. 2:4, 3:13, etc.). In sapiential humanism, as well as in prophetic and psalmodic Yahwism, the initiative is always divine. Whoever finds Wisdom finds life, but life is interpreted in the context of Israel's faith. The fear of Yahweh and the knowledge of God are the fruits of Wisdom (Prov. 2:5 ff.).

Wisdom is the feminine vehicle of spirituality through which Yahweh bestows his presence and its benefits.

> Do not abandon her, and she will keep thee safe.
>   Love her, and she will stand guard over thee.
> Cherish her,[40] and she will lift thee up.
>   She will honor thee whenever thou wilt embrace her,
> She will place a garland of grace on thy head,
>   and crown thee with magnificence
>
> (Prov. 4:4–8).

Man is pressed to welcome a reality which responds to his embrace because this reality initiates it. The analogy of love between woman and man rather than between man and woman corrects the implication of "male chauvinism," for it makes woman preeminent. Theologically, it introduces a dialectic of mutuality which makes any theory of salvation by work totally irrelevant.

The invitation of Wisdom is extended to all men, not just to a privileged class of court officials or intellectuals. Transposing —almost wrecklessly—the appeals of the goddess Ishtar to human beings,[41] the sapiential circles did not recoil from picturing Wisdom waiting at street corners and on hilltops (Prov. 8:2, etc.). As the sublime counterpart of the prostitutes in the mystery cults of the ancient Semitic world, Wisdom attempted to allure all those who passed by. Her call was addressed to the whole of humanity (Prov. 8:4). The universalism of the prophets and of the psalmists projected its own fulfillment to the end of history, but the universalism of the wise aimed at the present time. In her house, enigmatically built on seven pillars (Prov. 9:1 ff.),[42] Wisdom offers a sacramental meal of bread and wine that her guests may live (Prov. 9:5–6).

The theme of Wisdom's embrace persisted in the Hellenistic age. In *The Wisdom of Jesus ben Sirach* (*Ecclesiasticus*), *hokhmah* (wisdom) and *torah* (law) became explicitly identified (Sir. 24:1 ff.).[43] Nevertheless, even in the Siracide, Wisdom still extended her invitation to all: "Come to me, you who desire me, and eat your fill of my fruits" (Sir. 24:19). In the Hellenistic era of cultural openness, and before the Maccabean time of cultural withdrawal, Jewish teachers of wisdom were apparently eager to reach out toward the intellectuals of the cosmopolitan centers like Antioch and Alexandria.

The fragmentary Hebrew text of *The Acrostic Poem on Wisdom* which was discovered at Qumran[44] presents a strikingly different phrasing from that of the familiar Greek translation of Ecclesiasticus (Sir. 51:13–19). The Qumran recension (col. xxi, lines 11–17) contains an accumulation of sexual imagery which is quite devoid of reticence. Ben Sirach was not only a keen observer of the created world but also a passionate lover of wisdom. His love for wisdom was akin to a quasi-mystical immersion in the realm of divinity. He did not separate his reflective search for truth from a surrender to a presence which overwhelmed and possessed him. He sought wisdom, but it preceded him. He activated his search through his power of decision, but the initiative transcended his volitive faculties.

By comparing wisdom not just to a teacher and a suckling nurse but to a lover, Ben Sirach used the analogy of the feminine in humanity to describe the most pleasing and demanding element in divinity. Like Hosea and other prophets, he understood that the knowledge of God went far beyond doctrinal assent or the acquisition of information. To know is to be, and to be is to give oneself to another in a totality of devotion which knows no compromise and involves a surrender. Philosophical reflection grows from communion with transcendence, and this communion is comparable to an embrace with the feminine personification of the Godhead.

Almost two centuries later, the author of the *Wisdom of Solomon*[45] pursued a similar theme. As an emanation, mirror, and reflection of the high God, Wisdom makes herself visible to those who love her. To love Wisdom is to keep her laws, and to keep her laws is to be assured of incorruptibility. It is this incorruptibility which brings man near to his God (6:12 ff.)

The personification of wisdom as the daughter of God and the lover of men elicited an atmosphere of happiness which strangely ignored the tragic fate of Israel, although some sages had warned against the wiles of Dame Folly (Prov. 9:13 ff.). Poets of the sapiential circles, among whom may be included the Jobian rhapsodist, deliberately faced the enigma of suffering. Human evil and human misfortune, without apparent cause in history or character, prompted them to investigate the riddle of divine silence in the face of human agony.

It was in her garb of the mediatrix of presence that Wisdom influenced the early Christians in their attempt to articulate their new faith. They were convinced that Jesus, a human being

born of a woman, was comparable to divine wisdom, the bearer
of a divine presence in a human personality (Rom. 1:20 ff., Col.
1:12, Heb. 1:2 ff., etc.).[46]

A MASQUE OF REVOLT

Jewish and Christian tradition has placed the Book of Job in
the wisdom literature, but this unique document escapes strict
classification, for it presents a bewildering diversity of literary
genres: folktale, proverbial sayings, lament, hymn, invective,
prophetic confession, legal controversy, juridical oath, *onomas-
tica*, and theophany. In all probability, the poem of Job and his
comforters (3:1—42:6) was composed by a Jerusalem sage deported into Lower Mesopotamia,[47] who had been profoundly
influenced by Jeremiah, Habakkuk, and the psalmists at the turn
of the sixth century B.C.

From the time of David and Solomon, the story of the pious
man from the land of Uz, a foreigner, had been told at camp-
fires and in wisdom schools. A poet of singular genius borrowed the tale with its *dramatis personae* as a setting for a
discussion of spirituality under duress. He presented in effect
a paracultic drama, which was acted out and chanted with musical accompaniment before it was later written out by scribes.

The occasion for this *masque of revolt*[48] cannot be determined
with certainty, but it may have been the informal observance of
the autumn festival "by the rivers of Babel."[49]

Through the grimness of disaster, someone may have
thought that "the play of wisdom must go on," and that the *danse
macabre* of history might yet be transfigured by the contemplation of a creator who "gives songs in the night" (Job 35:10).

The hero had asked in the story: "Since we accept happiness
as a gift of God, why should we not accept hardship also?"
(1:10), but in the poem he lamented:

"Why did I not die in my mother's womb?"

(3:11.)

By using a dialogue form, which sages of Mesopotamia and Egypt had long favored to air unconventional ideas,[50] the poet found a way to go beyond the scandal of unexplicable pain and to probe an essentially theological problem. Does man dare to judge Deity?

In pursuing this question, the poet did not become a philosopher formulating a theodicy, but he made a contribution to the theology of presence. It is the theology of presence, not the problem of suffering, which lies at the core of the poem.

From the opening lament (3:1 ff.) to the closing confession (42:5–6), the argument moves on three levels. Presence is first beyond grasp and second beyond time. When it unexpectedly rushes in as "the voice from the whirlwind" (38:1 ff.), its obtrusiveness shatters man's imagination of God. Beyond grasp and beyond time, it now stands, most shockingly, "beyond honor."

Presence Beyond Grasp

Destitute, bereaved, excommunicated, the erstwhile paragon of selflessness in devotion to his God lost his composure and "cursed his day" (3:1). In a dozen soliloquies, the deterioration of the hero's faith was astutely depicted. The poison of pain may have at times vitiated his judgment, but his mind could also show clear thinking in the midst of frenzy, "la lucidité dans le délire."

In the prologue, Job had blessed God (1:21). In the poem, he accused God of caprice and sadistic cruelty:

"I was at ease when he broke me;
  he seized me by the neck and dislocated [my spine];
Then he set me up for target practice;
  his arrows fly all around me . . ."

(16:12–13).

Prophets and psalmists before Job had protested sickness, persecution, and ostracism. They had often turned their prayers of lament into prayers of bewilderment:

> "Why dost thou stand at a distance, O Yahweh?
> Why dost thou hide thyself in time of trouble?"
>
> (Ps.10:1.)

But they had not detected malevolence and irresponsibility at the heart of God. They had felt the dread of a silent God and an absent God but not an enemy God. Like Jacob at the Jabbok, they had fought in prayer,[51] but the *agon* motif was swiftly resolved into a new grace. For Job, on the contrary, divine hostility persisted night after night with no other prospect than the eventuality of his death. He was even deprived of hope in a resurrection (14:10–12). To die was for him better than to live, but he loved life fiercely and he refused the void without vindication.

The point at which his revolt exceeded the impatience of the prophets and the psalmists may be seen in a touch of black humor, when he played on the sound of his own name, "Job," and asked God:

> "Wherefore hidest thou thy face
> and holdest me for thy enemy?"
>
> (13.24.)

The word *'Iyyob* ('.y.b.), "Job," may have been a cognate of the word *'Oyeb* ('.y.b.), "enemy."

Never did the tormented man allude to a mythic power of evil distinct from the Godhead.[52] His monotheism was so stringent that it intensified the dilemma of his situation: "There is no God but God!" At the same time, he obstinately maintained that he was entirely in the right. Although he acknowledged peccadilloes of adolescence (13:26), he repeatedly proclaimed his

innocence of any crime. Since he also persisted in believing that
the divine power was neither divided nor limited, he was forced
to conclude:

"It is God who has taken away my right"

(27:2).

An awful misunderstanding kept them apart. Beyond the loss of
his children and his health, Job was racked by the experience of
a metaphysical solitude. His long familiarity with an ever-
present God had vanished. Starvation for the solace of God's
nearness led him to expand his self-respect into the pride of a
legendary giant and to ascribe to that God the most sordid
intentions.

Two centuries before Plato, but in a quite different mood,
this nonconformist Hebrew poet charged that man was but "a
plaything in the hand of God."[53] He did not mean, as Plato did,
that "this is the best thing about him." Rather, with the sarcasm
of a deceived lover, Job anticipated the now hackneyed ranting:

"As flies to wanton boys are we to the gods:
   They kill us for their sport."[54]

In a contradiction persistent throughout the poem, he hurled
his charges at the *Deus ludens* of his nightmares, but he still
appealed to the just Deity of his former faith:

"If only there were between us an umpire
   who might lay his hand upon us both!"

(9:33).

The appearance of God at a fair trial cannot be forced, and
his presence is beyond the grasp of man. Again and again
demanding an audience in order to argue his case directly (13:-
3) and to defend his ways to God's face even at the cost of his

own life (13:15),[55] the challenger had to fall back on the recognition of both his impotence and his loneliness:

> Oh that I knew where I might find him,
>   that I might come even to his throne!
> I would order my cause before him,
>   and fill my mouth with arguments.
> I would know the words which he would answer me,
>   and listen with care to what he would say to me ...
> If I go to the east, he is not there;
>   to the west, I cannot perceive him;
> To the north, where he works,[56] I have no vision of him;
>   to the south, where he hides himself, I cannot see him
>   (23:3–5, 8–9).

In man's extremity, God's presence is elusive and cannot be ordained, yet Job's ancient trust remained the underground source of his hope. He still expected that at some unspecified future an intervention from above would not fail him.

Presence Beyond Time

A glimmer of this expectation may be caught in Job's use of irony. Alluding to the myth of the cosmic fight by which the god of order triumphed over deified chaos, he taunted the creator:

> "Am I the Sea, or the Ocean Monster,
>   that thou placest a watch over me?"
>   (7:12).

In the Babylonian liturgy of the New Year, the god Marduk brought Tiamat down and posted a watch over her. Is then God playing with Job as if He were aping Marduk, or does a sick man on his pile of refuse pose a threat to "the mover of the world and all the stars"? The broad satire is not devoid of grandeur. By allowing himself to doubt both divine omnipotence and human finitude, Job reaffirmed in a perverted way his bond to the

Deity. It was his lingering faith which made him oscillate on the verge of blasphemy.

The element of play reappeared a few lines later when the sufferer reiterated his belief that God would someday come to his senses and relent—but too late. Like a mischievous child, Job said to the Most High, "You'll be sorry." Since he understood death as nonbeing, he turned his fear of annihilation into a jest at the expense of God:

"For now shall I sleep in the dust,
    and thou wilt seek me, groping in the gloom before dawn,
    but I shall not be!"

(7:21).

God himself will have to face the great void. A procrastinating Deity will be offered the spectacle of nothingness.

Once again, the hero basked in a pleasant reverie. The silent God will not ignore him forever. In a lyrical meditation on human mortality, a mortality which is far more drastic than the ephemerality of trees (14:1 ff.), he borrowed the language of oriental love poetry:

If thou wouldst hide me in Sheol,
    shelter me there until thy wrath would ease,
    and make a date with me to remember me!
If a strong man, once dead, could live again,
    all the days of my forced labor would I wait
    until the time of my relief!
Thou wouldst call, and I would answer;
    thou wouldst desire the work of thy hands!

(14:13–14.)

Abrupt return to the bleakness of reality (vss. 16 ff.) chased this phantasm, but the hope of a love call from God was implanted in the patient's mind. Presence was delayed, but it would surely come, even beyond time.

After Job's death, an unidentified "witness" will defend him against his divine murderer at a session of the heavenly council (16:21).[57] Far more extraordinary still is Job's certitude that the redeemer of his blood[58] will rise on the dust of his grave and vindicate his honor (19:25). The textual uncertainty of this pericope, typical of the manuscript corruptions which impair most of the so-called messianic passages, prevents a definite interpretation. Nevertheless, with the exception of the line which immediately follows (vs. 26a), a fairly safe rendering may be proposed:

And after this skin which is mine [?] is thus destroyed [?],
    within my flesh shall I see God!
It will be I, myself, who will contemplate him;
    my eyes will perceive him, and not a stranger;
    my desire burns within me

                                                    19:26–27).

The quadruple emphasis on the identity of the beholder, even after his death, but "within [his] flesh,[59] may well represent a turning point in Israel's traditional ignorance of an afterlife for the individual. In a post-mortem mode of being—perhaps brief, perhaps eternal—Job will at last see his God. By using the expression "within my flesh," he affirmed the concreteness and the fullness of his identity. This unambiguous credo, "And I know that my redeemer lives," followed by the unabashed announcement of the divine vision, played its part in the growth of the later belief in the resurrection of the dead. The mythic form of the belief polemized against the alien idea of the immortality of the soul—a disincarnate breath, a mere shadow of the human personality. Job waited, secure, without indulging in any doubt, for the rebirth beyond time of his corporeal personality. An anthropological realism of a similar kind inspired the Pauline formula of "a spiritual body" (1 Cor. 15:44).

Until the end of the poetic dialogue, Job never weakened in his expectation of seeing God, but he expected that this rapprochement would take place on his own terms, and he concluded his oath of innocence with an anticipation of assurance expressed in court style:

> Who will make sure that God hear me?
> Here is my signed statement: Let the Almighty answer me!
> If my opponent has written a bill of charge,
>   I shall carry it on my shoulder,
>   adorn my head with it as with a crown!
> I shall reveal the sum of my steps!
> As a prince I shall approach him!
>
> (31:35-37).

The royal majesty of the complainant was still intact. Throughout his quest for the presence, he asked only for the recognition of his rectitude. Unlike the poets of the Sumerian, Akkadian, and Hebrew laments, he never confessed any sin, begged for pardon, or even asked for healing. All he ever demanded, with unbent pride, was a verdict of acquittal.

Presence at last crashed in with the thunders, and the stance vanished. Job was invited to look at the world from the perspective of God.

Presence Beyond Honor

When the poet introduced the voice from the whirlwind, in a setting which echoed the theophanies of Moses and Elijah (38:1 ff.), no answer was ever given to the human questioner. On the contrary, it was the Deity's turn to ask questions,[60] not without irony.[61]

Was Job present at creation? At the end of the cosmic display, God insisted:

"Bind up thy champion's belt!
  I shall ask, and thou wilt instruct me.
  Wilt thou void my righteousness
  and call me evil to justify thyself?"

                                                    (40:8).

This question penetrated to the heart of the debate. Job had sought the presence for an egocentric aim. While his friends were engaged in rehearsing a purely didactic theodicy based on the traditional dogma of individual retribution, he had insisted on his rights to happiness. God was bound to respect these rights. The course of self-justification on which he had embarked inevitably entailed God's condemnation.

Orthodox wisdom practiced an intellectual form of idolatry, for the theodicy which it upheld was based on man's imagination of divine justice. The heterodox revolt of Job fell into a similar trap, although suffering rendered his error understandable. However perverted by the claims of his moralism, his faith carried him through the ordeal of a hell on earth. While the poet clearly showed that Job had not "feared God for nought" (1:9), he also succeeded in exhibiting a man who risked his whole being for the sake of a selfless gain: by passionately seeking the recognition of his moral integrity, he wanted to know, beyond religiosity, the divinity of God. From the vortex of the storm, he learned that God was God only when God was free from a man-made image. The Jobian poet anticipated Voltaire's witticism: "Dieu fit l'homme à son image, mais l'homme le lui a bien rendu."

By probing the theology of presence, the poet not only hinted at the insidiousness of intellectual idolatry but also exposed the corruptibility of the covenant theology. Like Job, whose inner greatness exceeded that of "all the sons of the East" (1:3), the people of Israel—elected by Yahweh for a unique mission in the history of the world—had tragically fooled themselves into assuming that they had acquired rights upon the Almighty.

Significantly, the Jobian poet used the same verb as Jeremiah's when he had Yahweh ask the question:

"Woudst thou void (*tapher*) my righteousness?"

(40:8).

In the Jeremianic indictment of Israel and Judah, Yahweh said:

"Their fathers ... have made my covenant void (*hepheru*)"

(Jer. 31:31).

Throughout the discussion between Job and his friends, the poet had showed himself to be an intimate follower of Jeremianic thought. Not only did he restate in a style of high lyricism Jeremiah's confession (Jer. 20:14 ff.) when he composed the opening soliloquy on the cursing of Job's birth (Job 3:1 ff.), but he also transposed many Jeremianic cries of despair, of doubt, and of remonstrance throughout the poetic controversy. Indeed, the prophet had engaged in a controversy (*rîbh*) with Yahweh (Jer. 12:1 ff.) before Job had.

The darkness of the theophany was a symbol of divine presence behind a mask.[62] While the evocation of Behemoth and Leviathan[63] did not offer a solution to the problem of evil,[64] the poet bypassed the enigma of suffering when he had the creator of the universe unveil for the lonely man the wonders of cosmic life and perhaps also confide in him some of his own perplexity in the face of cosmic evil.

To Jeremiah who had questioned his righteousness, Yahweh replied: "I have abandoned my own house, left my inheritance. I have delivered the darling of my being into the hands of her enemies" (Jer. 12:7). To Job who had questioned his governing of the world, Yahweh replied:

"Behold, I pray, Behemoth! I have made him as I have made thee!"

(40:15).

At the moment when history became meaningless for Israel,

Job was invited, almost tenderly, to contemplate the Creator at work.

At the rebirth of greenness with the autumn thunders, when dust that has been parched by the death of nature in the summer heat again became the soil of fertility (38:38), the bounty of the Creator transcended all forms of mercantilism in religion and in the destiny of man.

Although the poem of Job cannot be interpreted as a detailed allegory of the first Jews in exile,[65] its allusion to their theological plight cannot be missed.[66] The rise and fall of empires are the tainted fruit of political give-and-take. In the presence of a God who endows nature with both penury and luxury, the poem of Job views historical upheavals in their proper perspective.

The freedom of God was celebrated in Proverbs by the play of wisdom at creation. The freedom of God was celebrated in Job by the display of munificence in the cosmos, with a glance at the mythic monsters of evil. There is no place for anthropocentricity in nature, with its hint of holy waste. Rain falls on land "where no man is" (38:26).

In disclosing his labors in creating and maintaining the universe, Yahweh truly "answered Job" (38:1). He inclined himself toward a single creature whom history had rejected and with whom he shared the marvels of his act.

While the words "love" and "grace" are absent from the discourses of Yahweh, the realities which they represent should not be missed. In the presence of the holy, Job desisted, but his silence should not be interpreted merely as the submission of finitude to infinity. Modern critics who discern on his part an abject surrender show they do not understand the depth of the holy

"I had hitherto known thee by hearsay.
Now, my eyes have seen thee"

(42:5).

Job's honor no longer mattered. He was ushered for a moment into the realm of divinity. Presence beyond honor offered the solitary man an all-sufficient gift: the immediacy of God himself.

Of what crime, then, did he *repent?* He did not "repent."

> "Therefore I sink into the abyss and I grieve
>   On dust and ashes"
>
> (42:6).[67]

Job encountered the holiness of God in its fullness, without intermediary and without a protective armor. He reacted to the shattering power of the holy as the prophet Isaiah had, with the "woe is me" of human response to the *mysterium tremendum* (Isa. 6:5). In addition, Job's final word implies far more than the awareness of solidarity in guilt which seized the prophet. Job did not come to this moment in a spiritual vacuum. With the proud conscience of moral man, he had demanded an audience. He now discovered sinfulness not as moral transgression but as the pride of self-deification.

In his persistent claims for the vindication of his honor, the man from Uz had not spoken as a moral man aware of his finitude but as a moral man who had turned his morality into a lever for securing ultimate autonomy. He had unwittingly acted as a divine being associated with the creative activity of the sapiential myth (Prov. 8:22 ff.). Eliphaz of Teman had correctly detected in him this evidence of flirtation with the role of the *Ur-mensch* (15:7). Job had assumed the attributes of an infinite and eternal being. His bid for theodicy had led him to deny his humanity.

From the whirlwind, Yahweh reminded him of the irony of human finitude that plays with the illusion of infinity:

> "Put on majesty and grandeur!
>   Deck yourself with splendor and glory! . . .

Then, I myself will worship thee,
For thy right hand will have saved thee!

(40:10, 14.)

The confession of Job the sinner assumes, therefore, a most peculiar quality. He was not stained by a guilt which resulted from a rupture of the moral order in human society, nor had he violated any moral code. He had transgressed the limits of his creatureliness because he had passed judgment on the character of his Creator.

The poet did not have at his disposal a vocabulary suitable for the formulation of a theological hamartiology, but he succeeded in poetically communicating his intention. If Job had possessed the infinity of a divine being, Yahweh himself would have paid homage to him. Job did not "repent." He did not acknowledge moral turpitude. He, the moral man *par excellence,* grieved over his mythical pride—the pride which he had erected upon his morality.

Could it be that the poet intimated a further thought—that not only anthropodicy but even the noblest theodicy amounts to the most heinous of theological crimes? In any case, the Jobian theophany constitutes a scathing critique of religious subjectivism in all its manifestations, of egocentric flattery, either through the lull of ritual or the busyness of moral activism. In spite of darkness, presence induced illumination.

The *Masque of Job* began in revolt, but it ended in faith, without the old illusion about the self and with a new lucidity about God.

"MODEST DOUBT"

Many readers of the Bible have wondered why the Book of Qoheleth (Ecclesiastes), which reflects the mind of not so gentle a cynic,[68] has been included in the canon of the Hebrew Bible.[69] Part of the answer may be that it pierces the traditional delusions of religionists. In addition, by living through his modest doubt, Qoheleth developed a *modus credendi* which paradoxically maintained a sense of God's presence within the signs of God's absence.

The Threat of the Unknown

The name "Qoheleth" was a pseudonym[70] which concealed the identity of a Jerusalem sage[71] in early Hellenistic times (late fourth century B.C.).[72] The literary form of the book recalls the Egyptian genre of "royal testament," with its observations of the human scene. Its language is late Hebrew seasoned with Aramaisms and also bearing the marks of Phoenician.[73] There is no agreement on its structure;[74] although contemporary scholars increasingly recognize an inner unity which binds together its various parts.[75]

Seemingly skeptical, Qoheleth was a man of profound conviction. Like Job (42:5a), he doubted the validity of inherited beliefs, but the modesty of his doubt covered a deep attachment to some unshakable certainty. Qoheleth's doubt was modest, for he did not presume to corner the whole truth, nor did he arrogate to his mind the capacity to dissect, without also learning with his whole person the meaning of existence. Because he doubted, he looked at both sides of truth and was able to suspend his judgment in order to investigate the meaning of existence "under the sun." He thought without fear, ready to take on the threat of the unknown. For him, doubt was not only the *sine qua non* of science and philosophy but also the indispensable ingredient of religion. He loved both life and knowledge, even when he proclaimed that he hated life and that knowledge was inseparable from the willingness to question life and to confront the void. He understood that when faith refuses to look at death, it is unable to respond to life. It was as if he had known that

"modest doubt is call'd
The beacon of the wise, the tent that searches
To the bottom of the worst."[76]

In Elizabethan English, "tent" or "tint" was the lint with which surgeons probed a wound, cleaned it, and removed from it any impurities, a necessary procedure prior to healing. Qoheleth probed historical events and human nature "to the bottom of the worst," until he could discard the self-deceptive props of religion. He accepted the seeming immutability of phenomena in the universe. As a sage, he even admitted the futility of wisdom or at least the pain of awareness (1:18) and the illusion of pleasure (2:1),[77] if this awareness and this pleasure merely left man at the center of his world. He discerned the intricacy of the relationship between desire and mortality long before anyone had sketched the *eros-thanatos* syndrome, but he never gave up the quest for the supreme good in the midst of transitoriness. His recurrent theme was not the emptiness of all things, although he repeated more than a score of times, "Futility of all futilities, all is futility." Under a persiflage which never concealed the bruises or even the ravages of evil upon his being, his thought sprang from a cardinal belief, the theocentricity of all life.

The Theocentricity of All Life

The disabused approach of Ecclesiastes to the world has not led him to despair or rebellion. Unlike the Job of the poetic dialogue, he never tried to argue with the Deity. It would be wrong, however, to conclude that he was simply submissive to an impersonal fate. His many references to "times" and to "decrees" belong to the theocentric perspective of the entire book. Again and again he recognized God's activity behind every phenomenon of nature or every historical event.[78] He rejected orthodox wisdom with its traditional dogma of retribution,[79] but it cannot successfully be argued that this rejection led him to ascribe caprice and irresponsibility to God, as the Jobian hero had done in the controversy with his comforters. Like the Jobian poet of the theophany, he refused to think theologically in terms of human concepts of justice, which inevitably reflect the bounds of created finitude and historical relativity. He purged religion from the intellectual idolatry through which human ideals of ethics are blown up to the dimensions of infinity. He fought simplistic equations between destiny and character, but he could not be accused of reducing providence to blind necessity. He knew that life lay entirely within the hands of God, although he respected the freedom of man as much as the freedom of God. Implicitly, he suggested that the vicissitudes and even the horrors of human existence could not be ascribed to a malevolent creator: "[God] has made everything beautiful in its own time. Also, he has placed [the thought of] eternity in the mind of [men], but they have not discovered [the meaning of] the work which God accomplishes from beginning to end" (3:10-11). This passage comes close to the spiritual core of Qoheleth's thinking. Unfortunately, its interpretation is uncertain.[80] The Jerusalem sage seems to have maintained a dialectic between the benevolence of God's purpose in creation and the ignorance of man to discern it and to live by its implications. At the same time, Qoheleth reserved judgment about the source of this ignorance. He refrained from saying that man was responsible for his finitude and also from impugning the motives and the responsibility of the Creator.

"God has made everything beautiful in its own time." The word *yapheh*, "fair," "beautiful," acquired in late Hebrew a moral connotation not dissimilar to the Hellenistic overtones of *kalos kagathos*.[81] Every cosmic phenomenon or historical event (cf. 3:1-8) has its own appropriate time.[82] The whole of creation carries an appeal to which man might have responded with wonder, elation, and profit, had he seized the opportunity "at the proper moment" (*kairos*, as the LXX pointedly translated, vs. 10*a*).

For Qoheleth, the world was not the impersonal theater of human life. As the heir to the sapiential tradition of early Yahwism, and as a teacher of Jewish wisdom in the early Hellenistic era, he had been nurtured on the Torah and assumed that his auditors knew the creation stories. "And Elohim saw all that he had made. And behold, it was very good" (Gen. 1:30). For a reason which Qoheleth left unexpressed, man's epistemological faculties are so limited that he is unable to decipher the theological purpose of the universe or indeed to interact with nature in a dynamic relationship.

Qoheleth's dialectic between creation and mankind is further compounded by a tension within man. The contradiction between God's infinity and man's finitude is not foreign to human consciousness. God has placed in man's imagination the thought of eternity. Nevertheless (*mibbᵉli*), man does not discover the intention of the Creator (vs. 11*b*).

The traditional rendering of the word *'ōlām*, "eternity," has been generally repudiated by modern scholars. To be sure, the word carried a wide range of meaning, from "antiquity" to "continuous existence" (on earth), "future duration," and "the wholeness of time."[83] When it is applied to Yahweh or to Yahweh's activity, however, the word *'ōlām* always means "eternity" in the sense of a mode of being that transcends existential temporality.[84] Yahweh is the living God who stands beyond the risk of mortality.[85] Qoheleth did not state that man was created eternal. He had simply maintained that the creator had placed in the mind of men the thought of eternity.[86] While Qoheleth probably alluded to the theme of the *imago Dei* (Gen. 1:27) and to the motif of man's failure to obtain absolute knowledge (Gen. 3:5, etc.),[87] he carefully abstained from blaming anyone, God or man. Moreover, he did not believe that God in heaven and man on earth were totally and irremediably separated. He discerned in creation the veiled presence of God.

A Modus Credendi

Although the wise man who concealed his identity behind a *nom de plume* manifested no warmth of interest in ecstatic visions, the comforts of cultic presence, or even the emotional travails of prayer, he did not really rule God out of his existence as "the Great Absentee," for he was neither a determinist nor a deist. On the contrary, he was eager to discern God's gift to man in the enjoyment of existence and found a justification for man's devotion in awe before the face of God himself.

God's bounty in man's daily life is a manifestation of God's presence.

> I know that there is nothing good for [man] except to enjoy himself and to be happy as long as he lives. Moreover, when any man eats and drinks and finds happiness in his work, this is a gift of God. I know that all that God accomplishes will last forever. There is nothing to add to it or to substract from it. And God has made it so that man shall be in awe *before him* (italics added; 3:12–14).

One is not permitted to infer from Qoheleth's rejection of the traditional doctrine of retribution or from his aloofness from historical evidence of divine revelation that the fear of God differs from the fear of Yahweh. There is no ground for stating that religious fear in Qoheleth represents sheer dread of the unknown or unadulterated terror.[88] As elsewhere in Hebraic faith, the fear of Elohim represents man's ambivalent reaction to the nearness of the holy.[89] It may be an impulse of withdrawal from God's displeasure or pleasure (cf. 8:12, 13), just as for the psalmist it may be the fear of divine forgiveness (Ps. 130:4).

In a period of cultural transition, when old values are eroded and new realities beg for birth, traditional formulas of the faith lose their power and new expressions of theological certitude are wanting. Qoheleth found the inherited beliefs ineffectual, for they had ceased to ignite the faith he had received from his fathers. Nevertheless, he maintained in his somber way a definite *modus credendi*, which waited for a renewal of vitality in the words of his creed. His rude honesty was matched by his courage to survive, without hope, in the face of death. No commentator should hastily dismiss the religious stance of Qoheleth. In an age of the death of the gods, he was able to affirm God's presence in silence. His parting word may well have been: "Light is sweet, and it is pleasant for the eyes to behold the sun" (11:7).

Melville was more perspicacious than many biblical critics when he called the Book of Ecclesiastes "the fine hammered steel of woe."[90] With obstinacy, the old observer of the human scene and of his own depths held on to the strength of his faith—not a blind escape from reality but the power to face mortality as extinction and to fear God in his presence.[91] The vacuum of his cultural environment compelled him to reject easy affirmations. He would have admitted that

"There are, as in philosophy, so in divinity,
Sturdy doubts and boisterous objections
Wherewith the unhappiness of our knowledge
Too nearly acquainteth us ... "[92]

In the end, Qoheleth's "modest doubt" strangely coalesced with his "sturdy doubts" and it became what Marianne Moore named

the resolute doubt, —
dumbly calling, deafly listening—that
in misfortune, even death,
     encourages others
     and in its defeat, stirs
the soul to be strong".[93]

The play of Wisdom in the presence of the creator was never

free from the riddle of the human condition. No less than the Poem of Job or the Book of Ecclesiastes, the Book of Proverbs struck a note of threat. Wisdom called men in vain:

> "Since I have called you but you refused [to come],
>   I extended my hand, but no one noticed it.
> You rejected all my counsels,
>   and you would not [accept] my reproof.
> It will be my turn to laugh at your calamity,
>   and to mock when terror falls upon you. [...]
> Then, they will call but I shall not answer;
>   they will search for me agroping, without finding me,
> Because they have hated knowledge
>   and they have not chosen the fear of Yahweh"
>
> (Prov. 1:24–26, 28–29).

Wisdom danced and played (*saḥeq*) in the presence of Yahweh at the birth of the world. Wisdom will now laugh (*saḥaq*) at those who use their "free will"[94] in order to divorce themselves from "knowledge" and "the fear of Yahweh."

There were no *Magnalia Dei* at the Babylonian seizure of Zion in 587 B.C., but the first Jews saw a new form of the *Opus Dei* in their own lives. God was absent from history although he had been present for the fathers at the Sea of Reeds. The sages espoused the theological rigor of the prophets, but they went further. Although Amos and his successors had hailed Yahweh as the creator of heaven and earth, the sages shifted their attention from history—a stage now empty of God—to the theater of the universe, where they detected his presence.

Notes

1. Kenneth Clark interprets this figure as Eve about to be created in God's imagination (*Civilization* [New York, 1969], p. 129). The matter is more complex. By the time of the Renaissance, the Hebraic figure of Cosmic Wisdom had been incor-

porated into medieval Mariology as "the New Eve." See J. Klaczko, *Rome et la Renaissance* (Paris, 1898), p. 328; Ch. de Tolnay, *Michelangelo, II. The Sistine Chapel* (Princeton, 1969), p. 136. cf. the not altogether convincing refutation of H. Thode, *Michelangelo. Kritische Untersuchungen über seine Werke*, I (Berlin, 1908), p. 311 f.

2. J. Huizinga, *Homo Ludens: A Study of the Play-Element in Culture*, paperback ed. (Boston, 1955), p. 107.

3. H. Rahner, *Man at Play*, tr. by B. Battershaw and E. Quinn (New York, 1967), p. 65.

4. W. Zimmerli, "Zur Struktur der alttestamentlichen Weisheit," *ZAW*, LI (1933): 177 ff.; J. Schmidt, *Studien zur Stylistik der alttestamentlichen Spruchliteratur. Alttestamentliche Abhandlungen*, XII (1936); R. E. Murphy, "The Concept of Wisdom Literatur," *The Bible in Current Catholic Thought* (New York, 1962), pp. 46 ff.; *id.*, "Assumptions and Problems in Old Testament Wisdom Research," *CBQ*, XXIX (1967): 101 ff.; *id.*, "Form Criticism and Wisdom Literature," *CBQ*, XXXI (1969): 475 ff.; J. L. Crenshaw, "Method in Determining Wisdom Influence Upon 'Historical' Writing," *JBL*, LXXXVIII (1969): 129 ff.; G. von Rad, *Wisdom in Israel*, tr. by J. D. Martin (Nashville, 1972), p. 15 ff.; R. B. Y. Scott, "The Study of the Wisdom Literature," *In.*, XXIV (1970): 20 ff.; R. N. Whybray, *The Intellectual Tradition in the Old Testament* (Berlin, New York, 1974), pp. 2 ff.

5. See B. Gemser, "The Spiritual Structure of Biblical Aphoristic Wisdom," *Adhuc Loquitur* ([Collected Essays], Leiden, 1968), pp. 168 ff.; G. Fohrer, "Die Weisheit im Alten Testament," *Studien zur alttestamentlichen Theologie* (Berlin, 1969), pp. 242 ff.; von Rad, *Wisdom in Israel*, especially pp. 113 ff.; Whybray, *The Intellectual Tradition*, pp. 31 ff., 123 ff.

6. E. Schmitt, *Leben in den Weisheitsbüchern Job, Sprüche und Jesus Sirach* (Freiburg, 1954); W. Brueggemann, *In Man We Trust: The Neglected Side of Biblical Faith* (Richmond, Va., 1972), pp. 13 ff.

7. See A. Drubbel, "Le conflit entre la sagesse profane et la sagesse religieuse," *Biblica*, XVII (1936): 45 ff., 407 ff.; E. Gerstenberger, *Wesen und Herkunft des "apodiktischen Rechts"* (Neukirchen-Vluyn, 1965); W. Richter, *Recht und Ethos* (München, 1966); H. Duesberg et I. Fransen, *Les scribes inspirés*, 2d ed. (Maredsous, 1966); H. D. Preuss, "Das Gottesbild der älteren Weisheit Israels," *SVT*, XXIII (1972): pp. 117 ff.

8. See extended bibliographies in S. Terrien, "Amos and Wisdom," *Festschrift J. Muilenburg* (New York, 1962), pp. 108 ff.; Brueggemann, *In Man We Trust*, pp. 132 ff.; J. L. Crenshaw, ed., "Wisdom in the OT," *IDB, Suppl. Vol.* (Nashville, 1976), pp. 952 ff.

9. See N. Porteous, "Royal Wisdom," *SVT*, III (1955): 247 ff.; R. B. Y. Scott, "Solomon and the Beginnings of Wisdom in Israel," *ibid.*, pp. 262 ff.; W. McKane, *Prophets and Wisemen* (London, 1965), pp. 15 ff.; H.-J. Hermisson, *Studien zur israelitischen Spruchweisheit* (Neukirchen-Vluyn, 1968), pp. 97 ff.; "Weisheit und Geschichte," *Festschrift G. von Rad* (München, 1971), p. 136 ff.; C. Bauer-Kayatz, *Einführung in die alttestamentliche Weisheit* (Neukirchen-Vluyn, 1969), pp. 13 ff.

10. See J. F. Priest, "Humanism, Skepticism, and Pessimism in Israel," *JAAR*, XXXIV (1968): 311 ff.; H. D. Preuss, "Erwägungen zum theologischen Ort alttestamentlicher Weisheitsliteratur," *Ev. Th.*, XXX (1970): 393 ff.

11. See A. Lods, "Le monothéisme israélite a-t-il eu des précurseurs parmi les 'sages' de l'Ancien Orient?" *RHPR*, XIV (1934): 197 ff.; B. Couroyer, "L'idéal sapiential en Israël en en Égypte," *RB*, LVII (1950): 174 ff.; W. F. Albright, "Some Canaanite-Phoenician Sources of Hebrew Wisdom," *SVT*, III (1955): 1 ff.; G. Couturier, "Sagesse babylonienne et sagesse israélite," *Sciences ecclésiastiques*, XIV (1962): 293 ff.; S. Morenz, "Ägyp-

tologische Beiträge zur Erforschung der Weisheitsliteratur Israëls," *Les sagesses du Proche-Orient ancien* (Paris, 1963), pp. 63 ff.

12. See W. B. Couroyer, "L'origine égyptienne de la Sagesse d'Amenemopé," *RB*, LXX (1963): 208 ff.

13. See W. F. Albright, "The Goddess of Life and Wisdom," *AJSL*, XXXVI (1919–20): 258 ff.; id., *From the Stone Age to Christianity* (Baltimore, 1940), pp. 283 ff.; idem, "Some Canaanite-Phoenician Sources of Hebrew Wisdom," *SVT*, III (1955): 8; C. I. K. Story, "The Book of Proverbs and North-West Semitic Literature," *JBL*, LXIV (1945): 319 ff.; cf. critical observations of R. N. Whybray, *Wisdom in Proverbs* (London, 1965), pp. 83 ff.

14. See H. Conzelmann, "Die Mutter der Weisheit," *Festschrift R. Bultmann* (Tübingen, 1964), pp. 225 ff.

15. See H. Brunner, "Ägyptologie," *Handbuch der Orientalistik*, Vol. I–II (1952), p. 93; S. Morenz, *Egyptian Religion*, tr. by A. E. Keep (Ithaca, N. Y., 1973), pp. 113 ff.

16. See J. Plessis, *Étude sur les textes concernant Ištar-Astarté* (Paris, 1921), p. 57; G. Boström, *Proverbiastudien. Die Weisheit und das fremde Weib in Spr. 1—9* (Lund, 1935), pp. 156 ff.; Whybray, *Wisdom in Proverbs*, pp. 89 ff.

17. Job 28:1–28; Prov. 8:22–31; Sir. 7:1–20, 24:1–34, 51:13–14; Wisd. of Sol. 1:6–7, 7:22–30.

18. See W. Schencke, *Die Chokma (Sophia) in der jüdischen Hypostasenspekulation* (Christiana, 1913), pp. 78 ff.; H. Ringgren, *Word and Wisdom: Studies in the Hypostization of Divine Qualities and Functions in the Ancient Near East* (Lund, 1947); Whybray, *Wisdom in Proverbs*, pp. 78 ff.; M. Hengel, *Palestinian Judaism and the Hellenistic Age* (Philadelphia, 1974), pp. 153 ff.

19. See von Rad, *Wisdom in Israel*, p. 144.

20. For the wide variety of views on this point, see M. Löhr, "Hiob c. 28," *Festschrift P. Haupt* (1926), pp. 67 ff.; S. Terri-

en, *Job, Commentaire* (Neuchâtel, 1963), pp. 191 ff.; G. Fohrer, *Das Buch Hiob* (Gütersloh, 1963), pp. 389 ff.; M. Pope, *Job, The Anchor Bible* (Garden City, N. Y., 1973), p. xxvii.

21. Cf. vss. 20–21, with their progression of thought, in which Wisdom conceals herself from every living being. For the prophets, the self-concealing God shows thereby his disapproval of evil. For the wise, the hiddenness of Wisdom may help to explain or at least to point out human finitude.

22. The erotic overtones of the verbs, while absent from their literal meaning, were congruent with the imagery of Wisdom as a lover. The verb *saphar* in the *pi'el* means "to measure," "to count," "to recount liturgically," and "to celebrate" (Ps. 19:2, etc.). The verb *kûn* in the *hiph'il* means "to prepare," "to make ready," and the verb *haqar*, "to dig," "to excavate," "to search," "to penetrate."

23. *Contra* von Rad, who maintains that this wisdom is not a divine personification but simply the something implanted in creation "to be found somewhere in the world" (*Wisdom in Israel*, p. 148). The poem states specifically that wisdom cannot be found anywhere in the created cosmos, including the underworld and the primeval ocean.

24. "The fear of Adonay" (spelled out in most MSS of the MT rather than the tetragrammaton "Yahweh") designates the intimacy of living in the presence and is inseparable from love and knowledge. Both the fear of the Lord and the knowledge of the Lord are gifts of Wisdom (see Prov. 2:5 ff., etc.).

25. See R. N. Whybray, "Proverbs VIII 22–31 and Its Supposed Prototypes," *VT*, XV (1965): 504 ff.; C. Kayatz, *Studien zu Proverbien 1—9. Eine form-und motivgeschichtliche Untersuchung unter Einbeziehung ägyptisches Vergleichsmaterials* (Neukirchen-Vluyn, 1966); R. Stecher, "Die persönliche Weisheit in den Proverbien Kap. 8," *ZKT*, LXXXIII (1967): 95 ff.; M. Dahood,

"Proverbs 8, 22–31—Translation and Commentary," *CBQ* XXX (1968): 512 ff.; Ch. Bauer-Kayatz, "Die Weisheitsrede (Prov. 8)," in *Einführung in die alttestamentliche Weisheit* (Neukirchen-Vluyn, 1969), pp. 70 ff.; J. de Savignac, "Interprétation de Proverbes VIII 22–23," *SVT*, XVII (1969): 196 ff.; cf. *id.*, "La sagesse en Prov. 8, 22–31," *VT*, XII (1962): 211 ff.; N. C. Habel, "The Symbolism of Wisdom in Proverbs 1—9," *In.*, XXVI (1972): 131 ff.; G. M. Landes, "Creation Tradition in Proverbs 8:22–31 and Genesis 1," *Festschrift J. M. Myers* (Philadelphia, 1974), pp. 279 ff.; B. Lang, *Frau Weisheit. Deutung einer biblischen Gestalt* (Düsseldorf, 1975).

26. The verb *qanah* means "to possess," "to acquire," "to beget." It did not originally mean "to create," although it obtained such a sense in the Hellenistic period. Cf. the Greek translation of Sir. 1:4, 9; 24:8–9. Modern commentators who interpret the phrase "Yahweh created me," do so anachronistically and ignore the verbs of the context (vss. 24 f.) as well as its repeated emphasis on the preexistence of wisdom over the created world. On the complex range of scholarly opinion, see P. Humbert, " 'Qānā' en hébreu biblique," *Festschrift A. Bertholet* (Tübingen, 1950), pp. 259 ff.; C. F. Kraft, "Poetic Structure and Meaning in Prov. 8, 22–31," *JBL*, LXXII (1953): 7 ff.; W. F. Albright, "Notes on Psalms 68 and 134," *Festschrift S. Mowinckel* (Oslo, 1955), pp. 7 ff.; P. Katz, "The Meaning of the Root *qnh*," *JJS*, VI (1955): 126 ff.; H. Cazelles, "L'enfantement de la sagesse en Prov., VIII," *Sacra Pagina* (Gembloux, 1959), I, M. 511 ff.; W. A. Irwin, "Where Shall Wisdom Be Found?" *JBL*, LXXX (1961): 133 ff.; R. N. Whybray, *Wisdom in Proverbs*, pp. 150 f.; D. H. Weiss, "The Use of QNH in Connection with Marriage," *HTR*, LVII (1966): 244 ff.

27. Like Behemoth, in the later poem of Job 40 (vs. 19), Wisdom occupies a position of preeminence vis-à-vis the created cosmos. Unlike Behemoth and Leviathan, however, she is a divine daughter, "begotten, not made." She calls herself "first fruit of [God's] power," which may include procreation as well as creation (cf. the Ugaritic *d.r.k.t.*, "power in act"), but refers to a precreation achievement, since the parallel expression, "prelude of his works of old," unmistakably and perhaps polemically states that the coming of Wisdom into being preceded Yahweh's handiworks (*qedhem mippeʿalayw meʿaz*). Cf. de Savignac, "La sagesse en Prov. 8": pp. 222 ff.; *id.*, "Encore une fois Proverbes VIII 22," *VT*, VIII (1958): 90 ff.

28. The hapax legomenon *nissakhtî* is usually rendered, "I was set up" (from *nasakh III;* cf. Akkad. *nassaku*, "to install"), or "I was fashioned" (from *nasakh II;* cf. Arabic *nasaka*, "to weave"), or again "I was poured out" (from *nasakh I*, "to make a libation"). Some modern commentators favor the third interpretation because Near Eastern myths of "creation" through divine exudation (of tears, sweat, blood, or semen) were not uncommon. The meaning of *nasakh I*, however, argues against this exegesis, for it implies the actual flowing of water, wine, or oil. The nipheʿal of the verb probably indicates a passive voice in the sense of an impersonal act that is performed on the subject: hence, not "I was poured out," but "[someone] poured [something] on me." In all probability, the verb alludes to royal lustration or even unction. Cf. "I have consecrated (rather than "installed") my king on Zion" (Ps. 2:6); also the noun *neṣîkhîm*, "princes" (Jos. 13:21, Ps. 83:11 [Heb. 12], Mic. 5:4, Ezek. 32:30). If Wisdom displays a royal consciousness (cf. Prov. 8:15), the conjecture of an influence of the Isis myth, with its stress on "the Queen of Heaven," receives further support.

29. Literally, "In the nothingness of the fountains loaded with the burden of water."

30. Literally, "the dusts (pl.) of the universe."

31. Literary reminiscences of ancient Near Eastern cosmogonies in which a demiurge conquers and restrains the forces of chaos. Here, the abysses and the fountains of the deep are not preexistent (vss. 24, 28). There is no hint of even a qualified dualism (cf. Gen. 1:1, 2).

32. The hapax legomenon 'amôn has generally been read 'amman, "masterworkman," "architect," "artisan," "artificer" (cf. Song 7:2; from 'aman I, "to confirm," "to support" [e.g., "pillars"]; cf. Akkad. ummanu, "craftsman"; thus, LXX, Syr., et al., including many moderns). This meaning, however, does not fit the context in which Wisdom is a woman who plays and dances in the presence of Yahweh but takes no part in the planning or execution of his work. It is preferable to follow the rendering of Aquila, tithênoumenê, "darling daughter," "nursling," "foster-child," which respects the masoretic pointing ('amôn, also from 'aman I, "to support," in the sense of "to nurse," "to nourish"; cf. 'omen, "foster-father," and 'omeneth, "nurse": see Num. 11:12; Isa. 49:23; 2 Sam. 4:4; 2 Kings 10:1, 5; Ruth 4:16; etc.).

33. The participle pi'el meṣaheqeth means "playing," "making merry," "singing," "playing musical instruments," "making sport," "dancing," (2 Sam. 6:21; cf. the form meṣaheq, masc., used for the love-play of Isaac with Rebekah, Gen. 26:8). In Hellenistic times, the playing and dancing of Wisdom in the presence of Yahweh were interpreted as the celebration of a liturgy: eleitourgesa, "I officiated" (Sir. 24:10a). See O. Keel, "Die Weisheit spielt vor Gott. Ein ikonographischer Beitrag zur Deutung des meṣahäqät in Spr 8, 30 f.," Freiburger Zeitschrift für Philosophie und Theologie, XXI (1974): 1 ff.

34. A time differentiation is implied between Wisdom's playing at creation and Wisdom's enjoying delight with the sons of men. Some translate, "And

my delight was to be with the sons of men." The noun sha'ashu'îm (pl. of "intensity") reflects the palpel voice of the verb sha'a' II, "to sport," "to take pleasure," with a rhythmic connotation of caress, dance, and love-play.

35. Nicene Creed.

36. Prov. 8:1–11, 12–20, 32–36; 9:1–12; 1:20–33; 2:1–9; etc.

37. The stars of Ursa Minor ("The Little Dipper") were known in classical antiquity as "The Dancers" or "The Players" (Hyginus, Poetica astronomica, III, 1, and Germanicus, Scholia strozziana, according to H. Rahner, Man at Play [New York, 1967], p. 72, note 3).

38. Unless one were to explain that the word "creation" means "the creator as revealed in the created world." G. von Rad used the expression in an ambiguous way. See Wisdom in Israel, pp. 144 ff. On the one hand, von Rad looks at wisdom in Job, Proverbs, and Sirach as a quality immanent in creation, not a quality of God, a mysterious element through which the cosmic order turns itself toward man and enables him to live in an harmonious environment. On the other hand, von Rad admits that wisdom, immanent in creation, was differentiated from the "real" world of creation (p. 171). Since there is "an ontological separation of the phenomena within creation," one should also recognize that wisdom partakes of the divine realm.

39. The personification of wisdom as a woman was revolutionary. See E. Jacob, "Principe canonique et formation de l'Ancien Testament," SVT, XXVIII (Leiden, 1975), p. 17.

40. From salal I, in the pilpel, "to titillate," "to embrace," "to hug."

41. See Boström, Proverbiastudien, pp. 15 ff.; P. Humbert, "La femme étrangère du livre des Proverbes," RES, XXVII (1937): 49 ff.; id., "Les adjectifs zar et nokri et la femme étrangère des Proverbes bibliques," Mélanges syriens (Festschrift R. Dussaud), I (Paris, 1939), pp. 259 ff.

42. None of the many interpretations of this phrase has rallied a consensus.

43. See R. Smend, *Die Weisheit des Jesus Sirach* (Berlin, 1906), pp. 216 ff.; J. Hadot, "La 'volonté' dans Ben Sira: Son lien avec la Sagesse," in *Penchant mauvais et volonté libre dans la Sagesse de Ben Sira (L'Ecclésiastique)* (Bruxelles, 1970), pp. 201 ff.; J. Marböck, *Weisheit im Wandel. Untersuchungen zur Weisheitstheologie bei Ben Sirach* (Bonn, 1971), pp. 34 ff.; *id.*, "Gesetz und Weisheit. Zum Verständnis des Gesetzes bei Jesus ben Sira," *BZ*, XX (1976): 1 ff. Hengel, "Ben Sira and the Controversy with Hellenistic Liberalism in Jerusalem," in *Palestinian Judaism and the Hellenistic Age*, pp. 157 ff.

44. See J. A. Sanders, *The Psalms Scroll of Qumrân Cave 11 (11QPsᵃ)*, Discoveries in the *Judaean Desert of Jordan*, Vol. IV (Oxford, 1965), pp. 79 ff.; *id.*, *The Dead Sea Psalms Scroll* (Ithaca, N. Y., 1967), pp. 114 f.; *id.*, "The Sirach 51 Acrostic," *Festschrift A. Dupont-Somer* (Paris, 1971), pp. 429 ff.; M. Delcor, "Le texte hébreu du Cantique de Siracide LI, 13 et ss. et les anciennes versions," *Textus; Annual of the Hebrew University Bible Project*, VI (1968), 39 ff.; Marböck, *Weisheit im Wandel*, pp. 121 ff.

45. See J. Fichtner, ... *Weisheit Salomos* (Tübingen, 1938), pp. 25 ff.; G. Ziener, *Die theologische Begriffssprache im Buche der Weisheit* (Bonn, 1956), pp. 109 ff.; C. Larcher, *Etudes sur le Livre de la Sagesse* (Paris, 1969), pp. 179 ff.; J. M. Reese, *Hellenistic Influence on the Book of Wisdom and Its Consequences* (Rome, 1970), pp. 36 ff.

46. See below, Chapter X.

47. Recent commentators tend to place the origin of the poem before the restoration of the Second Temple. The date of the folktale is still an object of debate. See S. Terrien, "Introduction and Exegesis, The Book of Job," *IB*, III (1954): 877 ff.; *id.*, *Job: Commentaire* (Neuchâtel, 1963); *id.*, "Quelques remarques sur les affinités de Job avec le Deutéro-Esaïe," *SVT*, XV (1966): 295 ff. G. Fohrer, *Das Buch Hiob* (Gütersloh, 1963); R. Gordis, *The Book of God and Man: A Study of Job* (Chicago, 1965), pp. 209 ff.; J. Levêque, *Job et son Dieu: Essai d'exégèse et de théologie biblique*, I (Paris, 1970), pp. 128 ff.; M. H. Pope, *Job: A New Translation with Introduction and Commentary*, 2d Ed. (The Anchor Bible, Garden City. N. Y., 1973), pp. xxxii ff.

48. Cf. R. Frost, *A Masque of Reason* (New York, 1945).

49. The dates of religious feasts are usually observed in some way by inmates and deportees. How could the earliest Jews in exile keep the autumn feast, crown of the year? The poem was probably acted out with chant and musical instruments as part of a paracultic celebration of Tabernacles (Succoth) or even one of the first observances of the New Year (Rosh-Hashanah). Commentators have until recently missed the many allusions of the hero to himself as a mistreated king or royal figure. Like the monarch in the New Year ritual in Babylon, Job is divested of all honor and symbolically put to death. The poem evokes several times and especially in the climactic speech of Yahweh the autumn thunderstorms which are associated with the renewal of nature and the creation of the world (28:25–26, 36:26 —37:22, 38:31–38), while the autumn constellations rise over the horizon (9:9; cf. 38:31). Even in the folktale the heavenly council meets "at the turn" of the seasonal cycle (1:6; cf. vs. 5). See S. Terrien, "Le poème de Job: drame para-cultuel du Nouvel-An?" *SVT*, XVII (1969): pp. 220 ff.; *id.*, "The Yahweh Speeches and Job's Responses," *Review and Expositor*, LXVIII (1971): 497 ff.; *id.*, "Introduction au livre de Job," *Traduction oecuménique de la Bible: Ancien Testament* (Paris, 1975), pp. 1553 ff.

50. See "The Akkadian Acrostic on Theodicy" in W. G. Lambert, *Babylonian Wisdom Literature* (Oxford, 1960), pp. 63 ff., and "The Egyptian Dialogue of the Man Weary of Life" in A. Scharff; *Der Bericht über das Streitgespräch eines Lebensmüden mit seiner Seele* (München, 1937); also J.

A. Wilson, "A Dispute Over Suicide," *ANET*, pp. 405 ff.

51. Gen 32:30 ff.; cf. Hos. 12:5, etc. See above, pp. 85 ff.

52. Even in the folktale; Job was unaware of the mythical scenes in heaven (1:5 ff., 2:1 ff.) in which evil was instigated by "one of the sons of El," not "Satan" as in the traditional translations. The common noun, with the definite article, *has-saṭan,* "the prosecuting attorney," should not be confused with the anarthrous proper name, "Satan," of later Judaism and Christianity (cf. 1 Chron. 21:1 with 2 Sam. 24:1). In the poem, neither Job nor his friends allude to demonic forces in their search for an explanation of misfortune on earth.

53. Plato, *Laws*, 803 b, c; cf. 644 d, e.

54. Shakespeare, *King Lear*, iv, 1, 38.

55. The traditional rendering, "Though he slay me, yet will I trust in him," results from one of the eighteen corrections of the scribes (*tiqqune sopherim*). The oral form of the text understood the negative *lo'*, "not," rather than the personal pronoun *lô*, "to him." The meaning of the phrase was either "I have not any hope" or "I shall not tremble," which reflects an attitude of despair or defiance consonant with the immediate context. Synagogue and church piety preferred a reading which supported the image of a patient Job.

56. See R. J. Clifford, *The Cosmic Mountain in Canaan and the Old Testament* (Cambridge, Mass., 1972), pp. 57 ff.

57. The indefinite pronoun in vs. 21 refers to the witness of vs. 19. It is difficult to identify the "He" with God in the phrase "He will defend man against God."

58. The *go'el*, "vindicator," "avenger," "redeemer," designates the next-of-kin whose obligation is to avenge the honor of a victim of foul play, or "to redeem—purchase—his blood" (2 Sam. 14:14). It may also refer to the closest relative of a dead man who has the right to acquire his property (Ruth 2:20, etc.). *Mutatis mutan-*

dis, Yahweh has been for centuries called "the redeemer of Israel," by allusion to the freeing of the slaves from Egypt (Exod. 6:6, etc.), or the redeemer from oppression, death, or moral evil. Job's redeemer is neither human nor divine. His brethren, retainers, and tribesmen have rejected him (19:13 ff.). The context of 19:25–26 suggests that the redeemer is not God, since he will make the vision of God possible. The figure of the redeemer, like that of the witness (16:19), may have been borrowed from the mythology of the heavenly council. Cf. the "angel" of the later speeches of Elihu (33:23; and vs. 26.). See Terrien, *Job, commentaire,* pp. 149 ff. and notes.

59. *Contra* many moderns who translate "without my flesh," disregarding the syntax of the preposition *min*, which always means "from within" rather than "away from" when it is used with a verb of perception (cf. Ps. 33:13 f.; Song of Sol. 2:9). See Th. H. Meek, "Job XIX, 25–27," *VT*, VI (1956): 100 ff.

60. See M. Burrows, "The Voice from the Whirlwind," *JBL*, XLVII (1928): 117 ff.; W. Lillie, "The Religious Significance of the Theophany in the Book of Job," *ET*, LXVIII (1956–57): 355 ff.; R. A. F. MacKenzie, "The Purpose of the Yahweh Speeches in the Book of Job," *Biblica*, XL (1959): 435 ff.; S. Terrien, "The Yahweh Speeches and Job's Responses," *Review and Expositor*, LXVIII (1971): 497 ff.

61. See R. Voetzel, "Ironie biblique à l'égard de l'homme," *Foi et Vie*, LI (1953): 214 ff.; E. M. Good, *Irony in the Old Testament* (Philadelphia, 1965), pp. 234 ff.

62. See A. Dupont-Sommer, "Nubes tenebrosa et illuminans noctem," *RHR*, CXXV (1942): 66 f.; E. Beaucamp, "Orage et nuée, signes de la présence de Dieu dans l'histoire," *Bible et Vie chrétienne,* III (1953): 33 f.

63. See C. H. Gordon, "Leviathan, Symbol of Evil," in *Biblical Motifs*, ed. by A. Altman (Cambridge, Mass. 1966), pp. 1 ff.

64. Behemoth and Leviathan are earth and sea monsters, respectively, borrowed from the Northwest Semitic mythology. They do not suggest that pre-existent forces of evil limit divine omnipotence because they have been created (Job 40:19; Ps. 104:26). The poet reveals an attitude of sober agnosticism concerning the destructive aspects of nature. See Terrien, *Job, commentaire*, pp. 262 f.

65. Cf. E. E. Kellet, " 'Job': An Allegory?" *ET*, LI (1939–40): 250 ff.; M. Susman, *Das Buch Hiob and das Schiksal des jüdischen Volkes* (Zürich, 1946).

66. The conjecture which interprets the Jobian poem as a paracultic drama performed as "a masque" during the celebration of the autumn festival in exile should not be confused with others which view Job as a late imitation of a Greek tragedy. See H. M. Kallen, *The Book of Job as a Greek Tragedy Restored* (New York, 1918).

67. The exact meaning of the verb *'em'as*, "I sink into the abyss" (vs. 6a), is uncertain. Many translators render it by "I retract [my words]," "I repudiate [what I have said]," or "I despise [myself]." It is unlikely that we have here the common verb *ma'as*, "to despise," for elsewhere it is transitive, whereas it carries in this phrase no direct object. Most probably, this word is a variant of the intransitive verb *masas*, "to melt," "to dissolve" (cf. Job 7:5, 16; Ps. 58:8). The LXX attempted an approximation when it rendered *ephaulisa emauton kai etaken*, "I count myself as a vile man and I faint," while Symmachus on his own has rendered *kategnon emautou*, "I am reduced to fragments." E. Dhorme appears to be right when he translates, "Je m'abîme," "I sink into the abyss" (*La Bible, Bibliothèque la Pléiade, L'Ancien Testament*, II [Paris, 1959], p. 1346). The verb *niḥamtî*, "I grieve" (vs. 6a), should not be translated, "I repent" as if it were *shabhtî*, with its inevitable connotation of ethical behavior. Rather, the poet points to the intensity of grief,

the devastating sense of sorrow which undoes the self, for he uses the verb *niham* in the niph'al (cf. Judg. 21:6; Ps. 90:13, 106:45; Jer. 20:16; Joel 2:14; Zech. 8:12).

68. M. Jastrow, *A Gentle Cynic* (Philadelphia, 1919).

69. On the unity, date, composition, and canonicity of Qoheleth, see G. Barton, *Ecclesiastes* (I. C. C., Edinburgh, 1908); E. Podechard, *L'Ecclésiaste* (Paris, 1912); A. Allgeier, *Das Buch Prediger* (Bonn, 1925); G. Kuhn, *Erklärung des Buches Koheleth* (Giessen, 1926); R. Gordis, *Koheleth—The Man and His World* (New York, 1951); J. Steinmann, *Ainsi parlait Qohêlêt* (Paris, 1955); O. S. Rankin, "Ecclesiastes, Introduction and Exegesis," *IB*, V (1956), pp. 3 ff.; H. W. Hertzberg, *Der Prediger* (Gütersloh, 1961); W. Zimmerli, *Das Buch des Predigers Salomo* (Göttingen, 1962); R. B. Y. Scott, *Proverbs, Ecclesiastes* (Garden City, N. Y., 1965), pp. 191 ff.; A. Strobel, *Das Buch des Predigers* (Düsseldorf, 1967); A. Barucq, *Ecclésiaste—Qohélet. Traduction et commentaire* (Paris, 1968).

70. The name "Qoheleth" appears to be a feminine present participle *qal* of the verb *qahal*, "to assemble" (?), hence the LXX rendering *Ecclesiastes*, "Addresser of the Assembly." A possible allusion to Solomon (1 Kings 3:8; cf. 1 Kings 8:2, 14). See R. Tournay, review of A. Barucq, *Ecclésiaste*, in *RB*, LXXVI (1969): 454.

71. See H. W. Hertzberg, "Palästinische Bezüge im Buch Koheleth," *ZDPV*, LXXIII (1957): 113 ff.

72. The question of the affinities between Qoheleth and popular Greek and Hellenistic philosophy is still a matter of debate. See R. Braun, *Kohelet und die frühhellenistische Popularphilosophie* (Berlin, 1973); cf. E. Horton, "Koheleth's Concept of Opposites as Compared to Samples of Greek Philosophy and Near and Far Eastern Wisdom Classics," *Numen*, XIX (1972): 1 ff.; M. Hengel, *Hellenism and Judaism*, tr. by J. Owen (Philadelphia, 1974), pp. 115 ff.

73. See F. Zimmermann, "The Aramaic

Provenance of Qoheleth," *JQR*, XXXVI (1945): 17 ff.; *id.*, "The Question of Hebrew in Qoheleth," *JQR*, XL (1949–50): 79 ff.; R. Gordis, "The Original Language of Qoheleth," *JQR*, XXXVII (1946): 67 ff.; *id.*, "Koheleth—Hebrew or Aramaic?" *JBL*, LXXI (1952): 93 ff.; *id.*, "Was Koheleth a Phoenician?" *JBL*, LXXIV (1955): 103 ff.; *id.*, "Qoheleth and Qumran—A Study of Style," *Biblica*, XLI (1960): 395 ff.; M. Dahood, "The Language of Qoheleth," *CBQ*, XIV (1952): 227 ff.; *id.*, "Canaanite-Phoenician Influence on Qoheleth," *Biblica*, XXXIII (1952): 30 ff.; *id.*, "Qoheleth and Recent Discoveries," *ibid.*, XLIII (1962); 349 ff.; *id.*, "The Phoenician Background of Qoheleth," *ibid.*, XLVII (1966): 264 ff.; H. L. Ginsberg, "Supplementary Studies in Koheleth." *Proceedings for the American Academy of Jewish Research*, XXI (1952): 35 ff.

74. See H. L. Ginsberg, "The Structure and Contents of the Book of Koheleth," *SVT*, III (1955): 138 ff.; cf. G. Loretz, *Qohelet und das alte Orient* (Freiburg, 1964), pp. 212 ff.; see also G. Castellino. "Qoheleth and His Wisdom," *CBQ*, XXX (1968): 15 ff.; A. G. Wright, "The Riddle of the Sphinx: The Structure of the Book of Qoheleth," *ibid.*, pp. 313 ff.

75. H. H. Blieffert, *Weltanschauung und Gottesglaube in Buche Koheleth* (Rostock, 1938); B. Hessler, "Kohelet: The Veiled God," *The Bridge*, I (1955), pp. 191 ff.; H.-P. Müller, "Wie Sprach Qohälät von Gott?" *VT*, XVIII (1968): 567 ff.; L. Gorssen, "La cohérence de la conception de Dieu dans l'Ecclésiaste," *ETS*, XLVI (1970): 287 ff.; G. von Rad, *Wisdom in Israel*, tr. J. D. Martin (Nashville and New York, 1972), pp. 226 ff.; H. N. Bream, "Life Without Resurrection: Two Perspectives from Qoheleth," *Festschrift J. Myers* (Philadelphia, 1974), pp. 45 ff.; T. Polk, "The Wisdom of Irony: A Study of *Hebel* and Its Relation to Joy and the Fear of God in Ecclesiastes," *Studia biblica et theologica*, vi (1976): 3 ff.

76. Shakespeare, *Troilus and Cressida*, ii, 2, 15 ff.

77. See E. Glasser, *Le procès du bonheur par Qohélet* (Paris, 1970).

78. Eccl. 2:24 ff., etc. On the expression, "the work of God," see G. von Rad, "Das Werk Jahwes," *Festschrift Th. C. Vriezen* (Weigeningen, 1970), pp. 260 ff. Against the view of many moderns, von Rad insists on the positive aspect of Qoheleth's attitude. See *Wisdom in Israel*, pp. 229 ff.

79. See J. Pedersen, "Scepticisme israélite," *RHPR*, X (1930): 317 ff.; *ibid.*, XI (1931), 42 ff.; A. Lauha, Die Krise der religiösen Glaubens bei Kohelet," *SVT*, III (1955): 183 ff.

80. For the many interpretations of this verse, see in addition to the commentaries K. Galling, "Das Rätsel der Zeit im Urteil Kohelets (Koh. 3:1–15)," *ZTK*, LVIII (1961): 1 ff.; J. L. Crenshaw, "The Eternal Gospel (Eccl. 3:11)," *Festschrift J. Ph. Hyatt* (New York, 1974), pp. 23 ff.

81. Cf. Eccl. 5:17; Sir. 14:16, 32:15; Mishnah, *Zabim* 2:2, 3:1; etc.

82. The Greek ideal of "beautiful-and-good" appears in ancient Israel, with moral and aesthetic differences. See T. Boman, *Hebrew Thought Compared With Greek*, tr. by J. L. Moreau (London, 1960), pp. 84 ff.

83. See E. Jenni, *Das Wort ʿolam im Alten Testament* (Berlin, 1953); R. Martin-Achard, "La signification du temps dans l'Ancien Testament," *RTP*, IV (1954): 137 ff.; S. J. DeVries, *Yesterday, Today and Tomorrow: Time and History in the Old Testament* (Grand Rapids, Mich., 1975), pp. 31 f.

84. See Gen. 21:33, Isa. 40:28, etc.

85. See Deut. 5:28, etc.

86. The expression "to place in the heart of" meant "to plant an idea in the mind of," "to give a feeling to," "to suggest a certain course of action." Cf. Ps. 4:8, Exod. 35:34, Ezr. 7:27, Neh. 2:12. In all these passages, God is the subject.

87. Such appears to be the meaning of the expression, "to know good and evil."

This idiom, found thirteen times in Biblical Hebrew, alludes not to moral conscience but to the knowledge of the whole spectrum of possibilities. See J. Bottéro, "L'Ecclésiaste et le problème du mal," *Nouvelle Cléo*, VII–IX (1955–57): 133 ff.; C. C. Forman, "Koheleth's Use of Genesis," *JSS*, V (1960): 256 ff. 88. Cf. J. Fichtner, *Die altorientalische Weisheit in ihrer israelitisch-jüdischen Ausprägung* (Berlin, 1933), pp. 52 ff.; E. Pfeiffer, "Die Gottesfurcht im Buche Kohelet," *Festschrift H. W. Hertzberg* (1965), pp. 133 ff. 89. Cf. G. Nagel, "Crainte et amour de Dieu dans l'Ancien Testament," *RTP*, XXXIII (1945): 175 ff.; S. Plath, *Furcht Gottes. Der Begriff jr'im im Alten Testament* (Stuttgart, 1963); L. Derousseaux. *La crainte de Dieu dans l'Ancien Testament ...* (Paris, 1970); B. Olivier, *La crainte de Dieu comme valeur religieuse de l'Ancien Testament*

(Bruxelles, 1960); T. Polk, "The Wisdom of Irony: A Study of *Hebel* and Its Relation to Joy and the Fear of God in Ecclesiastes," *Studia biblica et theologica*, VI (1976): 3 ff.; G. T. Sheppard, "The Epilogue to Qoheleth as Theological Commentary," *CBQ*, xxxix (1977): 182 ff. 90. H. Melville, *Moby Dick*, ch. 96. 91. See E. Wölfel, *Luther und die Skepsis. Eine Studie zur Kohelet-Exegese Luthers* (München, 1958). 92. Sir Thomas Browne, *Religio Medici*. 93. Marianne Moore, "What Are Years?" *Collected Poems* (London, n.d., p. 99. 94. Observe the rare occurrence of the verb "to will," in the negative (vs. 26), and the stress on the refusal to choose (vs. 29). See Zimmerli, "Struktur": 187; Kayatz, *Studien zu Proverbien 1—9*, pp. 120 ff.; W. McKane, *Proverbs: A New Approach* (Philadelphia, 1970), p. 275; von Rad, *Wisdom in Israel*, p. 161.

8

The Final Epiphany

When Babylon crushed Jerusalem a second time, in 587 B.C., the kingdom of Judah died but Judaism was born. Instead of disintegrating among alien cultures, the Judahites (an ethnic and political group) became the Jews (an ethnic and religious society),[1] because they lived every day in anticipation of the final epiphany.

Hebraism had been founded on divine presence. Judaism arose from divine absence. The fathers had seen the *Magnalia Dei*. The sons knew only national dereliction. During the exodus, Yahweh had parted the Sea and thundered on the Mount. During the exile, the heavens were closed, but the first Jews still prayed to the *Deus absconditus* (Isa. 45:15), and the future only was their inheritance, their prerogative, and their passion. Deprived of sacred space, they discovered the sacrality of time. They transfigured the present by keeping weekly the day of the Sabbath. They erased the past by observing yearly the day of the Atonement. They lived in the future by expecting at any moment the day of the Lord.

The Day of the Sabbath

The origins of the day of the Sabbath are obscure.[2] Was it at first the day of the full moon observed by nomads in addition to the day of the new moon?[3] Or was it a day of rest from agricultural labor? Did it belong from the beginning to a weekly cycle—an hebdomad? Documentary evidence is fragmentary and conflicting.[4] During the exile, in any case, the day of the Sabbath assumed an unprecedented importance.[5]

The prophet Ezekiel in Babylon interpreted the hallowing of the Sabbath as a sign of communion between Yahweh and his people (Ezek. 20:12). The northern (E) tradition of the Mosaic decalogue had justified its observance on the ground of social ethics and humaneness toward slaves and animals of burden.[6] The descendants of the Jerusalem priests who moved in the Ezekielian orbit related the day of rest to the myth of creation (Exod. 20:8-11).

In effect, the priestly circles of Judah, undoubtedly influenced by the sages of the Jerusalem court,[7] presented the keeping of the Sabbath as an *Imitatio Dei*. Cessation from work on the seventh day amounted to a rite of communion with the cosmic creator. By setting the Sabbath apart and making it "holy," the worshippers of Yahweh participated in the divine rest that occurred when creation was completed (Gen. 2:1-4a).

Divine holiness and human repose were brought together in a ritual alchemy of interpenetration. Like Job, invited to share in the wondrous perspective of God's creative act, the average Jew was transformed from within as he articulated his life in relation to the rhythm of divine time. Finite attuning to the infinite actor inserted both human labor and human leisure into the *telos* of creativity. Like wisdom playing and dancing before the cosmic poet, the keeper of the Sabbath was making holy his labor and his rest.

The descendants of the Jerusalem priests went even further

than the liturgists, who recited the myth of cosmic creation (Gen. 1:1—2:4a). They spelled out Ezekiel's emphasis on the divine-human encounter that the Sabbath dramatically enacted every seven days. Like the prehistoric practice of circumcision,[8] the Sabbath became the sign of "an eternal convenant" (Exod. 31:16).[9]

The ceremonial evocation of the "genesis" of the universe (Gen. 1:1—2:4a) was told, not as a cosmogony destined to satisfy para-scientific curiosity, but as a proclamation of the holiness of the Sabbath within the creative act of God.[10] The story of the genesis of the universe does not belong to didactic or epic literature. It constitutes the opening of a living *Torah*. Because it climactically leads to the divine pronouncement of the sacrality of time, it ushers in a new mode of presence. The creator may seem to be absent from history, but he is present in the cosmos and offers man a means of participating in divine creativity. The Sabbath, whatever its prehistoric origins, became for the first Jews a sacrament of presence.

With the destruction of the temple, sacred space became obsolete. By keeping the Sabbath, the first Jews entered into an active "con-templation" of the *Opus Dei*. The Sabbath was now their temple, and became in effect a source of revelation. It was as if they had heard their God, absent from history, say to them on the Sabbath: "When two or three are gathered in my name, I am in the midst of them."[11] The prophetic theology of the name allied itself in exile with the sapiential theology of creation and radically transformed the priestly theology of cultic presence. The uniqueness of the holy place, through the Sabbath, became an interior and universal reality. The awareness of the sacrality of time enabled the first Jews to create the synagogue.[12]

Ancient Semitic cosmogonies had concluded in temple building. The proto-Canaanite liturgy of Baal,[13] as well as the Babylonian epic of *Enu-ma elish*,[14] conforms to this pattern. The priestly story of cosmic creation led not to the erection of a sanctuary but to the consecration of the Sabbath. Although the Jerusalem priests of the Ezekielian circle were immersed in the myth of Zion, they dared the most remarkable innovation when they substituted the Sabbath for the temple ideology.[15]

In spite of differences in terminology, the motif of divine rest (*shabbath*) called to mind that of Yahweh's "rest" (*menuḥah*), which designated the Jerusalem sanctuary (Ps. 132:8, 14, etc.). It is quite probable that the myth tellers presented the Sabbath as the climax of creation at a time when the temple lay in ruins. Consciously or not, they transferred to the Sabbath the element of dynamic vitality that was originally inherent in the theology of cultic presence. Yahweh's residence in the *hagios topos* was transfigured into Yahweh's presence in the *hagios kairos*.

Clearly, the notion of divine rest did not suggest a connotation of lethargic passivity anticipatory of philosophical deism. The faith of the fathers and of the prophets had always pictured Yahweh as a doer. Even if historical events precipitated a mood of national despair, the sixth-century Jews were not affected by a sense of cosmic solitude. Absent from history, Yahweh was present in the universe. A suspense of judgment maintained a cautious agnosticism vis-à-vis the *Gesta Dei* among nations, but the celebration of the Sabbath enabled the uprooted Jews to participate in the *Opus Dei*. Isaiah had compared the God of Israel to a vintner tirelessly tending his vineyard (Isa. 5:2). Those who rehearsed the myth of creation communed with the spirit of Elohim, striving over the face of the waters (Gen. 1:2). They also celebrated his rest (Gen. 2:1 ff.).

The seventh day did not call for a withdrawal of activity but for a renewal of vitality. "And the seventh day he rested and renewed his being" (*wayyinnaphash;* Exod. 31:17).[16] By comparison with the context of the six days, the seventh day alone was "open ended." It stood without an evening and without a morning (cf. Gen. 1:31 with 2:2–3). Linked to the completion of the universe, the Sabbath pointed to the *eschaton*, the final epiphany. Creation fulfilled is the new creation expected by the prophets and the psalmists. The Sabbath of God is recreation in both senses of the word. Wisdom dances and plays in the presence of the creator, and mankind celebrates the Sabbath in anticipation of the fulfillment of time.

By observing the Sabbath, man becomes "present to reality"[17] Not only his work but also his rest is transfigured into "an act of presence,"[18] which is the basis of all worship.[19]

When the second or third generation of the Jerusalem priesthood in exile pursued the task of revising and editing the legal traditions it had inherited from the era of the monarchy, it incorporated the Sabbath observance into the end of its description of the wilderness tabernacle—the exilic blueprint for a new theology of presence.[20] By a paradoxical twist of religious fluctuation, the Sabbath, which a few years previously had received a cultic meaning in the cultic vacuum of the Exile, now assumed a new significance within the ceremonial observances of the Second Temple. Associated with the ideology of "the rest of the people of God,"[21] it eventually lost the universal scope of its setting within the epic of creation. Inclusive and open, it became exclusive and closed, the restrictive "sign of an eternal covenant with Israel" (Exod. 31:17*a*).

The Day of the Atonement

The Jerusalem priesthood in exile prepared for an eventual return to the land of Judah. In his mature years (ca. 573 B.C.) the sacerdotal prophet Ezekiel initiated a ritualistic movement[22] which led to the codification of many ancient practices. Eventually, the laws of the Code of Holiness (in the Book of Leviticus) and the Priestly Code (especially in the Books of Exodus and Numbers)[23] took precedence over the ancient legislation.

After Cyrus of Persia conquered Babylon and allowed the repatriation of the deportees to their homelands (539–38 B.C.), priestly families and a comparatively small number of Jews—no doubt of a ritualistic persuasion—returned to Jerusalem.[24] Many remained abroad and eventually prospered under the relatively enlightened policies of the Persian empire.[25] A tension inevitably developed between the economically and culturally successful Diaspora and the sacerdotal community which built the Second Temple.[26]

As early as 549 B.C., Second Isaiah had foreseen a return to Zion, but he pictured such an event as a new exodus in the context of a new creation. A *via sacra* across a blossoming desert would lead directly from Babylon to Jerusalem, and the rebuilding of the sanctuary would usher in the final epiphany:

"The glory of Yahweh shall be revealed,
    and the whole of mankind shall see it"

(Isa. 40:5).

The old theology of glory was invoked, but only within the myth of a suprahistorical economy of human existence.[27]

The return did take place, but the hoped-for eschatology was delayed. In 520–19 B.C., the prophet Haggai sounded a note of urgency:[28]

". . . build the house,
that I may delight in it and appear in my glory, says Yahweh"

(Hag. 1:8).

At about the same time, the prophet Zechariah announced the imminence of Yahweh's advent[29] in a language reminiscent of the priestly description of the wilderness tabernacle.[30]

"Sing and rejoice, O daughter Zion,
    For, behold! I am about to come
    And I will sojourn in the midst of you, says Yahweh"

(Zech. 2:10 [Heb. 14]).

A new temple of modest appearence was at last erected in the ruins of the old (516 B.C.),[31] but the expected epiphany was again delayed *sine die*. Some of the old ceremonial was restored, but a profound change affected the new cult.

Ever since the first exodus, Israel had worshiped her divine savior with music, dance, and song. Immediately after the deliverance from the Egyptian army and the threat of the Sea of Reeds, tradition maintained that "the prophetess Miriam, sister of Aaron, took a timbrel in her hand and all the women went out after her with timbrels and they danced, and Miriam sang to them, 'Sing to Yahweh, for he is greatly exalted' (Exod. 15:20–21). The mood of rejoicing "in the presence of Yahweh" persisted in ancient Israel and Judah throughout the era of the conquest and the monarchy.[32] In time of national crisis, when fasting and mourning were decreed, holocausts (*'ôlôth*) were offered,[33] but in normal times the services of praise were held in high festivity. Communion sacrifices (*zebhaḥim* or *zebhaḥim shelamim* or *shelamim*),[34] the meaning of which varied in the course of the centuries,[35] were the occasions for communal banqueting and drinking. Before the exile, "to worship" was "to have mirth before Yahweh."[36]

The Babylonian disaster brought about a dramatic contrast. The inhabitants of the old territory of northern Israel, as well as the Judahites who had escaped deportation, made pilgrimages to the site of the ruined temple. With torn garments, shaved beards, and gashed bodies, they brought cereal offerings and incense to the hidden Lord of Zion (Jer. 41:4 ff.). Laments and ritual weeping could be heard on the roads leading to the holy place (Lam. 1:4). Years later, even after the return of some exiles from Babylon, the anniversary of the burning of the temple was still marked with fasting and mourning (Zech. 7:3 ff.). To worship was no longer "to rejoice before Yahweh" but "to make atonement" (*kipper*) for the guilt of the nation.

Expiatory sacrifices—the "sin-offering" (*hatta'th*) and the "guilt-offering" (*'asham*)—dominated the ceremonial.[37] Ritual features inherited from the ancient Northwest Semitic cults received official recognition.[38] Elements of apotropaic and prophylactic magic were subtly mixed with specifically religious concerns for forgiveness and reconcilation.[39]

The ambiguous character of the ritual which was performed on the Day of the Atonement (*yom kippur* or *yom hak-kippurim*) appears in the double meaning of the verb *kipper*, "to expiate" and "to atone."[40] Expiation pointed to the purification of the unclean, but it was never made clear whether the stain of ritual impurity was related to moral evil or to the violation of taboos that had been inherited from a pre-Hebraic past. Atonement was aimed at healing a breach ("at-one-ment") and reconciling the rupture between God and man.

While the slaughtering of the goat and the sprinkling of its blood on the one hand, and the release of the scapegoat into the wilderness on the other, represented the survival of magical techniques, the legislators insisted on the requirement that the whole ceremony be performed "in the presence of Yahweh" (Lev. 16:7 ff., etc.). Nevertheless, the stress was on human initiative. It was the high priest who "made atonement" (Lev. 16: 6, etc.).

In spite of its magical and amoral aspects, the ceremony of the Day of the Atonement fulfilled an important function. At the end of the sixth century B.C., the Second Temple community was clearly obsessed with collective fears and a pathological sense of national guilt. Expiatory rites attempted to make daily existence endurable. In addition, the ceremonial of the Day of the Atonement brought man into the very presence of God.

The testimony of Jesus ben Sirach, at the turn of the third century B.C., filled in the bareness of the legal prescriptions with the color of personal emotion. In praising the high priest of his time, Sirach described the concluding part of the ceremony in a style of lyrical hyperbole:

50:5 How glorious [the high priest] was
      when the people gathered around him
      as he came out of the house of the veil,
   6 Like the morning star among the clouds,
      like the moon when it is full!

  14 Completing the service at the altars,
      and placing the oblation before the Most High, the
         Almighty,
  15 He took the cup in his hand
      and poured the libation of the blood of the grape.

  17 Then all the people hastened together
      to prostrate themselves to the ground
      in order to worship their Lord, the Almighty, God Most
         High.

  20 At last [the high priest] came down and lifted his hands
      over the whole congregation of the sons of Israel
      To utter with his lips the benediction of the Lord
      and to pride himself in his name.

Through the intermediary of the high priest, the reality of presence was transmitted from a direct encounter in the Holy of Holies to the assembly (LXX, *ecclesia*) of the sons of Israel (vs. 20). Entering the innermost room (cf. vs. 5), the celebrant brought the blood of the slaughtered goat "within the veil" (Lev. 16:15). Not unlike Moses facing the numinous obscurity of the *'araphel* in the Sinai-Horeb theophany (Exod. 20:18), the high priest was alone with the Deity. As he emerged from "the house of the veil" (vs. 5), he carried with him the radiance of divine holiness (vss. 6 ff.).

The theology implied by this description is significant. The rite differed from the "apotheosis" or from the dramatically enacted "theophaneia" of the Egyptian, Mesopotamian, and

Greek temples, in which the statue of a god or goddess was actually brought forward in full view of the worshippers. True to its principle of imageless worship, Jewish faith introduced no gesture of "monstrance" into its cult. Nevertheless, the high priest was held to be the delegated representative of the Deity, and the temple served as the theater of a solemn dispensation. Cultus was not just the response of praise to the *anamnesis* of the past in anticipation of the final epiphany. It had become an event which proffered to the faithful a double commodity: a blanket assuaging of guilt and the comforts of reconciliation with a God who made his presence available to all.

The sight of pontifical sacrality was further enhanced by the potency of the benediction.[41] The combination of gesture and word objectified the reality which the benediction conveyed and perhaps contained. It also subjectified its appropriation by the assembly. Through the perception of the senses, "the sons of Israel"[42] received the sacrament of real presence. Since the formula of benediction was most probably the so-called Blessing of Aaron (Num. 6:22 ff.),[43] it is possible to spell out the words which the high priest uttered:

> The Lord bless thee and keep thee!
> The Lord make his face to shine upon thee
>   and be gracious unto thee!
> The Lord lift up his countenance upon thee
>   and give thee peace!
>
> (vs. 206.)

First, the blessing implied that the liturgical moment was continued in time, and that the benefits of the presence included protection from evil: "The Lord bless thee and keep thee." Second, the blessing implied a transfer of the radiance, not only from the Deity to the high priest but also from the high priest to the worshippers. In effect, the transfer of this radiance became a channel of divine grace: "The Lord make his face to shine upon thee and be gracious unto thee." Third, blessing implied the "at-one-ment" which resulted from the forgiveness of guilt, for it recalled the gesture of a judge signifying a verdict of acquittal, and its final fruit was peace. Divine peace (*shalom*) meant the growth of the individual and the health (*shalem*) of the community: "The Lord lift up his countenance upon thee and give thee peace."

Modern psychoanalysis may throw a light on the unconscious processes by which ritual acts have a therapeutic value. The collective aspect of participatory forgiveness, however, tends to dull the rigor of personal decision and the seriousness of behavioral commitment. Atonement ceremonial contains a built-in element of amorality. The sacral gesture, which draws upon the hidden memory of some archetypal unsconscious, may be a factor of unity and tolerance toward other cultures, but it also leads to a sense of false security and of pride. It tends even to blur the distinction between truth and error.

One may not go as far as Jean-Paul Sartre and maintain that "truth and fable are the same . . . Man is a ceremonial being."[44] Nevertheless, the positive gain of ritual in effecting reconciliation carries within it the seed of self-deception.

A far more serious danger in a theology of mediated presence lies in the corruptibility of the mediating agent. Unlike the ancient Near Eastern cults, Hebraic Yahwism had been free of sacerdotalism. In ancient Israel, priests were at first the keepers of the shrines and the preservers of the correct liturgy. They did not offer sacrifices on the behalf of ordinary people.[45] With the Deuteronomic reform (621 B.C.) and especially the crisis of the exile, the Jerusalem priesthood assumed a status of sacral uniqueness which led to a cultic separation between "a clergy" and "a laity." The Yahwist principle of priesthood for the entire nation (Exod. 19:6) was slowly eroded during the monarchy and eradicated during the exile. The levitical priests of the provincial sanctuaries were demoted as their descendants became "the Levites," or the cultic assistants to the Zadokites—the Jerusalem priesthood—who monopolized the sacerdotal function and status.[46] The "head priest" of the Jerusalem Temple, who was entrusted during the monarchy with the administration of the sacerdotal college, acquired an ontological sacrality during the exile. He became "the high priest," or *pontifex maximus*, of a theocratic hierarchy.[47]

Within the governmental structures of the Persian empire (538–333 B.C.) and later of the Hellenistic kingdoms, first Ptolemaic and then Seleucid (333–168 B.C.), the Second Temple community was in effect ruled by the high priests. It was the corruption of the high priestly office which brought about the persecution of Antiochus IV Epiphanes (168 B.C.). While the Maccabean revolt promised a new era, the collusion of the king and the high priesthood under the Hasmonean dynasty (161–67 B.C.) accelerated among the religious masses the spread of a deep suspicion against the temple and the sacerdotal authority. It was this suspicion which was largely responsible for the sectarian movements. In their opposition to official Judaism, many pinned their hopes on their belief in the imminence of the day of the Lord and his final epiphany.

THE DAY OF THE LORD

When and how did ancient Israel begin to speak of "the day of Yahweh"? This question is open to debate.[48] It is possible that the early Hebrews spoke of "the day of Yahweh" as they fought their enemies in the desert and in the land of Canaan.[49] Their descendants used the terminology of the Holy War when they looked forward to the end of history and hoped that, at last, Yahweh would have his day of triumph. Eventually, this nationalistic perspective was corrected by the theology of creation.[50] For the eighth- and seventh-centuries prophets, especially

Amos and Zephaniah,[51] the day of Yahweh would be the time when Yahweh would judge his own people as well as all the nations:

> "For he comes, for he comes to judge the earth.
> He will judge the world with righteousness,
> And the peoples with truth"
>
> (Ps. 96:13).[52]

A second temple was built in 516 B.C. but Yahweh did not come down to inhabit his "house." As the fierce desire for the final epiphany continued unabated, a deep-seated hostility toward the earthly sanctuary developed and eventually contributed to the growth of the myth of the heavenly Jerusalem.

Some disciples of Second Isaiah, at the end of the sixth century B.C., chose to maintain the prophetic ideal of a spiritual presence.

> Thus says Yahweh, Heaven is my throne,
> and the earth is my footstool.
> What house will you build for me,
> and what place for my rest?
> All these things my hand has made,
> and all these things are mine,[53] oracle of Yahweh.
> But this is the man to whom I will look,
> he who is humble and contrite of spirit,
> and who trembles at my word
>
> (Isa. 66:1–2).[54]

The anthology of Third Isaiah (Isa. 56–66) reflected the tensions which pulled Judaism apart at the end of the sixth century B.C. and which continued to produce a wide diversity of religious modes of thinking during the Persian, Hellenistic, Maccabean-Hasmonean, and Roman eras.

Opposition to an earthly temple[55] was related to the hope that the day of Yahweh would bring a radical transformation of nature and history. In the new Zion, the human and the divine realm would at last coalesce.[56]

At the turn of the fifth century B.C., the prophet Joel proclaimed that Yahweh would defeat his enemies, purify his people, and finally inhabit his temple. The new Jerusalem would then become in actuality the holy city (Joel 3 [Heb., 4]: 14–18).[57] In the following generation, an anonymous prophet known as Malachi ("my messenger") reaffirmed the advent of the Lord in his temple:

> "Behold, I am sending my messenger to prepare the way
> before me,
> And Yahweh, whom you seek, will suddenly come to his
> temple. . . .
> But who can endure the day of his coming,
> And who can stand when he appears?"
>
> (Mal. 3:1, 2.)

In the relative prosperity of Hellenistic times, the Jerusalem cult received wide approval, as shown by the favorable testimonies of Tobit (13:16 ff.) and Jesus ben Sirach.[58] With the horrors of the Maccabean wars and especially, a century later, under the duress of Roman oppression, many Jews found religious comfort in the apocalyptic literature.[59] For more than two hundred years (ca. 165 B.C. to A.D. 70), such writings as Daniel, 1 Enoch, the Assumption of Moses, 2 Baruch, 2 Enoch, 4 Ezra, the Apocalypse of Abraham, and 3 Baruch enabled the masses to endure national humiliation and personal hardship. Apocalyptic literature described the events of the end of time, the advent of the Messiah, the victory of the people of God over their enemies, and the establishment of the heavenly kingdom. It is significant that the themes of the new temple and of the heavenly Jerusalem occupied a central place in these expectations.[60]

Like most of the apocalyptists, the sectarians of Qumran rejected the authority of the high priests, and they thought of themselves as "the new temple." Since they respected the cultic aspects, in minute detail, of the Torah, one cannot say that they spiritualized the theology of presence; but they transferred the symbolism of the temple to their own community, which they called "a sanctuary" and "the holy of holies."[61] At the edge of their rocky cliffs overlooking the Dead Sea, "the servants of the presence of the glory"[62] waited for the final epiphany.

Typically, the word *Shekinah,* which the rabbis in post-biblical times[63] used to describe the presence of the Lord in the world—a presence which had been absent from the Second Temple—stood as a linguistic echo of the desert memories when Yahweh "sojourned" (*shaken*) in a nomadic tent.

For more than a thousand years, the religion of Israel was dominated by the experience, the memory, or the hope of divine presence.[64] Some of the psalmists were convinced that Yahweh was "near to all who call upon him" (Ps. 145:18), and one went so far as to express in song his fearful inability to escape the divine face (Ps. 139:7 ff.). The abstract word "omnipresence," however, is inadequate to describe their awareness of communion. The entire literature now preserved in the Hebrew Bible referred to specific "events" of divine manifestation in terms of time and space.

The national epic was structured on the stories of epiphanic visitations to the patriarchs and of the Mosaic theophanies. Yahweh was portrayed as descending from the heavens (Ps. 18:10; cf. 2 Sam. 22:10), going forth from Seir (Judges 5:4), marching in the desert (Ps. 68:8 f.), coming from Sinai, shining forth from Mount Paran (Deut. 33:2). The cultus of the early sanctuary and of the Jerusalem temples represented attempts to perpetuate the theophanic moments. It was a theology of cultic presence which informed the thinking of the prophets and of the apocalyptists, even when they were compelled to condemn temple worship. Both cult and law were channels of revelation, and both were corrected by wisdom and apocalyptic. The tension between the presence in creation and the presence in the temple was not resolved, nor was the tension between presence now and presence at the end of time.

At the dawn of the Roman Empire, a handful of Jews hailed from their own ranks a new prophet through whom they discerned a radically new mode of divine nearness. A man became for them the bearer of the presence.

Notes

1. See above, pp. 207 ff.

2. See M. Tsevat, "The Basic Meaning of the Biblical Sabbath," *ZAW*, LXXXIV (1972): 447 ff.; H. W. Wolff, "The Day of Rest in the Old Testament," *Concordia Theological Monthly*, XLIII (1972): 498 ff.; N.-E. Andreasen, *The Old Testament Sabbath. A Traditio-Historical Investigation* (Cambridge, Mass., 1972); id., "Recent Studies of the Old Testament Sabbath— Some Observations," *ZAW*, LXXXVI (1974): 453 ff.; B. E. Shafer, "Sabbath," *IDB, Suppl. Vol.* (1976), pp. 760 ff.

3. See A. Caquot, "Remarques sur la fête de la 'néoménie' dans l'ancien Israël," *RHR*, CLVIII (1960): 1 ff.

4. Cf. A. Lemaire, "Le sabbat à l'époque royale israélite," *RB*, LXXX (1973): 161 ff.

5. See above, p. 268. See H.-J. Kraus, *Worship in Ancient Israel*, tr. by G. Buswell (Richmond, Va., 1966), p. 87; G. von Rad, *Genesis*, tr. by J. Marks (Philadelphia, 1966), p. 60; cf. P. R. Ackroyd, *Exile and Restoration* (London, 1968), pp. 34 f.

6. See Deut. 5:12 ff., Exod. 23:12. The perspective of the northern tradition, reflected in the Deuteronomic preaching, was grounded on the cultic *anamnesis* of the *Magnalia Dei:* "Thou shalt remember that thou wast a slave in the land of Egypt" (Deut. 5:15).

7. G. M. Landes, "Creation Tradition in Proverbs 8:22–31 and Genesis 1," *Festschrift J. M. Myers* (Philadelphia, 1974), pp. 279 ff.; C. Westermann, *Genesis* (Neukirchen-Vluyn, 1968), pp. 230 ff.

8. The priestly emphasis on the theological character of circumcision (Gen. 17:9 ff., etc.) constituted a radical departure from the earlier practice. By linking circumcision to the "eternal covenant," the priests gave prominence to males and contributed to the cultic degradation of womanhood in Judaism.

9. See B. S. Childs, *The Book of Exodus* (Philadelphia, 1974), pp. 415 ff.

10. At the same time, the myth of creation in Genesis should not be viewed from the perspective of the modern conflict between science and religion. See G. von Rad, *Old Testament Theology*, I tr. by D. M. G. Stalker (New York, 1962), p. 148.

11. Matt. 18:20; cf. *Pirke Aboth* 3:3: "Two who sit together and occupy themselves with the words of the Torah have the *Shekinah* (The divine presence)."

12. See A. Menès, "Tempel und Synagogue," *ZAW*, L (1932): 268 ff.; J. Morgenstern, "The Origin of the

Synagogue," *Festschrift L. della Vida* (1956), II, pp. 192 ff.; J. Weingreen, "The Origin of the Synagogue," *Hermathena*, XCVIII (1964): 68 ff.

13. See H. L. Ginsberg, "Poems About Baal and Anath," *ANET*, pp. 137 ff.; C. H. Gordon, *Ugaritic Literature* (Rome, 1949), pp. 34 ff.

14. See E. A. Speiser, "The Creation Epic," *ANET*, p. 68 ff.

15. See von Rad, *Genesis*, pp. 59 ff.

16. This verb is related to the noun *nephesh*, commonly translated by "soul," which designates the totality of being-ness in an individual person. See J. Pedersen, "The Soul, Its Powers and Capacity," in *Israel, Its Life and Culture*, I-II (Oxford and Copenhagen, 1926), pp. 99 ff.; D. Lys, *Nèphèsh: Histoire de l'âme dans la révélation d'Israël au sein des religions proches orientales* (Paris, 1959); H. W. Wolff, *Anthropology of the Old Testament*, tr. by M. Kohl (Philadelphia, 1973), pp. 10 ff. Significantly, the editors of the priestly traditions now preserved in the Book of Exodus have inserted this special prescription on the Sabbath as a conclusion to the priestly description of the wilderness tabernacle—an exilic program for a new theology of cultic presence. See R. E. Clements, "The Crisis of the Exile and the Priestly Re-Interpretation of the Cult," in *God and Temple* (Philadelphia, 1965), pp. 111 ff.

17. N.-E. Andreasen, "Festival and Freedom," *In.*, XXXVIII (1974): 281 ff.

18. L. Lavelle, *The Dilemma of Narcissus*, tr. by W. T. Gairdner (London and New York, 1973), p. 74.

19. *id., ibid.*

20. J. Pieper, *Leisure. The Basis of Culture*, tr. by A. Dru (New York, 1952), p. 56.

21. Deut. 12:9 ff., 25:19; Josh. 21:43 ff.; 1 Kings 8:56; 2 Chron. 6:4 ff.; Ps. 95:11; cf. Heb. 3:11 ff., in which the rest of God and the rest of God's people are skillfully brought together. See G. von Rad, "There Remains Still a Rest for the People of God: An Investigation of a Bib-

lical Conception [1933]," *The Problem of the Hexateuch and Other Essays*, tr. by E. W. Trueman Dicken (Edinburgh and London, 1966), pp. 94 ff.

22. See above, pp. 212 ff.

23. See P. Grelot, "La dernière étape de la rédaction sacerdotale," *VT*, VI (1956): 174 ff.; R. E. Clements, "The Priestly Re-Interpretation of the Cult," *God and Temple* (Philadelphia, 1965), pp. 110 ff.; M. Haran, "The Priestly Image of the Tabernacle," *HUCA*, XXXVI (1965): 191 ff.; B. A. Levine, "The Descriptive Tabernacle Texts of the Pentateuch," *JAOS*, LXXXV (1965): 307 ff.

24. See the genealogical lists of Ezra 2:1–70, Neh. 7:6 ff.; cf. F. Michaéli, *Les livres des Chroniques, d'Esdras et de Néhémie* (Neuchâtel, 1967), pp. 256 ff.; J. M. Myers, *Ezra. Nehemiah* (Garden City, N. Y., 1965), pp. 14 ff., 223 ff. See also R. L. Braun, "The Message of Chronicles: Rally 'Round the Temple'," *Concordia Theological Monthly*, XLII (1971): 502 ff.

25. See P. R. Ackroyd, *Exile and Restoration. A Study of Hebrew Thought in the Sixth Century BC* (London, 1968), pp. 138 ff.

26. See H. Mantel, "The Dichotomy in Judaism During the Second Temple," *HUCA*, XLIV (1973–74): 55 ff.

27. Isa. 40:3 ff., 41:17 ff., 43:16 ff., 52:7 ff., etc. See Th. Chary, *Les prophètes et le culte à partir de l'exil* (Tournai, 1955), pp. 78 ff.; C. Stuhlmueller, *Creative Redemption in Deutero-Isaiah* (Rome, 1970), pp. 66 ff.

28. See P. R. Ackroyd, *Exile and Restoration* (1970), pp. 153 ff.

29. See L. G. Rignell, *Die Nachtgesichte des Sacharja. Eine exegetische Studie* (Lund, 1950), pp. 94 ff.; P. R. Ackroyd, *Exile and Restoration* (1970), pp. 171 ff.

30. Exod. 25:8 ff., 29:45 ff., 40:34 ff.; Lev. 26:11 ff.; etc. See B. S. Childs, *The Book of Exodus*, pp. 540 ff.

31. See A. Gelston, "The Foundation of the Second Temple," *VT*, XVI (1966): 232 f.; Ackroyd, *Exile and Restoration* (1968), pp. 142 ff.; R. de Vaux, "The Decrees of Cyrus and Darius on the Re-

building of the Temple," *The Bible and the Ancient Near East*, tr. by D. McHugh (London, 1972), pp. 63 ff.; D. L. Petersen, "Zerubbabel and the Jerusalem Temple Reconstruction," *CBQ*, XXXVI (1974): 366 ff.

32. 1 Sam. 2:1 ff., Deut. 12:7, etc.

33. See R. de Vaux, *Studies in Old Testament Sacrifice* (Cardiff, 1964), pp. 27 ff.; R. Rendtorff, *Studien zur Geschichte des Opfers im Alten Testament* (Neukirchen-Vluyn, 1967), pp. 74 ff.; B. A. Levine, *In the Presence of the Lord: A Study of Cult and Some Cultic Terms in Ancient Israel* (Leiden, 1974), pp. 22 ff.

34. Usage varied with nuances of meaning, from "slaughter" (*zebhaḥ*), to "communion meal" (*zebhaḥ shelamim*) to "communion" (*shelamim*). See de Vaux, *Studies*, pp. 31 ff., 37 ff., 42 ff.; Rendtorff, *Studien*, pp. 119 ff.

35. See Levine, *In the Presence*, pp. 27 ff., 45 ff.

36. See P. Humbert, "*Laetari* et *exultare* dans le vocabulaire religieux de l'Ancien Testament ..." *Opuscules d'un hébraïsant* (Neuchâtel, 1958), pp. 119 ff.

37. See de Vaux, *Studies*, pp. 91 ff.; Rendtorff, *Studien*, pp. 199 ff.; Levine, *In the Presence*, pp. 55 ff.

38. See A. Lods, "Eléments anciens et éléments modernes dans le rituel du sacrifice israélite," *RHPR*, VIII (1928): 399 ff.; R. Dussaud, *Les origines cananéennes du sacrifice israélite* (Paris, 1921).

39. See S. Landesdorfer, *Studien zum biblischen und Versöhnungstag Sündenbock* (1924); M. Löhr, *Das Ritual von Lev. 16* (1925); R. Schur, *Versöhnungstag und Sündenbock* (1934); E. Auerbach, "Neujahrs- und Versöhnungs-Fest in den biblischen Quellen," *VT*, VIII (1958): 337 ff.; R. Rendtorff, *Die Gesetze in der Priesterschrift* (Göttingen, 1963), pp. 59 ff.; Noth, *Leviticus*, tr. by J. E. Anderson (Philadelphia, 1965), pp. 117 ff.; Levine, *In the Presence* pp. 79 ff.

40. See Levine, "Kipper and the Israelite Blood Rites," *In the Presence*, pp. 67 ff.

41. See A. Murtonen, "The Use and Meaning of the Words Leᵇbarek and Beᵇrakah in the Old Testament," *VT*, IX (1959): 158 ff.; C. Westermann, *Die Segen in der Bibel und im Handeln der Kirche* (München, 1968); G. Wehmeier, *Die Segen im Alten Testament. Ein semasiologische Untersuchung der Wurzel brk* (Basel, 1970).

42. In the Second Temple, women were segregated in a special court.

43. See J. I. Durham, "Shalom and the Presence of God," *Festschrift G. Henton Davies* (Richmond, Va., 1970), pp. 286 ff.; D. N. Freedman, "The Aaronic Benediction (Numbers 6:24–26)," *Festschrift J. L. McKenzie* (Missoula, Mont., 1975), pp. 35 ff.; P. D. Miller, "The Blessing of God: An Interpretation of Numbers 6:22–27," *In.*, XXIX (1975): 240 ff.

44. J.-P. Sartre, *Les mots* (Paris, 1964), p. 69.

45. See A. H. J. Gunneweg, *Leviten und Priester. Hauptlinien der Traditionsbildung und Geschichte des israelitisch-jüdischen Kultpersonals* (Göttingen, 1965); A. Cody, *A History of Old Testament Priesthood* (Rome, 1969); P. J. Budd, "Priestly Instructions in Pre-Exilic Israel," *VT*, XXIII (1973): 1 ff.

46. See J. Bowman, "Ezekiel and the Zadokite Priesthood," *Glasgow University Oriental Society Transactions*, XVI (1955–56): 1 ff.; J. Mauchline, "Aaronite and Zadokite Priests: Some Reflections on an Old Problem" *GUOST*, XXI (1965–66): 1 ff.; P. D. Hanson, "The Rise of the Hierocratic Party of the Zadokites," in *The Dawn of Apocalyptic* (Philadelphia, 1975), pp. 220 ff.

47. See R. de Vaux, "Le grand prêtre," *Les Institutions del'Ancien Testament*, II (Paris, 1960), pp. 366 ff.; G. Fohrer, *History of Israelite Religion*, tr. by D. E. Green (Nashville and New York, 1972), pp. 180 ff.

48. See L. Černy, *The Day of Yahweh and Some Relevant Problems* (Prague, 1948); H. Weiss, "The Origin of the 'Day of the Lord'—Reconsidered," *HUCA*, XXXVII (1966): 29 ff.; A. J. Everson, "The Days of Yahweh," *JBL*, XCIII (1974): 329 ff.; J. Gray, "The Day of Yahweh in Cultic Experience and Eschatological Prospect," *Svensk Exegetisk Årsbok*, XXXIX (1974): 5 ff.

49. See G. von Rad, "The Origin of the Concept of the Day of Yahweh," *JSS*, IV (1959): 97 ff.; P. D. Miller, Jr., "The Divine Council and the Prophetic Call to War," *VT*, XVIII (1968): 100 ff.; cf. H.-M. Lutz, "Der 'Tag Jahwes'," *Jahwe, Jerusalem und die Völker; zur Vorgeschichte von Sach 12, 1–8 und 14, 1–5* (Neukirchen-Vluyn, 1968), pp. 130 ff.

50. See Ps. 24:1 ff.; F. M. Cross, "The Divine Warrior in Israel's Early Cult," in A. Altmann, ed., *Biblical Motifs* (Cambridge, Mass., 1966), pp. 11 ff.; *id.*, *Canaanite Myth and Hebrew Epic* (Cambridge, Mass., 1973), pp. 91 ff.

51. Amos 5:18 ff., Zeph. 1:15 ff.

52. The festival during the celebration of which this psalm was sung dealt with the kingship of Yahweh. It is not clear whether it was already the New Year festival. See S. Mowinckel, *He That Cometh* (Nashville and New York, 1954), pp. 145 ff. Cf. H.-P. Müller, *Ursprünge und Strukturen alttestamentlicher Eschatologie* (Berlin, 1967), pp. 16 ff., 72 ff.; F. Hecht, *Eschatologie und Ritus bei den "Reformpropheten". Ein Beitrag zur Theologie des Alten Testaments* (Leiden, 1971), pp. 71 ff., 108 ff.

53. With the LXX and Syr.

54. See J. D. Smart, "A New Interpretation of Isaiah lxvi, 1–6," *ET*, XLVI (1934–35): 420 ff.; J. Muilenburg, *IB*, V (1956): 757 ff. It is difficult to maintain that this poem merely aims at comforting the postexilic Jerusalem community for having failed to rebuild the temple at once. Cf. M. Haran, "The Divine Presence in the Israelite Cult and the Cultic Institutions" [A review article of R. E. Clements, *God and Temple*], *Biblica*, XLIX (1969): 267.

55. See R. G. Hamerton-Kelly, "The Temple and the Origins of Jewish Apocalyptic," *VT*, XX (1970): 1 ff.

56. See J. Bourke, "Le jour de Yahvé dans Joël," *RB*, LXVI (1959): 3 ff., 191 ff.; G. W. Ahlström, "The Day of Yahweh" in *Joel and the Temple Cult of Jerusalem* (Leiden, 1971), pp. 62 ff.

57. It is not easy to distinguish between "prophetic eschatology" and "apocalyptic eschatology." Both prophets and apocalyptists received visions and both waited for a new earth. While the prophets usually intervened in the affairs of their time, they did not really affirm "the historical realm as a suitable context for divine activity" for they all waited for a new creation and a supra-historical economy of human existence (cf. Hanson, *The Dawn of Apocalyptic*, p. 12). The difference between prophets and apocalyptists lies in their respective attitudes toward chronological time. The prophets were possessed by an eschatological fever, and they trusted the Lord of history to intervene at any moment. They did not offer a time table, a calendar, or a blue print for the events of the end. On the contrary, the apocalyptists proclaimed a "revelation" (*apocalypsis*) which, properly deciphered, enabled them to "read the signs of the times." Among the many studies that have been devoted to the relation of eschatology with history among the prophets, see E. Lipiński, "[Bahachit Hayyamim] dans les textes pré-exiliques," *VT*, XX (1970): 445 ff.; F. Hecht, *Eschatologie und Ritus bei den "Reformpropheten"* (Leiden, 1971); J. P. M. van der Ploeg, "Eschatology in the Old Testament," *OTS*, XVII (1972): 89 ff.; K.-D. Schunck, "Die Eschatologie der Propheten des Alten Testaments und ihre Wandlung in exilisch-nachexilischer Zeit," *SVT*, XXVI (1974): 116 ff.; J. G. Gammie, "The Classification, Stages of Growth,

and Changing Intentions in the Book of Daniel," *JBL*, XCV (1976): 192 ff.

58. See above, pp. 397 ff. See also Sir. 36:18 ff.

59. See B. Reicke, "Official and Pietistic Elements of Jewish Apocalypticism," *JBL*, LXXIX (1960): 137 ff.; D. Rössler, *Gesetz und Geschichte. Untersuchungen zur Theologie der jüdischen Apokalyptik und der pharisäischen Orthodoxie* (Neukirchen, 1960); D. S. Russel, *The Method and Message of Jewish Apocalyptic* (Philadelphia, 1964); J. Schreiner, *Alttestamentlich-jüdische Apokalyptik* (Müchen, 1967); O. Plöger, *Theocracy and Eschatology*, tr. by S. Rudman (Richmond, Va., 1968); H. D. Betz, "On the Problem of the Religio-Historical Understanding of Apocalyptic," *JTC*, VI (1969): 134 ff.; F. M. Cross, "New Directions in the Study of Apocalyptic," *ibid.*, 157 ff.; J. M. Schmidt, *Die jüdische Apokalyptik. Die Geschichte ihrer Erforschung von den Anfängen bis zu den Textfunden von Qumran* (Neukirchen-Vluyn, 1969); P. D. Hanson, "Jewish Apocalyptic Against Its Near Eastern Environment," *RB*, LXXVIII (1971): 18 ff.; *id.*, "Old Testament Apocalyptic Reexamined," *In.*, XXV (1971): 454 ff.; *id.*, "Prolegomena to the Study of Jewish Apocalyptic," *Festschrift G. E. Wright* (Garden City, N.Y., 1976), pp. 389 ff.; A. N. Wilder, "The Rhetoric of Ancient and Modern Apocalyptic," *In.*, XXV (1971): 436 ff.; K. Koch, *The Rediscovery of Apocalyptic: A Polemical Work on a Neglected Area of Biblical Studies and its Damaging Effects on Theology and Philosophy*, tr. by M. Kohl (London, 1972); M. E. Stone, "Lists of Revealed Things in the Apocalyptic Literature," *Festschrift G. E. Wright* (Garden City, N. Y., 1976), pp. 414 ff.

60. See A. Causse, "Le mythe de la nouvelle Jérusalem du Deutéro-Esaïe à la IIIe Sibylle," *RHPR*, XVIII (1938): 377 ff.; K. L. Schmidt, "Jerusalem als Urbild und Abbild," *Eranos Jahrbuch*, XVIII (1950): 207 ff.; S. Terrien, "The Omphalos Myth and Hebrew Religion," *VT*, XX (1970): 334. Cf. 1 Enoch 90:28 ff., Sib. Or. III, 616 ff., Wisd. of Sol. 9:8, 4 Ezra 10:44 ff., etc.

61. *Manual of Discipline*, 5:5 ff., 8:4 ff., 9:3 ff., etc.

62. See J. Strugnell, "The Angelic Liturgy at Qumran—4Q [...]" *SVT*, VII (1960): 337 ff.; cf. B. Gärtner, *The Temple and the Community in Qumran and the New Testament: A Comparative Study in the Temple Symbolism of the Qumran Texts and the New Testament* (Cambridge, 1965), pp. 16 ff.; R. J. McKelvey, *The New Temple: The Church in the New Testament* (London, 1969), pp. 36 ff., 46 ff.

63. See J. Abelson, *The Immanence of God in Rabbinical Literature* (London, 1912), pp. 261 ff.; A. M. Goldberg, *Untersuchungen über die Vorstellung von der Schekhinah in der frühen rabbinischen Literatur—Talmud und Midrasch* (Berlin, 1969); D. Moody, "Shekinah," *IDB*, Vol. R—Z (1962), pp. 317 ff.

64. See B. A. Levine, "On the Presence of God in Biblical Religion," *Festschrift E. R. Goodenough* (Leiden, 1968), pp. 71 ff.; W. Brueggemann, "Presence of God, Cultic," *IDB, Suppl. Vol.* (1976), pp. 680 ff.

9

Presence as the Word

The church began as a Jewish sect which hailed Jesus as the Lord, for it saw in him the human mirror of God himself. The word "Christianity" may have been in some respect a misnomer. The Greek word *Christos*, "Anointed One," translated the Hebrew *mashiªh*, "Messiah," which referred to a suprahistorical agent of the God of Israel on the Last Day. The historical figure of Jesus did not fulfill the messianic hope. Israel was not delivered from its Roman oppressors. History did not come to an end. Creation was not renewed. The kingdom of heaven did not descend upon earth. It was probably the early Christians who changed the meaning of the word "Messiah" when they applied it to the person of Jesus.[1] Early interpretations of this historical figure[2] were related to the ideology of messianism, but they sprang from the deeper roots of the Hebraic theology of presence.

In a witticism which has become notorious, Alfred Loisy correctly said, "Jesus preached the kingdom of God, but it was the church which came." Loisy probably did not know that he was thereby paying tribute to the power of Jesus in history, for it was the presence of God through Jesus, elusive as it may have been, which created the church. It was also the presence of God through Jesus which produced the literary structure of the gospels.

The words and the deeds of Jesus which were preserved in the oral tradition of the first Christians were eventually assembled and presented within a framework of three pivotal moments. At the beginning, a *preparatio evangelica* or "annunciation" introduced the public ministry of Jesus through the preaching of John the Baptist (Mark), the stories of the nativity (Matthew and Luke), or the prologue on the *Logos* (John). The center of the synoptics was provided by the scene of the transfiguration. The four gospels ended climactically with the stories of the resurrection.

In these three pivotal moments—annunciation, transfiguration, resurrection—the evangelists have presented an original interpretation of the Hebraic theology of presence. Interrelating the motifs of theophany, temple, and final epiphany, they interpreted the person of Jesus in the context of divine manifestation.

ANNUNCIATION

While the word "annunciation" has been traditionally reserved for the stories of the angelic visitation to Mary (Luke) or to Joseph (Matthew), it may legitimately be used in a wider sense, to include the preface of Mark on the presentation of John the Baptist as the forerunner of Jesus.

The Angel of the Presence

The preaching of John the Baptist was introduced by the earliest gospel[3] through the skillful blending of three texts from the Hebrew Scripture.

The beginning of the gospel of Jesus Christ,[4] even as it
is written in Isaiah the prophet,[5]
Behold I send my messenger before thy face,
who shall prepare thy way;
The voice of one crying in the wilderness:
Prepare the way of the Lord,
make his paths straight!

(Mark 1:1–3.)

The purpose of Mark is immediately apparent. He intends to
tell the "good news" (*euangelion*) of Jesus as the Christ, but he
draws his messianic interpretation primarily from the ideology
of the Mosaic theophany, from the prophetic expectation of
the new temple, and from the ambivalent hope in the final
epiphany.[6]

First, the evangelist quotes from the prophet Malachi:

"Behold, I send my messenger (*angelos*)
And he shall prepare the way before my face"

(Mal. 3:1).

The change from "my face" to "thy face" reflects the enigmatic
oracle on the angel of the presence in the traditions concerning
the Mosaic theophany, when Yahweh addressed Israel, saying:

"Behold, I send my messenger (*angelos*) before thy face,
to keep thee on the way"

(Exod. 23:20).

Second, the phrase "to keep thee on the way" becomes the
link of introduction for the theme of the new exodus in Second
Isaiah:[7]

"In the wilderness, prepare the way of Yahweh;
Make straight in the desert a highway for God"

(Isa. 40:3).

The new exodus will take place at the moment of the final epiphany. By quoting Second Isaiah from the Septuagintal translation, however, Mark omits with the Greek version the parallel phrase "in the desert" (vs. 3*b*) and relates the phrase "in the wilderness" to the preceding clause, saying: "The voice of one crying in the wilderness" (Mark 1:3). While preserving the angelic character of the voice, which in Deutero-Isaiah spoke from the heavenly council to proclaim the final epiphany, Mark was preparing his audience to identify "one crying in the wilderness" with the prophet John the Baptist, who preached "in the wilderness" (vs. 4).

Any pious member of the Jewish community who knew the Hebrew Scriptures in the first century A.D. would have at once caught the cluster of thematic associations which these biblical reminiscences summoned to mind.

In the first place, the "messenger" (*angelos*) of the final epiphany in Malachi was also the "angel" (*angelos*) of the Mosaic theophany. Malachi said:

> "And the Sovereign whom you seek
>   shall suddenly come to his temple.
> Behold, the angel of the covenant is coming
>   in whom you delight, says Yahweh of Hosts.
> But who will endure the day of his coming
>   and who will stand when he appears?" (Mal. 3:2.)

In the second place, the somber aspect of the day of Yahweh could not be missed, for the allusion to "the angel of the covenant" was inevitably related to the contextual sequence of the Exodus passage:[8]

> "Give heed to him and harken to his voice,
>   do not rebel against him,
> For he will not pardon transgression
>   because my name is with him" (Exod. 23:21).

In the third place, the theology of the name, thus evoked, not only called attention to the stringency of Yahweh's ethical demands but also prepared John the Baptist's preaching of repentance (Mark 1:4).

In the fourth place, however, the Markan exegesis also suggested the theology of the glory, for, although it was not explicitly quoted, the oracle of Second Isaiah continued the call to "prepare the way of the Lord" with the thrilling promise of the epiphanic presence:

> "And the glory of Yahweh shall be revealed,
>   And all flesh shall see it together" (Isa. 40:5).

The universal vision of the glory was reserved for the final epiphany, but the Last Day of history would also be the First Day of the new creation, when the presence of the Godhead in its fullness would no longer be elusive, but permanent, no longer veiled, but openly disclosed. Mark did not need to quote the text of this expectation. He wished to identify John the Baptist with "the voice in the wilderness," but he also maintained the ambivalence of the word "messenger," for he also waited for the angel of the presence in the context of the final epiphany.[9]

The Cloud of the Presence

Both in its form and content, the story of the annunciation to Mary (Luke 1:26–38) seems to differ widely from the Markan prologue. Nevertheless, its theme and method of scriptural exegesis are strikingly similar. Like Mark, Luke introduced the person of Jesus through the reinterpretation of the Hebraic theology of presence.

The Lukan story[10] assumes the form of an angelic vision couched in a dialogical style which echoes the epiphanic visitations to the patriarchs and the prophetic confessions of call. It also transposes elements of prophetic oracles concerning the final epiphany and alludes to the conception of the child in terms of the Mosaic theophany.

The angel Gabriel, "who stands in the presence of God" (Luke 1:19), hailed Mary with a *terminus technicus* of the eschatological expectation:

> And he came to her and said,
> Rejoice, thou, full of grace,
> The Lord is with thee.
> And she was greatly troubled at this word, and she considered
> in her mind what manner of salutation this might be.
> And the angel said to her,
> Fear not, Mary,
> For thou hast found grace with God.
>
> (Luke 1:28–30).

It is true that the Greek word *chaire*, "rejoice," was used as a popular form of greeting in Hellenistic times. However, the Septuagintal translation of the Bible never used this word to translate the familiar *"shalom"* but reserved it for the Greek rendering of the Hebrew "rejoice" in three poetic proclamations of the final epiphany.[11]

Moreover, one of these proclamations (Zeph. 3:15 ff.) contained, in sequence, several of the motifs which articulate the message of the angel Gabriel to Mary: "Rejoice, daughter Jerusalem!" (Zeph. 3:15; cf. Luke 1:28); "Fear not, Zion!" (Zeph. 3:16; cf. Luke 1:30); "The Lord thy God is in thy midst" (literally, "in thy womb," Zeph. 3:16; cf. Luke 1:31); "He will save" (Zeph. 3:17; cf. Luke 1:31, "Jesus"; the Zephaniah verb *yoshi*ᵃ', "he will save," is almost identical with the hypocoristic name *yeshu*ᵃ', "Jesus," "he will save.")

The Lukan story of the annunciation found in Zion—the tabernacle of presence—was a fit symbol for Mary, the maternal bearer of the child. The validity of this observation is confirmed by the final phrases of the angelic salutation:

And the angel said to her,
   The Holy Spirit will come upon thee
     and the power of the Most High will overshadow thee.
   Therefore the child to be born will be called
     Holy, the Son of God

(Luke 1:35).

The verb "overshadow" (*episkiazein*) has been used by the Septuagint to translate the "sojourning (*shaken*) of the cloud" over the tent of meeting, in the Sinai desert:[12] "Moses was not able to enter the tent of meeting, for the cloud sojourned over it and the glory of Yahweh filled the tabernacle" (Exod. 40:35).

The procreation of Jesus was symbolically described as the descent of Yahweh over the desert sanctuary. The theologoumenon of presence through the cloud, elsewhere associated with that of the thickdarkness, was now applied to the "Son of God." It carried with it the quality of the holy, the *mysterium tremendum* of divine nearness. It is significant that the Lukan story of the annunciation did not lay stress on the motif of the glory, although such a motif was associated with the tabernacle. The cloud created a shadow from which Moses himself was expelled. Divine presence in the humanity of Jesus belonged to the mask of the holy.[13]

The idea that God could have localized his presence in a man was indeed preposterous for Jewish monotheism in the first century A.D. Many historians of comparative religions have suggested that it represented the myth-making imagination of an Hellenistic environment. Like the Markan prologue, however, the Lukan story of the annunciation bears evidence of an extremely precise familiarity with the Hebrew Scripture. It also reveals that only a Jewish pattern of religious thinking, immersed in the Hebraic theology of presence, could have enabled the early Christians to formulate an interpretation of the historical figure of Jesus as the shrine of God. Similar remarks apply to the thoroughly Hebraic prologue of the Johannine gospel.

The Tent of the Presence

Traces of manifold influences have been detected in the Fourth Gospel, from the Hellenistic philosophers and Philo to the Gnostics and more recently the Qumran Sectarians.[14] Contemporary scholars rightly stress the Hebraic character of Johannine thought. It was chiefly through a fresh reading of the Torah, the Prophets, and especially the Sapiential Books that the evangelist interpreted the historical Jesus. In the prologue particularly (John 1:1–18), he looked at Jesus in the light of the feminine personification of Wisdom; but he fused this motif with the masculine personification of the Word, and he interpreted both of these in the light of the Hebraic theology of elusive presence:[15] "The Logos encamped among us" (vs. 14).

John presented this exegetical synthesis in a hymn of four strophes which he interspersed with comments on John the Baptist (vss. 6–9, 15, 17, 18).[16]

I

John 1:1 In the beginning was the Word,
    and the Word was in the presence of God,
    and the Word was God.
2 He was in the beginning in the presence of God.

II

3 All things came into being through him,
    and apart from him nothing came into being.
4 In him was life,
    and this life was the light of men.
5 The light shines in the darkness,
    and the darkness did not conquer it.

III

10 He was in the world,
       and through him the world came into being,
       but the world did not acknowledge him.
11 He came to his own,
       but his own did not receive him;
12 Yet all those who received him
       he empowered to become children of God.

IV

14 And the Word became flesh,
       and he pitched his tent among us,
   And we have seen his glory,
       the glory of an only son from [his] father,
       filled with grace and truth;
16 And from his fullness
       we have all received
       grace upon grace.

This is not the place for a detailed analysis. It should simply be observed that, although the hymn hails the incarnation of the Logos (vs. 14), it is the figure of Wisdom that is thus evoked in the key elements of the four strophes.[17] Like the young girl who was playing and dancing "in the presence of Yahweh"[18] "from the beginning,"[19] the masculine Logos was with God "in the beginning" (John 1:1). The poet insists that the Word was "in the presence of God" (vss. 1*b* and 2).

Again, the figure of Wisdom who moved in the realm of the divine found her delights with the sons of men (Prov. 8:31). Likewise the Logos "became flesh and sojourned as in a tent among us" (John 1:14).

The phrase *kai eskenosen en hemin*, "and he pitched his tent among us" or "he encamped among us," unmistakably suggested a temporary stay. Once more, the nomadic tent of the wilderness was used as an image of the elusive presence, but it referred this time to the swift passage of the historical Jesus on earth. The common rendering, "and he dwelt among us," following the traditional Vulgate, *"et habitavit in nobis,"* has received the connotation of an enduring quality which includes both the historical ministry of Jesus in the years 29–30 and the spiritual mode of divine presence which the church associated with the living Lord.[20]

In support of the time-honored notion of the indwelling Logos, commentators have pointed out the eschatological promise of an eternal presence which the postexilic prophets had expressed precisely in terms of the nomadic tent. Thus, the prophet Zechariah had transmitted the Lord's invitation to Zion:

"For behold I am coming to plant my tent in thy midst"
(Zech. 2:14)

and the prophet Joel had proclaimed an oracle which stated:

"You will know that I am Yahweh your God
    who encamps in Zion, my holy mountain"
(Joel 4:17, 21).[21]

Likewise, the sapiential writers used the same terminology for describing the presence of Wisdom among men:

Thus, the creator of the universe has given me orders:
    he who created me assigned a place for my tent, saying,
        Plant thy tent in Jacob,
            receive thy inheritance in Israel!
From eternity, in the beginning, he created me,
    and for eternity I shall not cease to be.
In the holy tabernacle I ministered in his presence,
    and thus I was settled in Zion
(Sir. 24:8–10).

A number of scholars have also appealed to the later rabbinical doctrine of the *Shekinah,* suggesting that the permanent manifestation of divine presence on earth corresponded to a belief which was common among first-century Jews and probably permeated Johannine thinking.[22]

One may easily admit that such ideas were "in the air" and may have played a part in the birth of the poetic process which finally produced the hymn. At the same time, it should not be forgotten that the Prologue alone speaks specifically of an incarnation. The verb "encamped" (vs. 14*b*) stands in close parallelism with the words "became flesh" (vs. 14*a*). Here lies the unprecedented character of the statement. That the Lord would dwell permanently in his new temple at the end of time or that Wisdom planted her tent in Jacob or in Zion does not affect the meaning of the Johannine use of the verb, for the situation envisaged by the Prologue was unique. When the hymnist sang "And we have seen his glory," he testified that "the Word" had lived on this earth at a particular time, and he confided that he had sensorially perceived[23] and psychologically apprehended the most extraordinary spectacle: Divine Wisdom inseparable in his mind from the Divine Word was seen in the flesh of a man. The presence of God was for a time contained in a human person.

Whether or not the poet of the prologue was consciously polemizing against nascent Docetism—which denied the reality of the humanity of Jesus—cannot be ascertained.[24] The thrust of the phrase, however, lies in an insistence on both the spatial and temporal reality of presence. This spatial and temporal reality had previously been related to cultic space and time, but it had never before been identified with a man.

Here indeed lay the stumbling block of the gospel. Eternal divinity had become temporal humanity. The Prologue did not promote a theology of eternal presence. On the contrary, presence remained elusive, for it was contained in the frailty, the finitude, indeed, the mortality of human flesh. It was that very frailty which carried a virtue, hidden to most, discerned by a few, and which the Johannine poet expressed through the theologoumenon of the glory. The fullness of the divine reality was present in a peculiar hiddenness.[25] The glory was not superimposed upon the carnal finitude. The body of a historical man was not a window through which the glory could be glimpsed. It was the body itself which at once concealed and revealed the glory. Only those who received him perceived with the sensorial apprehension of sight the quality in this man which set him apart from other men because it communicated the hidden reality of the divine. The verb "we saw" (*etheasametha*) did not mean a vision of spiritual ecstasy. It belonged to the realm of daily existence within the normal limitations of human finitude. Nevertheless, the word "glory" introduced an element of mytho-poetic thinking, which was, in its turn, the symptom of an existential transformation.

The movement of the Johannine prologue in its entirety brings together the inner life of the Godhead (1:1) and the inner life of the new community (1:16). It anticipates the Johannine theology of eucharistic presence[26] and parallels the Pauline theology of the spiritual temple.[27] The presence of the encamped Logos was necessarily elusive, but it engendered a new mode of communion between God and man.

In his annotations to the hymn, the evangelist inserted between the third and the fourth strophes a phrase destined to explain the mode by which those who welcomed presence as the Word were empowered to become the children of God. He wrote: "That is, those who had faith in his name" (1:12c). The theology of the name, long associated with the creative Word of the prophets,[28] appealed to the ethical ear. It was through the revelation of the name that Israel learned Yahweh's purpose in the cosmos and in history. Through the Logos encamped among men, the theology of the name coalesced with the theology of the glory. Those who received the Logos as presence received also the power to become children of God. The ethical ear allied itself to the mystical eye. To see the glory meant being born to sonship.

Three literary forms of the "annunciation" of Jesus, each in its own way, propose a steady movement from the divine reality to the human realm. "The angel of the presence," "the cloud of the presence," and "the tent of the presence" represent three different areas of Christian reflection on the mystery of the historical figure of Jesus. The use of three different sets of mythical imagery enabled the early church to narrow down its language as it sought to spell out this mystery. For the problem of interpreting the historical figure of Jesus was inseparable from that of expressing the experience of human transfiguration.[29] The various motifs of the Hebraic theology of presence —final epiphany, Mosaic theophany, cultic nearness—were summoned to introduce the gospel.

TRANSFIGURATION

Mark placed the scene of the transfiguration of Jesus[30] at the center of his "gospel" (Mark 9:2-13) for it represented a turning point in Jesus' attitude toward himself. The story closes the Galilean ministry and prepares for the journey to Jerusalem— and certain death. Was Jesus going to be a violent revolutionary as the Petrine confession may have implied? (Matt. 8:22-30.) The setting of the scene of the transfiguration was in all likelihood the Feast of Tabernacles, during which messianic fever often seized the crowds of worshippers.[31] It does not follow from this observation, however, that the story was created *in toto* by the early church or that it has been transferred from the traditions of the risen Christ.[32] In spite of its setting, the narrative does not suggest any heavenly confirmation of the messianic mission of Jesus. On the contrary, the three phases or movements of the scene are rooted in the early Hebraic understanding of divine presence, in contrast to the later expectation of a political Messiah.

The Radiance and the Light

The first movement sets the stage and makes the bare statement of the transfiguration. Pointedly, the narrator insists that Jesus selected only three of his friends, those who had been with him at the raising of Jairus' daughter (Mark 6:37) and whom he was going to invite, a few months later, to watch with him at the Garden of Gethsemane (Mark 14:33). From the start, the dynamics of the story warn the audience of the momentous character of the event soon to be told. The occasion may have been the Feast of Tabernacles, but Jesus ascended a high mountain with only three of his intimates:

> And after six days, Jesus took with him Peter, and James, and John, and he brought them up to a high mountain, apart by themselves. And he was transfigured in their presence, and his garments became glistening, exceeding white, as no fuller on earth can whiten them (Mark 9:2-3).

Even if the narrative mirrors in a stylized form the theological reflection of the early church, it appears to be based on a nucleus of a historical memory.[33] To the Markan account Luke added that "Jesus went up the mountain to pray" (Luke 9:28). He avoided the Markan verb *metemorphôthê*, "[Jesus] was transfigured," perhaps on account of his Hellenistic audience, which might have thought of the ritual of metamorphosis in the mystery cults.[34] Matthew preserved the Markan verb, but he added: "And his face did shine as the sun" (Matt. 17:2). Without waiting for the later mention of Moses and the cloud (Mark 8:4, 7), the Markan audience could not miss the parallel between the transfiguration of Jesus and the Horeb theophanies. Even the enigmatic note "after six days" (Mark 9:2) becomes clear as one remembers the tradition concerning Moses' ascent up the mountain with Aaron, Nadab, Abihu, and the seventy elders: "And the glory of Yahweh sojourned on Mount Sinai, and the cloud covered it six days; and the seventh day he called to Moses out of the midst of the cloud" (Exod. 24:16).

The radiant form of Jesus and the effulgence of his vestments recall the motif of glory over the tabernacle and the motif of the shining Moses (Exod. 34:29-35). Not unlike the man who spoke with Yahweh face to face, Jesus was "transfigured" by the proximity of the divine. The sequence of the narrative, however, introduced the quality of his uniqueness.[35]

Elijah with Moses

The second movement spelled out the special intention of the narrator.

> And there appeared unto them Elijah with Moses, and they were talking with Jesus. And Peter spoke and said to Jesus, "Master, it is good for us to be here. Let us make three booths, one for thee, and one for Moses, and one for Elijah." For he knew not what to say, for they had become sore afraid (Mark 9:4-6).

It is generally assumed that Elijah appeared because he was considered at that time the forerunner of the Messiah. Such an interpretation is not impossible, but it is unlikely. It does not account for the presence of Moses.[36] The linking of Moses and Elijah in the oracle of the prophet Malachi (4:4-5 [Heb. 3:22-23]) prepared the advent, not of the Messiah, but of Yahweh himself at the end of time. The peculiarity of the phrase "Elijah with Moses" (Mark 9:4) probably indicates a reminiscence of the two theophanies which bound these two men of the Hebraic faith on the same mountain. Moses was denied the vision of glory (Exod. 33:17 ff.), and Elijah was denied a display of thaumaturgical power in nature (1 Kings 19:9 ff.). Both of them learned, however, the theology of the name, by which the ear triumphs over the eye when man obeys the voice of a command. Had the original story of the transfiguration a similar purpose? This conjecture is probable, for it is precisely the way of death on the cross that is introduced by the scene.

Peter was unable to understand the situation, and Luke found it necessary to explain that the three witnesses had been heavy with sleep. Nevertheless, Luke also indicated clearly that they "saw his glory" (Luke 9:32), "fully awake," exactly as the hymnist of the Johannine prologue who "beheld his glory" (John 1:14). What kind of glory was this? It possessed a quality which Moses and Elijah, as prophets of the ancient faith, could not have known. By using a syntactic shift, which was surely not accidental, Luke pointedly said that the three disciples "saw his glory, and the two men that stood with him." Moses and Elijah were different from Jesus. It was Jesus who was "transfigured," not they. While "they appeared in glory" (vs. 31), the purpose of their intervention was a dialogue with Jesus. When Jesus conversed with these two men, who had conversed with God, he did not discover for the first time the meaning of his own death, but he may well have deepened his sense of obedience. True glory lay for him in abnegation for the sake of love. "They spoke of his exodus which he was about to accomplish at Jerusalem" (Luke 9:31). The Messianic ambiguity was dispelled. Jesus was to be, not the political deliverer of Israel from her Roman oppressors, but the human bearer of divine presence on earth. He was the reflector of the glory of God, but the reflection of this glory led to Jerusalem and to his own death. Such an interpretation is confirmed by the third movement of the story.

The Cloud and the Voice

The reminiscences of the two theophanies on Horeb, one to Moses and one to Elijah, are brought together in a dramatic climax. There was a cloud, like the cloud which descended over the mountain (Exod. 24:16) or the tent (Exod. 40:34), and there was a voice, like the voice which summoned Elijah after the sound of complete silence (1 Kings 19:13b).

And there came a cloud, overshadowing them, and there came a voice out of the cloud, "This is my beloved son: hear and obey him!" And suddenly looking round about, they saw no one any-more, save Jesus only with themselves (Mark 9:7-8).

The cloud was "overshadowing" (episkiazousa) them. The three evangelists used the same verb as that of the angelic word of the annunciation to Mary (Luke 1:35). The irradiating glory and the cloud combined to mean the power of the Most High (Luke 1:35; cf. 2:9), but the power of the Most High wrought its deeds in the darkness. The voice from the cloud said, "This is my beloved son" (ho huios mou ho agapêtos). The proclamation of divine sonhood (cf. Matt. 16:16b) connotes the uniqueness of the bond between God and Jesus on the one hand, and the pathos of divine fatherhood on the other. The Greek word agapêtos, "beloved," is used in the Septuagint to translate the Hebrew yahidh, "one and only."[37] As in the legend of Abraham, it carried with it the echoes of the heart of a father, torn by the gift of his only-begotten (monogenes) son for the sake of man-kind.[38] It answered the consciousness of Jesus himself, who referred to God as "my Father."[39]

The Lukan account of the transfiguration concluded by not-ing that the disciples who had seen the sight and heard the voice must have at least seized the ominous character of the scene: "And when the voice was past, Jesus was found alone, and they kept silent" (Luke 9:36).

The vision of the glory could not be divorced from the hear-ing of the voice. The three witnesses might well have asked:

> ... Was it a vision?
> Or did we see that day the unseeable
> One glory of the everlasting world
> Perpetually at work, though never seen... ?[40]

If the transfiguration was a portent of death, the disciples should have pursued their quest further, saying:

> ... Was the change in us alone,
> And the enormous earth still left forlorn,
> An exile or a prisoner?[41]

The literary structure of the Markan gospel provided a sequence which situated the transfiguration between the Petrine confession and the announcement of the passion. It is not possible to decide whether this master plan of the gospel constituted a theological statement of the early church, or followed a chronology of actual occurrences in the public life of Jesus. Even if the story of the transfiguration, as it now stands, represents Christian preaching in the middle of the first century A.D., it fits the impression which Jesus created among his followers. His humble living, punctuated by his retreats into solitary prayer, mediated the holy. Did Jesus, on the mountain top where he had retired at a time of festive celebration, enter into a traumatic fit of ecstasy? Was there an agony in the middle of his public career, like that which was narrated at its beginning in the desert temptation or at its end in the Gethsemane alternation between resistance and surrender? The intimates of Jesus, remembering him, knew that the holy in this human life was a transfiguration of obedience to a very present voice—glory in an overshadowing cloud, power in darkness.

It may have been in response to the kerygma of the transfiguration that Paul wrote to the Corinthians: "Beholding the glory of the Lord, we are being transfigured (*metamorphoumetha*) into his likeness ..." (2 Cor. 3:18): and that he admonished the

Roman Christians: "Do not be conformed to this world, but be transformed (*metamorphousthe*) by the renewal of your mind" (Rom. 12:2).[42] Paul could not have written these words, of course, without the memory of his own vision of the risen Jesus.

RESURRECTION

All historians of Christian antiquity admit that the followers of Jesus would have remained dispersed after his execution in A.D. 30 and slipped into oblivion had it not been for the rise of a faith in his resurrection from the dead.[43] While the problem of the historicity of the bodily resurrection of Jesus—by the very claim of its uniqueness—evades any historical investigation,[44] the faith of the early Christians in the presence of the living Lord Jesus is commonly accepted as historical fact.

The early Christians never related the actual occurrence of the raising of Jesus from the dead,[45] but they told stories about his appearances to women and men after his death.[46] The form of these manifestations varied, and literary analysis of the narratives has revealed problems of considerable complexity.[47] They display, however, one element in common. While the stories represent Jesus as "being seen" in bodily form, they all agree in implying the elusiveness of his presence in time and space. In addition, all of them lead to the spoken word. An appearance is never a mere "sighting." It is the channel of an exhortation, a command, or a commission. The presence of the risen Lord was "presence as the Word."

In reciting their own "literary" expressions of these experiences, the Christians of the first and second generations created a new literary genre, the "Christophany." In some respects, this term is misleading, for such stories described Jesus as "Lord" and especially as "the Son of God,"[48] not as the expected liberator from political oppression, which the word *Christos*, "Messiah," primarily implied. In view of the specifical-

ly "Christian" meaning of the word "Christ," however, the use
of the term "Christophany" may be accepted.

The *Gattung* of the Christophany, which differs from the literary genre of Hebraic theophany and from the theophanylike
stories concerning the public life of Jesus before his death,[49]
partakes both of epiphanic visitation to the patriarchs and of
prophetic vision.[50] The pattern of cultic presence in a shrine,
with the theologoumena of the cloud and the glory, is absent
from the synoptic stories of appearances, and so also is the
figure of personified Wisdom. Could it be that the cultic and
sapiential modes of presence, with their quality of mediating a
sense of permanence, were not fitted to convey either the elusiveness of these manifestations or the urgency of bringing the
gospel to the nations?

The Commission of the Eleven (Matt. 28:16-20)

The Gospel of Matthew ends with the report of a final appearance of the risen Lord.[51] It is devoid of circumstantial detail of
time or place, except for the vague indication of a Galilean
mountain, otherwise unidentified; but it introduces the words
of the so-called Great Commission, and it remains open-ended,
for it announces a mode of presence which will last for the
whole of historical time:

> As for the eleven disciples, they went to Galilee, to a mountain
> where Jesus had told them to meet him. And when they saw him,
> they worshipped, but some were in doubt. And Jesus came to
> them, and he spoke to them, saying, All power has been given me
> in heaven and on earth. Go ye therefore and of all the nations
> make disciples, baptizing them into the name of the Father, the
> Son, and the Holy Spirit, teaching them to observe all the things
> which I have presented to you. And behold, I am with you always,
> even until the end of time (vss. 16-20).

The literary type of prophetic vision, with its call and commission, has been inserted into the patriarchal-legend pattern of

epiphanic visitation.[52] It has thus been transformed into a new type, which may be called "divine delegation of power." The *Gattung* of epiphanic visitation to the patriarchs and to the judges, together with that of the prophetic vision, contains a number of basic elements which are present in the Matthean narrative: an introduction, an encounter, a response, a commission, a protest, a confirmation of support, and a conclusion.[53] The response and the protest have been combined in one phrase: "they worshipped, but some were in doubt" (vs. 17). The conclusion is missing, but its omission is charged with a theological implication of "extended temporality." The element of comfort includes the promise of presence "until the end of time" (vs. 20). In the Hebraic *Gattungen* of epiphanic visitation and prophetic vision, the encouragement of God to his envoy was limited to the historical activity of an individual appointee.[54] Now, the offer of communion still belongs to the realm of historical finitude, but it is marked with an eschatological urgency which paradoxically contains a built-in implication of delay. The end of time may be "not yet."

"I am with you always" (vs. 20*b*) introduces a mode of psychological communion which goes beyond the patriarchal or prophetic promises. The doubt of the disciples stresses the elusive character of all modes of presence, even that of an "appearance," and *a fortiori* that of a psychological awareness of companionship. A poetic *inclusio* on a grand scale embraces the entire gospel, since the affirmation of comfort, "I am with you always," constitutes a closing response to the Isaianic motif of the name *Immanuel*, "God is with us," with which the gospel began (Matt. 1:23).

The patriarchal and prophetic promises, in addition, offered promises to individuals, but the *Word* of the risen Lord addresses itself to the community. It reaffirms the corporateness which Matthew alone, among the evangelists, has preserved and has inserted into the middle of his gospel:

"Where two or three are gathered in my name,
There am I in the midst of them"

(Matt. 18:20)

The Hebraic theologoumenon of the name, which articulated the reality of presence in the hearing of the ear and the response of morality for the sake of corporateness, reappears in the context of the universality of the mission. The charge is not only to make disciples of *all nations* but also to baptize them *into the name* of the Father, the Son, and the Holy Spirit (vs. 19).

The simplicity, even the extreme sobriety of the entire narrative—as well as the unexpected candor of the reference to the doubt of some of the disciples—suggests an archaic stage of the tradition.

Hence, the so-called liturgical formula of the baptismal order should not be read in the light of a later, trinitarian, theology. In the middle of the first century, Paul would already speak of the Spirit of God in the same breath with his mention of Jesus as the Lord and of God himself (1 Cor. 12:3). He would also bring all three aspects of divinity into his salutation on grace, love, and fellowship (2 Cor. 13:14). The force of the preposition "into" confers upon the baptismal command a movement from without to within the universal church. Disciples from all the nations are incorporated into a body of presence for which the organic responsibility that emerges from the sense of oneness transcends all national and racial particularism. Presence as the Word brings out the worldwide horizon of the promise to Abraham. The church, through the presence of the risen Lord, is called to be a blessing to all the families of the earth.[55]

On the Way to Emmaus *(Luke 24:13–32)*

Whereas the Matthean Great Commission is open-ended, oriented to the outside world and to the future, the Emmaus legend represents theological reflection, in story form, on the

inner springs of the faith. It plays on the interrelationship between the elusiveness of vision and the simplicity of eucharistic
communion.[56]

The dynamics of the narrative are revealed by a series of key
words which are placed at strategic points. While the exegete
will not consider this material as an allegory, in which each
component part conceals a hidden meaning that requires de-
coding, he will pay attention to the method apparently used
by the storyteller. Modern commentators agree in believing
that Luke showed the birth of faith while sketching a concrete
scene.[57]

First, the story is anchored in a dialogue. Two men are walking away from a spiritual impasse, but they are engaged in a
theological discussion.

> And behold, two of them were going to a village. . . , and they
> talked of all the things which had occurred. And it came to pass,
> as they kept conversing and discussing together, Jesus himself
> joined them and walked along with them, but their eyes were
> closed and they did not recognize him (Luke 24:13–16).

Theological discussion has often been disparaged in favor of
mystical contemplation—with good reason. Such discussion
may well be concomitant with spiritual blindness. At the same
time, it may become a *preparatio evangelica*. "As they kept con-
versing and discussing, Jesus himself joined them." The human
word of the philosophical stance precedes the presence of the
living Word.

Second, the story moves on from dialogue to "trialogue."
Theological discussion will not by itself lead to any certitude,
because certitude requires the intervention of the divine teacher. Jesus asked, stirred, and extracted answers; he summoned
heuristically, and he finally disclosed a truth which enabled the
two men to live through the riddle of history.

And he said to them, What are these words which you exchange as you walk? Thereupon they stood still and somber. . . . And they said, We hoped that it was he who should redeem Israel . . . And he said to them, Insensate minds, slow to believe all that the prophets have declared, was it not proper for the Christ to suffer these things and to enter into his glory? And beginning from Moses and from all the prophets, he interpreted for them in all the Scriptures the things concerning himself" (vss. 17–27).

The living interpreter brought the written word and the event together. His exegetical method conformed to the midrashic methods of his time, but he drew unexpected conclusions. The risen Jesus dispelled the traditional view of the messianic prophet who would liberate Israel from Roman slavery, and he introduced the notion of a suffering and dying "Christ."

Third, the ministry of the living word constitutes a necessary prolegomenon to the birth of the new faith, but it remains insufficient if it does not convey the living presence.

"As they drew nigh the village whither they were going, he made as though he would go farther. But they constrained him, saying, Abide with us, for it is toward evening and the day is now far spent. And he went in to abide with them. And it came to pass, when he sat down with them to meat, he took the bread and blessed, and breaking it he gave to them. And their eyes were opened, and they knew him, and he vanished out of their sight" (vss. 28–30).

The story ends as a cultic legend of the Lord's Supper. The teacher on the road to Emmaus has become the actor at the Emmaus table. The Logos is both the Word and the Deed, true to the ambiguous inclusivity of the Hebrew term *Dabhar*. The blessing, breaking, and sharing of the bread are the means by which the presence makes itself available and discernible. But it is received at the very instant of its vanishing. Real presence is elusive. It is readily accessible but it remains beyond grasp. The common meal has become the *kairos* of communion, not only between the divine and the human, but also among men. The eucharistic notion of presence has hallowed the all-inclusive fellowship which the historical Jesus had portrayed and actualized when he ate with sinners and collaborationists (the tax collectors who betrayed Israel for the occupying forces of Rome).[58] The communion meal stems from the ethics of humane openness. The presence of the historical Jesus is transformed into the presence of the risen Lord. Communing with outcasts and outsiders belongs to the eucharistic mode of presence, at the center of the cultic activity of the church.

The eucharistic mode of presence is inseparable from the "sacrament" of the Word, for this is the conclusion of the story: "They told what had happened on the way and how they had recognized him at the breaking of the bread" (vs. 35). Instruction on the meaning of the cross, which made Jesus someone other than the prophet who would redeem Israel from political slavery, preceded the breaking of the bread. The preaching of the Word leads to the acting of the Word, which is the offering of the self. Both of them together open the eyes of the church. The presence remains elusive, for sight is temporary, but faith takes over, fills in, and holds on.

On the Road to Damascus (Acts 9:1–30).

The story of Saul's conversion[59] is not presented by the Book of the Acts of the Apostles as an appearance of the risen Lord, because the Lukan editor, alone among the New Testament writers, has adopted the scheme of the forty days (Luke 24:50–53, Acts 1:6–11). Nevertheless, after the Pharisee from Tarsus had preached the gospel for many years, he referred to his own experience on the road to Damascus, not as if it had been one of the ecstatic "visions" or "revelations" which carried him in rapture to the third heaven (2 Cor. 12:1 ff.), but as the last of the appearances of the risen Lord to the early followers of Jesus (1 Cor. 15:5–17).[60]

Like the epiphanic visitations to the patriarchs and like the prophets' visions, the story of Saul's conversion intimately binds the manifestation of presence and the commission to act:

Pursuing his journey [Saul] was approaching Damascus when, all of a sudden, a light from heaven enveloped him with its refulgence. He fell to the ground and heard a voice saying to him, Saul, Saul, why persecutest thou me? He asked, Who art thou, Lord? And he said, I am Jesus whom thou persecutest. But arise! Enter the city, and thou wilt be told what to do. His traveling companions had stopped, speechless with terror, for they had heard a voice but had seen no one. Saul rose from the ground, and while he had his eyes open, he could not see (Act 9:3–8).

The motif of the blinding light traditionally echoed the Hebraic theologoumenon of the glory, but the voice, with its self-asseverative declaration and its command, represented the Hebraic theology of the name.

Paul's companions heard the voice but they saw no one. In the second account of the event, they heard no voice (Acts 22:9), and in the third account, they saw the light (Acts 26:13). The three accounts differ but are interdependent.[61] Did Saul "see" the risen Lord? Or was the motif of the dazzling light emphasized precisely in order to indicate that he was blinded? Ananias was reported as saying, "The Lord . . . has appeared to thee" (Acts 9:17). The verb is the same as those used in the gospel traditions of Christophany. Saul himself told the apostles in Jerusalem that he saw the Lord (Acts 9:27). Years later, the Pharisee who had become the apostle Paul wrote to the Corinthians, "He has also appeared to me" (1 Cor. 15:8).

The second account of Saul's conversion amplifies the contents of the statement spoken by the heavenly voice, for Ananias is presented as saying to the blinded man:

The God of our Fathers has predestined thee to know his will and to see the Just One and to hear a voice from his mouth that thou art to be before all men the witness for him of what thou hast seen and heard (Acts 22:14-15).

The voice speaks more fully in the third account:

> I am Jesus whom thou persecutest. Arise, stand on thy feet! I have shown myself to thee to predestine thee to be a servant and a witness of what thou hast seen and of what I shall still show thee. I shall deliver thee from the people and from all the nations toward whom I send thee, to open their eyes, that they may turn from darkness to light (Acts 26:16-18a).

In this third version, which is part of his legal defense before King Agrippa, Paul uses the *Gattung* of the prophetic vision. It was Ezekiel to whom Yahweh had said, in the vision of the prophet's call, "Stand on thy feet!" (Ezek. 2: 1, 3). It was Jeremiah who had received the promise of deliverance from his enemies (Jer. 1:7). It was the Servant of Yahweh, in Second Isaiah, who had been called "to open the eyes of the blind" (Isa. 42:7). The apostolic commission reproduced the stresses and filled the molds of the prophetic commission, but it added the vital element of being a witness to all men for the sake of the risen Lord Jesus.

The appearance of the heavenly Lord to Saul did not occur in a historical vacuum. The element of hearing took precedence over that of seeing. Indeed, the sight at best was a distorted and blurred glimpse of infinity by a finite creature. The ethical ear overwhelmed the mystical eye. The purpose of the appearance was not just the conversion of the persecutor of Jesus. It was also his appointment as a witness not only to the members of the house of Israel but "to all men."

Paul himself always insisted on this close connection between his conversion and his appointment as a witness and an envoy. He remembered Jeremiah (1:5) when he wrote to the Galatians:

"The One who set me apart ever since my mother's womb and called me by his grace was pleased to reveal in me his Son in order that I might proclaim him to the nations" (Gal. 1:15).[62] The manifestation of divine presence through the appearance of the Son of God was spatially and temporally limited in Paul's experience, but it uncovered a reality which assumed, for him, the proportions of his existential destiny.

Paul thought that Jesus, having endured capital punishment, was the object of the malediction of God (Gal. 3:13; cf. Deut. 21:23). He had to accomplish the most radical and violent volte-face before he became apostle to the nations. The resurrection of Jesus, then, was for him inseparable from the death of his own self and the birth of his new life. The experience of presence as the Word generated his theology of the new creation.[63]

Why did the early church tell the stories of the annunciation, transfiguration, and resurrection—with their dimensions of sacral uniqueness—of an obscure Galilean executed for sedition by the Romans in or around the sixteenth year of Tiberius Caesar's reign? Why indeed was there such a historical event as the birth of the church? Why were the gospels recited, written, collected, and finally preserved?

Answers to these questions have been diverse and must remain tentative in view of the paradoxical mixture of paucity and complexity which marks the available evidence. One deceptively simple explanation has to do with the impression which the person of Jesus produced on his followers. They saw that God was present in Jesus, and that Jesus communicated divine presence to them.

For several decades, historians have admitted the impossibility of writing a biography of Jesus, even less of learning about his inner life, but several aspects of his character emerge from a critical sifting of the gospel traditions.[64] The result of these labors is significant. An element of continuity unites the memory of the historical Jesus to the faith of the early church in the exalted Lord.

In the Christian consciousness of the first generation, the presence of the Galilean healer and teacher had not gone away. The men and women who had known him still perceived the power of his openness toward humankind. It was the power of this openness to all sorts of people and conditions—the poor, the women, the outcasts, the "drop-outs," the collaborationists, the foreigners—which had lived again in their own renewal and in their triumph over misery.

A remarkable coherence sealed together the image of the itinerant prophet who was crucified and the vision of the Son of God in glory.[65] An integrated picture of the man who fits no formula arose from the heterogeneous bits of testimony which repeated his sayings and told his deeds—preserving them from oblivion against the vicissitudes and even the crises of the new communities. In his mortal existence, he had brought God's nearness to people in need. In his eternal life, his presence enveloped them and created them anew.

They remembered he had been a prophet at prayer. He had waited upon his God in solitariness. He had taught his intimates how to pray. Like an athlete, he had fought his own *agon*. He had engaged in combat with the powers of death.[66] He knew God as a son knows his father.[67] Divine sonship was the secret of his authority.[68] He had said, "Thou, follow me!" No wonder that they heard him make the appeal of ancient Sophia: "Come to me, all ye that labor and are heavy laden . . ."[69] Humaneness was the accent of his persuasiveness. It conferred upon his authority its own accreditation.

The synoptic gospels used the verb *splagchnizesthai*, "to be stirred by maternal compassion," when they showed Jesus being moved to the quick by the misery which surrounded him.[70] It was in his response to the plight of men and women, to the loss of their identity, and to their cosmic solitude that he most readily communicated presence as the word and the act of liberation.[71]

The spiritual alchemy which combined in him the awareness of sonship and the passion to save others from their extremity led him to humanize sacral institutions and therefore to reduce them to historical relativity while raising them to the level of a person-to-person adventure. Thus, in his own being, he appropriated the untouchable triad—the Torah, the elect people, and the temple.

He transcended the Torah on account of his humaneness, for he placed the rights and the obligations of human growth ahead of legal observances. Existential risk took precedence over institutional security. The Sabbath was made for man, and not man for the Sabbath (Mark 2:27).

He threw down the barriers of a racial and ritual covenant. He overcame separation between Jews and non-Jews as he praised the faith of a Syro-Phoenician woman, and even that of a Roman centurion, over the faith of Israel (Matt. 8:5). He envisioned pagans sitting down at the heavenly banquet (Matt. 8:11), and he spoke parabolically of a vineyard given to others (Mark 12:-9).[72]

He cleansed the temple as a sign of the new order.[73] The myth of sacred space had no function in the age to come.[74] The charge that he had announced the destruction of the temple reflected an accurate impression of his word.[75] The tradition correctly understood the meaning of his opposition to the temple when it said that the veil of the holy of holies had been rent asunder at the moment of his death.[76]

Jesus conveyed the presence when his call to personal allegiance was compounded with his resolution to face ultimate defeat. "I trust only," wrote Pascal, "those witnesses who lay their heads on the block." The *mysterium tremendum* of the temple was transferred into human flesh. The vague numinosity of the holy was concretized in a heart's beat. Thus, the gospel traditions said of the disciples: "They were on the road, going up to Jerusalem, and Jesus was walking ahead of them. They were filled with awe, and those who followed behind were plainly in dread" (Mark 10:32). The ancient prophets had spoken in the name of Yahweh. Jesus asserted, "But I say to you . . . " (Matt. 5:22). It was he himself who had become the *raison d'être* of ethics: "What you do to the least of these, my brothers, it is to me that you have done it" (Matt. 25:40). To live was "to confess him before men" (Luke 12:8; cf. Matt. 10:32).

When the first Christians tried to enunciate the nature of the bond which linked them to Jesus, they were still caught in eschatological fear and fever. They still waited for the end of the tragedy of man, but the quality of their waiting was altered, Jesus had come, and his presence had been elusive, but he would come again. They were possessed by this certitude because they had seen in him "the epiphany of God's desire to be known" (Ibn 'Arabi). In a new mode, his presence remained.

They searched for words and they used many symbols. The most potent among these was derived from the Hebraic theology of presence. They called Jesus "the new temple." Through a strange osmosis of the new faith, they took a bold step forward. They called themselves "the temple of the spirit."

Notes

1. It is not clear whether the notion of a suffering Messiah, attested to in the rabbinical literature of the second century A.D., had existed in Judaism before the time of Jesus, notably among the Qumran sectarians. See E. Jenni, "Messiah, Jewish," *IDB*, Vol. Q—R (1962), pp. 360 ff.; E. Rivkin, "Messiah, Jewish," *IDB, Suppl. Vol.* (1976), pp. 588 ff.; cf. H. Riesenfeld, "Le Messie souffrant," *Jésus transfiguré* (København, 1947), pp. 81 ff., and Appendix II, pp. 314 ff. See also M. de Jonge, "The Use of the Word 'Anoint-

ed' in the time of Jesus," *Festschrift G. Sevenster* (Leiden, 1966), pp. 132 ff.
2. In recent decades, scholars again took a moderate position toward the historicity of most traditions concerning the public ministry and the teaching of Jesus. See J. M. Robinson, *A New Quest for the Historical Jesus* (Naperville, Ill., 1959); G. Bornkamm, *Jesus of Nazareth*, tr. by I. and F. McLuskey with J. M. Robinson (London, 1960); R. H. Fuller, "The New Quest for the Historical Jesus," *The New Testament in Current Study* (New York, 1962), pp. 25 ff.;

N. Perrin, *Rediscovering the Teaching of Jesus* (New York, 1967); R. Slenczka, *Geschichtlichkeit und Personsein Jesu Christi* (Göttingen, 1967); O. Betz, *What Do We Know About Jesus?* (London, 1968); H. K. McArthur, "From the Historical Jesus to Christology," *In.*, XXIII (1969): 190 ff.; *id.*, ed., *In Search of the Historical Jesus* (New York, 1969); J. Jeremias, *New Testament Theology: The Proclamation of Jesus*, tr. by J. Bowden (New York, 1971); E. R. Schweizer, *Jesus*, tr. by D. E. Green (Richmond, Va., 1971); E. Trocmé, "Quelques travaux récents sur le Jésus de l'histoire," *RHPR*, LII (1972): 485 ff.; J. Dupont, *ed.*, *Jésus aux origines de la Christologie* (Gembloux, 1975), pp. 9 ff.; G. Aulén, *Jesus in Contemporary Research*, tr. by I. H. Hjelm (Philadelphia, 1976).

3. See E. P. Gould, *A Critical and Exegetical Commentary on the Gospel According to St. Mark* (Edinburgh, 1896), pp. 4 ff.; A. E. J. Rawlinson, *St Mark* (London, 1931), pp. 4 ff.; E. Klostermann, *Das Markusevangelium* (Tübingen, 1950), p. 5; S. E. Johnson, *A Commentary on the Gospel According to St. Mark* (London, 1966), pp. 33 ff.; W. Grundmann, *Das Evangelium nach Markus* (Berlin, 1965), pp. 25 ff.; V. Taylor, *The Gospel According to St. Mark* (London, 1966), pp. 152 ff.; E. Schweizer, *The Good News According to Mark*, tr. by D. H. Madvig (Richmond, Va., 1970), pp. 28 ff.

4. Several mss. add "the Son of God."

5. Some mss. read, "in the prophets." Scribes probably saw that the quotation from the Book of Isaiah was conflated with one from Malachi.

6. C. T. Ruddick suggested a dependence of Mark on the synagogal lectionary. See "Behold, I Send my Messenger," *JBL*, LXXXVIII (1969): 381 ff.

7. The Qumran sectarians justified their withdrawal to the wilderness of Judah by citing Isa. 40:3 (cf. 1QIsᵃ8:14). On the theme of the new exodus in Second Isaiah, see P. Volz, *Jesaiah II* (Leipzig,

1932), p. 4; J. Muilenburg, *IB*, V (1956), pp. 426 ff.

8. Cf. Exod. 14:19, 32:34, 33:2; Num. 20:26; Isa. 63:9. See B. S. Childs, *The Book of Exodus: A Critical, Theological Commentary* (Philadelphia, 1974), p. 487.

9. The identification of John the Baptist with the symbolic figure of Elijah (cf. Mark 1:6) further illustrates the kind of exegetical method that evokes themes through contextuality. The prophet Malachi had associated Elijah with the advent of Yahweh on the Last Day (Mal. 4:4 [Heb., 3:23]).

10. See A. Plummer, *A Critical and Exegetical Commentary on the Gospel According to S. Luke* (Edinburgh, 1901), p. 24; A. Loisy, *L'Evangile selon Luc* (Paris, 1924), pp. 88 ff.; M.-J. Lagrange, *L'Evangile selon St. Luc* (Paris, 1927), pp. 14 ff.; W. Grundmann, *Das Evangelium nach Lukas* (Berlin, 1964), pp. 54 ff.; K. H. Rengstorf, *Das Evangelium nach Lukas* (Göttingen, 1965), pp. 25 ff.; R. E. Brown, *The Birth of the Messiah* (Garden City, N.Y., 1977), pp. 292 ff.

11. See J. P. Audet, "L'annonce faite à Marie," *RB*, LXIII (1956): 346 ff., 364 f.; R. Laurentin, *Structure et théologie de Luc I–II* (Paris, 1957), pp. 73 ff.

12. Cf. LXX of Exod. 40:35; Pss. 90 (Heb. 91):4, 139 (Heb. 140):7; Prov. 18:11; see also Symmachus of Hos. 4:13 and Theodotion of Num. 11:25. J. Hen, "*Episkiazein*" Lk 1,35," *BZ*, XIV (1916–17): 147 ff.; A. Allgeier, "*Episkiazein*" Lk 1,35," *ibid.*, pp. 328 ff.; E. Burrows, *The Gospel of the Infancy and Other Biblical Essays* (London, 1940), p. 56, note 1.

13. The interpretation of Mary as the tabernacle of the Lord may have influenced also the Lukan story of the visitation (Luke 1:39–45). Elizabeth exclaimed, "Why is this granted me that the mother of my Lord should come to me?" (Vs. 43). When the ark had been carried to Jerusalem, David had said, "How can the ark of Yahweh come to me?" (2 Sam. 6:11). The parallelism is not fortuitous. Cf. also the span of "three months" dur-

ing which the ark was left at the house of Obed-edom (2 Sam. 6:11) and the "about three months" during which Mary remained with Elizabeth (Luke 1:56), with resulting benedictions in both cases. See R. Laurentin, *Structure*, p. 80.

14. See R. E. Brown, *The Gospel According to John I–XII* (Garden City, N.Y., 1966), pp. LII ff.; R. Bultmann, *The Gospel of John: A Commentary*, tr. by G. R. Beasley-Murray (Oxford, 1971), pp. 13 ff.; G. Richter, "Die Fleischwerdung des Logos im Johannesevangelium," *NTS*, XIII (1971): 81 ff.; *ibid.*, XIV (1972): 257 ff.

15. See J. Dillersberger, *Das Wort vom Logos. Vorlesungen über den Johannes-Prolog* (Salzburg-Leipzig, 1935), pp. 29 ff., 158 ff.; M.-E. Boismard, *Le prologue de Saint Jean* (Paris, 1953), pp. 66 ff., 165 ff.; F.-M. Braun, *Jean le théologien, III: Sa théologie, 1: Le mystère de Jésus* (Paris, 1966), pp. 21 ff.; Brown, John I–XII, p. 3 ff.; J. Jeremias, "The Revealing Word," *The Central Message of the New Testament* (London, 1965), pp. 71 ff.; H. Ridderbos, "The Structure and Scope of the Prologue to the Gospel of John," *NT*, IX (1965): 180 ff.; A. Feuillet, *Le prologue du Quatrième Evangile: Etudes de théologie johannique* (Bruges, 1968); R. Schnackenburg, *The Gospel According to St. John*, tr. by K. Smyth (London, 1968), pp. 221 ff.; H. Schneider, "The Word Was Made Flesh," *CBQ*, XXXI (1969): 344 ff.; E. D. Freed, "Some Old Testament Influences on the Prologue of John," *Festschrift J. M. Myers* (Philadelphia, 1974), pp. 145 ff.

16. The rhythmic and strophic structure of the Prologue, together with its affinities with Qumran and Christian hymns points to its Hebrew or Aramaic background and its early date. See Braun, *Jean le théologien*, pp. 224 ff.; P. Borgen, "Observations on the Targumic Character of the Prologue of John," *NTS*, XIV (1969–70), 288 ff.; J. Irigoin, "La composition rythmique du Prologue de Jean (I, 1–18)," *RB*, LXXVIII (1971), 501 ff.

17. See J. Rendel Harris, *The Origin of the*

Prologue of St. John's Gospel (Cambridge, 1917); *id.,* "Athena, Sophia and the Logos," *BJRL*, VII (1922–23): 56 ff.; R. Bultmann, "Der religionsgeschichtliche Hintergrund des Prologs zum Johannes-Evangeliums," *Eucharisterion [Festschrift H. Gunkel],* (Göttingen, 1923), II: pp. 10 ff.; G. Ziener, "Weisheitsbuch und Johannesevangelium," *Biblica*, XXXVIII (1957): 396 ff.; *ibid.*, XXXIX (1958), 37 ff.; Feuillet, *Le Prologue*, pp. 72 ff., 115 ff.; J. E. Bruns, "Some Reflections on Coheleth and John," *CBQ*, XXV (1963): 414 ff.; H. R. Moeller, "Wisdom Motifs and John's Gospel," *Bulletin of the Evangelical Theological Society*, VI (1963): 92 ff.; F.-M. Braun, *Jean le théologien, II: Les grandes traditions d'Israël et l'accord des Ecritures selon le Quatrième Evangile* (Paris, 1964), pp. 115 ff., Brown, *John I–XII*, pp. CXXII ff., 4 ff.

18. Prov. 8:23, 30; cf. Sir. 24:8 f., Wisd. of Sol. 6:22.

19. Prov. 8:22 ff., Sir. 24:9, Wisd of Sol. 6:22.

20. The desire to perpetuate the presence of Jesus and to transform its elusiveness into a permanent communion parallels in some respects the semantic evolution of the Hebraic word *shaken*, which at first meant "to sojourn as in a tent," later signified "to dwell," and led in the rabbinic period to the Aramaic notion of *Shekinah*.

21. In both texts (Zech. 2:14 and Joel 4:-17, 21), the LXX translated the Hebrew verb *shaken*, "to sojourn," by the Greek verb *kataskenoô*, "to pitch one's tent."

22. See J. H. Bernard, *A Critical and Exegetical Commentary on the Gospel According to St. John, I* (New York, 1929), p. 22; E. Burrows, "The Doctrine of the Shekinah and the Theology of the Incarnation," in *The Gospel of the Infancy and Other Biblical Essays* (London, 1940), pp. 101 ff.; L. Bouyer, "La Schékinah, Dieu avec nous," *Bible et vie chrétienne*, XX (1957–58): 8 ff.; A. M. Goldberg, *Untersuchungen über die Vorstellung von der Schekhinah in der frühen rabbinischen Literatur* (Berlin, 1969). The

imagery of the Shekinah tended to lose the dynamic character of the Hebraic theology of presence. For example, while Lev. 26:12 read in the Hebrew original, "I shall walk in the midst of you," the Targum of Onkelos translated, "I shall cause my Shekinah to be among you."

23. The Greek verb, "we saw," is used in this sense twenty-two times in the NT.

24. See Brown, *John I–XII*, p. LXXVI.

25. See Bultmann, *The Gospel of John*, p. 63; cf. p. 64; J. C. Meagher, "John 1, 14 and the New Temple," *JBL*, LXXXVIII (1969), 57 ff.; T. C. de Kruijf, "The Glory of the Only Son (John I:14)," *Studies in John (Festschrift J. N. Sevenster*, Leiden, 1970), pp. 110 ff.

26. See C. H. Dodd, "The Prologue to the Fourth Gospel and Christian Worship," in F. L. Cross, ed., *Studies in the Fourth Gospel* (London, 1957), pp. 9 ff.; J. A. T. Robinson, "The Relation of the Prologue to the Gospel of St. John," *NTS*, IX (1962–63): 120 ff.; J. L. Martyn, "... To the Presence of the Son of Man," in *History and Theology in the Fourth Gospel* (New York, 1968), pp. 120 ff.

27. Cf. 1 Cor. 3:16.

28. See Brown, "Appendix II: The 'Word'," *John I–XII*, pp. 519 ff.; and "Appendix IV: Ego Eimi—'I am'," *ibid.*, pp. 533 ff.

29. Cf. 2 Cor. 3:18.

30. See Ch. Masson, "La transfiguration de Jésus (Marc 9:2–13)," *RTP*, XIV (1964): 1 ff.; E. Schweizer, *The Good News According to Mark*, tr. by D. H. Madvig (Richmond, Va., 1970), pp. 180 ff.; H. C. Kee, "The Transfiguration in Mark: Epiphany or Apocalyptic Vision?" *Festschrift M. Enslin* (Valley Forge, Pa., 1972), pp. 135 ff.

31. See the evidence gathered by H. Riesenfeld, *Jésus transfiguré, L'arrière-plan du récit évangélique de la transfiguration de Notre-Seigneur* (København, 1947), pp. 265 ff.

32. See R. Bultmann, *The History of the Synoptic Tradition*, tr. by J. Marsh, (New York, 1963), pp. 259 ff.; M. Goguel, *La foi*

à la résurrection de Jésus dans le christianisme primitif (Paris, 1933), pp. 318 ff.; H.-P. Müller, "Die Verklärung Jesu. Eine motivgeschichtliche Studie," *ZNW*, LI (1960): 56 ff.; Ch. E. Carlson, "Transfiguration and Resurrection," *JBL*, LXXX (1961): 233 ff.

33. See H. Baltensweiler, *Die Verklärung Jesu* (Zürich, 1959); cf. E. Dabrowski, *La transfiguration de Jésus* (Rome, 1939); A. Feuillet, "Les perspectives propres à chaque évangéliste dans les récits de la Transfiguration," *Biblica*, XXXIX (1958): 281 ff.; J. M. Nützel, *Die Verklärungserzählung im Markusevangelium. Eine redaktionsgeschichtliche Untersuchung* (Würzburg, 1973).

34. See Apuleius, *Metamorphoses*, xi. Several examples are cited in Dabrowski, *La Transfiguration*, pp. 145 ff.

35. Moses was not "transfigured," and the disciples were aware of the difference (see Mark 9:4). Cf. A. R. C. Leaney, "Theophany, Resurrection and History," *Studia evangelica*, V, Part II (Berlin, 1968), p. 104.

36. See M.-J. Lagrange, *Evangile de Marc*, p. 229. "The Assumption of Moses" offers no messianic role to Moses. Its date, in any event, is later than the Christian era. The Samaritains used Deut. 18:15 as a messianic prophecy.

37. See Gen. 22:2, 12, 16, etc. Cf. G. H. Turner, "*ho huios mou, ho agapêtos,*" *JTS*, XXVII (1925–26): 113 ff.

38. See John 3:16; cf. Mark 1:11, 12:6.

39. See Matt. 11:27, 20:27, 25:34, 26:29. Cf. J. Jeremias, "*'Abbā* as an Address to God," *New Testament Theology: The Proclamation of Jesus*, tr. by J. Bowden (New York, 1971), pp. 61 ff.

40. Edwin Muir, "The Transfiguration," *Collected Poems, 1921–1951* (New York, 1954); p. 174.

41. *id., ibid.*

42. See below, p. 458.

43. See J. Moltmann, "The Historical Problem in Resurrection as Hope," *HTR*, LXI (1968): 129 ff.; C. F. D. Moule, *The Significance of the Message of the Resurrection*

for Faith in Jesus Christ (London, 1968); Ph. Seidensticker, Die Auferstehung Jesu in der Botschaft der Evangelisten (Stuttgart, 1968); B. R. Bater, "Towards a More Biblical View of the Resurrection," In., XXIII (1969): 47 ff.; K. Gutbrod, Die Auferstehung Jesu im Neuen Testament (Stuttgart, 1969); F. Mussner, Die Auferstehung Jesu (München, 1969); P. de Surgy, et al., La résurrection du Christ et l'exégèse moderne (Paris, 1969); C. F. Evans, Resurrection and the New Testament (Naperville, Ill., 1970); W. Marxsen, The Resurrection of Jesus of Nazareth (Philadelphia, 1970); H. C. Snape, "After the Crucifixion or 'The Great Forty Days'," Numen, XVII (1970): 188 ff.; U. Wilckens, Anferstehung. Das biblische Anferstehungs-Zeugnis historisch untersucht und erklärt (Stuttgart-Berlin, 1970); R. E. Brown, The Virginal Conception and Bodily Resurrection of Jesus (New York, 1973).

44. Some object to this view by maintaining that the historical method would not be "scientific" if it refused to investigate an "event" simply because it is unparalleled or unique. Cf. W. Pannenberg, Grundzüge der Christologie (Gütersloh, 1964), pp. 85 ff. It will be observed, however, that the faith in the resurrection of Jesus should not be confused with a belief in the resuscitation of corpses and the recapture of a new span of mortal existence. The faith in the resurrection of Jesus has to do with the transformation of a human being who had died into a "person" transcending space and time. Is not historical existence characterized by spatial and temporal finitude?

45. Matt. 28:2–4 implies the existence of such a story but does not include it. Cf. the Apocryphal Gospel of Peter, Fragment I, 35–42; see M. R. James, The Apocryphal New Testament (Oxford, 1950), pp. 91 f. The traditions of the "empty tomb" may have belonged to a later stage of the tradition, although a relatively early date should not be ruled out. See E. L. Bode, The Gospel Account of the Women's Easter Visit to the Tomb of Jesus (Rome, 1969); J. De-

lorme, "Résurrection et tombeau de Jésus; Marc 16, 1–8 dans la tradition évangélique," in P. de Surgy et al., La résurrection du Christ et l'exégèse moderne (Paris, 1969), pp. 105 ff.; I. Broer, Die Urgemeinde und das Grab Jesu. Eine Analyse der Grablegungsgeschichte im Neuen Testament (München, 1972); Brown, The Virginal Conception & Bodily Resurrection of Jesus, pp. 113 ff.

46. See Goguel, La foi à la résurrection de Jésus, pp. 235 ff.; C. H. Dodd, "The Appearances of the Risen Christ: An Essay in Form-Criticism of the Gospels," Festschrift R. H. Lightfoot (Oxford, 1957), pp. 9 ff.; A. R. C. Leaney, "Theophany, Resurrection and History," Studia evangelica, V, Part II (Berlin, 1968), pp. 107 f.; F. W. Beare, "Sayings of the Risen Jesus in the Synoptic Tradition: An Inquiry into their Origin and Significance," Festschrift J. Knox (Cambridge, 1967), pp. 164 ff.; J. E. Alsup, The Post-Resurrection Appearance Stories of the Gospel Tradition: A History-of-Tradition Analysis, with Text-Synopsis (Stuttgart, 1975).

47. For example, the narratives of the appearances which are preserved in the canonical gospels do not include some which are mentioned by Paul (1 Cor. 15:5 ff.). Was it that the evangelists did not know them or that they deliberately ignored them? The various accounts present conflicting locales (the vicinity of Jerusalem versus Galilee) and offer no discernible time schedule. The limit of forty days is found only in the Lukan writings (Luke 24:50–53; Acts 1:6–11). Paul himself included his own vision of the heavenly Lord within his list of other appearances (1 Cor. 15:8; cf. Acts 9:3–9).

48. See Martin Hengel, The Son of God: The Origin of Christology and the History of Jewish-Hellenistic Christianity (Philadelphia, 1976).

49. See A. R. C. Leaney, "Theophany, Resurrection and History," p. 107; J. E. Alsup, "Theophany in the New Testa-

ment," *IDB, Suppl. Vol.* (1976), pp. 898 ff.
50. See above, pp. 68 ff., 227 ff.
51. See W. C. Allen, *A Critical and Exegetical Commentary on the Gospel According to S. Matthew* (Edinburgh, 1907), pp. 305 ff.; A. H. McNeile, *The Gospel According to St. Matthew* (London, 1915), pp. 434 ff.; M.-J. Lagrange, *Evangile selon Saint Matthieu* (Paris, 1927), pp. 543 ff.; E. Klostermann, *Das Matthäusevangelium* (Tübingen, 1938), pp. 230 ff.; G. Bornkamm, "The Risen Lord and the Earthly Jesus: Matthew 28.16–20," *The Future of Our Religious Past, Festschrift R. Bultmann* (London, 1964), pp. 208 ff,; J. Schniewind, *Das Evangelium nach Matthäus* (Göttingen, 1964), pp. 275 ff.; J. Lange, *Das Erscheinen der Auferstandenen im Evangelium nach Matthäus. Eine traditions- und redaktionsgeschichtliche Untersuchung zu Mt 28, 16–20* (Würzburg, 1973); B. J. Hubbard, *The Matthean Redaction of a Primitive Apostolic Commissioning: An Exegesis of Matthew 28, 16–20* (Missoula, Montana, 1974).
52. Cf. Gen. 12:1–4*a*, 15:1–6, 17:1–4, 17:-15–27, 28:10–22, 35:9–15; Exod. 3:1–15, 6:2–13; Judg. 4:4–10, 6:11–24; 1 Sam. 3:1-19; 1 Kings 19:1–19*a*; Isa. 6:1–12; Jer. 1:1–10; Ezek. 1:1—3:15.
53. Cf. the promise of presence in Gen. 17:4, 26:3, 28:15; Jer. 1:8; also Deut. 31:-23.
54. See above, pp. 75, 235.
55. See above, p. 75.
56. See P. Schubert, "The Structure and Significance of Luke 24," *Festschrift R. Bultmann* (Berlin, 1954), pp. 165 ff.; P. Winter, "The Treatment of His Sources by the Third Evangelist in Luke XXI–XXIV," *Studia theologica*, VIII (1954): 138 ff.; R. Leaney, "The Resurrection Narratives in Luke (XXIV, 12–53)," *NTS*, II (1955–56): 110 ff.; W. Grundmann, *Das Evangelium nach Lukas* (Berlin, 1960), pp. 442 ff.; H. D. Betz, "The Origin and Nature of Christian Faith According to the Emmaus Legend (Luke 24:13–32)," *In.*, XXIII (1969): 32 ff.; J. Wanke, *Die Emmauserzählung. Eine Redaktionsgeschichtliche*

Untersuchung zu Lk. 24.13–35 (Leipzig, 1973).
57. See H. D. Betz, "The Emmaus Legend," pp. 34 and 38.
58. Cf. Matt. 9:11, 11:19; Luke 15:2, 19:1 ff.; see W. Marxsen, *Das Abendmahl als christologisches Problem* (Gütersloh, 1965), pp. 20 ff.; H. D. Betz, "The Emmaus Legend," p. 42.
59. Acts 9:1–39, 22:1–16, 26:12–18. See H. G. Wood, "The Conversion of St. Paul. . . ," *NTS*, I (1954–55); 276 ff.; W. Prentice, "St. Paul's Journey to Damascus," *ZNW*, XLVI (1955): 250 ff.; H. Conzelmann, *Die Apostelgeschichte* (Tübingen, 1963), pp. 57 ff.; J. Munck, *The Acts of the Apostles* (Garden City, N.Y., 1967), pp. 57 ff.; J. D. G. Dunn, "The Resurrection Appearance to Paul," in *Jesus and the Spirit: A Study of the Religious and Charismatic Experience of Jesus and the First Christians as Reflected in the New Testament* (Philadelphia, 1975), pp. 97 ff.
60. See W. O. Walker, "Postcrucifixion Appearances and Christian Origins," *JBL*, LXXXVIII (1969): 162.
61. *Contra* E. Hirsch, "Die drei Berichte der Apostelgeschichte über die Bekehrung des Paulus," *ZNW*, XXVIII (1929): 305 ff.
62. See Leaney, "Theophany, Resurrection and History," p. 111: J. Munck, "Paulus tanquam abortivus, I Cor. 15:8," *Festschrift Th. W. Manson* (Manchester, 1959), pp. 180 ff.
63. See H. R. Niebuhr, "The Solitary Exister," *Resurrection and Historical Reason: A Study in Theological Method* (New York, 1957), pp. 51 ff.; G. Siegwalt, "La résurrection du Christ et notre résurrection," *RHPR*, L (1970): 220 ff.; P. Siber, *Mit Christus leben. Eine Studie zur paulinischen Auferstehungshoffnung* (Zürich, 1972); cf. discussion of the theological interpretations of Pannenberg and Moltmann in P. C. Hodgson, *Jesus-Word and Presence: Essay in Christology* (Philadelphia, 1971), pp. 220 ff.; see also W. Marxsen, "Faith as a Venture," *The Resurrection of Jesus of*

Nazareth, tr. by M. Kohl (Philadelphia, 1970), pp. 149 ff.
64. See note 2 above. See also R. H. Fuller, "The Clue to Jesus' Self-Understanding," *Studia evangelica*, III, 2 (1964): 58 ff.; H. K. McArthur, *In Search of the Historical Jesus* (New York, 1969).
65. See I. H. Marshall, "The Divine Sonship of Jesus," *In.*, XXI (1967): 87 ff.; id., "Son of God or Servant of Yahweh—A Reconsideration of Mark 1.11," *NTS*, XV (1968–69): 326 ff.; H. D. Betz, "Jesus as Divine Man," *Festschrift E. C. Colwell* (Philadelphia, 1968), pp. 114 ff.; id., "The Concept of the So-Called 'Divine Man' in Mark's Christology," *Festschrift A. P. Wikgren* (Leiden, 1972), pp. 229 ff.; I. de la Potterie, "Le titre *kyrios* appliqué à Jésus dans l'évangile de Luc," *Festschrift B. Rigaux* (Gembloux, 1970), pp. 117 ff.; P. J. Achtemeier, "Gospel Miracle Tradition and the Divine Man," *In.*, XXVI (1972): 174 ff.; F. Hahn, *The Titles of Jesus in Christology* (London, 1969); Dunn, *Jesus and the Spirit*, pp. 15 ff.; M. Hengel, *The Son of God*, tr. by J. Bowden (Philadelphia, 1976). Of course, the notion of "Son of God" is also related to the ideology of the Davidic Son. See E. Schweizer, "The Concept of the Davidic "Son of God" in Acts and its Old Testament Background," *Festschrift P. Schubert* (Nashville, New York, 1966), pp. 186 ff.; see also, C. F. D. Moule, "The Christology of Acts," *ibid.*, p. 172.
66. See K. G. Kuhn, *Achtzehngebet und Vaterunser und der Reim* (Tübingen, 1950); A. R. George, *Communion With God in the New Testament* (London, 1953), pp. 31 ff.; W. Marchal, *Abba, Père! La prière du Christ et des chrétiens; étude exégétique sur les origines et la signification de l'invocation à la divinité du Père, avant et dans le Nouveau Testament* (Rome, 1963); T. Boman, "Der Gebetskampf Jesu," *NTS*, X (1963–64): 273 ff.; E. Lohmeyer, *The Lord's Prayer* (London, 1965); J. Jeremias, *The Prayers of Jesus* (London, 1967); R. S. Barbour, "Gethsemane in the Passion Tradition," *NTS*,

XVI (1969–70): 235 ff.; Dunn, "The Prayer Life of Jesus," *Jesus and the Spirit*, pp. 15 ff.
67. Matt. 11:27, Mark 10:22; see D. W. Davies, " 'Knowledge' in the Dead Sea Scrolls and Matt. 11, 25–30," *HTR*, XLVI (1953): 113 ff.; id., *The Setting of the Sermon on the Mount* (Cambridge, 1964), pp. 207 ff.; M. J. Suggs, *Wisdom, Christology and Law in Matthew's Gospel* (Cambridge, Mass., 1970), pp. 71 ff.
68. See H. F. D. Sparks, "The Doctrine of Divine Fatherhood in the Gospels," *Studies in the Gospels*, ed. D. E. Nineham (Oxford, 1955), pp. 241 ff.; H. W. Montefiore, "God as Father in the Synoptic Gospels," *NTS*, III (1956–57): 31 ff.; Jeremias, " 'Abba as an Address to God," *Theology of the New Testament*, pp. 61 f.; Dunn, *Jesus and the Spirit*, pp. 21 ff.
69. Matt. 11:28; cf. Prov. 8:1 ff., Sir. 24:1 ff.; see A. Feuillet, *Jésus et la sagesse divine d'après les Evangiles Synoptiques*," *RB*, LXII (1955): 161 ff.; F. Christ, *Jesus Sophia* (Zürich, 1970), pp. 81 ff.; Suggs, *Wisdom*, pp. 91 ff.; Dunn, *Jesus and the Spirit*, pp. 29 ff.
70. Matt. 9:36, 14:14, 15:32, 18:27, 18:33, 20:34, etc. The verb was almost absent from the LXX (cf. Prov. 17:5, 2 Macc. 6:-8), although the cognate noun was fairly common. The Hebraic thought-form, derived from the "longing of the womb," revealed the semantics of the feminine in the theological idiom. See S. Terrien, "Toward a Biblical Theology of Womanhood," *Male and Female; Christian Approaches to Sexuality*, ed. by R. T. Barnhouse and U. T. Holmes, III (New York, 1976), p. 21; cf. F. K. Mayr, "Patriarchalisches Gottesverständnis? Historische Erwägungen zur Trinitätslehre," *Theologische Quartalschrift*, CLII (1972): 224 ff.
71. See Hodgson, *Jesus-Word and Presence*, pp. 196 ff.
72. See B. Sundkler, "Jésus et les païens," *RHPR*, XVI (1936): 462 ff.; J. Jeremias, *Jesus' Promise to the Nations* (Lon-

don, 1967); id., *New Testament Theology*, pp. 245 ff.

73. See T. W. Manson, "The Cleansing of the Temple," *BJRL*, XXXIII (1951): 271 ff.; J. W. Doeve, "Purification du temple et dessèchement du figuier," *NTS*, I (1954–55): 297 ff.; Y. M.-J. Congar, *Le mystère du temple, ou l'économie de la présence de Dieu à sa créature de la Genèse à l'Apocalypse* (Paris, 1958), pp. 148 ff.; C. Roth, "The Cleansing of the Temple and Zechariah 14:21," *NT*, IV (1960): 174 ff.; E. Lohmeyer, *Lord of the Temple*, tr. by S. Todd (Edinburgh and London, 1961), pp. 36 ff.; B. Gärtner, *The Temple and the Community in Qumran and the New Testament* (Cambridge, 1965), pp. 99 ff.; R. J. McKelvey, *The New Temple: The Church in the New Testament* (London, 1969), p. 63.

74. Rev. 21:22. See Congar, *Le mystère du temple*, pp. 250 ff.; cf. O. Cullmann, "L'opposition contre le temple de Jérusalem," *NTS*, V (1958–59): 167.

75. See M. Goguel, *The Life of Jesus*, tr. by O. Wyon (New York, 1933), p. 510.

76. See G. Lindeskog, "The Veil of the Temple," *Coniectanea neotestamentica*, XI (1947): 132 ff.; D. Daube, "The Veil of the Temple," *The New Testament and Rabbinic Judaism* (London, 1956), pp. 23 ff.

10

The Name and the Glory

The early church came into being, not only because Jesus was remembered as the presence of God among men "once upon a time," but also because he was still known as the living presence "here and now" and he was expected to come again at the end of the age. It was a combination of this remembrance, knowledge, and expectation which enabled the Christians of the first hour to wait for the return of their Lord in glory. As they waited, however, they developed a *modus vivendi*. They gathered together in prayer, and they proclaimed their faith around them. In less than one generation they spread the gospel to the heart of the Empire. As they spoke to others or among themselves, the presence which animated them was necessarily articulated in words. Presence as "the Word" compelled them to assess, reflect, and find verbal expression for the "good news" they carried. Thus, the remembrance and the eschatological knowledge of Jesus as the living Lord had to be blended into theological interpretation.[1]

The thought-form which dominated one of the earliest methods of interpreting the person of Jesus was the temple ideology. Presence had been lifted from the realm of geography to that of humanity, and the ethical demands of the theology of the name were henceforth held in tension with the spiritual delights of the theology of the glory.

THE NEW TEMPLE

Among the homilies of the nascent church, the editor of the Book of the Acts of the Apostles gave particular attention to the speech of Stephen,[2] a Greek-speaking Jew (Acts 6:8—7:60).[3] This remarkable discourse represents the Lukan edition of an early source which reflects the thinking of one of the first theologians of Christendom.

Accused before the Sanhedrin of having spoken against the holy place and against the Torah, Stephen was summoned by the high priest to answer these charges (Acts 6:8—7:1). He replied by rehearsing the history of salvation, beginning with Abraham, Joseph, and Moses (Acts 7:2 ff.). Significantly, he made no mention of the covenant, and he called the Torah "the living words" (vs. 38), a formula which echoed the preaching of the apostles in the temple (Acts 5:20) and may have implied the prophetic quality of the Word, as opposed to the static finality of the written Law. In addition, Stephen stressed the rebelliousness of the fathers, which occurred as early as the sojourn in the wilderness (vss. 39 ff.), just as he had previously pointed out that the patriarchs had been envious of Joseph (vs. 9). He quoted the scathing words of the prophet Amos (Acts 7:42-43; cf. Amos 5:25-27), and he introduced at last the subject of the temple:

[David] found grace in the presence of God, and asked that he might [also] find a tent for the [God] of Jacob. But it was Solomon who built a house for him. And yet, the Most High does not dwell in [residences] built by human hands. As the prophet said,

> Heaven is my throne,
>   and the earth a stool for my feet.
> What kind of a house would you build for me, says the Lord,
>   and what could be the place of my rest?
> Is it not my hand which has created all these things?
>
> (Acts 7:46–50.)

To support his denunciation of Solomon, the temple builder, Stephen invoked the well-known oracle from the books of the Prophets (Isa. 66:1–2),[4] and by asserting that the Most High does not dwell in residences "made by human hands" (*cheiropoiêtois*), a word used in the Septuagint to designate idols, he implied that the holy place on Mt. Zion was a center of idolatry from which God was absent. His attitude, like that of Jesus before him, echoed an anticultic movement which developed in Judaism at the dawn of Christianity.[5]

It is not possible to ascertain whether Stephen would have also proclaimed that Jesus was "the new temple," for his discourse was interrupted by the anger of his opponents. The suggestion that he might have done so, however, is plausible, for he had begun his review of the *Heilsgeschichte* with the statement, "The God of glory appeared to our father Abraham" (vs. 2), and it was the ideology of glory which the narrator summoned for the concluding scene. The members of the Sanhedrin were exasperated by his words, "but he, filled with the Holy Spirit, kept his eyes fixed to heaven. He saw the glory of God, and Jesus standing at the right hand of God" (vs. 55). The theology of the name, with its ethical rigor and its prophetic critique of the cultic mode of presence, brought about the martyrdom of Stephen. The theology of the glory, with its spiritual delight, explained the courage of Stephen before the imminence of his death.

Like the prophet Ezekiel, for whom the heavens were opened (Ezek. 1:1), Stephen was engulfed in a vision of the divine glory. In view of the Lukan association of the temple with the glory, one may conclude that the narrative of Stephen's vision implied the motif of Jesus as "the new temple."[6] "Behold, I see the heavens opened, and the Son of man standing at the right hand of God" (Acts 7:56). The use of the expression "Son of man" was exceptional in the language of the early church. It alluded to the messianic saying of the Book of Daniel (7:13), which Jesus had quoted, according to the gospel tradition, in his answer to the high priest (Mark 14:6). In the vision of Stephen, however, the Son of man is neither "sitting" nor "coming down on the clouds of heaven," but "standing," as if he were momentarily poised between two worlds, perhaps rising to welcome his witness into the divine realm but not yet acting out his *Parousia* at the end of history.

In this incipient "Christology," one may discern the inauguration of the trend toward a "delayed eschatology." Jesus has come. He will come again. In the meantime, he keeps coming to his own people, "the temple of the Spirit."

THE TEMPLE OF THE SPIRIT

The problems of Christian life in Corinth offered Paul the occasion to develop the theme of the new temple, which Stephen had introduced twenty years previously (ca. A.D. 35). Most of the Pauline letters date from the middle of the first century (ca. A.D. 55). By that time, Christian communities had fanned out from many diaspora synagogues into the urban centers of Asia Minor, Greece, and Italy. These new communities faced the issue of their own distinctiveness, identity, and survival. Their position was far more delicate than that of the synagogues from which they had sprung, for they lacked the ethnic and ritual structures of Jewish separatism (such as racial origin, circumcision, Sabbath, and purity prohibitions). The universalism of the Christian vocation constituted a reverse risk of cul-

tural corruptibility. The local communities, so greatly frag-
mented, needed to be consolidated on a worldwide basis. Paul
alluded often to the universality of the *ecclesia*, and he described
the church with the help of several images: "people," "house,"
"body," and especially "temple."[7]

By the proclamation of the gospel, men and women of manifold races and creeds had been ushered into the presence of the
God of Israel. It was that presence—in the light of the attitude
of Jesus himself—which raised the status of women to the same
cultic level as that of men, eradicated the difference between
Jews and Greeks, and refused to distinguish between slaves and
freemen (Gal. 3:28). The presence welded them together into
a new people. Paul compared their corporateness to a sanctuary
where the presence of the living God beckons and empowers.
Each community was part of the larger community. The church
was the locale of the Spirit of God. The temple of the Spirit was
filled within and protected as well as commissioned without. As
in the Qumran sect, the temple was spiritualized into the community.[8]

The Shelter and the Guard (2 Cor. 6:14–18)

Possibly on account of its situation as a commercial and cultural meeting place between East and West, Corinth was notorious for its moral, intellectual, and religious experiments. The
Christians of Corinth were particularly susceptible to the idolatrous fascination of their Hellenistic ambience. Paul tried to
make them understand the ramifications of the word "idolatry,"
which embraced far more than image worship. Idolatry was the
latreia, or adoration, of the proximate for the ultimate. It may
have been, on the one hand, complacency in the security of
Jewish observance which tended to induce in the sons of the
chosen people a sense of proprietorship of the divine; or on the
other hand a yielding to the seduction of the many cults in which
mystical fusion with the life forces of nature and history pro-

duced illusions of infinity. The church was the sanctuary which sharply delimited the sacred from the profane.

> Is there anything in common between the temple of God
> and idols?
> For we are the temple of the living God; as God said,
> In the midst of them I shall dwell and march,
> I shall be their God and they will be my people.
> Therefore, get yourselves away from [non-believers],
> And keep yourselves apart, says the Lord,
> And touch nothing impure and I shall welcome you.
> I shall be for you a father,
> And you will be for me sons and daughters,
> Says the Lord Almighty.
>
> (2 Cor. 6:16–18)

By comparing the church to the temple of the living God,[9] Paul revealed the originality of his thinking. While he used the midrashic or exegetical methods of his time, he was able to bring out the vitality of the Hebraic theology of presence at the threshold of the new age, and to show that this theology concerned the whole of humanity. First, he linked together, perhaps under the influence of the Book of the Jubilees (1:17), the eschatological promise of the prophet Ezekiel (37:27) and the priestly picture of the desert tabernacle which the Ezekielian circles dreamed about at the end of the Babylonian captivity (Lev. 26:11 f.). Second, he summoned for his own purpose Deutero-Isaiah's warning to the priests, "touch nothing unclean"; but he omitted the words "you who carry the vessels of the Lord" (Isa. 52:11), for he applied the notion of priesthood to the entire community. Third, he returned to an Ezekielian oracle to proclaim the divine offer of welcome (Ezek. 20:34). Fourth, he broadened the Davidic promise from the Nathan oracle on filial kingship (2 Sam. 7:14) to embrace the entire community within the fatherhood of God. Fifth and finally, by borrowing the phrase "sons and daughters" from the same

Deutero-Isaiah (Isa. 43:6), he raised women to the status of men within the family of God, deliberately separating himself from the official cult of the Jerusalem temple, where women were segregated in a special court, and from the Qumran sect, which spiritualized the sanctuary but identified it with a male brotherhood—whether celibate or not.[10]

It was the treasure of divine presence, "dwelling and marching in the midst of them," which made the Christians into a spiritual temple, distinct from both Jews and pagans. The nomadic motif of "marching" was preserved because it suggested the desert tabernacle on the move rather than the sanctuary erected on the Zion rock. The spiritual temple was not an abstract idea, for it was incarnate in a worldwide community. The image of the tabernacle was singularly propitious, for it contained an element of liberation from static particularism without the risk of dilution into subjective individualism.

While religion may be what man does with his solitariness, Christian faith, on the contrary, is what happens to humankind —both men and women—when the presence of God bridges space and time by knitting sons and daughters of God into a tight but mobile society with a capacity for adaptation to historical change. The symbol of the spiritual temple suggests a corporate solidarity which never lets solitariness deteriorate into isolation. The spiritual temple is liberated from the restrictiveness of racial and ritual exclusivism, but it does not promote promiscuity with secular culture. On the contrary, it creates a distinctiveness of moral behavior. Viewed in the context of the Pauline letters, the exhortation to "touch nothing impure" (2 Cor. 6:14) alludes not to Jewish prohibitions of unclean food or bodily contact but to moral alertness. It is because God's temple is holy and the Spirit of God dwells in human beings individually as well as corporately that there are limits in social and especially sexual relations with nonbelievers. The image of the temple of God applies not only to the universal church but also to the body of each of its members, who are warned against sexual communion with pagans (1 Cor. 3:16–17). The temple of the Spirit is a shelter and a guard. Quite different from a vague feeling of divine omnipresence in nature or among all human-kind, the reality of the spiritual temple translated itself con-cretely into the life and the thought of the new community.

Paul was able to play on this particular aspect of the theology of presence because he knew the transformation which that presence could bring about in human beings. His notion of the temple of the Spirit was directly dependent on his idea of the new creature, transfigured daily by the reflection of glory.

The Reflection of Glory (2 Cor. 3:18)

The theologoumenon of the glory, which the Hebraic theol-ogy of presence opposed to the theologoumenon of the name both in the early traditions concerning the Horeb theophany and in the prophetic confessions of call until the time of Ezekiel, had come to assume a primary importance in Persian and Hel-lenistic Judaism.[11] The Lukan editor and the Prologue of John used the same motif in their attempts to interpret the person of Jesus of Nazareth.[12] By doing so, however, they altered its Hebraic meaning of pure transcendence by charging the word "glory" with the burden of the passion and the death of the Son of God in abasement. The apostle Paul contributed to this theo-logical development when he referred to Christians as mirrors of that glory:[13] "And all of us, with face unveiled, while reflect-ing as a mirror the glory of the Lord, are being transfigured into the same image, from glory to glory, by the Lord who is the Spirit" (2 Cor. 3:18).

Many commentators have detected here an expression of Hellenistic mysticism, in which the eye of vision triumphed over the ear of obedience. It has been maintained that Paul departed in this instance from Hebraic reticence about "seeing" God since he affirmed that Christians were able to "behold the glory of the Lord," whereas the Israelites were blinded by a veil over their mind. Such an interpretation, which has contributed to theological anti-Semitism in traditional Christendom, is not supported by the text. The exegete will admit, however, that the rhetorical movement of Paul's thinking, which is here unusually tortuous and elliptical, may lead to misapprehension.

The preceding context is clear enough. Some members of the Corinthian church, probably of Jewish origin, have challenged the apostle's credentials. With unconcealed passion, the missionary to the pagans—and to the Jewish diaspora—defends his ministry by appealing to the authenticity of his vocation: "Our sufficiency is of God" (2 Cor. 3:1-5).

In one of his few allusions to a new covenant, perhaps borrowed from the eschatological hope of Jeremiah under the influence of the Qumran sectarians,[14] Paul places the freedom of the Spirit above subservience to a written code. As shown by his disquisitions on legalism, in Galatians and elsewhere, the former Pharisee knows the risks of a written code: it may promote an empty formalism, dishonest casuistry, or egocentric pride. The Spirit transcends the written law (2 Cor. 3:6), for it creates responsible freedom in the presence of the living God. The Spirit respects the potentialities of human reaction to the urgency of the last days before the new age. The Spirit does not undermine the complexities of decision in unprecedented circumstances. The Spirit takes hold of the total person and animates the whole being. The Spirit gives life (vs. 7).

It is the thought of the immediacy of the presence which introduces the motif of glory. When Moses descended from the mountain, the radiance of his face was such that the Israelites could not bear to look at him, "on account of the glory" (vs. 7c). Moses veiled his face so that the Israelites would not see its brightness (vs. 13). By referring to this particular feature of the Mosaic theophany (Exod. 34:29-35), Paul in no way disparaged the person of Moses, but he defended himself against the Jews who attacked him: "Whenever they read Moses, a veil is upon their mind" (vs. 15). Obedience to the law is no substitute for the inner conflagration of death and renewal which marks the existential turmoil of a "turning about" or "con-version" to the Lord. The veil falls only from the faces of those who enter into a live relation of immediacy with the Most High God, although this Most High God is "seen" only under the image of the debased and humble Jesus.

Paul's argument was historically conditioned by the situation in which he labored. He did not attack Moses. Like the prophets of Israel and the poet of Job, however, he did pierce through the illusion and the arrogance of all forms of legalistic subservience. Subsequent history has shown that such an illusion and such an arrogance may be Jewish, Roman Catholic, or Protestant. They may include secular as well as clerical moralism, whenever the church or the state or any relative entity of the political right or left claims to be the ultimate reality.

Presence—elusive, intangible, unpredictable, untamed, inaccessible to empirical verification, outwardly invisible but inwardly irresistible—is the source of freedom from the written code. "For the Lord is Spirit, and where the Spirit of the Lord is, there is freedom" (vs. 17). Spiritual freedom, however, is barred from the eccentricities of individualism by the specific mode of presence from which it derives.

Now comes the most significant and controversial statement: "And all of us, with face unveiled, while we reflect as a mirror the glory of the Lord, we are being transfigured . . ." (vs. 18a). Discussion has arisen especially on account of the verb "we reflect as a mirror." Traditional versions have rendered it: "we behold."[15] This implies that Christians contemplate God himself through the mirror of the Lord's glory. Vision then becomes the source of *gnosis* and of transformation. There is little doubt, however, that the verb *katoptrizesthai*, in the middle voice, means not "to behold" but "to reflect as a mirror."[16]

There is no implication of cause and effect between this reflection and the transformation of those who reflect.

According to this translation, Paul declares that "all of us"—not just a few privileged individuals, charismatic leaders, or a sacerdotal college—are like Moses. With unveiled faces, Christians radiate the glory. A startling difference, however, separates them from Moses. They do not directly mirror the glory of God in its transcendent blindingness, but they transmit the subtle and subsumed splendor of God's abasement. Moreover, this reflection is not short-lived, for it does not refer to a temporary theophany. It is an attitudinal activity of long duration, as indicated by the participial form of the verb. It coincides with the slow, sometimes painful backtracking development of human transfiguration. As we reflect the glory to others, we are being transformed, literally, "metamorphosed" (*metamorphoumetha*),[17] into the image of God in Jesus. Paul does not refer to an ecstatic vision or to an esoteric *gnosis*. Rather, he is concerned with the growth of a new being. He has in mind the constancy of the inner progress which, little by little, conforms the Christian to the *imago Dei*.[18] It is not an act of contemplation which—through some spiritual technique or art—produces human transfiguration, for God remains the initiator, the agent, and the achiever. "It is he, himself, who has shined in our hearts in order to spread the splendor of the knowledge of his glory which radiates upon the face of the Christ" (2 Cor. 4:6). And Paul hastens to add, "but this treasure we carry in earthen vessels" (vs. 7a). It is as if he had thought that our mirror is quite tarnished. We may have our face unveiled, but what our face reveals is not the pure luminescence of the Deity. At best, we are dulled screens, obscured and distorted by the contradictions and tensions of our existential compromises. A silver or even a gold mirror always distorts the image which it redirects, just as our transfiguration represents only the beginning of a growth which awaits its completion.

Mystical ecstasy, from which Paul himself was not immune (2 Cor. 12:1 ff.), is short-lived and reserved for the few. But all of us, writes Paul to the Christians of Corinth, may have an inward perception of the person of Jesus on this earth, and enter into his outlook on humanity. In this sense, the traditional translation of the verb may receive a contextual justification. Man cannot see God, but there is a most distinctive kind of glory in the giving-up of the self, and this is the reflection of glory, which is accessible to all.

Salvador Dali has painted a large canvas for the Cathedral of Santiago.[19] He placed St. James on a gigantic horse which bears on its body the symbols of Ezekiel and the theology of glory. The horse is able to endure the splendor of the divine light. The saint, on the contrary, *even the saint*, must avert his face before the blinding brightness. Turning aside, he can look only at the rays of gleaming gold, which are diffused by the image of Jesus crucified.

The Name and the Glory (Phil. 2:5–11)

Whether Paul quoted an ancient hymn or composed it himself may never be ascertained.[20] If the poem represents the Greek translation of an Aramaic original,[21] it may have been sung in the churches of the first generation. In any case, the apostle introduces a hymn in order to show the indivisibility of ethics and spirituality. He exhorts the Philippians to bury their whims of egocentricity by cultivating the mind (*phronein*) of their Lord. He writes (Phil. 2:5): "Behave among yourselves according to the mind of the Christ Jesus,

I

2:6. Who, being in the form of God,
      Did not cling to his equality with God to exploit violence,

7. But he emptied himself.
   He took the form of a slave,
   And he assumed the likeness of men.

This is not the place for analyzing or even listing the manifold difficulties of this poem. It will be sufficient to suggest that no Hellenistic speculation is needed to explain its genesis. The poet asked himself obvious questions. What kind of man was Jesus, a just and compassionate healer who had been condemned to a dishonorable death? His presence continued to haunt and to heal men and women of many paths of existence. Could the simple and awesome holiness of his person mirror the very core of divinity? Is it possible that an innocent victim endured the shame and torture of the cross? Not only an innocent victim, but a man who carried with him a unique manner of being. His memory summoned the *imago Dei:* man, issuing forth, pristine and clean, out of the imagination of God. Could he be the Son of God, the mythical heavenly man, the Son of man of the Apocalyptic? Perhaps. Yes and no. He was not the royal messiah who would liberate Israel. Could he be the suffering slave of Yahweh who had been sung by the Deutero-Isaianic prophet of the Babylonian captivity?

The poet meditated on the origin of Jesus the man. By doing so, he went a step farther. He understood the ambiguity of the *imago Dei.*[22] Man is so much like God that he wants to ape the Deity, attempt to force the barriers of his finitude, evade the limitations of his humanity, snatch power, and even use violence in order to achieve his own brand of what he calls "the good." Above all, he desires to acquire the dimensions of eternity and to seize infinity in time. He wants to be exactly like God and therefore to be immortal. He eats the fruit of the tree of the knowledge of all things, "from good to evil." The irony of man's godlikeness is that man is so close to the divine status that he snatches divinity and immediately discovers his alienation, the brokenness of his selfhood, the loss of his own humanity, and a cosmic loneliness. Lusting for immortality, he merely confirms his mortality.

The poet imagined the decision of the son of the family who leaves home—a divine home—refusing to use his equality with God as a prize to be grasped and caught, a trophy to be stolen, a piece of booty to own as a way of self-aggrandizement or even usurpation. He knew the difference, enunciated in modern times by Gabriel Marcel, between "having" and "being." He proclaimed an authentic humanism, not the humanism of Protagoras, "Man is the measure of all things," but the humanism implied in the question of the psalmist, "What is man that thou shouldst remember him?" He discerned in Jesus the type of man who did not yield to the greed of deification through egocentricity. "He emptied himself" (*ekenosen*, vs. 7a). Theology is kenotic when it stresses the divine act of divesting oneself of prerogatives. The kenotic theology of the hymnist offers a prelude to the life of the man Jesus. It intimates in parallel fashion the "overshadowing" of the myth of the annunciation, the debasement of the baptism, when Jesus was immersed in the common guilt of the human race, the agony of his temptation to use power, in the desert and in the garden, and the taunting of the by-standers who said, before his last gasps of pain, "If thou be the Son of God, save thyself!"

The poet, in effect, sang the presence of the *Deus absconditus* at the crucifixion.

II

2:7d. Appearing in the fashion of a man,
   8. He became destitute,
      And his obedience led him to die,
      Even to die on a cross.

While the first strophe sought to discover words to express the divine radiance of the character of Jesus, the second strophe developed the historical significance of his incarnation. He was found in all respects to be the man who corresponded to the intention of the artist who had created him. *Ecce homo!* sang the theologian of the new anthropological dimension.

The hymnist proclaimed that the play of mankind is not a tragedy, for the knot is untied. The play has a *dénouement*. The infernal circle is exploded, the curse lifted, and the tension relieved. The play of man is the *divina commedia*, with the promise of plenitude. The mythical Son of God is a historical man. His marriage to poverty brings God and man together. The theology of presence is the anthropology of communion.

Faith overcomes alienation and revolt. It even exploits the scandal of suffering and uses it for a superior end. The agonies of man are transfigured by the agonies of God. Léon Bloy, in our time, thought of such a transfiguration, which early Christians, in ancient time, had attempted to express. He asked: "Do we not know at the very moment when we suffer some painful blow, that it is Jesus, covered with wounds, who is tumbling upon the muddy carpet of our souls, begging us, at the least, not to bristle too much against Him, and that thus we are filled to overflowing with the most unimaginable happiness?"[23]

III

2:9. Thus, God has highly exalted him
     And he has graced him with a name above any other
        name,
10. That at the name of Jesus every knee shall bend,
    In heaven, on earth, and in the depths,
11. And every tongue shall sing in praise
    That Jesus Christ is Lord
    To the glory of God the Father.

The hymn places the myth of the resurrection in its existential setting. It does not evoke the thought of Jesus *redivivus*, a mortal brought back for a season to a mortal existence, but it sings the exaltation of authentic humanity. The hymn echoes the Song of the Suffering Servant of Yahweh (Isa. 52:13; cf. 45:23),[24] and parallels the motif of a Qumran fragment in which it is said that "God wondrously caused his glory to draw near (to him) from among the children of the world to counsel him in the heavenly council."[25] In Second Isaiah, Israel was God's glory (Isa. 42:8, 43:7, 48:11). In Qumran, God's glory was the persecuted members of the sect. In the Pauline hymn, the obedient Jesus is manifested as the glory of God the Father. As in the Prologue of John (1:14), true glory lies in divine self-giving.[26]

The hymn brings together the two ideologies of cultic presence which had been found in ancient Israel. In the Elohistic traditions and in the Deuteronomic interpretation, Yahweh causes his name to sojourn in the sanctuary. In Ezekiel and the priestly school, Yahweh causes his glory to descend and to dwell in the shrine. In the Pauline hymn, the glory that was hidden in the man Jesus was also the shelter of the divine name. The apostle quoted the hymn in order to stress the meaning of the name *and* the glory. He called for a full accord and a oneness of mind among the Christians of Philippi, knowing that unity blossoms only from the expulsion of egocentricity and conceit (Phil. 2:2–3). He therefore concluded his exhortation with the words, "Let each one of you look not only to his own interests, but also to the interests of others. Cultivate among yourselves the mind which was in Christ Jesus, who. . . ." Then, the hymn follows (vss. 4–5, 6–11).

The unity of the church grows from the mutuality of service, but the power of love comes from association with the hidden glory. Paul does not stress any creedal conformism or ecclesiastical institution. What is important is conformity to the sacrificial mind of Jesus.[27]

The setting of the Philippians Hymn was in all probability the celebration of the eucharistic meal, during which the early Christians sang their faith, proclaimed in music and praise the remembrance of Jesus and "announced ritually" (*kataggelein*) his death in anticipation of his final epiphany.[28] The new temple was the temple of the Spirit, and therefore also, in terms of the Lord's supper, "the temple of his body."

THE TEMPLE OF HIS BODY

The cult of the first-century church was marked by an exuberance of joy (*agalliasis*, Acts 2:46).[29] The mood of the assemblies was mirthful, for it was dominated less by the remembrance of the past than by the expectation of the future.

The Breaking of the Bread

The earliest communities gathered for praise and prayer, for instruction and "the breaking of the bread" (Acts 2:42, 46; cf. 20:7). They met to worship "on the first day of the week" because it was "the Lord's day," the day of the resurrection of Jesus. In Greek, the expression could mean either "the day of the risen Lord" or "the day of Yahweh," the day of the final epiphany.[30]

In the first stage of the church's history, worship was inspired by an effervescence of hope in the nearly immediate return of the Lord. Its earliest liturgical word seems to have been *Maranatha!* "Come, Lord!" (Rev. 22:20; cf. 1 Cor. 16:22). The *Didache* (10:6) indicates that in the second century, the phrase was uttered at the end of the common meal. This practice must have issued from the first generation of Jewish Christians from the East, since the expression was preserved in its Aramaic original.

The gesture of the breaking of the bread was a rehearsal of the heavenly banquet, but it could not have received an eschatological significance unless it was preceded and motivated by a response to the reality of spiritual presence, intimately connected with the faith in the resurrection.

The story of Emmaus recalled that the two disciples recognized Jesus when he blessed the bread and broke it (Luke 24:-30).[31] It was during a common meal that Jesus appeared to the eleven (Luke 24:36; cf. John 21:12 ff.). The Jerusalem church "ate salt with him" (Acts 1:4). Peter affirmed that he was one of those "who did eat and drink with him after he rose from the dead" (Acts 10:40). The eucharistic meal was at first an Easter meal.[32] It stood as an event in "end-time," poised for a moment between the Lord's day and the day of the Lord (Rev. 1:10), for it coalesced the day of the Sabbath—harbinger of the final epiphany ("the day of the Lord")—with the day of the resurrection —harbinger of the *Parousia* ("the Lord's day). Through the mode of eucharistic presence, the Lord had already returned in the breaking of the bread.[33]

The Proclamation of the Death

A notable development occurred when the breaking of the bread—originally mentioned alone, without the drinking of the cup—came to be associated with the last supper which Jesus had eaten with his disciples before his arrest.[34] The synoptic gospels repeat in nearly identical terms the eschatological thrust of the blessing of the cup: "Verily I say unto you, I shall no more drink of the fruit of the vine until the day when I drink it new in the kingdom of God" (Mark 14:25; cf. Matt. 26:29, Luke 22:18). The eschatological thrust is still preserved, but the anamnesis of the death rather than of the resurrection tends to occupy the central place. "This is my body . . . This is the blood of the covenant which is poured out for many" (Mark 14:24; cf. Matt. 26:28, Luke 22:19, 20). The anamnesis of the death, to be sure, does not push the commemoration of the risen Lord into the background, for Paul declares: "Every time you eat this bread and drink this cup, you proclaim the Lord's death *till he come*" (1 Cor. 11:26).

The eucharistic meal, however, now includes the cup of the

covenant (1 Cor. 11:25). It has evolved into a rite of the union of all partakers with the presence which is in the new temple. The temple of the Spirit is also the risen Lord, the temple of his body: "The bread which we break, is it not a communion with the body of Christ? Since there is one bread, we who are many are one body" (1 Cor. 10:16–17).[35] Because the covenant meal is eschatological, a foretaste of the heavenly banquet, pre-enacted, so to speak, in anticipation of the day of the Lord, the body of Christ is indistinguishable from the spiritual body of the church.

Through the eucharistic advent of presence, the pluralism of the church is made homogeneous. Subsequent history, however, shows that Christendom has too often reversed this sequence of the apostle's thought. Many offshoots of the body of Christ, at one time or another, have decreed "closed communion," an exclusivistic exercise in esotericism, based on institutional and creedal conformism. In the early church, on the contrary, communion branched out in several dimensions. The presence of the risen Lord was believed to be the agent of unity in diversity.

It was this grasp of the multidimensional theology of presence which inspired the eucharistic prayer of the *Didache* (9:4): "As this broken bread was scattered like wheat on the mountains but was gathered and became one, so let thy church be gathered into thy kingdom from the extremities of the earth."

According to some interpreters, the dynamic character of memory as cultic reenactment and of anticipation as cultic pre-enactment, which informed the Hebraic celebration of the Feasts of Passover, Weeks, and Tabernacles, together with Paul's insistence on behavior-searching and intention-probing as a needed preparation for sharing in the eucharistic meal (1 Cor. 11:28), indicates that an event of divine manifestation is taking place which would not otherwise occur when the deeds of eating and of drinking are "properly" performed.

Such a view does not appear to be supported by the text—admittedly unclear and perhaps ambiguous—unless one isolates unintentionally the meaning of "body" from that of the risen Lord, which is the church, and divests this meaning of its eschatological thrust. Those who "do not discern the body" (vs. 29) are precisely those who, by their egocentric behavior, attitude of domination, or acts of social irresponsibility, disrupt the harmony of the church, which is the body of the risen Lord.

The self-discipline which is inspired by the compassion and the self-abnegation of Jesus constitutes a previous condition for sharing in the eucharistic meal. The words of Paul offer no justification for speculating on the efficacy or objectivity of the sacrament.

The Bread of Life

Do the daring words of the Johannine discourse on the bread of life (John 6:25—59) move in the same theological direction?[36] In the first part of the discourse (6:35–40), the invitation of the Lord who says "I am the bread of life" (6:35) is primarily colored by the figure of Wisdom (Prov. 9:5, Sir. 15:3),[37] who feeds her guests with the word which brings life, and even offers herself as food and drink (Sir. 24:19–21). Unlike Wisdom, however, whose sustenance is also a stimulant for further desire, the Johannine Jesus offers a grace which is sufficient and transcends the relativity of mortal existence:

I am the bread of life,
  No one who comes to me shall ever be hungry,
  And no one who has faith in me shall ever again be thirsty.

In truth, this is the will of the Father,
  That everyone who looks upon the Son
  And who has faith in him has eternal life,
  And I will raise him up on the last day

(John 6:35, 40)

The second part of the discourse (6:41–50) responds to the query of unbelief, "Isn't this Jesus, the son of Joseph?" (vs. 42), and compares the bread of life with the manna in the wilderness:[38]

"This is the bread that comes down from heaven,
    That any man may eat it and not die"

(vs. 50).

The third part of the discourse (6:51–58) develops the same theme in terms of the eucharistic "flesh" and "blood":

The bread that I give
Is my own flesh for the life of the world.

He who feeds on my flesh
And drinks my blood has eternal life,
And I will raise him up on the last day.

(vss. 51, 54)

The entire "midrash" or exegetical homily on manna is hinged upon faith in Jesus, who is wisdom in the flesh (John 1:14).

The Fourth Gospel, which omits the institution of the Lord's Supper, pictures Jesus as a naked slave who washes the feet of his disciples (John 13:1–20). The discourse on the bread of life places the eucharistic meal in the context of a faith in the man who took the form of a slave (Phil. 2:7; cf. John 13:16). It goes so far as to affirm that this faith is initiated by God. It is difficult to maintain, in the light of this theological affirmation, that faith may be sacramentally obtained. "No one can come to me unless the Father who sent me draws him" (John 6:44).

The Johannine Jesus who says, "I am the bread of life," also says, "I am the door" (John 10:9) and "I am the true vine" (John 15:1, 5). Large segments of Christendom have interpreted the expressions "feed on my flesh" and "drink my blood" in the light of pagan rituals, but they have done so by ignoring the theocentric structure of the Johannine discourse and the style of the Johannine gospel.[39]

For the early Christians, the eucharistic meal was not a sacrificial offering but a concrete gesture animated by the ritual word which exteriorized socially the inner mystery of sharing in the sacrificial life of Jesus.[40] Such a gesture deserves to be called a true symbol, for it carries within it the truth which it portrays. According to Martin Buber, the foremost meaning of sacrament is, "that the divine and the human join themselves to each other, without merging themselves in each other, a lived Beyond-transcendence-and-immanence."[41]

In the third generation of the church, the author of the Epistle to the Hebrews was compelled to state—no doubt in the face of contemporary abuses—that Jesus died "once and for all" (Heb. 9:12; cf. 1 Cor. 10:16).[42] It is easy to understand why the Johannine evangelist retold the story of the baptism of Jesus with the eucharistic word, "This is the lamb of God, which takes away the sins of the world" (John 1:29), and concluded his own account of the cleansing of the temple with another eucharistic word, "[Jesus] spoke of the temple of his body" (John 2:21).

The threefold theme of the new temple, the temple of the Spirit, and the temple of the body, pointed to the cultic reality of eucharistic presence, which in turn emerged from inner participation in the dying and the rising of the same Lord.[43]

Probably influenced by the Qumran sectarians,[44] and partly dependent upon the theology of the Passover, the early Christians celebrated in their common meal the thanksgiving (*eucharistia*) of their faith. This new rite enabled them to reenact with gratitude (*charis*) the whole life of Jesus, not just his death. It also announced the certainty of their hope in the fulfillment of creation. The certainty of this future event corresponded to the contemporaneity of the eucharistic presence. The presence was spiritual and therefore real. "It is the Spirit which gives life, the flesh is of no avail. The words that I have spoken to you are spirit and life" (John 6:63).

The meal was eucharistic, for it celebrated the presence of the risen Lord as an event of grace (*charis*). The gesture was a common meal, for it elicited oneness from the diversity of the participants. It was "the temple of his body" which made present the communality and the actuality of the invisible church in history.

DEUS ABSCONDITUS ATQUE PRAESENS

The foregoing survey has touched upon only a few high points in the literary deposit of biblical faith.[45] During more than twelve centuries of political, economic, cultural, and religious travail, Israel responded in diverse and often conflicting ways to the summons of a few "seers" who had not seen God but who had suddenly and unexpectedly[46] heard his command to act. Obedience to such commands always involved disruption and risk. From Abraham to Moses and from Amos to Second Isaiah, men obeyed in spite of their fears, for they were strong with the promise, "I will be with thee."

Presence perceived in an epiphanic visitation, a theophany, or the invaded solitude of a prophetic vision was "swift-lived," yet the acceptance of the promise it carried transformed those who received and obeyed the command. Faded presence became a memory and a hope, but it burnt into an alloy of inward certitude, which was *emunah,* "faith." When God no longer overwhelmed the senses of perception and concealed himself behind the adversity of historical existence, those who accepted the promise were still aware of God's nearness in the very veil of his seeming absence. For them, the center of life was a *Deus absconditus atque praesens.*

The erection of the tent and the ark in the wilderness, the sanctuaries in Canaan, and the temple in Jerusalem testified to the elusiveness of theophany and vision and stressed the paradox of a hiddenness which was not an absence. Prophets, psalmists, and wise men helped the people and perhaps even their priests to survive the destruction of the temple in the sixth century B.C., for they cultivated memory and hope in a mode of presence which transcended space. Judaism was born within sight of the final epiphany.

Christianity became distinct from Judaism when a handful of men and women saw the sign of the final epiphany not only in the teaching and the healing deeds of Jesus but also in the totality of his person, dying and alive. For them, the future had begun. While his historical existence had been short and the visionary exaltation which followed his death, like a theophany, soon faded, God's presence continued. It was at once an old and a new mode of presence. It was old because it was verified by the reading of Hebrew Scriptures, especially the Psalms, the Prophets, and Wisdom. It was new, because it was indissolubly linked to the memory of Jesus, the expectation of his return, and the contemporaneity of his inspiration to live.

Because Jesus discovered through the presence of his God a hermeneutic freedom which enabled him to read the Hebrew Scriptures in a universal and supralegal perspective, the early Christians soon included Jews and Gentiles, men and women, free men and slaves, who were all liberated and who lived at the edge of their faith. They knew the source of both their liberation and their oneness. It was a multidimensional reality which bound them to the living person of their Lord. The church in history was "the temple of his body," waiting for the new form of "time" when there would be no temple (Rev. 21:22).

Toward a Biblical Theology

Twentieth-century Christian students of the Hebrew Bible have attempted to discern and to explicate a principle of canonical continuity. Has the Old Testament a dynamic center? What is the secret which binds the early Yahwist traditions of the Late Bronze Age to the writings of Israel and Judah and especially those of nascent Judaism in Babylonian, Persian, Hellenistic, and Maccabean times?

Likewise, New Testament scholars have sought to delineate the thread which ties the Synoptic Gospels and Acts to the Pauline, Johannine, Petrine, and other writings of the first-century church.[47] At the same time, the critical assessment of the theological tension which holds these writings apart as well as together has seriously complicated the task of presenting the theological thrust of the New Testament as a whole. Although the span of historical time covered by its books is considerably smaller than the many centuries of the Old Testament literary growth, the diversity of the concrete situations from which the early Christian "theologies" arose has, in the eyes of some scholars, rendered any systematic exposition of New Testament theology an enterprise of questionable validity.[48]

The viability of a genuinely "biblical" theology—encompassing both Testaments—is *a fortiori* more problematic still, for it involves an informed, open, and eminently respectful attitude vis à vis the relationship of early Christianity to pre-rabbinical Judaism as well as an enlightened rigor of judgment on the exegetical (midrashic) and typological methods used by the first-century church when it read the Hebrew Scriptures.[49]

Recent discussion has shown the weakness of the various attempts to construct an Old Testament Theology on the covenant motif or around the "central" but in fact "peripheral"—or at least "partial"—notions of election, kingdom, the self-asseveration "I-Am-Yahweh," creation, redemption, community, and eschatology.[50] The last two decades have also revealed the difficulty of presenting as Old Testament Theology the various testimonies which Israel has recorded on the successive waves of historical challenge and response—however valuable and even brilliant the work of G. von Rad may have been.

Does the Hebraic theology of presence provide a legitimate approach to a genuine theology of the entire Bible? Contemporary trends in the study of wisdom as the main source of Christology suggest that this may well be the case.[51] The figure of personified Wisdom brings together the theologoumenon of the name, with its response of the ear,[52] and the theologoumenon of the glory, with its response of the eye.

Dancing before Yahweh at creation, Wisdom also seeks her delights with the children of men (Prov. 8:30–31). Through the use, not of mythology, but of mythical reflectiveness, Jesus ben Sirach and the author of the Wisdom of Solomon, as well as a few others, identified Wisdom with Torah and Temple.

Sophia became the visible embodiment of presence.

In their attempts to interpret the person of Jesus of Nazareth, the early Christians "saw" in him Sophia, Logos, and Nomos incarnate (John 1:14). In the hymns of the nascent church, Jesus was hailed not only as the master of wisdom but also the divine Wisdom, who could say,

"Come to me, all who labor and are heavy laden,
    And I shall give you rest

(Mt. 11:28).[53]

As Sophia and Logos, the figure of Jesus combined for the primitive church the masculine and feminine elements of the human understanding of the Godhead, without allowing for the alien mythology of an androgynous deity.[54]

The figure of personified Wisdom also offered a model for the paradox of presence in absence. Wisdom had not found a place where she could rest. Like the servant of Yahweh, she was rejected by men. She dwelt among men as the rain in the wilderness (Sir. 1:20 ff.; 1 Enoch 42:1 ff., 84:3; 4 Ezra 5:10; Syriac Baruch 48:36).

Blaise Pascal understood the paradox of presence in absence, which permeates the entire Bible, when he wrote: "A religion which does not affirm that God is hidden is not true" (*Pensées*, 586). Significantly, he added: "And a religion which does not offer the reason [of this hiddenness] is not illuminating." It was on account of Jesus, who "will be in agony until the end of the world," that he could appropriate with assurance and a certain wistfulness the expostulation of the Isaianic poet, *Vere tu es Deus absconditus* (Isa. 45:15a).[55] While the Latin version with its passive participle led to the often abused theme of "the hidden God," the Hebrew original, with its verbal reflexive, stressed divine freedom and sovereignty: "Verily, thou art a God that hidest thyself!"

Even in the Psalm of the Dereliction the cry "My God, my God, why hast thou forsaken me?" is an affirmation of presence, for it leads to the prayer, "Be not far, anguish is near" (Ps. 22:11 [Heb. 12]), which in turn is answered, since it culminates in the pledge, "I shall proclaim thy name to my brothers" (vs. 22 [Heb. 23]). The determination to praise in the presence of the community at worship presupposes the presence of divinity.[56]

The *theologia crucis* which haunts the heart of the Hebraic as well as Christian commitment to proclaim the name[57] is rooted in Jeremiah's rebellion, "I shall not speak any more in [Yahweh's] name" (Jer. 20:28). It also grows from the tenacity of "Job the Agnostic,"[58] and even from the disquieting acquiescence of Qoheleth the Skeptic, who refused "to pretend to certainty when none [was] to be had."[59] A case can easily be made for the uniqueness of Israel's evocation of "the play of wisdom," with its alternation between doubt and faith,[60] the indispensable vessel of the eucharistic celebration.

For the end of the twentieth century A.D. biblical theology may well have to be an intellectual exploration into the dance of wisdom through history, between lament and praise,[61] forerunner of the Christian festivity.[62]

The Servant of the Oikoumene

The failure of the so-called Biblical Theology Movement,[63] in no way precludes the dawn of a new era of scholarship when an ecumenical theology of the entire Bible will serve the various families of Christendom now divided.[64] The present stagnation of the official efforts toward a rapprochement cannot conceal the extraordinary work of dialogue, discussion, and mutual enlightenment which goes on among biblical scholars. Nor does it prevent the root-level communality of worship, service, and biblical study which, in many parts of the world, assembles Christians of separated traditions—Greek Orthodox, Roman Catholic, Anglican-Protestant.

An ecumenical theology of the Bible will approach the Old Testament with theological seriousness, for it has to reverse the nineteenth- and twentieth-century trend which reduces theology to Christology.[65] An ecumenical theology of the Bible will take the Old Testament seriously, for it will discern and describe those elements of theological truth which are common to Judaism and Christianity on the one hand, and Islam and Christianity on the other. An ecumenical theology of the Bible will assign for itself, however, a limited task, for it will not claim to propound a theological elucidation of Christian faith for the end of the twentieth century. It will only attempt to prepare the work of the systematic theologian.[66]

As a prolegomenon to an ecumenical theology of the Bible, the study of the motif of "the presence of God" may prove more fruitful than other motifs in providing a unifying and yet dynamic principle which will account not only for the homogeneity of the Old Testament literature in its totality,[67] including the sapiential books,[68] but also for the historical and thematic continuity which unites Hebraism and large aspects of Judaism with nascent Christianity.

The Elusive Presence

Under a radically different world view, the chief problem of contemporary theology remains what it was for the ancient Hebrews and the early Christians. From presence, remembered and anticipated, they received their interpretation of historical existence. From presence, they learned an uneasy equilibrium between their past and their future, and they obtained at once their condemnation and their liberation to live. Presence, as well as its modes, is at the root of the theological problem of revelation.

In biblical faith, human beings discern that presence is a surging which soon vanishes and leaves in its disappearence an absence that has been overcome. It is neither absolute nor eternal but elusive and fragile, even and especially when human beings seek to prolong it in the form of cultus. The collective act of worship seems to be both the indispensable vehicle of presence and its destroyer. Presence dilutes itself into its own illusion whenever it is confused with a spatial or temporal location. When presence is "guaranteed" to human senses or reason, it is no longer real presence.[69] The proprietary sight of the glory destroys the vision, whether in the temple of Zion or in the eucharistic body.

It is when presence escapes man's grasp that it surges, survives, or returns. It is also when human beings meet in social responsibility that presence, once vanished, is heard.

"The god comes when those in love recognize one another."[70]

In biblical faith, presence eludes but does not delude. The hearing of the name, which is obedience to the will and the decision to live now for an eternal future, becomes the proleptic vision of the glory.

Presence is articulated in the Word, but the Word is heard only by those who recognize the promise and already live by its fulfillment. In this sense, *Torah* is *Logos* made flesh.

Notes

1. See, "He Was Remembered, He Was Known Still, He Was Interpreted," in J. Knox, *Christ the Lord; The Meaning of Jesus in the Early Church* (Chicago, New York, 1945).

2. See B. W. Bacon, "Stephen's Speech," *Biblical and Semitic Studies* (New Haven, 1901), pp. 213 ff.; E. Jacquier, *Les Actes des Apôtres* (Paris, 1926), pp. 203 ff.; M. Dibelius, *Studies in the Acts of the Apostles* (London, 1956), pp. 138 ff.; B. Reicke, *Glaube und Leben der Urgemeinde* (Zürich, 1957), pp. 129 ff.; C. S. C. Williams, *A Commentary on the Acts of the Apostles* (London, 1957), pp. 12 ff., 100 ff.; A. F. J. Klijn, "Stephen's Speech—Acts vii. 2–53," *NTS*, IV (1957–58): 28 ff.; M. Simon, *Stephen and the Hellenists in the Primitive Church* (London, 1958), pp. 39 ff.; J. Bihler, *Die Stephanusgeschichte* (München, 1963), pp. 63 ff.; H. Conzelmann, *Die Apostelgeschichte* (Tübingen, 1963), pp. 45 ff.; E. Haenchen, *Die Apostelgeschichte. Neu übersetzt und erklärt* (Göttingen, 1965), pp. 227; T. Holz, *Untersuchungen über die alttestamentlichen Zitate bei Lukas* (Berlin, 1968), pp. 85 ff.; G. Stählin, *Die Apostelgeschichte übersetzt und erklärt* (Göttingen, 1968), pp. 105 ff.; M. Rese, *Alttestamentliche Motive in der Christologie des Lukas* (Gütersloh, 1969), pp. 78 ff.; J. Kilgallen, *The Stephen Speech. A Literary and Redactional Study of Acts 7, 2–53* (Rome, 1976).

3. See C. S. Mann, " 'Hellenists' and 'Hebrews' in Acts VI 1," in J. Munck, *The Acts of the Apostles* (Garden City, N.Y., 1967), pp. 301 ff.; A. Spiro, "Stephen's Samari-

tan Background," *ibid.*, pp. 285 ff.; M. H. Scharlemann, *Stephen: A Singular Saint* (Rome, 1968), pp. 17 ff.

4. See above, p. 402.

5. See M. Simon, "Saint Stephen and the Jerusalem Temple," *Journal of Ecclesiastical History*, II (1951): 127 ff.; O. Cullmann, "The Significance of the Qumrân Texts for Research into the Beginnings of Christianity," *JBL*, LXXIV (1955), 213 ff.; cf. Scharlemann, *Stephen*, p. 107.

6. See H. P. Owen, "Stephen's Vision in Acts VII.55–56," *NTS*, I (1954–55), 224 ff.; R. Pesch, *Die Vision des Stephanus, Apg 7, 55–56 im Rahmen der Apostelgeschichte* (Stuttgart, 1966), cf. Simon, *St. Stephen and the Hellenists*, pp. 70 f. K. Baltzer points out the Lukan awareness of the link which binds *doxa* (glory), Jesus, and the Heavenly Temple, in "The Meaning of the Temple in the Lukan Writings," *HTR*, LVIII (1965): 275, 277.

7. See P. Bonnard, *Jésus-Christ édifiant son Eglise* (Neuchâtel, 1948), pp. 28 ff.; P. S. Minear, *Images of the Church in the New Testament* (Philadelphia, 1961); J. Pfammater, *Die Kirche als Bau, Eine exegetisch-theologische Studie zur Ekklesiologie der Paulusbriefe* (Rome, 1961).

8. See M. Fraeyman, "La spiritualisation de l'idée du temple dans les épîtres pauliniennes," *ETL*, XXIII (1947): 378 ff.; O. Cullmann, "L'opposition contre le temple de Jérusalem, motif commun de la théologie johannique et du monde ambiant," *NTS*, V (1958): 162 f.; Y. M.-J. Con-

gar, Le mystère du temple (Paris, 1958), pp.
188 ff.; J. A. Fitzmyer, "Qumrân and the
Interpolated Paragraph in II Cor. vi.14—
vii.1," CBQ, XXIII (1961); 271 ff.; A.
Jaubert, "La communauté-sanctuaire,"
La notion d'alliance dans le judaïsme aux
abords de l'ère chrétienne (Paris, 1963), pp.
152 ff.; B. Gärtner, The Temple and the Community in Qumran and the New Testament
(Cambridge, 1965), pp. 49 ff.; R. J.
McKelvey, The New Temple: The Church in
the New Testament (London, 1969), pp. 93
ff.; J. C. Meagher, "John 1, 14 and the
New Temple," JBL, LXXXVIII (1969): 57
ff.; G. Klinzing, "Die Gemeinde als Tempel," Die Umdeutung des Kultus in der Qum-
rangemeinde und im Neuen Testament (Göttingen, 1971), pp. 50 ff.; J. Coppens,
"The Spiritual Temple in the Pauline Letters and Its Background," Studia evangelica, VI (1973): 53 ff.
9. See A. Plummer, A Critical and Exegetical Commentary on the Second Epistle of St.
Paul to the Corinthians (New York, 1915),
pp. 202 ff.; E.-B. Allo, Saint Paul, Seconde
Epître aux Corinthiens (Paris, 1956), pp.
187 ff.; Ph. E. Hughes, Paul's Second Epistle
to the Corinthians (Grand Rapids, Mich.,
1962), pp. 251 ff.
10. See M. Black, The Scrolls and Christian
Origins: Studies in the Jewish Background of the
New Testament (New York, 1961), pp. 27
ff., 83 ff.; G. Vermès, "Dead Sea Scrolls,"
IDB, Suppl. Vol. (1976), p. 214.
11. See above, pp. 138 ff., 171 ff., 259 ff.,
395 ff.
12. See above, pp. 421, 425.
13. See Plummer, Second Corinthians, pp.
93 ff.; J. Dupont, "Le chrétien, miroir de
la gloire divine d'après II Cor. III, 18,"
RB, LVI (1949); 392 ff.; id., Gnosis: la connaissance religieuse dans les épîtres de saint
Paul (Louvain, 1949), pp. 119 ff.; D. H.
Lietzmann u. W. G. Kümmel, An die Korinther I.II (Tübingen, 1949), pp. 112 ff.;
Allo, Seconde Epître aux Corinthiens, pp. 89
ff.; N. Hugedé, La métaphore du miroir dans
les épîtres de saint Paul aux Corinthiens (Neuchâtel, 1957); W. Schmithals, "Zwei

gnostische Stellen im Zweiten Korinther-
brief," Ev. Th., XVIII (1958): 552 ff.; S.
Schulze, "Die Decke des Moses. Untersuchungen zu einer vorpaulinischen Überlieferung in 2 Cor iii 7–18," ZNW, XLIX
(1958): 1 ff.; B. Rey, Créés dans le Christ
Jésus. La création nouvelle selon Saint Paul
(Paris, 1966), pp. 181 ff.; Hughes, Second
Corinthians, pp. 107 ff.; R. Scroggs, The
Last Adam: A Study in Pauline Anthropology
(Philadelphia, 1966), pp. 99 ff.; W. C. van
Unnik, " 'With Unveiled Face', An Exegesis of 2 Corinthians iii 12–18," NT, X
(1966): 153 ff.; C. K. Barrett, A Commentary on the Second Epistle to the Corinthians
(London, 1973), pp. 109 ff.
14. 2 Cor. 3:6; cf. 1 Cor. 11:25, 2 Cor.
3:14; cf. also Luke 22:20, Heb. 8:8, 9:15,
12:24. It will be observed that, in all these
passages, the notion of a new covenant is
always dependent on the primary reality
of presence, and that this notion does not
give rise to protracted development.
15. See Vetus Latina, Vulgate, Syriac,
KJV, RSV, etc. Yet, cf. RSV marg. In 1
Cor. 13:12, Paul uses the analogy of the
mirror to point to the imperfection of the
human vision. Those who render the
verb of 2 Cor. 3:18 by "we behold" or
"we contemplate," generally conclude
that Paul was influenced by Hellenistic
mystery cults. See R. Reitzenstein, Historia Monachorum und Historia Lausiaca
(Göttingen, 1916), pp. 244 ff.; cf., however, id., Die hellenistischen Mysterienreligion-
en (Leipzig & Berlin, 1927), p. 357.
16. See Plummer, Second Corinthians, pp.
105 f.; Allo, Seconde Epître aux Corinthiens,
p. 96; Dupont, "Le chrétien, miroir," p.
401.
17. See above, p. 423.
18. Cf. Rom. 6:3–11, 8:29; Col. 3:5–15;
etc. Paul alluded in many places to the life
of the Christian in terms of the Hebraic
theology of presence. See G. Wagner,
"Le tabernacle et la vie 'en Christ': exégèse de 2 Corinthiens 5:1 à 10," RHPR,
XLI (1961): 379 ff.; J. Murphy-O'Connor,

L'existence chrétienne selon Saint Paul (Paris, 1974).

19. See S. Terrien, *The Power to Bring Forth* (Philadelphia, 1968), p. 109.

20. See, in addition to the commentaries on Philippians, E. Lohmeyer, *Kyrios Christos, eine Untersuchung zu Phil.* 2.5–11 (Heidelberg, 1928); E. Lewis, "The Humiliated and Exalted Son—Interpretation and Doctrine," *In.,* I (1947): 20 ff.; J. Dupont, "Jésus-Christ dans son abaissement et son exaltation d'après Phil. 2, 5–11," *RSR,* XXXVII (1950): 500 ff.; L. Bouyer, "HARPAGOS," *RSR,* XXXIX (1951–52): 281 ff.; L. Cerfaux, "L'hymne au Christ-Serviteur (Ph 2, 7–11; Is 52,12—53,12)," *Recueil Lucien Cerfaux,* II (Gembloux, 1954), pp. 425 ff.; O. Cullmann, *Christology of the New Testament,* tr. by Sh. C. Guthrie and Ch. A. M. Hall (Philadelphia, 1959), pp. 174 ff.; B. Reicke, "Unité chrétienne et diaconie, Phil. ii 1–11," *SNT,* VI (Leiden, 1962): 203 ff.; D. Georgi, "Der vorpaulinische Hymnus Phil 2, 6–11," *Festschrift R. Bultmann,* ed. E. Dinkler (Tübingen, 1964), pp. 270 ff.; J. Coppens, "Les affinités littéraires de l'hymne christologique (Phil., II, 6–11)," *ALBO,* IV (1965): 32 ff.; A. Feuillet, "L'hymne christologique de l'épître aux Philippiens (ii, 6–11)," *RB,* LXXII (1965–6): 352 ff., 481 ff.; B. Rey, *Créés dans le Christ Jésus,* pp. 77 ff.; R. P. Martin, *Carmen Christi: Philippians ii 5–11 in Recent Interpretation and in the Setting of Early Christian Worship* (Cambridge, 1967); D. H. Wallace, "Heilsgeschichte, Kenosis and Chalcedon," *Oikonomia. Festschrift O. Cullmann* (Hamburg, 1967), pp. 248 ff.; E. Käsemann, "A Critical Analysis of Philippians 2:5–11," *JTC,* V (1968), 45 ff.; K. Gamber, "Der Christus-Hymnus im Philipperbrief in liturgiegeschichtlicher Sicht," *Biblica,* LI (1970): 369 ff.; J. G. Gibbs, "The Relation Between Creation and Redemption According to Phil. ii 5–11," *NTS,* XII (1970): 270 ff.; M. Black, "The Kyrios Christology," in "The Christological Use of the Old Testament

in the New Testament," *NTS,* XVIII (1971–72), 6 ff.; R. W. Hoover, "The Harpagos Enigma: A Philological Solution," *HTR,* LXIV (1971): 95 ff.; P. Grelot, "Deux notes critiques sur Philippiens 2, 6–11," *Biblica,* LIV (1973): 169 ff.; H. W. Bartsch, *Die Konkrete Wahrheit und die Lüge der Spekulation: Untersuchung über den vorpaulinischen Christushymnus und seine gnostische Mythisierung* (Frankfurt a. M./ Bern, 1974); E. S. Fiorenza, "Wisdom Mythology and the Christological Hymns of the New Testament," in *Aspects of Wisdom in Judaism and Early Christianity,* ed. by R. L. Wilken (Notre Dame, Ind., 1975), pp. 17 ff. J. Murphy-O'Connor, "Christological Anthropology in Phil. II, 6–11," *RB,* LXXXIII (1976): 25 ff.; L. Richard, "Kenotic Christology in a New Perspective," *Eglise et théologie,* VII (1976): 5 ff.; O. Hofius, *Der Christushymnus. Philipper 2, 6–11* (Tübingen, 1976).

21. See E. Lohmeyer, *Kyrios Jesus,* pp. 10 ff.; cf. J. Jeremias, "Zur Gedankenführung in den paulinischen Briefer," *Festschrift J. de Zwann* (Haarlem, 1953), pp. 152 ff.

22. See J. Jervell, *Imago Dei: Gen. 1.26 f. im Spätjudentum, in der Gnosis und in den paulinischen Briefen* (Göttingen, 1960).

23. Léon Bloy, *Pilgrim of the Absolute,* Selection by Raïssa Maritain, tr. by J. Coleman and H. L. Binsse (New York, 1947), p. 285.

24. See L. Krinetzki, "Der Einfluss von Is. lii,13–liii,12 Par. auf Phil. ii, 6–11," *Theologische Quartalschrift,* CXXXIX (1959): 157 ff., 291 ff.

25. See J. A. Sanders, "Dissenting Deities and Philippians 2 1–11," *JBL,* LXXXVIII (1969): 268.

26. As in the Johannine hymn, the figure of personified wisdom stands behind the motif of abasement and exaltation. See J. T. Sanders, *The New Testament Christological Hymns* (Cambridge, 1971), pp. 70 ff.

27. See Reicke, "Unité chrétienne," pp. 209 f.

28. See Lohmeyer, *Kyrios Jesus*, pp. 65 ff.; N. A. Dahl, "Anamnesis: mémoire et commémoration dans le christianisme primitif," *Studia theologica*, I (1947): 69 ff.; L. Cerfaux, "L'hymne au Christ," p. 129.

29. See O. Cullmann, *Early Christian Worship*, tr. by A. S. Todd and J. B. Torrance (Chicago, 1953), p. 15; A. B. du Toit, *Der Aspekt der Freude im urchristlichen Abendmahl* (Winterthur, 1965), pp. 56 ff.; F. Hahn, *The Worship of the Early Church*, tr. by D. E. Green (Philadelphia, 1973), p. 47.

30. H. Riesenfeld, "Sabbat et jour du Seigneur," *Festschrift Th. W. Manson* (Manchester, 1959), pp. 210 ff.; W. Rordorf, *Sunday; the History of the Day of Rest and Worship in the Earliest Centuries of the Christian Church*, tr. by A. A. K. Graham (London, 1960); C. W. Dugmore, "The Lord's Day and Easter," *Festschrift O. Cullmann* (1962), pp. 272 ff.

31. See above, p. 434.

32. See O. Cullmann, "The Breaking of Bread and the Resurrection Appearances," in "The Meaning of the Lord's Supper in Primitive Christianity," in O. Cullmann and F. J. Leenhardt, *Essays on the Lord's Supper*, tr. by J. G. Davies (Richmond, Va., 1958), pp. 8 ff.

33. See D. E. Aune, *The Cultic Setting of Realized Eschatology in Early Christianity*, SNT, XVIII (Leiden, 1972).

34. Among the many studies of the Last Supper and of the Lord's Supper in New Testament times, see Cullmann, "The Breaking of Bread"; C. F. D. Moule, "The Fellowship Meal and Its Development," in *Worship in the New Testament* (London, 1961), pp. 18 ff.; H. Lietzmann, *Mass and Lord's Supper—A Study in the History of Liturgy* (Leiden, 1953–69); M. Barth, *Das Abendmahl: Passamahl, Bundesmahl und Messiahmahl* (Zollikon-Zürich, 1964); G. D. Kilpatrick, "L'eucharistie dans le Nouveau Testament" *RTP*, XIV (1964): 193 ff.; E. J. Kilmartin, *The Eucharist in the Primitive Church* (Englewood Cliffs, N.J., 1965); J. Jeremias, *The Eucharistic Words of Jesus*, tr. by N. Perrin (London, 1966); *id.*,

"Das ist mein Leib ..." (Stuttgart, 1972); S. McCormick, *The Lord's Supper, a Biblical Interpretation* (Philadelphia, 1966); J.-M. Dufort, *Le symbolisme eucharistique aux origines de l'église* (Bruxelles & Montréal, 1969); N. A. Beck, "The Last Supper as an Efficacious Symbolic Act," *JBL*, LXXXIX (1970): 192 ff.; R. Feneberg, *Christliche Passafeier und Abendmahl ...* (München, 1971); G. Wainwright, *Eucharist and Eschatology* (London, 1971).

35. See A. Robertson and A. Plummer, *A Critical and Exegetical Commentary on the First Epistle of St Paul to the Corinthians* (New York, 1911), pp. 242 ff.; E.-B. Allo, *Première Epître aux Corinthiens* (Paris, 1956), pp. 239 ff., 285 ff.; A. Farrer, "The Eucharist in I Corinthians," *Eucharistic Theology Then and Now* (London, 1968), pp. 15 ff.; W. F. Orr and J. A. Walther, *I Corinthians* (Garden City, N.Y., 1976), pp. 249 ff., 265 ff.

36. See J. H. Bernard, *A Critical and Exegetical Commentary on the Gospel According to St. John* (New York, 1929), pp. 190 ff.; O. S. Brooks, "The Johannine Eucharist," *JBL*, LXXXII (1963): 293 ff.; P. Borgen, *Bread From Heaven*, SNT, X (Leiden, 1965); R. E. Brown, *The Gospel According to John I–XII* (Garden City, N.Y., 1966), pp. 268 ff.; extensive bibliography on pp. 303 f.; J. L. Martyn, "... To the Presence of the Son of Man," in *History and Theology in the Fourth Gospel* (New York, Evanston, 1968), pp. 120 ff.; F.-M. Braun, *Jean le théologien, III. Sa théologie, 2. Le Christ Notre Seigneur* (Paris, 1972), pp. 172 ff.

37. See above, pp. 81 f.

38. See Exod. 16:5, 15; cf. Wisd. of Sol. 16:20.

39. The expression "to eat flesh" alluded to the ancient sacrifice of communion in which the meat of the animal offered on the altar was partially eaten by the worshippers (see Exod. 16:12, Deut. 12:15, etc.). The drinking of blood, however, was strictly prohibited (Gen. 9:4, Deut. 12:16, etc.). Any concrete interpretation of the drinking of the wine as if it were the

blood of a sacrificial offering reflected some ritual of the Hellenistic cults. Cf. W. L. Dulière, "Un problème à résoudre: L'acceptation du sang eucharistique par les premiers chrétiens juifs," *Studia theologica*, XX (1966): 70 ff.

40. See Moule, *Worship in the New Testament*, pp. 40 f.; F. J. Leenhardt, "This is My Body," in O. Cullmann and F. J. Leenhardt, *Essays on the Lord's Supper*, tr. by J. G. Davies (Richmond, Va., 1958), p. 61; B. Reicke, "Worship in the New Testament," *Festschrift Th. W. Manson* (Manchester, 1959), p. 197.

41. *Hasidim* (New York, 1948), p. 117, quoted by M. S. Friedman, *Martin Buber: The Life of Dialogue* (New York, 1960), p. 140.

42. See C. F. D. Moule, "Sanctuary and Sacrifice in the Church of the New Testament," *JTS*, I (1950): pp. 36 ff.; L. Sabourin, "Liturgie du sanctuaire et de la tente véritable (Héb. VIII.2)," *NTS*, XVIII (1971–72): 87 ff.

43. See P. Bonnard, "Mourir et vivre avec Jésus-Christ selon saint Paul," *RHPR*, XXXVI (1956): 101 ff.; A. Feuillet, "Mort du Christ et mort du chrétien d'après les épîtres pauliniennes," *RB*, LXVI (1959): 481 ff.; R. C. Tannehill, *Dying and Rising with Christ* (Leiden, 1967), pp. 104 ff., 130 ff.; cf. J. Héring, "Les bases de l'humanisme chrétien," *RHPR*, XXV (1945): 18 ff.

44. See K. G. Kuhn, "The Lord's Supper and the Communal Meal at Qumran," in *The Scrolls and the New Testament*, ed. by K. Stendahl (New York, 1957), pp. 65 ff.; Black, *The Scrolls and Christian Origins*, pp. 102 ff.

45. Further investigation is required in several areas of the biblical literature, such as Chronicles, Ezra-Nehemiah, the Epistle to the Hebrews, the Epistles of Peter, and the Revelation of John the Divine.

46. See D. Daube, *The Sudden in Scripture* (Leiden, 1964).

47. It is generally understood that 2 Peter dates from ca. A.D. 150.

48. See A. Stock, *Einheit des Neuen Testaments. Erörterung hermeneutischer Grundpositionen der heutigen Theologie* (Köln, 1969).

49. See E. Käsemann, "The Problem of a New Testament Theology," *NTS*, XIX (1972–73): 235 ff.; A.-T. Nikolaien, "Comment structurer une vision globale de la théologie du Nouveau Testament," *SEÅ*, XXXVII–XXXVIII (1973): 310 ff.; E. Lohse, *Grundriss der neutestamentlichen Theologie* (Stuttgart, 1974); G. Strecker, "Das Problem der Theologie des Neuen Testaments," in G. Strecker, ed., *Das Problem der Theologie des Neuen Testaments* (Darmstadt, 1975), pp. 1 ff.

50. See above, p. 36. See also R. Smend, *Die Mitte des Alten Testaments* (Zürich, 1970), p. 57; G. E. Wright, "The Theological Study of the Bible," *IB, One Volume Commentary* (1971), pp. 983 ff.; Hasel, "The Problem of Center," p. 6. D. G. Spriggs, *Two Old Testament Theologies: A Comparative Evaluation of the Contributions of Eichrodt and von Rad to Our Understanding of the Nature of Old Testament Theology* (London, 1974); S. Amsler, "Pour éclairer le rapport entre les deux Testaments," *RSR*, LXIII (1975): 385 ff.; E. Jacob, "Principe canonique et formation de l'Ancien Testament," *SVT*, XXVIII (Leiden, 1975), pp. 16 ff.; J. Mays, "Historical and Canonical: Recent Discussion About the Old Testament and Christian Faith," *Festschrift G. E. Wright* (Garden City, N.Y., 1976), pp. 510 ff.

51. See J. Rendel Harris, "Athena, Sophia and the Logos," *BJRL*, VII (1922–23): 56 ff.; D. B. Botte, "La sagesse et l'origine de la Christologie," *RSPT*, XXI (1932): 54 ff.; W. L. Knox, "The Divine Wisdom," *JTS*, XXXVIII (1939): 230 ff.; A. Feuillet, "Jésus et la sagesse divine d'après les évangiles synoptiques," *RB*, LXII (1955): 161 ff.; id., *Le Christ, sagesse de Dieu* (Paris, 1966); J. W. Montgomery, "Wisdom as Gift: The Wisdom Concept in Relation to Biblical Messianism," *In.*,

XVI (1962): 43 ff.; J. C. Lebram, "Die Theologie des späten Chokma und häretisches Judentum," *ZAW*, LXX (1965): 202 ff.; P. E. Bonnard, *La sagesse en personne annoncée et venue: Jésus-Christ* (Paris, 1966); W. A. Beardslee, "The Wisdom Tradition and the Synoptic Gospels," *JAAR*, XXXV (1967): 231 ff.; F. Christ, *Jesus Sophia* (Zürich, 1970); B. L. Mack, "Wisdom Myth and Mytho-logy," *In.*, XXIV (1970): 46 ff.; *id.*, *Logos und Sophia. Untersuchungen zur Weisheitstheologie im hellenistischen Judentum* (Göttingen, 1973); M. J. Suggs, Wisdom, Christology, and Law in Matthew's Gospel (Cambridge, Mass., 1970); H. Conzelmann, "The Mother of Wisdom," in *The Future of our Religious Past. Festschrift R. Bultmann* [II], tr. by Ch. E. Carlston and R. P. Scharlemann (London, 1971), pp. 230 ff.; R. G. Hamerton-Kelly, *Pre-existence, Wisdom and the Son of Man* (Cambridge, 1973); R. A. Edwards, *A Theology of Q. Eschatology, Prophecy, and Wisdom* (Philadelphia, 1975); E. S. Fiorenza, "Wisdom Mythology and the Christological Hymns of the New Testament," in *Aspects of Wisdom in Judaism and Early Christianity*, ed. by R. L. Wilken (Notre Dame, Ind., 1975), pp. 17 ff.; J. M. Robinson, "Jesus as Sophos and Sophia: Wisdom Tradition and the Gospels," *ibid.*, pp. 1 ff.; P. J. Cahill, "The Johannine Logos as Center," *CBQ*, XXXVIII (1976): 54 ff.

52. See C. J. Bleeker, "L'oeil et l'oreille: leur signification religieuse," *The Sacred Bridge: Researches into the Nature and Structure of Religion* (Leiden, 1963), pp. 52 ff., especially p. 68; K. A. H. Hidding, "Sehen und hören," *Suppl. to Numen*, XVII (*Festschrift C. J. Bleeker*; Leiden, 1963): 69 ff.

53. In addition to the commentaries on Matthew, *in loc.*, see L. Cerfaux, "Les sources scripturaires de Mt 11, 25–30," *ETL*, XXX (1954): 740 ff.; *ibid.*, XXXI (1955), 331 ff.; A. M. Hunter, "Crux criticorum—Mt 11, 25–30," *NTS*, VIII (1961): 241 ff.; W. Grundmann, "Matth

11, 27 und der Sohn-Stellen," *NTS*, XII (1965): 42 ff.

54. Gal. 3:28. On the motif of divine Wisdom in Paul's theology, see H. Windisch, "Die göttliche Weisheit der Juden und die paulinische Christologie," *Festschrift G. Henrici* (Leipzig, 1914), pp. 220 ff.; H. Conzelmann, "Paulus und die Weisheit," *NTS*, XIV (1965–66): 231 ff.; A. Feuillet, *Le Christ, Sagesse de Dieu dans les épîtres pauliniennes* (Paris, 1966); *id.*, *Christologie paulinienne et tradition biblique* (Paris, 1973); A. van Roon, "The Relation Between Christ and the Wisdom of God According to Paul," *NT*, XVI (1974): 207 ff.

55. The context indicates that the divine selection of a foreign "Messiah" must have been deeply offensive to traditional piety (Isa. 45:1–11, 12–14). See R. Davidson, "Some Aspects of the Theological Significance of Doubt in the Old Testament," *ASTI*, VII (1970): 48 f. "The hiddenness of God is proclaimed and confessed as the obverse of his free sovereign choice of men" (K. H. Miskotte, *When the Gods Are Silent*, tr. by J. W. Doberstein [New York, 1963], p. 257).

56. Vide above, pp. 335 ff. Cf. P. Beauchamp, "L'analyse structurale et l'exégèse," *SVT*, XXII (Leiden, 1972), pp. 119 ff.

57. See J. A. Sanders, *The Old Testament in the Cross* (New York, 1961), p. 113.

58. See P. R. Ackroyd, "Job the Agnostic," *Context 1*, II (1968): 15 ff.

59. R. Gordis, *Koheleth—The Man and His World* (New York, 1955), p. 37.

60. See Davidson, "Some Aspects of the Theological Significance of Doubt," p. 51.

61. See C. Westermann, "The Role of the Lament in the Theology of the Old Testament," *In.*, XXVIII (1974): 20 ff.

62. The play of wisdom does not suggest "playfulness," even in the sapiential hymn on creation (Prov. 8:22 ff.). Its somber aspect of parody, sometimes accompanied by a "scapegoat" rite, ap-

pears in many cultures. This element may have influenced the Christian tradition concerning the mocking of Jesus by the soldiers. See D. L. Miller, "ἘΜΠΑΖΕΙΝ: Playing the Mock Game (Luke 22:63–64)," *JBL*, XC (1971): 309 ff.

63. See above, chapter I, notes 182 and 197. See also G. F. Hasel, "The Problem of the Center in the OT Theology Debate," *ZAW*, LXXXVI 1974): 5; J. Barr, "Biblical Theology," *IDB, Suppl. Vol.* (1976), p. 105; *id.*, "Trends and Prospects in Biblical Theology," *JTS*, XXV (1974), 265 ff.

64. See above, chapter I, note 210. See also A. Dulles, *Revelation and the Quest for Unity* (Washington and Cleveland, 1968); P. M. Minus, Jr., "Return to the Sources," *The Catholic Rediscovery of Protestantism* (New York, 1976), pp. 131 f.

65. Cf. D. Ritschl, *Memory and Hope: An Inquiry Concerning the Presence of Christ* (New York, 1967).

66. See J. H. Leith, "The Bible and Theology," *In.*, XXX (1976): 227 ff.

67. A few scholars have pointed out the motif of the presence of God as the key to the understanding of Old Testament Theology. See H. D. Preuss, " ' . . . ich will mit dir sein!'," *ZAW*, LXXX (1968): 139 ff.; J. A. Sanders, *"Mysterium Salutis,"* *Ecumenical Institute for Advanced Theological Studies* (Tantur), *Year Book* 1972–73, pp. 105 ff.; G. F. Hasel, "The Problem of Center," p. 81.

68. See W. Brueggemann, "Scripture and an Ecumenical Life-Style. A Study in Wisdom Theology," *In.*, XXIV (1970): 3 ff.; R. E. Murphy, "Wisdom and Yahwism," in *Festschrift J. L. McKenzie* (Missoula, Mont., 1975), pp. 117 ff.; J. A. ! nders, "Torah and Christ," *In.*, XXIX (1975): 372 ff.; A. de Pury, "Sagesse et révélation dans l'Ancien Testament," *RTPL*, XXVII (1977): 1 ff.

69. See R. Mehl, "Structure philosophique de la notion de présence," *RHPR*, XXXVIII (1958): 171, 173.

70. *"Theos gar kai to gignôskein philous,"* Euripides, *Helen*, 560.

Principal Abbreviations

	Alten und Neuen Testaments
HTR	Harvard Theological Review
HUCA	Hebrew Union College Annual
IB	Interpreter's Bible
IDB	Interpreter's Dictionary of the Bible
IEJ	Israel Exploration Journal
In.	Interpretation: A Journal of Bible and Theology
JAAR	Journal of the American Academy of Religion
JAOS	Journal of the American Oriental Society
JBL	Journal of Biblical Literature
JBR	Journal of Bible and Religion
JNES	Journal of Near Eastern Studies
JQR	Jewish Quarterly Review
JR	Journal of Religion
JSS	Journal of Semitic Studies
JTC	Journal for Theology and the Church
JTS	Journal of Theological Studies
LXX	Septuagint
NRT	Nouvelle revue théologique
NT	Novum Testamentum
NTS	New Testament Studies
OLZ	Orientalische Literaturzeitung
OTS	Oudtestamentische Studiën
PEQ	Palestine Exploration Quarterly
RB	Revue biblique
REJ	Revue des études juives
RGG	Die Religion in Geschichte und Gegenwart
RHPR	Revue d'histoire et de philosophie religieuses
RHR	Revue de l'histoire des religions
RSPT	Revue des sciences philosophiques et théologiques
RTP	Revue de théologie et de philosophie
SBT	Studies in Biblical Theology
SEÅ	Svensk exegetisk årsbok

SNT	Supplements to Novum Testamentum
ST	Studia theologica
SVT	Supplements to Vetus Testamentum
STU	Schweizerische theologische Umshau
Syr.	Syriac
TGUOS	Transaction of the Glasgow University Oriental Society
TLZ	Theologische Literaturzeitung
TR	Theologische Rundschau
TSK	Theologische Studien und Kritiken
TZ	Theologische Zeitschrift
VT	Vetus Testamentum
Vulg.	Vulgate
WTJ	Westminster Theological Journal
ZAW	Zeitschrift für die alttestamentliche Wissenschaft
ZKT	Zeitschrift für die katholische Theologie
ZTK	Zeitschrift für Theologie und Kirche

Index of Biblical References

Index of Authors

Index of Subjects